Historical Dictionaries of Asia, Oceania, and the Middle East

Edited by Jon Woronoff

Asia

1. *Vietnam*, by William J. Duiker. 1989. *Out of print. See No. 57.*
2. *Bangladesh*, 2nd ed., by Craig Baxter and Syedur Rahman. 1996 *Out of print. See No. 48.*
3. *Pakistan*, by Shahid Javed Burki. 1991. *Out of print. See No. 61.*
4. *Jordan*, by Peter Gubser. 1991.
5. *Afghanistan*, by Ludwig W. Adamec. 1991. *Out of print. See No. 47.*
6. *Laos*, by Martin Stuart-Fox and Mary Kooyman. 1992. *Out of print. See No. 67.*
7. *Singapore*, by K. Mulliner and Lian The-Mulliner. 1991.
8. *Israel*, by Bernard Reich. 1992. *Out of print. See No. 68.*
9. *Indonesia*, by Robert Cribb. 1992. *Out of print. See No. 51.*
10. *Hong Kong and Macau*, by Elfed Vaughan Roberts, Sum Ngai Ling, and Peter Bradshaw. 1992.
11. *Korea*, by Andrew C. Nahm. 1993. *Out of print. See No. 52.*
12. *Taiwan*, by John F. Copper. 1993. *Out of print. See No. 64.*
13. *Malaysia*, by Amarjit Kaur. 1993. *Out of print. See No. 36.*
14. *Saudi Arabia*, by J. E. Peterson. 1993. *Out of print. See No. 45.*
15. *Myanmar*, by Jan Becka. 1995. *Out of print. See No. 59.*
16. *Iran*, by John H. Lorentz. 1995. *Out of print. See No. 62.*
17. *Yemen*, by Robert D. Burrowes. 1995. *Out of print. See No. 72.*
18. *Thailand*, by May Kyi Win and Harold Smith. 1995. *Out of print. See No. 55.*
19. *Mongolia*, by Alan J. K. Sanders. 1996. *Out of print. See No. 42.*
20. *India*, by Surjit Mansingh. 1996. *Out of print. See No. 58.*
21. *Gulf Arab States*, by Malcolm C. Peck. 1996. *Out of print. See No. 66.*
22. *Syria*, by David Commins. 1996. *Out of print. See No. 50.*
23. *Palestine*, by Nafez Y. Nazzal and Laila A. Nazzal. 1997.
24. *Philippines*, by Artemio R. Guillermo and May Kyi Win. 1997. *Out of print. See No. 54.*

Historical Dictionary of Bangladesh

Fourth Edition

Syedur Rahman

*Historical Dictionaries of Asia, Oceania,
and the Middle East, No. 75*

The Scarecrow Press, Inc.
Lanham • Toronto • Plymouth, UK
2010

Published by Scarecrow Press, Inc.
A wholly owned subsidary of The Rowman & Littlefield Publishing Group, Inc.
4501 Forbes Boulevard, Suite 200, Lanham, Maryland 20706
http://www.scarecrowpress.com

Estover Road, Plymouth PL6 7PY, United Kingdom

British Library Cataloguing in Publication Information Available

Library of Congress Cataloging-in-Publication Data

Rahman, Syedur, Ph.D.
    Historical dictionary of Bangladesh / Syedur Rahman. — 4th ed.
        p. cm. — (Historical dictionaries of Asia, Oceania, and the Middle East ; 75)
    Rev. ed. of: Historical dictionary of Bangladesh / Craig Baxter and Syedur
Rahman.
    Includes bibliographical references.
    ISBN 978-0-8108-6766-6 (cloth : alk. paper) — ISBN 978-0-8108-7453-4
(ebook)
    1. Bangladesh—History—Dictionaries. I. Baxter, Craig. Historical dictionary
of Bangladesh. II. Title.
    DS394.5.B39 2010
    954.92003—dc22   2009046447

Printed in the United States of America

This edition is dedicated to those whose names are not the subjects of books or their lineage the subject of national pride; their uncommon valor is going far beyond their means to help others, to abide by the rules and live with dignity despite insurmountable challenges: *Abdur Rahman and Husnara Huque.*

It is also dedicated to those whose names are the subjects of books and their lineage a matter of national pride, but more because of their anonymous devotion to helping those who are not so fortunate and their humility for being so profoundly fortunate: *Mohammad Khosrowshahi and Mahin Boushehri.*

Contents

Editor's Foreword

Bangladesh is not a well-known Asian country, and what is known about it is often unfavorable. Reports stress its overpopulation and underdevelopment, and earlier its political instability. But there is much more to it than that: This land has a long and often proud tradition; it has produced writers and artists of genius; it is an important outpost of Islam; and, with a population of some 130 million, it is one of the more populated countries in the world. It therefore deserves to be known better by more people.

That is the purpose of this book, but it was not easy to achieve given the great age and considerable complexity of the place now called Bangladesh. It has been inhabited by people of different races and religions, and it has been ruled over by different leaders who imposed different regimes. Yet, with its many entries, enlightening introduction, and ample bibliography, this book will serve as an accessible point of entry for those new to the country and still be a source of useful information for more experienced readers.

This fourth edition of the *Historical Dictionary of Bangladesh* was written Dr. Syedur Rahman. The previous three editions were written by Dr. Rahman and Dr. Craig Baxter, a foreign service officer and then professor of politics and history at Juniata College. Dr. Rahman, who was born in Bangladesh and educated there and in the United States, has taught at the University of Dhaka and Pennsylvania State University. He has written on regional cooperation and economic development in Bangladesh, as well as the country's government, politics, and higher-education management. In his last position at Penn State, he was the director of International Programs in the College of Education. He was also president of the American Institute of Bangladesh Studies.

Jon Woronoff
Series Editor

Preface

This fourth edition of the *Historical Dictionary of Bangladesh*, while updating the substantial political entries of the earlier editions, also adds significant sociocultural entries. Previous editions emphasized pre- and postcolonial periods and the Pakistan era, but this edition hones in on events and personalities that significantly impacted Bangladesh. Understanding these events and personalities is crucial to understanding Bangladesh. I have attempted to record the firsts of any event. Bibliographic entries are now significantly supplemented by scholarship by Bangladeshi authors, thus bringing a different perspective to any review and analysis of Bangladesh.

A common dilemma in the entries is how to list names. For example, Abbasuddin Ahmed would normally be listed as AHMED, ABBASUDDIN. However, in Bangladesh it is most likely that it would be listed as ABBASUDDIN AHMED. In most cases I have listed the name as AHMED, ABBASUDDIN, but in a few cases I have listed the name as ABBASUDDIN AHMED since the person is better known by the first name than the last name.

Another issue is the specificity of records. In a number of cases, dates or the spelling of name are somewhat different in different sources. For example, when did Dhaka become a capital city? Some scholars think it is 1608 and others think it is 1610. I have made every effort to standardize information, while recognizing the controversy surrounding dates and events.

In justifying which entries I have chosen to include, I am reminded of a letter to the editor, someone who was looking for the name of a person in an encyclopedia and found a namesake rather than the person he was looking for. Instead of getting upset, he spent some time learning about the person he had found.

Finally, in the end, the responsibility for any errors or omissions is mine.

Acronyms and Abbreviations

ACC	Anti-corruption Commission
ADB	Asian Development Bank
AL	Awami League
AMI	Anjuman Mofidul Islam
ASA	Association for Social Advancement
ASEAN	Association of Southeast Asian Nations
ASF	Acid Survivors Foundation
ASHIS	Alokchitra Shilpi Sangsad
BAKSAL	Bangladesh Krishak Sramik Awami League
BADC	Bangladesh Agricultural Development Corporation
BARD	Bangladesh Academy of Rural Development
BDB	Bikalpa Dhara Bangladesh
BDR	Bangladesh Rifles
BKM	Bangladesh Khelefat Majlish
BLSP	Bangladesh Loko Sangeet Parishad
BNP	Bangladesh Nationalist Party
BRAC	Bangladesh Rural Advancement Committee
BSD	Bangladesh Samajtantrik Dal
CITES	Conservation on International Trade in Endangered Species
CMLA	Chief Martial Law Administrator
CML	Council Muslim League
COP	Combined Opposition Parties
CPI	Communist Party of India
CTG	Caretaker government
D8	Developing Eight Countries
EBDO	Elective Bodies (Disqualification) Order
EC	Election Commission
GDP	Gross domestic product

GNP	Gross national product
HUJI-B	Harkat-ul-Jihad-al-Islam–Bangladesh
HYV	High-yield varieties
ICDDRB	International Centre for Diarrhoeal Disease Research, Bangladesh
IDB	Islamic Development Bank
IDL	Islamic Democratic League
IDP	Islamic Democratic Party
IGA	Islamic Gono Andolon
IUCN	International Union for the Conservation of Nature and Natural Resources
JAGODAL	Jatiyatabadi Gonotantrik Dal
JMB	Jama'atul Mujahideen Bangladesh
JMJB	Jagrata Muslim Janata Bangladesh
JSD	Jatiya Samajtantrik Dal
KPP	Krishak Praja Party
KSJL	Krishak Sramik, Janata League (Peasants, Labor, People's League)
KSP	Krishak Shramik Party
LDP	Liberal Democratic Party
NAP	National Awami Party
NAP(B)	National Awami Party (Bhashani)
NAP(M)	National Awami Party (Muzaffar)
NAP(W)	National Awami Party (Wali)
NBR	National Board of Revenue
NGO	Non-governmental organization
NHRC	National Human Rights Commission
NUPF	National Union Parishad Forum
NWF	National Women's Federation
OIC	Organization of the Islamic Conference
PDP	Progressive Democratic Party
PKSF	Palli Karma-Sahayak Foundation
PPP	People's Party of Pakistan
PPP	Purchasing Power Parity
PRODA	Public and Representative Offices Disqualification Act
PSC	Public Service Commission
RAB	Rapid Action Battalion
RMG	Ready-made garment sector

SAARC South Asian Association for Regional Cooperation
SAPTA South Asian Preferential Trading Arrangement
SEATO Southeast Asia Treaty Organization
SJC Supreme Judicial Commission
TAC Truth and Accountability Commission
UF United Front
UN United Nations
UNESCO United Nations Educational, Scientific and Cultural Organization
USAID United States Agency for International Development
WCFFC War Crimes Fact Finding Committee
WHO World Health Organization

Chronology

1500 BC   Approximate date of arrival of Indo-Aryans in the Indus valley.

1000 BC   Approximate date of arrival of Bang tribe in the lower Ganges valley.

273–232 BC   Reign of Maurya emperor Asoka. Following his death the empire began to break up. Local chieftains ruled in Bengal.

AD 320–510   Reign of the Gupta dynasty, which extended its rule into portions of Bengal.

606–647   Reign of Harsha, a brief period often described as a revival of the Gupta Empire.

750   Founding of the Pala dynasty, a Buddhist dynasty that extended rule well beyond Bengal into northern India.

1095   Beginning of the Sena dynasty and the restoration of Brahmanical Hinduism.

1155   Fall of the Pala dynasty.

1202   Fall of the Sena capital, Nadia, to Khalji, a general representing the Ghurid dynasty of the Delhi Sultanate.

1336   Rebellion against the Tughluq dynasty of the Delhi Sultanate led by Fakhruddin Mubarak Shah.

1342   After a decade of turmoil, Shamsuddin Ilyas Shah founds the Ilyas Shahi dynasty.

1490   Overthrow of the Ilyas Shahi dynasty. Founding of the Husain Shahi dynasty.

1517   Arrival of the Portuguese in Chittagong.

1538   Conquest of Bengal by troops of the Mughal emperor Humayun.

1539   Rebels under Sher Shah Suri, an Afghan, take Bengal and rule until 1564.

1564   Rival Afghan Karrani dynasty wins control of Bengal.

1576   Conquest of Bengal by the Mughal emperor Akbar.

1608   Dhaka becomes capital of Mughal's Bengal province.

1650   Arrival of British in Bengal.

1690   British found Calcutta.

1704   Murshidabad replaces Dhaka as capital.

1756   Mughal governor Sirajuddaulah attacks Calcutta. Incident of the "Black Hole."

1757   British under Robert Clive defeat Sirajuddaulah at the Battle of Plassey.

1765   Clive becomes governor of Bengal.

1772   Warren Hastings becomes governor, then becomes governor-general in 1773.

1793   Permanent Settlement decreed by Lord Cornwallis. This made tax collectors de facto landowners (*zamindars*) and reduced the farmers to tenants.

1857   Sepoy mutiny.

1858   Transfer of power from British East India Company to the Crown. Queen Victoria proclaims that all subjects are equal under the law.

1861   India Councils Act permits the inclusion of Indians in the legislative councils of lieutenant governors and the governor-general.

1883   Local Councils Act permits limited election to local government boards.

1885 Indian National Congress is founded at Bombay.

1885 Bengal Tenancy Act alleviates some of the disabilities of the Permanent Settlement by giving tenants the right of occupancy and inheritance.

1894 India Councils Act expands those rights given in the 1861 act.

1905 Partition of Bengal into the province of Eastern Bengal and Assam and the province of Bengal, the latter including Bihar and Orissa.

1906 Muslim delegation meets Lord Minto at Simla. Muslim League founded in Dhaka.

1909 Government of India Act (Morley-Minto Act) grants the Muslim demand of separate electorates and further expands the powers of legislative councils.

1911 Annulment of the partition of Bengal. Capital of India is transferred from Calcutta to New Delhi.

1917 Montagu Declaration proposes ultimate "self-government" for India.

1919 Government of India Act (Montagu-Chelmsford Act) creates a system of dyarchy at the provincial level.

1935 Government of India Act provides for provincial autonomy and responsible government. Proposed changes at the federal level are not fully implemented, as Indian princes would not accept subordination to dyarchical system at that level.

1937 Provincial elections are held. Fazlul Haq becomes the first prime minister of Bengal.

1940 **23 March:** Muslim League passes at Lahore a resolution proposing that the partition of India may be necessary (often referred to as the "Pakistan Resolution" although the word "Pakistan" does not appear in the resolution). It is seconded by Fazlul Haq.

1941 Fazlul Haq leaves the Muslim League but his prime ministership continues.

1943 Muslim League ministry headed by Khwaja Nazimuddin is formed.

1945 Nazimuddin government falls; the governor assumes rule.

1946 New elections are held. Muslim League forms ministry headed by Husain Shahid Suhrawardy.

1947 **15 August:** Partition of India and the independence of dominions of India and Pakistan. Muslim League forms ministry in East Bengal headed by Nazimuddin.

1951 Nazimuddin becomes governor-general of Pakistan. Nurul Amin heads East Bengal ministry.

1952 **21 February:** Ekushey (Martyrs') Day held in memory of students killed in pro-Bengali language demonstrations in Dhaka.

1954 Muslim League is trounced by the United Front of the Awami League (Suhrawardy) and the Krishak Sramik Party (KSP) (Fazlul Haq). Fazlul Haq becomes chief minister briefly, but the central government imposes governor's rule (to 1956).

1955 East Bengal renamed East Pakistan.

1956 **23 March:** First Pakistani constitution.

1956–1958 United Front having broken apart, the Awami League and KSP alternate leadership of government during an increasingly tumultuous period.

1958 **7 October:** President Iskandar Mirza declares martial law. **28 October:** General Muhammad Ayub Khan dismisses Mirza and assumes the presidency.

1962 Ayub proclaims the second constitution, including the formalization of the system of basic democracies (operative since 1959). Martial law ends.

1965 **September:** War between Pakistan and India.

1966 **23 March:** Sheikh Mujibur Rahman (Mujib) announces the Awami League Six-Point Program.

1969 **20 January:** Asaduzzaman, a student of Dhaka University, is killed as police open fire on a procession in support of the 11-point demand of the Students Action Committee. **22 February:** Sheikh Mujibur Rahman, leader of the All-Pakistan Awami League, walks out of his prison cell in the Dhaka cantonment. **25 March:** Ayub resigns and turns the presidency over to General Yahya Khan. Martial law is reimposed.

1970   December: Elections are held in Pakistan. Awami League wins 160 of the 162 National Assembly seats from East Pakistan but none of the 138 from West Pakistan.

1971   25 March: Constitutional talks among Yahya Khan, Mujib, and Zulfiqar Ali Bhutto fail. Later in the evening the Pakistani army starts its campaign of mass killings against the Bengalis. **10 April:** Tajuddin Ahmed announces the formation of an interim Bangladesh government. **17 April:** The first government of Bangladesh is announced at Meherpur with Bangabandhu Sheikh Mujibur Rahman as the first president of the country. Vice President Syed Nazrul Islam is declared acting president and Tajuddin as prime minister. **November:** India enters the Bangladesh War of Liberation. **16 December:** Pakistan surrenders Dhaka to allied forces. **18 December:** Five political parties are banned in Bangladesh: the Muslim League and all its factions, Pakistan Democratic Party, Nezam-e-Islam, Jamat-e-Islami, and Peoples Party of Pakistan.

1972   10 January: Mujib, who has been in captivity in West Pakistan, returns to Dhaka. **16 December:** Bangladesh constitution is promulgated.

**1973   Elections to the Bangladesh Parliament give the Awami League 292 of 300 seats.

1975   15 August: Mujib is assassinated. Khondakar Mushtaque Ahmad becomes president. **3–5 November:** Insurrection led by Khalid Musharaf fails. Ziaur Rahman emerges as a key figure. A. S. M. Sayem is named president.

1977   21 April: Zia replaces Sayem as president. **30 May:** Zia wins a referendum to hold office.

1978   3 June: Zia is elected president and Abdus Sattar is appointed vice president.

**1979   Parliamentary elections give Zia's party 207 of 300 seats.

1981   30 May: Zia is assassinated. Sattar becomes acting president. **15 November:** Sattar is elected president.

1982 **24 March:** Sattar is overthrown in a military coup led by Hussain Muhammad Ershad.

1986 Parliamentary elections give Ershad's party a slight majority. Awami League and its allies win about one-third of the seats. Bangladesh Nationalist Party (BNP) boycotts the election.

1987 Awami League withdraws from parliament. In November, major demonstrations against Ershad take place, causing him to declare a state of emergency and dissolve the parliament.

1988 New elections to parliament are held and are boycotted by both the Awami League and the Bangladesh Nationalist Party. Ershad's Jatiya Party wins about 250 of 300 seats.

1990 Demonstrations against Ershad continue in 1989 and 1990 at a relatively low level, but in November 1990 they grow to major proportions. Two major parties, the Bangladesh Nationalist Party and Awami League, agree on ousting Ershad and holding "free and fair" elections under a neutral government. **4 December:** Ershad resigns, turning over the reins of government to Chief Justice Shahabuddin Ahmed.

1991 **March:** Elections give the Bangladesh Nationalist Party a small majority. Its leader, Begum Khaleda Zia, is sworn in as prime minister. Parliament approves a constitutional amendment ending the presidential system and establishing a parliamentary system of government. Parliament elects Abdur Rahman Biswas president; the position has mainly ceremonial duties. **29 April:** A cyclone and tidal surge along the coast of Bangladesh kill 138,000 people.

1994 **28 December:** Endemic opposition to Khaleda Zia in parliament and elsewhere leads the opposition to withdraw from parliament unless its demand for future elections to be held under neutral caretaker governments is met.

1995 **20 June:** Opposition seats are declared vacant as opposition members have not attended parliamentary sittings for 90 consecutive days. By-elections cannot be held, as the opposition declares it will boycott them. **24 November:** Parliament is dissolved by the president on the advice of the prime minister.

1996   15 February: Elections are held, resulting in an overwhelming BNP majority as the opposition boycotts amid increasing violence. The new parliament passes a constitutional amendment providing for future elections under a neutral caretaker government. **16 June:** A new election results in a plurality for the Awami League, which forms an alliance with the Jatiya Party. **23 June:** A new government led by Sheikh Hasina Wajid of the Awami League is formed. **12 December:** Bangladesh and India sign an agreement on the division of the waters of the Ganges River.

1997   Former president Ershad is released from jail on bail after more than six years in prison. The Awami League government repeals the indemnity bill passed by an Ershad-led government in 1986. Repeal is upheld by the Supreme Court. Government charges 25 people with the murder of Sheikh Mujibur Rahman and others. Government signs an agreement with dissidents in the Chittagong Hill Tracts that intends to end conflict with rebellious tribal groups.

1998   Awami League ends the coalition with the Jatiya Party that had been formed after the 1996 election. The breakup results from a disagreement over the peace agreement the government made with tribal groups in 1997. Bangladesh Nationalist Party forms an anti-government alliance with the Jatiya Party and Jama'at-i-Islami.

1999   Three-party alliance boycotts municipal elections. Government passes the Public Safety Act that permits arrest of "terrorists" and "enemies of the state." Arsenic is discovered in as much as 40 percent of Bangladesh's tubewells. Government signs an exploratory agreement with UNOCAL of the United States for gas. Government agrees to purchase eight MiG aircraft from Russia.

2000   High Court confirms the death penalty for 10 of the 15 people accused in the Mujib murder case. Four ministers in the Mushtaque Ahmed cabinet are indicted in the Dhaka jail killings case. High Court sentences Ershad to five years' imprisonment and a fine for corruption. Bangladesh Nationalist Party ends an 11-month boycott of parliament.

2001   20 January: Five are killed and 25 injured when a powerful bomb explodes at a rally of the Communist Party of Bangladesh in Dhaka. **April:** High Court confirms death sentences for 12 former army officers in the Mujib assassination. **June:** Parliament approves a bill providing protection to Prime Minster Sheikh Hasina and her sister. **July:** Hasina completes her term in office and hands over power to the caretaker government. **October:** National parliamentary elections are held and the Bangladesh Nationalist Party sweeps into power. BNP and its allies win 228 seats and hold the Awami League to 62 seats. The Awami League initially boycotts the parliament but soon decides to join, as it recognizes the increasing intolerance of the public for *hartals* and boycotts. Corruption charges are filed against Sheikh Hasina in connection with the MiG purchase agreement.

2002   21 June: A. Q. M. Badruddoza Chowdhury resigns as president of Bangladesh. **July:** President Musharraf of Pakistan expresses regrets over excesses committed by the Pakistani armed forces during the War of Liberation. **6 September:** Iajuddin Ahmed is sworn in as president of Bangladesh. **2 October:** The BNP government starts an anticrime initiative called Operation Clean Heart. **December:** Bomb blasts kill 17 people in Dhaka.

2003   January: Vietnam re-opens its embassy in Bangladesh. **January–March:** Union *parishad* elections are held in 4451 union parishads. **6 March:** A massive protest is held in Dhaka against the possible U.S. invasion of Iraq. International Republican Institute starts its operation in Bangladesh. **May:** Parliament amends the constitution of Bangladesh and increases the number of reserved seats for women from 30 to 45. **June:** Awami League boycotts parliament. **27 July:** An earthquake measuring 5.1 on the Richter scale hits Bangladesh. **November:** Hifazat Khatme Nabuwat Andalon leads the anti-Ahmadiyya movement, resulting in the killing of an Ahmadiyya imam.

2004   9 January: Government of Bangladesh bans the publication, sale, distribution, and preservation of all books and booklets on Islam published by the Ahmadiyya community of Bangladesh. **28 February:** Writer Humayun Kabir is stabbed. **3 April:** Ten truckloads of illegal armaments are seized in Chittagong. **8 May:** Ashanullah Master, an Awami League member of parliament, is assassinated. **16 May:** The Constitution (14th Amendment) Bill is passed. **19 May:** Bangladesh and the United States sign a Memorandum of Intent to implement the Personal Identification Secure Comparison and Evaluation System

(PISCES), sophisticated computer software, to document passengers traveling into and out of the country and check movement of suspected terrorists. **21 May:** British high commissioner to Bangladesh Anwar Choudhury is among about 70 injured in a powerful bomb blast, the second in five months, at Hazrat Shahjalal Shrine in Sylhet. **June:** Millions are homeless or stranded due to floods. **21 August:** Grenade attacks on opposition leader Sheikh Hasina's rally at Bangabandhu Avenue kill 22 people, including Awami League leader Ivy Rahman.

2005   27 January: Member of parliament and former finance minister Shah A. M. S. Kibria is assassinated in a grenade attack in his home constituency of Habiganj, Sylhet. **23 February:** Jagrata Muslim Janata Bangladesh (JMJB) is banned. **17 August:** Around 450 small bombs explode countrywide; JMJB claims responsibility. **November:** Bombs explode in Chittagong and Gazipur; Islamic militants claim responsibility.

2006   October: BNP completes its term of office and hands over power to the caretaker government led by President Iajuddin Ahmed, who announces parliamentary elections to be held in January 2007. **November:** Four-party alliance led by the Awami League seeks the removal of chief election commissioner M. A. Aziz, who eventually steps down. **December:** The national election date is set for 22 January 2007. Awami League and Bangladesh Khelafat Majlish sign the Election Alliance Accord.

2007   11 January: President Iajuddin Ahmed resigns as chief adviser and declares a state of emergency, suspending the fundamental rights guaranteed by articles 36, 37, 38, 39, 40, and 42 of the constitution. All election activities are suspended. Senior adviser Justice Fazlul Haque becomes acting chief adviser for a day. **12 January:** Fakhruddin Ahmed, a former governor of the Bangladesh Bank, becomes the chief adviser. **13 January:** Five new advisers are appointed: Barrister Mainul Hosein, Major General (retd.) M. A. Matin, Geeti Ara Safiya Chowdhury, Dr. Mirza Azizul Islam, and Tapan Chowdhury. **4 February:** The caretaker government of Fakhruddin Ahmed begins its anti-corruption drive by arresting major political and business leaders of Bangladesh. **10 June:** The voter registration with photographs, fingerprints, and national ID cards is started as a pilot project. **4 September:** Former Prime

Minister Khaleda Zia is arrested. **1 November:** The judiciary is made independent of the executive branch of government. The Election Commission, Anti-corruption Commission, Public Service Commission, and University Grants Commission are reconstituted.

2008 **10 January:** Five new advisers to the caretaker government are appointed. **11 January:** Gono Front Leader Kamal Hussain proposes a 10-point charter for national unity. **29 January:** The caretaker government approves the Supreme Judicial Commission Ordinance—Election Commission Secretariat Ordinance 2008. **4 February:** A new chief election commissioner is appointed to reconstitute the Election Commission for holding a free and fair election. **6 February:** High Court determines that former Prime Minister Sheikh Hasina cannot be tried for crimes supposedly committed prior to the imposition of a state of emergency under the emergency powers rule. **18 May:** Bangladesh High Court rules that children of Biharis awaiting repatriation to Pakistan have the right to Bangladeshi citizenship. **25 May:** Right to Voluntary Disclosure Ordinance 2008 is promulgated, permitting the establishment of a Truth and Accountability Commission and exempting people from prosecution in exchange for confession and surrender of fraudulently obtained wealth. **11 June:** Awami League President Sheikh Hasina is released from jail. After the state of emergency was declared on 11 January 2007, she was arrested after charges were filed against her on 6 July 2007. The caretaker government promulgates the Anti-Terrorism Ordinance. The death penalty is permitted under the ordinance for acts against the security of the country, terror financing, and other acts of mass terror. **18 June:** The caretaker government promulgates the Right to Information Ordinance. **9 July:** A nationwide digitized voter registration and national ID card system is completed, having registered 8.5 million voters in 11 months. **11 September:** Former Prime Minister Khaleda Zia is released from jail on bail. **17 December:** The caretaker government of Fakhruddin Ahmed lifts the state of emergency that was promulgated on 11 January 2007. **20 December:** Armed Forces of Bangladesh are deployed to ensure free and fair national parliamentary elections. **29 December:** The parliamentary elections are held under the leadership of the caretaker government of Fakhruddin Ahmed.

2009 **6 January:** Sheikh Hasina Wajid is sworn in as prime minister of Bangladesh. **11 January:** Bangladesh Nationalist Party and Bangladesh Jamaat-e-Islami begin to work independently, as their alliance was for election purposes only. **22 January:** The upazila parishad elections are held, although voter turnout is low. Awami League wins a majority. **12 February:** Zillur Rahman is sworn in as the 19th president of Bangladesh. **25 February:** Fifty-two officers of the Bangladesh army are killed as a result of a two-day mutiny by the Bangladesh Rifles (BDR), a paramilitary border security force. **16 July:** Four new Appellate Division judges are sworn. **19 July:** Interrogation of arrested militants points to an attempt to reorganize the banned militant group JMBJ in Rajshahi. **22 October:** Hizb-ut-Tahrir is banned.

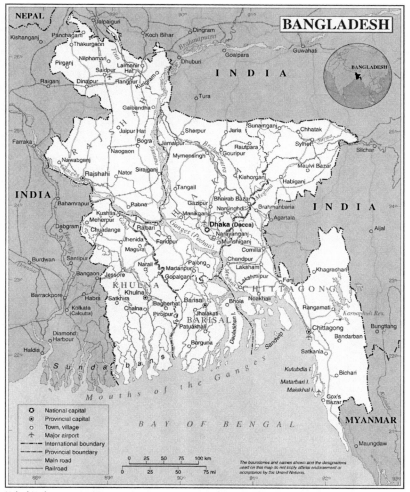

BANGLADESH

United Nations map no. 3711, rev. 2, January 2004. Dept. of Peacekeeping Operations, Cartographic Section.

Introduction

Bangladesh (literally, the land of the Bengalis) is the most recent addition (in 1971) to the independent nations of South Asia. The term "South Asia" is usually defined now as including the seven states that are members of the South Asian Association for Regional Cooperation (SAARC): Bangladesh, Bhutan, India, the Maldives, Nepal, Pakistan, and Sri Lanka. In academic usage and in the usage of the U.S. Department of State, the term may also include Afghanistan. These states are ones that were under British control or influence throughout much of the 19th and early 20th centuries. Those controlled directly by the British attained independence in 1947 (India and Pakistan) and 1948 (Sri Lanka, then Ceylon). In 1971 Bangladesh emerged out of Pakistan, not Britain. These countries therefore share a heritage in such areas as administration, legal systems, and many political structures. They also share a traditional background. Hinduism, which still dominates in India (and Nepal), has long since been superseded by Islam in Pakistan and Bangladesh, and by Buddhism in Sri Lanka.

The emergence of Bangladesh from Pakistan in 1971 and the partition of India in 1947 make it evident that there will be much overlap among the works in this series on the three countries. A further complication is that the term "Bangladesh" itself is a misnomer. While Bangladesh contains a majority of the speakers of the Bengali language, Bengali speakers also live in the Indian state of West Bengal, in the state of Assam, and in the smaller hill states of northeastern India.

LAND AND PEOPLE

Bangladesh is a compact country, comprising mainly the deltaic area formed by the mouths of the combined Ganges (Ganga) and

Brahmaputra Rivers that rise, respectively, in India and Tibet. To these rivers is added another major river, the Meghna, which rises in Assam. The confluence of the three rivers in one delta makes this delta unique, for most deltas of the world are formed by one river. Bangladesh is home to 1,500 rivers, but more than 1,250 have lost their existence. The remaining 250 rivers are simply struggling for survival. The region is thus an alluvial plain with but few exceptions. These include the hills in the northeastern portion (Sylhet region), where rainfall occurs at one of the highest rates in the world, and the southeastern area (Chittagong Hill Tracts region), with lower but still substantial rainfall. (It should be noted that the political units once known as "districts" have now been reclassified as "regions," and those formerly known as "subdivisions" as "districts," although no structure or functions have been assigned to the regions.)

The combination of the usually heavy monsoon rainfall and the flow from the rivers resulting from upstream snowmelt provides Bangladesh with a quantity of water that can be both a blessing and a curse. On the positive side, the annual flooding provides water for the growing of such water-demanding crops as rice and jute and also replenishes the fertile soil with deposits of silt brought from the Himalayas and the Tibetan plateau. The streams also provide an intricate network of routes for domestic travel and commerce. But, of course, at the same time they act as formidable barriers to the development of roads and rail transport. The continued migration of the rivers and streams makes bridging a difficult task, and the major rivers have also inhibited the distribution of electricity and of the natural gas that is abundant in the country. A major bridge to cross the Jamuna (Brahmaputra) has been constructed and will be a combination road and rail bridge that will also carry gas and electricity lines. Another serious "curse" is the frequent extensive flooding that washes away crops, kills animals and often people, and destroys villages.

Although there are dangers from an excess of water, Bangladesh is clearly heavily dependent on the flow of the rivers. The withdrawal of water from the Ganges by the upper riparian, India, has diminished the flow into Bangladesh. This has been demonstrated most clearly in India's construction of a barrage at Farakka, just upstream from the border, with the purpose of diverting Ganges water through the Bhagirathi and Hooghly Rivers to assist the city of Calcutta (Kolkata). In effect, the Farakka diversion would restore the Bhagirathi-Hooghly system as the principal distributary of the Ganges, which it was prior to the natural diversion in the 16th and 17th centuries that made the Padma (as the Ganges is called in Bangladesh) the principal distributary. An important and unresolved political dispute between India and Bangladesh has resulted, although there has been a temporary agreement to divide the water evenly during the low-flow period in April, May, and June. India has proposed a link canal to move water from the Brahmaputra (which usually carries more water than is needed for irrigation and navigation downstream) to a point on the Ganges upstream from Farakka to augment the low-season flow. In addition, the loss of land to the canal and its spoil bank would be serious in a land as densely populated as Bangladesh. Bangladesh has objected, as the canal would have both its intake and outflow under Indian control, but would flow for most of its length in Bangladesh. Bangladesh has proposed a tripartite arrangement that would include Nepal and result in additional storage dams on Nepali territory to regulate the flow of the Ganges and at the same time add to hydroelectric generation in Nepal and northern India. India opposes any multilateral agreement. The building of Farakka has had a severe negative impact on southwestern Bangladesh. The building of the Tipaimukh dam, a kilometer north of Jakiganj in Sylhet, threatens northeastern Bangladesh if the results of Farakka are replicated in the northeast.

The rivers flow slowly through Bangladesh. Dhaka, for example, is only 24 feet above sea level. Therefore there is but limited potential for hydroelectric generation. The only exception, so far, is the harnessing of the Karnaphuli River at Kaptai, upstream from Chittagong, for power.

Bangladesh is also subject to another climatic phenomenon, whose consequences are always destructive: the cyclones that arise in the Bay of Bengal and cause damage in Bangladesh as well as in eastern India. The great cyclone of 1970 may have killed as many as half a million people along the coastal areas and left countless more injured and homeless. Construction of homes from more permanent materials and the development of extensive early-warning programs are helping to ameliorate such widespread damage. The building of polders, with Dutch assistance, has also been effective in some areas. Major cyclones have struck as recently as 1991, 1993, and 2002. There is also a growing consensus among scientists that the earth is facing a period of global warming and its impact on Bangladesh and all the deltas of the world could be significant. It is estimated that if global warming causes a one-meter rise in sea level, approximately 15 percent of Bangladesh will be inundated, displacing 13 to 15 million people.

Bangladesh's borders are neither traditional nor natural. The shared land boundary is almost entirely with India, the exception being in the very southeastern end of the country where it borders on the Arakan area of Myanmar (Burma). As will be discussed below, the border with India was set in 1947 as part of the process of partitioning British India. The result has been enclaves on one side or the other of the border, creating another political problem between the two countries.

The southern boundary is the Bay of Bengal, but the exact location of that boundary is still a matter of dispute between India and Bangladesh. The appearance of new islands in the bay has complicated the negotiations, as has the Law of the Sea Agreement. Bangladesh, which forms an indendation, is not accorded an economic zone of 200 miles, as this zone must be plotted on a line that also respects the rights of Myanmar (Burma) and India. The determination of the ownership of new islands would affect the base points from which the economic zone is determined.

The more than 130 million people of Bangladesh are crowded into an area of 55,126 square miles (about the size of Wisconsin). This gives the country a population density of more than 2,400 people per square mile, higher than any state except for such city-states as Singapore and Hong Kong. There has been much progress in the family planning program; the growth rate, which was 2.5 percent (1960–1992), is expected to drop to 1.42 percent (2007–2008) and this rate is expected to continue till 2015. Nonetheless, the population was estimated to be 133.3 million in 2002 and 153.5 million in 2008, and will be around 161 million by 2015. Such overcrowding has, of course, important economic and social implications, which will be noted in the next section.

The rate of urbanization has been lower in Bangladesh than in most developing countries. More than 80 percent of the population is classified as rural. Dhaka, with 12.3 million (2007), is the largest city. Only two other cities have a population higher than one million, Chittagong with 3.7 million and Khulna with 1.4 million (2007). However, an urban population that was around 9.3 percent right after independence in

1971 is expected to be about 31 percent in 2015 and by some estimates nearly 50 percent by 2025.

The vast majority of the people are Bengalis, a branch of the Indo-Aryans who migrated to the eastern areas of the subcontinent after the earlier movement of the group from Central Asia to the region of the Indus River in the second millennium before Christ. Prior to their arrival, the region seems to have been populated by Dravidian groups, whose physical characteristics of shorter stature and darker skin are seen in the mixed population of Bangladesh. Evidence of some Mongoloid background can also be seen in eastern Bangladesh, especially in the regions of Sylhet and Chittagong.

About 88 percent of the Bangladeshis are Muslim, almost all of the Sunni branch. These include a small proportion of people who are descendants of Muslims who migrated from north India to serve as officers and soldiers of the Delhi Sultanate or the Mughal Empire and remained in Bengal. The bulk, however, were converted, usually through Sufi preachers, from among the population already resident in the area. For reasons that are not clear, the rate of conversion was higher in the eastern parts of Bengal than the western, and this was recognized when the united province of Bengal was partitioned in 1947.

Most of the remaining population (11 percent) is Hindu. Among them, the majority belong to the Scheduled Castes (a legal term for those formerly known as Untouchables). The bulk of the upper-caste Hindus fled to India by the early 1950s or at the time of the civil war in 1971. Generally, the western districts of Bangladesh have a higher percentage of Hindus than the eastern.

The other Bangladeshis are Christian (a few hundred thousand) or Buddhist. Many of each group are tribals. Christian tribals (e.g., Garos, Khasis) are often southern extensions of groups whose main territory is in the Indian state of Meghalaya, north of Bangladesh. Buddhist tribals are most often found in the Chittagong Hill Tracts (e.g., Chakmas, Tripuras). Many of the latter group had been in rebellion against the Bangladesh government, asserting that "flatlanders" had moved into the reserved hill areas. An agreement in 1997 has ended the rebellion. Some tribals, however, are Hindus or animists.

A special group among the Muslims is known as Biharis, who numbered about 600,000 at the time of the war of independence. These are Urdu-speaking Muslims who fled India in 1947 eastward to what was then East Bengal, rather than westward to what is now Pakistan, as most Muslim refugees did. Unable and perhaps unwilling to integrate with their Bengali-speaking co-religionists, the Biharis strongly supported the retention of a united Pakistan. They were therefore looked upon as a kind of fifth column by the Bangladeshi nationalists. Since 1971, some (usually younger persons) have been able to integrate and some have been sent to Pakistan or have made their own way there. While about 300,000 remain in camps awaiting transportation to Pakistan, the government of Bangladesh has given them Bangladesh citizenship, the result of a 2008 High Court ruling, and ordered the Election Commission to enroll them as voters.

Bangladesh is the only South Asian state that is unilingual; almost all Bangladeshis have Bengali as their mother tongue. The language is derived from the Magadha prakrit of Sanskrit, the most eastern of the Indo-European languages. It is written in a script that is a modification of the Sanskrit writing system and is akin to the script of Hindi. Early modern contributions to the rich Bengali literature have been mainly the product of Hindu writers, including the Nobel Prize–winner Rabindranath Tagore. More recently, Muslims have also added to the literary tradition with the works of such writers as Kazi Nazrul Islam. During the period of Sheikh Mujibur Rahman, great emphasis was placed on the Bengalization of all activity, but since then English has been revived as a key language of international communications and commerce, although it is often neglected in the state educational system. Private schools, usually enrolling the children of wealthier families, often teach in English.

EARLY HISTORY

One of the leading British historians of India said in the early part of this century: "No definite affirmation of any kind can be made about specific events in . . . Bengal before 300 BC." Since he wrote, there have been no discoveries that would change that statement. Unlike in the Indus valley in the western part of the subcontinent, where a developed civilization existed prior to the arrival of the Indo-Aryans, no archeological remains have been found to suggest the existence of a similar civilization in the lower Ganges valley. There are references to *Vanga* in early Sanskrit literature (the "b" and "v" are interchanged), and it is thought that an Indo-Aryan tribe, the Bang (or Vang), moved to the Bengal area in the beginning of the first millennium before Christ. The tribe, it is believed, gave its name to the area.

Bengal formed the eastern extremity of the empire built by Chandragupta Maurya in the fourth century BC and expanded by his grandson, Asoka, in the third century BC. A seaport (near Tamluk in West Bengal) was developed, and, in addition to its importance to trade, it may have served as the point from which Buddhism was spread to Burma, Sri Lanka, and Southeast Asia.

When the Mauryan empire collapsed shortly after the death of Asoka (c. 232 BC), Bengal was left very much on its own. Local rulers presumably held sway, although Bengal paid tribute to the Gupta empire in the fourth and fifth centuries AD. During this period, eastern Bengal was dominated by the kingdom of Samatata (the capital located near the present city of Comilla). In the seventh century, Samatata was drawn briefly into the short-lived Gupta revival empire of Harsha. In any event, during the long period from the Mauryas to Harsha, Bengal was very much a backwater as far as the rulers who dominated the northern heartland of India were concerned.

In 750, Bengal produced a dynasty that would spread its control over areas outside Bengal itself. This was the Pala dynasty, which ruled at times with difficulty until 1155. As its power moved westward, it faced challenges from other kingdoms in India that had the same goal of reconstructing the empire of Harsha. As it expanded, its base moved westward from Bengal and its capital became what is the present city of Monghyr in Bihar. The Pala capital within Bengal was Vikrampur in the neighborhood of Dhaka. The Palas were ardent Buddhists, descendants perhaps of those who had been converted from lower castes to Buddhism during the time of Asoka. As Pala power began to decline in the 11th and 12th centuries, it appeared that another group would inherit at least the Bengali portion of the empire. This came in 1155 when the last Pala (and Buddhist) ruler was overthrown by a tributary principality ruled by the Senas, a Hindu dynasty. In their brief career, the Senas worked to revive Brahmanism as the religion of Bengal, a task that alienated many of the common people who had welcomed casteless Buddhism and who would soon welcome equally casteless Islam in their aversion to the Brahmanical Hinduism of the Senas. In 1202, the last major Sena ruler was expelled from his capital at Nadia (now in West Bengal) by Muslims. Collateral branches of the Senas continued to rule for a short time in eastern Bengal, but the period of Islamic rule had begun in eastern India and would last until 1757.

ISLAMIC RULE

The Muslims had entered India in the eighth century in Sindh, but the major invasion that would change the political complexion of most of the subcontinent came at the beginning of the 11th century. Then Mahmud of Ghazni, a Turk, began a series of incursions from what is now Afghanistan. The Slave (Mamluk) dynasty was the first to rule from Delhi (1206–1290).

Ikhtiyaruddin Muhammad Bakhtiyar Khalji, representing the Ghurids (who had succeeded the Ghaznavids), attacked Bengal between 1198 and 1201, conquering Nadia in 1202. During the next 50 years, eastern Bengal would also come under control of the Slave dynasty of the Delhi Sultanate, and the surviving Sena rulers would be eliminated. Khalji established the capital of the region at Gaur, now a ruin site near Malda in West Bengal. Until Dhaka was established as the capital in 1608, Gaur and its neighbors Pandua and Tanda would serve almost continuously as the seat of government of Bengal.

Under the Khalji dynasty (1290–1320) in Delhi, Bengal remained a province of the sultanate. The sultanate reached its greatest power under the Tughluq dynasty (1320–1413), but the period also saw the beginning of the disintegration of the sultanate. During the early years of the reign of Muhammad bin Tughluq (1325–1351), the territory ruled by the sultanate reached its greatest extent, but by the time his reign ended much had been lost. Independent kingdoms were established in a number of areas, including Gujarat, the Deccan, Malwa, and Bengal.

The Bengal rebellion was begun in 1336 by Fakhruddin Mubarak Shah, who ruled the area somewhat tentatively for about 10 years. In the confused condition of Bengal, Shamsuddin Ilyas Shah came out the winner and established the Ilyas Shahi dynasty as independent rulers of Bengal. This dynasty was overthrown in 1490 by Alauddin Husain Shah. The Husain Shahi dynasty founded by him ruled until 1538.

A new force had arrived in Delhi that sought to reassemble the territories of the Delhi Sultanate and expand them. The decaying Lodhi dynasty in Delhi was defeated on 21 April 1526, at Panipat, north of Delhi, by Babar, the leader of the group that would found the Mughal Empire. Troops of his son, Humayun (reigned 1530–1540 and 1555–1556), conquered Bengal in 1538. However, Humayun faced a revolt from the Afghan Sher Shah Suri, whose troops took Bengal in 1539. Although Humayun regained the throne shortly before his death, the region of Bengal remained under the rule of the successors of Sher Shah until 1564. Bengal continued to remain separate from Delhi under a new Afghan dynasty founded by Taj Khan Karrani.

The Mughal emperor Akbar (1556–1605) brought Bengal under imperial control in 1576 when his troops defeated Daud Khan, the second and last sultan of Bengal in the Afghan dynasty. From then until 1971, when a portion of Bengal became independent, Bengal would be under the control of non-Bengal-based rulers.

Bengal became a province (*suba*) of the Mughal Empire and was ruled by a governor (*naib nazim*; later the governor was termed *nawab*) appointed from Delhi. The power exercised by the governor was dependent on the strength of the Mughal court. After the death of the emperor Aurangzeb in 1707, the empire steadily declined in power; conversely, the relative independence of the governors in Dhaka (where the capital had moved in 1608) tended to increase. Furthermore, the governorship became hereditary. The capital was moved from Dhaka to Murshidabad (now in West Bengal) in 1704.

In the 16th century, Europeans began to arrive in Bengal. The Portuguese made their first settlement in Chittagong in 1517 and added a station at Hooghly, on the river of the same name, in 1579. The Dutch arrived in 1602, followed by the British in 1650. The French and the Danes would follow. The British founded Calcutta in 1690.

So long as the governors were backed by some measure of Mughal strength, they were able to keep the Europeans in check and to regulate their activities reasonably well. In the early 18th century the system began to break down. A rebellion by Alivardi Khan, the deputy for Bihar to the governor, displaced the incumbent, and Alivardi became governor until his death in 1756. His grandson and successor, Sirajuddaulah, would see his brief rule bring the British into effective power.

THE BRITISH PERIOD

The British had become the dominant European power in India, in the south through their defeat of the French, and in Bengal through the decline of the Portuguese and the evident relative weakness of the French, the Dutch, and the Danes. The British expanded their station at Calcutta and built trading networks with the local merchants. Sirajuddaulah then attacked Calcutta on 20 June 1756 and took Fort William. According to British reports, the captured British were placed in a room (the "Black Hole") in the fort and 123 of the 146 prisoners died of suffocation. The British were determined to avenge the defeat and the deaths.

They were able to find persons in Sirajuddaulah's court, including a close relative, Mir Jafar, who would work with them. On 23 June 1757, at Plassey (Pilasi), a British force under the command of Robert Clive defeated Sirajuddaulah with the help of the treachery of Mir Jafar. Sirajuddaulah was executed on 2 July 1757; four days earlier the British recognized Mir Jafar as governor. In 1760, Mir Jafar was replaced by his son-in-law, Mir Qasim, but the latter was displaced in 1763 and Mir Jafar returned to office until his death in 1765.

In that same year, the British were granted the *diwani* (the right to collect and expend revenue) for Bengal, Bihar, and Orissa by the Mughal emperor. The Bengal government was not well organized until Warren Hastings was appointed governor in 1772. The following year, Hastings became the first governor-general of India, retaining the office of governor of Bengal and subordinating the other two major settlements, Bombay and Madras, to Calcutta. Calcutta would remain the capital of British India until 1911.

The dominance of Calcutta, however, tended to make the eastern portion of the province (the area that is now Bangladesh) a backwater. The Permanent Settlement initiated by Lord Cornwallis (governor-general, 1786–1793, and again briefly in 1805) also contributed to the slower development of eastern Bengal. Bengal under the Mughals and under the British had used a system of tax collectors (*zamindars*) who collected land tax from the *ryots* (tillers) and remitted an amount to the government after keeping a share for their services. Under the new system introduced by Cornwallis in 1793, the zamindar was recognized as owner of the land from which he had collected taxes. The ryots then, for all practical purposes, became his tenants. The system would not be fully abolished in East Bengal until after the independence of Pakistan. Most, but by no means all, of the zamindars in eastern Bengal were Hindus and most of the ryots Muslims. Gradually the zamindars became absentee landlords, and most migrated to Calcutta to participate in the development of that city, to the detriment of the rural areas of eastern Bengal.

Calcutta did indeed flourish. It became a center not only of government and commerce but also of the arts and literature and of reformist movements, leading eventually to the demand for Indian independence. Dhaka, which had ceased to be the capital in 1704, languished and saw much of its industry, especially the manufacture of Dhaka muslin, decline. Calcutta became the seat of a university in 1857; Dhaka not until 1921. As will be seen, there was a brief revival when Dhaka became a capital again after the first partition of Bengal in 1905.

The British Indian army (actually that of the British East India Company) was composed of three separate armies: Bengal, Bombay, and Madras. The troops (*sepoys*) were Indian; the officers British. There were also units of the British army stationed in India, but these were separate from the British Indian army. The British Indian army had faced several outbreaks of mutiny in the early 19th century, but these were relatively small affairs and were put down quickly.

In 1857, however, the British faced a large-scale mutiny by the Bengal army (Madras and Bombay did not join the mutineers). It broke out in Meerut on 10 May 1857, although there had been unrest elsewhere before. Delhi fell to the sepoys and eventually was recaptured. By early 1858, the mutiny was over, but two subsequent decisions would affect Bengal.

The British East India Company was formally wound up in 1858. It had been severely circumscribed by a series of acts passed by the British Parliament, beginning with the act that created the office of governor-general in 1773. In 1858, control of British India passed from the company to the British Crown. Queen Victoria (she would be designated Empress of India in 1877), in her proclamation, stated that all of her subjects would be treated equally before the law. Although this declaration was never fully implemented, it served as one step along the path of opening the system of governance to Indian participation. The governor-general would now also hold the title of viceroy.

A second outcome was the determination that India was populated by martial races and non-martial races. The Bengalis were in the latter category, as the British believed that the Bengalis were a major element among the mutineers. This meant that recruitment for the military was barred for Bengalis (except for some specialized personnel) and that the recruiting grounds moved to the northwest, primarily to the Sikhs and the Punjabi Muslims. One of the grievances of the East Pakistanis against the central government of Pakistan after independence in 1947 would be the small share of Bengalis in the military as Pakistan continued the policy of the British with but little change.

Bengal itself would be in the forefront of administrative changes made by the British. It and some other provinces saw Indians appointed to the legislative councils of the lieutenant governors under the provisions of the India Councils Act of 1861 and more under the next edition of the act in 1894. The viceroyalty of Lord Ripon (1880–1884), a liberal associate of William Gladstone, saw several changes (implemented first in Bengal), including the establishment of local boards at the subdivision level and district boards above them. Membership was elective, subject to rather strict franchise requirements. The bodies were permitted to raise and expend funds for such purposes as education and public works. Ripon also repealed the act that limited free expression in local-language newspapers and gave those newspapers equal status with those published in English. He attempted, but failed, to reform the judicial system so that Indian judges would have the same right to try Europeans as British judges did.

The Indian National Congress was founded in Bombay on 28 December 1885. The first president was a Bengali Hindu from Calcutta. For several reasons, Muslims did not associate with the Congress in large numbers. Part of this abstention came from the appeal of a leading Muslim educationist, Sir Syed Ahmad Khan, who sowed the seeds for the "Two Nation Theory" that would eventually be a source for the partition of India in 1947. Sir Syed and others who further developed the theory maintained that there was sufficient difference between the Hindus of India and the Muslims of India that they should be considered separate nations even though they inhabited the same territory. Sir Syed also feared that the departure of the British would result in a Hindu *raj* in which the Muslims would play a minor, if any, role and in which values held important by Muslims could be violated by a form of dictatorship of the majority. This theme would be replayed as Indian independence approached.

The introduction of the elective principle by Ripon through his act on local government also concerned the Muslims. Even in areas where Muslims might be a majority, they could be outvoted as a result of the stringent franchise rules, which generally involved either property ownership or educational attainments. Perhaps in no place more than eastern Bengal would the Muslims find meeting franchise qualifications so difficult.

Muslims throughout India recognized this problem. It was brought to a head when it became apparent that the viceroy, Lord Minto (viceroy, 1905–1910), and the secretary of state for India in the British cabinet, Lord Morley, were determined that further constitutional advance for India should be enacted. The Muslims would take two steps, a meeting with Minto at Simla and the formation of the Muslim League.

Before these two events occurred, however, another event of great importance for eastern Bengal took place. The governor-general/viceroy had been relieved of the direct administration of Bengal in 1854, when the province was placed under separate administration (the title for the head of the provincial government throughout India was then lieutenant governor, later to be changed to governor by the Government of India Act of 1909). Lord Curzon (viceroy, 1899–1905) determined that the large province of Bengal, which included Bihar and Orissa, was too unwieldy to be managed effectively. He partitioned the province so that Bengal itself was divided. The eastern portion of the province (roughly Bangladesh today) was joined with Assam into the province of Eastern Bengal and Assam; the remaining area became the province of (western) Bengal, which included Bihar and Orissa. Both Eastern Bengal and Assam, and Bengal had a lieutenant governor. Bengali Hindus objected to the change. In the first place, it created a Muslim majority province in the east (only one other, the Punjab in the northwest, existed at that time). With a view toward future elected governments at the provincial level, Hindus saw the danger of a Muslim raj much as Muslims saw the reverse on an all-India level. Second, those who spoke Bengali became a minority in the western province, being outnumbered by the total of the Hindi speakers of Bihar and the Oriya speakers of Orissa. Hindus reacted with measures that included violence and terrorism as well as less violent means such as a boycott of British goods. Noted Hindu Bengalis, including the poet Tagore and the future religious leader but then revolutionary Aurobindo Ghose, lent their voices and pens to the protest. The Muslims supported the partition, and Dhaka temporarily emerged from its backwater status to become a provincial capital.

The British eventually heeded the Hindu opposition and, to the great disappointment of the Muslims, revoked the partition of Bengal in 1911. The announcement was made during the imperial visit to India of King George V and Queen Mary. However, the annulment of the partition was coupled with an imperial decree transferring the capital of India from Calcutta to New Delhi. Under the new arrangement of provinces, Assam reverted to a separate status, eastern and western Bengal became the province of Bengal, and the remainder became the province of Bihar and Orissa (these two were later separated under the Government of India Act of 1935).

During the partition period, as noted earlier, the Muslims were active politically. A delegation led by the Aga Khan met Lord Minto at Simla in 1906 and proposed a system of separate electorates under which seats would be apportioned in legislative bodies between Muslims and "others" in proportion to the two groups' shares in the population. In the election, Muslims and "others" would vote separately and only for representatives of their own community. (As the system developed later, other religious groups such as Sikhs and Indian Christians would also gain separate representation and electorates.) The Muslim demand, a natural culmination of the Two Nation Theory, was incorporated into the Government of India Act of 1909 (the Morley-Minto Act). Separate electorates would continue in East Pakistan through the election of 1954.

In December 1906, a group of leading Muslims met in Dhaka at the invitation of Nawab Salimullah of Dhaka and the Aga Khan. There they founded the All-India Muslim League. The basic goals of the league were to support the Crown and to work for the interests of Muslims in India, but not to act against the interests of any other community. The league would follow an occasionally rocky path, but it would eventually lead the movement for the partition of India.

The act of 1909 established the elective principle for a portion of the provincial and national legislatures but retained most of the power in the hands of the governors and the officials. Indians began to enter the latter group as members of the Indian Civil Service; Bengali Hindus were well represented but the Muslims of the province were not. In education they continued to lag behind the Hindus.

In 1917, secretary of state for India Edwin Montagu declared that the ultimate goal of British rule in India was self-governance. After the war, this led to the act of 1919 (also called the Montagu-Chelmsford Act after the secretary of state and the viceroy). It expanded the Indian membership of the legislatures and set up a system of "dyarchy" at the provincial level. Under this system, the departments (ministries) that were related to development, such as education, health, agriculture, and public works, were placed under ministers who were responsible individually to the legislature. Departments that served the "steel-frame" method of rule (home, finance, and revenue) were headed by executive councilors who were appointed by and responsible to the governor. Several Bengali Muslims gained important experience during the period of dyarchy by serving as ministers. These included Fazlul Haq and Khwaja Nazimuddin.

The Muslim League in Bengal became more and more dominated by a group that would later be called the "national elite." This group was concerned primarily with the problems of Muslims on the broad canvas of India as a whole. Many of the group were descendants of Delhi Sultanate and Mughal Empire officials and used Urdu as a family language. Khwaja Nazimuddin (a member of the family of the Nawab of Dhaka) and the younger Husain Shahid Suhrawardy were among these, although the latter would later change his course. On the other hand, there were those of the "vernacular elite," individuals whose primary concern was the improvement of the status of the largely impoverished Muslims of Bengal, notably in the eastern region. They worked in Bengali rather than Urdu. Chief among these was Fazlul Haq, who prior to the 1937 election would form the Krishak Praja Party (KPP, Farmers' People's Party) to oppose the Muslim League in the Muslim seats and to try, with little success, to enlist peasants from the Hindu community as well. Fazlul Haq's platform was based on economic and social issues; the league's on communal matters.

The Government of India Act of 1935 confirmed the separate electorates despite strong opposition from the Indian National Congress led by Mahatma Gandhi. It also provided for fully responsible ministries in the provinces, although emergency powers were retained by the governors. Following the election of 1937, a coalition government was formed in Bengal under the prime ministership (this term was used until the independence of Pakistan and India, after which the title became chief minister) of Fazlul Haq but with support of the Muslim League and its leader, Nazimuddin.

Fazlul Haq and his fellow Muslim prime ministers from the Punjab and Assam, who were also not from the Muslim League, pledged their support to the Muslim League and Muhammad Ali Jinnah on national issues, with the understanding that provincial matters were to remain in their hands. This pledge, at Lucknow in 1937, was a boost to Jinnah, as the Muslim League had fared poorly in the 1937 election, especially in the Muslim-majority provinces. Fazlul Haq was also the author of one of several reports that condemned the behavior of Congress governments toward Muslims in the Muslim-minority provinces.

On 23 March 1940, in Lahore, the Muslim League passed a resolution often called the "Pakistan Resolution" although the word Pakistan does not appear in it. The resolution stated that if conditions for Muslims in India, especially in the Muslim minority provinces, did not improve, the Muslims would have no choice but to demand that separate states (plural, *sic*) be established as homelands for the Muslims of India. Fazlul Haq, who was a member of the Muslim League as well as leader of the KPP, was among the movers of the resolution. The acronym PAKISTAN, it should be noted, does not contain a letter for Bengal; all of the letters are derived from the northwest of India, present-day Pakistan. Fazlul Haq broke with Jinnah in 1941 over the former's membership in the viceroy's war advisory council. Haq resigned from the council as well as the league. The league withdrew its support from Haq's ministry, but he was able to continue until 1943 with Hindu assistance. In 1943, Nazimuddin set up a Muslim League ministry, which fell in early 1945 and was followed by a short period of governor's rule.

In the 1945–1946 election, Bengali Muslims voted overwhelmingly for the Muslim League, although Fazlul Haq was able to retain his own seat. Among Muslims, the league received 82 percent of the votes, the highest of any of the Muslim-majority provinces. Nazimuddin was not selected again as prime minister; the position went to Husain Shahid Suhrawardy. At his initiative, a meeting of Muslim legislators in New Delhi in 1945 decided that a single state of Pakistan should be formed rather than the two states contemplated in the Lahore resolution.

Suhrawardy waffled later and worked with some Hindus for the creation of a separate "united" Bengal as a third dominion on the subcontinent. He was prime minister during the Great Calcutta Killing in August

1946 but later worked with Gandhi to pacify the city as partition and independence approached. With almost undue haste the new viceroy, Lord Mountbatten, worked toward the end of British rule. This came on 15 August 1947—and the problems of Bengal would continue.

THE PAKISTAN PERIOD

The first independence day found the people of Bangladesh as residents of a province, East Bengal, of the dominion of Pakistan. Jinnah and the central leaders, angered at Suhrawardy's brief espousal of a united Bengal, managed his ouster from the prime ministership and replaced him with Nazimuddin, who became chief minister.

The boundaries of the new province were settled in two ways. The Assamese district of Sylhet contained a majority of Muslims. A plebiscite at the level of subdivision was held there, and four of the five subdivisions of the district voted to join Pakistan. For the division of Bengal itself, a commission headed by a British judge was appointed to determine the contiguous areas of Muslim majority. Some latitude was allowed and the final boundary did not follow precisely the contiguous area formula, but it was workable, with one major exception: the land boundary between the West Bengal district of Cooch Behar and the adjoining areas of Bangladesh remains in dispute.

It took little time for the disputes with West Pakistan that would lead to the dissolution of united Pakistan to appear. Before resuming the political history, it is best to look at these grievances. The government in Karachi seemed to Bengalis to be dominated by persons whose political activity had been either in the areas that remained in India (including Jinnah and the prime minister, Liaquat Ali Khan) or in the provinces included in West Pakistan. Originally only one Bengali, a Scheduled Caste Hindu, was included in the nine-member cabinet, although he was shortly joined by Khwaja Shahabuddin, a younger brother of Nazimuddin. His selection was clearly not from among the vernacular elite. In that group, Fazlul Haq was relegated to the post of advocate general, and Suhrawardy, who would soon join the group, remained in India, temporarily avoiding the wrath of Jinnah. With Jinnah's death in September 1948, Nazimuddin was appointed governor-general but clearly had much less influence than Jinnah. Later another person with remote connections to Bengal, Iskandar Mirza, would become in 1955 the last governor-general and in 1956 the first president of Pakistan. His connection, however, was with the family of Sirajuddaulah and Mir Jafar—the latter, of course, not held in high esteem.

It was not only in the political positions in government that the Bengalis had grievances. There were very few Muslim Bengalis in the higher civil service under the British. Consequently, few were taken into the central administration and many posts in the East Bengal provincial administration were filled by Muslims from India or West Pakistan or by reemployed British officers. Pakistan would make arrangements through preferences and quotas to attempt to redress the imbalance, but these had not even approached equality by 1971.

This imbalance was even greater in the military. As already noted, the British had practiced the doctrine of the martial races, which all but excluded Bengalis from military service. The practice, however, was continued by the independent Pakistan government: recruits still were very largely drawn from the Punjab and some districts of the Northwest Frontier Province (NWFP). An answer often given by West Pakistanis to the problem was that there was indeed no martial tradition in Bengal and there were few applicants for military positions. At the time of Bangladeshi independence there were but two Bengalis of general officer rank in the army. The issues that have been mentioned, along with the economy that will be discussed later, were important, but the one that aroused the highest emotional response was that of language. Jinnah and the other key persons in the government had determined that Urdu would be the national language of Pakistan. This decision was made in spite of Bengali being the language spoken by the majority of the people of Pakistan. Urdu is, furthermore, a language that is not native to Pakistan, its literary home being in Uttar Pradesh and Delhi in India. In addition, many of the contributors to the rich literary heritage of Urdu have been Hindus and Sikhs.

Jinnah, in March 1948, on his only visit to East Bengal after independence, declared that anyone opposing Urdu as the national language was an "enemy" of Pakistan. His views were supported by the then chief minister, Nazimuddin, but they were widely rejected by the Bengalis. The eventual downfall of the Muslim League can, in large measure, be attributed to this position of Nazimuddin and his ministry. The agitation continued and culminated in the demonstrations held in Dhaka in February 1952. On 21 February, several students were killed by the police. The day is still remembered as Martyrs' Day in Bangladesh. In recognition of the event UNESCO in November 1999 proclaimed 21 February as International Mother Language Day. Eventually, in September 1954, the constituent assembly of Pakistan decided that "Urdu and Bengali and such other languages as may be declared" shall be the "official languages of the Republic." It added that English would also be used as long as necessary. Although the language issue was decided in a manner acceptable to the Bengalis, it and the other grievances left a record that would fester and grow into the autonomy and then independence movements that would destroy the unity of Pakistan.

Pakistan took an inordinately long time in framing its constitution, being governed in the meantime by the Government of India Act of 1935 as amended by the India Independence Act of 1947, both acts of the British Parliament. These were acts that continued and preserved a viceregal form of government, one in which the governor-general would have ultimate power, as the viceroy had before 1947. That is, this would be the system unless the governor-general were a Bengali. During Nazimuddin's tenure (1948–1951), the locus of power moved to the prime minister, Liaquat Ali Khan. When Liaquat was assassinated in 1951, Nazimuddin stepped down from the governor-generalship to become prime minister himself. The new governor-general, Ghulam Muhammad, a civil servant before independence, dismissed Nazimuddin in 1953 without permitting the prime minister to test his support in the constituent assembly. Other Bengalis (Muhammad Ali Bogra, 1953–1955, and Suhrawardy, 1956–1957) would be prime ministers, but their power was subject to the whim of the governor-general. Iskander Mirza replaced Ghulam Muhammad as governor-general in 1955 and became the first president in 1956 when the constitution was adopted. He had a Bengali connection in that he was a relative of the family of the nawabs of Murshidabad.

A constitution for Pakistan was finally passed and became effective on 23 March 1956. However, it required the Bengalis to sacrifice their numerical majority in the population and agree to parity in the national parliament. There would be 300 members, 150 from each wing of Pakistan. The votes of Bengalis therefore counted for less than the votes of West Pakistanis. In an act passed prior to the constitution, West Pakistan (a term we have been using) was formally created by the merger of the provinces in the west wing. (The name of the east wing was changed from East Bengal to East Pakistan at the same time.) The creation of two provinces with equality in the parliament was the outcome of these actions. Bengal, led by Suhrawardy, was willing at the time to pay that price if similar parity could be achieved in other areas, including economic development and government employment. They were to be disappointed.

Before the constitution was passed, an election had been held in East Bengal. The position on the language issue was one factor in the growing discontent with the Muslim League. In 1949, Suhrawardy, returning from India, launched a new political party, which would become the Awami League. It was to be a non-communal party open to all residents of Pakistan. Meanwhile, Fazlul Haq had revived his earlier party under a slightly different name, the Krishak Sramik Party (KSP, Peasants' and Workers' party, but non-Marxist, unlike some other parties that have used a similar name). These two parties represented the vernacular elite. They decided to contest the 1954 election to the East Bengal legislative assembly as the United Front. The Muslim League was trounced; even Chief Minister Nurul Amin lost his seat.

The 21-point platform of the United Front was directed largely at provincial issues. A key matter was the recognition of Bengali as an official language of Pakistan. Foreshadowing the later Six-Point Program of Mujibur Rahman was a demand for provincial autonomy except in matters of foreign affairs, defense, and currency. There were also points regarding free trade with and travel to India, a newly and directly elected constituent assembly, and freedom of trade in jute.

Suhrawardy directed his attention to national affairs. He departed for Karachi and joined the cabinet of Muhammad Ali Bogra, who was then prime minister, also from East Bengal, but a Muslim Leaguer. Suhrawardy became prime minister in 1956. He had key lieutenants in Dhaka, notably Ataur Rahman Khan, who eventually became chief minister, and Sheikh Mujibur Rahman, the key party organizer. He also associated with Maulana Abdul Hamid Khan Bhashani, a leftist religious leader with whom he would split in 1957. Fazlul Haq and his KSP tended to look more toward the provincial arena. He became chief minister briefly in 1954, but the central government intervened and there was a period of governor's rule. Fazlul Haq had made some remarks during a visit to Calcutta that Karachi interpreted as treasonous in the sense that Fazlul Haq had referred generally to the unity of Bengalis.

By the time parliamentary government was restored in East Pakistan in 1956, the United Front had split, and the KSP held a slight edge in the provincial assembly. KSP leader Abu Husain Sarkar became chief minister. Fazlul Haq was named governor. The next two years saw the provincial assembly serve as a battleground between the Awami League and the KSP for control of the East Pakistan government. In 1956 Ataur Rahman Khan became chief minister over the opposition of Governor Fazlul Haq with the support of the central government, now headed by Prime Minister Suhrawardy. By 1958, the tussle became more complicated, with a split in the Awami League (see below) and changes in both the governorship and the prime ministership. As Pakistan moved toward military intervention, both Sarkar and Abdur Rahman Khan held the chief ministership during 1958. Turmoil on the streets moved into the assembly house itself to the extent that the deputy speaker died from wounds received on the floor of the assembly.

Meanwhile, as noted earlier, the language issue had been settled, West Pakistan had been unified, and a constitution had become effective on 23 March 1956. It was expected that elections would be held in 1958. Here again, the differences between East and West Pakistan were evident. West Pakistan favored the continuance of separate electorates (which Pakistan under Zia ul-Haq reinstated) on the grounds that these would reinforce the Two Nation Theory. East Pakistan—and here the Awami League and the KSP agreed—favored joint electorates in which there would be no distinction among communities. Their reasoning was fairly straightforward: Muslim votes might be split between the Muslim League and the Awami League, but Hindus (then about 20 percent of East Pakistan) would surely not vote for the Muslim League, a party they were not even permitted to join, and they would therefore be likely to support one of the members of the United Front, ensuring victory for the Front. It was decided in Karachi that each province could frame its own election law. It mattered little, for the elections were not held.

It has been mentioned earlier that Suhrawardy and Bhashani split. Bhashani disagreed with what he believed was a pro-West and pro-market economic stance by Suhrawardy. Bhashani withdrew from the Awami League in 1957 to form the National Awami Party with his followers and with some groups from West Pakistan. Several members of the provincial assembly followed him, and these would hold the balance in the body (as they did also in West Pakistan). The jockeying between Sarkar and Abdur Rahman Khan was complicated by the presence of this small but critical group.

On 7 October 1958, president Iskandar Mirza dismissed the parliament and the two provincial assemblies and the cabinets of Firoz Khan Noon at the center and those in the provinces and proclaimed martial law. Named as chief martial law administrator was General Muhammad Ayub Khan, the army commander in chief. On 28 October, Ayub dismissed Mirza and assumed the presidency himself.

Although the ending of the parliamentary era was initially welcomed as a relief from the tumultuous politics preceding martial law, it soon became a burden for East Pakistan. Many key oppositionists, including Suhrawardy, Mujib, and Fazlul Haq, were deprived of their political rights or jailed. Suhrawardy died in 1963, and the leadership of the Awami League in East Pakistan was taken by Mujibur Rahman. Ataur Rahman Khan eventually left the Awami League to form a splinter party. Fazlul Haq died in 1962, and his party has not since been a factor in East Pakistan or Bangladesh. Nazimuddin returned to politics to lead the Council Muslim League (CML) and the Combined Opposition Parties (COP) group, but he died in 1964. The COP opposed Ayub's reelection in 1965, nominating Jinnah's sister, Fatima, but Ayub won handily in West Pakistan and by a small majority in East Pakistan.

Ayub's newly proclaimed constitution of 1962 changed the electoral system. His form of local government, basic democracy, was based on earlier systems in that locally and directly elected members of the councils were given local administrative and development duties. The new element was that the union councilors would also serve as members of an electoral college for election of the president and the members of the national and provincial assemblies. There were 80,000 councilors, 40,000 in each province. It was clearly easier to control such a small number than the entire electorate. The Electoral College function came under constant attack from the opposition, which favored a system of direct elections by the entire electorate at all levels of government.

Ayub also envisaged a system that would be non-party. The first elections in 1962 to the national and provincial assemblies were held on this basis. But no sooner had the assemblies convened than parties were formed in them. Ayub, yielding to the inevitable, then convened a session of a party that would support him. This party became the Pakistan Muslim League (Convention). Other Muslim Leaguers formed an opposition group, the Council Muslim League. Still other parties began to function again, including, in East Pakistan, the Awami League led by Mujib, and the National Awami Party led by Bhashani.

After his reelection in 1965, Ayub's stock began to fall, for a number of reasons. Bengalis objected to the war with India in 1965 over Kashmir as, in their view, it left East Pakistan defenseless. The economy also turned downward and Ayub's health deteriorated. The upshot was a strong opposition move against him spearheaded by the newly formed People's Party of Pakistan (PPP) headed by Zulfiqar Ali Bhutto in West Pakistan and by the Awami League in East Pakistan.

In early 1966, Mujib had proclaimed a platform of Six Points. These were: (1) a federal government, parliamentary in form, with free and regular elections; (2) federal government control over only foreign affairs and defense; (3) a separate currency or separate accounts for each wing to prevent the movement of capital from the east to the west; (4) taxation only at the provincial level, with grants from the provinces to support the federal government; (5) the right of each province to enter into international trade agreements on its own initiative; and (6) each province could raise a militia. The key provision was not the last but the fourth: without a source of revenue under its own control, the federal government would be subject to the whim of either provincial government.

In the face of increasing demonstrations, Ayub resigned on 25 March 1969 and turned the government over to the commander in chief of the army, General Agha Muhammad Yahya Khan, who proclaimed martial law. Yahya promised to hold elections and did so in December 1970. The election rules for the national assembly scrapped both the system of separate electorates and the system of parity: of the 300 directly elected seats, East Pakistan would have 162 and West Pakistan 138. The election results displayed the polarity between the two wings. In East Pakistan, the Awami League won 160 of the 162; in West Pakistan, the PPP won 81 of 138. Neither party won seats in the other wing.

Yahya opened talks with both Bhutto and Mujib with a view toward forming a government agreeable to each and toward cooperating in the framing of a new constitution. With mounting pressure from his supporters, Mujib was forced to stand firmly on the Six Points as a basis for the constitution. This was adamantly opposed by both Yahya and Bhutto. Violent demonstrations began in East Pakistan. At the same time, Yahya increased greatly the number of troops (almost all of West Pakistani origin) in the east wing. No agreement was possible. Yahya ordered the troops into action against the Bengalis on 25 March 1971. Mujib was arrested and taken to West Pakistan, many Bengalis were killed in the initial assaults, and other Bengalis fled to regroup in India to become the government-in-exile and the Mukti Bahini (the national army). The Mukti Bahini fought a tenacious guerrilla war against the larger and far better equipped Pakistani army and by summer appeared to be getting the better of the struggle. India provided a haven and supplies and entered the war directly in late November. On 16 December, Dhaka fell to the forces of the Mukti Bahini and the Indians and Bangladesh became independent. Beyond the trauma associated with the end of the political system of united Pakistan and the damage to its economic system, the sheer magnitude of the loss of human lives in East Pakistan approached the dimensions of a holocaust. An estimate by *The National Geographic* (September 1972) placed the death toll in East Pakistan at about three million.

INDEPENDENT BANGLADESH

Sheikh Mujibur Rahman returned to a war-weary and badly damaged, but independent, Bangladesh on 10 January 1972, completing a process that started on 25 March 1971 when he was transferred by Yahya to West Pakistan and put in jail. Earlier, Bhutto, who took over the reign of Pakistan, under international pressure freed Mujib, who became prime minister of Bangladesh in an Awami League government. A constitution based on a parliamentary system became effective on 16 December 1972. It also enshrined the four principles of Mujibbad (Mujibism): nationalism, secularism, democracy, and socialism.

Mujib's associates in the cabinet had little experience in governing; they had been oppositionists during the 13 years of Ayub and Yahya. The transposition was not an easy task. Furthermore, the Bengali members of the Civil Service of Pakistan were often viewed almost as enemies during that period. Some had quickly joined the exile government, and many had remained at their posts in Dhaka. Some were posted in West Pakistan at the time the conflict began and were interned there. The military saw a similar division, although very few stayed at Pakistani posts in East Pakistan. Yet the work of government required personnel. Many persons were brought into the administration who had not taken or passed the entrance examinations; many of them were failures. When the repatriation of those detained in Pakistan took place in 1973, there was hesitation on the part of the Mujib government about reinstating them in the civil or military services. Bangladesh therefore suffered from poor administration as well as the vast problems of reconstruction and the food shortages, which peaked in 1974.

Opposition to Mujib began to increase as the problems mounted. Rapid nationalization of much industry caused severe setbacks in production. Corruption became a common occurrence. Although the Awami League won widely in the parliamentary election held in 1973 (292 of 300 directly elected seats), this did not confer legitimacy on what was seen by many as a failing and inefficient government. It was also said that the election was rigged, an allegation that was probably correct.

To meet the criticism, Mujib drew back from one of his pillars, democracy. On 25 January 1975, the constitution was amended to create a presidential system with Mujib as president and almost all power in his hands. On 6 June 1975, Bangladesh became a one-party state with the Mujib-led Bangladesh Krishak Sramik Awami League (BAKSAL) as the sole legal political grouping. The name was intended to combine the heritage of Fazlul Haq's Krishak Sramik Party and Suhrawardy's Awami League.

On 15 August 1975, a group of army officers, mostly majors, assassinated Mujib and much of his family (a daughter, Sheikh Hasina Wajid, was abroad and escaped to lead the Awami League later; see below). The majors chose a member of Mujib's cabinet, Khondakar Mushtaque Ahmad, to be president. Mushtaque promised new elections, abolished BAKSAL, and said he would work to restore democracy and faith in the government. However, he remained very much the tool of the majors.

The three days of 3–5 November 1975 were ones of utter confusion in Dhaka. A rebellion took place under the leadership of Brigadier Khalid Musharaf, who pledged to restore Mujibism. This uprising was put down by the main units of the army, many of which supported Major General Ziaur Rahman (Zia). Mushtaque resigned, was asked to return, but refused. Chief Justice A. S. M. Sayem became president and chief martial law administrator (CMLA). The key and rising person was Zia.

Zia became CMLA on 30 November 1976, while Sayem remained president. However, Sayem resigned the presidency on grounds of ill health and Zia became president on 21 April 1977. On 30 May, he held a referendum on his continuance in office, and although he gained overwhelming approval, it did not provide legitimacy for him because no alternative was presented. Having announced a new program (see below), he held a contested election on 3 June 1978. The major contenders were two who had played key roles in the civil war: Zia had commanded a unit of the Mukti Bahini and had, in fact, declared the independence of Bangladesh on 28 March 1971; his opponent, General M. A. G. Osmany, a retired Pakistani officer (as a colonel) had been the commander of the Mukti Bahini and later minister of defense. Zia was backed by the newly formed Jatiyatabadi Ganotantrik Dal (JAGODAL, the National Democratic Party); Osmany by a coalition among which the Awami League was most prominent. Zia's party was formally led by Justice Abdus Sattar, who was appointed vice president on the day of the election. Zia won with 76.7 percent of the vote to Osmany's 21.7 percent, the balance going to minor candidates.

Zia, looked upon as almost a fish out of water when he first gained power, developed into a charismatic leader. He traveled extensively, preaching his program of self-reliance to get development moving in Bangladesh. The key aspects of his Nineteen Points Program were increased food production and family planning, goals which were important for president Hussain Muhammad Ershad as well. Zia began to open up the political system and to curtail the socialist program of the Mujib period. A parliamentary election was held in February 1979. Zia's party, expanded and renamed the Bangladesh Jatiyatibadi Party (Bangladesh Nationalist Party—BNP) won 207 of the 300 seats in a poll generally judged as fair. The larger faction of a then divided Awami League won 39 seats and the revived Muslim League 20. Mashiur Rahman, who had been expected to become prime minister, died suddenly, and the post was given to Shah Azizur Rahman.

There were other accomplishments and some failures of the Zia regime. Among the former was his championing of the concept of cooperation among the countries of South Asia. He visited the other countries in the region, and eventually, after his death, seven countries (the others being India, Pakistan, Sri Lanka, Nepal, Bhutan, and the Maldives) agreed in New Delhi in August 1983 to form what is today called the South Asian Association for Regional Cooperation (SAARC). A summit meeting in Dhaka in December 1985 ratified the formation of SAARC. Annual summits have been held in the other capitals, and a permanent secretariat has been established in Kathmandu, Nepal.

On the other hand, Zia failed to establish his system firmly. It was dependent on him. When he was assassinated on 30 May 1981, he was succeeded by the aging vice president, Abdus Sattar, temporarily. The constitution required a new election. Infighting in the BNP did not permit the choice of a younger candidate. Sattar ran in the 15 November 1981 election and won, defeating his principal opponent, Kamal Hossain of the Awami League, by a margin of 65.5 percent to 26.0 percent.

Sattar's term turned out to be only an interlude. He was challenged by the army chief of staff, Hussain Muhammad Ershad, who took deserved credit for quelling the insurrection in which Zia was assassinated. Ershad called for the cleaning up of the corruption that undoubtedly existed but, more importantly, also demanded a regularized role for the military in the governance of the country. He asked specifically for a national security council, which would be dominated by the military. Sattar did reshuffle his cabinet but refused to accept the council. Ershad overthrew Sattar on 24 March 1982.

Ershad's martial law period was not as successful as Zia's in returning the country to some type of representative government. He did not assume the presidency until 11 December 1983. He also used the referendum pattern to gain support for himself and his program. He won what was reported to be a huge majority in the March 1985 poll, but most observers felt that the voting was rigged. His opposition clustered in three groups. The largest was a coalition led by the Awami League, headed by Sheikh Hasina Wajid (a daughter of Sheikh Mujibur Rahman). Another group coalesced around the BNP, led by Khaleda Zia, the widow of Ziaur Rahman. Much less important was a cluster around former president Mushtaque Ahmad, and some leftist and Islamic fundamentalist groupings. Ershad made a number of concessions and finally was able to convince the Awami League–led coalition to participate in elections in which it and Ershad's party, the Jatiya Dal, were the major contenders. The May 1986 election resulted in a slim majority of the 300 seats for the Jatiya Dal, with about 100 seats going to the Awami League and its allies. There were many reports of rigging and some switching of parties by winners so that the final party totals remained in some doubt. The BNP-led group boycotted the election.

Parliament first met briefly to hustle through a bill that would grant immunity to Ershad and his government for any acts taken during martial law. Hasina and her group boycotted that session. In the fall of 1986, she officially became leader of the opposition and began to participate, but the parting of ways between Ershad and Sheikh Hasina was soon to come.

Ershad had revamped the local government system, elevating the former subdivisions to the status of districts in a move intended to gain greater popular participation in development and, not incidentally, support for him and his Jatiya Party, as the Jatiya Dal had been renamed. His proposal to include military personnel in the councils was scuttled in the summer of 1987 by wide-scale demonstrations.

The success of these demonstrations apparently whetted the appetite of the opposition, for major demonstrations began in November 1987. Hasina had withdrawn her party from parliament. On 6 December 1987, Ershad dissolved parliament, having declared a state of emergency about two weeks earlier. New elections were held on 3 March 1988, but both the BNP and the Awami League boycotted them along with the smaller opposition groups. The Jatiya Party of Ershad won about 250 of the 300 seats, and Ershad appointed Moudud Ahmed as prime minister and Kazi Zafar Ahmad as his deputy. An amendment to the constitution was passed declaring that Islam was the state religion of Bangladesh but adding that other religions were free to practice their beliefs. Ershad went no further than this in creating an Islamic state.

Complaints by the opposition continued and reached their peak in the fall of 1990. Some changes were made in the Jatiya Party command structure: Moudud Ahmed was advanced to vice president and Kazi Zafar Ahmad was made prime minister. Ershad decreed that the vice president, previously appointed, would hereafter be elected jointly with the president. In March 1990, elections were held at the *upazila* (subdistrict) level and the Jatiya Party secured control of a bare majority; it was not a good sign to the party for future elections.

By October and November 1990, demonstrations against Ershad were so widespread that he resigned the presidency on 4 December (to be effective 8 December) and appointed Chief Justice Shahabuddin Ahmed as vice president so that he would become acting president when Ershad's resignation became effective. A factor in Ershad's fall was that the army seemed unwilling to support him. Shahabuddin Ahmed had, in effect, one task: to hold "free and fair" elections under a neutral caretaker government led by him. This he did in March 1991. Including the women's seats, the BNP achieved a small majority. Khaleda Zia became prime minister, but in a presidential system.

Ershad, who never approached the charismatic role of either Mujib or Zia, nonetheless accomplished a number of things in his presidency. Food production increased markedly and the effectiveness of family planning improved substantially, as did health delivery. He greatly extended the program of privatization and worked to open the economy of Bangladesh. Unfortunately for him, his aversion to democracy and the corruption of his government (allegedly touching him) were heavy factors on the negative side.

A NEW DEMOCRATIC SYSTEM

The Awami League's campaign called for the restoration of the parliamentary system; the BNP preferred a presidential system. However, after looking carefully at the election results, the BNP saw clearly that winning a presidential election on the basis of a popular vote was anything but a sure thing. The BNP switched its view and supported a constitutional amendment changing to a parliamentary system with a ceremonial president. With the amendment passed, Khaleda became "head of government," and Abdur Rahman Biswas was elected president and "head of state" by the parliament (not the people at large).

The path for Khaleda and the BNP was not easy. On 5 May 1994, the opposition began a boycott of parliament as it demanded a constitutional amendment that would require the resignation of the government and the appointment of a neutral caretaker government to conduct the elections. The boycott was followed by the mass resignation from parliament of the opposition on 28 December 1994. As a result of legal maneuvers, the resignations did not become effective until 20 June 1995.

The ferment initiated by the Awami League led by Sheikh Hasina Wajid has come to be called *hartal* (general strike) politics. Strikes were held frequently and often lasted for several days, disrupting the economy as well as the day-to-day lives of the citizens. Hartal meant the total cessation of work and transport and the closing of shops. Often violence occurred between supporters of the two principal parties and between the police and the demonstrators. Hartal politics would continue during the period Hasina was prime minister, although at a lower level. Now that Khaleda has returned as prime minister, Awami League hartals again plague the country, as did a boycott of the parliament by the Awami League that has now ended.

As the opposition said it would not participate in by-elections for the vacant seats, Khaleda was forced to ask for the dissolution of parliament on 24 November 1995. A new general election was held on 15 February 1996. As the opposition again refused to participate, the election was a farce in which the BNP won almost all seats. However, the new parliament passed a constitutional amendment that provided for a neutral government to conduct elections in the future, thereby meeting the demand of the Awami League. That done, the parliament was dissolved once again and a new election under a neutral caretaker government was held on 12 June 1996. The Awami League and others had stated that they did not trust the outgoing government to conduct the elections, as is the rule in most parliamentary systems. Despite this, the BNP government performed quite well in the economic sphere.

In the 12 June election, the Awami League fell just short of a majority of the seats, but it was able to form a government with the participation of the Jatiya Party in a coalition. This government headed by Hasina was able to serve its five-year term in full. The strong opposition used occasional boycotts and hartal politics in an attempt to unseat the government. Sheikh Hasina expended much energy on the glorification of her father, Sheikh Mujibur Rahman, known as Bangabandhu (literally, the friend of the Bengalis, but often said to mean the father of the country). In this, she had those accused of murdering Mujib placed on trial; most were convicted. The disruption that occurred during this government, as in the previous one, meant that little positive legislation was initiated and the economy remained in the doldrums.

With the expiry of Hasina's term, a new neutral caretaker government was formed to hold an election in October 2001. In what was clearly a repudiation of Hasina and the Awami League, a four-party alliance headed by the BNP won two-thirds of the seats in parliament and formed a new government headed by Khaleda Zia. The other members of the alliance were a faction of the disintegrating Jatiya Party, the Jama'at-i-Islami, and a small Islamic party. The Awami League, claiming election irregularities, boycotted the parliament. Their parliamentary participation was slim but their street agitation increased annually, especially after the passage of the constitution (14th Amendment) of May 2004. This amendment was viewed by the Awami League as a means of fixing future elections by ensuring that the chief adviser of the next caretaker government was a BNP supporter.

The BNP government, while winning a two-thirds parliamentary majority, managed to self-destruct. A power struggle between the younger members and the senior members of the party led to the resignation of President Badrudozza, a BNP founding member. The growth of militancy in the country, assassinations of key Awami League figures, and assassination attempts on the life of Sheikh Hasina coupled with the inability or unwillingness to pursue the perpetrators of these acts severely weakened the government's ability to function. Corruption that had become common in the public sector climbed to an unprecedented degree during the BNP rule and only became evident after the establishment of the caretaker government of Fakhruddin Ahmed further reduced the effectiveness of the BNP government.

The shenanigans around the selection of the chief adviser after BNP ended its five-year term in October 2006 caused president Iajuddin Ahmed to declare himself the chief adviser of the caretaker government that was itself questionable. Some political sanity was restored when, with the assistance of the Bangladesh armed forces, a state of emergency was declared in January 2007. A new caretaker government led by Fakhruddin Ahmed came to power and instead of tasking itself with holding a parliamentary election within 90 days, it gave itself two years to level the playing field. The Fakhruddin government made a number of significant changes between 2007 and the election of December 2008 that bode well for democracy. First the Election Commission was made independent and a new electronic voter list with photographs was prepared that allowed for a transparent election process to be established. Over 80 million voters were registered. Major changes were also made to political party registration and the code of conduct of individuals.

Second, an independent Anti-corruption Commission (ACC) actively pursued corruption in the higher echelons of the political process. The judiciary was separated from the executive branch and intensive effort was made to curb militancy in Bangladesh.

The end result was a smooth, free, and fair ninth parliamentary election. Once again the people of Bangladesh showed their maturity by switching their votes to support the Awami League and to punish the BNP for its mismanagement of the trust of the people. The supermajority that the Awami League obtained in December 2008 permitted it to form the government in 2009 with Sheikh Hasina as prime minister.

ECONOMY

In terms of per capita gross national product (GNP), Bangladesh is among the poorest nations of the world. According to data collected by the World Bank for 2001, GDP per capita was $1,570, calculated on the purchasing power parity (PPP) system. GDP per capita grew to as high as $2,300 in 2007 but went down to $1,400 in 2008. The total GDP in current prices for 1980 was $19.5 billion and is estimated to be $80.5 billion in 2008. Equity, as measured by income distribution for 2000, showed that the highest quintile received 42.8 percent of income, the second quintile received 20.8 percent, the third quintile 15.7 percent, the fourth quintile 12 percent, and the lowest quintile only 8.7 percent. Thus the income levels are very highly skewed. It is therefore not surprising that the number of persons living in poverty is 35.6 percent as reported in a 1995–1996 survey. Poverty is much greater in rural areas (39.8 percent) than in urban areas (14.3 percent). A study in 2000 reported that 36 percent of the population has a standard of living of less than $1 a day and 82.8 percent has a standard of living of less than $2 a day. Agriculture employs 63 percent of the labor force, industry 12 percent, and services 25 percent according to 2001 data. However, the higher rate of poverty in rural areas is clearly indicated by output information (contribution to GNP) data: agriculture contributes 21 percent, industry 27 percent (of which manufacturing accounts for 17 percent), and services 52 percent. Figures for 2007 show that the contribution of agriculture has gone down to 19 percent, while industrial and service contributions have gone up by 1.5 percent each.

The economy, so far as the high proportion of the population is concerned, is very much based on agriculture. For domestic consumption the key is rice; for export it was jute, a fiber used in such products as burlap and carpeting (as backing), but one that has a diminishing market, largely resulting from the development of synthetic fibers. The products are grown on very small plots of land. It is likely that with the "go green" renewable and sustainable development thrust of the 21st century jute will recapture a larger global market. According to the 1977 agricultural census, only 1.0 percent of Bangladeshi farmers owned more than 15 acres, and this group collectively held only 11.19 percent of the cultivated land. In 1983–84 those holding more than 15 acres fell to less than 0.06 percent and only 8.17 percent of cultivated land. The average farm holding among those who held land in 1993 was 2.2 acres, but when the landless are factored into this calculation the average holding is much less. The landless, if they have no other regular occupation, are dependent for income, in cash and kind, on farm labor opportunities. Of those who hold land by ownership or rental, 58.3 percent own all the land they till; about 0.5 percent rent all the land they farm. As the inheritance laws of both Hindus and Muslims tend to lead to rapid fragmentation of land holdings, the average 3.5-acre holding does not usually exist in a single consolidated piece. The 1977 census showed that most holdings contain six to nine fragments, and about 10 percent contain 20 or more. In 1996, farm holdings, as a percent of total holdings, were 66.0 percent, while non-farm holdings were 34 percent. Small farm holdings, anywhere between 2.49 acres to less than 0.05, are 80 percent of total holdings. Medium farms are approximately 18 percent and large farm holdings are 2.52 percent. Landless households are those with less than 0.2 hectares of land. Landless households were 46 percent in 1988 and increased to 49.6 percent in 1995. Nearly half of all rural households are considered landless and out of a total of 14 million agricultural households, 11 million possess no more than 0.05 hectares. In 1977, 55 percent of the land was single-cropped, while 38 percent was double-cropped and 7 percent was triple-cropped. By 2002–2003, only 36 percent was single-cropped, 51 percent was double-cropped, and 13 percent was triple-cropped. Irrigation is the key to multiple cropping. In 1977 about 30 percent of the holdings reported using irrigation water, covering about 31 percent of the cropped area. In 2003, 58 percent of net cropped area was irrigated.

Campaigns to intensify production, especially of rice, have had a major effect. Damage to the economic system resulting from the war of independence meant that the pre-war level of rice production was not reached until the 1973–1974 crop year. New seed research and application and more extensive use of fertilizers increased rice production. In the 10-year period from 1983–1984 to 1993–1994, rice production rose from 14 million tons to more than 18 million tons. By 2003–2004 the production of rice further rose to 26 million tons, leading to claims of a high degree of self-sufficiency in food production. Nonetheless, the production of this staple averages only about one pound per person per day and, even assuming equitable distribution, this means a nutritional deficiency. One more recent development is the expansion of wheat production, a cereal that was generally shunned by Bangladeshis during the Pakistan era. The 1977 agricultural census reported that 51 percent of landholders used chemical fertilizers, but also that this figure accounted for only 29 percent of the land. Between 1984–1985 and 1999–2000 fertilizer consumption went up from 1.2 million metric tons to 2.8 million metric tons. During the same period pesticide consumption went up from 7,000 metric tons to over 15,000 metric tons.

Industrial growth has been inhibited by a lack of raw materials, an untrained labor force, a shortage of investment capital, an early policy of nationalization, frequent periods of political instability, and a high level of corruption. More recently, the government has privatized some industrial units and has enacted a more liberal investment policy for both foreign and domestic investors, but so far this has had little effect on investment patterns. The failure of nationalized units to perform well, a situation often caused by mismanagement by government appointees, led the government to shut down the largest nationalized unit, Adamjee Jute Mill, in 2002. One sector that has shown remarkable growth is the manufacture of garments primarily for export; garments are a significant element in the export pattern of Bangladesh. Today the garment sector accounts for about 75 percent of the total export of Bangladesh, bringing about $10 billion to the economy. There has been some international criticism of employers in the garment industry in that they may be using minors in the workforce, although a report by the U.S. Department of State held that by the end of 2001 the use of child labor in the garment industry had been virtually eliminated.

A significant source of foreign exchange has been remittances from Bangladeshi workers in the Middle East. This has to a degree created shortages of trained personnel in the industrial and service fields. In 2001, external remittance was 1 percent of GDP, rising to 9 percent in 2008, when it contributed $10 billion to the Bangladesh economy. Over 800,000 Bangladeshi workers are in the international labor force.

Meanwhile the infrastructure is weak. The division of the country by rivers has made the linking of electrical and gas grids and road and rail transport lines difficult, although this has been overcome to some extent by the opening of a bridge over the Jamuna River. The rail system is outdated and the highway system is overcrowded and badly in need of repair and expansion. A proposal to build a beltway around Dhaka, if ever carried out, would make traveling to and from Chittagong to inland cities much more manageable than going, as now, through the heart of the capital. While there is extensive use of the river system for the movement of people and goods, heavy goods cannot safely be transported on small boats and the monsoon season disrupts river travel.

The future of the Bangladesh economy, particularly in view of the steadily growing population, is not bright. Bangladesh has an external debt of $20 billion and imports nearly 30 percent more than it exports. Even though the World Bank and the International Monetary Fund figures show that the economy grew at about 4.5 percent a year in the period 2002–2007, this, if correct, is well short of the 7 to 8 percent that the same organizations say is needed to pull Bangladesh out of its severe poverty. The International Monetary Fund estimates that in 2008 the growth rate for Bangladesh will be 6.9 percent and projects that the growth rate for 2009 will be 4.9 percent. Despite these estimations and projections, there are some hopeful signs that Bangladesh may be able to overcome some chronic development challenges. Mortality rate among children under five has dropped from 148 per 1,000 in 1990 to 73 in 2005. Fifty-three percent of the urban population of Bangladesh has access to improved sanitation and 74 percent of the total population has access to safe water, although arsenic poisoning is a major health issue.

Earlier in this introduction, the four principles of Sheikh Mujibur Rahman were mentioned: nationalism, secularism, democracy, and socialism. Nationalism remains strong and is unlikely to decrease.

Secularism has been dented by introducing some rather mild Islamic concepts into the constitution. Democracy is being hindered by the inability of the opposition to become a "loyal opposition" and by the failure of the governing coalition to accept the opposition as a potential partner in furthering the interests of the country. Socialism is no longer a major political goal but economic development still tends to be shortchanged.

Still, the future of democracy is safe, although the pace is slow. The changes made in 2007–2008 and the parliamentary election of December 2008 stabilized the democratic process. A market economy is emerging, but it needs significant facilitation by the public sector.

The Dictionary

– A –

ABDUL GHANI MIAN, NAWAB SIR KHWAJA (?–1896). A member of the **Nawab of Dhaka family**, he served as a member of the Bengal Legislative Council in 1866 and as a member of the legislative council of the governor-general. He is best remembered for donating the first waterworks in **Dhaka**. Abdul Ghani was succeeded as nawab by his son Nawab Khwaja **Ahsanullah Khan**.

ABDUL HAMID (1886–1963). Born in **Sylhet** district (then in **Assam**), he was a member of the Assam Legislative Council, 1924–1937, and served in various ministerial positions, 1929–1937. He was deputy leader of the **Muslim League** in the Assam Legislative Assembly from 1937 to partition, and he strongly supported the Pakistani position in the Sylhet plebiscite, which resulted in the transfer of most of Sylhet district to **East Bengal**. Abdul Hamid was minister of education in the Muslim League East Bengal government until its fall in the 1954 provincial election. *See also* SYLHET REFERENDUM.

ABDUL KARIM, MAULVI (1863–1943). A prominent educationist and **Muslim League** politician, he entered politics after serving in the Bengal Presidency Education Department. Abdul Karim was president of the Bengal Muslim League and a member of the Council of State and Bengal Legislative Council, 1926–1937.

ABDUL LATIF, NAWAB (1828–1893). A leading Muslim intellectual figure in **Kolkata** in the 19th century, a period when Muslims lagged well behind Hindus in **education**. He was an educationist, author, and later prime minister of the princely state of Bhopal in

1

Central India (1885–1886). Abdul Latif was born in Faridpur district and studied in **Calcutta**. He taught for some time and was then appointed deputy magistrate in 1849. He served in a number of positions, including presidency magistrate, before retiring in 1887. Abdul Latif was a member of the Bengal Legislative Council, 1862–1864 and 1870–1874. He was the founder of the Mohammadan Literary and Scientific Society in 1863, the goal of which was the education of Muslims and the dissemination of Western knowledge. Abdul Latif worked with Sir Syed Ahmed Khan to found the Muslim Anglo-Oriental College (now Aligarh Muslim University) and agreed with Sir Syed that Muslims would fare best under British rule in the face of the large Hindu majority in India. He was also a founder of the Central Mohammedan Association. *See also* AMIR ALI, SYED.

ABDUR RAHIM, SIR (1867–1947). A prominent Bengali Muslim political and legal figure. He was born in Midnapur, where his father was posted as deputy collector. He attended Presidency College and was later called to the bar from the Middle Temple in London in 1890. Abdul Rahim specialized in Muslim law, and his *Principles of Muhammadan Jurisprudence* (first published in 1911) is considered a classic on the subject. He practiced law, became involved in politics, and was one of the founding members of the **Muslim League** in 1906.

Abdur Rahim was also a member of the delegation of Muslim leaders that met with the viceroy, **Lord Minto**, at Simla earlier in the same year; the delegation proposed the creation of **separate electorates** for Muslims. In 1908, he was appointed a justice of the Madras High Court, where he served until 1920; during his service there, he was twice officiating chief justice. Also during that period, Abdur Rahim was a member of the Royal Commission on Public Service (1912–1915) and achieved recognition for strongly urging the rapid appointment of Indians to the highest levels of the civil service.

He was a member of the executive council of the governor of **Bengal**, 1921–1925, holding the portfolio of justice, and was then a member of the legislative council from 1926 to 1930. In 1931, Abdur Rahim was elected as an independent to the Central Legislative Assembly and presided over that body from 1935 to 1945. He also was a member of the Muslim portion of the Indian delegation to the

Round Table Conferences in the early 1930s. He is reported to have been opposed to the partition of Bengal, but he moved to East Bengal after partition and died soon thereafter.

Abdur Rahim's daughter was the first wife of **Husain Shahid Suhrawardy**, who supported the creation of a separate dominion for Bengal and **Assam**.

ABDUR RASHID, KAZI (?–1944). A pioneer in Muslim publishing in **Bengal**, he founded Bengal Moslem Provincial Library and associated publishing firms. He was born in **Dhaka** district and represented that district in the Bengal Legislative Council, 1937–1944.

ABDUR RASUL, MAULVI (1872–1917). He was born in Tippera (now **Comilla**) district and was educated at Oxford before being called to the bar from the Middle Temple in London in 1898. He began a lucrative practice at the **Calcutta** High Court, but also engaged in politics in the *swadeshi* and anti-partition movements. Abdul Rasul became a member of the **Muslim League** and was part of the group (working under **Muhammad Ali Jinnah**) that drafted the Congress-League accord at Lucknow in 1916 in which the Congress accepted the Muslim League demand for **separate electorates**.

ABU TAHER, COLONEL (1938–1976). Awarded *Bir Uttam* for bravery during the **War of Liberation**, he was executed during the regime of President **Ziaur Rahman** for his radical leftist beliefs and alleged treason. He joined **Jatiya Samajtantrik Dal** in 1974 and introduced to the party the concept of a people's army. Abu Taher was a major power broker during the coup and countercoup of August–November 1975 but later lost out to Ziaur Rahman. He joined the Pakistan army in 1960 and served in the Special Services group. He was decorated for his bravery during the **Indo-Pakistan War of 1965**. After the Pakistan army crackdown on the civilian population in East Pakistan, Abu Taher escaped from West Pakistan to join the War of Liberation. He was the first adjutant general of the Bangladesh army.

ABUL FAZAL (1903–1983). Adviser (i.e., minister) of education in the **Ziaur Rahman** regime, December 1975 to June 1977. Earlier he had taught at a number of institutions and he became vice-chancellor of **Chittagong** University in 1973. Abul Fazal was a founder of the Muslim Literary Society in 1923.

ABUL HASHIM (1905–1974). A member of the Bengal Assembly (1937–1947). He joined the **Muslim League** in 1937 and became general secretary of the provincial Muslim League in 1943. After the independence of Pakistan he remained in India until 1950, during which period he was the leader of the opposition in the West Bengal Assembly, until he left India for Pakistan. For his role as the president of the organizing committee of the language movement, Abul Hashim was arrested and jailed for a period of 16 months. In 1964 he formed the Khilafat-e-Rabbani Party in opposition to **Ayub Khan** and was its president until 1966. He was the first director of the Islamic Academy.

ABUL HUSAIN (1896–1938). Founder of the **Dhaka** Muslim Literature Society in 1923, he was one of the main proponents of the "freedom of thought" movement. He was involved with the **education** of the Muslims of Bengal. A liberal thinker, Abul Husain wrote a number of books, including *The Helots of Bengal*, *Religion of the Helots of Bengal*, and *The Development of Muslim Law in British India*.

ABYSSINIANS. The name given to African slaves who came to India. In Bengal in 1486, the Abyssinians led a revolt against the **Ilyas Shahi dynasty**. By 1490, an Abyssinian slave usurped the throne and took the name **Shamsuddin Muzaffar Shah**. His rule was despotic, and he was deposed in 1493 and succeeded by **Alauddin Husain**, founder of the **Husain Shahi dynasty**.

ACID SURVIVORS FOUNDATION (ASF). The Acid Survivors Foundation was established in 1999 to respond to the rising use of acid thrown at **women** when men feel they have been spurned. ASF works with **non-governmental organizations**, the government of Bangladesh, and the international community to prevent future attacks and to ensure survivors have free and better access to quality medical care. ASF also provides survivors with better access to Bangladesh's criminal and legal justice systems, and assists with the survivors' rehabilitation—access to **education**, training for new skills, and finding **employment**. These services have been made available in all parts of the country and victims are brought to the rehabilitation center in Dhaka. ASF also has a 15-bed hospital. Initial funding came from UNICEF and the Canadian International Development Agency.

ADAMJEE JUTE MILL. Located in Narayanganj in greater **Dhaka**, it was the largest such mill in the world. Before independence, it symbolized the domination of East Pakistani industry by West Pakistanis, as the Adamjee family was based in Karachi. In 1954 it was the scene of a major and violent labor dispute resulting from hiring practices that seemed to Bengali-speakers to discriminate against them in favor of Urdu-speaking **Biharis**. The strike contributed to the fall of the chief minister, **Fazlul Haq**, and some have alleged it was intended to do so. After independence, the mill, like many other West Pakistani–owned companies, was nationalized by the new government of Bangladesh. It, as well as many others, was a money-losing concern. This resulted in its closing by the government on 30 June 2002, and the loss of a substantial number of jobs.

ADISURA. Bengal literary tradition asserts that a ruler of this name became king of **Gaur** in the eighth century AD and attempted to revive Brahmanism. There are no contemporary records of him and he may not have existed. The name Adisura itself means "original Sura." *See also* SURA DYNASTY.

ADIVASI COMMUNITY. There are about 45 Adivasi (indigenous) communities in Bangladesh. Some of the more well-known communities are Garo, Manipuri, Chakma, Tripura, Santal, Malos, Bagdi, and Orano. There are 14 Adivasi festivals/celebrations in Bangladesh that can be considered major. Among these is the new year celebration, which the Chakmas call 'Biju' and the Marmas/Tripuras call 'Baisabi.' Santals and Oranos celebrate 'Karam Utshab' during 'Chaitra Shangkrani' (the last day of spring). Santals also have 'Baha Parab' or spring festival. Byoms have a splendid dance to usher in spring. Manipuris commemorate 'Dol Purnima.' Oranos have 'Phagoa Utshab.' Two organizations, the Research and Development

Collective and the Cultural Coordination Centre, Bangladesh, are involved in maintaining records of the society and culture of the Adivasi communities of Bangladesh. A number of issues impact the Adivasi communities of Bangladesh, including land rights, awareness by the majority, conversion, suppression of rituals and traditional cultures, and loss of **language**.

AFGHANISTAN. Bangladesh-Afghanistan relations were not close but were friendly prior to the communist takeover in Afghanistan in 1978. After the **Soviet** invasion of Afghanistan in 1979, the government of Bangladesh took a position similar to that of **Pakistan** and most other Islamic nations: it demanded the complete withdrawal of Soviet troops, the restoration of the non-aligned position of Afghanistan, and the establishment of a government in Afghanistan acceptable to the Afghan people. The Soviets withdrew in 1989. This touched off a struggle among competing groups in Afghanistan that culminated with the capture of Kabul by the Taliban (literally, "students") in September 1996. Pakistan supported the anti-Soviet forces and later the Taliban. Bangladesh took no active role, but generally supported the position of Pakistan and opposed India's position against the Taliban. As the Taliban became more extreme, whatever relationship that had existed cooled. After the attacks in the **United States** on 11 September 2001, by al-Qaeda, Bangladesh announced its support of the American fight against terrorism. With the ouster of the Taliban government relations between Bangladesh and Afghanistan have returned to being friendly, but they are not close or active. There has been speculation in the press, so far unproven, that some Afghans associated with the Taliban and al-Qaeda have made their way to Bangladesh. A few Bangladeshi organizations like the **Grameen Bank** are now working in Afghanistan in support of the North Atlantic Treaty Organization's mission.

AGA KHAN III (SIR SULTAN MUHAMMAD SHAH, 1877–1957). Born in Karachi, he was the spiritual leader of the Nizari Ismaili sect of Shia Muslims. He also played an important role in Indian-Muslim politics as leader of the Simla delegation to **Lord Minto** in 1906 and in the founding of the **Muslim League** in the same year. The Aga Khan was several times president of the Muslim League. As India's representative, he was president of the League of Nations in 1937. He had the status of an Indian prince although he ruled no territory. He died in Switzerland and was succeeded by his grandson, Prince Karim, as Aga Khan IV. Karim was born in Switzerland in 1936. Although the Aga Khan played a major role in Muslim India, there are very few of his Ismaili followers in Bangladesh.

AGARTALA CONSPIRACY CASE. Lodged against Sheikh **Mujibur Rahman** and others in 1968. It was alleged that Mujib and the others had plotted (in the Indian city of Agartala, the capital of **Tripura** state) with **India** to win the independence of **East Pakistan.** The trial was never completed, and the charges were dropped by **Ayub Khan** as a precondition placed by opposition leaders to meetings held between them and Ayub in early 1969. Those charged were the late Lt. Commander Moazzem Hossain (Navy); Steward Mujibur Rahman, LS (Navy); Sultan Uddin Ahmed, LS (Navy); Noor Mohammad (Navy); Ahmed Fazlur Rahman, CSP; Flight Sergeant Mofizullah, Corporal (Air Force); Abdus Samad, ABM (Air Force); Habilder Daliluddin (Army); Ruhul Kuddus, CSP; Flight Sergeant Md Fazlul Haque (Air Force); Bhupoti Bhushan Chowdhury alias Manik Chowdhury (political leader); Bidhan Krishna Sen (political leader); Subedar Abdur Razzaq (Army); Habildar Mujibur Rahman (Army); Flight Sergeant Md Abdur Razzaq (Army); Mohammad Khurshid, AB (Navy); Khan Mohammad Shamsur Rahman, CSP; Risalder Shamsul Haque (Army); Habilder Azizul Haque (Army); Mahfuzul Bari, SOC (Air Force); Sergeant Shamsul Haque (Air Force); Col. Shamsul Alam (Army); Maj. Mohammad Abdul Motalib (Army); Col. Khandker Nazmul Huda (Army); Brig. ANM Nuruzzaman (Army); Flight Sergeant Abdul Jalil (Army); Md Mahbubuddin Chowdhury (executive); Lt. MM Matiur Rahman (Navy); Subedar AKM Tazul Islam (Army); Mohammad Ali Reza (instructor, NIPA); Brig. Khurshid Uddin Ahmed (Army); and Commander Abdur Rouf (Navy).

AGRICULTURE. Agriculture accounts for 30 percent of gross domestic product, about 61 percent of employment, and about 33 percent of exports, according to data for 2007. Agricultural production is heavily dependent on the monsoon and is therefore vulnerable to weather fluctuations. Traditional agriculture is primarily rain-fed; modern **irrigation** facilities serve 25 percent of cultivated areas. The use of chemical fertilizer is both inadequate and unbalanced. Frequent droughts and floods in the 1980s and later have resulted in a series of crop failures.

Data from the 1996 Census of Agriculture report that about 8.3 million hectares (about 20.7 million acres) are cropped. This is a considerable drop from the cropped area reported in the 1977 census of 15 million hectares (37 million acres). According to the 1996 data, about two-thirds of the cropped land is owned by the farmer. The climate permits much of the land to be double-cropped and some to be triple-cropped so that the actual acreage cropped during a year is closer to 10.6 million hectares (26.7 million acres). The cropping rate is reported as 176 percent. About 80 percent of the cropland is used for annual crops and about 7 percent for orchards and other permanent plantings. The remainder was fallow at the time of the census.

Rice is the most important crop, accounting for approximately 79 percent of the cropped area; wheat accounts for 5.7 percent, a sizable increase from 4 percent in 1977; jute is the next largest crop at about 5 percent. Other crops taking more than 1 percent of the cropped land are rape and mustard seeds, potatoes, chilies, and sugarcane. The principal permanent crops are bananas, mangoes, jack fruit, and coconuts.

The average annual growth in value added of the Bangladeshi agricultural sector was only 2.3 percent for the period 1990–1999. Rice production in 1999 was 20.2 million metric tons, increasing to 26 million tons in 2003–2004, and further increasing to 28.8 million tons in 2005–2006. Claims of food self-sufficiency are made although **population** increases and natural disasters continue to undermine per capita rice consumption. Despite a steady increase in food grain production, the increase is less than the increase in population, resulting in continuing food imports. Food security at the household level continues to remain precarious, and agricultural productivity remains low. While increased productivity is pursued through irrigation, high-yield varieties (HYV) of seeds, and fertilizer technology, only 0.83 million hectares (a bit more than 2 million acres) utilize groundwater irrigation, compared to a potential of about 2 million hectares (5 million acres). Surface-water irrigation is used at less than 50 percent of capacity. Fertilizer application has increased significantly; most nitrogenous fertilizer is now manufactured in Bangladesh, utilizing the country's extensive natural gas resources. Approximately 60 percent of the areas suitable for HYV seed usage continue to use local seed varieties.

Fish, which is the most important source of animal protein, provides substantial employment and export earning. However, inland fish production has declined in recent years. At the same time, cultivated fishing has increased and is contributing to overall agricultural production. Improvement in livestock through genetic means, along with an efficient supply of feed and fodder, and small business development in poultry have increased the supply of meat. More than 78 percent of farmers also raise poultry. There are also more than 20 million head of cattle. Overexploitation of forest resources for fuel and cultivation has created serious ecological and **environmental** problems, especially in southern Bangladesh and the **Chittagong Hill Tracts**. Reforestation of forest reserves and forestation with community participation are in progress to arrest further damage and initiate recovery. *See also* LAND FRAGMENTATION.

AHAD, ABDUL (1918–1994). A noted lyricist and composer, he was a disciple of Ustad Bali and Ustad Manju Sahib and in 1936 he won the All Bengal Competition in *thumri* and *ghazal*. He was the first Bengali Muslim to receive a full scholarship from Shantiniketan, a school of learning established by **Rabrindranath Tagore** in 1901. Abdul Ahad studied directly under him. Some of his well-known compositions include *Ami shagorer o neel, Amar desher matir gondhey, Onek brishti jhorey tumi eley,* and *Bhramarer pakhna jotodur jak na.* Abdul Ahad wrote a number of books on Tagore and Bengali music. In 1978 he received the Swadhinita Padak. *See also* MUSIC.

AHMED, ABBASUDDIN (1901–1959). A disciple of **Kazi Nazrul Islam,** he spent about 20 years with him. He was a master of at least two varieties of folk songs: *bhawiya* and *palligeeti.* He influenced the resurgence of Bengali Muslims and, with poet **Jasimuddin,** was instrumental in popularizing folk songs. Abbasuddin is credited with having popularized Islamic songs and is also known for using a two-string musical instrument (*duo tara*). He received Pakistan's

Pride of Performance award. Abassuddin's autobiography is entitled *Amar Shilpa Jeban*. *See also* MUSIC.

AHMED, ABUL MANSUR (1897–1979). A journalist and politician. He was the editor of the *Daily Ittehad*, 1945–1950. In the 1920s he participated in both the **Khilafat** and the non-cooperation movements. He first joined the Swaraj Party, then the Congress Party, and in 1944 he joined the **Muslim League**. In 1954 he became the minister of health in the **United Front** government. Abul Mansur was the education and commerce minister when the **Awami League** was in power in 1956. From 1958 to 1962 he was placed under arrest. After his release in 1962 he did not return to politics but became a well-known columnist, writing for such papers as *Ittefaq* and *Observer*. Abul Mansur wrote a number of books in Bengali. In English, his *End of a Betrayal and Restoration of Lahore Resolution*, published in 1975, is a valuable look at the period between 1940 and 1971.

AHMED, FAKHRUDDIN (1940–). Dr Fakhruddin Ahmed was born in Munshiganj. He graduated from **Dhaka University** with a bachelor's and master's degree in economics. He received another master's degree in development economics from Williams College in the **United States** and then his Ph.D. in economics from Princeton University. He started his career as a lecturer of economics at Dhaka University. Later, he joined the civil service of **Pakistan**. He served the government until 1978, when he joined the World Bank. He served there until 2001, and then from 2002 to 2005 he served as governor of Bangladesh Bank. Prior to becoming the chief adviser of the **caretaker government**, he was the managing director of the Palli Karma-Sahayak Foundation (PKSF), a micro-finance organization.

AHMED, FARRUKH (1918–1974). A poet and journalist, he was born in Jessore and studied in Calcutta. He was on the staff of *Mohammadi* before partition and then worked with Dhaka radio until 1972. In college, he was influenced by the radical humanist movement of M. N. Roy, but broke away from humanism and became an ardent Muslim. This change is reflected in his poetry.

AHMED, GULZAR UDDIN, COLONEL (?–2009). A member of the Bangladesh army, in 2004 he was assigned to the **Rapid Action Battalion (RAB)** – 3, to manage and improve law and order in Bangladesh. Within two months of his appointment, he was assigned to a government committee charged with investigating the grenade attack on the British high commissioner to Bangladesh. In 2005, he was appointed the head of the Intelligence Unit of RAB and spearheaded the investigations and operations against Jama'atul Mujahideen Bangladesh (JMB) and Harkatul Jihad Al Islami. He was instrumental in apprehending JMB chief Sheikh Abdur Rahman, and second-in-command Siddiqul Islam, also known as **Bangla Bhai**, who was executed by the **caretaker government** in 2007. Colonel Gulzar was deputized to the **Bangladesh Rifles** in 2006 but because of his knowledge about **terrorism** and **militancy** in Bangladesh, the caretaker government moved him back to RAB as its director general. Colonel Gulzar was instrumental, in November 2008, in directing RAB's seizure of 70 kg of explosives, 40 kg of nitric acid, and 150 cases of improvised grenades stockpiled by JMB. In January 2009, the new government of **Sheikh Hasina Wajed** made him the commander of the Sylhet sector of the Bangladesh Rifles. On 26 February 2009, he and all sector commanders of Bangladesh Rifles attended the annual gathering of the Bangladesh Rifles in **Dhaka,** where, as a result of a servicemen mutiny, he along with all the sector commanders were assassinated. The mutineers called him out by name, suggesting that he was singled out for his role as a principal investigator of terrorism and militancy. During the **War of Liberation** Colonel Gulzar's father, Anwar Uddin Ahmed, was killed by Pakistani armed forces on 4 April 1971. His father was a civil servant working at the Gazipur Ordinance Factory who, along with 20 other civilian officers, was taken to the parliament building in Dhaka and killed.

AHMED, IAJUDDIN (1931–). Elected president of Bangladesh, 5 September 2002. He was born in what was then **Dhaka** district in the subdivision (now district) of Munshiganj. He received a Ph.D. from the University of Wisconsin and then joined the faculty of **Dhaka University** as a biologist in 1963, rising to professor in 1973. From 1991 to 1993, he was chairman of the Public Service Commission (PSC). He has been the vice-chancellor of the public sector State

University in the Mohammadpur section of Dhaka. On 29 October 2006, he became the chief adviser of the **caretaker government**, charged with conducting a national election upon completion of the term of office of the BNP government led by **Khaleda Zia**. He resigned from that position on 11 January 2007. On 12 January 2009, he left the office of president and was succeeded by **Zillur Rahman**.

AHMED, KAZI ZAFAR (1940–). A **trade unionist** and member of the **National Awami Party**, he joined **JAGODAL** in support of president **Ziaur Rahman**. He served briefly in 1978 as minister of education. He changed parties to join the **Jatiya Party** of **Hussain Muhammad Ershad** and, as a member of the cabinet, held various portfolios, including commerce, education, and information and broadcasting. In November 1988, Kazi Zafar was designated deputy prime minister, and in September 1989, he was appointed prime minister and remained in that position until the fall of the Ershad regime in December 1990. He remains a key member of the Jatiya Party.

AHMED, MOUDUD (1940–). Active in the 1971 liberation movement, he later broke with Sheikh **Mujibur Rahman** and worked as a civil rights lawyer. He held ministerial posts under **Ziaur Rahman**, 1977–1980, and was elected to parliament in 1979. Even though he had earlier been jailed by the **Hussain Muhammad Ershad** regime, he was appointed to the Ershad cabinet in 1985 and named deputy prime minister in 1986, a post he held until becoming prime minister in March 1988. Moudud Ahmed was nominated vice president in September 1989 but resigned in December of that year to make way for the appointment of **Shahabuddin Ahmed** as vice president and then successor to Ershad when the latter resigned. He was elected to parliament from Noakhali in 1986, 1988, and 1991. In 1996, he joined the **Bangladesh Nationalist Party** but was defeated in the election that year. Successful in the 2001 election, he was appointed minister of law and justice. His wife, Husna, the daughter of poet **Jasimuddin**, was also elected in 1988, but has not run again since. Moudud Ahmed has written several books on the politics and constitutional development of Bangladesh.

AHMED, MOYEZUDDIN (MODHU MIAN) (1855–1920). A journalist and writer who lived in Jessore. He published several journals that appealed to the Muslim middle class and wrote several books on Islam.

AHMED, MUZAFFAR (?–1972). The leader of the pro-Soviet faction of the **National Awami Party.** He was one of the first political leaders to ask for elections after the independence of Bangladesh. He argued that the 1970 election through which the **Awami League** came to power had been held under conditions that pertained prior to independence, and therefore the mandate required reconfirmation.

AHMED, NAIBUDDIN (1925–2009). A well-known photographer of rural landscapes, rivers, and ordinary people engaged in their daily lives, he was able to dupe a Pakistani army photographer and use his camera to capture the Pakistani army atrocities in the Mymensingh area in 1971. The photographs were smuggled to India with the assistance of Colonel **Abu Taher.** The story of the atrocities really broke when one of the pictures was published in the *Washington Post*. A documentary on his **War of Liberation** photos was produced by Ahmed Zaki. The title of the short documentary is *71: In Frame and Out of Frame*.

AHMED, SHAHABUDDIN (1929–). A member of the judicial service, he rose to become chief justice of Bangladesh. During the rioting that led to the resignation of president **Hussain Muhammad Ershad,** Shahabuddin was selected by the opposition to become vice president. The then vice president, **Moudud Ahmed,** resigned, and Shahabuddin was appointed to that position by Ershad on 6 December 1990. He became acting president on 8 December, when Ershad resigned the post. His primary task was to hold a "free and fair" election for a new **parliament.** Shahabuddin accomplished this in February 1991. The new parliament amended the **constitution** to provide for a parliamentary system to replace the presidential system. Another amendment permitted Shahabuddin to return to his position as chief justice. This he did when **Abdur Rahman Biswas** was elected president and assumed office on 8 October 1991. Shahabuddin retired as chief justice in 1994. However, when the **Awami League**

formed a government after the June 1996 election, parliament elected Shahabuddin as president. He served until October 2001. *See also* ELECTIONS.

AHMED, SHAMSUDDIN (1889–1969). He was born in Kushtia and received a law degree from **Kolkata**. He took an active part in the non-cooperation movement and the **Khilafat movement**. He was elected to the Bengal Legislative Council as a member of Congress in 1927 and to the Bengal Legislative Assembly as a member of the **Krishak Praja Party** in 1937. Shamsuddin joined the **Muslim League** in 1944, but after independence formed the Socialist Party of Pakistan. He also served as Pakistan's ambassador to **Burma**.

AHMED, SULTANUDDIN (1902–1977). Governor of **East Pakistan** in 1958. A lawyer and pre-independence legislator, he also served as ambassador of Pakistan in **Burma**, **China**, and Indonesia.

AHMED, SYED ISHTIAQ (1932–2003). One of the originators of the concept of the **caretaker government** that led to of the promulgation of the 13th Amendment, he served as attorney general of Bangladesh and also as a member of the Council of Advisers of two caretaker governments of Bangladesh. In 1954 he was called to the bar from Lincoln Inn in England and also received a graduate degree in economics from the London School of Economics. He served as chairman of the Bangladesh Institute of Law and International Affairs and was twice elected president of the Supreme Court Bar Association. In *Anwar Hossain vs. the State*, also known as the 8th Amendment case, he was successful in challenging the constitutionality of creating several divisional benches in different parts of the country. He also won a number of cases against the government, especially those related to the government ban of newspapers. For his activities regarding **human rights** and the rule of law he was imprisoned by the **Hussain Muhammed Ershad** government in 1983 and 1987. His support for the language movement in 1952 and his opposition to the governor-general's rule in East Pakistan in 1954 earned him jail time. He is the principal architect of the separation of the judiciary from the executive that the caretaker government of **Fakhruddin Ahmed** implemented in 2008.

AHMED, TAJUDDIN (1922–1975). He headed the first provisional government of Bangladesh. He was a close confidant of Sheikh **Mujibur Rahman** during negotiations with both the **Muhammad Ayub Khan** and the **Yahya Khan** regimes. During the Mujib regime, he held the portfolios of defense (1972), finance (1972–1974), forests, fisheries, and livestock (1974), information and broadcasting (1972), jute (1973–1974), and planning (1972–1974), often heading more than one ministry at a time. Preferring closer ties with the **Soviet Union**, Tajuddin fell into disgrace when Mujib felt that circumstances required a closer relationship with the **United States**. He was one of the four political leaders who were assassinated following the **Khalid Musharraf** coup of November 1975. *See also* DHAKA JAIL KILLINGS.

AHSAN, ABUL (1937–2008). He was the first secretary general of the **South Asian Association for Regional Cooperation**, a foreign secretary of Bangladesh, and Bangladesh ambassador to the **United States**. As an assistant secretary of the Ministry of Foreign Affairs, he was a key member of the Bangladesh negotiating team at the Tripartite Conference among Bangladesh, Pakistan, and India that dealt with issues of prisoners of war, a war crimes tribunal, the division of assets, and other matters related to the 1971 **War of Liberation** and the separation of Bangladesh from Pakistan.

AHSAN-UL-HUQUE (1919–?). His father, Sir **Muhammad Aziz-ul-Huque**, was a prominent Muslim Bengali political figure before independence, but Ahsan-ul-Huque was engaged principally in commerce and industry. Ahsan-ul-Huque served as a Pakistan ambassador under **Ayub Khan** and was a member of the cabinet formed by **Yahya Khan** in 1969 in the latter's unsuccessful effort to gradually civilianize the martial law government.

AHSANULLAH (1873–1965). Born in Satkhira in Khulna district, he was the first Indian to be appointed to the Indian Education Service. He ended one aspect of discrimination on the basis of religion by assigning numbers rather than using names in examinations. Ahsanullah also worked to improve the quality of education in the Muslim *madrasas* (primary schools) so that graduates of the madrasas could be admitted to secular colleges. He established libraries and publishing houses.

AHSANULLAH KHAN, NAWAB KHWAJA (1846–1901). Son of Nawab Khwaja **Abdul Ghani Mian**, he succeeded his father as nawab of Dhaka in 1896. He was a member of the legislative council of the governor-general in 1890 and 1899. His philanthropic donations included the **Dhaka** Mitford Hospital and the Dhaka Electric Supply organization. Ahsanullah was succeeded as nawab by his son, Nawab Sir **Salimullah**.

AID. Bangladesh depends heavily on foreign aid for its development programs. Since its independence in 1971, Bangladesh has received more than $40 billion in grants and loans from multilateral organizations such as the World Bank, the Asian Development Bank, and the United Nations Development Programme, and bilateral assistance from many countries, including, among the major donors, the **United States**, Japan, and Saudi Arabia. Of this amount, about $20 billion has been disbursed. These grants initially were largely for recovery from the 1971 **War of Liberation** and food assistance. Now grants are largely for social projects and loans are for infrastructure and industrial development. In 2002, Bangladesh received a total aid package of $1.56 billion. On an average year Bangladesh continues to receive approximately $2 billion of international aid assistance. Additional substantial sums have been received as gifts from **nongovernmental organizations** (NGOs). These funds are used for a variety of purposes, including **education**, **health delivery**, and job training.

AKRAM KHAN, MAULANA MUHAMMAD (1870–1968). A founding member of the **Muslim League** in 1906. He founded the newspaper *Daily Azad* in 1936 as a journal to support the Muslim League. He was the president of the provincial Muslim League and vice president of the All-India Muslim League and Pakistan Muslim League. Akram Khan was also a social activist and a litterateur and was given the Pride of Performance in **Literature** award by the government of Pakistan.

ALAOL (c. 1607–1680). An important medieval Bengali poet, he was born in **Chittagong** district, but he did most of his work while a counselor to the king of **Arakan**. A number of his works have been discovered. Among these are several drawn from Persian and Arabic sources written between 1660 and 1669. *See also* LITERATURE.

ALAUDDIN HALWAI SWEETMEAT SHOP. It is generally acknowledged that the two sweet makers Mathar Baksh and Alauddin came to Dhaka from Lucknow in the late 19th century. In 1896, Alauddin opened the first sweet shop called Aluddin Halwai in the Chawkbazar area of Dhaka, where it still stands. These sweetmeat shops are an important part of the Dhaka culture. Other well-known sweetmeat shops were Kalachand Gandha Banik and Sitaram Mistanno Bhandar of Islampur, Latmiar Islamia Mistanno Bhandar in Nayabazar, and Maranchand Gosh and Co. in Nababpur Road. Many of the Hindu-owned shops like Kalachand Sitaram and Latmia closed down at the time of the **War of Liberation** because the owners sought refuge in India.

ALAUDDIN HUSAIN SHAH (?–1519). The sultan of Bengal from 1493 to 1519 and the founder of the **Husain Shahi dynasty**, having overthrown Sultan **Shamsuddin Muzaffar Shah**, an **Abyssinian** ruler. As Alauddin was a Sayyid of Arab descent, the dynasty is sometimes known as the Sayyid dynasty (not to be confused with the Sayyid dynasty of the **Delhi Sultanate**). Alauddin proved to be a very successful and popular ruler, beginning with the restoration of order and the expulsion of the Abyssinian mercenaries. He extended the sultanate to the borders of Orissa and retook Bihar from the rulers of Jaunpur (now in Uttar Pradesh). His invasion of Assam was unsuccessful in that he did not add any territory to his realm. He was a builder and erected many monuments in his capital, **Gaur**.

ALI, A. F. M. ABDUL (1932–2008). Popularly known as Lalu Bhai (Brother Lalu), he was a comedian and actor. He was a child artist of Mymensingh and his first play was *Palli Samaj*. Unil his move to Dhaka in 1962, he was considered a cultural icon of Mymensingh. His first movie role was in *Shurjo Snan*. After that he acted in over

100 movies. He also participated in Bangladesh Betar (Radio Bangladesh) and Bangladesh TV. His *Kainchain Dehi* was a popular program on radio. *See also* FILM.

ALI, AHMED (1904–2008). Also known as Rupa Miah, was made famous by poet **Jasimuddin** in his dance drama *Nakshi Kanthar Math*. The poet observed Ahmed Ali in a local dispute and based his dance drama on that particular incident.

ALI, MAHMUD (1919–2006). Leader of the **Ganotantrik Dal**, a constituent of the **United Front** that swept the 1954 election to the East Bengal Legislative Assembly. Although he had won one of the two non-**Awami League** seats in the 1970 **election**, after Bangladeshi independence he chose to move to **Pakistan** and held a variety of posts under both the **Zulfiqar Ali Bhutto** and Zia ul-Haq regimes.

ALI MARDAN KHALJI (?–1230?). Appointed governor of Bengal by Sultan Qutbuddin of the Mamluk series of rulers of the Delhi Sultanate in 1206, he revolted on Qutbuddin's death in 1210 and attempted to set himself up as an independent ruler. He was defeated by Sultan Iltutmish of Delhi in 1230.

ALI, MUHAMMAD KORBAN (1924–1990). Political figure first associated with the **Awami League** and later with the **Jatiya Party**. He was elected to the provincial assembly in 1954 and to parliament in 1973, 1986, and 1988. A senior vice president of the Awami League, Korban Ali changed parties in 1984 and joined the cabinet of the regime headed by **Hussain Muhammad Ershad**.

ALI, SYED MURTAZA (1903–1981). Born in **Sylhet** (then a part of **Assam**), he studied in **Calcutta** and entered the Indian Civil Service. After retirement as a divisional commissioner in 1959, he headed the Bangla Academy. Murtaza Ali published a number of books, including *History of Chittagong* (1964).

ALIM, ABDUL (1931–1974). Folk singer. He migrated from India after the partition of India and joined Dhaka Radio. He recorded his first songs by the age of 14. He recorded songs for the first Bangla movie, *Mukh O Mukhosh*. He was well known for his rendition of Bhatiali, a folk song genre from the Bhati region of Mymensingh and some parts of Sylhet district of Bangladesh. *See also* FILM; MUSIC.

ALINAGAR, TREATY OF. A treaty signed between Nawab **Sirajud-daulah** and the British, represented by **Robert Clive**, on 9 February 1757, following the British recapture of **Kolkata**. The terms imposed by the British were stiff, although the violations of the treaty that occurred were by the British and not the nawab. These included entering into a conspiracy against the nawab with **Mir Jafar**. This led to the **Battle of Plassey** on 23 June 1757, and the defeat and death of Sirajuddaulah.

ALIVARDI KHAN (c. 1678–1756). His original name was Mirza Muhammad Khan. He was appointed to positions of power by Nawab Shujauddin (nawab, 1727–1739). Shujauddin's son, Sarfraz Khan, succeeded his father. Alivardi Khan became Shujauddin's deputy for the Bihar region of the Bengal province of the Mughals in 1733. Taking advantage of the confusion in Delhi caused by the raid of the Persian Nadir Shah in 1739 and with the help of dubious documents, he claimed that he had been chosen to replace the incumbent governor. He defeated Sarfraz Khan at Giria and became governor. He was assisted by the banker **Jagat Seth**. Alivardi's term in office was relatively peaceful as he successfully met the challenges presented by the British. An exception to this was the constant struggle with the Marathas in Orissa beginning in 1742. In 1751 Alivardi made peace with the Marathas by agreeing to pay one-quarter of the revenue from Orissa to the Marathas and to pay an annual tribute. He died in **Murshidabad** and was succeeded by his daughter's son, **Sirajuddaulah**.

AL MAHMUD (1936–). He was the first Bangladeshi poet to heavily use colloquial words from local dialects in his poems. His poetry almost always dealt with nature and rural community and is often compared to the work of Jibanananda Das and Poet Jamimuddin. He published more than 50 books of poems, short stories, and novels. Among his greatest works are *Shonali Kabin*, *Lok Lokantor*, *Bakhtiyarer*

Ghora, *Nodir Bhitorer*, and *Kaler Kalosh*. For his contributions to Bengali **literature** he has received the Ekushey Padak, Bangla Academy Award, and Sufi Motaher Hossain Literary Gold Medal. Born and raised in a conservative Muslim family, he is a great believer in secularism. *See also* LITERATURE.

AL MAMUN, ABDULLAH (1941–2008). Pioneer of the **theatre** movement of Bangladesh. He is a playwright who delved deeply into the lives of the poor and downtrodden. He wrote over 20 plays and acted in more than 15 of those plays. He was a founding member of the theatre group called Theatre. He shaped the theatre and TV world in Bangladesh after the **War of Liberation**. His major plays are *Akhono Kritodash*, *Tomrai*, *Kokilara*, and *Meraj Fakir-er Maa*. The first TV play he directed was *Ektola Dotola*. His first theatre production was *Subachan Nirbasan*. In 1997 he won the National Film award for his documentary on the career of Ferdousi Majumdar. He made his first movie in 1972 and was critically acclaimed for the **film** *Sareng Bou*. For his contributions to the world of **literature** and entertainment he received the Ekushey Padak and the Bangla Academy Award. *See also* FILM; THEATRE.

ALOKCHITRA SHILPI SANGSAD (ASHIS). Established as a training institute for photography in 1978, its facilities are located on public property donated through the auspices of the deputy commissioner of **Mymensingh**. In addition to providing a three-month course on photography, it also organizes photographic exhibitions and competitions, seminars, and workshops to advance knowledge and skills in classical and modern photography.

AMAR EKUSHEY GRANTHAMELA (ETERNAL TWENTY-FIRST BOOK FAIR). Honoring the **language movement**, it has become one of the most significant book fairs in the country. In 1972, in remembrance of 21 February 1952, a book sale was arranged on the premises of Bangla Academy by Chittaranjan Saha. In 1971 he supported the Bangladeshi scholars who escaped to **Kolkata**, India, to write about the **War of Liberation** and founded the publishing house of Muktadhara. By 1978, a number of other publishers joined in the book sale that was then taken over by the Bangla Academy and renamed "Amar Ekushey Granthamela" in 1984. It is now a month-long book fair. In 2008 Chittaranjan Saha was recognized at the book fair for his contribution.

AMENA-BAKI RESIDENTIAL SCHOOL. A residential model school located at Chichirbandar, in the district of **Dinajpur**, which started its operation in 2001 and was funded by freedom fighter and orthopedic surgeon Dr. Amjad Hossain to memorialize his parents. In a developing country like Bangladesh, where the more modern schools are normally set up in the capital, Amena-Baki school is an outstanding demonstration that with appropriate funding, leadership, and teaching, excellent schools from outside of the major urban centers can also produce outstanding results. The school started with 19 teachers and approximately 400 students in grades one through seven. The teacher-student ratio is 1 to 19–25. When evening remedial classes are required, both the teachers and students are provided evening meals. The national curriculum is supplemented with mandatory computer **education**. Students are taught communal harmony, self-help, and personal hygiene. Emphasis is placed on service learning through environmental study tours and tree-planting activities. Within a very short time Amena-Baki students are performing well in student competitions and receiving a large number of talent pool scholarships.

AMIR ALI, SYED (1849–1928). A Bengali Shia, he wrote extensively on **Islam**. He was born in Cuttack, Orissa, and educated in India before being called to the bar from the Inner Temple in 1873. He was the first Muslim barrister at the **Kolkata** High Court and was law lecturer at several colleges in Kolkata. He was a judge at the Kolkata High Court, 1890–1904, the first Muslim to sit on the bench.

Amir Ali had been active in politics prior to being named to the court and had founded the National (later Central) Mohammedan Association in 1877, a body created to put forward the ideas of Muslims in Indian politics. Amir Ali was influenced by Sir Syed Ahmad Khan, whom he had met during his stay in England. In 1882, the association presented a memorial to the viceroy, Lord Ripon, demanding greater representation of Muslims in government service.

Amir Ali reentered politics after his retirement from the bench and was a member of the Simla delegation to **Lord Minto** in 1906 and led a **Muslim League** delegation to **Lord Morley**, the secretary of state for India, in London in 1909. He was a champion of the cause of **separate electorates**. Amir Ali was active in the Muslim League, presiding over its third session in Delhi in 1910.

After his retirement from the High Court, he lived in London and represented the Muslim League there. Amir Ali was also the first Indian appointed to the Judicial Committee of the Privy Council, serving from 1908 until his death in 1928. Although a Shia, he supported retention of the caliphate during the **Khilafat movement**. Amir Ali published a number of books on Islam, the most noted being *The Spirit of Islam* (first published in 1922). He also wrote extensively on Islamic law.

ANJUMAN ARA, BEGUM (1942–2004). A vocalist, she was considered one of the most popular artists of her time. She was one of the pioneers of the Golden Age of Music of East Pakistan and continued her career well into independent Bangladesh. She sang for film soundtracks and performed on stage. During the height of her radio career she performed during the morning, evening, and night programs. Her repertoire included light modern songs, Nazrul *geeti*, folk songs, semi-classical songs, patriotic songs, and *ghazal*. Her more outstanding Bengali songs include "*Tumi Ashbe Boley*," "*Akasher Hatey*," "*Key Swaraner Prantore*," "*Khokonshona*," "*Chadni*," "*Brishti Johon*," "*Shathi Ronger*," "*Obhimaan koro na*," "*Key biro- her prantoray*," and "*Sathti ronger majhey aami mil khunje na pai*." She also made a film soundtrack in Urdu. Her Urdu song "*Chandni bheegi bhieegi hawa na jani tum kaha*" was an instant hit. For her contribution to music she received the **Ekushey Padak** in 2003. Her father, Dr. Kasiruddin Talukdar of Bogra, was killed by the Pakistani army during the **War of Liberation**. A number of members of her extended family like Zeenat Rahana and Runa Laila are also prominent singers of Bangladesh. *See also* MUSIC.

ANJUMAN MOFIDUL ISLAM (AMI). Established in Calcutta in 1905 by Ibrahim Mohammad Duplay with the primary goal of providing burial services for unclaimed Muslim bodies, it began operation in **Dhaka** in 1947. It primary services are providing access to ambulances for poor patients and burying the unclaimed dead. Between 1992 and 2004, the AMI provided ambulance services to over 65,000 patients and buried over 30,000 people. Its primary source of financing is individual donations and income from renting some houses and shops. It also receives an annual grant from the government of Bangladesh. AMI has also traditionally operated separate boys' and girls' orphanages. Over the years it has expanded its services to include a vocational and technical training institute and a girls' school. It now has branches in 26 of the 64 districts of Bangladesh. Its most ambitious project to date is a projected $17 million hospital for which the Bangladesh government has donated land.

ANTI-CORRUPTION COMMISSION (ACC). Reconstituted in February 2007 under the Anti-corruption Commission Bidhimala (rules) of 2007 and empowered to independently pursue cases of **corruption** that have permeated the social fabric of Bangladesh, it evolved from an enforcement branch established in 1943 under the police department to monitor and pursue corruption in the food-rationing system. Through the Anti-corruption Act of 1947 it was placed under the Criminal Investigation Division (CID) of the police department. In 1957 it was reorganized as the Bureau of Anti-corruption under the Anti-corruption Act of 1957. After 1971, depending on the system of government in place, it came under control of the president's secretariat or the prime minister's office. In 1983 it was provided independent power of hiring. The ACC was created in 2004 through an act of parliament. It is still dependent on the government of Bangladesh for its budget and therefore is subject to political interference.

ANWARUL HUQUE, KAZI (1909–2001). A member of the Indian Police Service, he became inspector general of police in 1958 and later, in 1961, chief secretary of **East Pakistan**. Anwarul Huque joined the cabinet of **Ayub Khan** in 1965 and remained until 1969. After Bangladeshi independence, he was a member of the cabinets of **Sayem, Ziaur Rahman**, and **Sattar**.

ARAKAN. The province of **Burma** adjacent to Bangladesh on the Bay of Bengal, now known as Rakhine. Rulers of Arakan controlled the **Chittagong** region from the 15th to 17th centuries. The area troubled British and Bengali commerce for many centuries because it served as the base of pirates operating in the bay. Arakanese pirates were often associated with or allies of **Portuguese** adventurers. Arakan was an independent kingdom until 1784, when it was conquered by the Burmese. Many Arakanese fled to Chittagong and used the city as a base for attempts to re-create an independent Arakan. In 1820, the Burmese attacked **Assam** and Manipur, prompting the outbreak of the first Anglo-Burmese war in 1824. In the treaty of Yandaboo ending the war in 1826, Arakan was among the territories ceded to the British and British control of Manipur and the affected areas of Assam was reestablished.

There is a sizable Muslim minority in Arakan, known as Rohingyas, meaning "native born." However, they are thought by some to be descendants of Muslim soldiers of the **Suri dynasty** who fled there when the **Mughals** defeated the Suri usurpers and restored Humayun to the throne of Delhi in 1555. The Rohingyas have felt oppressed by the Burmese government and twice have fled to the southern parts of Chittagong district, in the late 1970s and again in the late 1980s. Some Rohingyas remain in Bangladesh, but most have been repatriated to Burma. While in Bangladesh they were cared for by the government of Bangladesh, the United Nations High Commissioner for Refugees, and international relief agencies.

ARCHEOLOGY. Organized archaeology began with the Europeans in the early 18th century. The British founded the **Asiatic Society of Bengal** in 1784. There is a wealth of archeological sites in Bangladesh, most dating from the medieval period, both Muslim and non-Muslim, although there are other sites that date back as far as the second and third centuries BC. Many of these sites have not been fully explored. In 1971, the government of Bangladesh began a systematic survey of the unexplored areas. Many sites are of the **Pala**, **Chandra**, and **Deva** periods. Other sites are from the **Mughal** and other Muslim periods. Important sites include **Paharpur**, **Mahasthangarh**, **Mainamati**, **Sonargaon**, and several sites in **Dhaka**.

Few international teams have undertaken archaeological research in Bangladesh. An exception is the French-Bangladeshi team working at Mahasthangarh. *See also* ARCHITECTURE; BANERJI, RAKHALDAS; COMILLA.

ARCHITECTURE. The building art of Bangladesh can be classified into four distinct periods. The first period, identified through **archeology** and extending from the third century BC to the 12th century AD, is the ancient period. **Buddhist** monuments at **Paharpur** and **Mainamati**, and Buddhist and **Hindu** temples at **Mahasthangarh** define this period. Although these ancient monuments are not as spectacular as those discovered in other parts of the subcontinent, they provide sufficient clues to the historical importance of Bangladesh as a crossroads of different cultures.

The second period is that of the **Delhi Sultanate**. This period witnessed the development of terra cotta floral motifs, delicate stone carvings, and the curvature of the cornice. The architectural design was similar to that of the Tughluq architecture of Delhi. Some of the more noted sites include the tombs of Ghiyasuddin Azam Shah at **Sonargaon** and Khan Jahan Ali at Bagerhat. Mosques that are representative of this period include the Shair Gumbad mosque in **Khulna**, the Sura mosque in **Dinajpur**, the Chhota Sona mosque in **Rajshahi**, and the Kherua mosque in **Bogra**.

The third period is that of the **Mughal Empire**. This period is characterized by the dominant central dome, the tall central entrance, and the straight horizontal skyline. During the early part of the Mughal period, a blending of the Sultanate and Mughal styles was seen in such buildings as the Atia Jami mosque in Tangail and the Shah Muhammad mosque in **Mymensingh**. Distinctive Mughal architecture is concentrated in **Dhaka** in such monuments as the Bara and Chhota Katras, the Lalbagh Fort, the tomb of Bibi Pari, the Hussaini Dalan, and the river forts of Munshiganj, Hajiganj, and Narayanganj.

The fourth period is that of the British, who brought with them the European Renaissance style seen in the first churches. Public buildings such as the former State Bank building in Dhaka and private structures such as Ahsan Manzil, residence of the **Nawabs of Dhaka**, are noted from the British period. As the Sultanate and Mughal periods blended earlier, there was also blending between the Mughal and British periods. Examples of this are seen on the campus of **Dhaka University** in Curzon, Salimullah, and Fazlul Haq Halls.

While Muslim architectural design dominates modern Bangladesh, affluent Hindu *zamindars* (landlords) made an important contribution to continuing the ancient art form through their patronage of temples. Examples of these include the Govinda temple in **Rajshahi**, the Mathurapur Deul in **Faridpur** and the Satararatna temple in **Comilla**. Buddhist architectural design continues in Bangladesh, resulting from the influx of Magh tribals from **Myanmar (Burma)** into the Cox's Bazaar region. The Khyangs of Cox's Bazaar and the Ramu and Chitmorong temples near Kaptai are excellent examples.

Modern architecture is heavily influenced by Mazharul Islam, whose works integrate structures and their culture and context. He believes that modern architecture should blend the rural and urban environment such that there is no difference between the two. *See also* KHAN, FAZLUR RAHMAN; SHAKHARI BAZAR.

ARMANITOLA HIGH SCHOOL. The first high school in the country was founded in 1848 by J. G. Nicholas Pogose, an **Armenian**. It is still in use and is operated by an Armenian family. *See also* EDUCATION.

ARMED FORCES. Bangladesh armed forces are organized in the usual pattern of army, navy, and air force and generally follow, like other Commonwealth countries, the British model. The army consists of approximately 200,000 personnel organized into seven infantry divisions and a division each of armored, artillery, and engineering. It also has a commando brigade. The navy is designed primarily for coastal patrolling. Among its vessels is a recently acquired South Korean–built frigate. With offshore drilling rights disputed by both India and Burma, and fishing boundary challenges, the navy is undertaking a major expansion program in 2009 to deal with such border disputes. The air force, which was almost without aircraft at independence, has expanded significantly with the acquisition of 12 T-37 jet trainers from the **United States** in 1995 and the transfer of four C-130Bs as a gift from the United States under the Excess Defense Articles program. In 2002, Bangladesh ordered eight MiG-29 fighters from **Russia**. It has also obtained Chinese F-7 interceptors and A-5 ground support aircrafts.

The army participated in the Gulf War in 1991 with a detachment of 2,300 troops. Bangladesh has been an important contributor to **United Nations peacekeeping operations** in such places as East Timor and Sierra Leone.

There are other defense- and security-related organizations. Under the Home Ministry, rather than the Defense Ministry, are the Bangladesh Rifles, designed primarily for border patrolling, and a newly formed Coast Guard. Volunteer organizations include the Ansars (named for the companions of the prophet Muhammad) and village defense parties.

The major supplier of defense equipment has been **China**. Bangladesh inherited some equipment from the defeated Pakistan armed forces, but presumably all of this has been discarded. Initial personnel of the services were drawn from the **Mukti Bahini** and from Bengalis who had been interned in **Pakistan**.

Although the Bangladesh armed forces are constitutionally and legally subject to civilian control, they have interceded into the normal activities of the civilian government on a number of occasions. The first occasion was in 1975 when they were involved in the assassination of Sheikh **Mujibur Rahman,** and the second was the 1981 assassination of **Ziaur Rahman**. In 1982, they forcibly removed a sitting president and brought into power **Hussain Muhammad Ershad**, the chief of staff of the Bangladesh army. The army once again interceded in 11 January 2007 when president **Iajuddin Ahmed** declared a state of emergency. At times, it has mutinied against its own. Most recently in February 2009, the **Bangladesh Rifles** mutiny led to the assassination of 52 officers of the Bangladesh army. Nonetheless, its international peacekeeping role and the changing culture of the last two army chiefs have significantly reduced the likelihood of further direct intervention of the armed forces. *See also* BOGRA MUTINY; CARETAKER GOVERNMENT; MAJORS; WAR OF LIBERATION.

ARMENIANS. Armenians, based in Persia, were an important trading community in South Asia and in Bengal in particular. The East India

Company recognized the "Armenian nation" through an agreement in 1688 that granted the "nation" special trading privileges. In Bengal, there were sizable Armenian settlements in Dhaka and Calcutta. In Dhaka, there remains an Armenian church, but most Armenians in South Asia have left.

ARSENIC CONTAMINATION. It has been determined that 46 percent of "shallow" tube wells (those with a depth of less than approximately 500 feet) in Bangladesh are contaminated with naturally occurring arsenic in excess of the standard established by the World Health Organization (WHO). These wells supply water to an estimated 57 million people. The affected wells are in the southern and southeastern areas of the country, primarily in the **Dhaka**, **Chittagong**, and **Khulna** regions. In the northern areas, which are generally higher in elevation, the incidence of arsenic is significantly less. The recommendation of the WHO and others studying the situation is the use of tube wells with a depth in excess of 500 feet. Tests have shown that water from such wells does not generally exceed the WHO standard. *See also* POLLUTION.

ART. Modern Bangladeshi painting draws from the ancient traditions of terra cotta plates. Many aspects of mythology, folklore, and nature were expressed in terra cotta works. Perhaps the most noted modern painter is **Zainul Abedin**, who depicted the plight of the Bengalis during the 1943 **famine**. Others well known for their contributions to painting include S. M. Sultan, Qamrul Hasan, and Shafiqul Amin. Since 1971, many Bangladeshi artists have expressed themselves through the landscape of the **War of Liberation**.

ARTICLE 70 CONSTITUTION OF BANGLADESH. An effort to ensure stability in the parliamentary system of government by eliminating the ability of members of **parliament** to switch their allegiance to any other party. Article 70 was part of the 1972 **Constitution of Bangladesh**. Article 70(1) states, "A person elected as a member of parliament at an election at which he was nominated as a candidate by a political party shall vacate his seat if he resigns from that party or votes in parliament against that party." Further restrictions and elaborations to Article 70(1) were made by amendments such as the Constitution (Fourth Amendment) Act of 1975 and the Constitution (Twelfth Amendment) Act of 1991. Article 70(1), along with the explanations, is considered a stabilizing force for democratic institution-building but also an impediment to a member of parliament's freedom of expression.

ASIAN DEVELOPMENT BANK (ADB). Headquartered in Manila, the purpose of the ADB is "[to fight] poverty in Asia and the Pacific." In Bangladesh its projects have been principally in rural infrastructure, including roads and bridges, and in several flood-control and water-logging programs in southwestern parts of the country. It also assists in urban **health** care, especially for **women** and children.

ASIATIC SOCIETY OF BANGLADESH. An outgrowth of the Asiatic Society of Bengal, an association of learned men interested in oriental studies. It was founded by **Sir William Jones** in 1784 and supported by governor-general **Warren Hastings**. Its initial task was to inquire "into the history, civil and natural, the antiquities, arts, sciences, and literature of Asia." Today, the society in Bangladesh maintains an extensive library of books and manuscripts. In 1951, the Asiatic Society of Pakistan was formed by Dr. **Mohammad Shahidullah**. When Bangladesh became independent in 1971, the organization was renamed the Asiatic Society of Bangladesh. In addition to lectures and seminars, it maintains an excellent program of publications.

ASIATIC SOCIETY OF BENGAL. *See* ASIATIC SOCIETY OF BANGLADESH.

ASOKA. The third emperor of the **Maurya dynasty** who reigned from c. 272 to c. 232 BC. He ruled Bengal, which had been conquered by the founder of the dynasty, his grandfather, Chandragupta (reigned c. 322 to c. 298 BC). The Bengali port of Tamluk (now in West Bengal) served as the major export and import center for the Mauryas as well as a point from which **Buddhism** could be disseminated to Sri Lanka and Southeast Asia.

ASSAM. As it is adjacent to Bengal, there has been much interaction between Assam and Bengal. In the pre-Islamic period, portions of western Assam (then called Kamarupa, a site mentioned in the *Mahabharata*) were controlled by Bengal dynasties such as the Senas. In the 16th century, the Koches, the rulers of **Cooch Behar**, extended their territory into Assam and Bengal, primarily in **Rangpur**, which appears to have remained under Koch rule until 1498, when it was captured by the Muslim rulers at Gaur who also invaded Assam in 1527. There had been earlier and less permanent Muslim invasions in the 13th century. During the 17th century as the **Mughals** expanded eastward there were further conflicts, resulting in the cession of western Assam to Aurangzeb in 1662.

British control of Bengal was extended to Assam and in 1838 it was formally incorporated into Bengal. A separate chief commissionership was set up in 1874. The **partition of Bengal** in 1905 led to the creation of the province of Eastern Bengal and Assam. This was revoked in 1911 and Assam was reestablished as a separate area, rising to the status of province in 1919. The province included the district of **Sylhet**. At the independence of **India** and **Pakistan**, a referendum was held in 1947 in Sylhet, a Muslim majority district, and the voters in four of the five subdivisions voted to join Pakistan. *See also* SYLHET REFERENDUM.

ASSOCIATION FOR SOCIAL ADVANCEMENT (ASA). Established in 1979, the ASA, a **non-governmental organization** (NGO), emphasizes social action, promoting legal rights, awareness, and social justice for the poor. In 1991, the ASA made major changes in its vision and programs, shifting to a nearly exclusive focus on providing financial services for poor **women** in rural areas. It is managed by a governing body of eight people. The ASA operates 830 branches in 61 districts and has 1.23 million members, of whom 1.22 million are active borrowers. Savers are borrowers and have accumulated about $22 million. The membership is 94 percent female. The repayment rate is 99.74 percent. Members can borrow small amounts of the equivalent of about $200 to $240. The members receive training in leadership and management. The ASA is associated with the Women's World Banking network, which has affiliates in 34 nations.

ATAUR RAHMAN KHAN (1907–1991). He became a member of the **Awami League** at its inception in 1949. He acted as president of the **East Bengal** Awami League several times when the head of the provincial organization, **Maulana Bhashani**, was in jail. He was elected to the East Bengal Assembly in 1954 and was leader of the Awami League part of the **United Front**. After representative government was restored to the province in 1956, Ataur Rahman served as chief minister of **East Pakistan** throughout much of the period from 1956 to 1958 (when **Ayub Khan**'s coup displaced him), with the exception of short periods when the **Krishak Sramik Party** leader **Abu Hussain Sarkar** was able to form a government.

After the death of Awami League founder **Husain Shahid Suhrawardy** in 1963, Ataur Rahman Khan's relations with Sheikh **Mujibur Rahman** became difficult, and in the 1970 election Ataur Rahman Khan formed the Pakistan (later Bangladesh) National League. He was defeated in 1970 but won election to the Bangladesh Parliament in 1973 (and was leader of the opposition in 1975 when Mujibur Rahman imposed one-party rule) and led the opposition again in 1979. On 30 March 1984, Ataur Rahman was appointed prime minister by the martial law president, **Hussain Muhammad Ershad**, and held that office until 7 January 1985, when Ershad reshuffled the entire cabinet.

ATISH DIPANKAR SRIGYAN (982–1054). One of a number of Bengali **Buddhist** scholars who transmitted Buddhist ideas to Tibet. He came from **Vikrampur**, a major Buddhist center, and also studied at Nalanda in Bihar. In Tibet, he gathered and copied Sanskrit manuscripts, which he sent to Bengal, and Tibetan manuscripts for use in India. His masterpiece is *Lamp for the Way of Enlightenment*. Bangladesh awards the Atish prize for scholarship and service to education.

AUGUST COUP. The first coup by the Bangladesh army took place on 15 August 1975. This coup led to the assassination of Sheikh **Mujibur Rahman** and the collapse of the first democratically elected government of Bangladesh, although by this time the regime of Mujib had become autocratic. The coup was led by junior-ranking members of the army, including two lieutenant colonels and five majors. The August coup was followed by the November 1975 coup and countercoup in which **Khalid Musharraf** was killed and **Ziaur Rahman** became the key person in the government. *See also* ARMED FORCES.

AUROBINDO. *See* GHOSE, AUROBINDO.

AWAMI LEAGUE. Founded in June 1949, as the Awami ("People's") Muslim League by **Husain Shahid Suhrawardy** as a vehicle for his political ambitions and as a political party that would be an alternative to the **Muslim League.** Suhrawardy opposed the clause in the Muslim League constitution that prohibited non-Muslims from becoming members, stating that this would cause continued divisions in Pakistan; hence the word Muslim was soon dropped from the new party's name. The party developed little strength in West Pakistan, but emerged as the strongest party in **East Pakistan.** It joined with the **Krishak Sramik Party** and some smaller parties in the **United Front** of 1954, which won the legislative election in East Bengal from the Muslim League.

Among those closely associated with Suhrawardy were **Ataur Rahman Khan,** chief minister for most of the period from 1956 to 1958; Sheikh **Mujibur Rahman,** organizational leader during the same period and, after the death of Suhrawardy, de facto leader of the party; and **Maulana Abdul Hamid Khan Bhashani.**

Bhashani differed with Suhrawardy on domestic and international issues and left the party in 1957 to form the **National Awami Party (NAP).** The program of the party on economic matters was middle of the road, although after Bangladeshi independence Mujibur Rahman, as prime minister and later as president, pursued a strong program of nationalization of industry and trade. Before independence, Mujib supported a high degree of autonomy for the provinces of Pakistan; this was embodied in the **Six-Point Program** Mujib proclaimed in 1966.

In the 1970 **elections** the Awami League swept both the East Pakistan segment of the National Assembly and East Pakistan Provincial Assembly polls. After Bangladeshi independence, the Awami League held office until mid-1975, when it merged into **BAKSAL.**

After independence the program of the party was expressed in **Mujibbad**: democracy, nationalism, secularism, and socialism. The creation of a single-party state following what are widely believed to have been rigged elections in 1973 made a mockery of democracy and made the Awami League seem concerned with the single goal of retaining power.

After the November 1975 coup and after political parties were permitted to return to activity, the party was revived. It supported **Muhammad Ataul Ghani Osmany** for the presidency in 1978 and participated in the 1979 parliamentary elections, winning about 10 percent of the seats and becoming the official opposition to the **Bangladesh Nationalist Party (BNP)**. In the presidential election in 1981, following the assassination of **Ziaur Rahman**, the Awami League candidate, **Kamal Hossain**, finished second to the BNP's **Abdus Sattar**.

In May 1981, the almost leaderless Awami League called upon Mujib's daughter, **Sheikh Hasina Wajid**, who had been in exile, to assume the leadership post. She had no previous political experience, but the party felt that her familial association with Mujib would draw additional membership to the weakened party.

The Awami League was banned again after the coup led by General **Hussain Muhammad Ershad** in 1982, but the party revived once again to finish second in the 1986 parliamentary elections to Ershad's **Jatiya Party**. (The BNP did not participate.) When Ershad had parliament pass an indemnity act that forbade any legal challenge to his martial law actions in 1987, the Awami League withdrew from parliament. The party did not participate in the 1986 presidential election, which was won by Ershad, or the 1988 parliamentary election.

The Awami League favors a Westminster form of parliamentary government, but it has dropped the socialist economy platform and now favors a market economy, albeit somewhat mildly. It remains strongly secular in its stance.

The present leader of the party (and now leader of the opposition in parliament since the Awami League's defeat in the 2001 election) is Sheikh Hasina Wajid. In the February 1991 election the Awami League won the second-largest number of seats. In 1994 and 1995, the Awami League pressed for an amendment to the constitution that would provide for elections to be held under a **caretaker government** similar to those held in 1991. The Awami League parliamentarians and those of other opposition parties resigned from parliament on 28 December 28 1994.

Parliament was dissolved in November 1995. A new election was called for February 1996. The Awami League and most other opposition parties boycotted this election and the BNP gained an overwhelming majority. The new parliament passed a constitutional amendment providing for a caretaker government as demanded by the opposition in the previous parliament, and then dissolved the parliament. Another election was held in June 1996 in which the Awami League gained a plurality (but not a majority of the seats). It formed a new government with the support of the Jatiya Party with Sheikh Hasina Wajid as prime minister.

When this parliament ended its term, a new election was held in October 2001 in which the Awami League was soundly defeated, winning less than one-third of the seats. The new government was formed by the BNP and its electoral associates. The Awami League's defeat came as no surprise to observers of the Bangladesh political scene. The party had performed poorly, especially in economic affairs, and was viewed by many as **corrupt**. Sheikh Hasina seemed to many to be more concerned with keeping alive the memory of Mujib than with governance. An example of this was the passing of an act that would permit Hasina to live in the prime minister's residence in perpetuity. Needless to say, this act was repealed on the assumption of power by the BNP.

During 2001–2006 the party struggled to bring down the BNP government by mass demonstrations and non-participation in the parliamentary process, challenging the BNP government on its inability to curtail militancy, manage the **economy,** and, above all, curb corruption. In 2007–2008, the Awami League played an initially supportive role in the caretaker government of Fakhruddin Ahmed but increasingly distanced itself from any close cooperation. The return to power through the ninth parliamentary election is seen as a vindication of its principled stand on democracy. The Awami League's "A Charter for Change" 2008 election manifesto, consisting of 23 national needs, highlighted its desire to (1) have a stronger Anti-corruption Commission; (2) have 5,000 megawatts of power by 2011;

(3) have free education up to the undergraduate degree level; (4) institute permanent pay and wage commission; (5) provide jobs for one youth per family; and (6) place war criminals on trial. *See also* JAMA'AT-I-ISLAMI.

AWAMI LEAGUE—BANGLADESH KHELAFAT MAJLISH ELECTION ALLIANCE ACCORD. On 23 December 2006, an accord between the **Awami League,** the acknowledged secular political party, and an Islamic party gravely damaged the reputation of the Awami League. The Bangladesh Khelafat Majlish is an insignificant political party, but this accord compromised the secular nature of the Awami League, especially its acceptance of the clause that no law in Bangladesh will be formulated that contradicts the holy Qur'an. The major clauses of the accord are as follows: 1) No law will be formulated that contradicts the holy Qur'an, the Sunnah (of the prophet), and the Sharia; 2) Qaumi Madrasah certificates will be provided their due; and 3) Laws enacted will acknowledge that Prophet Muhammad is the last and the greatest of the messengers, that certified knowledgeable clerics will have the right to issue *fatwa* and anyone without certification will not be able to issue any *fatwa*, and that criticism and vilification of prophets and *sahabas* (companions of prophets) are punishable crimes. *See also* ISLAM.

AYUB KHAN, MUHAMMAD (1907–1974). President of **Pakistan,** 1958–1969, he was a career military officer in the Indian and Pakistani armies, having been commissioned from Sandhurst in 1928. He reached the rank of major general in 1948 while he was in command of the troops stationed in **East Bengal.**

In 1951, having reached the rank of lieutenant general, he was appointed the first Pakistani to be commander in chief of the army (his predecessors since independence in 1947 had been British officers seconded to the Pakistani army). Ayub was additionally minister of defense in the "cabinet of talents" headed by **Muhammad Ali Bogra** from October 1954 to August 1955 and during this time was a key person in the negotiation of military assistance from the **United States** to Pakistan.

On 7 October 1958, he became chief martial law administrator (until 1962) following the dismissal of the civilian government by

President **Iskandar Mirza**; Ayub then deposed Mirza on 28 October and became president (until 25 March 1969). Rioting in opposition to his rule began in West Pakistan in September 1968 and quickly spread to **East Pakistan**. Despite Ayub's offer to restore parliamentary rule and his withdrawal of the **Agartala Conspiracy Case** against **Mujibur Rahman** and others, he was forced by leaders of the military to resign the presidency to General **Agha Muhammad Yahya Khan**.

While Ayub's period of rule oversaw considerable economic growth in East Pakistan, the growth in West Pakistan was much more rapid, leading to a marked increase in the economic disparity between the two provinces. He generally supported private investment, but he did little to **privatize** enterprises already owned by the government.

Ayub attempted to bring government closer to the people through a program called **Basic Democracy**. In the international field, his ill-fated conflict with **India** over Kashmir in September 1965 resulted in a cease-fire but didn't accomplish Pakistan's objective of "liberating" Kashmir. He was, in effect, forced to go to the Tashkent conference called by the **Soviet Union** that resulted in a return to the status quo. Although he was the foreign minister at the time, **Zulfiqar Ali Bhutto** strongly opposed Ayub, which contributed to Ayub's eventual downfall. *See also* AZAM KHAN.

AZAD, MUHAMMAD ABDUS SAMAD (1922–2005). From **Sylhet**, he has long been associated with the **Awami League**. Azad was a member of the cabinet of **Mujibur Rahman** as minister of foreign affairs (1972–1973) and agriculture (1973–1975). He was minister of foreign affairs again in the cabinet of **Sheikh Hasina Wajid** (1996–2001).

AZAM, GOLAM (1922–). He was the *amir* (leader) of the **Jama'at-i-Islami** from 1992 to 2001. He was born in **Dhaka** and educated at Dhaka University, where he was actively involved in student politics. Golam Azam taught at Carmichael College in Rangpur and joined the Jama'at in 1955. He was elected president of the **East Pakistan** Jama'at in 1969 and has served several jail terms for his activities.

Golam Azam was accused of collaborating with the **Pakistan** army in 1971 and was stripped of his Bangladeshi citizenship in 1973 as a result. He returned to Bangladesh from exile to assume the leadership of the Jama'at. Golam Azam's citizenship was restored by a Supreme Court decision in 1994. This brought protests from many in Bangladesh and demands for his trial on charges of murder during 1971. One group, of which **Jahanara Imam** was a prominent member, held a mock trial and "convicted" him.

AZAM KHAN, MUHAMMAD (1908–1994). Appointed the administrator of Martial Law Zone B, which included the whole of West Pakistan except Karachi, when General **Muhammad Ayub Khan** took over in 1958. He was given high credit for his reorganization of the Ministry of Refugees and Rehabilitation. In 1960, Azam Khan was appointed governor of **East Pakistan**. He became a very popular governor because of his untiring effort to reach the people. His popularity was seen as a threat to President Ayub, who removed him in 1962. He came to prominence once again when he joined the opposition and supported the presidential candidacy of Fatima Jinnah against Ayub Khan in 1964. Azam Khan continued to oppose Ayub, but he became quite inactive after Ayub's ouster.

AZIZ-UL-HUQUE, SIR MUHAMMAD (1892–1947). A lawyer by profession, he served as a member of the Governor-General's Executive Council, 1943–1946. Earlier he was the Indian High Commissioner to Great Britain (1942–1943). His efforts in the field of **education** are well recognized. As vice-chancellor of **Calcutta** University from 1928 to 1942, he established the first Department of Islamic History and Culture. He was elected to the Bengal Legislative Council in 1929 and was education minister, 1934–1937. Elected to the new Bengal Legislative Assembly in 1937, Aziz-ul-Huque was chosen Speaker and served until his appointment as high commissioner in London in 1942 in succession to **Malik Firoz Khan Noon**. He was an active member of the **Muslim League** and supported the League's decision to accept the **Cabinet Mission Plan**. He wrote the book *Man behind the Plough*, published in 1939. His son, **Ahsan-ul-Huque**, served in the **Pakistan** cabinet and as a Pakistani ambassador.

AZIZUR RAHMAN, SHAH MOHAMMAD (1925–1988). Secretary general of the All-India Muslim Students Federation and All-Bengal Muslim Students League from 1945 to 1947. He became the joint secretary of the East Pakistan Muslim League in 1947 and was the general secretary from 1952 to 1958. He joined the **Awami League** in 1964. In 1969, he was the deputy leader of the party in the Pakistan National Assembly. During the **War of Liberation** Shah Aziz remained out of politics, but reemerged when the Bangladesh **Muslim League** was permitted to operate in 1976. In 1979, he was elected a member of the parliament and became the prime minister of the country. Shah Aziz joined the **Bangladesh Nationalist Party (BNP).** He continued as the prime minister until December 1981. After the assassination of President **Ziaur Rahman** in May 1981, Shah Aziz remained with the BNP until he was expelled from the party for "disciplinary reasons" in 1985.

– B –

BACKERGANJ. *See* BARISAL.

BADRUDDUJA, SYED (1900–1974). A Muslim politician from Murshidabad district, he remained in India after partition. He was associated with both the **Muslim League** and the **Krishak Praja Party (KPP),** having been elected to the Bengal Legislative Assembly in 1937 on the Muslim League ticket and losing in 1946 on the KPP ticket. Badrudduja was mayor of **Kolkata** from 1943 to 1944. After independence he served at various times as a member of the West Bengal Legislative Assembly and the Lok Sabha. One of Badrudduja's daughters, Razia Faiz, has been a member of the Pakistan National Assembly and the Bangladesh Parliament as a Muslim League member from Khulna.

BADRUNNESSA AHMAD (1929–1974). She served as minister of education in the Sheikh **Mujibur Rahman** government that was formed after the parliamentary election of 1973. She was a member of the East Bengal Legislative Assembly from 1954 to 1958. Badrunnessa served as the vice president of the Mahila Samity (**Women's**

Organization) of **East Pakistan** and later of Bangladesh from 1959 to 1972. A member of the **Awami League**, she actively participated in the **War of Liberation** by promoting the Bangladeshi cause. Like many of her contemporaries, Badrunnessa was arrested during the **language movement**.

BAKSAL. An acronym for Bangladesh Krishak Sramik Awami League, the name chosen by Sheikh **Mujibur Rahman** for the single party in Bangladesh decreed by him in June 1975. The name combined the names of two of the parties, the **Awami League** and **Krishak Sramik Party,** which had joined to form the **United Front** in 1954. Not all Awami Leaguers agreed to join the new party; those who did not were technically out of politics. BAKSAL was dissolved following the assassination of Mujibur Rahman on 15 August 1975, and the installation of a new government under **Khondakar Mushtaque Ahmed**. A small group has continued to use the name and won five seats in parliament in the 1991 election, but it has not won seats in subsequent elections.

BALDAH GARDEN. A private botanical garden established in 1909 by Narendra Narayan Rai Chowdhury, who owned Baldah estate. After his death in 1936, a private trust took over the management of the garden. In 1964, it was taken over by the public sector. It is now part of the national botanical garden system. The garden has two parts—Psyche (soul) and Cybele (mother of the goddess of nature). Psyche is a collection of plants from over 50 countries which Narendra Chowdhury had visited. Cybele comprises the propagated species of the plants in Psyche. Baldah Garden is spread over 3.38 acres of land, including over 18,000 trees covering more than 600 species, 335 genera, and 87 families. The baobab plant (*Adansonia digitata*), *Camelia japonica* from Japan, *Pothos* from Indonesia, *Salix* from Afghanistan, maranta, and *Anthurium* are some of the unusual types of plants in the garden. **Rabindranath Tagore** composed his famous poem "Camelia" when he visited the garden. Currently the garden suffers from lack of proper maintenance.

BANDE ALI MIAH (1906–1979). He was born in Pabna district. His published works include more than 80 books of poetry, prose, and plays. In 1927, he published his first book, *Char-Jamai*. His most renowned poem, entitled "*Maynamotir Char*," was published in 1931, and was praised by **Rabindranath Tagore** as one of the finest depictions of rural life of the people living by the river Padma. Noteworthy books included *Anurag* (1933), *Padma Nadir Char* (1933), *Shapno Shadh* (1936), *Madhumatir Char* (1946), *Jagrato Jouban* (1949), *Tasher Ghar* (1954), *Moner Mour* (1956), and *Aranno Godhuli* (1958). He also wrote a number of books for children, including *Megh Kumari, Jongoler Khabar, Jangaler Raja* and *Shishuder Bishad Shindhu*. While primarily known for his poetry and prose, he was also a painter and used his brush to vividly depict rural life. He spent considerable time in Kolkata, India, but moved back to Bangladesh after the partition of India in 1947. From 1964 till his death he served as a scriptwriter at Radio Rajshahi. *See also* LITERATURE.

BANERJEA, SURENDRANATH (1848–1925). An important Bengali moderate political figure. He entered the Indian Civil Service in 1871, one of the first Indians to do so, but he was dismissed for "procedural irregularities," a euphemism for his nationalist views, in 1875. Banerjea devoted himself to education and nationalist politics, serving as president of the Indian National Congress in 1895 and 1902. Opposed to what he considered to be extremism in the Congress, Banerjea and others formed the National Liberal Federation in 1918. He was a founder of Ripon College in **Calcutta**.

BANERJI, RAKHALDAS (1886–1930). A noted historian and archeologist, he was born in Murshidabad district, now in West Bengal. He worked first as an archeologist in the Indus valley, but later studied the **Pala dynasty** and worked at **Paharpur**. Among Banerji's works are *Palas of Bengal, The Origin of the Bengali Script*, and *Eastern India School of Medieval Sculpture*.

BANG TRIBE. Believed to have been the first Indo-Aryan group to have migrated to the lower Ganges valley and to have given its name to Bengal. (In Sanskrit, the tribe is Vang and the area **Vanga**.)

BANGALEE SHAMAGRA GALLERY. A private gallery that displays portraits of important personalities of Bangladesh and West

Bengal who have contributed to the sociocultural development of Bangladesh. These portraits are grouped in four categories: 1) language, **literature, education**; 2) society, politics, economics; 3) **music, theatre, film**, sports; and 4) science, **architecture**, fine arts. The gallery also displays the original manuscripts, diaries, works, and personal belongings of those whose portraits are displayed. There is also a collection of newspapers and magazines, and a new section of interviews of critical personalities on videotape is being developed. The gallery is built around 52 portraits and opened in 2004.

BANGLA BHAI (1970–2007). He used a number of aliases, including Siddiqul Islam and Azizur Rahman, and is primarily known for conducting terrorist activities in Rajshahi district. In the late 1980s he is supposed to have fought in **Afghanistan** as a *mujahidin*. He became a member of **Jagrata Muslim Janata Bangladesh** (JMJB) and was responsible for intimidating and torturing those who he decided were not following **Islamic** practices, as well as other minorities. He is considered one of the masterminds of the 17 August 2005 countrywide bombing. He was the commander of the militant wing of JMJB and also became a member of its decision-making body, the *Majlish-e-Shura*. On 6 March 2006 he was captured by the **Rapid Action Battalion** in Mymensingh and for his terroristic activities he was sentenced to death in May 2006. He was executed on 30 March 2007 along with five other militants.

BANGLA KEYBOARD. In 1988 Mostafa Jabbar created the software program *Bijoy* and patented a computer keyboard that used Bangla. After a two-decade patent challenge, his computer company, Ananda Computer, was assessed to have the patent rights to the Bangla keyboard.

BANGLADESH ACADEMY OF RURAL DEVELOPMENT (BARD). The name now used by the former **East Pakistan** unit of the **Pakistan** Academy of Rural Development was established in 1959 in **Comilla**. It was originally known as the Comilla Rural Academy and later as the East Pakistan unit of the Pakistan Academy of Rural Development. Its purpose was to apply social science theories to practical problems of administration and to promote rural development. In the beginning, under an agreement with the United States Agency for International Development (USAID), the project was aided by Michigan State University. The Comilla district was used as a living laboratory to test projects which could then be applied to other parts of the country. The four major project areas were an improved model for rural administration, a model for reconstruction and expansion of rural infrastructure, a model for utilization of surface and ground water for irrigation, and a new, two-tier cooperative system. BARD undertakes evaluations of rural projects and offers advisory and consultancy services. The academy also offers a wide range of courses on rural matters to resident scholars. As a result, Comilla is often used as a model for rural development in the international development community. The late **Akhtar Hameed Khan** is credited with the success of the program. After Bangladeshi independence, he returned to Pakistan. Much of the research was undertaken in the Matlab Thana of Comilla district. One of the projects that resulted was the Cholera Research Laboratory in **Dhaka** (now named the **International Centre for Diarrhoeal Disease Research, Bangladesh**).

BANGLADESH JAMA'AT-E-ISLAMI. *See* JAMA'AT-I-ISLAMI.

BANGLADESH KRISHAK SRAMIK AWAMI LEAGUE. *See* BAKSAL.

BANGLADESH LOKO SANGEET PARISHAD (BLSP). The Bangladesh Folk Song Committee was formed under the leadership of Indra Mohan Rajbangshi in 1998 for the purpose of promoting the folk **music** heritage of Bangladesh. It now has 35 branches in six districts. Since its inception it has held 82 programs on folk music. In 2003 it brought together 120 folk singers and held a three-day musical festival called *Shoto Moromi Kobir Gaan.*

BANGLADESH MUSLIM LEAGUE. An outgrowth of the Pakistan **Muslim League**, itself an outgrowth of the All-India Muslim League, which was established in 1906. The Pakistan Muslim League was the governing party in **East Pakistan** until the provincial election of 1954, when it lost heavily to the **United Front**. In the 1960s the Pakistan Muslim League broke into two factions: the **Pakistan Muslim League (Convention)** and the **Council Muslim League.** After the independence of Bangladesh, both factions were banned. These two factions cooperated after the passing of the Political Parties Regulation Ordinance of 1976 and formed the Bangladesh Muslim League. In 1978 this party split into two factions. The more conservative group was led by **Abdul Sobur Khan** and the more liberal wing by **Shah Azizur Rahman.** Azizur Rahman later joined the **Bangladesh Nationalist Party**, and after Sobur's death the remainder of the party factionalized to the extent that it is now all but nonexistent and it has not participated in recent elections under that name. *See also* ELECTIONS.

BANGLADESH NATIONALIST PARTY (BNP). The BNP was originally formed in 1978 as the political vehicle for the associates of the then-president, **Ziaur Rahman.** Zia had been elected in June 1978 as the candidate of **JAGODAL** (an acronym for the Bengali equivalent of "People's Party"). Besides JAGODAL, the party included elements from the leftist **National Awami Party**, the conservative **Bangladesh Muslim League**, and several other smaller parties and groups. The party supported the **Nineteen Points Program.** The titular leader of the party was Justice **Abdus Sattar**, who succeeded Ziaur Rahman as president when the latter was assassinated in 1981. The BNP won more than two-thirds of the parliamentary seats in the 1979 elections.

Since Zia's assassination and the coup that ousted Sattar in 1982, the party has been led by Ziaur Rahman's widow, **Khaleda Zia.** It boycotted the 1986 and 1988 parliamentary elections. Before and after the elections it saw many key members defect, usually to support president **Hussain Muhammad Ershad** and his **Jatiya Party.** However, in November and December 1990, the BNP joined with the **Awami League** and other smaller groups to lead demonstrations against Ershad, which led to his fall in December and the installation of a **caretaker government** under chief justice **Shahabuddin Ahmed** that had as its primary charge the holding of elections. The BNP gained a majority in parliament through the February election and Khaleda Zia became prime minister on 20 March 1991. This parliament was dissolved in November 1995.

In the election held in June 1996, the BNP finished second and became the principal opposition to the governing Awami League. As the Awami League had during the preceding BNP government, the BNP boycotted much of the 1996–2001 parliamentary sessions. However, when the term of that parliament expired, the BNP and its allies won a two-thirds majority in the 2001 election. Khaleda Zia again became prime minister. BNP's 36-point "Save Country Save People" 2008 election manifesto declared, among many changes, the following: (1) Deputy speaker would be selected from the opposition; (2) Speaker and deputy speaker have to quit party posts; (3) There would be an independent secretariat under Supreme Court; (4) All-party Jatiya Sangshad would appoint the Anti-corruption Commission and University Grants Commission chiefs; (5) Health insurance for the poor and unemployment allowances would be provided; and (6) A job would be ensured for at least one youth per family. However, in the election of December 2008, the BNP lost, primarily due to mismanagement and corruption during its tenure from 2001 to 2006 and its inability to curb growing militancy in the country. Its close relationship with the Bangladesh Jama'at-i-Islami party is viewed by many in the party as a major drawback.

Since its founding, the party has been considered to be somewhat right of center. For example, it opposed the socialization program of the Awami League (which has now discarded that pillar of **Mujib-bad**). The BNP in office has modified the secular approach held by the Awami League and, like the Jatiya Party, has moved toward the recognition that the vast majority of the Bangladesh population is Muslim. As a result of the actions of the two parties, **Islam** has become the state religion of the country. *See also* AWAMI LEAGUE—BANGLADESH KHELAFAT MAJLISH ELECTION ALLIANCE ACCORD.

BANGLADESH RIFLES (BDR). A paramilitary force, its primary role is to protect the 4,500-kilometer border of Bangladesh. Its origin can be traced to the Ramgarh Local Battalion formed in 1795. Between 1891 and 1920, it was renamed the Bengal Military Police and was charged with border protection. In 1920, the Eastern Frontier Rifles was formed, which in turn became the East Pakistan Rifles in 1947. During the **War of Liberation** members of the East Pakistan Rifles fought against the Pakistani armed forces. Two of the seven recipients of the highest military awards for bravery (Bir Srestha) were members of the East Pakistan Rifles. In 1972, the Bangladesh Rifles was established. Its officer corps is drawn from the Bangladesh army. In February 2009, for reasons still unknown, the Bangladesh Rifles soldiers mutinied and killed 52 military officers. *See also* ARMED FORCES.

BANGLADESH RURAL ADVANCEMENT COMMITTEE (BRAC). Now formally known as BRAC, it is a private-sector development organization that has been operating in Bangladesh since 1972. BRAC implements a number of multisectoral programs to achieve its two major goals of alleviating poverty and empowering the poor. BRAC programs cover more than 60,000 villages in all districts, benefiting more than 110 million people. It has also begun operations in some urban slums. BRAC's objectives are to make the program participants aware of their own problems, to provide them with tools to unite into organized groups, and to increase their capacity to exercise their legal and civic rights. It has a loan program under which in the first six months of 2002 it lent $140 million, bringing the cumulative value of its loans to $1.6 billion.

These small loans are made to 3.5 million members and have a repayment rate of 99.12 percent, according to BRAC reports. The lent funds support many sectors of **agriculture** such as **poultry**, livestock, sericulture, and fisheries. BRAC arranges for the export of vegetable crops to Europe and Southeast Asia in particular. It claims to be the largest **non-governmental organization** in the world. Its total workforce is over 100,000, a majority of them **women**. It has also established BRAC University in **Dhaka** and has opened a **bank**. BRAC also operates in neighboring Sri Lanka, Afghanistan, and in several countries of Africa.

BANKING. Following independence the **Awami League** government nationalized all domestic banks. Foreign banks, of which there were several, were permitted to continue operations, and the number of foreign banks has since increased. During the **Hussain Muhammad Ershad** regime, the denationalization of some banks took place and several privately owned banks were permitted to begin operations. Central banking is performed by the Bank of Bangladesh.

BARA BHUIYAN. Literally the "twelve landowners," the Bara Bhuiyan were a group of chieftains who resisted **Mughal** rule in the late 16th century. The principal leader was **Isa Khan**, who controlled territory in **Comilla, Dhaka,** and **Mymensingh** districts from his base near **Sonargaon.** Another key person among them was **Pratapaditya,** whose lands were in the region of **Khulna.** In 1584 the Bara Bhuiyan, led by Isa Khan, inflicted a major naval defeat on the Mughals and followed with almost continuous land combat. In 1594 the Mughal emperor Akbar appointed **Raja Man Singh** governor of Bengal in the hope of controlling eastern Bengal. Another naval defeat in 1597 tempered that hope, but Isa Khan died in 1598. Man Singh established a military headquarters in **Dhaka** in 1602. By the time Man Singh retired as governor in 1606, the rebellion had been quelled.

BARISAL. A region, district, and district town. The district was formerly part of Backerganj, which was divided into Barisal and **Patuakhali** in December 1969. Barisal town was the headquarters of Backerganj district. The area had formed a part of the kingdom of **Vanga** or **Samatata** in ancient times. In the 16th century, it was under one of the chieftains of the **Bara Bhuiyan;** this chieftain had a marriage alliance with **Pratapaditya.** The area was subject to raids by the **Maghs** of **Arakan** in the 17th and 18th centuries. It then passed into the hands of Agha Bakar, for whom the village of Backerganj is named. The **Mughals** established a fort, no longer standing, near Barisal to control the region. The British gained the district in 1765 when they obtained the **diwani** from the Mughal governor of Bengal.

Barisal is a river port, lying on a branch of the Arial Khan River, about 70 miles south of Dhaka and 100 miles from the Bay of Bengal. Trade is largely in rice, jute, and fish. The city is also home to a curiosity, the "Barisal guns," an unexplained noise similar to a cannon firing. It is the home of **Fazlul Haq.** When the **Hussain Muhammad Ershad** government made subdivision districts, the former Barisal district was divided into Barisal, Jhalakati, and Pirojpur districts.

BARKATULLAH, MOHAMMAD (1889–1975). A member of the Indian Civil Service, he served in a number of positions but is best known for his role in organizing the Bangla Academy.

BASIC DEMOCRACY. The term used for local government during the **Ayub Khan** regime. Insofar as local government itself was concerned, it was not a radical change from previous systems. Local (union) councils of 7 to 15 members were elected by direct franchise, each member to represent about 1,000 persons. **Parity** was applied so that there were 40,000 basic democrats from each wing. Local duties included some powers of taxation, administration, adjudication, and development. Higher levels of government were also covered by the system at the *tehsil* (West Pakistan) and *thana* (East Pakistan) tiers and at the district level. The significant innovation by Ayub was that the 80,000 basic democrats would also serve as an electoral college for the office of the presidency and the national and provincial assemblies. This last aspect was strongly opposed by the **Combined Opposition Parties** and other opposition groups. These groups favored a system of direct elections at all levels of government (and, generally, also favored a parliamentary system).

BASIC PRINCIPLES REPORT. The working draft that culminated in the 1956 **constitution of Pakistan**. The report was first published in 1950 and was criticized by the **United Front** for, among other things, its proposition that Urdu be the national language of Pakistan. *See also* LANGUAGE MOVEMENT.

BAU-KUL FRUIT FARMING. Two research scientists from the Germ Plasma Center of Bangladesh Agricultural University, Professors A. M. Faruq and M. A. Rahmin, collected a local variety of *kul* (a type of fruit), as well as samples from the Philippines, Somalia, Taiwan, Thailand, and India to develop a fast-growing variety that could generate income for small farmers. Their research started in 1999 and was completed in 2003 when the adaptation trials were completed. In 2005, the National Seed Board registered the fruit as FTIP BAU-*kul*. Fruits are borne within three months of planting. Fruit output the first year is expected to be about 10 kilograms, to nearly quadruple by the second year, and to continue to increase as the tree matures. It is citric, with a meaty flesh and a central pit. The ripe fruit can be eaten fresh, cooked, dried, and in pickle form. This type of agricultural research is new in Bangladesh and is instrumental in contributing to the economic improvement of the rural small-business sector.

BAULS. A rustic group of troubadours who travel from one area to another, singing devotional songs. They often use a one-string instrument (*ektara*) for their **music**. Described as a mystical sect, the group practices a combination of **Islam** and **Hinduism**. The Bauls emphasize freedom from compulsion, doctrine, caste, and formal worship. The word "Baul" originated from "Bawra"—meaning people who do not associate with traditional lifestyles or norms. Bauls are not followers of any stated religion or religious communities. They believe in the religion of "humanity." Searching for the "higher being" through love, peace, and harmony among fellow human beings is their conviction. Local singers of religious songs (*Nabitatwa Gaan*), their instruments of choice are the two-string *dotara* and s*horaj*. The Bauls also use the *dhol* and *tabla* (drums) and the flute, violin, and mandolin. They tend to follow ascetic and austere lifestyles, although as their songs are becoming more popular some of them are becoming more materialistic in their outlook. Some master the art of making music with their tongues, known as *jibra*. Other art forms include the *palta-palti* and *sawaal-jawaab* (question-answer) sung as duets. The Bauls are increasingly highlighted on Bangladesh TV, and are making their presence felt in nontraditional cultural events such as those held by the diplomatic communities. UNESCO proclaimed the traditional Baul songs of Bangladesh as one of the 43 masterpieces of oral and intangible world heritage. *See also* MUSIC.

BAYAZID BASTAMI. A Persian who was born in the ninth century and settled in **Chittagong**. He was a preacher, and there are numerous myths and legends about him. He converted a large number of **Hindus** and **Buddhists** to **Islam**. Bayazid's tomb in Chittagong is an important pilgrimage site. The tomb is near a small pond that is known for its numerous large tortoises, suggesting that the site may have an older Hindu connection. This shrine is now considered a national heritage site of Bangladesh.

BAYAZID SHAH. Titular ruler of Bengal, 1412–1414, who was overthrown by **Raja Ganesh**.

BENGAL FAMINE (1943). The **famine** of 1943, at its height from July to December, is estimated to have caused between 1.5 and 3.5 million deaths. It is sometimes described as "man-made," although nature also played a part. There was a decline in food production in **India** and an increase in population. Imports to Bengal from the usual source, **Burma**, were unavailable because of the Japanese conquest, and, at the same time, the British feared a major invasion of India and were prepared to deny food to the potential invaders by a scorched earth policy in eastern Bengal. The governments of Bengal and India had failed to anticipate and prepare for the replacement of the imports and failed in the distribution of what was available.

BENGAL, PARTITION OF (1905). The then-viceroy, **Lord Curzon**, determined that the province of Bengal (which then included approximately the present territory of Bangladesh and the Indian states of West Bengal, Bihar, and Orissa) was too large to be administered efficiently. Curzon decreed a partition in 1905. One new province, named Eastern Bengal and **Assam**, joined what is roughly Bangladesh today with the area north and northeast of it. It had a Muslim majority and the capital was **Dhaka**. The other province was named Bengal, and included western Bengal, Bihar, and Orissa. It had a **Hindu** majority, but the Bengalis were no longer the majority group, being outnumbered by the combined Biharis and Oriyas. The capital was **Calcutta**. Bengali Hindus objected strongly to the partition, and this was expressed through written protests, speeches, demonstrations, boycotts of British goods, violence, and terrorism. Bengali Muslims were, expectedly, pleased with the prospect of a province in which they would be a majority, especially as new constitutional reforms by the British were expected to include provincial elections (the **Government of India Act of 1909** was already under discussion). The British finally heeded the Hindu objections, and the partition was annulled in 1911. Bengal was reunited, Assam separated, and Bihar and Orissa joined in a single province (they were separated in 1936). Accompanying the annulment was the British decision to transfer the capital of India from Calcutta to New Delhi.

BENGAL, PARTITION OF (1947). The partition of India in 1947 also required the partition of two provinces: the Punjab and Bengal.

A commission headed by a British judge, Sir Cyril (later Lord) Radcliffe, was charged with the task of determining the boundaries. The basic rule was that contiguous areas with Muslim majorities would go to **Pakistan**. Some leeway was permitted in the decision. In dividing Bengal, the commission decided that **Khulna** district, despite its **Hindu** majority, would go to Pakistan, and **Murshidabad** district, despite its Muslim majority, would go to **India**. One reason for this decision was that West Bengal would have been split into two parts if a connecting area in Murshidabad were not given to India. Some other districts, such as Malda and **Dinajpur**, were divided between the two countries. The **Sylhet Referendum** was also held to decide the boundary between East Bengal and Assam.

BENGAL TENANCY ACT (1885). The act was intended to provide security to tenants by giving them the right of occupancy and inheritance. Tenants who held land in the same village could not be evicted. It also limited rent paid by an "occupancy" tenant to one-fifth of the produce. While intended to provide security to the tenants, the act also gave landlords the opportunity to contest matters in the courts, a path that was not available to the nearly destitute tenants.

BENGALI. *See* LANGUAGE.

BERUBARI ENCLAVE. A small piece of territory awarded to **East Bengal** in the partition of 1947 that is surrounded by India. Pakistan (and later, Bangladesh) and **India** have been unable to sort out the question of territory in north Bengal. The enclaves result primarily from the remnants of the former princely state of **Cooch Behar**. A portion of the disputed territory, Tin Bigha (literally, three *bighas* or one acre), was transferred by India to Bangladesh in 1992. *See also* BENGAL, PARTITION OF (1947).

BHADRALOK. Literally, this means respected people or gentlemen. They are socially privileged, educated members of society who have distinct speech, dress, housing, and eating habits. The *bhadralok* abstain from manual labor. The term is infrequently used in Bangladesh, as it is linked primarily to the **Hindu** caste system.

BHASHANI, MAULANA ABDUL HAMID KHAN (1885–1976).
A leader of the **Muslim League** in **Assam** before independence, although originally from Tangail district of eastern Bengal. He returned to **East Bengal** after independence and became a founding member of the **Awami League** in 1949 and president of the East Bengal provincial unit of the party. Although holding the Islamic title "maulana," Bhashani was often viewed as a leftist in politics, espousing the cause of the peasantry against the holders of power in the villages and, in international affairs, opposing the West and favoring closer ties with **China**, a product, as he saw it, of a peasant revolution. It was principally over international issues that Bhashani broke with **Husain Shahid Suhrawardy** in 1956, when Suhrawardy supported Pakistan's growing ties with the **United States**. Bhashani and his associates from the Awami League formed the **National Awami Party** in 1957, bringing his East Pakistani group into association with the Pakistan National Party of West Pakistan. In **East Pakistan** and in national politics Bhashani continued to play a prominent role in opposition (except on **Ayub Khan**'s policy of opening relations with China) until his death. Bhashani opposed **Mujibur Rahman**, most notably when he led protests against the **India-Bangladesh treaty** in 1972 and against **Farakka barrage**.

BHUTTO, ZULFIQAR ALI (1928–1979). A member of a prominent Sindhi family, he began his political career when he was appointed a minister in the first cabinet of **Ayub Khan** in 1958. He was foreign minister, 1963–1966. Resigning from the cabinet over differences with Ayub Khan on relations with **India**, he founded the **Pakistan People's Party (PPP)** in 1967 and remained its chairman until his death. The PPP won the majority of seats from West Pakistan in the National Assembly elected in December 1970, but won none in **East Pakistan**. In the negotiations following the election, Bhutto maintained that there were two majorities in Pakistan: his in West Pakistan and that of the **Awami League** led by **Mujibur Rahman** in East Pakistan. His actions, along with those of President **Yahya Khan**, are credited with bringing about the impasse that led to the breakdown of negotiations and the outbreak of civil war in March 1971. With the defeat of the Pakistani forces in December 1971,

Yahya Khan resigned and turned the government over to Bhutto and the PPP. Bhutto was president of Pakistan from 1971 to 1973, and, after a new constitution was adopted, served as prime minister from 1973 to 1977. He was overthrown in a coup led by General Muhammad Zia ul-Haq on 5 July 1977. Charged with complicity in a murder, Bhutto was convicted and hanged on 4 April 1979.

BIHARIS. The term used to describe those Muslim refugees, principally from Bihar, who fled eastward to **East Bengal** in 1947. The refugees were Urdu-speaking and found it difficult to integrate with the Bengali speakers in whose midst they found themselves. The term may also be derived from *baharis* (Urdu for "outsiders"). Generally, they were strong supporters of the Pakistan idea and many supported the **Pakistan** army during the 1971 **War of Liberation**. There were about 600,000 Biharis at that time. After independence, they were often shunned by Bangladeshis, and their plight made international news. Since then, many have gone to Pakistan, legally or illegally; a large number, perhaps 300,000, remain in camps, and many younger Biharis have integrated into Bangladeshi society. In May 2008, the Bangladesh High Court ruled that children of Urdu-speaking refugees, awaiting repatriation to Pakistan, have the right to Bangladeshi citizenship. Others also have the right to acquire citizenship and vote.

BIRANGANA. A term used to denote those **women** who were raped during the **War of Liberation** by members of the **Pakistan** armed forces. They also refer to those women who, during the war, lost their husbands and family breadwinners. The literal meaning of the term is heroine, symbolic of honor and courage rather than disgrace and shame. Although there is no exact count of their numbers, a consequence of rape during the war is the war babies. The government of Bangladesh established on 18 February 1972 the Bangladesh Women's Rehabilitation Board (BWRB) to address challenges faced by the affected women. To address the issue of war babies, especially for national and international adoption, the Bangladesh Abandoned Children (Special Provisions) Order 1972 was promulgated. On 21 July 2008 a special program was organized to remember one such person, Hasna Banu, who stated, "My village didn't accept me, neither did my husband. I had to take shelter in the near-by woods. However, my mother was sympathetic and secretly brought me food, though it was once a day, in the darkness of night usually. This is how I lived until a rehabilitation centre took me in."

BISWAS, ABDUL LATIF (1892–1964). A leader of the **Krishak Praja Party**, he was later the secretary of the **Krishak Sramik Party**. Between 1926 and 1945 he was a member of the Bengal Legislative Council and the Bengal Legislative Assembly. In 1954, Biswas was the minister of land revenue in the **United Front** government and became the central minister for food and agriculture in 1955. At his death he was a member of the National Democratic Front in opposition to **Ayub Khan**.

BISWAS, ABDUR RAHMAN (1926–). President of Bangladesh, from October 1991 to June 1996. He was a member of the cabinet of **Ziaur Rahman**, holding at various times the portfolios of jute, and health and population control. After the February 1991 election, he became speaker of **parliament**. Biswas was elected president after the parliament adopted an amendment to the **constitution** changing the governmental system from a presidential to a parliamentary one. He did not participate in the 2001 election.

BLACK HOLE. The name of a small room in old **Fort William** in **Calcutta** in which 146 British prisoners were allegedly kept in captivity by Nawab **Sirajuddaulah** after his capture of Calcutta on 20 June 1756. Some accounts state that 123 prisoners died of suffocation, although there is some question about the numbers involved. Other accounts have it that there were 64 prisoners, of whom 43 died.

BLUE MUTINY. In 1859, peasants refused to grow **indigo**, claiming that it was unprofitable for them. The peasants broke their contracts with the dealers and violence broke out between the two groups. In 1860, a government commission ruled that the payments were too low. They were increased and by 1861 production was restored. As noted in the entry on indigo, the development of synthetic blue dyes has meant that indigo is no longer produced.

BOGRA. District and district town on the banks of the **Karatoya River**, a branch of the Ganges. The river divides the district into two distinct geological zones: to the east is the alluvial soil typical of deltaic areas; to the west is the heavier clay of the Barind region (the name is derived from Birendra or **Varendra**). The river at one time formed the boundary between the Assamese kingdom of Kamarupa and the area of **Pundra**. It then came under the rule of the **Palas** and later the **Senas**, before being taken over by the **Delhi Sultanate**. Near Bogra city is the archeological site of **Mahasthangarh**. The upgrading of subdivisions in the **Hussain Muhammad Ershad** regime has resulted in the division of the former Bogra district into Bogra and Sherpur districts. Sherpur town was a Mughal outpost under **Raja Man Singh**.

BOGRA, MUHAMMAD ALI (1901–1963). A member of a leading landowning family in eastern Bengal, he was a grandson of **Syed Nawab Ali Choudhury**. He was elected to the Bengal Legislative Assembly in 1937 and 1946 and was appointed a parliamentary secretary in the **Khwaja Nazimuddin** government in 1943 and a minister in the **Suhrawardy** cabinet in 1946. After independence, he held high diplomatic posts (although he retained his membership in the constituent assembly): ambassador to **Burma** in 1948; high commissioner to Canada in 1949; and ambassador to the **United States** in 1952. Bogra was summoned back from the latter post to become prime minister in 1953, following the dismissal of Nazimuddin from that post by Governor-General **Ghulam Muhammad**. His first cabinet was political, but he reorganized the cabinet in 1954 to form a "cabinet of talents," including, among others, General **Ayub Khan** as minister of defense. Bogra was dismissed in 1955 and returned to the United States as ambassador from 1955 to 1958. Inactive in the first part of Ayub's regime, Bogra became minister of foreign affairs in 1962, holding the post until his death, when he was succeeded by **Zulfiqar Ali Bhutto**.

BOGRA MUTINY. One of the more significant coup attempts during the regime of President **Ziaur Rahman**. An army tank regiment in Bogra attempted to seize the local air force base in order to negotiate the freedom of Lieutenant Colonel Farook Rahman, who was one of the majors who had led the first army coup in Bangladesh that led to the assassination of Sheikh **Mujibur Rahman**. The Bogra mutiny started on 30 September 1977, and spread to **Dhaka** on 2 October 1977. The Dhaka phase of the coup attempt coincided with the unrelated hijacking of a Japan Airlines aircraft by the Japanese Red Army. The aircraft landed at Dhaka airport. The Dhaka phase, staged largely by air force personnel against senior air force officers who were at the airport directing Bangladeshi actions against the hijackers, led to 11 air force officers being killed. As a result of the coup attempt a large number of military personnel were executed. Amnesty International protested the summary executions. *See also* ARMED FORCES.

BOSE, SIR JAGDISH CHANDRA (1858–1937). Born in Dhaka district, he was educated in **Calcutta** and at Cambridge. He was noted for his work in both physics and plant physiology, publishing widely in both fields. He taught at Calcutta University and founded the Bose Research Institute in Calcutta. In physics, Bose worked primarily in the field of electrical radiation. In 1994, Bangladesh honored Bose by establishing a museum in his home village of Rarikhal.

BOSE, SUBHAS CHANDRA (1897–1945). A Bengali political leader who earned from his followers the title *netaji*, which means leader. He passed the examination for the Indian Civil Service, but he resigned almost as soon as he had joined in 1921 and became active in the Indian National Congress. He worked with **Chittaranjan Das** and with Gandhi, but was often to the left of the important leaders of the Congress. Nonetheless, he became president of the Congress in 1938 and was reelected in 1939. Opposition from Gandhi and others forced Bose to resign before completing his second term. He did not agree with Gandhi's concept of the renunciation of violence. Frequently jailed, Bose was able to escape **India** in January 1941, when he made his way to **Afghanistan** and eventually to Germany. In 1943, he was transported by a German submarine to Singapore and began to organize Indian prisoners of war held by the Japanese into the Indian National Army to fight alongside the Japanese against **Great Britain**, principally in **Burma**. Bose proclaimed the provisional government of India. After Japan's defeat, Bose flew from

Singapore to Japan, but the aircraft crashed and he was killed in Taiwan, although members of the Bose cult maintain he survived.

BRAHMAPALA. Founder of the Pala dynasty in Kamarupa (**Assam**) about AD 1000. This dynasty is not to be confused with the almost contemporaneous **Pala dynasty** in Bengal. The Kamarupa Pala dynasty ended in the first half of the 12th century.

BRAHMAPUTRA. The river of about 1,800 miles that rises in Tibet (there known as the Tsangpo), flows through **Assam** as the Brahmaputra, and enters Bangladesh, where it is known as the Jamuna. Along its way, it picks up a number of tributaries in Tibet, Arunachal Pradesh, and Assam. Among its tributaries in Bangladesh is the **Tista**. It joins the **Ganges** at Goalundo and these two rivers join the **Meghna** near Chandpur to flow to the Bay of Bengal. Until the end of the 18th century, the Brahmaputra flowed through the center of **Mymensingh** district to join the Ganges near Bhairab Bazaar. But early in the 19th century this route silted up, and the river migrated westward so that it now forms the western boundary of Mymensingh district. The river drains an area of about 360,000 square miles. At high flood its flow is estimated at 500,000 cubic feet per second. During less heavy flow, the river and its tributaries form an essential part of Bangladesh's water transportation system; the river is navigable to Dibrugarh, Assam.

BRAHMO SAMAJ. A religious movement formally established by Debendranath Tagore (grandfather of **Rabindranath Tagore**) in **Kolkata** in 1843, but founded on the base of the beliefs of **Raja Ram Mohan Roy**. It used a form of congregational worship and thus was formed at least partly to counteract conversions to Christianity.

BUDDHISM. The small Buddhist population in Bangladesh is largely in the **Chittagong Hill Tracts** and in groups of migrants from the hills. The 2001 census shows that approximately 0.62 percent of the population of Bangladesh are Buddhists, of whom an overwhelming majority lives in the Hill Tracts; the remaining live in the neighboring **Chittagong** region. These Buddhists are almost invariably members of one of the tribal groups residing in the area. There are no restrictions on employment, private or public, placed on Buddhists, and their principal holidays are national or regional holidays.

This small remnant, however, obscures the historical impact of Buddhism in Bengal. The religion was presumably brought to Bengal by the **Mauryas** in the third century BC. It flourished under the **Pala dynasty** (about AD 750–1155), as for much of that period it was the equivalent of a state religion. The **Sena dynasty**, which overcame the Palas in the middle of the 12th century and ruled parts of Bengal until about the middle of the 13th century, attempted to reinstate Brahmanism in Bengal. The importance of non-caste Buddhism is seen as a factor in the rapid conversion of much of eastern Bengal to **Islam** when the Muslims arrived. The period has left many monuments that travelers frequently visit. *See also* ARCHITECTURE; TRIBES.

BUDGET. The Bangladesh budget is divided into two major categories: the revenue budget based on internal resources, such as taxes, and the development budget based on external resources, namely loans and grants. In the overall budget the major sources of revenue are taxes (56.8%), nontax internal revenue (12.6%), domestic borrowing (17%), and foreign financing (13.6%), as recorded in the 2008–2009 budget. Major areas of expenditure are education and information technology (12.8%); **transportation** (12.7%); social security, welfare, and public administration (12.2%); **local government** (21.2%); **health** (8.9%); **agriculture** (8.5%); defense (8.0%); and energy and power (15.7%). The fiscal year runs from July 1 to June 30.

BULBUL CHOUDHURY (1919–1954). A renowned dancer and writer. His real name was Rashid Ahmad Choudhury. He first achieved prominence because of his work in one of **Rabindranath Tagore**'s dance dramas. In 1937, he founded the Oriental Fine Arts Association in **Calcutta** and made original contributions to understanding and propounding fine arts. During the period of 1943–1948, Bulbul joined the civil service and worked as a public information officer in the Ministry of Information. In 1948 he resigned from the service and founded his own dance group. In 1950, Bulbul moved to **Dhaka** from Calcutta. Between 1950 and 1952 he visited a number of European countries, performing with his dance group. In 1955 he established the Bulbul Academy of Fine Arts, which continues to be a major center of fine arts in the country. He also wrote several plays.

BURMA. Now called Myanmar, Burma is the only country other than **India** to share a border with Bangladesh. The land border was undemarcated prior to 1985, when an agreement was reached between the two countries. The sea border has yet to be determined. Relations between the countries have been generally cordial, with the exception of events pertaining to the movement of Rohingyas. In 1976 a substantial number (estimated variously at 100,000) of Rohingyas fled from Arakan into Bangladesh, apparently as a result of the application of a new citizenship law in Burma that would have left the Arakanese Muslims in a legally subordinate position. Negotiations between the two countries resulted in the return of most of the refugees to Burma and the restoration of cordial relations. However, in the late 1980s, there was another influx of Rohingyas and a deterioration of relations between Bangladesh and Burma (by then officially Myanmar). Some of the refugees have returned to Burma, but many remain in camps in Bangladesh and are unsure of the conditions they would find were they to return. They are being assisted by the **United Nations** and other international groups.

Other than the Rohingya issue, relations between the two countries have been normal but not close. However, in January 2001 it was discovered that Burma had begun building an embankment on its side of the Naaf River, which forms the agreed boundary at the very southern reach of Bangladesh. Such building was prohibited under the boundary agreement of 1985, as it was determined then that an embankment by either side would divert water from the river to the detriment of the other side.

Although Burma has been a major producer and exporter of rice, Bangladesh most often imports rice when it is needed from Thailand. Burma's membership in the Association of Southeast Asian Nations (ASEAN) turns Burma's interests eastward rather than westward toward Bangladesh, although there are signs of closer relations between **India** and Burma.

There is a proposal for Burma to export natural gas to India through a pipeline that would pass through Bangladesh rather than a northern route that would run directly from Burma to India. This proposal appears, however, unlikely to be implemented in the near future, if at all. In 2008 and 2009, two outstanding issues—the Rohingyas and the sea boundary—have raised tensions between the two countries. *See also* ARAKAN; SEA BOUNDARY.

BUXAR, BATTLE OF. Although the battle took place in Bihar, it had a major impact on British control of Bengal. On 22 October 1764, British forces faced the combined forces of Mughal emperor Shah Alam II, the Nawab of Oudh, and the Bengalis under **Mir Qasim**. The British, although severely outnumbered, won. The victory confirmed that the British were rulers of Bengal and that the Mughal emperor would become a puppet.

– C –

CABINET MISSION PLAN. Proposed by a three-member team of the British cabinet that visited India in 1946. Although not the leader, Sir Stafford Cripps was the most prominent member. The plan called for a three-tier government for a united India in which the powers of the federal (central) government would be limited to foreign affairs, defense, currency, and communications. All other powers would devolve to the provinces. The provinces would be grouped into three zones: (1) Bengal and Assam (Muslim majority); (2) the Punjab, the Northwest Frontier Province, Sindh, and Baluchistan (Muslim majority); and (3) the other provinces (Hindu majority). The provinces could delegate upward such powers as they chose to the zonal groupings. A possible example might have been inland waterways in group one, Assam and Bengal. Minority rights would be guaranteed. The **Muslim League** accepted the plan, but the Congress accepted with such reservations that it was taken by the Muslim League to be a rejection. The plan was therefore discarded.

CALCUTTA (KOLKATA). Calcutta was founded in 1690 by the British East India Company under Job Charnock on the bank of the navigable Hooghly River to serve as a trading station. It became the capital of the Bengal presidency in 1700, being called **Fort William**. It was captured by the nawab (Mughal governor) of Bengal,

Sirajuddaulah, in 1756, but retaken by the British in 1757. In 1773, the British governor of Bengal, **Warren Hastings**, was named governor-general of the company's territories in India, making the governors of Madras and Bombay subordinate to the governor-general in Calcutta. Calcutta remained the capital of British India until 1911, when the seat of the viceroy/governor-general was moved to New Delhi. Calcutta was the capital of Bengal (including other territories at various times and excluding **Eastern Bengal and Assam** during the period that it was a separate province) until 1947, when India was partitioned and the city became the capital of the Indian state of West Bengal. Long the principal commercial and industrial center of India, it has now been eclipsed by Bombay (Mumbai). Nonetheless, it remains a city of highest importance in commerce and industry and in the arts and culture. Its university, founded in 1857, was a magnet for students from all parts of Bengal, even after the founding of Dhaka University in 1921. The West Bengal government has changed the spelling of the name of the city to Kolkata. *See also* ALINAGAR, TREATY OF.

CARETAKER GOVERNMENT. A demand raised by the opposition led by the **Awami League** and the **Jatiya Party**, who were joined by the **Jama'at-i-Islami** and smaller opposition parties in 1994, was to establish a neutral caretaker government to oversee the transfer of power by conducting free and fair **elections**. The demand was raised in response to allegations that the ruling **Bangladesh Nationalist Party (BNP)** had acted improperly in a by-election in which the BNP was declared to have won a seat long held by the Awami League. The demand was that a constitutional amendment be passed that would require the ruling party to resign prior to a general election and turn the reins of government over to a neutral government whose primary task would be the conduct of the election. The precedent for this was in the election held in 1991 following the resignation of **Ershad**. The BNP refused to accept the demand. The opposition resigned en masse from parliament on 28 December 1994. The opposition took the demand to the streets, using demonstrations and *hartals* (general strikes).

The resignation of the opposition forced the dissolution of parliament in November 1995. A new election in February 1996 resulted in a walkover by the BNP as the opposition boycotted the poll. The unrepresentative parliament, however, passed a constitutional amendment providing for future elections to be held under neutral caretaker government. The primary purpose of the caretaker government was to hold a national parliamentary election within 90 days of the end of term of the last government. The parliament was then dissolved and a new election was held in June 1996, in which the opposition participated. Similarly the 2001 election was held under a neutral caretaker government. In October 2006 when the BNP government completed its term of office, a major dispute arose in determining the chief adviser. The Awami League did not want the last chief justice to become the chief adviser, as they felt that he was a BNP-allied person. President **Iajuddin Ahmed**, in an attempt to surmount the obstacle, took over the office of chief adviser himself. This caused further consternation and he was forced to resign when a state of emergency was promulgated on 11 January 2007. A new caretaker government was established on 12 January 2007 under the leadership of **Fakhruddin Ahmed**, former governor of Bangladesh Bank. Due to the state of emergency, the caretaker government of Ahmed took two years to hold the parliamentary election, in the process developing a new electronic voters list and reorganizing a number of critical governmental organizations. *See also* ANTI-CORRUPTION COMMISSION; ELECTION COMMISSION; ELECTIONS.

CAREY, WILLIAM (1761–1834). Originally a shoemaker by trade, he came to Srirampur, in Danish territory near Calcutta, in 1793 as a Baptist missionary. While preaching Christianity, he also studied languages and produced the first translation of the Bible into Bengali. He also translated the Bible or portions of it into Oriya, Assamese, Hindi, Marathi, and Sanskrit. Carey also wrote prose in Bengali of such quality that one writer has called him "the father of Bengali prose." He campaigned against *sati*, infanticide, child marriage, and other causes that later would be taken up by **Raja Ram Mohun Roy** and the **Brahmo Samaj**. In 1801 he became professor of Sanskrit and Bengali at Fort William College, a post he held until his death. *See also* KEITH, JAMES; MARSHMAN, JOHN.

CASTE. Caste is the hereditary and hierarchical division of society in **Hinduism**. The term is also used loosely in **Islam** on the subcontinent despite the fact that Islam is an egalitarian religion. Probably a holdover from the pre-Islamic period, caste as used by Muslims is often important in status assignments and in such rites as marriage, especially in rural areas.

CHAITANYA (1486–1533). A Brahmin who popularized Vaishnaism, specifically the Krishna cult, in Bengal. His birth name was Vishvambara Mishra. An excellent Sanskrit scholar, he left his family at the age of 24 and took up the life of a *sanyasin* (a wandering mendicant). He emphasized the role of love and devotion (*bhakti*), that is, a personal relationship between man and god. He emphasized the joint worship of Krishna and the milkmaid Radha, a still-popular form of **Hindu** worship. Nonetheless, Chaitanya preached to all castes and religions, and the hymns (*kirtans*) that he wrote remain an important part of the Bengali heritage.

CHAKRABORTY, DEBDAS (1933–2008). He was born in Faridpur district and graduated from **Dhaka University**. From 1958 to 1970 he served as the senior designer of the Information Directorate of the Ministry of Agriculture. From 1970 to 1980 he was assistant professor of the Department of Fine Arts of Chittagong University. During the **War of Liberation** he served as designer to the Mujibnagar government and his painting inspired the freedom fighters.

CHANDRA DYNASTY. Local chieftains in eastern Bengal who assumed control in the area after the decline of the rulers of **Harikela** during the 10th century. The headquarters of the dynasty appear to have been at **Karmanta**, near **Comilla**, and at **Vikrampur**, near **Dhaka**. The dynasty seems to have ended during the latter part of the 11th century, when there was a period of **Pala** rule, followed by the establishment of the **Varman dynasty**.

CHANDRANAGORE. *See* FRENCH EAST INDIA COMPANY.

CHARS. See COASTAL ISLANDS.

CHATTERJI, BANKIM CHANDRA (1838–1894). Bengali novelist who was also in government service. His works were viewed as anti-

Muslim by Muslims, especially his best-known novel, *Anandamath.* Chatterji also wrote the nationalist song *"Bande Mataram"* ("Hail Motherland"), also seen as opposed to the Muslims. Nonetheless, he is considered the greatest novelist in Bengali of the 19th century. *See also* LITERATURE.

CHINA. Initially, relations between the People's Republic of China and Bangladesh did not exist on a formal basis, as China supported the Pakistani position that Bangladesh was an illegal creation. China exercised its veto in the Security Council to exclude Bangladesh from membership in the **United Nations**. The recognition of Bangladesh by **Pakistan** through the good offices of members of the **Organization of the Islamic Conference** rendered the Chinese position null. China and Bangladesh established diplomatic relations in 1976, following the assumption of power by **Ziaur Rahman**. Relations have continued to improve. There have been a number of high-level visits, China has provided limited military and economic assistance, and, to a degree, trade has developed. A contributing factor, no doubt, has been the cooling of relations between Bangladesh and **India**, encouraging China to maintain closer relations with India's neighbors, although China's relations with Bangladesh do not approach those between China and Pakistan.

CHINSURA. Established in 1653 by the **Dutch East India Company** as a trading station. A Dutch challenge to the British East India Company was fought off by the British in 1769. The town remained in Dutch hands until 1825, when it came under British control in return for British cession of territories in Sumatra.

CHITTAGONG. (Also known in history as Chattagram, Chatgaon, and Chatigana.) The leading seaport of Bangladesh at the mouth of the **Karnaphuli River** and the country's second-largest city. Improvements to the seaport and cargo handling are planned and a long-term project may be to return Chittagong to its former role as the port of entry and shipment for Assam and the smaller states of northeastern India. It is also the seat of a university.

The city was known to the West in the early centuries of the Christian era and was used by Arab traders as early as the 10th century.

Chittagong had been a part of the **Hindu** kingdom of **Tripura** (now reduced to a state in India), which also ruled much of the districts of **Comilla** and **Noakhali**. It was conquered by the **Buddhist** king of **Arakan** in the ninth century and by the Muslims in the 13th century, but came under the control of Arakan again in the 16th century. The district was ceded to the **Mughal** Empire by the king of Arakan in 1666 after the Mughals defeated the Arakanese. Much involved in the struggle between Arakan and the Mughals were the **Portuguese**, who first arrived in 1538. They were traders, missionaries, and, eventually, pirates who raided along the coast as far west as **Barisal** and beyond, sometimes in cooperation with and sometimes against the Arakanese (or **Maghs**). The district was ceded to the British by **Mir Qasim** in 1760. When Arakan was captured by the Burmese in 1784, many Arakanese fled to Chittagong and their descendents comprise the Buddhist Magh community today.

Chittagong contains a number of shrines, such as those of **Bayazid Bastami** and Hazrat Bader Aulia. There are also Buddhist and Hindu temples of **architectural** note, and there are a number of Muslim shrines in Maizbhandar, about 25 miles from Chittagong. Nearby is the industrial town of Kalurghat, developed by **Abul Kasem Khan**. Cox's Bazaar in the south of the district, with its excellent beach, has the potential to be developed as a **tourist** site. With the reorganization of **local government** under **Ershad**, Cox's Bazaar has become a separate district.

The Arakanese Buddhists in Chittagong and surrounding areas are known as Maghs.

CHITTAGONG HILL TRACTS. Located in the southeast corner of Bangladesh and bordering on both **India** and **Burma**, it lies between **Chittagong** district and the Lushai hills of India. The area was set aside by the British as an area for tribal groups, including such tribes as the Chakmas and Maghs. About 75 percent of the population is **Buddhist**. Under the British, land ownership in the region was not permitted to non-tribals. Since independence there has been some influx of plains people to the Hill Tracts. This has been opposed, often violently, by the tribals, and a low level of guerrilla warfare has been endemic to the region. Bangladesh has asserted that India lent assistance and asylum to the tribal groups opposing Bangladesh, although this ended prior to the agreement mentioned in the next paragraph.

Some land was lost to the tribals through the building of the **Karnaphuli** hydroelectric station and the ponding of water behind the dam. The Hill Tracts district has now been divided into three districts: Rangamati, Bandarban, and Khagrachari. Negotiations during the **Hasina Wajid** ministry resulted in an agreement that met many of the demands of the people in the tracts, but not all, and some violence has continued. A tribal council was established to oversee the tracts and to deal with the central government.

CHOUDHURY, A. K. M. FAZLUL QADER (1919–1973). A lawyer by profession, he served the **Muslim League** in numerous capacities after joining the party in 1938. He was the general secretary of the All-India Muslim Student Federation. He was an elected member of the East Bengal Legislative Assembly in 1954 and a member of the National Assembly of Pakistan in 1962. A member of the **Muhammad Ayub Khan** cabinet in 1962, Fazlul Qader later was speaker of the National Assembly, 1963–1966. During the movement to oust President Ayub he remained loyal and was the president of the **Pakistan Muslim League (Convention).** Fazlul Qader opposed the liberation of Bangladesh, and for his association with the **Razakar Bahini** and the **Peace Committees,** he was arrested after the liberation of Bangladesh. He died while he was in jail. His son, Salahuddin Qader Choudhury, has been active in Bangladesh politics as a member of parliament and as a leader in the **Bangladesh Nationalist Party.**

CHOUDHURY, A. Q. M. BADRUDDOZA. *See* CHOWDHURY, A. Q. M. BADRUDDOZA.

CHOUDHURY, ABDUR RAHMAN (1926–1994). Lawyer and Supreme Court justice. He was born and educated in **Dhaka.** He was actively involved in the **language movement.** He was the first Bengali to be elected general secretary of the Pakistan Bar Council. Choudhury was a justice of the Supreme Court of Bangladesh, 1978–1983, and later chairman of the Bangla Academy.

CHOUDHURY, HAMIDUL HAQ (1903–1992). A lawyer, political figure, and newspaper owner (of the former *Pakistan Observer*, now *Bangladesh Observer*, published in **Dhaka**). He was elected to the Bengal Legislative Council in 1937 and to the legislative assembly in 1946, serving as a minister in the **Nurul Amin** cabinet until 1949, when he faced proceedings under the Public and Representative Offices Disqualification Act (PRODA) and was disqualified from holding office. Hamidul Haq was also elected a member of the constituent assembly in 1946 and, despite disqualification, again in 1955. He was foreign minister in 1955 in the cabinet of Chaudhury Muhammad Ali and again in the cabinet of **Firoz Khan Noon** in 1958. He was banned from politics for seven years under **Ayub Khan**, but when his disqualification ended Hamidul Haq became a member of the **Democratic Action Committee** opposing Ayub in 1969. He opposed the separation of East Pakistan and remained for several years in Karachi, but later returned to Dhaka and had his properties, including the newspaper, restored to him.

CHOUDHURY, MAJOR GENERAL MAHMUDUR RAHMAN (1928–1999). Graduated from **Calcutta** Medical College in 1951, he was commissioned into the **Pakistan** Army Medical Corps in 1951. For a time he served as the executive director of the Pakistan National Health Laboratories. In 1976, he established the Bangladesh Armed Forces Institute of Pathology and Transfusion. In the same year he also organized the Bangladesh Society for Microbiologists. As a result of his initiative in microbiology, **Dhaka University** established the Department of Microbiology. For his contributions he received the highest civilian award of Bangladesh—the Independence Day Award.

CHOUDHURY, MOAZZAM HUSSAIN (LAL MIA) (1905–1967). From Faridpur, he studied at Aligarh Muslim University and became central minister for health, labor, and social welfare in 1965. Prior to that he was the chief whip of the **Muslim League** and member of the National Assembly of Pakistan. Earlier, Lal Mia participated in the non-cooperation movement and the **Khilafat movement** (both in the early 1920s) and was jailed by the British. He joined the Muslim League in 1943. He was also a poet and published two books of poems. He changed his name later to Abdullah Zahiruddin, but was known by the nickname Lal Mia. He was the brother of **Yusuf Ali Choudhury**.

CHOUDHURY, MUNIR (1925–1971). He obtained a master's degree in linguistics from Harvard University. Fluent in English and Bengali, he was a faculty member at both **Dhaka University** and Rajshahi University. In 1943 he formed the Writers Association. He joined the Communist Party in **Calcutta** in 1948. After moving to **East Pakistan**, Choudhury actively participated in the **language movement** to make Bengali one of the national languages of **Pakistan** and was jailed several times between 1952 and 1955. Some of his major works were written while he was in jail, including the play *Kobor* (*Grave*). He received a number of awards, including the Sitara-i-Imtiaz in 1966, which he renounced in 1971. Choudhury also developed the Bengali typewriter. He was one of the intellectuals who were murdered by the Pakistani forces 11–14 December 1971, just prior to the surrender of the Pakistani army. *See also* WAR OF LIBERATION.

CHOUDHURY, SHAMSUL HUDA (1920–?). From Mymensingh, he was educated at **Kolkata** and Aligarh Muslim University. He spent his career in broadcasting, until he was appointed by **Ziaur Rahman** as minister of information and broadcasting. Shamsul Huda later served as speaker of the parliament elected in 1988.

CHOUDHURY, SYED NAWAB ALI (1863–1929). A prominent *zamindar* (landowner) from Mymensingh, he was part of the delegation that met the viceroy, **Lord Minto**, at Simla to demand **separate electorates** for Muslims and was one of the founders of the **Muslim League**. Nawab Ali was a nominated member of the East Bengal and Assam Legislative Council, 1906–1911; an elected member of the Bengal Legislative Council, 1912–1916 and again 1920–1929; and a member of the Governor-General's Legislative Council, 1916–1920. Nawab Ali was the first Muslim to be named a minister in Bengal in 1921. He was born in Dhanbari Tangail. He was one of the founding members of Dhaka University. He also established 38 educational institutions in the Tangail and Mymensingh area. His grandson, **Muhammad Ali Bogra**, was prime minister of Pakistan.

CHOUDHURY, YUSUF ALI (MOHAN MIA) (1905–1971). He was a provincial minister in the **United Front** government. He started his political life as a member of the **Faridpur** municipality and later became the chairman of the Faridpur District Council. He was also a member of the Bengal Legislative Assembly before 1947. Mohan Mia was an active member of the **Muslim League**, serving as the chairman of the Faridpur district Muslim League and in 1952 becoming the president of the East Pakistan Muslim League. He was ousted from the Muslim League in 1953. He then joined the **Krishak Sramik Party** of **A. K. Fazlul Haq** and became its general secretary in 1957. In the 1960s, Mohan Mia joined the National Democratic Front and was a member of the National Democratic Movement, which was formed to oust the government of **Ayub Khan**. He became a member of a faction of the Muslim League once again in 1969. Mohan Mia was opposed to the freedom movement of Bangladesh. He started a charity organization called the Khademul Islam (Servants of Islam) and the paper *Daily Millat*. He was the brother of **Moazzam Hussain Choudhury (Lal Mia).**

CHOUDHURY, ZAHUR AHMED (1916–1974). He joined the **Awami League** in 1949 and served as its labor secretary in 1957. He was elected to the Bengal Provincial Assembly in 1954, to the **East Pakistan** Provincial Assembly in 1970, and to the National Assembly of Bangladesh in 1973. According to the Awami League version of the declaration of independence of Bangladesh, Zahur Ahmed Choudhury carried the declaration from Sheikh **Mujibur Rahman** and gave it to **Ziaur Rahman** to be announced over **Chittagong** radio on 25 March 1971. According to this version, Zia made the announcement but also declared himself acting president of Bangladesh.

CHOWDHURANI, FAIZUNNESSA (1834–1903). Although a woman, she was awarded the title nawab by Queen Victoria for her work in improving the lot of women and the poor. She established the Faizunnessa Girls School in **Comilla** in 1873, and the Faizunnessa Women's Hospital in 1893.

CHOWDHURY, A. Q. M. BADRUDDOZA (1932–). Fifteenth president of Bangladesh. He was a well-established professor of medicine before he went into politics and in 1978 became the founding general secretary of the **Bangladesh Nationalist Party** (BNP). As a medical professional he served at Rajshahi and Sylhet Medical College and Salimullah Medical College. For his contribution to the field of medicine, in 1993 he was awarded the Swadhinata Puraskar (Independence Award). From 1979 to 1982 he was senior deputy minister and in charge of the Ministry of Health and Population in the **Ziaur Rahman** government.

During the BNP rule of 1991–1996 he once again became a cabinet minister in charge of the Ministry of Education, Science, Technology, and Culture. He initially joined the BNP cabinet in 2001 as foreign minister, and he became the president of Bangladesh in November 2001. He resigned as president on 21 June 2002 because of his disagreements with BNP's view of the role of the president. He formed the Bikalpa Dhara Bangladesh (BDB) on 11 March 2004. He merged BDB with the Liberal Democratic Party (LDP) in October 2006 but in June 2007 decided to delink BDB from LDP. Prior to the ninth parliamentary **election** of December 2008 he attempted to form an electoral alliance with the Gono Forum of Dr. **Kamal Hossain**, but that alliance did not materialize. His party won one seat in the parliamentary election of 2008.

CHOWDHURY, ABU SAYEED (1921–1987). President of Bangladesh from January 1972 till December 1973. Earlier he had been a justice of the Dhaka High Court and a vice-chancellor of Dhaka University. Out of **Pakistan**, attending a meeting of the **United Nations** Commission on Human Rights in March 1971, Abu Sayeed Chowdhury was able to play a key role as a roving ambassador in Europe and the **United States** on behalf of emerging Bangladesh. He was briefly foreign minister in 1975, but thereafter he remained out of politics. His eldest son Kaiser Chowdhury became the state minister for foreign affairs during the Awami League government of 1991–1996.

CHOWDHURY, ABUL FAZAL MOHAMMAD AHSANUDDIN (1915–2001). Appointed president of Bangladesh by **Hussain Mu-**

hammad Ershad in March 1982. He resigned the office in December 1984, when Ershad himself assumed the presidency. Earlier he had been a jurist, retiring from the Supreme Court in 1977.

CHOWDHURY, ANWARA BAHAR (1918–1987). A leading figure in **women's** education, both before partition in **Calcutta** and after it in **Dhaka**. She was a cofounder of the Bulbul Academy of Fine Arts and also began schools in dancing and in music. *See also* BULBUL CHOUDHURY.

CHOWDHURY, HASAN MASHHUD (1948–). General Mashhud was commissioned in the Pakistan army (infantry) in 1969 and joined Bangladesh army in 1974. He graduated from Defense Services Command and Staff College in 1979. He served as commandant at the School of Infantry and Tactics, Defense Services Command and Staff College, and National Defense College. He is also a graduate of the U.S. Army War College, class of 1992. He attended training courses at naval post-graduate school in Monterrey, California, and the Asia Pacific Center for Security Studies in Hawaii in the **United States**. He completed a master's degree from Shippensburg University in Pennsylvania, U.S. He commanded the Bangladesh military contingent in Saudi Arabia during operation Desert Shield/Desert Storm in 1990–1991. He was the chief of general staff during 1997–2000. He served as Bangladesh's ambassador to the United Arab Emirates in 2001–2002. He was the chief of staff of the Bangladesh army during 2002–2005. After retiring from the army Hasan Mashhud Chowdhury served as adviser of the **caretaker government**. He was appointed as **Anti-corruption Commission** chairman in February 2007 and resigned from his post in April 2009. As Anti-corruption Commission chairman, he was instrumental in bringing about a sea change in how Bangladesh curtailed and managed corrupt practices that impregnated Bangladesh politics and **economy**. An honest, upright, and transformational leader, he was instrumental in strengthening army training, professionalizing the army forces for the **United Nations peacekeeping** mission, and reorienting the army mission away from politics.

CHOWDHURY, MIZANUR RAHMAN (1928–2006). Prime minister of Bangladesh under president **Hussain Muhammad Ershad**, he was a member of the **Pakistan** National Assembly from 1962 to 1969. He was for a time the acting general secretary of the **East Pakistan Awami League**. During the movement to oust the regime of President **Ayub Khan**, he was one of the organizers of the **Combined Opposition Parties**. Mizanur Rahman was elected twice to the Bangladesh parliament, in 1970 and 1973, and served in the government of Sheikh **Mujibur Rahman** as a cabinet minister (1972–1973). After the assassination of Sheikh Mujibur Rahman, Mizanur Rahman split with the main body of the Awami League and headed his own faction of the league in opposition to that of **Abdul Malik Ukil**. He joined President Ershad's party, the **Jatiya Dal**, in 1983 and was named prime minister in 1986. Mizanur Rahman was replaced by **Moudud Ahmed** in March 1988. He remained a key person in the Jatiya Party till his death.

CHOWDHURY, MUHAMMAD YAKUB ALI (1888–1940). Writer and journalist. He was born in Faridpur and studied in **Calcutta**, after which he became a schoolteacher. He was jailed for his activities in the **Khilafat movement**. He then took up journalism in **Kolkata** and was the editor of the monthly literary journal *Kohinoor*.

CHOWDHURY, MUZAFFAR AHMED (1923–1978). Born in Noakhali, he was educated at **Dhaka** and the London School of Economics. He taught at **Dhaka University** and served as a constitutional adviser to the government of **Pakistan**, 1955–1956. During the civil war he served as the head of the planning cell for the government-in-exile in **Mujibnagar** (**Calcutta**) and later was the first post-independence vice-chancellor of the University of Dhaka. Muzaffar Ahmed later was minister of education in the **Mujibur Rahman** and **Mushtaque Ahmed** governments. He was a theorist for the **Awami League** and the author of a number of works on politics and administration in Pakistan and **East Pakistan**.

CHOWDHURY, SALAH UDDIN SHOAIB (1965–). Editor of the weekly *Blitz*, he is considered by many to be an Israeli sympathizer for his writings on anti-Israeli and anti-Semitic sentiments in Islamic nations. He was arrested in 2003 while trying to go to Israel and in 2004 was charged with sedition. He is an ardent supporter of interfaith dialogue but faces significant challenges as he also propounds a friendly relationship between Bangladesh and Israel. He has received international recognition for his tenacious stance on journalistic freedom and freedom of thought. In 2007 he published the book *Injustice and Jihad*, in which he denounces radicalism and extremism. Earlier in his career he was a correspondent for TASS and later ITAR-TASS of Russia.

CHRISTIANITY. The Bangladesh censuses of 1981, 1991, and 2001 show that the Christian community is approximately 0.31 percent of the total population. Most of the Christians live in three regions of Bangladesh—**Mymensingh**, **Dhaka**, and **Khulna**. The Christians in Mymensingh are principally members of tribal groups, such as the Garos, whose main center of population is in the Indian state of Meghalaya to the north of Mymensingh. This group tends to be Protestant, most often Presbyterian. In the metropolitan areas of Dhaka, the Christians belong generally to two groups: Bengali converts and Eurasians (often described as "Anglo-Indians"). In the latter group Roman Catholicism predominates. Missionaries began to arrive in the 17th century and in British territory in the 19th century. The missions played and continue to play an important role in education and medical services. There is freedom to propagate religion, but donations from abroad to missions and missionaries are regulated by the government.

CITY CORPORATION ELECTION 2008. Elections for four city corporations and nine municipalities were held on 4 August 2008. With the city corporation election, the Election Commission started the process of returning the country to civilian rule. Elections were conducted in the city corporations of Rajshahi, Khulna, Barisal, and Sylhet, and in the municipalities of Manikganj Sadar, Chuadanga Sadar, Shariatpur Sadar, Naohata of Rajshahi, Dupchanchiya of Bogra, Sripur of Gazipur, Fulbaria of Mymensingh, Golapganj of Sylhet, and Sitakunda of Chittagong. Over 5,500 local election observers monitored the election and 119 observers came from 16 foreign countries. This is a sharp increase from the 2002 election, when there were only 19 foreign observers. Approximately 1.9 million voters were registered for the city elections and 2.7 million for the nine municipalities. For the elections in the city corporations 46 candidates vied for the 4 mayoral seats, 752 for the 118 councilor seats, and 194 for the 39 councilor seats reserved for women. In the 9 municipal elections, 59 candidates competed for the 9 mayoral seats, 429 for the 81 councilor seats, and 120 for the 27 councilor seats reserved for women. The **Awami League** won all four city corporation mayoral seats and eight out of the nine municipal mayoral seats. **BNP** won only one mayoral seat.

CLIMATE. Located on the Tropic of Cancer, Bangladesh has a semi-tropical monsoon climate. The seasons are a hot summer period from March to June; a warm, very humid monsoon period from June to September, during which about 80 percent of the rain occurs; a brief, dry, hot period from the end of the monsoon to mid-November; and a cooler, dry winter period from November to February.

There is a wide variation in rainfall; in 1984 it ranged from 188 inches at a station in Sylhet region in the northeast to 60 inches at Ishurdi in the northwest. The weather system often includes violent storms, especially the **cyclones** that arise in the Bay of Bengal. A cyclone in 1970 is believed to have claimed as many as a half-million lives in the affected areas along the coast and resulted in the postponement of the scheduled general **election** from October to Decembert until January 1971.

In 1988, 1989, and 2002 the region suffered the worst **floods** in its history; in 1988 more than 25 million people were made homeless. In 2002 heavy rains on the eastern subcontinent caused heavy damage and loss of life in Bangladesh, Nepal, and eastern India. *See also* GLOBAL WARMING.

CLIVE, ROBERT (BARON CLIVE OF PLASSEY, 1725–1774). The victor for the British at the **Battle of Plassey** (1757) and governor of Bengal (1765–1767). He returned to England during 1760–1765, and was given the title of baron. Disturbances in India, in which **Mir Qasim** was a major actor, caused the East India Company to return Clive to Bengal as governor. Before Clive arrived, Mir Qasim and his allies, the Mughal emperor Shah Alam II, and the nawab of Oudh, had been defeated at the battle of **Buxar** (1764). Clive's task then was to arrange a settlement, the most important part of which was the acquisition of the *diwani*, that is, the right of revenue collection for Bengal, Bihar, and Orissa, which was granted by the Mughal emperor. Clive earlier had earned a reputation as an administrator and a military leader in Madras. Subjected to a parliamentary inquiry on his return to England, Clive eventually committed suicide.

COASTAL ISLANDS (*CHARS*). Low-lying islands created by the silt that is carried by the **Meghna** estuary and other rivers emptying into the Bay of Bengal. They are subject to extreme damage when **tidal bores** arrive and during **cyclonic** storms.

Among the major islands are Hatia and Sandwip in the Meghna estuary and Dakhin Shahbazpur in **Barisal**. One of the worst storms struck Hatia in 1876 and killed about 30,000 people, more than half of the people on the island. This storm serves as a benchmark for destruction and loss of life. Sandwip was noted for its shipbuilding, even, assuming the report is correct, building ships for the Ottoman sultan. It was often contested by the Portuguese and the Arakanese, either together or in opposition to each other. Dhakin Shahbazpur has been hit frequently by cyclonic storms. The coastal islands' very existence, in larger terms, is now being threatened by **global warming**.

COMBINED OPPOSITION PARTIES (COP). A term that has several meanings, but the one used most often is that for the group that opposed **Ayub Khan** in the 1960s. The group included the **Council Muslim League**, the **Jama'at-i-Islami**, the **Nizam-i-Islam**, the Pakistan Democratic Party, and other smaller groups. The initial leader of the group was **Khwaja Nazimuddin**. The COP supported the candidacy of Fatima Jinnah, sister of **Muhammad Ali Jinnah**, in the 1965 election for the presidency. She lost to Ayub Khan. The COP had ceased to function by 1968 and was superseded by the **Pakistan Democratic Movement**.

COMILLA. A district and district town, about 50 miles southeast of **Dhaka**, located on the Gumti River. The district was formerly known as Tippera and was for a time ruled by the raja of Tippera (present spelling: **Tripura**, now a state in India). The British took control of the territory in 1765, but, in an odd arrangement, the raja maintained temporary possession of a portion of the area for which he paid tribute to the British.

The territory of Comilla and neighboring **Noakhali** are associated with the early region of **Samatata**, which is mentioned in the inscription of Samudragupta. The region was known as **Harikela**, perhaps a synonym for **Vanga**, in the ninth century. It was ruled by the **Chandras**, the **Varmans**, the **Senas**, and the **Devas** from the 10th to the 13th centuries. After that, the territory was under the rule of the raja of Tippera, who faced frequent Muslim raids until most of the area was incorporated into the Mughal province of Bengal in 1733. The present boundary with "hill" Tippera, the raja's territory, was set by the British. Noakhali was separated from Comilla in 1822.

Comilla city and its environs are important centers of **archeology**, most notably nearby **Mainamati** in the Lushai hills. A more recent site is that of the Satararatna temple. The city is also the seat of the **Bangladesh Academy of Rural Development**. With the **local government** changes during the **Ershad** regime, Brahmanbaria and Chandpur became districts. Chandpur is a major port on the **Meghna** River. *See also* GUPTA DYNASTY.

COMMONWEALTH OF NATIONS. Often referred to as the British Commonwealth, this group is a loose association of **Great Britain** with its former colonies (and in a few cases, protectorates, such as the Maldives). In South Asia, it includes Bangladesh, **India, Pakistan**, Sri Lanka, and the Maldives Islands. Pakistan at times has been suspended from membership, usually as the result of a military takeover. It is interesting to note that Bangladesh has also experienced military takeovers but has not been suspended.

The members of the Commonwealth recognize the British monarch as head of the Commonwealth and the monarch presides over the biennial sessions known as the Commonwealth Heads of Government Meetings (CHOGM). These meetings are policy-making bodies to the extent there is agreed policy among the members. Only a few of the members still recognize the British monarch as the head of state. If so, the monarch is represented by a governor-general as in Canada, Australia, and New Zealand. Most members have become republics, having their own heads of state but still recognizing the

British monarch as head of the Commonwealth. A few, such as Malaysia, have their own monarchs.

A Commonwealth Secretariat was established in 1965 and performs such duties as are prescribed by the CHOGM. Ministerial meetings are held to discuss common interests. There is also a Commonwealth Fund for Technical Cooperation that uses voluntary contributions from member countries for training programs.

Bangladesh has been a member of the Commonwealth since 1974 and participates in all activities of the organization.

COMMUNIST PARTY OF BANGLADESH. An outgrowth of the Communist Party of Pakistan, which itself is an outgrowth of the Communist Party of India. The Communist Party of Pakistan was established in 1948 but was banned in 1954. The party existed in an underground form until 31 December 1971, when it was given legal recognition by the new government of Bangladesh. Led by **Moni Singh**, the party was "pro-Moscow" in its orientation and called for political and economic reforms in social institutions that could lead to the establishment of socialism. It cooperated with the **Awami League** but was banned by **Ziaur Rahman** during the early part of his regime. The Communist Party of Bangladesh was allowed to resume its legal existence in November 1978. Although sharply factionalized, the party won five seats in the 1991 parliamentary election, but it has won none since that election.

CONSTITUTION OF BANGLADESH, 1972. The Bangladesh constitution adopted a parliamentary system of government with a ceremonial president and a governing prime minister and cabinet. It was modeled very much on the constitution of **India** (1950), but without the federal concepts, which were obviously not needed in the unitary Bangladeshi system. The constitution also enshrined the four pillars of **Mujibbad**: nationalism, secularism, democracy, and socialism. The constitution was modified first in January 1975, when an amendment was passed transforming the system to a presidential one with **Mujibur Rahman** as president. It was changed again in June 1975, when provisions were made for a one-party state. Military rulers, including **Ziaur Rahman** and **Hussain Muhammad Ershad**, also made changes so that the Bangladeshi political system became one in which the cabinet and parliament were subordinate to the president. After the **election** of 1991, the constitution was again amended to restore a parliamentary system of government with the prime minister as the head of government and the president as head of state, a primarily ceremonial position. An additional important amendment in 1996 provided that elections would be held under a **Caretaker Government**.

CONSTITUTION OF PAKISTAN, 1956. Pakistan's first constitution was effective on 23 March 1956. Its adoption followed more than eight years of debate. It provided for a parliamentary system of government with a single house at the center and single-chamber provincial assemblies in **East Pakistan** and West Pakistan. The system was said to be federal, but the bulk of the powers were given to the central government. A point of particular concern to the East Pakistanis was that of **parity**. The constitution of 1956 was abrogated by the martial law decree of 7 October 1958. Elections were never held under this constitution.

CONSTITUTION OF PAKISTAN, 1962. The 1962 constitution of Pakistan was the second for the country. It was not passed by a constituent assembly but rather was promulgated by President **Ayub Khan** as his own "gift" to the nation. It provided for a strong presidential system with an indirectly elected national assembly. The president and the members of the national and provincial assemblies were to be elected by basic democrats. Governors of the two provinces were appointed by the president and served according to his pleasure. The cabinet was also appointed by the president and was not responsible to the assembly. The **parity** system was continued so that East Pakistani votes counted for less than West Pakistani votes. *See also* BASIC DEMOCRACY.

CONVENTION MUSLIM LEAGUE. *See* PAKISTAN MUSLIM LEAGUE (CONVENTION).

COOCH BEHAR. A princely state during British rule and now a district of West Bengal, it lies mainly in the valley of the **Tista** River. The name is apparently derived from the name of a tribal group, the

Koches. In the 16th century, the ruler, Nara Narayan (r. 1540–1584), extended the territory of the state over much of **Assam** and south into the present district of **Rangpur** in Bangladesh. Nara Narayan was defeated by **Isa Khan**. The territory came under the control of the **Mughals** at the end of the 16th century and was recognized as a princely state by the British in 1772, when the British intervened on behalf of Cooch Behar in a conflict with the Bhutanese. After Indian independence, a problem arose between India and first Pakistan and then Bangladesh over exclaves of Cooch Behar (Indian territory) inside Pakistan/Bangladesh. *See also* BERUBARI ENCLAVE.

COOPERATIVES. There are literally thousands of cooperative organizations in Bangladesh, some sponsored by the government and others privately organized. They cover almost all aspects of human endeavor and economic activity, from such things as prenatal care services and children and **women** to **agriculture**, slum clearance, and electricity generation. A 1994 report stated that there were more than 130,000 cooperatives with more than 7 million members.

The British rulers recognized the importance of cooperatives by passing the Indian Cooperative Law as early as 1904. The first cooperative was organized the next year in Bengal. Additional legislation was passed by **Pakistan**. An **East Pakistan** Cooperative Bank was established in 1964. Cooperatives were founded under the auspices of the organization now known as the **Bangladesh Academy of Rural Development**. Other organizations mentioned in this dictionary that have set up cooperative organizations are the **Association for Social Advancement, Bangladesh Rural Advancement Committee**, and **Grameen Bank**.

CORNWALLIS, CHARLES, FIRST MARQUESS (1738–1805). In the United States he is remembered as the commander of the British force that surrendered to George Washington at Yorktown in 1781. His reputation in Britain was not tarnished and he served twice as governor-general of India, from 1786 to 1793, and again in 1805. During his first term, Cornwallis introduced major reforms in the civil services of the **East India Company** that separated the governing role of the service from the private commercial activities of the company's officers. He also instituted the **Permanent Settlement** system for the lands in the Bengal presidency (province).

CORRUPTION. One of the major deterrents to foreign investment and to economic development in general is the high level of corruption reported for Bangladesh. This is not only a frequently heard complaint for both Bangladeshis and foreigners, but it has also been recognized by Transparency International, which rated Bangladesh as the most corrupt state among the 102 countries it surveyed in both 2000 and 2001. Transparency International focuses on the misuse of public office for private gain. Actions taken in 2007–2008 by the **caretaker government** of **Fakhruddin Ahmed** significantly reduced the incidence of corruption. *See also* ANTI-CORRUPTION COMMISSION.

COSSIMBAZAR (KASIMBAZAR). Now an industrial suburb of Berhampur, the district headquarters of **Murshidabad** district in West Bengal, Cossimbazar was a major trading point in the 17th and 18th centuries owing to its proximity to Murshidabad. An English factory was established in 1658. The town was captured by Nawab **Sirajuddaulah** in 1757, but was restored to British control after the battle of **Plassey** the same year. It has never fully recovered, mainly because of the westward shifting of the Bhagirathi River.

COUNCIL MUSLIM LEAGUE (CML). The name applied to a **Muslim League** group opposed to **Ayub Khan**'s **Pakistan Muslim League (Convention)**. When parties were formed after the 1962 election, a group made up of members of the Muslim League that existed before parties were banned by Ayub in 1958 called a meeting of the council of the league (hence, the name of the new party). They revived the league through the revived council.

Conversely, Ayub called a convention of Muslim Leaguers, bypassing the old council, to form his party. The CML became part of the **Combined Opposition Parties (COP)**. Its first leader was **Khwaja Nazimuddin**. After his death, the principal figure was Mian Mumtaz Muhammad Khan Daultana of the Punjab. The CML contested the 1970 **election** and won nine national assembly seats in

West Pakistan but none in **East Pakistan**. It does not exist as such in either Pakistan or Bangladesh today.

CROCODILE FARM. The first crocodile-rearing farm was set up in Bangladesh in 2003 in the Bhaluka upazila, in the **Mymensingh** district. The farm is built on approximately 13 acres consisting of 12 specially designed ponds and two lagoons. The farm does not procure crocodiles from the wild and adheres to the laws and regulations of the International Union for the Conservation of Nature and Natural Resources (IUCN) and Conservation on International Trade in Endangered Species (CITES). It is a self-contained breeding farm. It imported crocodiles from Malaysia and modern incubator equipment from Australia. The farm has the potential to earn Bangladesh approximately $1 million per year. It will serve as a center for breeding threatened species, research, and recreation. It also expects to become a center for breeding tortoises and snakes. Approximately 6,000 different kinds of plants can be viewed on the farm.

CULTIVABLE LAND. In 1971, the population was 75 million and the cultivable area was 9.9 million hectares. In 2008 the population was 150 million but cultivable land was only 6.6 million hectares. A variety of reasons including erosion of land, increasing homesteads, industrialization, and transportation development has resulted in the shrinking of available cultivable land. This loss will only be exacerbated by **global warming**.

CURRENCY. The unit of currency is the *taka*, a word that means money. This replaced the Pakistani rupee. The exchange rate floats so that there are frequent changes. In 2009 the exchange rate is about 70 taka to the dollar. The taka has slowly but steadily lost value in dollar terms over the years.

CURZON OF KEDDLESTON, GEORGE NATHANIEL CURZON, FIRST MARQUESS (1859–1925). A British statesman, viceroy, and governor-general of **India**, 1898–1905. Among his goals in India was the improvement, as he saw it, of the administrative system. One act taken in this direction in 1905 was the partitioning of the province (or presidency) of Bengal. He also extended the railway and irrigation systems and established the first national police force. Curzon left India as the loser in a quarrel with Lord Kitchener, then commander in chief of the Indian army. Curzon also made a major contribution to the preservation of Indian antiquities. His major post after leaving India was British secretary of state for foreign affairs, 1919–1924. *See also* BENGAL, PARTITION OF (1905).

CYCLONE. Because of its location at the head of the Bay of Bengal, Bangladesh is a frequent location for cyclonic storms. In 1970, a cyclone caused extensive damage and resulted in a reported 500,000 deaths. Since 1981, 19 violent storms have hit the **coastal islands** and have gone much farther inland. Winds have been as strong as 140 miles per hour and have created sea surges as much as 25 feet. For example, in 1970 the water rose by as much as two feet as far inland as **Khulna**, flooding a considerable area in a land as low and flat as Bangladesh. Bangladesh has tried to meet the danger in two ways: the building of more solidly constructed homes, often using cement blocks, and the erecting of *polders* as in the Netherlands. *See also* CLIMATE.

– D –

DACCA. *See* DHAKA.

DANCE. Folk dance is one of the main forms of performing art. These folk dances are generally specific to particular groups or regions. The Chakmas of the **Chittagong Hill Tracts** have the *visu sankranti* dance. *Lal Hara Uba* is a dance of another tribal group, the Manipuris, while a third tribal group, the Garos, have the *pisa dima dima* performed during the harvest season. Santals, Tripuras, and **Maghs** also have traditional dances. From these and other folk dances comes the performing art dance. Major dance-teaching institutions are the Bulbul Academy and the Chhayanat. *See also* ADIVASI COMMUNITY; ALI, AHMED; BULBUL CHOUDHURY; CHOWDHURY, ANWARA BAHAR; DAS, JOGESH; JAMIL, GOUHAR; *JATRA*; MANIPURI DANCE; MUSIC; WANNA FESTIVAL OF GARO.

DANISH EAST INDIA COMPANY. Founded in 1616, its first and only factory in Bengal was at Srirampur (Serampore), now a suburb of **Kolkata**, founded in 1755. The town was an operating base for many **Christian** missionaries, including **William Carey** and **John Marshman**, when missionary activity was banned in the territory controlled by the British **East India Company**. The factory never prospered, and it was sold to the British company in 1845.

DAS, CHITTARANJAN (1870–1925). A noted lawyer and politician who went into full-time politics in 1920 to join Gandhi's noncooperation movement. He entered the legal profession after failing to pass the examination for the Indian Civil Service. In 1923, he was elected mayor of **Kolkata**, with **Husain Shahid Suhrawardy** as deputy mayor and **Subhas Chandra Bose** as chief executive officer. He became president of the Indian National Congress in 1922, but he broke with Gandhi on the issue of boycotting elections. Das and some others, including Motilal Nehru, formed the Swaraj (Independence) Party with the goal of contesting elections and "noncooperating" from within the system created by the **Government of India Act of 1919**. The Swaraj Party won sufficient seats in the Bengal Legislative Council that it was able to prevent the formation of ministries in Bengal as stipulated in the act. Das attempted to solve the Muslim complaint that Muslims were denied a fair share of government jobs by signing the **Das-Haq pact** with **Fazlul Haq** in 1923. He was honored with the title *deshbandhu* (friend of the country).

DAS, JIBANANDA (1899–1854). Poet. He was born in **Barisal** and studied in **Calcutta**. He was a college professor and a journalist. His poetry concentrated on urban themes and the vulnerability of urban life. *See also* LITERATURE.

DAS, JOGESH (1926–2008). He started dancing at the age of 17 and for the next six decades performed, taught, and directed classical dances. He directed dance sequences in *Mahua*, *Nakshi Kanthar Math*, *Rakhal Bandhu*, *Kabor*, *Janani-Janmabhumi*, *Mayar Khela*, *Shyama*, *Chitrangada*, and many more.

DAS, SAMAR (1929–2001). A musician, he served in a number of capacities, including as **music** director of the first South Asian International Music Conference in Dhaka in 1954. He later was director of the *Swadin Bangla Betar Kendro* (Independent Bangla Radio Centre) during the **War of Liberation**. He also composed a number of songs, including "*Kando Bengalee Kando*" ("Cry Bengali Cry"), which was important during the independence war as a rallying point. He scored numerous folk and religious songs.

DAS-HAQ PACT. An agreement in 1923 between the principal Muslim political figure in Bengal, **Fazlul Haq**, and the leader of the Swarajist faction of the Indian National Congress, **Chittaranjan Das**. They agreed to limited cooperation to permit the system of dyarchy to work in the province and also to informal quotas to permit increased Muslim employment in government posts.

DASTIGAR, PURNENDU (1909-1971). A labor leader with a revolutionary background. He had been arrested by the British in 1930 for involvement in the **Chittagong** Armory raid. Dastigar organized labor, peasant, and student groups in Chittagong and was arrested again during the martial law of **Ayub Khan**. He was a member of the East Pakistan Provincial Assembly, 1954–1958.

DATTA, DHIRENDRA NATH (1886–1971). Member of the Bengal Legislative Assembly (1937–1947), the Constituent Assembly of Pakistan (1946–1954), and the East Bengal Legislative Assembly (1947–1958). He was assassinated by the Pakistani army in 1971. His most memorable speech was delivered at the Constituent Assembly of Pakistan in 1948 in defense of Bangla as a state **language**.

DAUD KHAN (r. 1573–1576). The successor of Bayazid Karrani of the Afghan **Karrani** dynasty. He was the last ruler in this dynasty. When he succeeded his brother in 1573, he claimed to be the independent ruler of Bengal. The **Mughal** emperor, Akbar, contested this and his armies began a campaign against Daud Khan in 1574, which ended in 1576 with the death of Daud Khan at the battle of Rajmahal and the full incorporation of Bengal into the Mughal Empire.

DEB, RADHAKANTA (1783–1867). A strong advocate of the modernization of the Indian educational system, he urged the teaching of English as beneficial to India. He also supported an increasing role for Indians in the administration. He supported **education** for **women**, but contrarily he opposed the banning of *sati* and child marriage. He favored the introduction of Western means of teaching medicine, including the dissection of corpses.

DEBT. *See* EXTERNAL DEBT.

DEEN, SALEEM AL (1949–2008). Considered one of the three foremost playwrights of Bangla literature, he was born in Feni in 1949. He obtained his master's degree from **Dhaka University** and his Ph.D. in Bangla literature from Jahangirnagar University in 1995; he became a professor of the Department of Drama and Dramatics at Jahangirnagar University, which he established. In 1968 he published his first article, "Negro Literature," in *Dainak Pakistan*. In 1969 his first radio drama, *Biporit Tomoshay*, was broadcast and in 1970 his first TV drama, *Ghum Nei*, was presented. He was the founding member of Dhaka Theatre and Bangladesh Gram Theatre. He also compiled the only anthology on Bangla drama, *Bangla Natyakosh*. Bangla drama literature is defined as having three distinct periods, one of which is know as the Selim period. The two others are the Girish era and Shishir era. For his accomplishments he received the Ekushey Padak, Bangla Academy Literature Award, and the National Film Award.

DELHI SULTANATE. The name applied to the Muslim kingdoms based in Delhi from 1206, when Turkish rulers first established a permanent base in India, to 1526, when the last dynasty was defeated in the battle of Panipat by the founder of the **Mughal Empire**, Babar. There were five dynasties: Slave (or Mamluk) (1206–1290), Khalji (1290–1320), Tughluq (1320–1413), Sayyid (1414–1451), and Lodhi (1451–1526). Before the establishment of the capital at Delhi, the **Sena** kingdom based in Nadia in Bengal fell in 1202 to a general of the **Afghan** sultanate based at Ghor. Bengal remained under at least the nominal control of Delhi until 1336, when **Fakhruddin Mubarrak Shah** rebelled against the Tughluq dynasty. In 1346, Bengal became independent and remained so for almost two centuries, mainly under the **Ilyas Shahi** and **Husain Shahi** dynasties. In 1538, forces of the Mughal emperor Humayun conquered Bengal, which became dependent on Delhi once again, but as part of the successor empire to the Delhi Sultanate, the Mughal Empire.

DEMOCRATIC ACTION COMMITTEE. Formed in January 1969, principally composed of the **Awami League**, the **National Awami Party** of Wali Khan, and the **Jama'at-i-Islami**. The committee was set up to oppose the rule of President **Ayub Khan**. Its purpose was the full and complete restoration of democracy in Pakistan. It issued an eight-point manifesto that included, among other points, the establishment of a federal parliamentary system of government, direct election by adult franchise, and the release of popular leaders such as Sheikh **Mujibur Rahman** and **Zulfiqar Ali Bhutto**.

DEMOCRATIC LEAGUE. Organized by defectors from the **Awami League** in August 1976. This party was established after the enactment of the Political Parties Regulation Act by President **Ziaur Rahman**. It was headed by **Khondakar Mushtaque Ahmed** with the support of Mainul Hussain, who was the proprietor and managing editor of the *Ittefaq* newspaper. In mid-1977 the Democratic League split into two factions. The Democratic League experienced a resurgence in 1980 after the release of Mushtaque Ahmed from jail. In 1983 the Democratic League organized a national united front composed of right-wing opposition parties. It has since faded from politics. *See also* TOFAZZUL HUSSAIN (MOHAN MIA).

DEMOCRATIC PARTY. Formed in December 1980 by the members of the **National Awami Party** and led by **Maulana Bhashani**, it was a dissident faction of the United People's Party and two other participants in the 1979 Democratic Front: the Jatiya Gana Makti Union and the Gono Front. The Democratic Party was organized by Mirza Nurul Huda (not the same person for whom there is an entry in this dictionary), who subsequently joined the **Bangladesh Nationalist Party**.

DEV, GOVINDA CHANDRA (1907–1971). Educationist. He was born in **Sylhet** and studied in **Kolkata**. He remained with **Dhaka**

University after partition and published a number of works on philosophy. In his search for the meaning of life he took the basic tenants of Shri Ramakrishna, Vivekanda, **Buddha**, Spinoza, and Copernicus and blended them to form his own ethical standards. He began his teaching career at Surendranath College in Calcutta. When Surendranath College moved to Dinajpur in Bangladesh, he moved with the college. He joined Dhaka University in 1953. He was bayoneted and shot to death by the Pakistani army on 26 March 1971 at his Dhaka University residence.

DEVA DYNASTY. A dynasty that ruled in southeastern Bengal, probably in the latter part of the eighth century. Information about the dynasty comes from copper plates found at **Mainamati** on which there is no decipherable dating. The dynasty is thought to have been preceded by that of the **Khargas** and succeeded by that of **Harikela**.

DEVAPALA (r. c. 810–850). The third ruler of the **Pala dynasty**, succeeding **Dharmapala**, he extended the territories controlled by the Palas to their greatest extent. The domains stretched from **Assam** in the east to the borders of Kashmir in the west and from the foothills of the Himalayas in the north to the Vindhyas in the south. He was a patron of **Buddhism** and, particularly, of the university at Nalanda in Bihar.

DEVELOPING EIGHT COUNTRIES (D8). An association of Bangladesh, Egypt, Indonesia, Iran, Malaysia, **Pakistan**, Thailand, and Turkey, it was inaugurated in June 1997 following a conference in October 1996 in Istanbul. It is intended to help the members improve their positions in the world economy. This is to be done through the exchange of technical information and the holding of conferences and seminars in a variety of areas including **trade**, **industry**, telecommunications and information, finance, **banking** and **privatization**, and rural development.

DHAKA. The capital and largest city of Bangladesh is on the Buriganga River. There is **archeological** evidence that may indicate rule by the **Pala dynasty** at Sabhar, Mahona, and Dakuri, places located near Dhaka. Before Dhaka became a capital there were rulers at nearby **Sonargaon**.

It first became a capital in 1610 when the **Mughals** made it the headquarters of the province of Bengal, but in 1574 it had become a military headquarters of the Mughals as a means to suppress the revolt of **Isa Khan**. The move of the capital was largely made to control eastern Bengal, especially from the challenges by the Ahoms in **Assam** and the **Maghs** and **Portuguese** in the **Chittagong** area. At the time it became the provincial capital it was renamed Jahangirnagar in honor of the then Mughal emperor. It remained the capital until **Murshid Quli Khan** moved the headquarters to **Murshidabad** in 1702. After that time and until the independence of **Pakistan** and **India**, it was a district headquarters, except for the period 1905 to 1911, when it was the capital of the short-lived province of **Eastern Bengal and Assam**. With Pakistani independence in 1947, it became the capital of **East Bengal** and **East Pakistan**. With the independence of Bangladesh, it became the capital of the newly independent state.

The British established a branch factory in Dhaka to trade in the fine muslin and silks manufactured in Dhaka. Dhaka is noted for *chikan*, fine muslin intricately embroidered with silk. The city thrived as a trading station and a river port, but the transfer of the capital, a series of **famines**, and a decreased demand for the hand-woven cloth caused a sharp decline in the city's prosperity in the 18th and 19th centuries. When it became the capital of Eastern Bengal and Assam, the city began to grow again and became the second city of Bengal after **Calcutta**. The establishment of Dhaka University in 1921 added to its **educational** stature. Today, with a population exceeding 12 million, it is the administrative, economic, and educational center of Bangladesh.

Dhaka preserves much **architecture** from its past, including the Lalbagh Fort begun in 1678 by Azam Shah, a son of the Mughal emperor Aurangzeb. The most interesting building in the fort is the tomb of Bibi Pari, a grandniece of the Mughal empress Nur Jahan, consort of Jahangir. Other Mughal buildings include the Bara Katra (1664), the Chhota Katra (1663), and the Shia mosque, Hussaini Dalan (1642). Of **Hindu** temples, the most notable is that devoted to Dhakeshwari, from whom the city may have gotten its name.

In trade Dhaka was best known for its fine cotton muslin cloth known as *jamdani.* Today the city and its suburb, Narayanganj, are the center of industrial and financial activity in Bangladesh. Dhaka district has now been divided into Dhaka, Narayanganj, Narsingdi, Gazipur, Manikganj, and Munshiganj districts. *See also* BENGAL, PARTITION OF (1905).

DHAKA JAIL KILLINGS. These resulted in the death of **Tajuddin Ahmed, Syed Nazrul Islam, Mansur Ali**, and **A. H. M. Kamruzzaman** on 3 November 1975. Tajuddin Ahmed had been jailed during **Mujibur Rahman**'s regime, and the others following the **August coup**. Responsibility for the orders permitting the murders has not been fixed, although popular belief often assigns it to the **majors.** A day after the killing, deputy inspector general of police Abdul Awal filed a case with Lalbagh Police Station against four persons, one of whom was Risaldar (retd.) Muslemuddin. On 15 October 1998, after 23 years, police submitted a charge sheet against 23 people. The Metropolitan Sessions Judge's Court in Dhaka passed the verdict in the case on 20 October 2004, sentencing 3 people to death and 12 to life in prison. On 29 June 2008, the High Court (HC) acquitted six former military men, including Syed Farook Rahman, Sultan Shahriar Rashid Khan, Bazlul Huda, and A. K. M. Mohiuddin Ahmed of charges in the Jail Killing Case. It upheld the death sentence of Risaldar (retd.) Muslemuddin. Of those cleared, Dafadar (dismissed) Marfat Ali Shah and Dafadar (dismissed) Abdul Hashem Mridha had been sentenced to death by trial court and Lt. Col. (dismissed) Farook, Lt. Col. (retd.) Shahriar Rashid, Major (retd.) Huda, and Major (retd.) Mohiuddin to life for their role in killing four national leaders inside Dhaka Central Jail.

DHAKA, NAWAB OF (FAMILY). The family of the Nawab of Dhaka has produced a number of important political leaders in the region now comprising Bangladesh. The title is hereditary, but as a *zamindar* (landlord), not as a ruling prince. Among the members of the family have been Nawab **Salimullah**, a founder of the **Muslim League**; Khwaja Sir **Nazimuddin**, whose last official position was prime minister of Pakistan; and Khwaja **Shahabuddin**, Nazimuddin's younger brother, who served in several Pakistan cabinets. The last nawab in the Pakistan period was **Hasan Askari**. The family was part of the **national elite** and has not been active in politics in independent Bangladesh, although many collaborators are active in the administration. For example, General Khwaja Wasiuddin, son of Khwaja Shahabuddin and a former Pakistani army officer, has been a Bangladeshi ambassador. Another collaborator, Khwaja Khairuddin, went to Pakistan as the leader of a splinter of the Muslim League. *See also* VERNACULAR ELITE.

DHAKA STREET POTTERY. An area near the Dhaka University science campus called Doel Chattar has become the biggest market for pottery and terracotta pieces. Traditional pottery was available in small rural fairs and was on the decline for many decades. In the early 1980s, a few traders opened makeshift shops to sell pottery, primarily plain pots for plants. Today there are about 70 shops selling decorative terracotta sculptures, figures, vases, candle and pen stands, and ashtrays. Most pottery is produced in Barisal, Comilla, Faridpur, and Dhaka division localities of Dhamrai, Savar, and Nabinagar. Besides pottery, some wood products are also sold, and these come primarily from Bogra and Rangpur. Demand for pottery and traditional wooden carvings is linked to the development of professional interior decorators (for private homes and businesses) and a return of pride in Bangla culture. Traditional pottery and wooden items are highlighted during festivals such as ***Poheila Boishakh*** (Bangla New Year), and often utilized by those in the theatre and film industries.

DHAKA UNIVERSITY. Established in 1921 so that students from East Bengal, who were primarily Muslims, would have access to higher **education**, it became a center of academic excellence rivaling other well-established universities of **India**, especially that of the University of **Calcutta** (Kolkata). After the partition of India in 1947, Dhaka University became the principal institution of higher education in **East Pakistan**. It also quickly emerged as the center for social change when students of Dhaka University played a leading role in the movement to make Bangla one of the national **languages** of Pakistan. While it maintained its academic leadership by graduating high-quality students, it also facilitated student initiatives against dictatorship and the tyranny of governance and government. In 1971, its faculty, students, and staff played a pivotal part in the independence movement of Bangladesh.

After 1971, the faculty of Dhaka University proposed the 1973 Dhaka University Ordinance Order as a way of improving its governance system, ensuring accountability, and creating separation from government interference. While it succeeded for a while, the politicization of faculty and staff made Dhaka University dysfunctional. At the same time, pressure on recruitment and the politicization of student leadership further challenged the institution, causing severe stress on academic standards and integrity. Unless significant changes are made in both faculty governance and student recruitment, Dhaka University is likely to lose its academic standing in the higher education system.

DHARMAPALA (r. c. 770–810). Considered the greatest king of the **Pala dynasty**, he extended the power of the dynasty beyond the boundaries of Bengal and Bihar. His conquests in northern **India** were consolidated by his successor, **Devapala**. He was an ardent **Buddhist** and supported a number of Buddhist establishments, including the Somapura Vihara near **Paharpur** in **Rajshahi** district.

DHOLAIKHAL. Located near the Buriganga River in Old **Dhaka**, it was one of many canals in and around Dhaka city. Since 1960 the banks of the canal have became a repair and service center for buses and trucks. It is the primary salvage yard for all types of vehicles. Over the years it has become known for local non-mechanical spare parts production and is known today for the relatively complex manufacturing of engine parts. Trading houses and wholesale dealers of Japanese cars, as well as dealers from **India**, Singapore, Thailand, and **China**, have set up shops in this area. The area currently has over 5,000 shops and employs between 35,000 and 45,000 people.

DINAJPUR. A district and district town in northwestern Bangladesh. The town lies on the Punarbhaba River. The district is dominated by the Barind, a somewhat elevated tract, in what is otherwise a flat plain.

Tradition associates the area of Dinajpur with Matsyadesa of the **Hindu** epic *Mahabharata*, the place where the Pandhavas of the epic took refuge during their exile and the place of exile of Sita, the wife of Rama of the epic *Ramayana.* Valmiki, the author of the *Rama-yana*, may have been born in Dinajpur and is reputed to have bathed in Tarpur Ghat in Nawabganj. Nearby is a mound said to have been the home of Sita. It was a part of **Varendra** and later came under the rule of the **Palas**, who have left **Buddhist** monuments, and the **Senas**. Stone pillars perhaps date from the Pala period, including a monolith at Dhibar. Copper plates have also been found from this period. Dinajpur was the home territory of **Raja Ganesh**, who interrupted the rule of the **Ilyas Shahi dynasty** in 1415 and is said to have founded the town of Dinajpur.

Among the **architectural** sites are the Sura mosque in Dinajpur and the Vishnu temple of the 18th century in Kantanagar. Much of the limited trade between Bangladesh and India passes through the border village of Hili in the district. Dinajpur district now comprises Dinajpur and Thakurgaon districts.

DIRECT ACTION DAY. 16 August 1946 was a day set aside by the **Muslim League** for work stoppages (*hartals*) and demonstrations to emphasize the league's demand for the partition of India. The day had been agreed on at a meeting of Muslim League legislators in New Delhi on July 27, following the Congress rejection of the **Cabinet Mission Plan**. The meeting also endorsed a single state of **Pakistan** as opposed to the plural "states" used in the **Lahore Resolution**. The day was peaceful except in **Calcutta**, where serious violence between Muslims and **Hindus** occurred. **Husain Shahid Suhrawardy** was prime minister of Bengal at the time. He and Gandhi worked together to quell the violence.

***DIWANI* OF BENGAL.** Granted to the British East India Company by the **Mughal** emperor Shah Alam II in 1765. It gave the company the right to collect taxes in the province of Bengal, with portions going to the emperor and to the nawab at **Murshidabad** (successors to **Mir Jafar**) and the remainder being used by the British. Collection by the British actually began in 1772. As the collection of revenue was inseparable from the governing of the province, the British became rulers of Bengal in fact.

The term *diwan* appears to have been used first under the caliph Omar as a record of financial transactions. Later it was sometimes used to describe the government at large, but under the Mughal emperor Akbar it was used for financial matters, especially the collection of revenue.

DUDU MIA (1819–1860). His real name was Muhammad Moshini, and he was the son of Haji **Shariatullah**. He furthered the organizational setup of the **Faraizi movement** by dividing East Bengal into a number of regions and appointing persons to head each of the regions. He was able to keep himself well informed about all forms of suppression and to take countermeasures against them. Dudu Mia propagated the idea that land belongs to Allah and that no one has permanent rights over it. He worked extensively for the equality and welfare of the poor. For his activities, Dudu Mia was arrested a number of times and was tried but never convicted of any crime. He was imprisoned in 1857 and died in 1860.

DUTCH EAST INDIA COMPANY. The company was founded in 1602. Its impact on Asia was mainly in present-day Sri Lanka, Malaysia, and Indonesia, although, like other European trading companies, it also established factories in Bengal. *See also* CHINSURA.

DUTT, MICHAEL MADHUSUDAN (1824–1873). Poet and playwright, the first Bengali poet to use the sonnet technique in his poems. In 1843 he converted to Christianity. In 1849 two significant works—*Captive Lady* and *Vision of the Past*—were published. Much of Dutt's early writing was in English, but his best-known poem, "*Meghanadvadh*," was in Bengali. He was called to the bar from London in 1866 and joined the Calcutta bar. A college bearing his name is located in his birthplace, **Jessore**. *See also* LITERATURE; THEATRE.

DUTT, ROMESH CHANDRA (1848–1909). He entered the Indian Civil Service in 1871, and added to a distinguished administrative career with the publication of a number of historical works. His most noted work, *Economic History of India*, was published in two volumes in 1902 and 1904. Dutt retired to England in 1897, but he returned to India to serve as president of the Indian National Congress in 1899.

DUTTA, GURUSADAY (1882–1941). Born in **Sylhet**, he studied in **Calcutta** and London and passed the examination for the Indian Civil Service. While he was district magistrate in **Mymensingh** he began a program for the reconstruction of villages. This led to the founding of the Rural Heritage Preservation Society of Bengal.

DYARCHY. The term used to describe the system of provincial government created by the **Government of India Act of 1919** (the Montagu-Chelmsford Act). Elected members became a majority in the legislative councils of the provinces, and they controlled, as in a parliamentary system, the ministers heading the "nation-building departments." The control, however, was individual and not collective; the ministers did not form a cabinet. These departments included **education, agriculture**, public works, and health. The other departments, which represented the "steel frame" of British rule, including home, finance, and revenue, remained under the control of the governor through executive councilors appointed by and responsible to him. In operation, however, many of the executive councilor posts came to be held by Indians, most of whom had previous experience as ministers. Dyarchy was abolished at the provincial level in 1937 by the **Government of India Act of 1935**, which created a system of provincial autonomy.

– E –

EARTHQUAKE. Bangladesh has had major earthquakes in the past. Three critical ones were the 1885 Bengal earthquake, also known as the Manikganj earthquake because of its epicenter, the 1762 Bengal-Arakan earthquake with its epicenter in the **Chittagong Hill Tract**, and the 1918 earthquake with its epicenter in the Srimongol/Kishoreganj area. The 1897 Great Assam earthquake that directly impacted Bangladesh also must be considered in assessing the potential for earthquake impact. The 1897 earthquake was determined to be above 8.0 on the Richter scale and the Manikganj was between 7.0 and 8.0. There are indications that the Highlands (*Gar*) of Madhupur and the Hoars of Sylhet are a result of earthquake activities and that the flow of rivers such as the Tista and Brahmaputra have changed due to seismic activities in Bangladesh and the surrounding areas. Between 2007 and 2008 earthquakes hit Bangladesh near **Chittagong** (6.0) and **Dhaka** (5.6 and 3.0), causing experts to discuss the potential of a significant quake that would correspond to a 135-year cycle. Faults have been identified in the hills of the Chittagong and Khagrachari districts and neo-faults along the Dhaleshwari and Buriganga Rivers near Dhaka. The Earthquake Disaster Risk Index developed at Stanford University identifies Dhaka as having the highest potential for damage among the 20 cities identified in the study.

EAST BENGAL. The official name of the territory that is now Bangladesh from independence in 1947 to the enactment of legislation that consolidated the provinces in the west wing. This consolidation created a single province ("one unit") in 1955 as part of the process of adopting the **Constitution of Pakistan of 1956**. The Indian portion of the pre-1947 province of Bengal was (and is) designated West Bengal, with its capital at **Calcutta**.

EAST INDIA COMPANY. The company was founded as a trading company in 1600 and was disbanded in 1858. During that period, the company was transformed from a trading company to an administrative and military organization as it expanded British territory in India and ruled over that territory as if it were a truly colonial regime. The transfer of power from the company to the Crown in 1858 barely changed the system of governance as far as the governed in India were concerned. This entry will note briefly the role of the company in Bengal.

The first factory of the company was in Surat, on the west coast of India, established in 1612. The company set up a factory in **Calcutta** in 1690 and created other trading stations in such cities as **Chittagong** and **Dhaka**. Calcutta was captured by **Sirajuddaulah** in 1756, but the city was retaken by a company force led by **Robert Clive** in 1757. The company then became the de facto ruler of Bengal, a situation that was confirmed by the acquisition of the *diwani* **of Bengal** in 1765. This gave the company the right to collect taxes in Bengal on behalf of the **Mughal** emperor (then Shah Alam II). As tax collection and general administration were for all practical purposes inseparable, the nawab of Bengal (already a British puppet) became little more than an ornament. The company also recognized the importance of Bengal by designating the governor of Bengal, **Warren Hastings**, as governor-general of all of its Indian territories in 1773. Calcutta then became the capital of the company's possessions.

As the company changed from a trading institution to a governing body, the British parliament increased its interest in the company's activities and began to exercise greater control over its activities. Lord North's Regulating Act of 1773 and William Pitt's India Act of 1784 gave Westminster the greater control that it desired. The company lost its monopoly on trade with India in the early 19th century through the Charter Acts of 1813 and 1833. Thus by the time of the company's abolition in 1858, it had long ceased to perform its initial objective of trade with the East.

EAST PAKISTAN. The official name for the territory that now comprises Bangladesh from 1955 until Bangladeshi independence in 1971. The territory was often also referred to informally as the "east wing."

EASTERN BENGAL AND ASSAM. A province created as a result of the **partition of Bengal in 1905**. It included the districts in the divisions of **Dhaka**, **Rajshahi**, and **Chittagong**, along with **Assam**. The remainder of the province of Bengal retained that name and included Bihar and Orissa. In 1911, the partition of Bengal was revoked. The Bengali districts in East Bengal and Assam were joined with the Bengali districts of the western part of Bengal to form the new province of Bengal. Assam was separated as a chief commissionership, and later elevated to a province. The areas of Bihar and Orissa were joined to form the province of Bihar and Orissa, and later, under the Government of India Act of 1935, divided into two separate provinces.

ECONOMY. In many ways Bangladesh remains a colonial-type economy. During the period of British rule, and to some extent before, it was a producer of raw materials that were shipped elsewhere for processing. The most notable of these commodities was **jute**. It was produced mainly in eastern Bengal and then sent to **Calcutta** or Scotland for manufacturing into such things as sacking and rope.

The growers were tenant farmers working land owned by landlords (*zamindars*) who reaped most of the profits and who usually resided in Calcutta and not on the land. This ownership arrangement was alleviated somewhat by the **Bengal Tenancy Act of 1885** that conferred some security to the farmers. Another crop, introduced in the 19th century, was **tea**. These plantations were usually owned by the British. Today the demand for jute has declined markedly as it has been replaced by synthetic fibers. Tea remains an important export and the plantations are now owned by Bangladeshis.

Another aspect of colonial-type rule is the importation of raw materials that are then fabricated into materials for export, taking advantage of the lower wage rates in Bangladesh. In earlier times, cotton was imported and the famed **Dhaka muslin** was exported. Today the modern counterpart of this is the import of textiles that are then made into exportable **garments**.

Until the relatively recent discovery of abundant natural gas, Bangladesh had no exploitable mineral resources. Limited amounts of poor-grade coal do exist, but mining is difficult in areas where the water table is high. The recently discovered gas supplies might be exported to **India** and earn a significant amount of hard currency, but political opposition based on the long-term needs of Bangladesh (based, it seems, on the belief that no more gas would be recovered from what international companies believe to be a very high amount of reserves) has stymied proposals for exportation. Energy could be exported either as gas by pipeline or as gas-generated electricity through an international grid system. The **Awami League** is the principal opponent of exportation. Some might say that exportation would be a return to the role of a colonial-type supplier of a resource, with gas replacing jute as the commodity. Domestically gas is used in electricity generation and in the manufacture of nitrogenous fertilizers.

Despite the potential of natural gas, the economy was and is heavily based on **agriculture**. In 2006, agriculture accounted for 21 percent of the gross domestic product (GDP), while **industry** accounted for 28 percent and the balance was the catch-all category of services. The importance of agriculture to the population is more sharply shown in that 63 percent of the labor force is engaged in agriculture, while industry absorbs 17 percent and services 25 percent. With the bulk of the employed population working in agriculture or in the generally low-paying service sector, Bangladesh remains one of the poorest countries in the world. In 2000 its per capita GDP was $1,570 on a purchasing power parity basis. It moved to as high as $2,300 in 2007, but with the global economic downturn it moved down to $1,400 in 2008.

Significant gains have been made in the production of food, the principal component being rice. Rice production in 1999 was 20.2 million metric tons. It is currently at 28.8 million metric tons. The land, generally well watered, is naturally conducive to growing rice, often in two or three crops a year. The rate of cropping is 176 percent. Rainfall is abundant, although crops can sometimes be destroyed by **floods** caused by excessive rainfall. A crop that has not been historically important in Bangladesh is wheat, the quantity of which has grown significantly. It is used primarily in bread products. As already mentioned, jute and tea are crops for export. Much of the cereals grown is used at the subsistence level, with any surplus going to urban and nonfarming populations. The usual cause for cereal importation is the failure to produce a sufficient surplus for this nonfarming population. The harvesting of fish, a significant source of protein in the Bangladeshi diet, and of shellfish is an important and growing industry. Fish farming has been taken up enthusiastically. Much of the shellfish is frozen and exported. Livestock and poultry are also major agricultural endeavors.

In 2000, exports totaled $5.9 billion and imports $8.1 billion, leaving a substantial **trade** deficit. More than 75 percent of the exports are from the **garment industry**. As noted earlier, the traditionally largest export, jute, has dropped significantly in earnings. Other exports are leather, jute goods, frozen fish and shellfish (especially shrimp), tea, urea fertilizers, pharmaceuticals, newsprint, and ceramics. In 1999, approximately one-third of exports were to the **United States**. Today, Bangladesh is the sixth-largest exporter of garments to the United States. Several countries of the European Union are also important destinations. Import sources are more diversified and are led by India and Singapore. Imports include petroleum, textiles (most often for the garment industry), grains, chemicals, vegetable oils, and food.

Industry is centered on the manufactured items exported from Bangladesh. Other industries include the processing of tea (for domestic consumption and export) and sugar, newsprint, leather tanning, pharmaceuticals, and fertilizer. Steel is produced in a mill in **Chittagong** using scrap from the ship-breaking industry. Much industry occurs in small establishments which can be described as cottage industries. Cottage industry production is not recorded but includes such activities as weaving, sewing, pottery, and **handicrafts**.

Industrial development and efficiency are greatly hindered by the failure to **privatize** much of the industrial structure. Bangladesh nationalized assets owned by **Pakistanis** at the time it achieved independence. Government officials have been assigned the task of running these corporations, which have almost unanimous money-losing records. One reason for the failure to privatize has been the opposition of labor unions, as they fear (probably correctly) that jobs would be lost in the increased efficiency of the private sector. The money-losing record caused the closure in 2002 of the largest industrial employer, the **Adamjee Jute Mill**.

The **banking** system, too, remains primarily under government ownership and is largely dysfunctional. This impedes foreign investment and economic growth. Investors, both domestic and foreign, are reluctant to put money in Bangladesh when the financial sector is in such disorganization and is often accused, along with other sectors, of **corruption**. An exception to this is the investment made by foreign firms in natural gas, but many of these are disenchanted by bureaucratic and political inaction. *See also* EMPLOYMENT; HIGH TECHNOLOGY; INDUSTRY; NATURAL RESOURCES; PLANNING; REMITTANCES; SHIP BREAKING; SHIP BUILDING; STEEL RE-ROLLING INDUSTRIAL SECTOR.

EDUCATION. Education is not compulsory but is free at the primary level beginning at age five and continuing for five years. It is reported that 77 percent of the children aged five to nine attend primary school. This figure is probably inflated, as it appears to include children who attend for any portion of the school year rather than just those who attend the entire school year. At the secondary level, attendance of those aged 10 to 14 was reported to be 22 percent, perhaps a more accurate figure. The state school system operates on the basis of five years of primary school, five years of secondary school, and two years of higher secondary school. The government is concentrating on the extension of primary education, especially in the rural areas.

As of mid-2006, there are 27 government universities in Bangladesh and 51 private universities, although some of the latter may not be operating fully, and some may not prove to be viable in the long run. An estimate states that 83 percent of the university attendees are male and 17 percent female.

Educational enrollment figures for 2006 show that approximately 24 million students are enrolled in the K–12 system and an additional 153,000 are enrolled in higher education. Thus, like most developing countries, access to higher education is extremely limited. Education expenditures by the government are just over 2 percent of gross domestic product and are very highly concentrated in the primary and secondary areas. In 2008, however, 12.8 percent of the revenue **budget** was allocated for education and information technology.

For those who can afford the tuition fees or receive scholarships, much of the pre-university education takes place in privately operated schools rather than state schools. These private institutions, which often conduct classes in English, vary widely in quality from the very good schools often run by Christian mission groups to those at the other end of the scale, often operated by entrepreneurs for profit. The vocational education system can best be described as very weak. There are also a substantial number of Islamic primary schools (*madrasas*) of varying quality that are attached to mosques and other religious endowments.

Latest available census figures show that literacy rates are about 41 percent for males and 34 percent for females, for an overall rate of about 38 percent. *See also* DHAKA UNIVERSITY.

EIGHTEEN POINTS. A program that was announced by president **Hussain Muhammad Ershad** in March 1983 for the economic and political revival of Bangladesh. Economic self-sufficiency, democratization of the political system, and decentralization of the administrative system provided the major thrust of the program. The latter point was carried out by raising subdivisions to the level of district and designating the former districts as regions. *See also* LOCAL GOVERNMENT.

EKUSHEY PADAK. An annual award of the Ministry of Culture, it recognizes the contribution of outstanding personalities in a variety of fields including journalism, arts and **literature**, social service and **education**, and science and engineering. It is the highest cultural award of the country. *See also* MARTYRS' DAY.

ELECTIONS. There have been a number of elections that are of importance to the history of Bangladesh. This entry provides a comment on each election held since the passage of the **Government of India Act of 1935**, with the exception of the indirect **basic democracy** elections held during the **Ayub Khan** period. District level results for each election through the 1996 election are contained in tables in Craig Baxter, *Bangladesh: From a Nation to a State* (Boulder, Colo.: Westview Press, 1957). Constituency results for the 2001 and 2008 elections can be obtained from the Bangladesh Election Commission website.

Bengal Legislative Assembly Election of 1937. The results of this election, the first under provincial autonomy, can be described only as inconclusive. Of the 119 seats of the 250 in the entire assembly allotted to Muslims under the **separate electorate** system, the **Muslim League** won 39, the **Krishak Praja Party (KPP)** 36, the Tippera Krishak Samiti (a small party based in **Comilla**) 5, and independents 39. (Two additional Muslim independents won seats reserved for industry and Dhaka University graduates.) The largest party was the Congress with 52. The Muslims worked out a coalition between the Muslim League and the KPP, with **Fazlul Haq** as prime minister and **Nazimuddin** as his second in command. Five non-Congress Hindus were included in the ministry.

Bengal Legislative Assembly Election of 1945–1946. This election was held under the system of separate electorates. It was considered by the Muslim League to be a referendum on the question of the partition of India—a strong vote for the League would be interpreted as strong support for partition. In the Muslim seats located in what is now Bangladesh, the Muslim League won 82.04 percent of the vote and its principal rival, the Krishak Praja Party (KPP), only 5.98 percent, with the remainder going to smaller parties and independents. In terms of seats, the Muslim League won 92 of the 98 Muslim seats in the future East Pakistan and Bangladesh; the KPP, 4; and independents, 2. The popular vote in this electorate province for the Muslim League was the highest in this election of any Muslim-majority area (the others being the Punjab, Sindh, and the Northwest Frontier).

East Bengal Legislative Assembly Election of 1954. A legislative assembly election had been due in 1951, but as it seemed clear that the Muslim League was rapidly losing ground over the language issue and other concerns, it was delayed until 1954. The election showed clearly that the Muslim League had lost its support among Muslim voters. The election was again held on the basis of separate electorates. The **United Front**, comprising the **Awami League** and the **Krishak Sramik Party (KSP)**, won a major victory in the Muslim seats, winning 223 of the 237 seats and reducing the Muslim League to 10 seats. The United Front gained 65.72 percent of the Muslim vote and the Muslim League 19.57 percent.

East Pakistan Vote for the National Assembly of Pakistan of 1970. The martial law government headed by **Yahya Khan** held elections for the National Assembly of Pakistan and the Provincial Assembly of East Pakistan in December 1970 and January 1971. The results were overwhelming victories for the Awami League, now led by Sheikh **Mujibur Rahman**. In the National Assembly voting the Awami League won 160 seats of the 162 contested; the others were won by **Nurul Amin** of the **Democratic Party** and an independent. The Awami League received 75.22 percent of the popular vote, far ahead of the second place **Jama'at-i-Islami** with 6.08 percent and no seats. The 160 seats gave the Awami League a majority in the 300-seat assembly even though it won no seats in West Pakistan.

East Pakistan Provincial Vote of 1970. The results for the Provincial Assembly were similar. The Awami League won 288 of the 300 seats contested with a similar proportion of the popular vote.

Bangladesh Parliamentary Election of 1973. As the Bangladesh Parliament had been formed after independence by a merger of the members of the Provincial Assembly and those Bangladeshi members of the Pakistan National Assembly who remained in Bangladesh, a new election for a parliament was held in 1973. It confirmed overwhelmingly the strength of the Awami League, although there were also reports of substantial rigging of the polls. The Awami League won 291 of 300 seats with 73.18 percent of the popular vote.

Referendum of 1977. President **Ziaur Rahman** sought to legitimize his assumption of the presidency. A referendum on his continuance in office gave him 98.9 percent of the valid votes. As there was no alternative in the referendum, the goal of legitimacy was not met.

Presidential Election of 1978. President Ziaur Rahman then called for a national election for the presidency. Although there were a number of candidates, the principal opponent was General **Muhammad Ataul Ghani Osmany**, who was supported by a number of parties, including the Awami League. Zia polled 76.63 percent; Osmany, 21.70 percent. The election was viewed as generally free and fair.

Parliamentary Election of 1979. With the presidency securely in his hands, Ziaur Rahman called a parliamentary election in 1979. His party, the **Bangladesh Nationalist Party (BNP)**, won 207 of the 300 seats contested, with the Awami League faction led by **Abdul Malik Ukil** winning 39, and the Muslim League–**Islamic Democratic League** alliance winning 20. The BNP polled 41.16 percent of the popular vote; the Awami League–Malik, 24.52 percent. The vote has been characterized as "free and fair."

Presidential Election of 1981. On the assassination of Zia in May 1981, vice president **Abdus Sattar** became acting president pending an election for the presidency to be held within 180 days. The BNP nominated Sattar and the Awami League nominated **Kamal Hossain**; there were other candidates as well. Sattar won the election with 65.5 percent of the vote to Hossain's 26.0 percent.

Referendum of 1985. President **Hussain Muhammad Ershad** called for a referendum on his continuance in office. It was reported that there was a 72 percent turnout and that 94 percent voted in favor of Ershad. It did not bestow legitimacy on the Ershad regime.

Parliamentary Election of 1986. Ershad called for a parliamentary election in 1986 despite statements by the principal opposition parties, the BNP and the Awami League, that they would not participate. Ershad eventually convinced the Awami League to join the election. Despite widespread reports of rigging, Ershad's **Jatiya Party** barely scraped through to a majority of 152 seats in the 300-seat house. The Awami League won 70 seats and with its allies formed a block of about 100 seats. The BNP did not participate.

Parliamentary Election of 1988. Ershad dissolved parliament in 1987 after there had been rioting and called a new election. The

Awami League, which had resigned from parliament, joined the BNP and other parties in boycotting the election. The result, which was hardly a reflection of political opinion in the country, was a parliament almost entirely composed of members of Ershad's Jatiya Party and a few scattered representatives of small parties prepared to work with Ershad.

Parliamentary Election of 1991. Following the fall of Ershad in December 1990, a general election was held under a **caretaker government** for a new parliament. The BNP, led by **Khaleda Zia**, won 168 seats of the 300 directly elected; the Awami League, 88; the Jatiya Party, 35; and the Jama'at-i-Islami, 20; other parties and independents won the remaining 19. When 30 indirectly elected seats for **women** were included, the BNP total increased by 28 to 196 and that of the Jama'at by 2 to 22. In terms of the popular vote, the BNP won 30.6 percent; the Awami League, 30.6 percent; the Jatiya Party, 11.8 percent; and the Jama'at, 12.1 percent. However, if the votes of Awami League allies in seats that were not contested by the Awami League are added to the League's total, the percentage received by the League and its allies was 33.6 percent.

Parliamentary Election of February 1996. An election was held in February 1996, following the resignation of opposition members. The opposition, led by the Awami League, the Jatiya Party, and the Jama'at-i-Islami, boycotted the election, demanding that an election must be held under a neutral caretaker government. The result of the election was meaningless as almost all seats were won by the Bangladesh Nationalist Party. The new parliament passed a constitutional amendment providing for future elections to be held under a neutral caretaker government. It was then dissolved and a new election scheduled for June 1996. (As the election was all but uncontested, the district level results are not given in the Baxter book mentioned above.)

Parliamentary Election of June 1996. Following the dissolution of parliament, a new election was called for on 12 June 1996. The result of the election gave the Awami League a plurality of seats with 146, but not a majority. The Bangladesh Nationalist Party (BNP) won the second largest number of seats, 116. To form a government, the Awami League gained the support of the Jatiya Party, the party that finished a distant third in the polling, with 32 seats.

Parliamentary Election of October 2001. The election resulted in a rout by the BNP. It and its allies (the Islamic Unity Front and a small faction of the Jatiya Party) won 199 seats while another ally, the Jama'at-i-Islami, won 17, giving the alliance a total of 216 seats, more than a two-thirds majority. The Awami League won 62 seats. Other winners were the Jatiya Party headed by Hussain Muhammad Ershad with 14, another faction of the Jatiya Party, 1, the Krishak Sramik Janata League, 1, and independents, 6. Complete constituency results are available by entering "Bangladesh Election Commission" in a search engine. The leader of the Awami League, **Sheikh Hasina Wajid**, claimed that the election was rigged, but independent observers, including foreign observers, maintained that the election was free and fair.

Parliamentary Election of December 2008. The national parliamentary election was held on 29 December 2008. For the first time a computerized voter registration roll was developed and each voter was issued a registration card with photo identification. The total number of registered voters in Bangladesh was determined to be 81 million. Under the Representation of the People Order, any political party wanting to take part in the parliamentary election had to register with the Election Commission. A total of 107 political parties, of which 22 were religious, applied for registration. Thirty-eight political parties participated in the election. The four major parties, Awami League, Bangladesh Nationalist Party, Jatiya Party, and Bangladesh Jama'at-e-Islami Party, received 95 percent of votes cast. Eighty-seven percent of registered voters participated in the election.

The Awami League won 230 of the 300 parliamentary seats. Its archrival the Bangladesh Nationalist Party won 30 seats, followed by the Jatiya Party with 27 seats. Other parties that won seats included Jatiya Samajtantrik Dal (3), Bangladesh Jama'at-e-Islami (2), Workers Party of Bangladesh (2), Liberal Democratic Party (1), Bangladesh Jatiya Party (1), and independents (4). The Awami League received 34.5 million votes and the Bangladesh Nationalist Party received 23 million votes. The Jatiya Party received 4.6 million votes.

In the ninth parliament, the Awami League will have a three-fourths majority. The combined religious parties (nine) received 4.4 million votes, which is approximately 6.31 percent of the electorate; of these votes the Bangladesh Jama'at-e-Islami received 3.2 million.

Islamic-oriented parties won a total of two seats. Success of the ninth parliament will depend on the ability of the Awami League to be inclusive in its legislative deliberations, and the constructive engagement of the Bangladesh Nationalist Party, neither of which has much precedence in Bangladesh political institution building.

ELECTION COMMISSION (EC). Established under Article 118 of the Constitution of Bangladesh, it is an independent body. Article 126 of the constitution and Articles 4 and 5 of the Representation of the People Order (RPO), 1972, provide that it shall be the duty of all executive authorities to assist the Election Commission in the discharge of its functions. The EC is principally charged with conducting a free and fair election at all levels of government. The presidential election is guided by the Presidential Election Act of 1991. The parliamentary election guidelines have changed over time as they are influenced by political developments. The ninth parliamentary election was guided principally by the Representation of the People (Third Amendment) Order of 2008 and the Representation of the People Order of 1972. The local government (*upazila parishad*) election was guided by the Upazila Ordinance of 2008.

One of the principal functions of the EC that came into existence in February 2007 was to prepare a comprehensive voter list as part of planning for a free and fair election. The voter list preparation started on 10 June 2007; a pilot project was officially inaugurated on 14 August 2007 and was completed by 9 July 2008. In 11 months Bangladesh had developed its first nationwide digitized voter registration and national ID card system, registering 81.1 million voters. Over 10,000 army personnel were involved in the registration process and the operational code name was Operation *Nabojatra* (New Journey). Through RPO other changes were made by the EC. These included such regulations as mandatory registration for **political parties** intending to participate in any parliamentary election. Under the Delimitation of Constituencies Ordinance of 1976, the EC redistricted the 300 constituencies among the six divisions of Bangladesh and allocated seats to **Dhaka** (94), **Chittagong** (58), **Barisal** (21), **Khulna** (34), **Rajshahi** (72), and **Sylhet** (19). It also changed the boundaries of 133 of the total 300 constituencies before the ninth parliamentary election because of changes in the population. Of the country's 64 districts, 17 districts saw changes in the number of constituencies, with Dhaka gaining the most—seven new seats. This was the first major redistricting of constituencies since 1984, although some adjustments were made in 1995. With the approval of the Election Commission Secretariat Ordinance of 2008, the EC secretariat was separated from the Office of the Prime Minister, making the EC a fully independent body. *See also* ELECTIONS; ELECTION LAWS.

ELECTION LAWS. The 1972 **Constitution** of Bangladesh provides the legal constructs for the Election Commission in Articles 118 and 119. The operational rules and procedures are determined by various laws and ordinances, principle among them are the Representation of the People Order of 1972, the Conduct of Election Rules of 1972, the Election Officials (Special Provision) Ordinance of 1990, Election Officials (Special Provision) Act of 1991, the Code of Conduct of 1996, and the Representation of the People Order of 2001. The Representation of the People (Amendment) Ordinance of 2008 and the Representation of the People Order (Second Amendment) of 2008 are the latest iteration, determining the procedures for the holding of a fair and free election under an independent election commission by amending the Representation of the People Order of 1972. The most important provision of the 2008 amendment was a requirement for the registration with the **Election Commission** of any **political party** intending to participate in the ninth parliamentary election. Other provisions were introduced to strengthen the overall rules and procedures for participation in a national election, such as ensuring financial transparency, severing relationships with front organizations and overseas units, implementing more stringent measures for disqualifications, placing a three-year limitation on retired bureaucrats and army personnel, limiting the number of seats from five to three from which a single candidate can participate, and providing for the first time a "no vote" option.

ELECTIVE BODIES (DISQUALIFICATION) ORDER (EBDO). Issued in April 1959, during the regime of **Ayub Khan**, its purpose was to inquire into allegations of misconduct by any person who held any public office or position, including membership in any elective body in the country. Persons appearing before the EBDO tribunal were not allowed the assistance of counsel. Proceedings were held under the Code of Civil Procedure and not the Code of Criminal Procedure. A number of officials were disqualified under the order from participating or holding public office for seven years. The order was repealed in December 1960, but pre-existing disqualifications continued until the end of 1967.

EMPLOYMENT. A study in 2000 found that **agriculture** employed 63 percent of the workforce in Bangladesh. **Industry** employed 12 percent, and the balance was employed in the catch-all sector of service. A similar survey in 2005 found that agriculture contributed 51 percent of employment in Bangladesh and industry an additional 11 percent. The 2000 survey did not report the gender composition of those employed, but the 1995–96 Labor Force Survey estimated that about 62 percent were male and 38 percent were female. In a similar survey in 2005 it was estimated that the total number of persons employed in Bangladesh was 46.5 million, of which 37 million were male and 9.5 million were female. Ten million were employed in the urban areas and 36 million in the rural areas. In 2008, it was estimated that nearly 70 million Bangladeshis are in the labor force. The share of agriculture was 19 percent of the GDP. The contribution of industry to the GDP was 28.5 percent and the service-sector share was 52.3 percent.

Bangladesh has seen a steady decline in employment in the primary sectors of agriculture, forestry, and fishing. In 1961, 84.6 percent of the labor force was employed in agriculture. In 2000, the number had declined to 63 percent, although not surprisingly it remains the largest sector of employment in the rural areas. In the same period, employment in the industrial sector increased from 5 percent to 12 percent. A substantial increase was seen in the service sector: from 10.4 percent to 25 percent. The service-sector employment is currently estimated to be over 50 percent. *See also* GARMENT INDUSTRY; TRADE UNIONS.

ENVIRONMENT. The most important environmental problems for Bangladesh have to do with water. Much of the water used for drinking and other purposes is drawn from the many rivers and streams that are invariably polluted, as they are the ultimate repository of human and animal waste and, in general, of garbage. They also serve as disposal points for industrial waste, at least some of which is toxic. Cholera and other intestinal diseases are endemic.

An alternative to water drawn from streams is water drawn from wells. One problem with this is the high water table that often means waste has not been filtered by the soil. However, the greatest danger is the naturally occurring **arsenic** in the soil of much of Bangladesh. The World Bank estimates that at least 25 percent of the wells are affected by arsenic.

Another environmental danger is that of overcutting the extensive forests of the **Chittagong Hill Tracts**. There is no effective means of control over the logging.

The air is becoming increasingly affected by **pollution.** Increased industrialization and use of internal combustion engines contribute to pollution, as does the use of wood and dung as fuel.

ERSHAD, HUSSAIN MUHAMMAD (1930–). A regular army officer, he rose to the rank of lieutenant colonel in the Pakistani army. During the civil war of 1971, he was posted in Pakistan and detained there, returning to Bangladesh only in 1973. He reached the rank of major general in 1975 and was appointed deputy chief of staff. Ershad succeeded **Ziaur Rahman** as chief of staff in 1978, when the latter resigned from the army. Ershad was promoted to lieutenant general in 1979.

Ershad led a coup against the elected government of **Abdus Sattar** in March 1982 and became chief martial law administrator. He assumed the presidency in December 1984. He was elected president in a referendum for a five-year term in October 1986; he ran as a civilian, having resigned from the army, as the candidate of the **Jatiya Dal**, of which he was the chairman. Ershad's title as chief martial law administrator was abolished in November 1986 with the ending of martial law. His government held a parliamentary election in 1986 in which his party barely scraped by to a majority. In that election the **Awami League** became the official opposition, with **Sheikh Hasina Wajid** as leader. Ershad was challenged in November 1987, when both the Awami League and the **Bangladesh Nationalist Party (BNP)** demanded free and fair elections. By that time, the Awami League had walked out of the parliament. Ershad dissolved parliament and called new **elections** in 1988, which were boycotted by both the Awami League and the BNP. The election resulted in a parliament that was overwhelmingly led by the Jatiya Dal.

Demonstrations in November and December 1990, in which the Awami League and the BNP cooperated, led to the resignation of Ershad in December. He was placed in jail on a number of charges, many of which, in the view of some observers, were frivolous at best. He contested the 1991 election from jail and won all five of the seats he contested, having then to resign four of them, as well as be denied the right to take a seat in parliament. He was elected to parliament again in June 1996 and did take his seat. He was barred from participating in the 2001 election as a person convicted in a criminal case. Following the June 1996 election his party supported the Awami League government and some party members were included in the cabinet. Ershad himself did not enter the cabinet. In the December 2008 election he once again supported the Awami League and floated the idea of his becoming the president of Bangladesh but nothing materialized; he remains the president of Jatiya Party.

EXTERNAL DEBT. The external debt of Bangladesh in June 2000 was $17 billion, compared with $12.8 billion in 1990. This amounts to 8 percent of gross domestic product (GDP). Much of this is long-term and much that is owed to governments may be forgiven. External debt in 2007 has gone up to $21.23 billion, amounting to 10.19 percent of GDP. The per capita debt is $153 and nearly 83 percent of the population lives on less than $2 a day.

– F –

FAKHRUDDIN MUBARRAK SHAH (?–1346). He led a rebellion against the Tughluq dynasty of the **Delhi Sultanate** in 1336. On the death of the governor in 1336, Fakhruddin proclaimed himself the independent ruler of **Sonargaon**. In 1346, he was superseded by the **Ilyas Shahi dynasty**.

FAKIR, LOKMAN HOSSAIN (1934–1991). A lyricist, composer, and vocalist, he established several schools, including the Begum

Momtaz Girls School and the Fakir Mainuddin High School. Lokman Hossain was the cultural secretary of the **Bangladesh Nationalist Party (BNP)** from 1979 to 1984 and again from 1988 until his death in 1991. *See also* MUSIC.

FAMILY LAW ORDINANCE OF 1961. Proclaimed by the **Ayub Khan** government, it greatly strengthened the powers of **women**. It banned polygamy and vastly increased the rights of women in the case of divorce. Special family courts were established that, through a simplified procedure, considered questions relating to marriage, dower, divorce, and the custody of children. The ordinance also required the registration of marriages and divorces. To reduce the cases of divorce, arbitration councils were set up to attempt reconciliation between the disputing parties. Procedures were also established to determine the allocation of the properties of a divorcing couple.

FAMINE. While Bangladesh is often marginally deficient in food production, this shortfall has been made up by imports and famine has been avoided for almost four decades. Bengal, along with Punjab, was seen as the food basket of northern India during the pre-Mughal and **Mughal** periods. However, in more modern times two severe man-made famines have occurred. The first was during World War II in 1943, when there was a great food shortage.

The second came in 1974, resulting from the destruction of farmlands by the Pakistanis during the **War of Liberation**. This famine was delayed as such food stocks as remained were consumed. The competence of the initial Bangladesh government in restoring the **economy** was minimal. A major effort by foreign donors assuaged the famine eventually, but the number of deaths was substantial. There are varying estimates that between 450,000 to 1.5 million people perished as a result of the famine. *See also* BENGAL FAMINE.

FARAIZI MOVEMENT (FARAIDIYYAH). A Bengali Muslim movement that had its antecedents in the Wahhabi movement in Arabia. It was founded by Haji **Shariatullah** of Faridpur in 1818, and it preached the oneness of Allah and opposed any deviations from a strict interpretation of the Qur'an and Sunna, such as the syncretism of the **Sufis** and Shia and the universalism of some **Hindu** elites.

Shariatullah declared that India under the British was a *dar al-harb* (an abode of war, i.e., not a proper place for Muslims to reside) and said that Friday congregational prayers and the celebration of the two great *eids* (festivals commemorating the end the fasting month of Ramadan and the sacrifice day ending the Hajj) were forbidden so long as the British ruled. Shariatullah was followed by his son, **Dudu Mia** (1819–1860), whose violent actions in opposition to Hindu land-lords and British officials and planters of indigo ended in his arrest in 1841 on charges of murder. But in this trial, as in all others, he was acquitted for lack of evidence, as witnesses would not testify against him. The movement weakened after Dudu Mia's death, although fol-lowers remain.

FARAKKA BARRAGE. The dam is at the core of the **Ganges** waters dispute between Bangladesh and **India**. The idea of a barrage near Farakka was first considered in the early 20th century. The barrage would divert water from the Ganges River through canals and the Bhagirathi and Hooghly Rivers to reduce salinity in the Hooghly at **Calcutta** and to augment its flow. This would assure Calcutta a greater supply of drinking water and would lessen the silting of Calcutta harbor. After Indian independence, India revived the idea and built the barrage, which was completed after Bangladesh became independent. Bangladesh claims that it needs the water withdrawn to reduce salinity and improve irrigation in **Khulna** division.

Significant soil damage is occurring because of the diversion of the water. The western districts of Bangladesh are experiencing both shortages of water for **agriculture** and increases in soil salinity. While Bangladesh is dealing with the problem with India in bilateral talks, it is also trying to raise the issue in international forums. India objects to the latter as an inappropriate place to discuss what it deems to be a bilateral issue.

India has proposed that a link canal be built that would transfer water from the **Brahmaputra** River to the Ganges above Farakka so that adequate flow would be available both for Calcutta and Khulna division. Bangladesh has countered with a plan that would entail additional storage dams in Nepal to regulate better the flow of the Ganges during the low-flow season (April–June); at other times the flow is usually sufficient for both India and Bangladesh. The two countries reached an interim agreement on sharing the water during the low-flow period in 1978, but a final agreement has not been made. The interim agreement expired in 1988, but another agreement providing for sharing during the period of low flow has been made. *See also* GANGES WATERS TREATY.

FARID AHMAD (1923–1971). He resigned from government service because of his support for the **language movement** of 1952. He was the leader of the **Nizam-i-Islam** political party. He served as a member of the Pakistan Constituent Assembly in 1955 and was a member of the National Assembly in 1962. In 1964, Farid Ahmad joined the **Combined Opposition Parties** and was elected as a representative of the party to the National Assembly. He joined the opposition in its movement to oust President **Ayub Khan** in 1969. Farid Ahmad was opposed to the **War of Liberation** and collaborated with the Pakistani armed forces. He was an adviser to the **Razakar Bahini** and a leading member of the **Peace Committees** that were set up to coerce Bengalis to continue the idea of a united Pakistan.

FARIDPUR. A district and district town, it is named for a Muslim saint, Farid Shah, whose shrine is in Faridpur city. The area now comprising Faridpur was a part of **Vanga** or **Samatata**, and was a base for the rebellion of the **Bara Bhuiyan** against **Man Singh**. The ruins of the fort of Raja Sita Ram Rai are at the village of Kilabari. Faridpur is an important rail center lying on the line between Goalundo (where the **Ganges** and **Brahmaputra** meet) and **Calcutta**. The city is also the site of the Hindu structure Mathurapur Deul. With the **local government** changes during the **Ershad** period, the former district was divided into Faridpur, Gopalganj, Madaripur, Shariatpur, and Goalundo.

FAST FOOD OF OLD DHAKA. Different types of food are available to the rich and poor of old Dhaka. Some are served on the roadside, others in small cabins serving as restaurants. The food of Old Dhaka is a mixture of Persian, Mughal, Portuguese, British, French, Dutch, Greek, and Armenian foods. *Bakhorkhani* is flour-based, oven-baked, semi-toasted bread. It is an early morning food, and also a specialty during the month of fasting. Three types are available depending on the type of baking – *gao jobon*, *shuki*, and *nimshuki*. A combination of rice, meat (chicken, beef, or lamb), potato, and dried plums or raisin meal is also sold as a main lunch or dinner meal. Called *biriyani*, it is of Persian and Mughal origin. A more composite meal known as the *torabondi pila* is a combination of different types of *biriyani*, different types of *kababs*, and different types of breads and cheese. Some of the breads are *Baghdadi* and *bon roti*, and *khasta* and *sohali parata*. Besides the local sweets, two types of sweets known to come from Old Dhaka are *sheerberenj* and *sheer-e-faluda*. The base of the first is course-ground rice, while the second is made from rice vermicelli. Other ingredients include milk, sugar, raisin, pistachios, honey, fruits, rosewater, and spices like cardamom and cinnamon.

FAUJDARHAT CADET COLLEGE. Established in the late 1950s and then known as the **East Pakistan** Cadet College, its mission was to serve as a feeder school for future East Pakistan army officers for the Pakistan armed forces. The first principal of the school was Colonel William M. Brown, an air force officer from New Zealand. The school became operational with the arrival of the first batch of students in 1958. A total of four batches were recruited in 1958. Entry to the school was through competitive examinations. It became known for excellence in both academics and extracurricular activities. After Bangladesh's independence, there was a period of turmoil as to the name and direction of the school. It eventually overcame the challenges and is today considered one of the premier schools of Bangladesh.

FAXIAN (?–c. 418). Also spelled Fa-hsien. A Chinese **Buddhist** monk who traveled to **India** to survey the original sites of **Buddhism**. His surviving record is of great value to historians of South Asia, including those of Bengal.

FAZILATUNNESSA (1899–1977). Born in Tangail, she was the first Muslim woman to earn a master of arts degree at **Dhaka University**. She also studied in **Great Britain** and taught in **Kolkata**. After partition, Fazilatunnessa was principal of Eden Girls College in **Dhaka** from 1948 to 1957.

FAZLUL HAQ, (MOULVI) ABUL KASEM (1873–1962). Fazlul Haq was born in **Barisal** district and educated in the law at Calcutta University. Before his first election to the legislative council, he practiced law in Calcutta, taught in Barisal, and edited several Bengali magazines. He became a protégé of Nawab Sir **Salimullah** of Dhaka, a founder of the Muslim League, who assisted him in winning his first election. Fazlul Haq is known as "Sher-e-Bangla," the lion of Bengal. He was the leading Bengali Muslim political figure in the pre-independence period and for many years after independence and was a member of the Bengal Legislative Council constituted under the **Government of India Act of 1909**, 1913–1920, and again under the **dyarchy** system established by the **Government of India Act of 1919**, 1921–1935. He was minister of education in 1924. He was a member of the **Muslim League**, 1913–1942, until his membership was ended in a dispute with **Muhammad Ali Jinnah.**

After the elections following the passage of the **Government of India Act of 1935**, Fazlul Haq served as prime minister of Bengal, 1937–1943, first (1937–1941) in coalition with the Muslim League, whose leader, Khwaja Sir **Nazimuddin**, Fazlul Haq had defeated in the election. During this period he was, for all practical purposes, a member of both the **Krishak Praja Party** and the Muslim League. He was also the mover of the **Lahore Resolution** in 1940. After the collapse of the coalition with the Muslim League, he formed another coalition with the Hindu Mahasabha and other parties that lasted until 1943.

It was during his prime ministership in 1942 that he broke with Jinnah and left the Muslim League. The viceroy had invited the provincial prime ministers to join a military advisory council. Fazlul Haq and two other Muslim prime ministers (of Punjab and **Assam**) who were also members of the Muslim League, although the leader from Punjab was, like Fazlul Haq, a member also of a local party, accepted the invitation. Jinnah, infuriated, stated that each had violated party discipline and insisted they resign from the viceroy's council. Fazlul Haq did.

Fazlul Haq was the founder (in 1927) of the Krishak Praja Party, leading it in the 1937 and 1946 elections. In the latter, the party was badly defeated by the Muslim League, although Fazlul Haq retained his own seat. The party was then dissolved.

After independence, Fazlul Haq was advocate general of **East Bengal**, 1947–1954, but he resigned to revive his party under the altered name **Krishak Sramik Party** and to enter the **United Front** with the **Awami League**. The Front swept to victory and Fazlul Haq became chief minister briefly in 1954, but his government was dismissed by the central government of Pakistan, which accused him of wanting to declare an independent Bengali state, drawing on a statement he was alleged to have made while visiting **Calcutta** just after the election. It was also alleged that the great strike at the **Adamjee Jute Mill** was "arranged" to embarrass the incoming chief minister. Following a partial settlement with the central government, he became a central minister, 1955–1956, and governor of **East Pakistan**, 1956–1958. He retired from politics after the coup of **Ayub Khan** in 1958.

FAZLUR RAHMAN (1905–1966). A lawyer from **Dhaka**, he was a prominent **Muslim League** political figure both before and after independence. He was elected in 1937 and 1946 to the Bengal Legislative Assembly and became a minister in 1946. Fazlur Rahman was a member of the cabinet of Pakistan, 1947–1953, but he was removed by the governor-general, Ghulam Muhammad, largely because of his advocacy of Bengali positions on such issues as **language** and economic parity, despite his remaining in the Muslim League. He was reelected to the constituent assembly in 1955. After martial law was proclaimed by **Ayub Khan** in 1958, Fazlur Rahman continued to be associated with the Muslim League (the **Council Muslim League** in his case after 1962) until his death in an automobile accident.

FILM. The first full-length film to be made in what is now Bangladesh was *Mukh-o-Mukosh* (*Face-to-Face*) in 1956, adapted from a play by Abdul Jabbar Khan. While a vast number of films are now made, few can be described as classical, as the scripts are no longer based on social issues, but are drawn from fantasy and romance and appeal to a much wider audience. The East Pakistan (now Bangladesh) Film Development Corporation was established in 1959. Its studio has facilities permitting the production of 50 to 100 films a year. In the early 1980s a film archive was founded. A film festival is held annually in **Dhaka**.

FLAG. The official description of the Bangladesh national flag is that it will be bottle green and rectangular in size in the proportion of length to width 10:6, bearing a red circle on the body of the green. The red circle will have a radius of one-fifth of the length of the flag. Its center will be placed on the intersecting point of the perpendicular drawn from the nine-twentieth part of the length of the flag and the horizontal line drawn through the middle of its width. The specification of the colors are as follows: (a) the green base of the flag will be of Procion Brilliant Green H-2RS, 50 parts per 1000, and (b) the red circular part will be of Procion Brilliant Orange H-2RS, 60 parts per 1000. The flag was created by artist Quamrul Hasan. An early version of the flag had the map of Bangladesh in the center. This particular flag was first shown by A. S. M. Abdur Rab, vice president of the **Dhaka University** Students Union, on 3 March 1971 on the premises of Dhaka University. The same flag was unfurled on 7 March 1971 at a historic speech given by Sheikh **Mujibur Rahman** at Ramna Race Course in **Dhaka**. Some have disputed the symbolism of green in the Bangladesh flag. To some it signifies youth and vitality and to others it represents **Islam**.

FLOODS. Floods are both a curse and a blessing to Bangladesh. The country is crossed by three heavy-flow rivers, the **Ganges**, **Brahmaputra**, and **Meghna**, as well as such tributary rivers as the **Surma** and **Tista**, which flow into the larger rivers. As this is the case, annual flooding is almost inevitable. Moderate flooding is beneficial in that the rivers not only provide water but also replenish the fertility of the soil as silt is deposited. However, in many years the flooding is extensive, causing loss of life and property to a large degree. Flooding also occurs when **cyclones** move inland from the Bay of Bengal, causing damage from the wind as well as the water. In 1971, one of the most destructive cyclones caused the delay of that year's election. Other major storms occurred in 1974, 1988, and 2002.

Following the 1988 flood, a project entitled the Bangladesh Flood Alteration Plan was begun under the aegis of the World Bank working with 15 donor countries. The plan contemplated the construction of about 5,000 miles of embankments, although little has actually been done. In 1991, another major storm struck and relief efforts were assisted by U.S. Marines returning from Operation Desert

Storm. In 1998, another storm killed about 1,400 and stranded perhaps 30 million. Between 1954 and 2004, Bangladesh faced floods about 41 times. Flood losses are estimated to be about $4 billion a year. In recent years, the flood of 1987 covered almost 40 percent of the country and the 1988 and 1998 floods were record-breaking in terms of total rise of water. Bangladesh witnessed two medium-sized floods in 1989 and 1993, and a flood in 2000 covered the entire southwest. Floods are major disaster phenomena in Bangladesh and the earliest record of serious flood was in 1781.

FOOD. The staple foods of Bangladesh are rice, lentils, fish, and vegetables. Meat and poultry have become more available. Varieties of lentils are cooked primarily as soups while fish, meat, and poultry are made into different forms of curries and kabobs prevalent throughout the subcontinent of **India**. Seasonal fruits of Bangladesh include mangos, pineapples, bananas, and watermelons. Other local fruits include *bon-koi, lotka, amra, ataphal, paniphal*, and *kul-boroai*. Bangladesh has achieved a level of self-sufficiency in rice production and while overall food production has increased, the per capita caloric intake remains very low and is unlikely to see any rapid improvements. *See also* BAU-KUL FARMING; FAST FOOD.

FOREIGN POLICY. At the time of independence, the foreign policy of Bangladesh was focused on two major issues: emergency assistance to help with rebuilding a country that had been heavily damaged by war and faced severe food shortages, and gaining recognition by the international community as an independent state.

Several states recognized Bangladesh almost immediately, such as **India** and the **Soviet Union**. The **United States** delayed until February 1972 and within a few months most states had recognized Bangladesh as independent. **Pakistan** and its close associates in this matter, many Muslim states and **China** delayed much longer. When the **Organization of the Islamic Conference (OIC)** met in Lahore in February 1974, many of the other Islamic states persuaded Pakistan to recognize Bangladesh. The members of the OIC did and China followed quickly. Bilateral and multilateral **aid** began to flow almost immediately. The initial aid can best be described as relief, but as time went on aid was increasingly aimed at developmental and social projects, as it is today. At times, however, relief is again needed when natural disasters such as **floods** occur.

Following recognition by Pakistan and the lifting of the Security Council veto by China, Bangladesh was admitted to the **United Nations** in 1974. Bangladesh was elected to the Security Council in 1978 and 2000. In 1985, its foreign minister, Humayun Rashid Chowdhury, was elected president of the General Assembly. In its international role, Bangladesh is a member of most of the UN-related agencies. It has also provided forces to **UN peace-keeping operations**.

Bangladesh is a member of the Non-aligned Movement and of the Group of Seventy-seven. It is also an active member of the Organization of the Islamic Conference. Bangladesh is a member of the (British) **Commonwealth of Nations**.

Economic issues continue to be dominant in the foreign policy of Bangladesh. International assistance is still required in substantial amounts for economic, social, and technological development. Bangladesh also tries to improve conditions under which its international **trade** is conducted, looking, for example, for free trade agreements and for fewer restrictions on its key exports such as textiles and ready-made **garments**. Foreign direct investment is sought, but other ministries than the Foreign Ministry often have rules that inhibit investment or at least present a climate that discourages potential foreign investors. They are also discouraged by **corruption**.

Foreign policy is very much the realm of the prime minister. Both recent prime ministers, **Hasina Wajid** and **Khaleda Zia**, have traveled extensively to other states and to international forums to present Bangladesh's views. The foreign minister, finance minister, and commerce minister are also heavily involved. The Bangladesh Foreign Service is a professional, career service and higher positions such as ambassadorships are usually drawn from its personnel. As in most countries there are occasional political appointees to major countries, sometimes with results that are not advantageous to Bangladesh.

The official statement on the foreign policy of Bangladesh includes two fundamental principles: 1) The state shall base its international relations on the principles of respect for national sovereignty and equality, non-interference in the internal affairs of other countries, peaceful settlements of international disputes, and respect for international law and the principles enunciated in the United Nations Charter, and on the basis of those principles shall a) strive for the renunciation of the use of force in international relations and for general and complete disarmament; b) uphold the right of every people freely to determine and build up its own social, economic, and political system by ways and means of its own free choice; and c) support oppressed peoples throughout the world waging a just struggle against imperialism, colonialism, or racialism; and 2) The state shall endeavor to consolidate, preserve, and strengthen fraternal relations among Muslim countries based on Islamic solidarity. *See also* AFGANISTAN; BURMA; CHINA; INDIA; MIDDLE EAST; PAKISTAN; RUSSIA; UNITED STATES.

FORT WILLIAM. The fort built during the period 1696–1715 to protect **Calcutta**. It was captured by Nawab **Sirajuddaulah** in 1756 but retaken by the British in 1757. The original site, near the present Dalhousie Square, was vacated in 1819. New buildings were later built there. The present fort is on a different site.

FOUR-POINT DEMAND. In September 2008, the BNP along with its alliance members demanded that unless the following conditions were met, it would not participate in the ninth parliamentary election: (1) withdrawal of the state of emergency, (2) scrapping of the Representation of the People Order (RPO) (Amendment) of 2008, (3) holding of an *upazila* (subdistrict) election after the national polls, (4) withdrawal of **corruption** cases, and (5) release of all political leaders held without specific charges. On 18 November 2008 the BNP changed its five-point demand to a four-point demand. These demands were a watered-down version of the earlier demands. The four points were that (1) the state of emergency be lifted immediately, (2) "objectionable" clauses in the amended RPO be suspended, (3) an *upazila* election be held one month after the ninth parliamentary election, and (4) the parliamentary elections be rescheduled so that *hajis*, who were to return to Bangladesh by 12 January 2009, could participate in the election. The **caretaker government** held the ninth parliamentary election on 29 December 2008, acceding only to the demand to lift the state of emergency, and the BNP, despite its demands, participated in the election.

FRENCH EAST INDIA COMPANY. It was founded as a trading company by the French mercantilist Jean-Baptiste Colbert in 1662. In Bengal, it established a trading station at Chandernagore in 1690. The company was dissolved in 1795, but its possessions in India remained French enclaves. Chandernagore was transferred to India on 2 February 1951.

FYZENNESSA, NOORUNNAHAR (1931–2004). A champion of women's rights and an educationist, she received her undergraduate degree in **education** from the Dhaka Teacher's Training College. She received her graduate degree in political science from **Dhaka University**. She went on to receive an Ed.D. from the University of Northern Colorado. She joined the Institute of Education and Research, Dhaka University, in 1969. In 1985 she was the first woman member of the Dhaka University Syndicate, the highest policy-making body. She served as the provost (head) of Rokeya Hall, the first women's dormitory of Dhaka University. Her radio program *Khela Ghor* (Play House) was an important children's program, as *Sesame Street* is in the United States. She established the Rokeya Foundation at Dhaka University to provide scholarships to meritorious students. She also established a senior center, the Begum Rokeya Probeen Abash, and much earlier the day care center Chhayaneer. In addition, she was a champion hurdler at a time when women were not in the forefront of sports in Pakistan.

– G –

GANESH, RAJA. A noble from **Dinajpur**, he rose to be the most powerful person in the court of the sultan, Ghiyasuddin Azam (r. c. 1393–1410). At the sultan's death a succession struggle took place and Ganesh assumed rule in 1414. He fought off an invasion from Jaunpur and died in 1418. His elder son, Jalaluddin, who had converted to **Islam**, ruled until 1431. Jalaluddin's son, Shamsuddin Ahmad, was a tyrant and was murdered in 1442, leading to the restoration of the **Ilyas Shahi** dynasty.

GANGA-KOBADAK IRRIGATION PROJECT. Conceived in the 1950s (i.e., prior to the building of **Farakka Barrage** in India), the project was intended to be the largest lift-irrigation project in Asia. The concept was to pump water from the **Ganges** and into channels that would serve irrigation needs in **Kushtia, Jessore**, and **Khulna** districts amounting to more than 500,000 hectares (1.25 million acres). In addition to irrigation, an equally important purpose of the project was to counteract the salinity infiltration from the Bay of Bengal through the **Sundarbans**. The pumping station would be just south of the Hardinge Bridge next to the international border. It was intended to increase cropping intensity from 60–70 percent to 220 percent. The supply of water has not reached the intended amount and as a result rivers and channels in the system have dried up to the extent that only some areas in Kushtia district can be served. *See also* GORAI RIVER.

GANGES RIVER (GANGA). The river rising in the Himalayas and fed by other rivers rising in the same mountains as well as other streams from the south is worshipped by **Hindus** as a goddess. The most sacred city of the Hindus, Varanasi (Benares), is located on the river and the confluence of the Ganges; mythical Saraswati at Allahabad is another sacred place. The river itself is 1,557 miles long. Until the latter part of the 16th century, the principal distributary of the river was the Bhagirathi-Hooghly route. At that time, the route turned east to the present primary distributary through Bangladesh.

In Bangladesh the river is known as the Padma. Its enormous flow of water during most seasons provides the **flooding** that enriches the fertile soil of Bangladesh with the silt carried by the river. Flooding, which is often beneficial, can also be extraordinarily destructive, especially in areas where the flow of the Ganges is combined with that of the **Brahmaputra** at Goalundo and the **Meghna** at Chandpur.

During the months of January to May the flow of the river is low. The construction by **India** of the **Farakka Barrage** to divert Ganges waters to **Kolkata** has made the flow during that period insufficient for the operation of irrigation works in southwestern Bangladesh and to curtail the salinization of that region resulting from the infusion of sea water. The barrage and its results are the major point of dispute between Bangladesh and India. *See also* GANGES WATERS TREATY.

GANGES WATERS TREATY. There have been several agreements between Bangladesh and India on the division of the waters of the **Ganges River**, especially during the low-flow season from January to May. The latest treaty was concluded in 1996, soon after the beginning of the **Sheikh Hasina Wajid** ministry. This perhaps was done in haste and many feel that India gained the upper hand in the agreement. It has been noted that, in comparison with the agreed flow amounts in 1977, India has received an increase in each of the 15 10-day periods in which allocation is to be monitored while Bangladesh has received a decrease in eight days of those periods. (It is assumed that the total flow will be greater.)

GANOTANTRIK DAL. A short-lived political party led by **Mahmud Ali**. It was leftist and attempted to be non-communal. It gained its only (and very small) electoral success when it was part of the **United Front** in 1954.

GARMENT INDUSTRY. A relatively recent arrival on the Bangladesh industrial scene is the manufacture of garments for the export market. The industry has grown extensively, mainly with medium-sized operations. The industry was initially dependent on imported fabrics that were then made into garments according to the purchaser's specifications. Bangladesh is now the fifth-largest supplier of imported garments to the United States and is also a major exporter to the European Union.

Known as the Ready-made Garment Sector (RMG), this sector within a span of 25 years has become the main driver of economic growth in Bangladesh. In 1978 Bangladesh entered the RMG exporting goods worth $69 thousand. In the early 1980s, when RMG contributed about 1 percent of total exports, a new industrial policy provided the growth impetus to this sector. In 2007–2008, with a total export of $10 billion, it is nearly 75 percent of the total export of Bangladesh. The total number of manufacturing units in 2008 stood at 4,750, together employing approximately 2.5 million workers. Of the total units, 1,500 are knitwear units that contribute 39 percent of total exports. In the period 1985–1990, the cumulative average growth rate was 40 percent. The end of the Multi-Fibre Agreement, which provided market protection for Bangladesh products, did not lead to the expected slowdown of this sector in Bangladesh. The growth of the apparel sector in Bangladesh was facilitated domestically by public sector policies that included no tariffs on machinery, rebates on power, freight, and income tax, as well as tax holidays and cash assistance. Low labor costs also contributed to the growth of this industry. Around 80 percent of the demand for accessories used in exportable garment and knit items is now locally met, as there are more than 100 accessory manufacturing industries. These industries have an average annual growth rate of 20 percent. Approximately 90 percent of the knitwear is backward linked in Bangladesh while for other woven goods the backward linkage is only 25 percent. Backward-linked manufacturing products such as packaging and accessories are also exported and earn approximately $1.5 billion a year.

The industry has come under criticism for using young female employees who were employed before completing school. The issue appears to have been settled through negotiations in which the International Labor Organization, the Bangladesh government, foreign governments, and the manufacturers were involved. Attendance at schools is considered the paramount activity for the young employees. *See also* ECONOMY.

GAS. *See* NATURAL RESOURCES.

GAUR (GAUDA). This place was also known as Lakhnauti, and earlier as Lakshmanavati, when the city and its region were under Hindu rule. Now in ruins, it is located in Malda district, West Bengal. It was the capital of **Sasanka** in the seventh century and was the **Sena dynasty**'s capital in the 11th and 12th centuries. The name Lakshmanavati is derived from the Sena ruler **Lakshmana Sena**. The city was captured by an army of the **Delhi Sultanate** led by **Ikhtiyaruddin Muhammad Bakhtiyar Khalji** in 1202 and made the capital of the province of Bengal in 1220. The city was destroyed in 1538 by **Sher Shah Suri** but restored and occupied when the **Mughals** retook Bengal in 1576. It and its neighboring sites of **Pandua** and **Tanda**

served as capitals during various periods of Muslim control of Bengal from the beginning of the 13th century to the latter part of the 16th century. A shift in the flow of the **Ganges** in 1564 caused Gaur to be abandoned as a capital in favor of Tanda, which was closer to the main stream, but there were other times when Gaur was occupied. In the 18th century, the city was little more than a place of ruins, and in the 1870s much of the city was plowed for agriculture. Many of the buildings were used as a source of brick and tiles. Several ruins, however, are of historical and **tourist** interest. Among these are the Great Golden Mosque (also known as the Bara Darwaza, for its 12 doors), the Small Golden Mosque, the Tantipara Mosque, and the Kadam Rasul Mosque of 1530, the last of which is in good condition and in use.

GHASITI BEGUM (fl. c. 1720–1770). The eldest daughter of **Alivardi Khan**, she was caught up in the intrigues surrounding the succession of Alivardi's grandson, **Sirajuddaulah**, as nawab. She supported another nephew in the succession, who eventually was killed by Sirajuddaulah in 1756. After the death of her husband, Ghasiti Begum allegedly had an illicit relationship with another relative, who was also killed by Sirajuddaulah. She entrusted her wealth to another courtier, who eventually fled with the funds and joined the British in the conflict between the British and Sirajuddaulah. She died in oblivion, and her residence, Motijheel, is a ruin.

GHAZNAVI, SIR ABDUL HALIM (1876–1953). This politician and social activist was a *zamindar* (landlord) from **Mymensingh** (now Tangail) district. He was educated in **Calcutta**. He actively participated in political, economic, and educational movements in India. In 1929, Sir Abdul Halim was the president of the All-India Muslim Conference, a short-lived rival of the **Muslim League**. He participated in the Round Table Conference in London. He was not associated with the Muslim League and appealed to Lord Wavell in 1945 to add non–Muslim League Muslims to the viceroy's council. Sir Abdul Halim served both as chairman of the Calcutta Chamber of Commerce and as the sheriff of Calcutta. He was a brother of Sir **Abdul Karim Ghaznavi**.

GHAZNAVI, SIR ABDUL KARIM (1872–1939). Educated outside India, he was a politician and social activist. He was a member of the Imperial Legislative Council, 1909–1916. As a representative of the British raj he went to Syria, Palestine, Egypt, and Saudi Arabia. Sir Abdul Karim was a member of the Bengal Legislative Council, 1926–1929, and a minister in 1924 and 1927. From 1929 to 1934 he was an executive councilor in Bengal. While giving evidence before the Reforms Commission in 1924, Sir Abdul Karim expressed doubt about India's ability to accept democratic institutions. He was the author of *Moslem Education in Bengal.* He was a brother of Sir **Abdul Halim Ghaznavi.**

GHORAGHAT. Located in **Dinajpur** region on the **Karatoya River,** its ruins are connected to the *Mahabharata.* It is believed that the ruins belonged to Raja Virat, who gave refuge to Yudhishthira and his brothers and their wives. There is also a military outpost ascribed to **Alauddin Husain Shah.**

GHOSE, AUROBINDO (1872–1950). He first gained prominence as a scholar, studying in England as well as Bengal, but on his return he became engaged in politics and is often known as a revolutionary. Aurobindo actively opposed the partition of Bengal in 1905 and spent time in jail. He changed direction in 1910 and founded an ashram (a religious retreat) in French-controlled Pondicherry. From this base, he wrote extensively on **Hindu** philosophy.

GHOSE, JOGESH CHANDRA (1887–1971). One of the **Hindu** intellectuals killed by the Pakistani army at the beginning of the **War of Liberation.** He had been a professor of chemistry and also the principal of Jagannath College, Dhaka. A scholar of ayurvedic medicine, Ghose founded a company to manufacture ayurvedic medicines in 1914.

GHULAM HUSAIN KHAN TABATABAI, SYED (LATE 17th–EARLY 18th CENTURY). A noted historian who was a cousin of **Alivardi Khan.** He worked at the **Mughal** court in Delhi and at the court of the nawab of Bengal. He represented Nawab **Mir Qasim**

in **Kolkata** and later was employed by the **East India Company**. Tabatabai's works on the decline of the Mughal Empire and the rise of the British are noted near-contemporary accounts of the events of the 17th and 18th centuries.

GHULAM MUHAMMAD (1895–1956). Governor-general of **Pakistan**, 1951–1955. Although he was born in Lahore, his family home was in East Punjab (now part of India). Before independence, Ghulam Muhammad was a civil servant and later in business. He was finance minister of Pakistan prior to succeeding Khwaja **Nazimuddin** as governor-general.

GLOBAL WARMING. In 2007, the Global Climate Risk Index identified Bangladesh, North Korea, and Nicaragua as the countries most impacted by extreme weather conditions. Bangladesh has suffered significant loss of life and direct economic loss estimated to be $10 billion. A 2009 **United Nations** Intergovernmental Panel on Climate Change reports that sinking deltas and rising seal level will cause severe disasters in many parts of the world. Bangladesh is impacted by both these phenomena. The Ganges delta of Bangladesh has been placed in a category just below the highest level of vulnerability among the 33 deltas of the world. While sea level was earlier estimated to rise between 7 and 26 inches, it is now expected to rise by 39 inches by the beginning of the 22nd century. In the case of Bangladesh, melting glaciers in the Himalayas and the possible rupturing of closed lakes in the Tibetan plateau will add to the intensity of floods in Bangladesh. Consequently Bangladesh will continue to see increases in the severity of its flooding and more intense storms and cyclones. It is expected that 45–50 million people will be impacted by such global changes.

GOLAM MUSTAFA (1897–1964). A major Bengali Muslim poet. He began his career by very much imitating the style of **Rabindranath Tagore** to the extent that he was criticized by Muslim writers as being "Hinduized." His major work was *Rakta Rag* (1924), which received high praise from Tagore. He became known as the poet of the Muslim Renaissance. Mustafa's *Bishwanabi* (published in 1942) is considered "a masterpiece." Of his other writings, *Raktoraag* (published in 1924), *Hasnahena* (1927), *Khushroze* (1929), and *Sahara* (1935) are more well known. Mustafa also wrote *The Musalman* and *The Star of India*. *See also* LITERATURE.

GONO FORUM. A political party led by former foreign minister **Kamal Hossain**, it is always in the forefront of political reform and social justice. It was established in August 1993 with the explicit purpose of making politics violence-free. It also focused its energy toward economic progress for the average Bangladeshi. During the caretaker government of **Fakhruddin Ahmed**, Gono Forum proposed a 10-point charter to guide political reform.

- Equal rights and **human rights**
- Uniform system of **education** for all
- An effective **parliament**
- Building the country
- Administration system accountable to the people
- Free and fair **elections**
- Upholding citizens' right to information
- Freedom of press and expression
- National dialogue on timely issues
- No abuse of religion for political purposes

See also MANIK, SAIFUDDIN.

GOPACHANDRA. The first of three kings who ruled over **Vanga** in the early sixth century during the period of decline of the **Gupta** empire. The other two rulers were Dharmaditya and Samacharadeva. The information about them is primarily numismatic.

GOPALA I. The founder of the **Pala** dynasty. He ruled from about 750 to 770. In a period of anarchy in Bengal and Bihar, he appears to have been selected as king by common consent.

GORAI RIVER. The first major distributary of the **Ganges River** on the right bank inside Bangladesh from the Indian border and **Farakka Barrage** and an integral part of the **Ganga-Kobadak Irrigation Project**. The decrease in water flow caused the river to dry up from 1988 to 1989. It was once also a major inland waterway but is now unusable. However, the Gorai River Restoration Project is planned to restore flow and reduce the rate of salinization in the **Sundarbans** and possibly restore some level of navigation.

GOVERNMENT OF INDIA ACT OF 1909. Also known as the Morley-Minto Act after **Lord Morley**, secretary of state for India in the British cabinet, and **Lord Minto**, viceroy-governor general of India. The act was a major step along the route toward Indian self-government. The act admitted Indians to the executive councils (i.e., cabinets) of the governor-general and the governors of the provinces. It provided for election of Indians to the legislative councils at the central and provincial levels, although a majority of the members (including some Indians) were appointed. The act also introduced the system of **separate electorates** for Muslims and "others" (primarily **Hindus** but not all in this category were Hindu).

GOVERNMENT OF INDIA ACT OF 1919. Also known as the Montagu-Chelmsford Act after Edwin Montagu, secretary of state for India in the British cabinet, and Lord Chelmsford, the viceroy-governor general. At the central level, the act created two legislative houses, the (upper) Council of State and the (lower) Central Legislative Assembly. In each house, elected Indians would form a majority. However, the final powers continued to be held by the viceroy, and no concept of parliamentary responsibility was introduced. The viceroy's executive council of seven would have three Indian members. At the provincial level, the legislative councils would also have a majority of elected Indians. A limited admission of the principle of responsibility at the provincial level was the system of **dyarchy**.

GOVERNMENT OF INDIA ACT OF 1935. The last such act passed by the British Parliament before independence. At the provincial level, the act provided for autonomy in the sense that responsible governments were introduced in each of the provinces. The prime minister (as he was then designated—the title would become "chief minister" after independence in both India and Pakistan) and his cabinet must enjoy the confidence of the legislative assembly. "Legislative assembly," as a term, replaced "legislative council," although in a few provinces, including Bengal, there was also an upper chamber, which retained the name "legislative council."

In the provinces, in the case of a breakdown of the cabinet or government, or in a financial emergency (e.g., failure to pass a budget), the governor retained powers to act to permit government to continue. At the center, a federal system was contemplated that would include the princely states. The princes did not agree to this arrangement, so the system of **dyarchy**, which was to have been introduced at the center, was never adopted. Power, therefore, was distributed as under the **Government of India Act of 1919**. The 1935 act, as amended by the **India Independence Act of 1947,** served as the "constitution" of both India and Pakistan until each adopted its own constitution.

GRAM SARKAR. It was a village government scheme introduced by President **Ziaur Rahman** in 1980. It was based on the local government scheme of **Muhammad Yunus**. Each Gram Sarkar was to be responsible for a number of activities, including family disputes, population control, food production, and law and order. A 12-member committee was to head the unit, with two members coming from each of the following groups: landless peasants, women, landed peasants, shopkeepers, and fishermen/artisans. The chairman and the secretary were to be chosen by these 10 members, completing the body of 12 members. *See also* LOCAL GOVERNMENT.

GRAMEEN BANK. The outcome of an experimental project undertaken by **Muhammad Yunus** in one village, Jobra, it has become one of the most creative models of development **banking** for the poor. The bank began operations in 1976 on the model of **Gram Sarkar**. Its five primary purposes were (1) to extend banking facilities to poor men and women; (2) to eliminate exploitation by moneylenders; (3) to create opportunities for self-employment for underutilized and unutilized manpower; (4) to bring the disadvantaged into an organizational format; and (5) to reverse the age-old cycle of low income, low savings, and low investment and replace it with "low income, injection of credit, investment, more income, more savings, more investment, more income," setting up a continuous program that would lead to a higher standard of living. Its success can be measured by the fact that in 2009, 7.3 million individuals have borrowed from the bank and 97 percent of the borrowers are women. It has disbursed $8.26 billion and borrowers have paid back $7.34 billion. Its success can also be measured by the fact that the program has been copied in a number of countries. For his contribution to international development, Professor Yunus was awarded the World Food Prize in 1994 and the Nobel Peace Prize in 2006.

Several subsidiaries have been opened by the bank. These include a telecom company that makes cell telephones available to **women** in local areas which they often operate as an effective long-distance system. There is also a program to make renewable energy available in villages where there is no electricity.

GREAT BRITAIN. Two dates, 4 February 1972, and 18 April 1972, mark the starting point of Bangladesh and Great Britain's foreign relationship. Great Britain recognized Bangladesh in February and in April, Bangladesh became a member of the Commonwealth of Nations. But an even more important date was 9 January 1972, when Sheikh **Mujibur Rahman** arrived from **Pakistan** after being in a Pakistani prison for nine months during the **War of Liberation**. Mujibur Rahman met with prime minister Edward Health and thanked him for British support during the war. Britain is also home to nearly 500,000 people from Bangladesh, many of whom are now British citizens. Bangladesh-born Anwar Chowdhury became the British ambassador to Bangladesh in 2004. A week after his arrival he went to **Sylhet** to visit the shrine of **Shah Jalal**, where a bomb exploded and injured him. That did not deter the friendly relationship that exists between Bangladesh and Great Britain.

Although Great Britain is not one of the top five countries for imports from Bangladesh, it has for a number of years received approximately 10 percent of the total export of Bangladesh. The United States and Germany are the two countries that receive a higher percent of Bangladesh exports. The primary exports to Great Britain are **garments**, shrimp, and **jute**. Bangladesh exports to Great Britain have increased from $400 million in 1997–1998 to $ 1.3 billion in 2007–2008. Imports on the other hand declined from $1.78 million in 1997–1998 to $1.70 million in 2007–2008. Britain is one of the largest sources of foreign direct investment. In 2008 this investment was $205 million, primarily in gas and oil exploration. Bangladesh is also the second-highest recipient of British development assistance, after **India**.

Bangladesh and Great Britain cooperate in a large number of areas and in numerous forums like the **United Nations**. In September 2008, Bangladesh and Great Britain organized a climate change conference in London. Other areas of close cooperation include the Millennium Development Goals, **human rights**, and peacekeeping operations.

GUHA, AJITKUMAR (1914–1969). Writer and educationist. He taught in the Bengali department of **Dhaka University**. In 1952, he was jailed with others during the **language movement**. He wrote extensively on Bengali.

GUPTA DYNASTY. Founded by Chandragupta I in about 320, the dynasty ruled much of northern India until about 510. The dominion of the empire included Bengal. It appears, however, that Gupta control over all of Bengal was not firm. In an inscription from the reign of the second Gupta ruler, Samudragupta, **Samatata** in southeastern Bengal is referred to as a frontier state.

GUPTA, SAMUDRA (1946–2008). His real name was Abdul Mannan but he took the pen name in the early 1960s. He was known for his anti-communalism and fundamentalist stands and his works represented these positions. He has 13 poetry books to his credit and his poems have been translated into English, Chinese, French, Japanese, Urdu, Hindi, and Norwegian. His works include *Rode Jholshano*, *Swapnamongol Kaybo*, and *Chokhey Chokh Rekhey*. For a time he was the general secretary of the National Poetry Council. For his contribution to poetry and his role as a freedom fighter he was buried at the Martyred Intellectuals Graveyard. His ultimate demonstration of cynicism about communalism and fundamentalism was changing his Muslim name to a Hindu name. *See also* LITERATURE.

– **H** –

HABIBULLAH, ABUL BARKAT MUHAMMAD (1911–1984). A well-known historian and educationist who was the president of the **Asiatic Society of Bangladesh** and the Bangladesh History Association and served two terms as the curator of the Dhaka Museum. Habibullah wrote a number of books, including *The Foundation of Muslim Rule in India* (1975). For his research in Bengali **literature** he was awarded the Bangla Academy award in 1980.

HAFIZ, MIRZA GHULAM (1920–2002). A lawyer, he was earlier considered to be a leftist, as exemplified by his presidency of the Bangladesh-China Friendship Society. He joined the cabinet of **Ziaur Rahman** in July 1978 as minister of land administration and land reform. Following the 1979 parliamentary election, Ghulam Hafiz was elected speaker of parliament. In the first **Khaleda Zia** government he was minister of law and justice.

HAJI AHMAD (fl. EARLY 18th CENTURY). Brother of **Alivardi Khan**, whom he helped in gaining control of Bengal. His youngest daughter was the mother of Nawab **Sirajuddaulah**.

HAJI ILYAS. *See* ILYAS SHAH, SHAMSUDDIN.

HAKALUKI HOAR. This is one of the major wetland areas located in the eastern part of Bangladesh. It contains 235 small and large water bodies and is spread over 45,000 hectares, 70 percent of which is in the Moulvibazar district and the remaining is in the Sylhet district. The different water bodies are known as *beels*. Some well-known *beels* include Malaambeel, Joyabeel, Chatlabeel, Hawabeel, and Futbeel. Some of the native aquatic plants include *koroch*, *borun*, *makna*, *singari*, *zarul*, and *shaluk*. Hakaluki Hoar is one of the major bird sanctuaries of Bangladesh, falling in the path of the north-south migration of birds from Russia to Australia. Many species of migratory birds (between 40 and 50) use the hoar, including the northern pintail, northern shoveller, graganey, blue-winged teal, mallard, gadwall, wigeon, common teal, tufted duck, ferruginous pochard, common pochard, ruddy shell duck, cotton pygmy goose, fulvous whistling duck, lesser whistling duck, falcated duck, gray-leg goose, common shell duck, Indian-pond heron, grey heron, cattle egret, great egret, large egret, little egret, intermediate egret, purple swamphen, pheasant-tailed jacana, little grebe, great-crested grebe, little cormorant, great cormorant, Asian openbill, common coot, pintail snipe, marsh sandpiper, little ringed plover, golden plover, wood sandpiper, green shank, red shank, red-wattled lapwing, brown-headed gull, and black-headed gull. This area was declared an ecologically critical area in 1999 by the government of Bangladesh and systematic attempts are being made to bring back the wetland to its natural state. In 2007 more than 60,000 saplings of native plants like *koroch* and *hizol* were planted on 1,800 acres of the wetland. Serious attempts are also being made to develop local awareness of the importance of the wetlands and biodiversity among plants, fowls, and other wildlife inhabitants. *See also* ENVIRONMENT.

HALHEAD, NATHANIEL BRASSEY (1751–1830). Grammarian. Already fluent in Arabic and Persian, he came to India with the East India Company in 1772. At the request of **Warren Hastings**, Halhead prepared a book on Hindu law entitled *Code of Gentoo Laws*. In 1778 he wrote a grammar of the Bengali **language**.

HAMDARD LABORATORIES (WAFQ) BANGLADESH. Founded in Delhi by Hakim Abdul Majid in 1906, it provides health-care services to the poor. Hamdard opened two branches in **Dhaka** and **Chittagong** in 1953. By 2005 the number of centers exceeded 100. It primarily provides herbal medicine at a cheaper rate. It is also involved in charities and social work.

HAMOODUR RAHMAN COMMISSION AND REPORT. The report of the commission was withheld by the government of **Pakistan** until a purported copy of it was published by the Indian weekly *India Today* in December 2000. What is said to be the complete report was then released by the government of Pakistan, although the press has speculated that some secret documents were withheld.

The commission was appointed by Pakistani president **Zulfiqar Ali Bhutto** in 1972 to look into the political and military causes of the loss of **East Pakistan**. The head of the commission, Hamoodur Rahman, himself a Bengali who chose to remain in Pakistan, was a retired chief justice of the Supreme Court.

The report was highly critical of military leaders, both for their strategic and tactical actions and for their treatment of the Bengali population. It criticized Bhutto's claim that there were "two majorities" in Pakistan, as his People's Party had a large majority of seats from West Pakistan and the **Awami League** won almost all the seats in East Pakistan. The commission termed Bhutto's concept as suited for a confederation and not a federation. It noted that the Awami League held a two-thirds majority in the new assembly and therefore could impose a constitution based on the **Six Points** articulated by **Mujibur Rahman.**

In addition to criticizing the "generals," the report suggested that **Yahya Khan** and "his companions" should be tried for the illegal usurpation of power from **Ayub Khan** in 1969.

It must be noted, however, that no action has been taken on the report. The full text is available by entering the name in a search engine.

HANDICRAFTS. The government classifies handicrafts into 20 different categories. Many of the handicrafts are made of cloth, including the *nakshi kanthas*, quilts that depict mythological, pastoral, and other scenes, and have been quite popular with tourists. Folk paintings, wood carvings, baskets, cane and bamboo crafts, terra cotta earthenware and pottery, folk **musical instruments**, brass, copper, metal utensils, bone carvings, and jute items are among the many handicraft items available for domestic and tourist sales, although in some cases they are challenged by machine manufacturing. *See also* ART; *KANTHA.*

HAQUE, ANWARUL (1918–1981). Artist. He studied in **Kolkata** and taught at a number of **art** schools. In 1948, he worked with **Zainul Abedin** and other artists to establish the **East Pakistan** Art Institute. Many of his works are on display at the **Dhaka** Museum.

HAQUE, MAZHARUL (1911–1974). He was born in **Noakhali** and studied economics at **Dhaka University** and the London School of Economics. In addition to teaching, Mazharul Haque was an adviser to the government on a number of economic issues, including tariffs, small and cottage industries, and agricultural loans.

HAQUE, MUHAMMAD ENAMUL (1902–1982). From **Chittagong**, he studied in **Kolkata**. He taught at a number of institutions and was vice-chancellor of Jahangirnagar University. Enamul Haque was a senior fellow at the **Dhaka** Museum and worked with the Bangla Academy. His work was on Bengali **language** and various aspects of **Islam**, including **Sufism**.

HARIKELA. The rulers of this place seem to have dominated eastern Bengal during the ninth century, possibly succeeding the **Deva dynasty**. There is some indication from copper plates that the third ruler, the only one given royal titles, may have been the grandson of the last Deva ruler, Bhavadeva. There is speculation that Harikela may be a synonym for **Vanga** or that it may refer to **Sylhet**. By the beginning of the 10th century the rulers of Harikela were superseded by the **Chandra dynasty**.

HARTAL **POLITICS.** The term used to describe the political use of general strikes (*hartals*) to attempt to force the current government to take an action, including resignation. The process was used frequently during the first **Khaleda Zia** government by the **Awami League**, which extended these actions to include a boycott of **parliament**. They were then used by the **Bangladesh Nationalist Party (BNP)** against the Awami League, as was the boycott, when the latter ruled. Both were used again by the Awami League against the BNP ministry that was elected in 2001, although the Awami League eventually joined parliament. These events are extremely disruptive to the **economy** and to the general populace and, in addition, rarely if ever accomplish the goal for which they have been called.

HASAN ASKARI, NAWAB KHWAJA (1921–1984). The last nawab of **Dhaka** during the **Pakistan** period. He assisted the Pakistani army during the **War of Liberation** and stayed in Pakistan. A military officer by profession, he joined the Indian armed forces as a commissioned officer and served on the **Burma** front during World War II. From 1948 to 1961, Hasan Askari was in the Pakistani army after independence. In 1962 he became a member of the Pakistan National Assembly and later the communication minister of **East Pakistan**. He died in exile in Pakistan.

HASINA WAJID. *See* SHEIKH HASINA WAJID.

HASTINGS, WARREN (1732–1818). He came to **India** in 1750 as a clerk in the East India Company and rose to become the first governor-general of India in 1773. He had been named the governor of Bengal in 1772. He abolished the *diwani* set up by **Lord Clive** and began to collect revenue directly. Payments to the **Mughal** emperor were also discontinued. Hastings had a remarkable knowledge of Indian languages and sponsored many scholarly activities such as the Royal Asiatic Society and the **Kolkata** *madrasa* and supported the work of Sir **William Jones**. He left India in 1780. Hastings was accused by his opponents of financial improprieties, but his attempted impeachment by the British Parliament ended in acquittal on all counts.

HAWA BHABAN. A rental property that was initially the political office of Prime Minister **Khaleda Zia,** it became notorious for housing the office of the eldest son of Khaleda Zia, **Tarique Rahman**. To many this house represented all that was evil and negative in political leadership and politics of Bangladesh. To some it became an alternative center of power and often competed with the formal public sector in the operation and management of the country. To others it became the center of **corrupt** practices and injustices. After the ninth **parliamentary election**, this **Bangladesh Nationalist Party** office was closed.

HEALTH DELIVERY. The health delivery system of Bangladesh can best be classified as weak. In 2005, the total number of physicians in Bangladesh was 42,000, increasing to 45,000 in 2006. The per capita ratio was 1:3,317 and 1:3,125 respectively. These data refer to the country as a whole. But there is a strong bias toward urban areas, and therefore there is much lower medical coverage in the rural areas. Infant mortality was 60 per 1,000 in 2001. In 2001 life expectancy at birth was 58 for both males and females. It improved to 63 in 2005 and 66 in 2007. Life expectancy for females in 2007 was 67.9 per 1,000 births and 64.5 for males.

The country is subject to a number of the debilitating diseases often associated with tropical areas and with areas in which the availability of safe drinking water and the provision of adequate sewage facilities are rare. Most prevalent are diarrheal diseases, including cholera, that are among the principal causes of the high infant mortality rate. Malaria is also endemic. The government is placing a high priority on health delivery and is utilizing foreign assistance as well as its own resources to improve conditions. It was estimated in 2002 that approximately 14,000 persons were infected with HIV/AIDS. In 2004, it was estimated that per 100,000 people, fewer than 100 had HIV, 54 had malaria, and 435 had tuberculosis.

There remain problems in the area of nutrition. An estimated 10 to 15 percent of the population does not receive an adequate and balanced diet. This is to a large extent the result of a shortage of protein. Malnutrition then further increases the incidence of disease and worsens overall health conditions.

However, one disease that had been a scourge, polio, is coming under control by wide administration of the polio vaccine through programs of the World Health Organization and Rotary International. In 2002, no cases of polio were reported. *See also* ARSENIC CONTAMINATION; POLLUTION.

HEBER, REGINALD (1783–1826). Anglican bishop of Calcutta, 1822–1826. He traveled extensively, as his diocese included all of British India. The travels are described in his *Journey through India* (published in 1828), which has been described as one of the best early British accounts of life in India. Heber was a founder of Bishop's College in Calcutta and the writer of many hymns, including the well-known missionary hymn "From Greenland's Icy Mountains."

HERITAGE IN RUINS. The Department of **Archeology** of the government of Bangladesh has identified nearly 400 heritage sites. Many of these sites are in ruins and the Department of Archeology has neither the manpower nor the resources to take proper care of them. Twelve of these sites are in **Dhaka,** the capital city. These are Bara Katra, Chhoto Katra, Hosseni Dalan, Lalbagh Fort, Hazi Khaza Shabaz Mosque, Khan Mohammad Mridha Mosque, Ruplal House, Sankhanidhi House, Sat Masjid, North Brook Hall, Rose Garden, Old Eidgah Matth (field), Radha Krishan Temple, and Bhajahari Lodge. Some selected sites in ruins due to lack of **architectural** restoration include the following:

Shib and Dol Mandir in Jhenaidah, 16th century
Kapileswar Shiva Temple in Tarash, Sirajganj, 17th century

Nayabad Mosque in Kaharol, Dinajpur, 17th century
Kherua Mosque, in Sherpur, Bogra, 16th century
Shiv Temple in Puthia, Rajshahi, 19th century
Binat Bibi Mosque in Narinda, Dhaka City, Dhaka, 15th century
King Kanak Palace in Sharsha, Jessore, 15th century
Atia Jam-e-Mosque in Delduar, Tangail, 17th century
Mathurapur Deul in Madhukhali, Faridpur, 17th century
Rakhine Buddhist Temple in Patuakhali, Barisal, 19th century

HIGH TECHNOLOGY INDUSTRY. Two companies, one export-based and the other promoting internal growth, lead the high technology industrial growth of Bangladesh. Japanese-owned Sanko produces high-quality camera lenses, as well as lenses for fax machines, security cameras, scanners, and projectors. The lens factory was established in 1990. Currently located in an Export Processing Zone in **Chittagong**, it employs 1,400 female workers and has an annual production of 18 million lenses, earning $8 million a year. As the production method is labor intensive and Bangladesh labor is more competitive than that of **China**, Singapore, or Malaysia, there is great possibility that other high technology industries may move to Bangladesh. Solar energy is another growing sector that is affecting rural economic development in Bangladesh. Solar energy is especially important in off-grid areas of Bangladesh. It is spurring small business development by reducing the cost of business and expanding the number of hours that businesses can remain open, as well as reducing the consumption of kerosene and supporting agricultural production. It has particularly affected the growth of the poultry farms in rural areas. It is expected that by 2015 over a million households in Bangladesh will have access to solar energy through the Solar Home System (SHS).

HIGHEST PEAK IN BANGLADESH. *Keokradong* is officially the highest peak in Bangladesh and it rises to a height of 3,161 feet. However, in 2008, a group of Bangladesh mountaineers climbed the *Tlangmoy Swapnachura* peak near the Bangladesh-Myanmar border and utilizing a GPS was able to determine that the *Tlangmoy Swapnachura* peak was approximately 300 feet higher than the *Keokra-*

dong peak. The group is seeking official recognition for *Tlangmoy Swapnachura* as the highest peak in Bangladesh.

HINDUISM. Hinduism, as defined most broadly, was presumably the religion of all Bengalis prior to the expansion of **Buddhism** during the **Pala dynasty**. With the **Sena dynasty**, Brahmanical Hinduism revived briefly before the advent of **Islam** in the 13th century. According to the 1991 census, there were about 11.2 million Hindus in Bangladesh, comprising 10.5 percent of the population. This showed a considerable decrease from the last, pre-independence census, that of 1961, when the Hindu population was recorded as 18.4 percent of the population. The substantial out-migration to India during the 1971 civil war was not offset, by any means, by the return of the Hindu refugees. The regions (former districts) with the highest ratios of Hindus in the 1981 census (comparable data for 1991 and 2001 are not yet available) were Khulna (27.2 percent), Dinajpur (21.9 percent), Jessore (19.6 percent), Faridpur (18.8 percent), and Sylhet (18.0 percent).

Although **caste** census data were not reported in 1981, it is widely believed that the majority of the Hindus in Bangladesh belong to the Scheduled Castes (the group once described as "untouchables," or in Gandhi's term, Harijans, i.e., children of God). In the 1961 **Pakistan** census, caste Hindus were enumerated separately and represented 53.2 percent of all Hindus. As a basis for comparison, the 1961 census of India indicated that 12.6 percent of Indian Hindus were from the Scheduled Castes. It is clear that the two major out-migrations of Hindus, in the early 1950s and in 1971, comprised primarily caste Hindus. In the 1954 election, Hindus voted separately from Muslims under the system of **separate electorates**. In elections since then, the system of joint electorates has been used. Hindus are under no legal restrictions, and several have served in parliament and in the cabinet. Data appear to show that Hindu voters have favored the **Awami League**.

HOMEGUTI KHELA. A traditional game played in some areas of Mymensingh district of Bangladesh, it involves one group of villagers hiding the *guti*, a 30-kilogram brass ball, which then has to be found by another group of villagers. It is played on the last day of the Bengali month of *Poush*. The day is locally known as *Pahura* or *Poush Sangkranti*. This game ends when the *guti* is found and can last for many days.

HOSSAIN, KAMAL (1937–). A British-educated barrister who was a close associate of Sheikh **Mujibur Rahman**. He was elected to the National Assembly in a by-election in 1971. After independence he served in the Mujib cabinets as minister of law and then as minister of foreign affairs. In the former post, Kamal Hossain piloted the constitution bill. After Mujib's assassination, he went into self-imposed exile in England, but he returned to run for the presidency in 1981 as the candidate of the **Awami League**, when he was defeated by **Abdus Sattar**. He has since ended his association with the Awami League and has formed a new political group called the Gono Forum (People's Forum). This group participated in the June 1996 **election** with a few candidates, including Kamal Hossain, none of whom were successful. It did not take part in the 2001 election. The group had no formal organization and operated more as a discussion body, which it now remains on a much reduced scale.

HOSSAIN, ROKEYA SAKHAWAT (1880–1932). She and her sister, Karimunnessa Khanam, were early champions for the **education** of Muslim **women**. She founded the Sakhawat Memorial School in **Calcutta** and, in 1916, the Muslim Women's Society to assist distressed Muslim women and girls. *See also* WOMEN.

HOSSAIN, SUFI MOTAHAR (1907–1975). A poet, he was born in **Faridpur** and studied in **Dhaka** before becoming a government officer and teacher. He was inspired by **Kazi Nazrul Islam** and wrote a large volume of poetry. *See also* LITERATURE.

HUDA, MIRZA NURUL (1919–1991). In 1949 he received his Ph.D. in agricultural economics from Cornell University and joined **Dhaka University**. Prior to going to the United States he had joined the Bengal Civil Service. He had a long and successful career at Dhaka University and served in various leadership positions, including the head of the Department of Economics. He also served in a number of national commissions such as the Planning Commission of **Pakistan**, which was charged with drafting the first and second five-year plans. From 1965 to 1969, he was the minister of planning of **East Pakistan**. He was a member of the Pakistan **Muslim League** delegation to the roundtable conference held by **Ayub Khan** in 1969, in opposition to the **Democratic Action Committee**. In March 1969, he was governor of East Pakistan for two days, and resigned when General **Yahya Khan** declared martial law in the country. He was called back to public service in 1975 and till 1979 served variously as the minister of agriculture, commerce and industries, planning, and finally finance. In 1981, he became the vice president of Bangladesh during all but the last few days of the presidency of Abdus Sattar and left this position when General **Hussain Muhammad Ershad** took over power in 1982. He is the son-in-law of **Tamizuddin Khan**.

HUMAN RIGHTS. Part two of the **Constitution** of Bangladesh states that Bangladesh is a democracy that guarantees fundamental human rights, freedoms, and respect for the dignity and worth of the individual. Part three of the constitution lists the specific rights, starting with equality before the law, no discrimination on the basis of religion, right to life and personal liberty, safeguards against arrest and detention, freedom of movement and assembly, freedom of speech and conscience, and other rights normally associated with a modern state. However, in practice sufficient evidence exists that there is disregard for human rights and at times suppression of all rights. Political interference in the activities of law enforcement, actions taken by the **Rapid Action Battalion** (RAB), and a weak judicial system that is subject to executive pressures are the major factors that reduce constitutional guarantees of human rights to deceptive and dishonest practices.

Recent institutional changes that strengthen the **Anti-corruption Commission** (ACC), the introduction of the **National Human Rights Commission** and the **Right to Information Ordinance**, and the separation of the judiciary from the executive, in addition to the formation of **women's** groups like Ain O Shalish and human rights organizations like **ODHIKAR**, are likely to improve human rights practices in Bangladesh.

HUQ, MUHAMMAD SHAMSUL (1910–2006). A noted educationist who was vice-chancellor of **Rajshahi** University (1965–1969), he served also in the **Pakistan** cabinet of **Yahya Khan** (1969–1971) and in the Bangladesh cabinets of **Ziaur Rahman** (1977–1981) and **Abdus Sattar** (1981–1982). In the Bangladeshi cabinets, Shamsul Huq was minister of foreign affairs. He was instrumental in bringing to fruition the goal of Zia to form the **South Asian Association for Regional Cooperation (SAARC)**. It is reported that Shamsul Huq was offered the presidency by **Hussain Muhammad Ershad** in 1982, but he refused in opposition to the military coup that ousted the elected civilian government of Sattar. After leaving office, he headed the Bangladesh Institute of International and Strategic Studies, an important and influential think tank. He was a special adviser on **education** and the author of several studies of Bangladesh **foreign policy**.

HUQ, OBAIDUL (1911–2007). Editor of the *Bangladesh Observer* from 1972 till 1980. He also served as chairman of the Press Institute of Bangladesh and was on the Board of Trustees of *Danik Bangla* and *The Bangladesh Times*. He received a graduate degree in philosophy from **Dhaka University** and a law degree from **Kolkata**. In addition, he was the first Bengali Muslim to write, produce, and direct a feature **film**. The movie was entitled *Dukkhe Jader Jibon Gara* (Tragedy Defines Their Lives). For his accomplishment as a playwright he received the Bangla Academy Award in 1964. For his accomplishment as a journalist he received the UNICEF Medal and the Ekushey Padak. *See also* FILM; THEATRE.

HUQ, WAHEEDUL (1933–2007). A social organizer, journalist, politician, and cultural activist, he is well known for organizing Chayanat in 1961. Nearly 20 years later in 1980, he organized the National Rabindra Sangeet Conference. Other organizations he founded include *Khontoshilon* to promote recitation, *Anondodhani* for teaching music, *Shishu-Tirtha* for children's recitation, and *Chalachitra Sanshad* to promote quality art **films**. His most successful column was "*Avoy Baje Hridoy Mazhe*," written for the newspaper *Janakantha*. He also worked for *The Bangladesh Observer, The Morning News, The People, The New Observer*, and *The Daily Star*, where he served as a joint editor.

Huq also had a political career. He was the district organizer of the leftist **National Awami Party** (NAP) and was elected as a member of the **Basic Democracy** during the reign of **Ayub Khan**. The NAP also nominated him for a parliamentary seat. He had a deep commitment to Bangla culture and society and saw secularism as a force against fundamentalism and communalism. He immersed himself in public service devoted to building a just society. While he received the Ekushey Padak for **music**, he will be remembered for his uncompromising efforts to uphold all essential elements of Bangla society and culture.

HUQUE, MAHMADUL (1941–2008). After the partition of India and at the age of ten he moved from **Kolkata** to **Dhaka**. He was unfamiliar with the Bangla dialect used in Dhaka, and therefore found it difficult to assimilate in school. While at school he was physically abused because he did not wear a Jinnah cap. These two childhood experiences he worked into his writings. His characters were alienated men or men who were passive, perhaps the result of his migration from India and observations of the society of his adopted country. In 1976, he wrote his first novel, *Jekhane Khonjona Pakhi*. The trauma of the **War of Liberation** was a constant in his writing. His first novel after the 1971 war was entitled *Nirapod Tondra in 1974*, followed by *Jibon Amar Bone* (1976). He took the title from Boris Pasternak's poem, "Sister My Life." His writing underwent another transformation after the war when he focused on rural life rather than city life. His novels *Kalo Borof* (1977), *Matir Jahaj* (1977), and *Khelaghar* (1978) are written in rural settings. His characters narrated stories of their daily lives, through which he explored events and their impact on individuals and society. By the time he was in his forties he stopped writing. His was disillusioned by the literary community he associated with and moved to Narshindi, where he spent the rest of his life. He also managed his family business, Tasmen Jewellers. *See also* LITERATURE.

HUSAIN SHAHI DYNASTY. Ruled Bengal from 1494 to 1538. The dynasty was founded by **Alauddin Husain Shah**, from whom it derives its name. The first ruler extended the kingdom to the borders of Orissa and into northern Bihar. He also recaptured **Chittagong** from the **Arakanese**. The period was one of great building at **Gaur** as well as the patronizing of **literature**. The Husain Shahis, for example, sponsored the translation of the **Hindu** epic *Mahabharata* into Bengali. The dynasty ended in 1538 when the last ruler, Ghiyasuddin Mahmud Shah, was defeated by **Sher Shah Suri**.

HUSAIN, SYED ANWAR (1947–). He was born in Bogra district. After graduating from **Dhaka University** with a degree in history in 1968 and obtaining a master's degree in modern history in 1969, he received an M.A. from Edinburgh University in 1975 and his Ph.D. from London University in 1978. He held numerous post-doctoral research appointments in various universities in the United States. He joined the department of history at Dhaka University in 1970. He served as director general of Bangla Academy during 1997–2001 and as vice-chancellor of Darul Ihsan University during 2004–2005. He was also president of the Bangladesh Itihash Samity (historical society), general secretary of Bangladesh Asiatic Society, and founding president of the Bangladesh Association for American Studies and Bangladesh Association for International Studies. He has authored 28 books and 93 essays.

HUSSAIN, QAZI MOTAHAR (1897–1981). He was a founder, in 1921, of the Muslim Sahitya Samaj, an organization of educated Muslim youth. He also was instrumental in launching the Free Thinking Movement and was the editor of its journal, *Shikha*.

– I –

IBRAHIM KHAN (fl. LATE 17th CENTURY). Mughal governor in Bengal, 1689–1697, whose weak rule allowed the placement and fortification of European settlements in Bengal. His predecessor, Shaista Khan, had driven the English out of Bengal, but Ibrahim Khan invited them back and permitted the settlement of what became **Calcutta** in 1690. He also permitted the English, French, and Dutch to fortify their settlements. He was dismissed by Aurangzeb in 1697.

IBRAHIM KHAN (1894–1978). An educationist, litterateur, and social activist, he participated in the non-cooperation movement and the **Khilafat movement** in the early 1920s. He joined the Congress in 1920 and the **Muslim League** in 1937. He was a member of the Pakistan National Assembly in 1962. Ibrahim Khan established a number of schools and colleges, of which the Korotia College in Tangail, which he managed after it was founded with the financial assistance of **Wajid Ali Khan Panni**, is the best known.

IBRAHIM, MUHAMMAD (1894–1966). A member of the judicial service and a firm believer in parliamentary democracy, he was appointed a justice of the Dhaka High Court in 1950, vice-chancellor of **Dhaka University** in 1956, and the central law minister in 1958 during the **Ayub Khan** government. It was during Ibrahim's leadership of the law ministry that the Muslim **Family Law Ordinance** was promulgated in 1962.

IHTISHAMUDDIN, MIRZA SHEIKH (18th CENTURY). In 1765, he was the first educated Indian to visit England; he brought a letter from the Mughal emperor, Shah Alam II, to King George II. He also visited France. Although he was asked to remain in Europe to teach Persian, he returned to India. The written account of his journey has not been critically published, although an unauthorized edition was published in 1827. It is thought that there may be additional material written by Ihtishamuddin.

ILYAS SHAHI DYNASTY. It ruled Bengal from 1342 to 1490. It was founded by Shamsuddin Ilyas Shah following a period of turmoil during the previous decade as local Bengali chiefs overthrew the rule of the governor of the Tughluq dynasty of the Delhi Sultanate. Shamsuddin was able to repulse an attack by the Tughluqs during the 1350s, and he established his capital at **Pandua**, near **Gaur**. He captured eastern Bengal in 1352 and repulsed attacks from the Delhi sultan Firuzshah Tughluq. The rule of the dynasty was interrupted by the seizure of power by a Hindu minister, **Raja Ganesh**, in 1417, but the dynasty was restored in 1437. The dynasty was overthrown in 1490 by the **Abyssinians**.

IMAM, JAHANARA (1929–1994). An educationist, she gained acclaim as the author of *Of Blood and Fire*, her diary of the **War of Liberation** of 1971, during which one son was killed and her husband died. She was born in **Murshidabad** district (now in West Bengal) and educated in **Calcutta** and **Dhaka** and in the United States, the last as a Fulbright scholar. Jahanara Imam was an important leader of a group opposing the restoration of the citizenship of **Golam Azam**, the amir of the **Jama'at-i-Islami**, and demanding his trial for collaboration with the Pakistani army in 1971.

INDIA. India contributed greatly to the independence of Bangladesh by providing refuge, sanctuary, supplies, training, and arms to the **Mukti Bahini**, the Bangladeshi personnel in rebellion against **Pakistan**. In late November 1971 (early December according to Indian sources), India intervened directly in the conflict and, with the Mukti Bahini, defeated the Pakistani forces. The latter surrendered at Dhaka on 16 December 1971, in a ceremony that excluded representatives of the Mukti Bahini and Bangladesh government-in-exile. This began a series of events that cooled relations between the two countries. Others included the commissioning by India of the **Farakka Barrage**, the overstaying (from a Bangladeshi perspective) of Indian troops in the **Chittagong Hill Tracts**, and the taking of Pakistani military equipment and prisoners to India. Nonetheless, during the period of Sheikh **Mujibur Rahman** relations were close, culminating in the signing of a 25-year treaty of friendship between the two nations in 1972. Strong opposition to the treaty developed in Bangladesh and it was not renewed when it expired in 1997.

India, under Indira Gandhi, took the assassination of Mujib in August 1975 as an event aimed against India. India supported insurgents under an opponent of **Ziaur Rahman**. Although relations improved under Morarji Desai (1977–1979) in India and **Hussain Muhammad Ershad** in Bangladesh, a number of problems remain. Chief among these is the unresolved Farakka dispute; an interim agreement was made during the Morarji Desai period in 1978, but it was not renewed in 1988. However, another agreement on the sharing of the water during the low-flow period was made in 1996. Other disputes include the land and maritime boundaries, **trade** relations in which Bangladesh has a sizable deficit, the migration of Bangladeshis into West Bengal and Assam and other northeastern states of India, and occasional firing across the borders by border forces of each country. India would also like to utilize transit facilities on the rivers and railroads in Bangladesh so that its goods can reach northeast India more easily.

India has accused Bangladesh of harboring dissidents from its northeastern provinces and has also accused Bangladesh of working with the Pakistani Interservices Intelligence (ISI) to destabilize the northeastern areas. These accusations have become sharper since 2002. Another complaint by India against Bangladesh is that a vast number, sometimes stated as 18 million, of Bangladeshi nationals have migrated to India in violation of Indian immigration regulations. Since 2003, India has become more vocal about Bangladesh harboring dissidents from India like members of the United Liberation Front of Assam, India, and militants from Pakistan, Sri Lanka, and even Burma. The responses of both the BNP and the caretaker government of Fakhruddin Ahmed to such allegations were lukewarm. After the election of 2009 and the return of the Awami League to power there is sufficient evidence that India's allegations to a large extent are correct. Although the relationship between Bangladesh and India has improved, especially since India immediately provided 100 megawatts of power to the new Awami League government, some old problems like the Tin Bigha Corridor, **Talpatty Island**, and illegal immigration remain. New problems, especially those associated with the building of another dam (Tipaimukh dam) in Manipur right across from the northwest border of Bangladesh, may hold back improved trade relationships between the two countries. Bangladesh would like to see India import additional Bangladesh goods while India seeks transit rights to its eastern provinces and also the use of Chittagong port for Indian imports.

One long-range project that has been discussed is the reopening of the Chittagong-Assam rail line that has been closed since 1947. The capital costs for this project would be very high. Gas export to India is another item on the countries' agendas.

Both countries are members of the **South Asian Association for Regional Cooperation**. The five principal Bangladeshi leaders (**Mujibur Rahman, Ziaur Rahman, Hussain Muhammad Ershad, Hasina Wajid,** and **Khaleda Zia**) have made official visits to India and Indian leaders have reciprocated these by visiting

Bangladesh. *See also* ASSAM; BERUBARI ENCLAVE; GANGES WATER TREATY; INDIA-BANGLADESH TREATY; NATURAL RESOURCES; SEA BOUNDARY; TALPATTY ISLAND; TRIPURA.

INDIA INDEPENDENCE ACT OF 1947. This act of the British parliament provided for the independence of **India**, its partition into India and **Pakistan**, and the continuance of governance under the **Government of India Act of 1935**, with the provisions of this act extended to the central governments until each state enacted its own constitution.

INDIA-BANGLADESH TREATY. A 25-year agreement between the two countries contracted in March 1972. It was formally termed a treaty of friendship, cooperation, and peace. It was signed as India completed its withdrawal from Bangladesh, and it was seen by some as a quid pro quo for the removal of Indian troops from the **Chittagong Hill Tracts**. The treaty, which in itself is not exceptional within the general class of treaties between neighbors, was seen by some Bangladeshis as substituting Indian dominance for that of Pakistan. In the June 1996 **election**, the major parties pledged that the treaty would not be renewed when it expired in 1997. As promised, the **Awami League** did not renew the treaty.

INDIAN COUNCILS ACTS. The Indian Councils Acts of 1861 and 1892 were passed by the British parliament prior to the first major constitutional reform, the **Government of India Act of 1909**. Each of these was intended to permit and increase Indian representation in the executive and legislative branches of the British Indian government. The Indians who were associated were appointed and not elected.

INDIGO. A plant native to South Asia (hence its name) producing a blue dye. Known in ancient times as a product of India, it was grown extensively on a commercial basis for export by the **East India Company** during the 19th century. Exploitation of farmers resulted in conflict between planters and farmers in mid-century. The development of a synthetic dye in Germany in 1897 ended the plant's commercial cultivation. *See also* BLUE MUTINY.

INDO-PAKISTAN WAR OF 1965. This was a conflict over Kashmir. Pakistani forces attacked Indian troops in Kashmir; India responded by attacking along the Punjab border and farther south. The war on the Punjab boundary began on 6 September, and a cease-fire on all fronts came in three weeks. Although there was no conflict involving territory in **East Pakistan**, East Pakistanis were nonetheless concerned that the concentration of Pakistani troops in the west wing left them vulnerable to an Indian attack. This formed a basis for the last of the **Six Points** announced by Sheikh **Mujibur Rahman** in January 1966, that of separate militias for each of the provinces of **Pakistan**.

INDO-PAKISTAN WAR OF 1971. An outgrowth of the **War of Liberation** in **East Pakistan** that began on 26 March 1971. **India** provided, early on, sanctuary and training areas for the **Mukti Bahini** and a home for the Bangladesh government-in-exile. It also served as a home for a large number of refugees (some estimates are as high as 10 million) and as a source of arms for the Mukti Bahini. In late November, Indian forces began to operate with the Mukti Bahini against Pakistani troops. Indian troops captured **Dhaka** on 16 December, ending the conflict in the east. There were also actions in December in the west between Pakistan and India, but a unilateral cease-fire declaration by India was accepted by **Pakistan** on 18 December. *See also* WAR OF LIBERATION.

INDUSTRY. The industrial sector produces a small portion of the gross domestic product: 27 percent in 2001 and 28.7 percent in 2008. The industrial sector grew at an annual rate of 3.9 percent from 1990 to 1999. The annual rate of growth dipped to only 1.8 percent in 2003 but increased to 6.5 percent in 2005, further increasing to 7.2 percent in 2007. In 2008, it reached a high of 8.4 percent. Large-scale manufacturing enterprises provide jobs for only 20 percent of the industrial labor force, although they contribute 58 percent of the value added. The bulk of employment is provided by small and cottage industries.

Sustained industrial growth is constrained by the small size of the domestic market and especially by the small size of what might be called the middle class with disposable income.

Jute processing and cotton textiles are the largest industries. However, the declining demand for jute has left the industry with excess capacity. Since the early 1980s, the **garment industry** has been a growth industry with high demand externally. Bangladesh is the fifth-largest supplier of cotton apparel to the **United States**. Breaking up ships supplies most of Bangladesh's steel requirements; the scrap is processed in **Chittagong**. Other industries include sugar refining, **tea** processing, leather, newsprint, pharmaceuticals, and fertilizers.

The nationalization of industries during the **Mujibur Rahman** period was a hindrance to industrial growth. A policy of **privatization** was instituted by the **Hussain Muhammad Ershad** regime and was continued in effect by the succeeding governments, but has not been effective. Only a few large concerns have been denationalized. Much of this ineffectiveness results from the desire of government employees to continue control of enterprises, many of whom have profited from exercising their control. Foreign investment has had some success, primarily in new industrial undertakings, but the record of **corruption** has discouraged many potential investors. **Banking** has been partially freed from government ownership. There are no limits on foreign investment other than the lack of demand, raw materials, and trained labor, and a concern about political stability and corruption. *See also* HIGH TECHNOLOGY INDUSTRY; LIGHT ENGINEERING; SHIP BREAKING; SHIP BUILDING; STEEL RE-ROLLING INDUSTRIAL SECTOR.

INSTRUMENT OF SURRENDER. On 16 December 1971, the Pakistan armed forces surrendered to the joint command of the Indian armed forces and the **Mukti Bahini**. The surrender instrument was signed by Lieutenant-General Jagjit Singh Aurora on behalf of the Indian and Bangladesh forces and by Lieutenant-General Amir Abdullah Khan Niazi on behalf of the Pakistani forces. The surrender ceremony was held at the Ramna Race Course in **Dhaka**.

INTERNATIONAL CENTRE FOR DIARRHOEAL DISEASE RESEARCH, BANGLADESH (ICDDRB). Located in **Dhaka**, it is commonly referred to as the Dhaka Cholera Hospital. It was founded in 1960 as the Cholera Research Hospital under the initial auspices of the Southeast Asia Treaty Organization (SEATO). It is recognized internationally as a leading center for the study and treatment of cholera and is working to develop an effective and safe immunization for the disease as well as treatments for it. Much of its research has been centered on the Matlab *thana* of **Comilla** through its **Health** and Demographic Surveillance System. Funding is now provided by governments, including the **United States**, international organizations, and many private organizations and corporations.

IRRIGATION. Most of the crops in Bangladesh utilize water either from wells and rain or from relatively small channels from water courses that can direct water to a field during the high-flow period. An exception to this small-scale irrigation is the **Ganga-Kobadak** scheme. Only one large-scale dam exists in Bangladesh, on the **Karnafuli River** near **Chittagong**, and its purpose is to produce hydroelectricity. *See also* AGRICULTURE; RICE.

ISA KHAN (?–1598). The chief member of the **Bara Bhuiyan** (12 landlords) who resisted **Mughal** rule in the late 16th century and was based at Katrabo near **Sonargaon** and controlled much of **Comilla**, **Dhaka**, and **Mymensingh** districts. He inflicted a number of defeats on the Mughals, including naval defeats in 1584 and 1597. His exploits against the Mughals have made Isa Khan a symbol of the eastern Bengalis' resistance of the Mughals, which at the present time can be transmuted into "Pakistanis." He also defeated Nara Narayan, the ruler of **Cooch Behar**. He was succeeded by his son, Daud Khan, but the Mughals consolidated their hold under **Man Singh**, who established a Mughal military headquarters at Dhaka not far from Sonargaon. Isa Khan's descendants were major landlords in Mymensingh known as the Diwan Sahibs of Haibatnagar and Jangalbari.

ISLAM. Islam is professed by about 88 percent of the population of Bangladesh. Almost all Bengali Muslims are Sunni, with a small number of Ithna Ashari Shia and Ismaili Shia. Most who adhere to the latter two sects are descendants of non-Bengalis who migrated to Bengal during the period of Muslim rule from Delhi or later. With about 123 million Muslims, Bangladesh ranks after Indonesia and with India and Pakistan as a state with the largest number of Muslims. This has given Bangladesh an important position in the **Organization of the Islamic Conference**.

Leadership among Muslims includes the local mullah or imam; the *maulana*, who is presumed to be learned in Islam (a member of the ulema); and the pirs, who preside over shrines usually dedicated to deceased **Sufi** saints. Among Sunnis there is no designated hierarchy. The Islamic leadership is generally confined to religious matters. Political activity has been limited; although there are parties demanding an Islamic state, such as the **Jama'at-i-Islami**, their electoral importance has been minor. As a result, there is no significant fundamentalism in Bangladesh. Rather, Islam is generally considered to be a personal matter, and there is no state enforcement of Islamic law or custom, although Islam has been declared the state religion. Nonetheless, Islam in the personal sense is deeply rooted in the country.

Bengali Muslims formally eschew **caste**, as do all subcontinental Muslims, but in practice, hereditary groupings are recognized and in rural Bangladesh are important in such rites as marriage. Within the Muslim society certain distinctions are admitted: the *ashraf*, the upper class and often members of the **national elite**; the *ajlaf*, an urban and rural middle class that has included many of the leaders of the **vernacular elite**; and the *arzal*, the lower classes. *See also* MILITANCY; TERRORISM.

ISLAM, BEGUM SULTANA (1939–2003). Founder of the National Women's Federation (NWF) of Bangladesh, she is the granddaughter of **Sir Abdur Rahim**. She was raised by her grandmother in **Kolkata**, who initiated her into public service. While a student she launched the monthly magazine *Jagaron* (Awakening) and became its first editor. She was also the first Muslim to receive an honors degree in Bengali from Bankura **Christian** College and later studied English at Calcutta University. From 1949 to 1960 she served as treasurer, secretary, and vice president of the all-**Pakistan Women's** Association. In 1953 she received the Queen's Coronation Award for her contribution. After the **War of Liberation** she worked closely with Mother Teresa to rehabilitate the children of war. She also worked to repatriate Bangladeshis stranded in Pakistan. In 1972 she founded the NWF. Her public service was devoted to the needs of the poor and the helpless, especially women and children. She initiated projects to improve women's literacy and primary school, and to provide a hospital dialysis unit for children. She was one of the early proponents of collateral-free loans. She devoted her life to resolving those challenges facing women in Bangladesh. She participated in the 1985 Nairobi Third World Conference on Women and the 1995 Beijing Fourth World Conference on Women.

ISLAM, MOHAMMED NURUL (? – 2007). He graduated from B. M. College of Barisal and joined the civil service of Pakistan in 1950. During his career he concentrated in the area of exports and imports. For his expertise and integrity he was twice offered ministerial positions, in 1982 and 1991, which he refused. He served as governor of Bangladesh Bank, prior to which he served as chairman of the Trading Corporation of Bangladesh (TCB) and National Board of Revenue (NBR). He introduced innovative projects in the "Deferred Payment Scheme," under which he was able to maintain the flow of imports when the foreign reserve position of Bangladesh was very weak. He introduced a financing scheme for small apartments up to 1,500 square feet, financing up to 90 percent of the cost with a 5 percent interest rate on a 30-year repayment schedule.

ISLAMIC DEMOCRATIC LEAGUE (IDL). Formerly an ultraconservative **political party** composed of members of the **Nizam-i-Islam**, the **Jama'at-i-Islami**, and two smaller parties, the People's Democratic Party and the Islamic Ganotantrik Dal. It was established in 1976. Its leader, Maulana Abdur Rahim, contested the 1981 presidential election without success. The party stood against Westernization and secularism and aimed to make Bangladesh an Islamic republic. One of its demands was that the national anthem of Bangladesh be changed because it was written by **Rabindranath Tagore**, who was a Hindu. The party has since broken up.

ISLAMIC DEMOCRATIC PARTY (IDP). It was established in 2008, with the explicit goal of running the country under the Charter of Medina (propounded by Prophet Muhammad), which, according to conveners of the IDP, provides equal rights to all citizens irrespective of **religion** or ethnicity. They also want to introduce Sharia laws for the Muslims of Bangladesh. Non-Muslims will be permitted to follow the law of the land and norms of their communities. Sharia will be imposed if the party receives an electoral mandate, but only through a change in the **constitution**. One of the IDP conveners, Sheikh Abdus Salam, was also associated with Harkatul-ul-Jihad-Islami, Bangladesh (HUJI-B), which was established in 1992 and banned in 2005. After HUJI-B was banned, a small group formed the Islamic *Gono Andolon* (IGA), another political party. In 2006, the IGA renamed itself *Sacheton Islami Janata*. IDP is the third iteration of some of those who originally started HUJI-B. Kazi Azizul Huq and Sheikh Abdus Salam are two prominent members of the IDP.

ISLAMIC DEVELOPMENT BANK (IDB). Loosely associated with the **Organization of the Islamic Conference**, the **bank**'s members include representatives from all Muslim-majority countries, as does the OIC. It has a variety of programs in Bangladesh. One of the more interesting is the assistance given to the establishment of polytechnic institutes for **women**. These are to be located in **Chittagong**, **Khulna**, and **Rajshahi**. The IDB also supports the establishment of rural clinics and the construction of primary schools and *madrasas* (schools with an Islamic curriculum).

ISMAIL, KHAN BAHADUR MUHAMMAD (1871–1945). He received the title of Khan Bahadur from the British. He was a contemporary of Nawab Sir **Salimullah**. He organized the **Krishak Praja Party** in **Mymensingh** district of Bangladesh. Ismail was actively involved with the Mymensingh district council, serving as its vice chairman from 1906 to 1920 and as its chairman from 1920 to 1929. He was a lawyer by profession.

ISPAHANI FAMILY. A Shia Muslim business family that originated in Iran, as the name indicates. The family moved to India in the 18th century. Based first in Madras, the family achieved prominence in Bengal before 1947. After Pakistani independence, the group maintained headquarters in Karachi and **Dhaka**. Activities included **tea** processing, **jute** manufacture, insurance, and **banking**. The group also established Orient Airlines, the predecessor of the nationalized

Pakistan International Airlines. In the 1960s, the group was ranked eighth among Pakistani business houses in assets. **Mirza Abol Hasan Ispahani** was a prominent political figure as well as a part of the managing group of the family. Since 1971 the family has maintained holdings in both Bangladesh and **Pakistan**.

ISPAHANI, MIRZA ABOL HASAN (1902–1981). A member of the important business house of the **Ispahani family**, he was a close associate and later a biographer of **Muhammad Ali Jinnah**. He was a member of the Bengal legislature before independence (1937–1947) and the constituent assembly of Pakistan (1947–1955). Ispahani was the first Pakistani ambassador to the **United States** (1947–1952) and later high commissioner to **Great Britain** (1952–1954) and a central minister (1954–1955). In politics, he represented the small Muslim commercial and industrial community in Bengal, having been president of the Muslim Chamber of Commerce, **Calcutta**, 1945–1947, and opposed the **Awami League** and **Husain Shahid Suhrawardy** in their regionalist goals. Ispahani was therefore a member of the **national elite**.

– J –

JAGAT SETH. This title, meaning "banker of the world," was conferred on Fatehchand by the **Mughal** emperor Muhammad Shah in 1723. The **banking** house, whose members originally came from Marwar in Rajasthan, had its headquarters in **Murshidabad** and branches in **Dhaka** and Patna. It functioned almost as a central bank for the Mughal province of Bengal. At Fatehchand's death in 1744, the title passed to his grandson, Mahatabchand. He and his cousin and partner, Maharaja Swarupchand, had great influence during the governorship of **Alivardi Khan**, but they were alienated by Alivardi Khan's grandson and successor, **Sirajuddaulah**. They joined a conspiracy with the British to overthrow Sirajuddaulah, providing much financial assistance both before and following the battle of **Plassey** (1757). Jagat Seth's (Mahatabchand's) influence was restored during the rule of **Mir Jafar**, but it fell again when **Mir Qasim** became governor. Mir Qasim caused the cousins to be killed in 1763. Successors to the title Jagat Seth continued to use the title until the early 20th century, but they were persons of little influence.

JAGODAL. An acronym for Jatiyatabadi Ganotantrik Dal or National Democratic Party, a **political party** formed largely by non-political figures to support President **Ziaur Rahman**. In 1978, it merged into the broader **Bangladesh Nationalist Party (BNP)**, although a small group retaining the name JAGODAL remains.

JAGRATA MUSLIM BANGLADESH JANATA (JMBJ) (Awakened Muslim Bangladesh Mass). A Bangladesh vigilante **terrorist** group formed in 1998 in the northwest part of Bangladesh (especially Rajshahi). The two principal leaders were Abdur Rahman and Siddiqur Rahman, also known as **Bangla Bhai**. This group was banned in 2004 by the **Bangladesh Nationalist Party** government. Most of their leaders were arrested in July 2006 and sentenced to death. The **caretaker government** of **Fakhruddin Ahmed** executed them in April 2007. Abdur Rahman was also the leader of Jama'atul Mujahideen Bangladesh (JMB), a related militant, terror group. The JMB was also banned in 2004. Other names used to identify those who are involved in this type of violence are Mujahidin Alliance Council, Islami Jalsha, and Muslim Raksha Mujahidin Oikya Parishad. After the execution of its leaders in 2007, JMBJ went into hiding but in 2009 was attempting to reorganize itself under the new name Islam O Muslim.

JAHAN ALI, KHAN (?–1459). A military officer under Sultan Nuruddin Mahmud Shah of the **Ilyas Shahi dynasty** who fought rebellious non-Muslim landlords in the region of **Jessore** and **Khulna** districts. Local legend adds that he tried unsuccessfully to cultivate the **Sundarbans**. In his old age Jahan Ali renounced the world and became an ascetic. He died at Bagerhat, Khulna, where his tomb attracts pilgrims. He is also honored at Bidyanandakati, Jessore, where a pond reportedly excavated by Jahan Ali is the site of an annual fair.

JALALUDDIN AHMAD, MOLLAH (1926–1979). A close friend of Sheikh **Mujibur Rahman**, he was a lawyer by profession. A member of the **Muslim League** student organization during the movement for

Pakistan, he was a very active participant and worked extensively during the **Sylhet Referendum**. He left the Muslim League to join the **Awami League** in 1949. Jalaluddin Ahmad was, for nearly 29 years, a member of the Working Committee of the Awami League. He actively supported the **War of Liberation** and after the independence of Bangladesh held a number of ministerial positions. Jalaluddin Ahmad was among the few members of the Awami League who were elected to the National Assembly of Bangladesh in 1979.

JALIL, M. A. (?–1989). He was a freedom fighter in 1971 and later a political figure. In politics, he was at first associated with the **Jatiya Samajtantrik Dal** but changed groups as that party factionalized. At his death, Jalil was the president of the newly formed Jatio Mukti Andolan, which then dissolved.

JAMA'AT-I-ISLAMI. A **political party** generally described as Islamic fundamentalist. It was founded in India in 1941 by Maulana Syed Abu Ala Maududi. It supports the return of the political system to that of the period of the first four caliphs (AD 632–661) and opposed the creation of **Pakistan**, as it believed the Europeanized leaders of the **Muslim League** such as **Muhammad Ali Jinnah** would create a secular state that would be a homeland for the Muslims of India but would not be an Islamic state. For similar reasons, the Jama'at opposed the breakaway of Bangladesh, as it feared the **Awami League**, led by Sheikh **Mujibur Rahman**, would do the same thing. Members of the Jama'at in East Pakistan supported the military action taken by the Pakistan army in 1971. While Maududi's writings and his emphasis on religious purity have had an impact throughout the Islamic world (for example, on the Muslim Brotherhood in Egypt), the party has had but little success in Pakistani elections. Its principal base was in West Pakistan.

In Bangladesh it is among the lesser political groups in electoral terms but has some influence through the network of Islamic organizations. The Jama'at won 20 seats in the 1991 parliamentary **election** and added two more in the separate election for 30 seats for women. It supported the **Bangladesh Nationalist Party (BNP)** in the women's election and thereby permitted the BNP to win the remaining 28 and gain an absolute majority in **parliament**. In 1994, however, it joined with the **Awami League** and the **Jatiya Party** in the opposition's demand that a **caretaker government** be installed prior to the next general election. In the June 1996 election for parliament the party saw a marked decline in the number of seats won, dropping to three. In the 2001 election the Jama'at joined the alliance led by the Bangladesh Nationalist Party along with a faction of the Jatiya Party and a smaller Islamic party and won 17 seats. The alliance as a whole won more than two-thirds of the seats and formed the government. The Jama'at was allotted two seats in the cabinet. In order to participate in the 2008 election it had to change its name to Bangladesh Jama'at-i-Islami and also to change its **constitution** and state the supremacy of secular laws. Bangladesh Jama'at-i-Islami's 2008 election manifesto focused on the following: (1) religious rights for all but criticism of other religions not acceptable; (2) mass education in all religious institutions with an emphasis on *forkania madrasa*; (3) military training under the supervision of armed forces for all between the ages of 20–30; (4) improved financial packages for public servants; (5) write-offs for agricultural loans; and (6) the strengthening of oil and gas exploration. It received only 3.2 million of the total votes and only two of its candidates won the **parliamentary** election. *See also* AZAM, GOLAM.

JAMIL, GOUHAR (?–1980). He was the founder of the Jago Art Centre, an institute of dance, in 1959. He was an expert in Bharatya Natyam and Kathak **dance**. Originally a **Hindu** named Ganesh, he converted to **Islam**.

JASIMUDDIN (1903–1976). A noted Bangladeshi author. He is principally known for his collection of traditional stories about village life, turning them into ballads depicting the joys and sorrows of the Bangladeshi countryside. Jasimuddin's daughter, Husna, is married to **Moudud Ahmed**. *See also* LITERATURE.

JATIYA DAL, JATIYA PARTY. Originally called the Jatiya Dal, the Jatiya Party was formed to support president **Hussain Muhammad Ershad**. The party drew members primarily from the **Bangladesh Nationalist Party (BNP)**, which had been formed to support **Ziaur Rahman**. It also drew some members from the **Awami League**. It is a centrist party and favors **privatization** of many industries that were nationalized during the period of **Mujibur Rahman**. As is the case with most parties formed around an individual, it is weak in organization. The Jatiya Party won a slight majority in the **parliamentary election** of 1986 and an overwhelming majority in the 1988 election, which was largely uncontested by the principal opposition parties. Its parliamentary leader, **Mizanur Rahman Chowdhury**, became prime minister and was later succeeded by **Moudud Ahmed** and **Kazi Zafar Ahmed**.

After the fall of Ershad in December 1990, many of the leaders, including Ershad, were arrested or, at least, sought by the police. Nonetheless the party contested the 1991 election and won 35 seats in parliament, making it the third largest party after the BNP and the Awami League. Mizanur Rahman Chowdhury acted as leader of the party while Ershad was in jail and Moudud Ahmed led the party group in the parliament that was dissolved in November 1995. In the June 1996 election, the Jatiya Party finished a distant third, but it supported the Awami League government. The party has since split into three factions. One faction joined the BNP-led alliance and won two seats in parliament. Moudud Ahmed had defected earlier to the BNP and became a minister in the **Khaleda Zia** ministry in 2001. In the 2001 election Jatiya Party won only 14 seats. Jatiya Party in its 2008 election manifesto expected (1) undertake administrative restructuring to divide the country into eight provinces with provincial assemblies and cabinets; (2) relocate 50 percent of head offices from the capital to other parts of the country; (3) introduce the upazila system of local governments and associated courts; (4) control population and distribute free birth control supplies; (5) register the poor for free distribution of basic foods like rice pulses and edible oil, as well as free medical treatment at the local level; and (6) establish energy security by emphasizing the use of coal. In the 2008 election it once again supported the Awami League alliance and finished third with 27 parliamentary seats.

JATIYA JUKTA FRONT (NATIONAL UNITED FRONT). An alternative political alliance to counter the two major political alliances, one led by the **Awami League** and the other by **Bangladesh Nationalist Party**, the National United Front was formed in

November 2008. This alliance was led by former president **A. Q. M. Badruddoza Chowdhury**, who after resigning from the presidency formed the Bikalpadhara Bangladesh, and Dr. **Kamal Hossain**, who after resigning from the Awami League formed the **Gono Forum**. Other alliance members were the Bangladesh Kaylan Party of Major General (retd.) Syed Muhammad Ibrahim of *Islami Shashantantra*, the Liberal Party, the Zaker Party, and the Forward Party. The National United Front sought to bring about a qualitative change in politics and free the country from three scourges: **corruption**, **terrorism**, and poverty. The alliance had another partner, Krishak Sramik, Janata League (Peasants, Labor, People's League) (KSJL) led by Abdul Kader Siddiqui. The KSJL pulled out of the alliance because of a disagreement over the name *Jukta* Front.

The attempt to form a United Front alliance is of some historical significance. The first **United Front** was a political alliance set up in 1954 and it was a dominant force in the East Pakistan provincial political system. Another United Front was formed in 2005 by Dr. Kamal Hossain, Kader Siddiqui, and A. S. M. Abdur Rob to forge a third-party alliance that did not continue because of differences of opinion and direction of the three leaders. Disagreement over the participation of the Progressive Democratic Party (PDP) of controversial political leader Ferdous Ahmed Qureshi, as well as between Gono Forum and Bikalpadhara Bangladesh, resulted in the breakup of National United Front of 2008.

JATIYA SAMAJTANTRIK DAL (JSD). Established in October 1972, the JSD was organized by Abdur Rab and Shajahan Siraj, who were student leaders at **Dhaka University** and also members of the **Awami League**. Two distinguished members of the Bangladesh army, Colonel **Abu Taher** and Major **M. A. Jalil**, also provided leadership to the party. It opposed the Awami League's **Mujibbad**. The JSD is a socialist and left-leaning **political party** intent on introducing scientific socialism in Bangladesh, and it has comparatively young leaders. It came into prominence as a result of its influence in the army through such units as the Biplobi Sainik Sangsthan (Revolutionary Soldiers Organization) and Biplobi Gana Sena (Revolutionary People's Army). Abu Taher assisted **Ziaur Rahman** in his rise to power. Ziaur Rahman later disassociated himself from Abu Taher and reduced the influence of the JSD within the army. Abu Taher was later executed for alleged treason.

After 1977, the party was banned, but it reemerged in 1978 favoring the **parliamentary** system. It has been characterized as an anti-Indian, anti-**Soviet**, and pro-**Chinese** political party, but this is simplistic. Like many other political parties of Bangladesh, the JSD split into two factions in 1980. One splinter group was called Bangladesh Samajtantrik Dal (BSD) and the other retained the original name. It has since divided further. One of the factions won a single seat in the 1991 election and one in the June 1996 poll. It won no seats in 2001. However in the 2008 election it won three seats.

JATIYO RAKKHI BAHINI (RAKKHI BAHINI). Established by Sheikh **Mujibur Rahman** in mid-1972 as a village paramilitary security force. However, it soon came to be known as the personal security force and political enforcement body of the **Awami League**. It functioned out of the presidential secretariat and reported directly to Sheikh Mujibur Rahman. Deemed by the Supreme Court of Bangladesh to be an organization that functioned without any rules of procedure or code of conduct, it was disbanded after the first military coup, which took place in **August 1975**.

JATRA. A theatrical form of folk opera using **music** and **dance**. The term is also applied to spoken drama. The content is most often devoted to the Krishna legend and to the devotion described in the adha-Krishna **literature**. Some of the plots are drawn from the writings of **Chaitanya**. The usual instrumental accompaniment is a drum, a flute, and a harmonium.

JAYADEVA (JAIDEV). A poet at the **Sena** court in the late 12th century. He was the author of the still popular *Gita Govinda*, a lyrical work based on the story of Radha and Krishna, the milkmaid and the god. *See also* CHAITANYA.

JESSORE. A district town in western Bangladesh located on the Bhairab River. Jessore in Bangladesh was formed from four subdivisions of the former Jessore district of united Bengal (the four subdivisions are named in the last sentence of this entry). Vikramaditya, a counselor of **Daud Khan Karrani**, was awarded a land grant that included the area of Jessore. According to legend, Vikramaditya named the place Yasohara ("glory depriving"), as he said it decreased the prestige of the Karrani ruler. Yasohara was corrupted to Jessore. **Pratapaditya**, one of the **Bara Bhuiyan**, was the son of Vikramaditya. An earlier village, Kasba, was formally renamed Jessore when it became a district town about 1790. There are some older buildings, including the Rajbari of Chanchra and the shrines of pirs Bahram Shah and Gharib Shah. A local college is named for **Michael Madhusudan Dutt**, as the writer was born in Jessore. Bidyanandakati has a tank that is a festival site for **Jahan Ali Khan**. Bara Bazaar was once a center for **Buddhist** studies. At Muhammadpur (originally Mahmudpur) are the remains of buildings, including a temple to Krishna erected by Sitaram Roy, one of the **Bara Bhuiyan**. With the reorganization of **local government** during the **Hussain Muhammad Ershad** regime, Jessore district was divided into Jessore, Narail, Magura, and Jhenidah districts.

JINNAH, MUHAMMAD ALI (1876–1948). Known also as Quaid-i-Azam (great leader) by his admirers in **Pakistan** and in the **Muslim League**, he was the leader of the league in its struggle for the partition of **India** and the formation of a separate Pakistan. A London-trained barrister, he entered politics as a member of the Indian National Congress but joined the Muslim League as well in 1913. He was a key figure in the negotiation of an agreement between the Congress and the league in 1916 on the question of **separate electorates** for Muslims, which, through the agreement, the Congress then accepted. Jinnah left the Congress in 1920 and, except for some time in the early 1930s, continued to work for a special status for the Muslims whom he saw as a nation in India separate from the **Hindus**.

With independence in 1947, Jinnah became governor-general of Pakistan, a post he held until his death on 11 September 1948. Jinnah visited East Bengal only once as governor-general (in March 1948) and he angered many East Bengalis by stating, among other things, that Urdu would be the only official language of Pakistan. The statement touched off the **language movement**. Although his goal was a separate state for the Muslims of India, he at no time supported the concept of an Islamic state; in religious matters, Jinnah was a secularist.

JONES, SIR WILLIAM (1746–1794). He studied Hebrew, Arabic, and Persian at Oxford, but for personal financial reasons took up the study of law and became a commissioner for bankruptcy, for which he was knighted. He went to India in 1783 as a judge of the Supreme Court. In 1784, he founded the Asiatic Society of Bengal. He studied Sanskrit to improve his understanding of Hindu traditional law and used Arabic to study Muslim law. His studies resulted in two works: *Muhammadan Law of Inheritance* (1792) and *Institutes of Hindu Law* (1794). His studies helped him see similarities in Greek and Sanskrit, leading him to postulate that the two languages had a common origin. He is thus considered the founder of comparative philology. He translated a number of works from Sanskrit to English, such as Kalidasa's *Shakuntala*. He clearly earned his title "Oriental Jones." *See also* ASIATIC SOCIETY OF BANGLADESH.

JUTE. A fibrous plant grown extensively in Bengal that yields a fiber used for cordage and sacking. The **East India Company** encouraged its production and export by the end of the 18th century. Prior to the partition of 1947, the bulk of the production was in eastern Bengal, and the processing factories were in the **Kolkata** region or abroad in such cities as Dundee in Scotland. Principal areas of production are in Rangpur, Pabna, Dhaka, Mymensingh, Faridpur, and Comilla. After 1947, East Bengal erected processing factories such as the **Adamjee Jute Mill**, the world's largest. As it had been owned by a West Pakistan–based concern, it was nationalized after Bangladeshi independence. Continued operational losses led the government to close the mill on 30 June 2002. More recent uses for the fiber have been found in carpet backing. Development of plastic sacking significantly reduced the demand for jute as a container but with increasing demand for green products demand for jute in the world market is likely to increase. In 2008, Bangladesh produced 5.1 million tons of jute in 4.9 million hectares of land. However new product research and marketing is essential for the revival of jute as a major export product. *See also* AGRICULTURE.

– K –

KABIR, ALAMGIR (1938–1989). He was the first president of the **Film** Institute, which he founded in 1969. A student of electrical engineering at Oxford University in the late 1950s, he went on to become a major figure in the world of filmmaking in Bangladesh. England changed him in two major ways. He became interested in filmmaking and leftist movements. Ingmar Bergman's film *The Seventh Seal* channeled him into films and filmmaking. During his stay in **Great Britain** he joined the Communist Party. A reporter for the *Daily Worker*, he was credited with interviewing Fidel Castro of Cuba. He also joined the wars of liberation of Palestine and Algeria. The French government jailed him for eight months. While in London he formed the **East Pakistan** House and the East Bengal Liberation Front. Kabir returned to East Pakistan in 1966 and promptly involved himself in the leftist movement and was jailed for his activities. Between 1966 and 1971 he became a reporter for the *Pakistan Observer* and later an editor of the weekly *Express*. His specialization was reviewing and critiquing films. During the **War of Liberation**, he worked as the chief reporter for the Bangladesh government-in-exile. He was the English newscaster on Swadhin Bangla Beter (Independent Bangladesh Radio). In 1973, he pioneered a new trend in Bangladeshi cinema through his first film, *Dhire Bahe Meghna* (Quietly Flows the Meghna). Among his short films of note are *The Liberation Fighter* and *Pogrom in Bangladesh*. He authored *Films in East Pakistan* and *Films in Bangladesh*. He died in a road accident. *See also* FILM.

KABIR, HUMAYUN (1906–1969). From **Faridpur** district, he was a member of the Bengal Legislative Council, 1937–1947, and was deputy leader of the **Krishak Praja Party (KPP)** under **Fazlul Haq**. He was educated in **Kolkata** and at Oxford. Kabir was closely associated with Maulana Abul Kalam Azad, the Congress Party president, for whom he served as secretary during the Simla Conference in 1946. He chose to remain in **India**, where he became educational adviser to the government (1952–1956) and minister of education in the central government (1958–1965) after Azad's death. Kabir wrote extensively on literature and history. Perhaps his most noted volume was *Muslim Politics, 1906–42*, first published in 1944. He was also involved in the preparation of Azad's *India Wins Freedom* and followed Azad's instructions to withhold parts of the book until after Jawaharlal Nehru's death; the withheld portions have since been published. Kabir's brothers took different directions at independence: Jahangir remained in India and became a member of the Bengal Legislative Assembly; Alamgir and Akbar held official positions in **East Pakistan** and Bangladesh.

KABIR, KHAIRUL (?–1997). He was the founder of the National Press Club, for which he was accorded the first lifetime membership of the club. He was also the founder-editor of the *Daily Shangbad.* He was one of the authors of the Awami League Six-Point Program that is the foundation document for the provincial autonomy demand of **East Pakistan** and a key document in the independence march of Bangladesh.

KAIKOBAD (1857–1951). He was given the title of great poet for his work entitled *Mohashoshan* (or Great Funeral Pyre). His actual name was Muhammad Kazem Al-Quarashi. He received numerous awards and was the president of the Bengal Muslim **Literature** Society.

KAISAR, SHAHIDULLAH (1927–1971). Journalist and novelist. He was born in Feni district and educated at Presidency College, **Calcutta**. After partition in 1947, he worked for the *Weekly Ittefaq*, edited by Maulana **Bhashani**, and later for *Sangbad* until his death at the hands of the pro-Pakistani group Al-Badr. Kaisar's novels earned him an award from the Bangla Academy. *See also* LITERATURE.

KAISER, KHAWJA MUHAMMAD (1918–1985). A member of the Indian Police Service, he joined the **Pakistan** Foreign Service in 1950. He served as Pakistani ambassador to Switzerland, Denmark, and Norway and was high commissioner to Australia and New Zealand. As ambassador to **China** in 1971, Kaiser switched his allegiance from Pakistan to Bangladesh. From 1976 to 1982 he was the permanent representative of Bangladesh to the United Nations. He resigned from service in 1982 but was later called on by Bangladesh to be its ambassador to China. Kaiser was instrumental in improving the relationship between China and Bangladesh. He was offered the presidency of Bangladesh by General **Hussain Muhammad Ershad** but refused.

KAMRUZZAMAN, A. H. M. (1926–1975). Assassinated in what is known as the **Dhaka jail killings**, he was president of the **Awami League** in 1974. A member of the first provisional government of Bangladesh, he also served as the Bangladesh commerce minister. Kamruzzaman was elected to the National Assembly of Pakistan in 1962.

KANAI, PAGLA (1809–1889). A legendary folk (*baul*) singer who started to write songs at a very early age, he is recognized for his devotional songs and his spirituality and mysticism. A total of 419 of his songs exist, although these need to be properly preserved or they will be lost. His songs are identified as *jari*, *dhua*, *pala gaan*, *kobi gaan*, *murshidi*, *marfati*, and *Islamic*. He had many disciples and numerous scholars have carried out research on his life and mysticism. Pagla Kanai was born in Madhabpur village in Jhenidah district and his burial site is considered a *mazaar* (shrine) where an annual festival is held in his memory. *See also* MUSIC.

KANSA (BELL-METAL). A traditional industry in Tangail district for producing home utensils like dinner plates, bowls, and pitchers, and also some decorative artwork and musical instruments, it is dying primarily due to dramatic fall in demand. Competition is primarily from similar articles produced from glass, ceramic, melamine, and steel. The Kansa products were produced in family-owned blacksmith shops. In the last decade of the 20th century there were over 100 Kansa shops, but in 2009 there were only two. Some of the more prominent areas of Tangail where Kansa articles were made included Kagnari, Kalipur, Mogra, and Charabari.

KANSAT MOVEMENT. This is a peasant movement that emerged in the township of Kansat, in Chapai Nawabganj district of Rajshahi, from September 2005 to April 2006. The peasants were seeking redress from power shortages and irregularities and **corruption** of the Rural Electrification Board. When the peasants formed a committee

(The Action Committee for Rural Power Development) to put forth their demands and took to the streets of Kansat, they were fired upon on three different occasions by the police, resulting in the death of more than 20 people. Once the male leaders of the protest were arrested, the movement became primarily a **women**'s movement (both leadership and participants). The initial demands for an adequate supply of electricity were later extended to a greater supply of diesel, fertilizers, and seeds, the reduction of the price of essential goods, and political freedom. In order to contain the movement, the government of Bangladesh acceded to the demands, although it is difficult to assess to what extent these concessions were implemented.

KANTHA or *KATHA*. An elaborately embroidered quilt used by **Buddhist** monks, **Hindu** yogis, Muslim fakirs, and **Baul** syncretists, as well as ordinary folk. It is made of several pieces of cloth stitched together to be used as a cover or shawl. From a utilitarian craft it has become a work of art known as *nakshi kantha* (artistic quilt). The art form became better known when the poet **Jasimuddin** published his well-known work *Naksha Kathar Math* (The Fields of the Embroidered Quilt). Samples of the quilts can be found in several places, including the **Dhaka** Museum and in the private collection of the family of **Zainul Abedin**. The oldest kantha dates from about 1850. Designs include animals, trees, leaves, flowers, and abstract forms.

KAPTAI HYDROELECTRIC STATION. *See* KARNAPHULI RIVER.

KARATOYA RIVER. Rises in Jalpaiguri district of West Bengal and flows through **Rangpur** and **Bogra** before flowing into the **Brahmaputra**. It bisects the Bogra region and serves as an important source of irrigation water and as a major waterway.

KARIM, ENAYET (1927–1974). A member of the **Pakistan** Foreign Service, he was deputy chief of mission and the highest-ranking Bengali officer in the Pakistan embassy in Washington in 1971. Although ill with heart disease, he led the Bengali officers who defected from the embassy. Karim was foreign secretary of Bangladesh at the time of his death.

KARIM, NAZMUL (1922–1982). Educationist. He studied at **Dhaka,** Columbia University, and the London School of Economics. His work as a sociologist and political scientist was well received in academic circles. Karim's major work was *The Dynamics of Bangladesh Society.*

KARMANTA. In present-day **Comilla** district, the city was a capital of the **Chandra dynasty.**

KARNAPHULI RIVER. It rises in **Burma** and flows through the **Chittagong Hill Tracts** to the port of **Chittagong.** That city is 12 miles from the mouth but the river's depth is sufficient for ocean-going vessels. For smaller draft vessels, the river is navigable to Rangamati in the Hill Tracts. On the river is the Kaptai hydroelectric station, the only significant hydroelectric plant in Bangladesh.

KARRANI DYNASTY. Established in 1563 by its leader, Taj Khan Karrani, brother of a Karrani ruler of southern Bihar. They were north Indian Afghans who fled to Bengal after the recapture of Delhi by Humayun, the **Mughal** emperor, in 1554. Taj Khan defeated the remnants of the Suri dynasty who had maintained control in Bengal. Taj Khan died in the same year as his victory and was succeeded by his brother, Sulaiman Khan, who ruled until 1573. Mughal armies during the reign of Akbar defeated the Karranis in 1575. **Daud Khan**, the last Karrani sultan (1573–1575), however, made one more attempt against the Mughals and was defeated, captured, and executed in the battle of **Rajmahal** in 1576. *See also* SHER SHAH SURI.

KASTIGAR GIRLS HIGH SCHOOL. Located in **Chittagong**, it is the first girl's school of Chittagong. In 2007 it celebrated its 100th year. Among it alumni are revolutionaries like Pritilata Waddedar, Kalpana Dutta (Joshi), Nibedita Nag, and Joshanara Rahman, the wife of language movement hero Mahbub Ul Alam Chowdhury; authors like Moitreyi Devi and Umar Tul Fazal; and politicians like Ivy Rahman, who was killed on 21 August 2005 when hand grenades were thrown at a public meeting of the Awami League. **Sheikh Hasina Wajed**, leader of the Awami League, was injured.

KAZEM ALI MIAN (1852–1926). An educationist, he was responsible for the founding of several schools in **Chittagong**, including a middle school and a high school using English as the medium of instruction. Kazem Ali was also a member of the Central Legislative Assembly in the 1920s.

KAZI, BEGUM ZOHRA (1912–2007). She finished secondary school in 1926 and was admitted to the Aligarh University, where she completed her intermediate examination in science with distinction. She was the first Muslim female who received a stipend from the university as a reward for her academic excellence. In 1935, she received a medical degree from the Lady Harding Medical Collage for **Women**. The first medical college for women in Asia was established by the then-viceroy of India, Lord Harding, and named after his wife. As she obtained first class first in Bachelors of Medicine, Bachelors of Surgery (MBBS), the British government awarded her the prestigious Viceroy's Medal. She also received a scholarship from the central government of what was then India. Zohra's only sister, Shirin Kazi, was also a physician.

Zohra started her profession as a voluntary gynecologist at Sebashram, a charity organization established by Mahatma Gandhi that provided free medical care for the poor. Later, in 1949, she received another proposal to join Dhaka Medical College as their resident surgeon. She agreed and joined as the only Bengali Muslim doctor. In 1964 the **Pakistan** government conferred Zohra with the title "Taghma-e-Pakistan" for her contribution in the **health-care** field. Being the first female Bengali doctor of the country, she had many opportunities to work in different areas within health care. She became the head of the gynecology department of Dhaka Medical College and Hospital. Zohra also worked as an honorary colonel of the Combined Military Hospital and taught as an honorary professor of Holy Family Hospital and Bangladesh Medical College. The Bangladeshi government awarded her the Begum Rokeya Padak while the Bangladesh Medical Association honored her with a gold medal for her outstanding contribution to humanity and medical services.

KEITH, JAMES (1784–1822). Grammarian and missionary. He came to **Calcutta** in 1816 as a member of the London Missionary Society.

His Bengali work, *A Grammar of the Bengalee Language Adapted to the Young in Easy Questions and Answers* (1820), was the first grammar in Bengali. It was used widely in the schools.

KENDRIYA KHELA GHAR ASAR. Established on 2 May 1952, it is the oldest organization for showcasing children's talents. Since 1971, its mission has also been to make children knowledgeable about the philosophy and ideology of the **War of Liberation** and to prepare children to take a leadership role in the future development of the country. In 2008, a special effort was made to give the organization a national scope by attracting new membership from all parts of the country.

KHAFILUDDIN AHMAD (1899–1972). He joined the **Muslim League** in 1926 but resigned from the party in 1939 because of the domination of the **Nawab of Dhaka family**. He was law minister in the 1954 **United Front** cabinet. In 1956, Khafiluddin joined the **Awami League** and was arrested by the martial law authorities in 1958. He reemerged in politics in 1970 when he was elected a member of the National Assembly of Pakistan. During the liberation movement, Khafiluddin was a member of the Bangladesh provisional government-in-exile.

KHAIRAT HUSAIN (1911–1972). A founding member of the **Awami League**. He participated as a member of the **Muslim League** in the Lahore session of the Muslim League in 1940, which called for a separate state for the Muslims of India. For his support of the **language movement**, he was jailed by the government of **Pakistan** for 18 months. During the first martial law period in Pakistan beginning in 1958 he was placed in custody. In 1962 Khairat Husain established the National Democratic Front. In 1970 he served as the secretary of the Pakistan National League, which was founded by **Ataur Rahman Khan**.

KHALEDA ZIA (1945–). Prime minister of Bangladesh from March 1991 to March 1996 and again from October 2001 to October 2006, she was born 29 August 1945 in Jalpaiguri (now in West Bengal), although her family is from Feni district in Bangladesh. She attended school in **Dinajpur**. She married **Ziaur Rahman**, an officer in the Pakistani army, in 1960. She was kept under house arrest by the Pakistani authorities during the 1971 **War of Liberation**, in which her husband played a leading role in the **Mukti Bahini**. She entered politics after Ziaur Rahman's assassination, joining the **Bangladesh Nationalist Party (BNP)** on 3 January 1982. In March 1983 Khaleda Zia was named senior vice chairperson, and on 10 May 1984, chairperson of the party.

Khaleda Zia was consistent in her opposition to the regime of **Hussain Muhammad Ershad**, and the BNP did not participate in the **elections** held in 1986 (as the **Awami League** did) and 1988 during Ershad's rule. She was arrested seven times. Following the fall of Ershad in December 1990, a general election was held in February 1991. The BNP won a majority of seats in parliament and she became prime minister on 20 March 1991. She resigned the office on 24 November 1995, in the face of the opposition demand for new elections to be held under a **caretaker government**. In the June 1996 election the BNP finished second to the Awami League, which formed the new government with the support of the **Jatiya Party**, and Khaleda became the leader of the opposition. In the October 2001 election the BNP and its allies won a two-thirds majority in parliament and Khaleda again became prime minister.

It is known that following the 1991 election Khaleda favored a continuance of the presidential form of government modifying the dictatorial system to which the presidential form had evolved during the Ershad regime. However, the results of the election in which the BNP fell short of a majority of the popular vote made the direct election of a president, Khaleda herself, doubtful, and she accepted a return to the parliamentary system and retained the office of prime minister. In her current role as prime minister she has clearly shown that she has a stronger grip on governance and at the same time appears to rely on her cabinet ministers to a greater extent. She, however, let her eldest son **Tarique Rahman** play an increasingly larger role both in party affairs and in governance, which negatively impacted her ability to govern. The 2001–2006 BNP government was riddled with charges of **corruption**. For nearly a year during the **caretaker government** (2006–2008) period she was jailed for charges of corruption. There was a serious attempt on the part of the caretaker government to remove her from politics and exile her to Saudi Arabia. Khaleda Zia resisted all such attempts. In the election of 2008, BNP won only 30 seats and she once again became the leader of the opposition. *See also* MINUS TWO POLITICS.

KHALIQUZZAMAN, CHAUDHURY (1889–1973). A **Muslim League** politician from the United Provinces (now Uttar Pradesh), where he gained prominence. He migrated to **Pakistan** in 1948 and succeeded **Muhammad Ali Jinnah** as president of the Muslim League later that year. He was governor of **East Bengal**, 1953–1954.

KHALJI, IKHTIYARUDDIN MUHAMMAD BAKHTIYAR (?–1206). A leader in the army of the Slave dynasty of the **Delhi Sultanate**. He defeated the last **Sena** king in 1202 at Nadia and brought Bengal under the control of the sultanate. His later excursion through **Assam** toward Tibet ended in failure in 1205.

KHAN, ABUL KASEM (1905–1991). He headed the largest Bangladeshi industrial establishment. The A. K. Khan group was the only indigenous East Pakistani group ranked among the 30 largest Pakistani industrial, commercial, and financial houses in the 1960s. After Bangladeshi independence, many holdings were nationalized during the regime of Sheikh **Mujibur Rahman**, but the group has remained important and some properties were returned during the regime of **Hussain Muhammad Ershad**. A. K. Khan himself was a minister from 1958 to 1962 in the **Ayub Khan** regime.

KHAN, AKHTAR HAMEED (1914–1999). He began his career as a member of the prestigious Indian Civil Service, but his interests soon were centered on the development of poorer areas in newly independent **Pakistan**. In 1959, he was sent to **East Pakistan** to establish what is now known as the **Bangladesh Academy of Rural Development (BARD)**. His work was recognized internationally and he was a recipient of the Magsaysay Award. After Bangladesh independence he moved to Karachi, where he became the head of the urban Karachi program known as the Orangi Pilot Project.

KHAN, ASHRAFUZZAMAN (1910–2008). A former director general of Bangladesh Betar (Bangladesh Radio), he is recognized for his rebelliousness in leaving the Dhaka Radio station to protest the decision of the East Pakistan government not to air the historic 7 March 1971 speech of Sheikh **Mujibur Rahman**.

KHAN, ENAYETULLAH (1939–2005). He is the founder-editor and publisher of the daily newspaper *New Age* (2003) and the editor-in-chief of the weekly *Holiday* (1965). He started his journalism career as a cub reporter for the *Pakistan Observer* in 1959. From 1975 to 1977 he was also the editor of the *Bangladesh Times*. He was also a president of the National Press Club. Two days after the end of the **War of Liberation** on 16 December 1971, he formed a committee to investigate the assassination of Bangladeshi intellectuals by the armed forces of **Pakistan** and their local collaborators like the groups Al-Badr and Al-Shams. An activist with an imposing personality, he was associated with **Maulana Bhashani**'s Farakka March and worked against all forms of communalism. During the Sheikh **Mujibur Rahman** era he opposed the extremes of Rakkhi Bahini. He also served as a minister under the military rule of General **Ziaur Rahman** and as Bangladesh ambassador to **Myanmar**, Cambodia, North Korea, and **China**.

As a student leader he served as the general secretary of the Ananda Mohan College Student Union of **Mymensingh**, as vice president of Dhaka Hall, and as a member of the **Dhaka University** Students Union. His father was Justice Abdul Jabbar Khan, who served as speaker of the Pakistan National Assembly.

KHAN FAMILY OF BRAHMANBARIA. A lineage of musicians starting with Aftabuddin Khan (1862–1933), who earned the title *faqir* (in this case, saint). He had the ability to bridge classical and folk **music**. He was joined by two brothers: Ustad Alauddin Khan (d. 1972) and Ustad Ayat Ali Khan (1884–1967). The two brothers modernized **musical instruments** such as the *chandra sorong*, the *mantranad*, and the *monohara*. The brothers also introduced several new *ragas* and were pioneers in bringing the classical music of the subcontinent to the West. They established the Alauddin Music

College in **Comilla** and Brahmanbaria. Other members of the family include Bahadur Hossain Khan (1931–1991), the son of Ayat Ali, and Khadem Hossain Khan (1922–1990).

KHAN, FAZLUR RAHMAN (1929–1982). Architect and structural engineer, he is best known for his design of the Sears Tower in Chicago. He studied at what is now the Bangladesh University of Engineering and Technology and in the **United States**. Khan developed the "tube in tube" design that is used in most modern skyscrapers.

KHANDAKAR, MUKARRAM HUSSAIN (1922–1972). Educationist. Born in **Dhaka**, he was educated in Dhaka and Durham, England. A chemist, he did major research in plastics, food, and road and building materials.

KHARGA DYNASTY. It ruled in the **Vanga** and **Samatata** regions of southern and eastern Bengal in the latter part of the seventh century. Badkamta in the **Comilla** district appears to have been the royal seat.

KHILAFAT MOVEMENT (1919–1925). A Muslim movement after World War I in which many Indian Muslims demanded that the status of the caliph, who was also the sultan of Turkey, be unchanged following the defeat of the Ottoman Empire in the war. The principal leader of the movement was Muhammad Ali Jauhar. Mahatma Gandhi brought the Indian National Congress into the movement as well in an effort to strengthen Hindu-Muslim unity. Differences between the two communities, however, were so great that the net result may have been an increase in communal friction. Although a Shia, **Syed Amir Ali** supported the Khilafat movement. The question became moot when the Turks, led by Kemal Atatürk, settled the question by ending both the caliphate and the sultanate.

KHULNA. A city and regional and district headquarters, Khulna is the third-largest city in Bangladesh, with a population of about 1.5 million. Khulna lies on the Bhairab River. Nearby is the port of Mangla, a manmade anchorage that serves as the second port of Bangladesh after **Chittagong**. The anchorage was originally situated at Chalna, about 26 miles from Khulna, and opened in 1950. In 1954, the anchorage was shifted to Mangla, about 12 miles from Chalna. In practice the two names are used interchangeably. Khulna itself is an important river port and is connected with **Barisal**, Madaripur, Narayanganj, and **Dhaka**.

In ancient times, Khulna was a part of **Vanga** or **Samatata**. Local traditions associate Khulna with Khanja Ali (also known as Khan **Jahan Ali**), who obtained a *zamindari* in the area in the mid-15th century from the rulers of **Gaur**. Khulna is the home district of **Pratapaditya**, one of the **Bara Bhuiyan** who rebelled against **Mughal** rule in the latter part of the 16th century. **Architectural** monuments in Bagerhat (formerly a subdivisional headquarters and now a district headquarters) include the Sathgumbad Mosque and the tomb of Khan Jahan Ali. In Khulna is the Navaratna temple.

With the **local government** reorganization during the **Hussain Muhammad Ershad** regime, the former Khulna district was divided into the Khulna, Bagerhat, and Satkhira districts. Satkhira before 1947 had been a subdivision of the Twenty-Four Parganas district, now in West Bengal.

KIBRIA, SHAH A. M. S. (1933–2005). Member of **parliament**, he was assassinated in a grenade attack in his electoral constituency of Habiganj, Sylhet, on 27 January 2005. He was one of the university students who were jailed during the **language movement** of 1952. He joined the foreign service of **Pakistan** in 1954. During the **War of Liberation** he was in Washington, D.C., as a member of the Pakistan Embassy. He left the Pakistan Embassy in support of Bangladesh and in 1972 he became the foreign secretary of Bangladesh. In 1978 he once again became the foreign secretary. He served as high commissioner to Australia and also the permanent representative of Bangladesh to the **United Nations** agencies in Geneva. While there, he became the chairman of the Group of 77. From 1981 to 1992 he became the executive secretary of the United Nations Economic and Social Commission for Asia and the Pacific. He joined the **Awami League** and became the finance minister from 1996 to 2001. After the Awami League lost the parliamentary election of 2001, he continued to be a member of the Advisory Council of the Awami League but also became the founder-editor of a weekly magazine,

Mridubhasan (Softly Spoken), that allowed him to speak on behalf of the country. *See also* FOREIGN POLICY.

KOLKATA. *See* CALCUTTA.

KRISHAK PRAJA PARTY (KPP) (PEASANTS' AND PEOPLE'S PARTY). The political vehicle of **Fazlul Haq** before Indian independence. It was founded in 1927 and formally structured prior to the 1937 elections. Intended to be non-communal, the KPP, in fact, received little non-Muslim support. The KPP found its base among the peasants, principally in eastern Bengal, and it opposed the landlord system. The difficulty of the time was that the restrictive franchise rules made most of the peasants, many of them tenants, ineligible to vote. The KPP also opposed the landlord-dominated **Muslim League**. The party won about one-third of the seats in the Bengal Legislative Assembly but was able to form a coalition with the Muslim League and govern Bengal until 1941. The Muslim League withdrew in that year, but the KPP joined with non-Congress Hindus and others and continued in office until 1943. At that time, a Muslim League–led ministry replaced it. In the 1945 election the party did poorly, although Fazlul Haq retained his seat. The party disappeared at the time of independence in 1947. Haq, however, formed the **Krishak Sramik Party (KSP)** after independence.

KRISHAK SRAMIK PARTY (KSP) (PEASANTS' AND WORKERS' PARTY). A revival by **Fazlul Haq** of the **Krishak Praja Party (KPP)**. Fazlul Haq became advocate general of East Bengal briefly after independence, and he had temporarily dropped out of party politics. With the approach of the provincial assembly elections in 1954, he returned to active politics and formed the KSP. The party continued to champion the cause of the peasants who had, in many cases, gained ownership of their land through *zamindari* abolition. Also, this election, unlike pre-independence elections, would be held under universal adult franchise, although **separate electorates** would remain. The KSP joined with the **Awami League** in the **United Front**, which trounced the **Muslim League** in the election.

The KSP leader was chosen as the first chief minister under the United Front, but Fazlul Haq was soon ousted from office by the central government. With the revival of the suspended assembly in 1956, **Abu Hussain Sarkar** of the KSP became chief minister, but the United Front had divided, and Sarkar and **Ataur Rahman Khan** of the Awami League alternated chief ministerships until martial law was imposed in October 1958. Fazlul Haq died in 1962, about the same time that party activity was again permitted. KSP continued to exist for a time after his death, but it was a small, unimportant group.

KUNDU, NITAN (1935–2006). Artist and sculptor, he was well known for his innovation and creativity. Among his most important works are the *Shahbash* Bangladesh (Well Done Bangladesh) at Rajshahi University, *Shampan* (a type of boat) in Chittagong, and **South Asian Association for Regional Cooperation** and *Kadamphul* (a type of flower) Fountains in **Dhaka**. In his works he attempted to push the youth of Bangladesh toward higher achievements, to integrate traditional culture with modernity, and to highlight progress and advancement through the use of symbols and representation. During the **War of Liberation** he served as the chief designer of posters and banners at the **United States** Information Service and in that capacity he assisted numerous artists and students. He created works of art that helped to strengthen the struggle for independence. His poster of a young working-class Bengali holding a rifle is viewed as the standard-bearer of the revolution and is an inspiration to the youth of Bangladesh. While at heart an artist and sculptor, Kundu was also a very accomplished businessman. In 1974 he started a furniture company, Otobi, which is one of the leading furniture manufacturing firms of Bangladesh. He used a combination of wood and metal in his design and manufacture of furniture. For his contribution to the world of art, he received the **Ekushey Padak** in 1997.

KUSHTIA. Kushtia district was a part of Nadia district (now a district in West Bengal) prior to the partition of 1947. With the reorganization of **local government** during the **Hussain Muhammad Ershad** government, it was divided into three districts: Kushtia, Chuadanga, and Meherpur, the three subdivisions that had been part of Nadia. It is the home district of **Haji Shariatullah** of the **Faraizi movement**, and of **Lalon Shah**, whose tomb is at Sevria, near Kushtia town.

The Kushtia area, along with Jessore, is the base of the **Ganges-Kobadak** pump irrigation project through which water is pumped from the Ganges just inside the Bangladesh border with India to water fields. The project is threatened by the shortage of water during the dry season by the **Farakka barrage** erected by India.

– L –

LAHORE RESOLUTION. Passed on 23 March 1940, by the **Muslim League**. It is often called the **Pakistan** resolution, although the word Pakistan does not appear in the document. The resolution stated that, if conditions for the Muslims of **India** did not improve, the league would have no alternative but to call for the creation of independent states in the eastern and northwestern Indian areas that had a Muslim majority in the population. The plural "states" was used in 1940, with the implication that there would not be a single Muslim state. At a meeting of Muslim League legislators, this was modified in 1946 to the singular "state" and a single state was created by the partition of India in 1947. **Fazlul Haq** was among the movers of the resolution in 1940; **Husain Shahid Suhrawardy** supported the alteration in 1946.

LAILI, QAMRUNNAHAR (1937–1984). One of the earliest female lawyers, she entered the **Dhaka** bar in 1963 and in 1973 was the first **woman** member of the council of the Bangladesh bar. Laili was also one of the founders of the **National Awami Party**.

LAKNAUTI, LAKSHMANAVATI. *See* GAUDA.

LAKSHMANA SENA. The last member of the **Sena dynasty** to rule from Nadia. He ascended to the throne in about 1184 and shortly afterward subdued Kamarupa (**Assam**). He was a patron of the arts; the poet **Jayadeva** wrote the *Gita Govinda* at his court. He and his governance, however, declined, and his capital was taken by an army of the **Delhi Sultanate** led by **Ikhtiyaruddin Muhammad Bakhtiyar Khalji** in 1202. Lakshmana Sena fled to eastern Bengal, where his successors reigned for about 50 years until all of Bengal came under Muslim rule.

LALMAI. *See* MAINAMATI.

LALON SHAH (?–1890). A syncretistic folk poet and composer. His poetry and songs are considered treasures of Bengali **literature**. A district gazetteer stated that he "combined in himself all that was best in **Hinduism** and **Islam**." At his tomb at Sevria, near **Kushtia**, his disciples assemble for an annual festival of music and poetry. His songs describe the lives of ordinary people going about their daily lives of cultivating and fishing. **Rabindranath Tagore** acknowledged that he was greatly influenced by Lalon. Verses of Lalon are known as *Kalaams*. In many of his verses Lalon focused on how to go beyond the physical to the metaphysical state. Estimates of the number of songs composed by Lalon varies from 2,000 to a high of 10,000, of which only about 800 songs are generally considered authentic Lalon and even those are disputed. Lalon Shah's tunes are also the subject of controversy but it is generally accepted that the Akharai tradition is authentic. Those who sing his songs have also blended classical and Western music into their presentation.

LAND FRAGMENTATION. This phenomenon results primarily from Islamic inheritance rules. In the usual pattern, on the death of a landholder the land is divided among his children, with sons receiving a full share and daughters a halfshare. As the land inherited is not of uniform quality, an effort is made to share the land so that each inheritor will receive shares of the best, the middling, and the poorest land. The outcome is that an heir may receive three or four or more small parcels of land as an inheritance. The result over several generations is evident. Government data (1977 agricultural census) indicate that most holdings contain six to nine fragments, and about 10 percent contain 20 or more. In 1983–1984 the average holding (of those who owned land) was 2.2 acres; if the landless were included in the calculation, the average holding would be much less. Fragmentation was not addressed in the 1996 agricultural census.

Related to land fragmentation is the size of land holdings. Eighty percent of land holdings are less than 2.49 acres and over 50 percent of households involved in agricultural production are landless, which is defined as owning less than 0.05 hectares of land. Less than .05 percent of the landholders held 25 or more acres. *See also* LAND REFORM.

LAND REFORM. The **Permanent Settlement** of 1793 converted tax-farmers into landowners (*zamindars*). Most land in Bengal was owned by zamindars (often absentee), and most tillers were either sharecropping tenants or landless laborers. After Pakistani independence in 1951, an East Bengal Land Reform Act was passed that limited holdings of a cultivating family to 100 *bighas* (33 acres). In September 1984, the **Hussain Muhammad Ershad** regime decreed a new land reform ordinance under which the maximum permissible holding was reduced generally to 60 bighas (20 acres). Surplus land was to be distributed to the landless and to very small holders, but the amount of surplus land was estimated at less than half a million acres. *See also* LAND FRAGMENTATION.

LANGUAGE. Bangladesh is, for all practical purposes, a unilingual nation and is therefore unique among the nations of South Asia. All primary and much secondary and higher **education** is taught in Bengali, locally known as Bangla. Other languages used in Bangladesh include English and several tribal languages.

Bengali belongs to the easternmost branch of the Indo-European family of languages known as Indo-Aryan. Its direct ancestor is Magadhi Prakrit, which descended from Sanskrit and is also the ancestor of Bihari, Assamese, and Oriya. While Sanskrit remained the language of culture and **literature** for centuries, the spoken language varied considerably from region to region in northern India. By no later than the middle of the 10th century a distinctive Bengali language had developed. Little literature remains from this period.

At present, Bengali has two literary styles: *Sudhobhasa* ("elegant language") and *Chaltibhasa* ("daily language"). The former continues the literary style of Middle Bengali of the 16th century. The latter is largely a creation of the 20th century and is based on the cultivated dialect spoken by residents of **Calcutta** and its region. The difference between the two as literary styles is not sharp. The vocabulary is largely the same; the difference lies mainly in the forms of the pronoun and the verb. Sudhobhasa has the older forms, while Chaltibhasa uses lighter and more modern forms. Sudhobhasa shows a partiality for lexical words and for compound words similar to Sanskrit. Chaltibhasa was first seriously taken up at the urging of **Rabindranath Tagore** during the early years of the 20th century.

Soon after, Tagore all but discarded Sudhubhasa, and Chaltibhasa is now generally favored by writers. The script is based on that of early Sanskrit (*devanagiri*) although the variation is significant. The present form can be dated from the first casting of type by Charles Wilkins in 1778, although since then there have been some changes. *See also* LANGUAGE MOVEMENT.

LANGUAGE MOVEMENT. One of the defining moments in the political development of Bangladesh, the **language** movement of 1952 was intended to establish Bengali as one of the national languages of **Pakistan**. The movement had its origins as far back as 1948 when **Muhammad Ali Jinnah** announced in **Dhaka** that Urdu, and only Urdu, would be the national language. At that time the Student Action Committee of **Dhaka University** demanded that Bengali be declared the official language of **East Pakistan**. The central government in 1952 attempted to introduce the Urdu script (modified Arabic) for Bengali, leading to violent reactions by students. During the language movement in 1952 a number of people, including university students, were killed. A monument, the Shahid Minar, has been erected on the spot where police fired on 21 February 1952, now known as **Martyrs' Day**. The language controversy ended in 1954 when the Pakistan **Parliament** declared both Urdu and Bengali to be official languages, but the hard feelings on this and other issues would eventually lead to the independence movement, culminating in civil war and independence in 1971. *See also* AMAR EKUSHEY GRANTHAMELA; LANGUAGE MOVEMENT MARTYRS; LATIF, ABDUL.

LANGUAGE MOVEMENT MARTYRS. Five people shot on 21 February 1952 are generally considered the **language movement** martyrs. They are Salam, Jabbar, Barkat, Rafiq, and Shafiqur. Jabbar and Rafiq were killed immediately while the others died later on. Not much is known about these five. Rafiquddin Ahmed was born in Paril under Singair upazila in Manikganj on 30 October 1926. He was the first to be martyred during the language movement in 1952. Abdul Jabbar was born in 1919 in Gafargoan, **Mymensingh**. At a young age he managed to get to Rangoon, Burma, where he became a sailor. After five years of sailing, he returned to Rangoon in 1939. Later he received training to join the Royal British Navy but could not as he broke his knee during training. After the partition of **India**, he joined the Ansar brigade. He was in **Dhaka** to see his ailing mother-in-law at Dhaka Medical College when he was shot dead.

LATIF, ABDUL (1927–2005). In 1952 he wrote the song *Ora amaar mukher kotha kaira nitey chaye* (they want to snatch away my language) and set the lyrics for *Amaar bhaiyer rakte rangano ekushey February* (my brothers blood brightened the 21st of February), both defining songs of the 1952 language movement. He wrote over 1,500 songs. His first song was *Shamal baran meyeti.* He refused the Tamgha of the **Pakistan** government. His publications include *Duare Aisache Palki, Bhashar Gaan, Deshar Gaan,* and *Dilrobab.* In 1979 he was a recipient of the Ekushey Padak, honoring those who made a significant contribution to the language movement, and in 2002 he received the Swadhinata Padak (Independence Day Award).

LEGAL FRAMEWORK ORDER. Issued by **Pakistani** President **Yahya Khan** in 1970 to set parameters for the operation of the constituent assembly to be elected in October of that year (later postponed to December because of a major cyclonic storm that struck **East Pakistan**). The principal points were: (1) a federal state; (2) Islamic principles would be paramount; (3) direct and regular elections; (4) fundamental rights guaranteed; (5) independent judiciary; (6) maximum provincial autonomy, "but the federal government shall also have adequate powers, including legislative, administrative and financial powers, to discharge its responsibilities"; and (7) disparities between the provinces will be removed. The order was in major part a response to the **Six Points** of **Mujibur Rahman**. The major conflict in the two documents was between Yahya's sixth point and Mujib's fourth, in which the latter stated that all power of taxation would be at the provincial level and the provinces would grant sums to the federal government to carry out its duties. *See also* PARITY.

LEVIN, LEAR. A U.S.-based filmmaker who in 1971 filmed a group of Bangladesh singers as they traveled from one camp to another to encourage refugees and freedom fighters. The group was called Bangladesh Mutki Shangrami Shilpi Shanhgstha (Bangladesh Revolutionary Artists Group). In 1990, Bangladeshi filmmakers Tareque and Catherine Masud met Lear Levin in New York, where they were provided with Levin's 1971 uncut film footage. In 1995, an edited version of the original footage entitled *Muktir Gaan* (freedom's songs) was first screened. In 2008, the film was screened to honor Lear Levin and most members of the original group attended the event.

LIAQUAT ALI KHAN (1895–1951). Although from a prominent east Punjab family, he gained his political experience in the United Provinces (now Uttar Pradesh, India). He served in the provincial legislative bodies, 1926–1940, and in the Central Legislative Assembly, from 1940 until its dissolution in 1947, and he was leader of the **Muslim League** group in that body. He was also a member for finance in the interim cabinet, 1946–1947. Liaquat was **Muhammad Ali Jinnah**'s principal lieutenant as general secretary of the league from 1936 until independence, when he became prime minister. Liaquat was assassinated in Rawalpindi on 16 October 1951.

LIGHT ENGINEERING. Since 1971 Bangladesh has had significant growth in this sector. Industrial policy changes in 1984 and 2005 provided the framework for growth in this sector. The light engineering sector has the capacity to produce about 10,000 items and employs about 6 million workers and professionals. There are about 40,000 small-scale light engineering manufacturers and repair and refurbishing business enterprises. Exportable goods produced by light engineering include bicycles, iron chain, dry cell batteries, generators, instant power supply (IPS) devices, copper wire, telephone sets, fishing reels, garment-cutting tables, light garment machinery, electric fans, and GI pipe. Bangladesh is able to manufacture machinery needed for the ready-made garment sector, as well as manufacture power looms, some automobile spare parts, ammunition boxes, and machinery for the paint industry. It also produces the machinery needed to make ballpoint pens, bakery equipment, and CD and DVD covers. *See also* INDUSTRY.

LITERATURE. The earliest extant work in Bengali is a pre-12th-century collection of lyrics found in Nepal. In this period and the time up to the mid-14th century almost all extant literature is in Sanskrit and not **Bengali**. Writers include **Jayadeva**, the author of the popular *Gita Govinda*.

In the medieval period, roughly 1360 to 1800, Bengali is most often used and the works are mainly verse intended to be sung and transmitted orally. Except in the very late part of that period, almost all literature has to do with **Hindu** subjects such as aspects of the Hindu classics *Ramayana* and *Mahabharata* and such devotional themes as Radha-Krishna. The best known of the authors is **Chaitanya**, but there were many lesser writers whose works have survived.

As **Islam** entered Bengal, there were many works by **Sufi** writers celebrating the Divine Being. Examples include *Yusuf-Zulakha* by Shah Muhammad Saghir, *Nasihat Name* by Afdal Ali, and *Ghazivi-jaya* and *Rasul Vijaya* by Faizullah. These poets flourished in the 15th and 16th centuries. Among Muslim poets **Alaol** is perhaps the best known; he drew on the earlier works of Daulat Kazi (fl. c. 1630). However, the form continues in such modern poets as **Jasimuddin**.

The modern period saw the development of prose literature that was stimulated by the work of **William Carey** and his and **John Marshman**'s development of textbooks for use in colleges and lower schools. Marshman also began newspaper publishing. However, the person credited with being the father of Bengali prose is **Isvarchandra Vidyasagar**. Novels by such writers as **Bankim Chandra Chatterji** and Bhibutibhusan Bannerji appeared; perhaps the best-known work of the latter is *Pather Panchali*, which was made into a prize-winning film directed by Satyajit Rai. Playwrights such as **Michael Madhusudan Dutt** brought Bengali into the theatre. The key person in the modern period is, of course, **Rabindranath Tagore,** who wrote prose and poetry in both Bengali and English. He was awarded the Nobel Prize for Literature in 1913 and was knighted by the British (although he later renounced the knighthood). Although younger than Tagore, **Kazi Nazrul Islam** became the voice of the Muslims in Bengali literature.

During the later period of British rule, literature often contained themes of resistance to the British. After the independence of **Pakistan**, a new resistance theme developed based very much on the denigration of Bengali in favor of Urdu. A number of poets wrote on the protection of Bengali culture. Among these were Shamsur

Rahman, Alauddin al Azad, Mauzarul Islam, and Zillur Rahman Siddiqui. During the 1960s, as antipathy toward West Pakistan and Bengali nationalism began to take the shape that would lead to war and Bangladeshi independence, other poets wrote on these themes, including Abul Hasan, Humayun Kabir (not the person included in this dictionary), Asad Chowdhury, Altaf Hossain, Farhad Mazhar, Rafiq Azad, and Abdul Mannan Syed. After the **War of Liberation**, poetry assumed an air of dissolution in the face of political and manmade instability. Other contributors to modern literature include Akhtaruzzaman Ilias, Makbula Manzoor, Selina Hossain, and Hasan Hafizur Rahman.

Some literature, including folk tales, has been translated into English, such as *Folktales of Bangladesh* by Jasimuddin. There is little literature written originally in English. Bangladeshi authors like Niaz Ali are increasingly translating Bengali literature into English. Bangladeshi authors have not yet enjoyed the international popularity of writers from other South Asian countries, especially India, who use English as their medium.

In December 1978, the World Literature Center (Bishwa Sahitya Kendra) was established to facilitate the study of Bangladeshi literature, philosophy, and **music** by students. *See also* ABUL HUSAIN; ALAOL; AL MAHMUD; ALI, AHMED; BANDE ALI MIAH; CHATTERJI, BANKIM CHANDRA; DAS, JIBANANDA; DEEN, SALEEM AL; GOLAM MUSTAFA; GUPTA, SAMUDRA; HABIBULLAH, ABUL BARKAT MUHAMMAD; HOSSAIN, SUFI MOTAHAR; HUQUE, MAHMADUL; JASIMUDDIN; KABIR, HUMAYUN; KAIKOBAD; KAISAR, KHAWJA MUHAMMAD; LANGUAGE; LITTLE MAGAZINES; MONIRUZZAMAN, MOHAMMAD; MOTHAR HUSAIN, KAZI; MUSHARRAF HUSAIN, MIR; NASRIN, TASLIMA; RABEYA KHATUN; RAHMAN, SHAMSUR; SEN, DINESH CHANDRA; SHARIF, AHMED; WALIULLAH, SYED; ZAFAR, SIKANDER ABU.

LITTLE MAGAZINES. Originating from the European concept of publishing high-quality innovative literary works not found in mainstream journals, the Bangladesh little magazine sector took off during the repressive military rule of **Ayub Khan** in the 1960s. Among all the 1960s publications, Abdullah Abu Sayeed's little magazine

Kanthoswor is the best known. Others include *Chhotogolpo* (1966), S*aptak* (1962), and *Sampratik* (1964). Little magazines provided first-time authors an outlet for their works. *Purbalekh, Rupsa, Pratidhwani, Samaswar, Polimati, Kranti,* and *Tridhara* were the other little magazines of the 1960s that earned some reputation. While little magazines were primarily in **Dhaka**, their popularity spread throughout **East Pakistan**. *Karnaphuli* of **Chittagong**, *Bipratik* of **Bogra**, and *Sandeepan of* **Khulna** were renowned for their quality. **Rangpur, Jessore**, Netrakona, and **Mymensingh** also published little magazines. These magazines emerged during a period of repressive action by the national government. The trend continues, but it was in the 1960s that this form of literary expression first found its creative outlet. *See also* LITERATURE.

LOCAL GOVERNMENT. The basic form of governance in the subcontinent until the 6th century BC, when large kingdoms came into existence, is generally assumed to have been local government (the idealized "village republics" of Mahatma Gandhi). While not much is known about local governance in ancient Bengal, the first census conducted by the British in the Bengal presidency in 1872 suggests strong village organizations in eastern Bengal (present Bangladesh). Local governance in Bengal was affected by such legislation as the **Permanent Settlement** Act of 1793, the Chowkidari (village watchmen) Act of 1870, and the Local Self-Government Act of 1885. The last established a three-tier system that included a district board, a local board at the subdistrict level, and a union committee at the village level. Local government in Bangladesh conforms to this basic structure.

Since 1971, three major attempts have been made by three successive governments to supply public services to the people through strengthening local government. In the first experiment, during the regime of **Mujibur Rahman**, Bangladesh was divided into 61 districts, each of which would be headed by a governor. Although the stated purpose was to devolve some power to local governments, the clear purpose was to bring about political control over district administration, a critical issue in the Bangladeshi administrative system, political **economy**, and local government system. The first experiment did not affect the local government system because the Mujib regime ended shortly after the announcement of the plan.

The second experiment, linked to the democratization of the **Ziaur Rahman** regime, set up rural local government consisting of *zilla* (district), *thana* (subdistrict), and union *parishads* (councils), and *pourashavas* (municipal corporations) in the urban areas. The system was dominated by the bureaucracy as the elections to the local bodies that were integral to the system were never held. The concepts of **Gram Sarkar** (village rule) and *swarnirvar* (self-reliance) were introduced as major building blocks for local government strengthening and autonomy. The purpose was to mobilize people at the village level for development work. Decision-making was to be based on consensus, and all groups were to be represented at the village level. Gram Sarkars were to be organized around increasing **food** production, expanding mass literacy programs, promoting family planning activities, and maintaining law and order. Mobilization, participation, and involvement were other critical issues that were to be addressed in strengthening the local government system.

The third experiment, also linked to a process of democratization of a military government, took place during the regime of **Hussain Muhammad Ershad**. It upgraded the 464 thanas to *upazilas* (subdistricts) and the 64 former subdivisions to districts. The upazilas were to be the center of all development activities, policy planning, and implementation. Each upazila had a council that was partly elected and partly appointed. All central administrative units that had offices at the upazila level came under the upazila council. A separate staff functioned as the secretariat for the upazila council. This plan for strengthening local government brought together for the first time two conflicting elements—popular participation and merit-based administrative units—in the implementation of development plans. The purpose was to pull together the cooperative and relative strength of two key forces in the economic development of Bangladesh. Local government units at the union level were retained but with reduced powers. Pourashavas in the urban areas were also retained.

This experiment continued until the upazila parishads were abolished in 1992 by the **Khaleda Zia** government. Before this government could reassess the nature and structure of local government, the government of **Sheikh Hasina** came to power and restored the upazila system. The **Awami League** government did not prepare a clear vision of local government during its tenure.

The return of the **Bangladesh Nationalist Party** to power in October 2001 led to the introduction of a Gram Sarkar bill in February 2003. This bill was passed to reintroduce Ziaur Rahman's concept of Gram Sarkar, but it was not implemented. The BNP did not like the upazila system and rolled back most of its people-oriented units, bringing back the thanas to "govern" local administration. When the Awami League came to power it went back to the name *upazila* and reinstated a few public services there, but did not establish an elected upazila parishad. The appointed *thana nirbahi* officer (TNO) declared by the BNP government was renamed *upazila nirbahi* officer (UNO). The last BNP regime did not pay much attention to the local government system. Probably the most serious attempt to develop an independent and sound local government system was enacted through an ordinance promulgated by the caretaker government of **Fakhruddin Ahmed**, but the Awami League government of Sheikh Hasina amended the ordinance and restored the ability of the member of **parliament** to not only influence but also determine the operation of upazila administration.

In assessing local government in Bangladesh, it is possible to identify four factors detrimental to the effective institutionalization of local government: (1) tinkering with the process by each new administration; (2) lack of standardization of the structure; (3) utilization of the system for partisan and personal political gains; and (4) micro-management from the higher echelons. Factors that would be conducive to better local governance include (1) local leadership that encourages the community and sets the tone for innovation and change; (2) resources for projects which are mobilized from a variety of sources; (3) local management practices that may not apply to higher levels of government; (4) local projects which clearly benefit residents; (5) projects that lead to further, often secondary, projects; and (6) local government that cooperates with other local organizations, including those that are not part of the government structure. No local government system will become independent unless it has its own viable source of income and separation from both national bureaucracy and parliament members.

LOHANI BROTHERS. Fateh (1923–1975) and Fazle (1929–1985) were involved in the **film** and television industries. Fateh Lohani was one of the first Bengali Muslim filmmakers, and Fazle Lohani was a television performer. A younger brother, Kamal Lohani, is now working in films and television.

– M –

MACAULAY, THOMAS BABINGTON, FIRST BARON (1800–1859). The great British historian, essayist, and political figure spent a part of his career in **Calcutta** as law member of the governor-general's executive council. He had earlier been a member of the Board of Control of the **East India Company**. Macaulay arrived in India in 1834. He is perhaps best known in Indian history for his "Minute on Education" of 1835. Macaulay argued for a Western (i.e., British) system of education in English, in opposition to the "orientalists" who espoused teaching in local languages. Although Macaulay has been criticized for this (for example, as creating a group of "brown sahibs"), his view was that Indians educated under his proposal would eventually demand representative institutions. In the interim, Britain would rule by the sword. Macaulay, as law member, changed the legal system so that British and Indians would be tried under a single court system.

MAGHS. The term applied locally to Buddhist migrants from **Arakan**. They settled generally in **Chittagong**, **Noakhali**, **Barisal**, and the **Chittagong Hill Tracts**. In the last, they are considered one of the several tribes of the tracts. Many fled when Arakan was conquered by **Burma** in 1784, but others had arrived earlier when the Arakanese and the **Portuguese** raided along the coast of the Bay of Bengal and up the **Meghna** estuary. Many Maghs are famed as cooks.

MAHASTHANGARH. An **archeological** site in the district of **Bogra**, it is identified with the Pundranagara mentioned in the records of the **Maurya** empire and the **Gupta**, **Pala**, and **Sena** dynasties. This old ruined city is situated near the **Karatoya River**. The city is surrounded by 11-foot-thick defense walls 500 feet long on two sides and 450 feet long on the other two sides. Limited excavation has revealed closely packed dwellings and temples of Hindu and Buddhist origin. Excavations have also resulted in the discoveries of copper, bronze, and gold jewelry, pendants, badges, and coins. This area was later conquered by Muslim generals. It is the site of the mazar (grave) of Saint Shah Sultan Baki Mahisawar. The city is mentioned by Huien Tsang, the third-century Chinese Buddhist pilgrim.

MAHIPALA I. A ruler of the **Pala dynasty** who reigned about 978–1030, under whom the disintegration of the dynasty took place. Southwestern Bengal came under the rule of the **Sena dynasty** and eastern Bengal under the **Chandras**. He also fought losing battles with the Cholas, a south Indian dynasty that penetrated to the Ganges in 1023, and the Kalachuris, who ruled in central India. Mahipala is remembered, however, for public works at Nalanda, the Buddhist university in Bihar, and for irrigation works in north and west Bengal.

MAHMUD, ALTAF (1930–1971). One of the many intellectuals killed by the Pakistani army. He was a singer and composer whose best-known song was one paying tribute to those killed during the **language movement** in 1952. He popularized *gono-sangeet* and inspired Bengali nationalism through his compositions. Although **Abdul Latif** composed the song *Aamar bhai–er roktey rangano*, it was Altaf Mahmud's recomposition of the song that made it popular. In 1977, he was awarded the Ekushey Padak (posthumously). *See also* MUSIC.

MAINAMATI. Five miles west of **Comilla** town, contains the **archeological** sites of Mainamati and Lalmai. These two sites are thought to be the remains of the one-time political and cultural center of this region. Excavations show that the structures spread along the Lalmai ridge for a distance of 11 miles. The structures are **Buddhist** monasteries and stupas often inset with characteristic terra cotta plaques. They date from as early as the seventh century. Archeological finds here have increased knowledge of southeastern Bengal dynasties such as the **Khargas**, **Devas**, **Chandras**, and **Varmans**, but much of their histories remain speculation.

MAJORS. This refers to the leaders of the **August coup** of 1977. They were Lieutenant Colonels Syed Farook Rahman and Sultan Shahriar Rashid and Majors Shariful Huq Dalim, Abdul Nur Chowdhury, Abdul Hafiz, Badrul Rashid, and Muhammad Huda. After they were ousted in November 1977, they, along with a number of other officers, were forced to leave the country. Some of them were later permitted to join the Bangladesh Foreign Service. All have been permitted to return to Bangladesh. Two other coup attempts are linked to this group, including the **Bogra Mutiny**. Lieutenant Colonel Syed Farook Rahman returned to Bangladesh and, in 1986, he took part in the presidential **election** that was won by Lieutenant General **Hussain Muhammad Ershad**. Farook organized a political party, the Freedom Party, which won no seats in the 1991 election and no longer exists.

During 1996, when the **Awami League** took office, the case was revived as the Bangabandhu (Sheikh **Mujibur Rahman**) Murder Case. The trial court delivered its verdict on 8 November 1998, finding the officers and eight others guilty of murder and ordering that they be hanged. The case was appealed to the High Court. A number of the judges on this court recused themselves from the case, but in April 2001 the High Court upheld the convictions of 12 of the 15, following a split decision of the High Court on 14 December 2000. In December 2002 it was appealed to the Appellate Division of the Supreme Court. The case lay dormant from 2002 to 2007. On 23 September 2007, an Appellate Division bench allowed five death row convicts to appeal on five grounds: whether 15 August 1975 was a mutiny in the army; whether delay of 21 years in filing of the first information report was justified under law; whether a civilian court can try army personnel; whether conspiracy was properly established; and whether disjointed depositions of witnesses can be utilized as testimony. When the Awami League returned to power in January 2009, president **Zillur Rahman** appointed four judges to the Supreme Court, making it possible for the Appellate Division to form a new bench to review the case. In October 2009 the Appellate Division began its review.

MAJUMDAR, CHARU (1915–1972). Born in **Rajshahi**, he turned to socialism while studying in **Pabna** and worked to organize farmers.

He joined the Communist Party. In 1969, he formed the Communist Party of India—Marxist-Leninist. Some of Majumdar's followers were known as Naxalites (from Naxalbari, where they operated), a rural terrorist group in West Bengal that has lent its name to similar groups in South Asia. Majumdar was arrested in 1972 and died in jail 12 days later.

MAJUMDAR, PHANI BHUSHAN (1901–1981). A follower of **Subhas Chandra Bose**, he was a member of the Revolutionary Communist Party from 1930 to 1938. He spent a considerable amount of time in jail during the British era in **India**. He was elected a member of the East Bengal Legislative Assembly in 1954. From 1954 until 1962, Majumdar was under arrest by the **Pakistani** government. In 1970, as an **Awami League** nominee, he was elected a member of the Pakistan National Assembly. During the **War of Liberation** he was a member of the advisory board of the provisional Bangladesh government-in-exile. Majumdar was a member of the cabinets of **Mujibur Rahman** and **Mushtaque Ahmed**, 1972–1975.

MAJUMDAR, ROMESH CHANDRA (1888–1980). Historian. Born in **Faridpur**, he studied in **Calcutta** and taught in Calcutta and **Dhaka**. With Sir **Jadunath Sarkar**, he edited the monumental *History of Bengal*. Majumdar also edited the multivolume *History and Culture of the Indian People*, published by the Bharatiya Vidya Bhavan; later volumes were edited by his son, Ashok.

MALIK, ABDUL MUTTALIB (1905–1977). Appointed governor of East Pakistan by **Yahya Khan** in November 1971, during the civil war, in an attempt to civilianize the embattled Pakistani regime. He had earlier been appointed a minister in the central government by Yahya in 1969. An ophthalmologist by training, Malik entered politics as a member of the Bengal legislature (1937–1947). After **Pakistan**'s independence he served as a cabinet minister and as ambassador to a number of countries. He played no role in independent Bangladesh.

MALLICK, AZIZUR RAHMAN (1918–1998). A historian, he received his Ph.D. in 1953 from the University of London. In 1965 he became the first vice-chancellor of **Chittagong** University. During the **War of Liberation** he visited many universities in the **United States** and Europe to gain support for Bangladesh. He served as president of the Liberation Council of Intelligentsia. After the independence of Bangladesh, he served as the first **education** minister and was also the finance minister, replacing **Tajuddin Ahmed**.

MAMUN MAHMUD (1929–1971). Entering the police service in 1947, he served as superintendent of police in **Chittagong** and **Khulna**. He was also the deputy inspector general, **Rajshahi**. He raised the black flag of protest on 4 March 1971, against the military rule of President **Yahya Khan**. On 26 March 1971, a day after the beginning of the civilian massacre by the **Pakistani** army, Mamun was summoned by a Brigadier Abdullah and was never heard from again.

MAN SINGH, RAJA. A Rajput from Amber (Jaipur) who entered the service of the **Mughal** emperor Akbar in 1562. He was among the principal **Hindu** supporters of the Mughals and served the empire until his death in 1614. Among the positions he held was governor of Bengal, 1594–1606, during which period he extended Mughal control eastward in Bengal from his capital of **Rajmahal**.

MANIK, SAIFUDDIN (1939–2008). He was born in Jalpaiguri, India, although his family is from Feni, Bangladesh. At the time of his death he was the general secretary of the **Gono Forum**. He was one of the founding members of Gono Forum in 1993. He was involved in the student movements of 1962 and 1966 and the political movements of 1969, 1971, and 1990. His other political leadership roles include serving as president of the Communist Party of Bangladesh (1987) and as general secretary (1973). He was elected a member of the central committee of the Communist Party of Bangladesh in 1972. He is the founder of one of the most recognized cultural groups of Bangladesh—Chhayanaut.

MANIPURI DANCE. Held on temple premises, the traditional Manipuri **dance** is based on *Lai Haraba* (Joy of God). These dances are held all through the night. A more modern form with a faster rhythm and short sequence is gaining ground and it held for public entertainment. This type of dance is prevalent in **Sylhet**. One of the prominent proponents of this dance form is Anil Kishan Shingha, who has been associated with Manipuri dance since the early 1960s. Another form of dance in Bangladesh is the Kaththak dance.

MANIRUZZAMAN, TALUKDER (1938–). Political scientist. In 1966 he received his Ph.D. in political science in Canada and joined Rajshahi University. From 1974 to 2001 he was a professor of political science at **Dhaka University**. His major contribution was in political institution building, the role of the military, and security issues. In 2005 he became a National Professor in recognition of his lifetime contribution to educational excellence.

MANSUR ALI (1919–1975). Assassinated during the **Dhaka jail killings**, he was the last prime minister of Bangladesh during the presidency of Sheikh **Mujibur Rahman**. He was also the general secretary of **BAKSAL**. A lawyer by profession, he was elected president of the Pabna Lawyers Association three times. Mansur Ali was a vice president of the Pabna District **Muslim League** from 1946 to 1950. He joined the **Awami League** in 1951 and had his first ministerial appointment in 1956 in **Ataur Rahman Khan**'s cabinet. In 1969 he became the vice president of the Awami League. Mansur Ali served as finance minister in the provisional Bangladesh government-in-exile. After the independence of Bangladesh and before he became prime minister in 1975, Mansur Ali served in a number of ministries, including commerce, finance, and industries.

MANSUR ALI KHAN (1829–1884). He had the dubious distinction of being the last person to hold the title nawab nazim of Bengal. The nawab nazim title resided in **Murshidabad**. When the ceremonial status of the title was reduced and his appeal in London was unsuccessful, Mansur Ali resigned the title in 1880.

MANZUR, MAJOR GENERAL MUHAMMAD ABUL (1940–1981). Awarded the *Bir Uttam* (the highest military decoration) for bravery during the **War of Liberation**. In 1957 he joined the **Pakistan** army and by 1971 was a brigade commander. During the War of

Liberation, Manzur escaped from Pakistan and actively participated in the war as a sector commander. In 1973, he became the military attaché of Bangladesh in New Delhi. He later was appointed the chief of the general staff of the Bangladesh army. In 1977 he was transferred as the general officer commanding the 24th Division based in Chittagong. Manzur was the commander of the 24th Division when he became involved in the coup attempt. He was first a friend and later a foe of President **Ziaur Rahman**. He was one of the leaders of the coup attempt that led to the assassination of Ziaur Rahman in May 1981. Following the failure of the coup he was arrested and killed. The Manzur case was reopened in 1995 as part of a general review of the assassination of Ziaur Rahman.

MARIUM BIBI. One of the earliest recipients of a **Grameen Bank** loan, she was a resident of the village of Jobra, located at Hathazari upazila of Chittagong, when she received her loan of 1,500 taka. Other recipients with her were Sufia Khatun, Manjura Begum, Hafizur Rahman, Anjuman Ara Begum, Monwara Begum, Noor Pakhi, Firoza Begum, Tahera Begum, and Marium Begum. A poor woman, mother of five, she bought a cow to begin her journey toward financial stability. She paid off her loan and obtained other loans. Through one of these loans she was able to send one of her sons abroad. In 2006 three of her sons were working in Saudi Arabia. In 2006, her net worth included a one-story building and five shops at the village bazaar.

MARSHMAN, JOHN. A **Christian** missionary associated with **William Carey** in Srirampur (Serampore) and later in **Kolkata**. He started the journal *The Friend of India*, which advocated reform of such institutions as *sati* (widow burning) and child marriage. The publication was later merged with the *Statesman*, a Calcutta-based newspaper still being published.

MARTIAL RACES. A term introduced by the British following the mutiny of the Bengal army in 1857. The Bengal army was comprised mainly of soldiers (*sepoys*) recruited from the lower **Ganges** basin. The British were aided in quelling the rebellion by Sikh and Muslim Punjabi troops and some other groups from northern India. After the mutiny the British decided to recruit only from those groups that had supported them; these were designated "martial races." The peoples of the former recruiting grounds in the lower Ganges basin were described as "non-martial races" and were not recruited. The designations continued to operate in practice to a large degree even after Pakistani independence and resulted in an army in which the Bengalis were very much underrepresented.

MARTYRED INTELLECTUALS DAY. On 12 December 1971 the Pakistani armed forces and their local collaborators systematically killed a number of Bengali intellectuals in order to destroy the intellectual capacity of Bangladesh. Some of those assassinated include Professor Munir Chowdhury, Dr. Alim Chowdhury, Professor Muniruzzaman, Dr. Fazle Rabbi, Sirajuddin Hossain, Shahidullah Kaiser, Professor G. C. Dev, Professor J. C. Guha Thakurta, Professor Santosh Bhattacharya, Mofazzal Haider Chowdhury, and journalists Khandaker Abu Taleb, Nizamuddin Ahmed, S. A. Mannan, A. N. M. Golam Mustafa, Syed Nazmul Haq, and Selina Parvin.

MARTYRS' DAY. Celebrated annually on 21 February, it honors those who lost their lives during the **language movement** to make Bengali a national language of **Pakistan**. The incident occurred on 21 February 1952, near the Dhaka Medical College, when police fired upon students demonstrating against the plan to make Urdu the sole national language of Pakistan. A number of students were killed as a result. A monument, called the Shahid Minar, has been erected near the place where the students were killed.

MASHIUR RAHMAN (1928–1979). A prominent parliamentarian, he started his political career as a member of the **Muslim League**. In 1957 he joined the **National Awami Party** and became a leading member of the organization. He was a member of the **Pakistan** National Assembly in 1962 and deputy leader of the opposition. He was again elected to the National Assembly in 1965 but resigned in 1969 when the movement to oust president **Muhammad Ayub** started. Mashiur Rahman became the general secretary of the East Pakistan National Awami Party. During the **War of Liberation** he first left for **India** but later surrendered to the Pakistani armed forces and opposed the liberation forces.

After the liberation of Bangladesh, Mashiur Rahman was arrested as a traitor but was later released. After the death of **Maulana Bhashani**, he became the leader of the National Awami Party in 1977. During the presidency of **Ziaur Rahman**, his faction of the National Awami Party joined the **Bangladesh Nationalist Party**, and he became the senior minister of Ziaur Rahman's cabinet and minister of railways. In the 1979 **election** he was elected as a member of the **parliament** once again. It was believed that Mashiur Rahman would be the prime minister, but he died suddenly just before the cabinet was announced. **Shah Azizur Rahman** became the prime minister in his stead.

MAURYA DYNASTY. Founded by Chandragupta Maurya in about 322 BC, the dynasty quickly controlled all of northern India, including Bengal, and in the west up to the present Northwest Frontier Province. The most noted ruler of the dynasty was Chandragupta's grandson, **Asoka**.

MEDIA. Bangladesh has more than 1,000 national, regional, and local newspapers and periodicals, including 142 daily newspapers. Some of the more prominent daily national newspapers are *Ittefaq*, *Inquilab*, *Sangbad*, *Dainik Bangla*, *Ajker Kagoz*, and *Bhorer Kagoz*. Among the English-language dailies are the *Bangladesh Observer*, *Bangladesh Times*, *Morning Sun*, and *Daily Star*.

Radio Bangladesh has nine stations and an external service that is broadcast in seven languages. Radio Bangladesh can be heard throughout South Asia and in the Middle East. Television was introduced in 1964 and now has a number of private channels. Bangladesh TV also permits transmission of Cable News Network (CNN) and the British Broadcasting Corporation (BBC).

The media in Bangladesh have been relatively free although the country has been under military rule for much of its existence. Press freedom has expanded since the fall of the **Hussain Muhammad Ershad** regime in 1990. *See also* FILM.

MEGHNA. A river that becomes quite large when it is joined by the already combined **Ganges** and **Brahmaputra** at Chandpur, about 80 miles from the Bay of Bengal. It rises in the Indian state of Megalaya, near the town of Cherrapunji, reputed to be the rainiest place in the world. The Meghna drains the exceptionally rainy areas of **Sylhet**. Some of its channels comprise sections of the "old" Brahmaputra before that river changed course. The seasonal changes in flow mean that at no place are its banks clearly defined. There are four principal mouths. These enclose the islands of Hatia, Sandwip, and Dakhin Shahbazpur. *See also* COASTAL ISLANDS.

MIDDLE EAST. Relations between Bangladesh and most nations in the Middle East did not exist prior to the Lahore meeting of the **Organization of the Islamic Conference** in 1974, when several of the Arab delegates persuaded **Pakistan** to invite Bangladesh to the meeting. Thereafter, during the early part of the **Ziaur Rahman** regime, most Middle Eastern countries recognized Bangladesh and established formal diplomatic relations. Several countries, especially Kuwait and Saudi Arabia, have provided economic **aid** to Bangladesh. Many countries also serve as hosts to Bangladeshi migrant labor. This has generated as much as $8–10 billion per year in **remittances** to Bangladesh. There have also been objections by some Middle Eastern countries, notably Saudi Arabia, to the principle of secularism contained in the Bangladeshi constitution. This provision was modified by Zia to provide that Muslims in Bangladesh would be able to order their lives in accordance with the Sunna while retaining provisions allowing freedom of **religion**. **Hussain Muhammad Ershad** declared **Islam** to be the state religion, but this again did not diminish the rights of non-Muslims. *See also* MUJIBBAD.

MILITANCY. On 6 March 1999, during the cultural program of Udichi's 12th annual national conference, two bombs exploded at Munshi Meherullah Maidan (field) in Jessore. Ten people died as a result of the explosions and over 200 were injured. This incident is considered the beginning of militancy in Bangladesh. The following is a list of the major bombings since then:

6 March	1999	Jessore	Social program
8 October	1999	Khulna	Ahmediyya Mosque
20 January	2001	Dhaka	Political rally
14 April	2001	Dhaka	New Year Celebration
3 June	2001	Gopalganj	Christian church

16 June	2001	Narayanganj	Political party office
23 September	2001	Bagherhat	Political rally
26 September	2001	Sunamganj	Political rally
28 September	2002	Satkhira	Movie theatre
6 December	2002	Mymensiingh	Movie theatre
17 January	2003	Tangail	Local fair
12 January	2004	Sylhet	Shahjalal Mosque
15 January	2004	Khulna	Journalist
8 May	2004	Tongi	Assassination MP
21 May	2004	Sylhet	Shahjalal Mosque
21 August	2004	Dhaka	Political rally
27 January	2005	Sylhet	Assassination MP
17 August	2005	Bangladesh	Countrywide
14 November	2005	Barisal	Judges
3 May	2007	Dhaka	Explosions in 3 railway
		Chittagong	stations
		Sylhet	

Three other incidents, the 21 May 2004 explosion that wounded the British high commissioner along with 70 others at the Shahjalal Mosque in **Sylhet**, the 21 August 2004 explosion at the **Awami League** (AL) rally that wounded Sheikh Hasina, and the 17 August 2005 incident when 459 small bombs exploded in 63 of the 64 districts of Bangladesh, are viewed as the most intense periods of recent Bangladesh militancy.

The grenade attacks on the Awami League rally on Bangabandhu Avenue on 21 August 2004 killed 24 people, including Ivy Rahman, wife of the 19th president of Bangladesh Zillur Rahman; 200 others, including AL chief **Sheikh Hasina**, were injured. Bangladesh Nationalist Party lawmaker Abdus Salam Pintu and Harkat-ul-Jihad-al-Islam, Bangladesh (HUJI-B) chief Mufti Abdul Hannan were charged. Twenty others were co-conspirators. The 12 accused in jail are Hannan's brother Mohibullah alias Mafizur Rahman alias Ovi, Sharif Shahidul Islam alias Bipul, Maulana Abu Sayeed alias Dr. Abu Zafar, Abul Kalam Azad alias Bulbul, Jahangir Alam, Maulana Abu Taher, Shahadatullah Jewel, Hossain Ahmed Tamim, Mufti Moinuddin Sheikh alias Abu Zandal alias Masum Billah, Arif Hasan

Sumon, Rafiqul Islam Sabuj, and Mohammad Ujjal alias Ratan. The eight remaininging accused are Pintu's brothers Maulana Tajuddin and Maulana Liton, Anisul Mursalin and his brother Mahibul Muttakin, Iqbal, Maulana Abu Bakar alias Selim Howlader, Jahangir Alam Badar, and Khalilur Rahman.

By October 2008 as many as 283 cases were filed in connection with the 459 bomb blasts across the country on 17 August 2005 against 822 Jama'atul Mujahideen Bangladesh (JMB) leaders and activists. The investigators have so far submitted charge sheets in 241 cases, accusing 743 of their involvement in the serial blasts.

Much-delayed action by the BNP government to arrest the major militants and their subsequent execution by the Fakhruddin Ahmed government in 2007 has significantly reduced the incidents of militancy. However, there was a growing rise in militancy in 2009. *See also* TERRORISM.

MILITANT ISLAMIC ORGANIZATIONS OF BANGLADESH. Shahadate-Al Hiqma, Jama'atul Mujahideen Bangladesh (JMB), Jagrata Muslim Janata, Bangladesh (JMJB), and Harkatul Jihad al Islami, Bangladesh (HUJI-B) have been banned by the government for **terrorism** in the name of **religion**. Other parties, groups, and associations involved in militancy include the following: Hizb-ut-Towhid, Allahr Dal, Islami Samaj, al Harat al Islamia, Jama'atul Faliya, Towhidi Janata, Biswa Islami Front, Juma'atul al Sadat, Shahadat-e-Nobuat, Jama'at-e Yahia al Turat, Joyshe Mostafa Bangladesh, al Jihad Bangladesh, Woarat Islamic Front, Jamaat-as-Sadat, al Khidmat, Harkat-e-Islam al Jihad, Hijbullah Islami Samaj, Muslim Millat Shahria Council, World Islamic Front for Jihad, Joysh-e Mohammad, Hijbul Mahadi, Kalemar Dawat, Islami Dawati Kafela, al Islam Martyrs Brigade, Dawat-e Islam, Tanjim, Hizb e Abu Omar, and Jadid al-Qaeda Bangladesh. The newly formed **Islamic Democratic Party** is also included in this category because it was formed by those who formed HUJI-B.

MINTO, GILBERT JOHN ELLIOT-MURRAY-KYNYNMOUND, FOURTH EARL OF (1845–1914). The viceroy of **India**, 1905–1910. (He was great-grandson of the first earl, who was governor-general of India, 1806–1813.) Minto was governor-general of Canada, 1898–1904. He was required to restore the authority of the office of governor-general, which had been lowered in the dispute between his predecessor, Lord **Curzon**, and the commander in chief, Lord Kitchener. He was successful in doing this. Minto came to office at a time when changes in the constitutional arrangements for India were imminent. He worked with Lord **Morley**, the secretary of state for India, in framing the **Government of India Act of 1909**. A key aspect of this process was the question of **separate electorates** for Muslims. Minto received a Muslim delegation headed by the **Aga Khan** at Simla in 1906. The delegation pressed for separate electorates, which were ultimately incorporated into the 1909 act.

MINUS TWO POLITICS. A political strategy initiated by the **caretaker government** of **Fakhruddin Ahmed**, with the support of the Bangladesh **armed forces,** to set in motion steps that would prevent the heads of the **Awami League** and the **Bangladesh Nationalist Party** from participating in the politics of the party. They felt that the political development of Bangladesh was severely handicapped due to the inflexibility and antagonism of the two leaders. The initial attempt was to keep the former Prime Minister **Sheikh Hasina** from returning to the country and sending former Prime Minister **Khaleda Zia** to exile in Saudi Arabia. When neither strategy worked, both were detained and charges were brought against them for abuse and **corruption.** When this strategy also failed, both were released under bail and allowed to participate in the December 2008 parliamentary **election.** After the election Sheikh Hasina became the prime minister and Khaleda Zia the leader of the opposition.

MIR JAFAR (?–1765). He remains a symbol of treachery in Bengal. He was a brother-in-law of **Alivardi Khan** and used his treachery on Alivardi's grandson and successor, **Sirajuddaulah**. In this he was associated with the banker, **Jagat Seth**. At the battle of **Plassey** in 1757 between Sirajuddaulah and the British under **Clive**, Mir Jafar deserted Sirajuddaulah, contributing to the latter's defeat. Mir Jafar was rewarded with the governorship of Bengal but was soon displaced (in 1760) by his son-in-law, **Mir Qasim**, at the insistence of the British. Mir Jafar was returned to the governor's post in 1763 by the British following Mir Qasim's defeat at **Buxar** and he held the position until his death.

MIR QASIM (?–c. 1777). A son-in-law and successor as governor of Bengal to **Mir Jafar**. He was installed as governor in 1760 at the insistence of the British, at the same time ceding the districts of **Chittagong**, Midnapur, and Burdwan to the **East India Company**. His actions to curb the private trade of British company officers led to a worsening of relations between Mir Qasim and the company. He is said to have perpetrated a massacre of the British at Patna. In 1764, the British attacked Mir Qasim, defeating him at the battle of **Buxar** on 22 October 1764. Mir Qasim fled and died in poverty in Delhi about 1777.

MIRZA, ISKANDAR (1899–1969). A collateral of the family of the nawabs of **Murshidabad**, he was in 1919 the first Indian cadet to graduate from Sandhurst, but he served his career primarily in the Indian Political Service. After independence he was defense secretary (1947–1954), governor of **East Bengal** (1954), a central minister (1954–1955), and governor-general (1955–1956). Mirza then became the first president of **Pakistan** in 1956. On 7 October 1958, he ended parliamentary government and proclaimed martial law, but he was dismissed on 28 October by the chief martial law administrator, **Ayub Khan**; Mirza left Pakistan on 2 November for London. He died in exile in London and was buried in Tehran.

MITRA, DINBONDHU (1830–1873). Playwright born in Nadia. His most famous play, *Neel Dorpon*, depicts the exploitation of poor farmers by the British **indigo** planters. *See also* THEATRE.

MODABBER, MOHAMMAD (1908–2008). Born in West Bengal, he was the editor of the daily newspaper *Azad* when it was published in **Kolkata** and later in **Dhaka**. He was a veteran anti-British movement leader, for which he was jailed a number of times. He also systematically criticized the government of **Pakistan** for its anti-Bengali **language** stance. Known as *Baghban Bhai*, he was instrumental in the *Mukul* Child Movement espousing the rights of children. He believed in the role of the youth in eliminating injustice and ensuring democratic society. *See also* LANGUAGE MOVEMENT.

MOHAMMADULLAH (1921–1999). President of Bangladesh from January 1974 to January 1975, when **Mujibur Rahman** assumed the presidency. After Mohammadullah stepped down from the presidency, he was minister of land administration and land reform until August 1975, when the regime of Mujibur Rahman was overthrown. Mohammadullah was named vice president by **Abdus Sattar** in March 1982 just prior to the coup by **Hussain Muhammad Ershad**.

MOHSIN, HAJI MOHAMMAD (1732–1812). A philanthropist and social activist, he was a lifelong bachelor who withdrew from an active life at age 32 to become a *fakir*, in which capacity he visited Egypt, Turkey, Iran, and Saudi Arabia. In 1906 he donated all of his property for the **education** of Muslims in India. Mohsin was the founder of the Hooghly College in **Kolkata** and established *madrasas* (religious schools) in **Dhaka**, **Rajshahi**, and **Chittagong**. He also established the Moshin Scholarship Fund for Higher Education for meritorious students. Today, when someone donates a large sum, that person is called Haji Mohsin in honor of Haji Mohammad Mohsin.

MONDAL, GURUDASHI (1951–2008). She represents the ordinary citizens of Bangladesh who suffered the atrocities of Pakistani armed forces during the **War of Liberation** of 1971. She and her family fled to India at the start of the 1971 war but came back to Bangladesh (East Pakistan) when the Pakistan government announced amnesty for those who had fled to India. In June 1971, her husband, two sons, and two daughters were killed by the **Razakar Bahini** as they found out that Gurudashi and her family were assisting the **Mukti Bahini**. She was kept a prisoner at a camp and was finally freed on 6 December 1971 when the Mukti Bahini and the Indian armed forces freed southern Khulna. For her support of the freedom fighters she was buried with national honor.

MOMEN, NURUL (1908–1990). A practicing lawyer at the **Kolkata** (India) High Court, he later taught at the Department of Law of **Dhaka University**, and was also known as a poet and a playwright. In 1944 he wrote the one-act play *Nemesis*, which is considered a classic in the annals of Bangladesh **theatre**. Other significant plays include *Rupantar*, *Ruplekha*, and *Alo Chayya*. For his contributions to Bangladesh theatre, he was given the title of *natyaguru* (expert of Bangladesh drama). He was also known as the father of modern

Bangla drama. For his contribution he was awarded the Bangla Academy award in 1961, the Sitara-e-Imtiaz in 1967, and the **Ekushey Padak** in 1978.

MONEM KHAN, ABDUL (1899–1971). A member of the **Muslim League** since 1935, he was the founder-secretary of the **Mymensingh** district Muslim League. He was a member of the Constituent Assembly of Pakistan until 1954. A protégé of **Nurul Amin**, Monem Khan was a mid-level political leader of **East Pakistan** who did not have the stature or the personality of leaders such as **Abul Kasem Fazlul Haq** or **Hussain Shahid Suhrawardy**. Nonetheless, he was a shrewd politician who spoke the language of the people. Elected as a member of the National Assembly of Pakistan in 1962, he was brought into the national limelight by President **Ayub Khan**, first as central minister of health, labor, and social welfare, and then as governor of East Pakistan, 1962–1969. Monem Khan was assassinated in 1971, during the **War of Liberation**.

MONI SINGH (1901–1994). Chairman of the **Communist Party of Bangladesh**. His participation in anti-British movements and his leadership in organizing the peasant movement brought him to the forefront of politics. For these activities, Moni Singh was arrested a number of times by the British. During the Pakistani period he was also frequently under arrest. He was associated with the freedom movement of Bangladesh and was a member of the Consultative Committee of the Bangladesh provisional government-in-exile. After independence, Moni Singh cooperated with the Sheikh **Mujibur Rahman** government.

MONIRUZZAMAN, MOHAMMAD (1936–2008). A lyricist, poet, and cultural activist, he joined the Department of Bangla, **Dhaka University**, in 1962. He wrote more than 50 books and over 1,500 songs. Among his critical translations are the writings of Emily Dickenson. Songs written by him that are considered classics in Bangladesh include *Amar desher matir gondhey*, *Tumi ki dekhechho kobhu*, *Asru diye lekha e gaan*, *Protidin tomaye dekhi shurjolokey*, *Premer naam bedona*, *Holud bato mehdi bato*, and *Charagachhe phul phuitachhe*. A number of his poems focused on the **War of Liberation**. These include *Kobita-e aar ki likhbo/ Jokhon buk-er roktey likhechi/ Ekti naam/ Bangladesh*. As a faculty member his research publications on Bangla **literature** and poetry include *Bangla Kobita-e Chhondo*, *Adhunik Bangla Sahitya*, *Bangla Sahitya-e Bangaali Chetona*, and *Adhonik Bangla Kobita*. Some of his well-acknowledged collections of poetry are *Durlobh Din, Shankito Alokey, Protonu Protyasha Biponno Bishad*, and *Bhashamoy Projapoti*. He was bestowed the Bangla Academy Award and the **Ekushey Padak**.

MONTAGU, EDWIN SAMUEL (1879–1924). He became acquainted with **India** as parliamentary secretary in the India office under **Viscount John Morley** and his successor, Lord Crewe. Montagu visited India in 1912. He became secretary of state for India in 1917 and in the Montagu declaration of that year stated that the goal of Britain was the "progressive realization of responsible government" in India. He worked with the viceroy-governor general, Lord Chelmsford, to take steps toward that goal in the act that is often referred to by their names, the **Government of India Act of 1919**.

MONTAGU-CHELMSFORD ACT. *See* GOVERNMENT OF INDIA ACT OF 1919.

MORLEY, VISCOUNT JOHN (1838–1923). A British literary and political figure whose place in politics was enhanced by a close relationship with William Ewart Gladstone, whose biographer Morley became. He served in several liberal cabinets and became secretary of state for India in 1905 in the Balfour cabinet and continued in the Campbell-Bannerman and Asquith ministries. It was in the last that he accepted the concept of **Lord Minto** that a means should be found to increase Indian representation in the governing of India, and he also accepted the provision for **separate electorates** for Muslims. He is reported to have said earlier that India was unfit for self-government.

MORLEY-MINTO ACT. *See* GOVERNMENT OF INDIA ACT OF 1909.

MOTHAR HUSAIN, KAZI (1897–1981). Granted the title of National Professor in 1975 for his contribution to science. In 1926 he organized the Muslim **Literature** Society and he became the president of the Pakistan Literature Society in 1952.

MOUNTBATTEN OF BURMA, LOUIS MOUNTBATTEN, FIRST EARL (1900–1979). The son of Prince Louis of Battenberg (later Mountbatten) and Princess Victoria of Hesse (a granddaughter of Queen Victoria), he was viceroy of India in 1947 and governor-general of India, 1947–1948. Mountbatten's task was to facilitate the withdrawal of British power from India and (reluctantly) arrange for the partition of the British dominions between India and Pakistan. His son-in-law, Lord Brabourne, was governor of Bengal, 1937–1939.

MUGHAL EMPIRE. The Mughal Empire (1526–1857) was the successor to the **Delhi Sultanate**. Babar, the founder of the dynasty, defeated the last Lodhi sultan at the battle of Panipat in 1526. The dominion of the Mughals soon spread from **Afghanistan** to Bengal and as far south as the Deccan. The principal rulers were the first six: Babar (1526–1530), Humayun (1530–1540 and 1555–1556), Akbar (1556–1605), Jahangir (1605–1627), Shahjahan (1627–1658), and Aurangzeb (1658–1707). Thereafter, the dynasty declined and was, in effect, under British control from the early 19th century until the final collapse in 1857 following the sepoy mutiny.

With respect to Bengal, control was taken by the Mughals under Humayun in 1538, but it was lost a year later to **Sher Shah Suri**, whose descendants ruled Bengal until 1564. A short non-Mughal period followed until 1576, when the Mughals regained control under Akbar. Mughal governors (nawabs) ruled from **Dhaka** and **Murshidabad**, and in 1765 the emperor Shah Alam II granted the *diwani* to the British. *See also* KARRANI DYNASTY; MARTIAL RACES.

MUJIBBAD (MUJIBISM). The term used for the four pillars espoused by Sheikh **Mujibur Rahman** as the key principles on which the government of independent Bangladesh would be based: nationalism, secularism, socialism, and democracy. They form part of the **1972 constitution**. Mujibbad follows closely the four principles attributed to Jawaharlal Nehru of **India**: non-alignment, secularism, socialism, and democracy.

MUJIBNAGAR. The name given to the temporary capital of Bangladesh during the **War of Liberation**. It was first located at the village of Baidyanath near the Indian border in the subdivision of Meherpur in **Kushtia** district (Meherpur is now a district in its own right).

In fact, very quickly the capital was moved to **Calcutta** to remove the possibility of attack by **Pakistani** forces. The name Mujibnagar was retained for the Calcutta location.

MUJIBUR RAHMAN (?–1940). A prominent Bengali Muslim journalist who also involved himself in politics. He was an editorial writer for the *Mussalman*, an important weekly that began its publication in 1906 in reaction to the **partition of Bengal**. Mujibur Rahman also was a member of the **Muslim League**, and as such his major impact was his strong opposition to Muslim League association with the Simon Commission (1928), a British parliamentary commission sent to survey the operation of the **Government of India Act of 1919**. Many Indians, including the Congress Party, objected to the exclusion of Indians from the commission.

MUJIBUR RAHMAN, SHEIKH (1921–1975). Prime minister (1972–1975) and president (1975) of Bangladesh. He began his political career as a student in **Calcutta** in 1940 with the Muslim Students' Federation, an arm of the **Muslim League**. He was a founding member with **Husain Shahid Suhrawardy** of the **Awami League** in 1949. Mujib was the principal organizer of the party in **East Bengal**, later **East Pakistan**. He was minister of commerce in East Pakistan, 1956–1957, but he was more respected for his party organizational abilities than for his administrative skills, a factor that would make his management of Bangladesh difficult.

After Suhrawardy's death in 1963, Mujib became de facto national leader of the Awami League, although his official position pertained only to East Pakistan. In this role, he proclaimed the **Six-Point Program** in 1966. Mujib led the Awami League to an overwhelming victory in the 1970 **elections** in East Pakistan, but his party was unable to win any seats in West Pakistan. Following the negotiations among Mujib, **Bhutto**, and **Yahya Khan** in early 1971, Mujib came under increasing pressure to declare independence, rather than autonomy within Pakistan, as the goal of the Awami League. When the army took action in March 1971, Mujibur Rahman was arrested and held in West Pakistan until after the surrender of the Pakistan army in East Pakistan. Much of this time was spent under the threat of death, but Bhutto, who replaced Yahya Khan after the defeat, released Mujib and permitted him to return to Bangladesh.

He arrived on 10 January 1972 and assumed the prime ministership. Under his leadership the parliament enacted a constitution that called for a parliamentary system and embraced what came to be called **Mujibbad**. However, the administration was very poorly run, and, under increasing opposition, Mujib obtained parliamentary approval for a presidential system with himself as president in January 1975. In June 1975 he dissolved the Awami League into **BAKSAL**, which became the only legal party in Bangladesh.

Mujib was assassinated along with many members of his family by disgruntled army officers on 15 August 1975. His daughter, Sheikh **Hasina Wajid**, was not in Bangladesh at the time and has since become leader of the Awami League and leader of the opposition in parliament following the 1986 and 1991 **elections**. She became prime minister in 1996. However, in the 2001 election the Awami League was defeated and she again became leader of the opposition. In 2008, she once again became the prime minister.

MUKTADHARA. A publishing house established in **Kolkata** during the **War of Liberation**. It supported the writings of the Bangladeshi scholars and journalists who had escaped to India. It published 32 books on the war during the war. The founder of the Muktadhara also was instrumental in establishing the **Amar Ekushey Granthamela** fair held annually.

MUKTI BAHINI. Literally this means "freedom force." It was initially an ad hoc fighting force formed after the beginning of military operations against the civilian population of Bangladesh by units of the Pakistani army in March 1971. It was mainly composed of Bengali personnel serving in the Pakistani army, the East Bengal Rifles, the East Pakistan Police, and civilians who took arms against the Pakistani army. The Mukti Bahini received Indian assistance in small arms and training. Some members of the Mukti Bahini were incorporated into the **Jatiyo Rakkhi Bahini** after independence. *See also* WAR OF LIBERATION.

MUKUL, M. R. AKHTAR (1929–2004). A journalist employed by the newspapers *Daily Azad* and *Daily Ittefaq*, he was also the Dhaka bureau chief of United Press International. An activist, like many he was involved in the 1952 **language movement** and the 1969 mass movement against President **Ayub Khan**. His highest recognition came as a result of his role in the **War of Liberation**. During the 1971 war he ran a radio program from the *Swadhin Bangla Betar* (Free Bangla Radio) not only denouncing the barbaric and **terroristic** acts of the **Pakistani** army and the military and civilian leaders but also chiding them for their cowardly acts. He used the local Dhakia dialect and took on the character of *Chokku Mia* of Bakshi Bazar, a **Dhaka** neighborhood settled by Mughal and Persian rulers, craftsmen, and soldiers. His radio program was the most satirical denunciation of the Pakistani actions in Bangladesh. For his services to the nation he became the press minister at the Bangladesh High Commission to **Great Britain**. He wrote a number of books on such topics as the 1971 war, the **language movement**, and Sheikh **Mujibur Rahman**.

MURSHED, SYED MAHBUB (1911–1979). A nephew of **Abul Kasem Fazlul Haq**, he was a barrister who became a judge in 1955 and chief justice of the Dhaka High Court in 1964. He resigned in 1968 to enter politics and was a member of the **Democratic Action Committee** that negotiated with **Ayub Khan** in 1969. Murshed announced himself a candidate for the presidency in the election of 1969, a vote that was not held.

MURSHID QULI JAFAR KHAN (?–1727). A Persian who was a **Mughal** government official and who had risen to the post of *diwan* (collector of revenue) of the Deccan under Aurangzeb. He was appointed diwan of Bengal in 1700 by the emperor, Aurangzeb. He performed so well that he was made independent of the governor and moved the revenue offices from **Dhaka** to the town that would bear his name, **Murshidabad**, in 1701. He was raised to the governorship of Bengal, Bihar, and Orissa in 1707, but a year later was transferred to the Deccan as governor. He was perhaps born a Brahmin and was purchased and adopted by Haji Shafi Isfahani, presumably a Persian, hence the origin of Quli Khan as his name. He secured quasi-independent status in 1717 (i.e., was no longer a slave of Isfahani).

MURSHIDABAD. A city on the Bhagirathi River in West Bengal. It was already a substantial commercial town when **Murshid Quli Jafar Khan** moved the headquarters of the *diwan* to it from Dhaka in 1704. As Murshid rose from diwan to nawab of Bengal, Murshidabad became the capital of Bengal until 1773. Administratively, the city was superseded by **Calcutta**, but many important monuments remain. Murshidabad is separated from Bangladesh by the river Padma. A number of prominent Bengali Muslim families come from Murshidabad. *See also* MIRZA, ISKANDAR.

MUSEUMS. There are a number of museums in Bangladesh. The leading museum is the Bangladesh National Museum in **Dhaka**, which has an outstanding collection pertaining to the early periods of Bengal history as well as more modern items. The museum of the **Asiatic Society of Bangladesh**, also in Dhaka, has a wide range of historical artifacts. More specialized museums include the Folk Art and Crafts Foundation Museum in **Sonargaon** and the Ethnology Museum in **Chittagong**. Most of the sites for **archeology** have museums at the sites. The **Varendra** Research Society museum in **Rajshahi** is important for that area of Bangladesh.

MUSHARAF HUSAIN, NAWAB (1871–1966). A businessman, politician, and philanthropist, he was given the title of nawab in 1926. In 1918 he was a member of the Bengal Legislative Council and became **education** minister of Bengal in 1927. He was responsible for passing the first education bill calling for free primary education in Bengal. Musharaf Husain was law minister in the **Fazlul Haq** cabinet in 1937. He established a number of schools and *madrasas* (religious schools).

MUSHARRAF HUSAIN, MIR (1847–1912). Proclaimed as the "father of Bengali literature," he was an advocate of Hindu-Muslim unity. His book *Go-Jivan* (The Life of Cattle), in which he opposed cow slaughter, was, to say the least, controversial and led to some Muslim opposition to him.

MUSHARRAF, KHALID (?–1975). A Bengali major in the Pakistani army in 1971, he came to prominence as a hero during the **War of Independence**. He was an ambitious officer who was promoted to brigadier by Sheikh **Mujibur Rahman**. Pro-Indian in his outlook, Khalid Musharraf masterminded the countercoup of 3 November 1977 that resulted in the ouster of **majors** who were responsible for the **August coup**. He himself was overthrown and killed by a popular uprising in the army on 7 November 1977. *See also* ARMED FORCES.

MUSHTAQUE AHMED, KHONDAKAR (1918–1996). President of Bangladesh from August 1975 to November 1975. Active in the **language movement**, he was also a founding member of the **Awami League**. In 1954 he served as the chief whip of the **United Front** government. During the 1969 political movement to oust President **Ayub Khan** he was the convener of the East Pakistan **Democratic Action Committee** and participated in the roundtable conference held at that time. Mushtaque was elected to the National Assembly in 1970. During the **War of Liberation** he was the foreign minister and minister for law and parliamentary affairs in the Bangladesh government-in-exile. He was a member of the cabinet of **Mujibur Rahman**, 1972–1975. Mushtaque became president of the country after Mujibur Rahman was assassinated, but gave up the presidency when a countercoup led by **Khalid Musharraf** took place in November 1975. He was arrested in 1976 and released in 1980. He was characterized as a conservative, Western-oriented politician. Mushtaque headed the now defunct **Democratic League**.

MUSIC. All genres and emotions are found in Bangladeshi music: ecstasy, romance, folklore, moroseness, social commentary. Many of the folk songs are associated with boatmen. These often express the longing of the traveler for a loved one. Some of the music is taken from the **Bauls**. Other pieces remind the musician of the past, such as the sad music of *jarigan*, which is drawn from the martyrdom of Muhammad's grandson, Hussain, at Karbela in Iraq. *Poonthigaan* is also historical in content, celebrating the legends of the invading Arabs and Persians. Songs based on the writings of **Rabindranath Tagore** (*Rabindra sangeet*) and **Nazrul Islam** (*Nazrul geeti*) are popular. A musical drama form, known as *jatra*, is based on historical, mythological, and religious episodes and is popular at festivals. *See also* DANCE; KHAN FAMILY OF BRAHMANBARIA; THEATRE.

MUSICAL INSTRUMENTS. There are a number of instruments associated with folk **music** that are used in modern and classical music. The *ektara* is a one-stringed instrument that provides a drone to folk music. The *dotara*, despite its name meaning two strings, is actually a four-stringed instrument in which the strings act in pairs. There are several varieties of drums, including the *dhol*, the most popular folk percussion instrument. Cymbals and bamboo flutes are used, as are bracelets of small bells usually tied around the ankles of dancers.

MUSLIM LEAGUE. A political party formed in **Dhaka** in December 1906. Its initial goals were to support the Crown and to further the cause of the Muslims of India without opposing the other groups in India. Its founding followed the Simla meeting of Muslims with Lord **Minto**. The Muslims demanded **separate electorates**. This demand was met in the **Government of India Act of 1909** and accepted by the Indian National Congress in an agreement with the Muslim League signed in 1916 at Lucknow. The league gained its most important member when **Muhammad Ali Jinnah** joined in 1913. He led the Muslim League negotiations with the Congress at Lucknow. The Congress soon retracted its acceptance of separate electorates and worked to end the system from the 1920s to partition in 1947. Jinnah agreed in 1928 to yield on the issue if other safeguards for the Muslim minority were given; this was not done by the Congress or the British.

The league contested **elections** as a single body first in 1937. It did well in the Muslim-minority provinces but poorly in the Muslim-majority provinces. It was seen by many Bengali Muslims as the party of **Calcutta** Muslims and of those Muslims who belonged to the **national elite**. At a session of the league in Lucknow later in 1937, four of the Muslim prime ministers (including **Fazlul Haq**) agreed to support the league in national matters in return for a free hand in their own provincial affairs. This greatly strengthened Jinnah's position and that of the Muslim League.

On 23 March 1940, the **Lahore Resolution** was passed, expressing the possibility of a demand for partition. In the 1946 election the Muslim League won handsome majorities in the Muslim seats in all the Muslim-majority provinces except the Northwest Frontier Province. Jinnah took this as a mandate to press for partition. The demand was accepted, and Pakistan was created on 14 August 1947. After independence and the death of Jinnah (1948), the league began to weaken. It was defeated badly in the election to the **East Bengal** provincial assembly in 1954 and shortly thereafter split in West Pakistan. All parties were banned by **Ayub Khan** when martial law was declared in October 1958. In 1962, Ayub resurrected the **Pakistan Muslim League (Convention)**; some of his opponents formed the **Council Muslim League**. Both parties did poorly in the 1970 election; neither won a seat in East Pakistan. In Bangladesh the party was banned during the period of **Mujibur Rahman**, but was permitted to return during the period of **Ziaur Rahman**. The party, led by **Abdul Sobur Khan**, won 20 seats in the 1979 parliamentary election but has since splintered and is of small consequence. *See also* BANGLADESH MUSLIM LEAGUE.

MUSLIN. A cloth for which **Dhaka** became famous. The Dhaka variety is handwoven of very fine cotton. Muslin was traded extensively in India and later to Europe as one of the valuable exports of Bengal. The skill to make Dhaka muslin seems to have been lost and now textiles in Dhaka tend to be machine made and therefore not of the fine quality produced earlier.

MUZAFFAR AHMED (1889–1973). Born in **Chittagong**, he was one of the early members of the Communist Party of **India** (CPI). As such, he was involved in a number of conspiracy cases brought by the British colonial government. With others, including **Kazi Nazrul Islam**, he organized the Bengal Peasants and Workers Party in 1925, which was merged with the CPI. Muzaffar Ahmed wrote extensively on the communist movement and the party, and his publications are important primary sources for the study of Indian communism. He remained in India after partition.

MYANMAR. *See* BURMA.

MYMENSINGH. A district and district town. The city lies on the banks of the old channel of the **Brahmaputra**, the river having diverted its main channel westward in the early 19th century so that it now forms the boundary between Mymensingh and **Pabna**, **Bogra**, and **Rangpur**. Mymensingh town was formerly known as Nasirabad.

The area was under the control of Kamarupa (**Assam**) in ancient times and a series of rulers after that, including the **Senas** just prior to Muslim control. In 1351 Mymensingh was taken by **Shamsuddin Ilyas Shah** as he united Bengal. The region was subject to rebellions, most notably in the latter part of the 16th century when **Isa Khan** and the **Bara Bhuiyan** led a revolt against **Man Singh** and **Mughal** rule.

Mymensingh city is the seat of the Bangladesh **Agricultural** University. During the **Hussain Muhammad Ershad** period **local government** reorganization resulted in the creation of three districts: Mymensingh, Netrakona, and Kishorganj. Earlier, two other subdivisions, Jamalpur and Tangail, had been elevated to district status. Most of the Madhupur jungle reserve lies within the present Mymensingh district. The jungle contains the Bara Tirtha, allegedly built by Bhagadatta, who fought in the battle of Kurukshetra recorded in the Hindu epic *Mahabharata*. Bhairab Bazaar, in Kishorganj district at the junction of the Old Brahmaputra and the **Meghna**, is a major river port. **Isa Khan** founded the family of landlords known as the Diwan Sahibs of Haibatnagar and Jangalbari.

– N –

NABADWIP. A town, formerly known as **Nadia**, located in Nadia district of West Bengal. It was founded in 1063 by a ruler of the **Sena dynasty** that was beginning to consolidate his rule over territories of the **Pala dynasty**. It was at Nabadwip, then known as Nadia, that **Lakshmana Sena** was defeated by **Ikhtiyaruddin Khalji** in 1202. Nabadwip is the birthplace of **Chaitanya**.

NADIA. A district in West Bengal in which **Plassey** is located. It is also the site of the **Farakka Barrage**. Three distributaries of the **Ganges**

flow through Nadia district, of which the major one is the Bhagarathi, through which the waters diverted at Farakka flow. In the district is **Nabadwip**. At the partition of India in 1947, Nadia lost the subdivisions of **Kushtia**, Meherpur, and Chuadanga to the newly formed district of Kushtia in East Bengal.

NAKSHI KANTHA **(EMBROIDERED QUILTS).** *Nakshi kantha* is a traditional craft with creative designs made by the housewives in Bangladesh in their leisure period. Depending on the type of stitching, it has a variety of names such as *dal foure, chain foure, kamal foure, shujoni, dubadubi, jessori, mushuri kadam, moy par, jora par, hashia taaga, anas taaga, kolshi par, phool par, borfi tip par, mukta dana par*, and fly stitch. In 1929, the poet **Jasimuddin** acknowledged this art form when he wrote his famous poem, *Nakshi kanthar maath.* After independence, this **art** form was patronized by the fashion house Aarong. The stitch patterns are no longer limited to quilts but are also embroidered in *saris, kurtas*, bed covers, wall hangings, lamp shades, and jewelry boxes.

NANDI, ARUN (1940–2008). He is best known for drawing the attention, primarily of Indians and Western countries, to the plight of the Bangladeshi during the **War of Liberation**. He swam in a lake in **Calcutta** for 90 hours. In the process he broke the world endurance record in swimming held by B. C. Moore, an American swimmer. For his unique role in the 1971 conflict, he was awarded the National Sports Award in 1996.

NASRIN, TASLIMA (1962–). A physician and author, she attracted international attention when her novel *Lajja* (Shame) was banned by the government in 1993 as being offensive to the religious sensibilities of many Bangladeshi Muslims. The work condemned Muslim religious leaders for their persecution of **Hindus** in Bangladesh. An ardent feminist who had been criticized earlier for similar writings, Taslima was sentenced to death by fundamentalist religious leaders and charged by the government of offending religious sensibilities. She first hid from arrest but then reported to the court. She fled to Sweden in August 1994, but she has occasionally visited Bangladesh from her Swedish base. Her attempt to settle in India in 2007 failed. *See also* LITERATURE.

NATIONAL AWAMI PARTY (NAP). Formed in **East Pakistan** by **Maulana Abdul Hamid Khan Bhashani** when he withdrew in 1957 from the **Awami League**. Bhashani objected to the program of then prime minister **Husain Shahid Suhrawardy**, which he saw as too pro-Western and too market-economy oriented. Bhashani's party incorporated several West Pakistani leaders of small parties that were either regional or leftist or both. In the 1960s the party split, with one branch, often incorrectly referred to as "pro-China," remaining with Bhashani (called the NAP[B]). The other splinter was headed nationally by Khan Abdul Wali Khan of the Northwest Frontier Province (the NAP[W]) and in East Pakistan by **Muzaffar Ahmed**.

Both factions in East Pakistan failed to attract appreciable support in the 1970 election. After independence and especially the death of Bhashani in 1976, the NAP(B) splintered many times and has since ceased to exist. Some members even joined the **Bangladesh Nationalist Party**, including **Mashiur Rahman**, the presumptive prime minister in 1979 (he died as the election results were coming in). The Muzaffar Ahmed group, reinitialed NAP(M) after 1971, has also been of little consequence since independence, although it has won an occasional seat. Muzaffar strongly supported **BAKSAL** in 1975 as a means of political survival. A party bearing the initials NAP(M) won one seat in the 1991 election, but none in succeeding elections.

NATIONAL ELITE. A term applied to those in Muslim Bengali leadership who tended to use Urdu as a family **language** (hence they are also known as the Urdu elite) rather than Bengali. This distinguished them from the **Hindu** elite of Bengal, but also had several other consequences. The members were often descendants of **Mughal Empire** or **Delhi Sultanate** officers who had been sent to Bengal to govern and whose families remained in the region. Often, they were also Muslim *zamindars* (landowners), for example, the **Nawab of Dhaka**. In the **Muslim League** they tended to support national issues rather than Bengali issues. Among these were such leaders as **Khwaja Nazimuddin**. Their use of Urdu detached them from the mass of Bengalis and permitted such **vernacular elite** leaders as **Fazlul Haq** to achieve prominence. After Pakistan's independence, this group continued to support the Muslim League, even to the extent of supporting Urdu as the Pakistani national language. Their power was destroyed in the East Bengal election of 1954, in which the Muslim League was trounced by the **United Front**. To a limited degree, the national elite also supported the **Pakistan Muslim League (Convention)** formed by **Ayub Khan**.

NATIONAL HUMAN RIGHTS COMMISSION (NHRC). Formed in 2008 by the caretaker government of **Fakhruddin Ahmed**, the NHRC investigates reports and complaints regarding human rights violations and maintains the standards of prisons and other correctional facilities. The NHRC will also examine the Bangladesh constitution and laws and regulations to ensure compliance and to remove any loopholes. It will also align Bangladeshi human rights rules and regulations with international human rights covenants.

NATIONAL SOCIALIST PARTY. *See* JATIYA SAMAJTANTRIK DAL.

NATIONAL UNION PARISHAD FORUM (NUPF). An association of union *parishads*, its membership is limited to union parishad chairs, general members, and members elected to reserved seats. NUPF organizes public discussions, press conferences, mail campaigns, and other activities on issues impacting local government. It is focused on improving governance through better participation of its citizens, meeting its obligations and responsibilities, and improving its financial resources. It seeks a greater role in development projects and wants to reduce the role of the local member of parliament.

NATOR. Early in the 18th century, the *zamindari* of Rajshahi was granted to Ramjivan, the founder of the Nator family. The Nator holdings stretched from Bhagalpur in the west to **Dhaka** in the east, although the major portion of the zamindari was in **Rajshahi** district. The gazetteer of the province of Eastern Bengal and Assam states: "Rajshahi presents an example of the process by which a native zamindari has been molded into a British district." When the management of the land came under Rani Bhawani, about 1780, she reduced the land through charitable grants and impoverished the assets. Indebtedness followed and gradually the hereditary property was sold and the estate ended. The palace of the Nator rajas is in Nator town, now the headquarters of a district of the same name.

NATURAL GAS. *See* NATURAL RESOURCES.

NATURAL RESOURCES. Bangladesh has few exploitable natural resources. Petroleum reserves were estimated at less than 60 million barrels in 2000. There is some low-quality coal in the north-central area, but extensive mining is so far not feasible owing to the high groundwater levels. There are no known metallic minerals that can be commercially exploited.

The major exception is natural gas, which will be in abundant supply when fully developed. Natural gas was first exploited in Jalalabad in **Sylhet** district, but it has since been found in large quantities in such places as **Chittagong** and the districts along the Bay of Bengal and may be found offshore as well. Estimates are that 80 trillion cubic feet of gas may be available, an amount greatly in excess of the likely requirements of Bangladesh for many years. The principal use within Bangladesh has been in the manufacture of nitrogenous fertilizers and also to a limited degree in domestic and industrial fuel.

American and British firms, among some others, have been prepared to invest to exploit the gas reserves. Because the reserves are so large, there has also been discussion of exporting the gas, either as gas or as gas-generated electric power, to the Indian state of West Bengal, which is power short. Foreign firms have been frustrated by what appears to them to be indecisiveness on the part of the government of Bangladesh. Another proposal that would require the use of Bangladesh territory has come from **Burma** (Myanmar) for the export of its gas via a pipeline through Bangladesh to West Bengal, a route that is thought to be more easily and safely developed than one through **Assam** and the smaller states in India's northwest.

In general, there has been minimal movement in developing the natural resources of the country.

NAUSHER ALI, SYED (1891–1972). Born in Jessore district, he was educated in **Kolkata** and became an advocate. Before independence, he was associated with the **Krishak Praja Party**, but after independence, he remained in **India**, where he had close connections with the

Communist Party of India (CPI). Nausher Ali served in the Bengal Legislative Council, 1929–1936, and in the Bengal Legislative Assembly, 1937–1946, in both cases being elected from Jessore. From 1943 to 1945, he was speaker. After independence, he was a member of the Rajya Sabha, 1952–1956 and 1962–1968, associated as an independent with the CPI.

NAZIMUDDIN, KHWAJA (SIR) (1894–1964). A member of the **Nawab of Dhaka family.** He was educated at Aligarh Muslim University and Cambridge University. He was a member of the Bengal Legislative Council, 1923–1934, and the Bengal Legislative Assembly, 1937–1945, until the assembly was dissolved by the governor. During the period 1934–1937, Nazimuddin was a member of the governor's executive council. Earlier, he was minister of education, 1929–1934. As a member of the legislative assembly of Bengal, he served as home minister, 1937–1941, under the premiership of **Abul Kasem Fazlul Haq** during a coalition between the **Krishak Praja Party** and the **Muslim League.** With the breakup of the coalition, Nazimuddin became leader of the opposition, 1941–1943, but he became prime minister in 1943, serving until the ministry was terminated by the governor in 1945. After the 1946 elections, Nazimuddin was denied a return to the premiership, as he was defeated by a rival Muslim Leaguer, **Husain Shahid Suhrawardy.** However, after independence in 1947, he became chief minister of East Bengal, where he served until he was appointed in 1948 to succeed **Muhammad Ali Jinnah** as governor-general.

When **Liaquat Ali Khan** was assassinated in 1951, Nazimuddin stepped down from the governor-generalship to become prime minister, remaining in office until he was dismissed in 1953 by Governor-General **Ghulam Muhammad,** although it was not demonstrated that Nazimuddin had lost the confidence of the constituent assembly. Nazimuddin remained a member of the constituent assembly and parliament, though he was less active, until the imposition of martial law in October 1958 by president **Iskandar Mirza.** When **political parties** were again permitted to function in 1962, Nazimuddin became president of the **Council Muslim League** and was a leader of the **Combined Opposition Parties** in opposition to **Ayub Khan** until he died in 1964.

Nazimuddin's brother, **Khwaja Shahabuddin**, was also prominent in politics. Although they were often rivals, Nazimuddin, Fazlul Haq, and Suhrawardy are buried in adjacent graves in a **Dhaka** park.

NAZRUL ISLAM, KAZI (1899–1976). A Muslim poet, born in Burdwan district, whose principal writings were between 1919 and 1941. He served in the British Indian army, 1917–1919, and wished to use that training in his opposition to British rule in **India**. During the British period his writing was frequently proscribed, and he was arrested several times. Nazrul Islam's political views were much to the left. He was associated with **Muzaffar Ahmed** in the founding of the Bengal Workers and Peasants Party, which later was absorbed into the Communist Party of India. He wrote love songs, drawing often on the legends and myths of Bengal, but he also composed revolutionary poetry, which drew the negative attention of the British. Nazrul Islam suffered from a neurological disease in 1942, which ended his literary career and left him incapacitated. Although he lived most of his life in **Kolkata**, he moved to Bangladesh at the invitation of Sheikh **Mujibur Rahman**. He was buried on the campus of **Dhaka University**. *See also* LITERATURE.

NAZRUL ISLAM, SYED (1925–1975). As a student leader in his youth, he actively participated in the language movement. He joined the **Awami League** in 1953 and rose through the ranks to be the senior vice president of the Awami League. He was a close confidant of Sheikh **Mujibur Rahman** and headed the Bangladesh government-in-exile in 1971 when Mujib was in jail in Pakistan. It was during his tenure as minister of industry that a large number of **industries** and **banks** were nationalized. In 1975 Nazrul Islam became vice president of Bangladesh. He was assassinated in the **Dhaka jail killings**.

NIJERA KORI. Established in 1981 as a non-governmental organization (NGO), it attempts to engender individual and group awareness about social, political, and economic challenges facing **women** and the downtrodden. Through its work it seeks an accountable and democratic society where sustainable development is facilitated. The organization focuses on victims of exploitation, social marginalization, oppression, and poverty. It especially focuses on wage laborers, sharecroppers, and small and marginal farmers, as well as tradespeople such as potters, cobblers, blacksmiths, and weavers. Nijera Kori also works with indigenous peoples of Bangladesh.

NINETEEN POINTS. A program outlined by **Ziaur Rahman** in 1979. Zia provided, through the nineteen points, his ideas of the direction that Bangladesh should be taking in the economic, political, and social sectors. Affirming such fundamental constitutional principles as faith and reliance upon Allah, democracy, nationalism, and social development, he wanted to set up a self-reliant Bangladesh. Participation, **food** self-sufficiency, enhanced provision of services including **health** and shelter, **privatization**, and decentralization were some of the other program goals.

NIZAM-I-ISLAM. A small conservative Muslim political party led by **Farid Ahmad** established in 1953. It was said to have been influenced by **Abul Kasem Fazlul Haq**. Nizam-i-Islam supported the concept of a government based on **Islam** and wanted separate electorates. This party joined the **United Front** government in **East Pakistan**. It opposed the martial law regime of President **Ayub Khan**. It did not support the Bangladesh freedom movement led by the **Awami League**. After the independence of Bangladesh it was banned. Nizam-i-Islam reemerged after the passing of the Political Parties Regulation in 1976. It later merged with the **Islamic Democratic League**.

NIZAMUDDIN AHMED (1929–1971). A journalist who was killed by collaborators with the Pakistani army four days before the surrender of the army. He was born in Munshiganj and educated in **Dhaka**. As general manager of the Dhaka office of Pakistan Press International, Nizamuddin avoided censorship and sent many pictures and documents out of Bangladesh during the **War of Liberation**.

NOA MIA (1852–1883). Second son of **Dudu Mia**, he was named Abdul Ghafar Noa Mia. In 1864 he became the leader of the **Faraizi movement**. Like his father, he stressed **religion** rather than politics or economics.

NOAKHALI. A district in southeastern Bangladesh that became well known in 1946 when Mahatma Gandhi traveled there to help relieve the communal violence that was occurring. Gandhi achieved some success and then moved to other areas, including **Calcutta** and Bihar, to attempt to accomplish the same results.

The history of Noakhali is closely entwined with that of **Comilla**. Noakhali was created as a district separate from Comilla (then known as Tippera) in 1822. The reorganization of **local government** during the **Ershad** government resulted in the detaching of Feni as a separate district.

Noakhali has a long coastline with the **Meghna** estuary and is often subject to tidal bores and to cyclones originating in the Bay of Bengal. Hatia and Sandwip are in the district. *See also* COASTAL ISLANDS; SUHRAWARDY, HUSAIN SHAHID; TRIPURA.

NON-GOVERNMENTAL ORGANIZATIONS (NGOs). One of the major recent trends in Bangladesh has been the large increase in the number of NGOs active in supporting social, economic, and political development. Some estimates are as high as 30,000 NGOs, but a more likely number is 15,000. The difference in estimates is largely a question of definition.

One of the earliest was the **Bangladesh Rural Advancement Committee** founded in Sylhet in 1972. Other major NGOs include the **Grameen Bank**, the **Association for Social Advancement**, and Proshikha. The activities of the NGOs include involvement in **poverty** alleviation, empowerment, and social sector programs. Several NGOs are active in group-based credit provision; others focus on women, such as **Nijera Kori**.

A number of factors have been identified as key to the success of NGO activities and to the proliferation of NGOs as a means of providing services to the mass of people who do not benefit from public sector programs. In the work of the NGOs, partial management responsibility is placed with the recipient group, including training in basic financial management which can lead eventually to full management responsibility. Issues such as the role of NGOs relative to the traditional role of government in development, the sustainability of the work of the NGOs, and the impact of religious beliefs (some NGOs are Christian-supported) are causing some friction. Nonetheless, NGOs have attained a significant amount of political power owing to the perception that they, as a group, have made a significant contribution to the overall welfare of the country. *See also* ODHIKAR.

NOON, MALIK FIROZ KHAN (SIR) (1893–1970). A prominent Punjabi political figure who held many positions in the Punjab and central governments before independence. He was Indian high commissioner to London (1936–1941) and a member of the viceroy's council (1941–1945). After independence, in addition to being a member of the constituent assembly, Noon was governor of **East Bengal** (1950–1953), serving during some of the more difficult periods of the Bengali language agitation. Noon, nonetheless, was popular personally, and a school bearing his wife's name (Viqaranessa) still operates in **Dhaka**. He later was chief minister of the Punjab (1953–1955), foreign minister under **Husain Shahid Suhrawardy** (1956–1957), and prime minister (1958) until the imposition of martial law in October 1958.

NUNCOMAR (NANDA KUMAR RAY) (1721–1775). Deputy governor of Bengal, c. 1765, and served under **Warren Hastings** after the latter's arrival in India in 1772. In 1773, when Hastings was named governor-general, Nuncomar had charge of governing Bengal. In 1775, he brought charges against Hastings for **corruption**, but he himself was charged with forgery, convicted, and hanged.

NURUL AMIN (1897–1974). He was born in **Mymensingh**, where he practiced law after completing studies in **Calcutta**. He first entered the legislature as a member of the Bengal Legislative Council in 1942, was elected to the Bengal Legislative Assembly in 1946, and was chosen speaker. At independence, Nurul Amin became a member of the **Khwaja Nazimuddin** cabinet in **East Bengal** and succeeded Nazimuddin as chief minister when the latter became governor-general in 1948. Both he personally and the **Muslim League** as a party were defeated in the **United Front** sweep in the 1954 **elections**. Nurul Amin remained leader of the Muslim League in **East Pakistan** until parties were banned after the coup of **Ayub Khan** in 1958.

In 1965 he was elected to the National Assembly as a member of the National Democratic Front. In 1969 Nurul Amin played a prominent role in the negotiations that ended with the resignation of Ayub Khan. In 1970, as a candidate of the Pakistan Democratic Party, Nurul Amin was one of only two non–Awami Leaguers elected to the National Assembly from East Pakistan. He strongly opposed the separatist position taken by the Awami League in 1971 that led to the breakup of Pakistan. He remained in Pakistan and became vice president in 1971 under **Zulfiqar Ali Bhutto**, who was president. Nurul Amin held the office until the parliamentary constitution of Pakistan took effect in 1973.

– O –

ODHIKAR (RIGHTS). A human rights organization formed in 1994 with the explicit goal of ensuring that citizens are made aware of their civil and political rights. It aims to improve the public sector human rights record by highlighting civil and political rights abuses in its annual report. It is an advocacy group for the protection of human rights. It is also involved in election monitoring to ensure that electoral candidates and voters are able to participate freely in the election process. Odhikar is a registered non-governmental organization and it conducts its advocacy from its headquarters in **Dhaka**. For countrywide information it depends on 150 trained human rights advocates who provide information on human rights abuses. Its annual report is an important source of information on the state of human rights in Bangladesh. *See also* HUMAN RIGHTS.

ORGANIZATION OF THE ISLAMIC CONFERENCE (OIC). King Faisal of Saudi Arabia called a summit meeting of the heads of Islamic states in Rabat, Morocco, in September 1969. King Faisal's request followed the arson attack on the al-Aqsa mosque in Jerusalem the previous month, and was intended to create solidarity among Islamic countries and to establish a level of security.

This led to the founding of the Islamic Conference in 1971. In its charter, adopted in 1972, the OIC stated the following aims: to promote Islamic solidarity, coordinate efforts to protect Islamic holy places, support the Palestinian struggle for national rights, and increase social, cultural, and economic cooperation among members. The secretariat of the Organization of the Islamic Conference is located in Jidda, Saudi Arabia, and funding is principally from Saudi Arabia.

Over the years several subsidiary organizations have been created, several of which are of importance to Bangladesh. These include the International Red Crescent, the **Islamic Development Bank**, and the Islamic Institute of Technology.

The second summit of the OIC was held in Lahore, **Pakistan**, in February 1974. Bangladesh was not initially invited to the meeting. Through the efforts of several Muslim heads of state, Pakistani prime minister **Zulfiqar Ali Bhutto** was prevailed upon to invite **Mujibur Rahman** to attend. Pakistani recognition of Bangladesh as well as that of most Arab nations dates from this meeting, although formal diplomatic relations were not established with most of these countries (including Pakistan) until after the death of Mujib. Bangladesh has been active in the OIC and presented an unsuccessful candidate for the secretary generalship in 1985.

OSMAN, SHAWKAT (1917–1998). His real name was Sheikh Azizur Rahman and he was one of the leading authors of Bangladesh. He wrote primarily against fundamentalism and chronicled stories of oppressed peoples. Two of his most noted works are *Kritodasher Hanshi* and *Janani*. For his contribution to Bangla **literature** he was awarded the Bangla Academy Award in 1962 and the Independence Day Award in 1997. *See also* LITERATURE.

OSMANY, MUHAMMAD ATAUL GHANI (1918–1984). He commanded the **Mukti Bahini** during the Bangladesh **War of Liberation** in 1971. He had joined the British Indian army in 1939 and retired from the Pakistani army in 1967 with the rank of colonel. He became active in politics, associating with the **Awami League**, and he was elected to the National Assembly in the 1970 election. After the independence of Bangladesh, Osmany was promoted to general and made commander in chief of the Bangladesh army, a post he held until April 1972. He then retired and returned to politics, and he was a member of the cabinet of **Mujibur Rahman**. In January 1975 he resigned his parliamentary seat in protest of Mujibur Rahman's creation of **BAKSAL** as the sole party in the country. Osmany formed a separate party in 1977 and in 1978 he was the candidate of most of the opposition in the presidential **election**, standing against **Ziaur Rahman**. Osmany was soundly defeated. He also ran for president in 1981, but not as a consensus opposition candidate, and again lost. *See also* ARMED FORCES.

– P –

PABNA. A district and district town. There is speculation that the name may have been derived from **Pandua**. The present district was separated from **Rajshahi** in 1832, and its early history is closely connected with that of Rajshahi. The other subdivision (now a district, as is Pabna), Serajganj, was added to Pabna from **Mymensingh** in 1855 as a result of the shift in course of the **Brahmaputra**. Agrarian riots in Pabna in 1873 were a major prelude to the enactment of the **Bengal Tenancy Act** of 1885.

At Shahzadpur there is the tomb of an important 17th-century **Sufi** leader, Makhdum Shah Daulat Shahid, as well as tombs of a number of his followers. Other historic sites include the **Hindu** temple of Jor Bangla and the palaces of Sitlai and Taras Rajbari.

PAHARPUR. A **Buddhist archeological** site located near **Rajshahi**. This site, with its massive central *vihara* (monastery) measuring about 1,000 feet on each side, is the largest monastery south of the Himalayas. It contains 177 monastic cells in the walls that enclose the courtyard. There is an elaborate northern gateway and numerous votive stupas, minor chapels, and extensive ancillary buildings within the 22-acre courtyard. In the center of the courtyard is a towering pyramidal temple. It was built during the **Pala dynasty**.

PAKISTAN. Relations between Pakistan and Bangladesh were, to say the least, strained after Bangladesh attained independence from Pakistan in December 1971. Pakistan proclaimed a doctrine under which it would break diplomatic relations with any state recognizing Bangladesh, a policy that became impractical when the major nations did so. Pakistan, with the aid of the veto of **China**, kept Bangladesh from membership in the **United Nations**. The Lahore summit of the **Organization of the Islamic Conference (OIC)** in 1974 began a reversal of this policy, as Pakistan was persuaded by other Islamic countries to accept the fait accompli of Bangladeshi separation from Pakistan. Pakistan recognized Bangladesh and withdrew its opposition to Bangladeshi membership in the United Nations and other bodies, although the formal exchange of ambassadors did not occur until 1976.

Bangladesh and Pakistan as separate entities retain the fear of **Hindu** (now **Indian**) hegemony in South Asia that led Bengali Muslims to support so strongly the Pakistan concept in the 1946 election. The two countries cooperate in the OIC and in the **South Asian Association for Regional Cooperation** and often take almost identical positions on international issues (e.g., on **Afghanistan** and Cambodia in opposition to India, and on Palestine). One outstanding issue, the division of the assets and liabilities of united Pakistan, is unlikely ever to be resolved and has recently been ignored. Another issue is the continued presence of **Biharis** in Bangladesh who demand to be sent to Pakistan.

Bangladeshi leaders have visited Pakistan although the reverse has been much rarer. However, in July 2002, the Pakistani president, General Pervez Musharraf, visited and expressed his "regret" for the actions of the Pakistani troops and civilian leaders against civilians in what was then **East Pakistan**. Several agreements were signed, including ones that permitted the duty-free export of **jute** and **tea** from Bangladesh to Pakistan. A broader free trade agreement was deferred for later discussion. An additional agreement covered scientific and cultural relations. The **caretaker government** of **Fakhruddin Ahmed** maintained a close relationship with Pakistan, although the relationship between Bangladesh and Pakistan tends to diminish during any Awami League–led government. *See also* HAMOODUR RAHMAN COMMISSION.

PAKISTAN DEMOCRATIC MOVEMENT. The term applied to a group of opposition parties that challenged the continued rule of **Ayub Khan**. Most, but not all, opposition parties were formal members of the movement. However, other parties were also represented at the roundtable discussions in early 1969. These included the Pakistan People's Party of **Zulfiqar Ali Bhutto** and the **Awami League**, led by **Mujibur Rahman**.

PAKISTAN MUSLIM LEAGUE (CONVENTION). The name generally given to the political party formed to support **Ayub Khan**. The name derived from a convention of Muslim Leaguers called by Ayub following the 1962 elections to the national and provincial assemblies. Among the **East Pakistanis** who supported the Ayub League were **Abdul Sobur Khan** and **Khwaja Shahabuddin**. Shahabuddin's brother, **Nazimuddin**, supported the rival **Council Muslim League**. Neither party won a seat in East Pakistan in the 1970 election.

PAKISTAN RESOLUTION. *See* LAHORE RESOLUTION.

PALA DYNASTY. It ruled Bengal from about 750 to about 1155. The dynasty received its name from all the rulers' names, which ended in "-pala." In appendix 1, the names of all the rulers and approximate dates of their reign are shown. At its peak, the kingdom extended well into present-day Uttar Pradesh in India. Pala rule in Bihar lasted until the Muslim conquest in 1199. The capital of the dynasty was Pataliputra (Patna), but it was transferred to Monghyr by **Devapala**. The empire's decline set in during the reign of **Mahipala I** with pressure from the Chola rulers from south India and the Kalachuris from central India. Control of the "home" of the Palas, Bengal, was lost to the **Sena dynasty** in the 12th century.

The rulers were **Buddhists** and patronized the scholars of that religion. Much was expended on the Buddhist universities at Nalanda (near present Rajgir, Bihar) and Vikramasila (Bhagalpur district of Bihar). The dynasty also supported Buddhist missionary activities in Tibet. It patronized **art** and **architecture**, though little remains of this patronage. Irrigation works in **Dinajpur** district are credited to the Palas. *See also* ATISH DIPANKAR SRIGYAN.

PANDUA. Located in the present Malda district of West Bengal, Pandua lies on the banks of the Mahananda River near its confluence with the Kalindri River, a main stream of the **Ganges**. It was probably founded as an outpost of **Gaur**. The port of Pandua had a large trade with Europeans in the 18th century in silk and cotton fabrics. English Bazaar is the headquarters of the district, signifying the importance of British trade. Gaur is about 10 miles from English Bazaar and about 20 miles from Pandua. Pandua succeeded Gaur as the capital of Bengal around 1340, but in 1455 Gaur became the capital again and Pandua declined. The 14th-century Adina and Sona (also known as Kutbshah) Mosques survive. The Adina Mosque was built by Sikandar Shah of the Ilyas Shahi dynasty in 1370 as a copy of the Jama Masjid in Damascus.

PANNI, WAJID ALI KHAN (1869–1936). An educationist, philanthropist, and social activist, he belonged to the **national elite**. He was a *zamindar* (landlord) who was credited with establishing a number of educational institutions, small hospitals, and dispensaries, and with building roads and canals. Among the educational institutions is Karotia College in Tangail district. He participated in the non-cooperation movement against British rule and was jailed for 15 months. Panni's family has remained active in politics and administration. His sons Khurram Khan Panni and Humayun Khan Panni were legislators and ambassadors.

PARITY. A term associated with the **Constitution of Pakistan, 1956**. **East Pakistanis** agreed to accept the equality (or parity) of membership in the national parliament, 150 members each from the east and west wings. This diluted the value of a vote from East Pakistan, as East Pakistan had the greater population. The quid pro quo for this was that the government of Pakistan would also commit itself to working for parity in the administrative services and in the **economy**. Although steps were taken to try to redress the imbalance in the services, it was not possible to convince investors or to divert government investment funds to lessen the economic imbalance. Although the East Pakistani economy grew between 1956 and 1971, it grew at a slower rate than that of West Pakistan, so the disparity increased rather than decreased. The legislative parity was continued in **Ayub Khan**'s 1962 **constitution of Pakistan**, but was discarded by **Yahya Khan** when he called for **elections** in 1970. At that time elections were held on a population basis: East Pakistan had 162 directly elected seats in the national assembly and West Pakistan had 138.

PARLIAMENT. The Bangladesh Parliament is unicameral with 300 members elected from single member constituencies. Any citizen over the age of 21 is eligible for election and to vote. The only significant reason for disqualification from candidacy is criminal conviction, a basis for the disqualification in 2001 of **Hussain Muhammad Ershad.** Voters must live in the electoral district in which they vote, but candidates are not required to live in the constituency in which they run. In fact, many candidates run in more than one constituency. If elected by more than one, the individuals may choose which constituency they will retain and resign from the others, in which a by-election will take place. By-elections are also required when a member dies, resigns, or is disqualified.

The parliaments resulting from the 1991 **election** and the two elections in 1996 had, in addition to the 300 directly elected seats, 30 seats reserved for **women,** although women were permitted to and did run for the general seats as well. These 30 seats were elected by the holders of the general seats in parliament on a winner-takes-all basis. For example, in 1991 the **Bangladesh Nationalist Party (BNP)** was short of a majority in the parliament. It made an agreement with the **Jama'at-i-Islami** under which both parties would vote together for the women's seats, resulting in 28 being won by the BNP and two by the Jama'at. The result gave the BNP a majority of the seats in parliament.

The parliament serves as the electoral college for the **presidency.** It also elects its speaker, who serves as acting president when the office of president is vacant. Bangladesh does not now have the office of vice president. The parliament must also give a vote of confidence to the prime minister and the cabinet. A vote of no confidence results in the fall of the cabinet. If no other combination can be found that can receive a vote of confidence, the parliament is dissolved by the president and a new election called.

In what is somewhat of an oddity, not all members of the cabinet must be members of parliament. This provision is meant to permit the appointment of specialists to the cabinet. Sessions are run generally in accordance with the practices of the parliamentary systems in the British Commonwealth, including such things as the question hour. However, the parliaments elected since the restoration of parliamentary government in 1991 can perhaps best be described as tumultuous. Boycotts by the opposition have occurred in each of the parliaments except the second in this series (now of four) and that exception was simply because the opposition boycotted the election. *See also* WOMEN, OPEN PARLIAMENTARY SEATS.

PATUAKHALI. A district formed in 1969 by the division of Backer-ganj into **Barisal** and Patuakhali. The history of Patuakhali is covered in the entry for Barisal. The district has since been divided into Patuakhali and Barguna districts.

PEACE COMMITTEES. Set up in 1971 in various cities of Bangladesh and in localities within each city. The civilian government set up the committees, but they were actually part of a system run by the **Pakistani** military authorities to attempt to counteract the influence of the **Mukti Bahini**. The purpose of the committees was to persuade the Bangladeshis to accept the idea of maintaining a united Pakistan.

PERMANENT SETTLEMENT. Promulgated by Lord **Cornwallis** in 1793. Cornwallis designated the tax collectors (*zamindars*) as owners of the land from which they raised revenue. Previously these persons were, in effect, tax farmers who collected revenue from the farmers (*ryots*). With Permanent Settlement, the ryots became tenants of the zamindars, who were new landlords. As it turned out, most, but not all, of the zamindars in eastern Bengal were **Hindus**. This led to challenges from such leaders as **Fazlul Haq** and his **Krishak Praja Party** in the 1930s. The system, however, was not changed until after the independence of **Pakistan** by land reform acts passed by the provincial assembly.

PITHA **(RICE CAKE).** A mixture of rice and molasses, it is an integral part of rural culture. *Pithas* are primarily made during the short winter season. The most noted types of pithas are steamed, filled with coconut or cream, and fried or stewed in milk. Pithas are given a variety of names. Some of them are *bhapa, pakon, shaipuli, nakshi pitha, khejur pitha, poa, puli, rosh goja, bibikhan,* and *patishapta. See also* FOOD.

PLANNING. Planning is an integral part of public sector management philosophy in Bangladesh. The first five-year plan covered the years 1973 to 1978 and targeted a growth rate of 5.5 percent. The actual growth rate during the period was 4 percent. A two-year plan followed with a target of 5.6 percent; it achieved 3.5 percent. Five-year plans have followed for 1980–1985, 1985–1990, 1990–1995, and 1995–2000. In none of these plans was the anticipated growth rate achieved.

The fifth plan for 2000–2005 focused on poverty alleviation, increased agricultural production, development of local-level institutions for participatory rural development, **population planning**, human resources development, **education**, private sector development, export-led industrialization, employment and income generation, micro credit, and resources mobilization. Some of these functions are also carried out by **non-governmental organizations**. During the Bangladesh Nationalist Party rule from 2001 to 2006 there was no five-year planning. After the Awami League regained power in 2009, it started the process of formulating the sixth five-year plan. The strategic direction for the sixth plan includes reducing poverty from its current level of 40 percent to 15 percent by the year 2021. It attempts to bring about growth parity by concentrating its resources in Barisal, Khulna, and Rajshahi, as they have sustained economic growth. This plan emphasizes infrastructure building and foreign investments from the private sector.

The Planning Commission is the highest planning body and is entrusted with the responsibility of preparing overall national plans and programs of socioeconomic importance. Other units involved in the planning process include the National Economic Council and the Project Evaluation Committee. *See also* ECONOMY; PRIVATIZATION.

PLASSEY (PILASI), BATTLE OF. This battle between the British, led by **Robert Clive,** and the Bengal forces under Nawab **Sirajuddaulah** occurred on 23 June 1757. The British had lost **Kolkata** to the nawab in 1756 and, although the city was regained earlier in 1757, the British wished to replace him with a more pliable governor of Bengal. Sirajuddaulah's forces numbered about 50,000; Clive's about 3,000. Aided by the treachery of **Mir Jafar,** the British routed the Bengali force. Sirajuddaulah was killed and replaced as governor by Mir Jafar.

POHEILA BOISHAKH. Celebrated in Bangladesh on 14 April as the first day of the New Year, it originated during the era of the Mughal emperor Akbar. It was linked to tax collection and the celebration following payment of taxes. During the **Pakistani** era, Poheila Boishakh was viewed as a form of political protest against the Pakistani attempt to suppress local Bangla culture. In 1965, Chhayanat, a cultural organization, protested the Pakistani government's ban of **Rabindranath Tagore** songs and welcomed the New Year by singing them. After 1971, it took on a life of its own and is celebrated with nationalistic fervor, an upholding of Bangla culture. From a rather insignificant informal celebration of culture it has become an epitome of Bangladesh independence. A related celebration in rural areas is the Nabanno festival, which is increasingly a part of urban and national culture. Nabanno is a celebration of the harvest of the new crop and is held on 15 November of each year.

POLITICAL PARTIES. Political parties in post-independence Bangladesh have generally been weak in organization because they are built around personalities.

Although the **Awami League** existed before independence and had, for some time, a dominant leader in **Husain Shahid Suhrawardy**, in the few years before and after independence, until his assassination, it depended on the dominating personality of Sheikh **Mujibur Rahman**. With his death, after a short, almost leaderless interval, the mantle fell upon his daughter, Sheikh **Hasina Wajid**, although she had no previous political experience. Currently she, like her father before her, dominates the party to the extent that there is no obvious alternative leader.

Similarly, the **Bangladesh Nationalist Party (BNP)** is a personality-dominated party in that it was specifically designed to be a political vehicle for **Ziaur Rahman**. With his assassination, his charismatic leadership could not be continued, until the party looked to his politically inexperienced widow, **Khaleda Zia**. As with the Awami League, there is no apparent rival for Zia's current leadership in the BNP.

The **Jatiya Party**, too, was designed to be a political vehicle, this time for **Hussain Muhammad Ershad**. With the loss of political standing by Ershad and his being banned from running in elections, the raison d'etre for remaining together was gone and the party has divided into at least three factions. The **Jama'at-i-Islami** is an exception possibly because it, unlike the other principal parties, is organized around an idea and has within its party individuals who are dedicated to that idea.

A unique aspect of the political institution–building process of Bangladesh is the number of political parties. In 2008, 107 political parties applied for registration with the Election Commission of Bangladesh. Of them only 37 parties were deemed eligible to participate in the ninth parliamentary election. In the eighth parliamentary election 39 political parties participated. In the first national election, held in 1973, only 14 of the 2,008 registered parties participated. The largest number of political parties to participate in a national election was in February 1996 when 43 parties contested the sixth parliamentary election. *See also* ELECTION COMMISSION; ELECTIONS; CARETAKER GOVERNMENT.

POLITICAL PARTIES ESTABLISHED AFTER STATE OF EMERGENCY 2007. The following political parties were established during the **caretaker government** of **Fakhruddin Ahmed**: National People's Party of Sheikh Shawakat Hossain Nilu, Progressive Democratic Party of Firdaus Ahmed Quarishi Bangladesh, Guardian Party of A. T. M. Shafiuddin, Bangladesh Welfare Party of Major General (retd.) Syed Muhammad Ibrahim, and Jago Bangladesh of Golam Muhammad Sorowar.

POLLUTION. A **United Nations** study describes pollution in Bangladesh and its neighbors as the "Asian Brown Cloud." Partly this is the result of the most frequently cited sources: the burning of wood and dung, industrial smoke emissions, and the use of internal combustion engines in motor vehicles and farm equipment. The study also found particulate pollution such as ash and soot. Moreover, the study estimates that half a million premature deaths occur each year. It recommends the use of more efficient stoves and arresters of carbon dioxide on engines, and greater use of solar and other clean sources of energy.

Water pollution is also a serious problem. Waste, human and animal, is generally flushed into waterways without any attempt at treatment. There are also runoffs from fertilizers used in **agriculture**. Water for domestic and industrial use is often drawn from streams or wells and is used without treatment. Water-borne diseases such as cholera are endemic. *See also* ARSENIC CONTAMINATION; ENVIRONMENT.

POPULATION PLANNING. The high density of population (1,146 people per square km.) and the still rapid rate of population growth (2.0 percent in 2006) have made population planning a key aspect of government policy. The population of Bangladesh increased to 153 million in 2008 from 132 million in 2000 and from the 1992 population of 114 million. Population policy is designed to influence demographic behavior through **education**, information, and motivation, and through the delivery of family planning services. The policy recognizes that long-term success will depend on socioeconomic factors such as **employment**, education, **health delivery**, reduction in infant and maternal mortality, and, most of all, by the participation of **women** in development.

Efforts by the government and **non-governmental organizations** raised the use of contraceptives by families from 5 percent in 1975 to 43 percent in 2002, according to a statement by the Ministry of Health and Family Welfare in June 2002. The report went on to say that if the rate rose to 70 percent, the fertility rate could drop from 3.3 to 2.2. Contraceptive use among those 15–49 years old in 2007 was estimated to be 54 percent. Efforts by Bangladesh were recognized by the **United Nations**, which awarded a prize to president **Hussain Muhammad Ershad** for his government's promotion of family planning.

Despite these efforts, the growth rate in 2002 was 1.75 percent, and even the growth rate of 1.0 percent in 2008 continues to add significant population annually. This continues the pressure on land, employment, and other indicators of social and economic development.

PORTUGUESE IN BENGAL. The main thrust of Portuguese power in India was on the west coast. Goa, Daman, and Diu remained Portuguese colonies until 1961, when they were forcibly incorporated into India. In Bengal, the Portuguese were the first European traders to arrive, visiting **Chittagong** and Satgaon (on the Hooghly River) beginning about 1530. By the end of the 16th century they were well established at Hooghly, which the Portuguese had founded in 1537 to replace Satgaon, whose estuary has silted up. In the early 17th century, some Portuguese were active as pirates, operating from **Arakan**, Chittagong, and islands near the mouth of the **Meghna**. In retaliation for the piracy, Hooghly was attacked by Mughal troops in 1632 and many Portuguese were killed or captured. The Portuguese were permitted to return to Hooghly in 1633, but the city was granted to the British East India Company in 1651, thereby ending Portuguese use of territory in Bengal.

POULTRY INDUSTRY. It has become a very high-growth sector of the **economy**, employing directly or indirectly over 5 million people. This sector initially began as backyard coop production and has progressed to where today there are approximately 1.5 million chicken farms of various sizes. Large-scale poultry farming began in Bangladesh only in 1980. Approximately 70 percent of the chicken outputs are still produced by the backyard coop process. The total production is 220 million chickens and 37 million ducks, contributing about $1 billion to the GDP of Bangladesh. During 2007–2008, this sector was hit by the avian bird flu, resulting in the culling of over one million chickens and one million eggs. Bird flu negatively impacted 271 farms located in 78 *upazilas* in 43 of the 64 districts. *See also* AGRICULTURE.

POVERTY. Two terms define the poverty level in Bangladesh: the chronic poor, who are in long-term poverty often spanning generations, and the extreme poor, who live in deep poverty and are considered at the bottom of the poverty ladder. About 20–30 million Bangladeshi are chronically poor. For 1995–1996, 35.6 percent of the population lived below the poverty line. In rural areas the figure was 39.8 percent and in urban areas 14.3 percent. The same source noted that 77.8 percent had incomes below $2 per day. Reports published in 2007 state that about 24 percent of the population are living in extreme poverty. In rural households, 19 percent cannot have three meals per day. Another 10 percent live on two meals or less per day. Approximately 31 percent of the rural population lives in a state of chronic poverty. Many steps have been taken to try to overcome poverty, but the limits of economic productivity have stymied any significant decrease in the percentage of people living below the poverty line. Government programs and, perhaps more important, programs of **non-governmental organizations** are used in the attempt to alleviate poverty.

PRATAPADITYA (?–1576). A local hero of the **Jessore** area, he refused to pay taxes to the government of the Emperor Akbar after the conquest of Bengal by Akbar's forces in 1576. He defeated a **Mughal** army, but he was eventually captured and sent to Delhi for trial. He died en route to Delhi. *See also* BARA BHUIYAN.

PRESIDENT. Under the **constitution** of Bangladesh the president is the head of state. However, since independence there have been presidents who also were heads of government during times when there was a presidential system or the country was under military rule. Under the present **parliamentary** system, the **prime minister** is head of government. The office of president is largely a ceremonial one.

Under the present system of government, the president is elected by the parliament for a five-year term. In case of the death or resignation of a president, the speaker of the parliament acts as president until a new election can be held. The person elected in this by-election has a full five-year term. Thus the terms of the president and of the parliament are not linked.

The first president, Sheikh **Mujibur Rahman**, was selected by the provisional government in **Mujibnagar (Calcutta)**. As he was jailed in Pakistan, **Syed Nazrul Islam** was designated acting president. When Mujib returned to Bangladesh, he was declared president, but said the government was a parliamentary one and he became prime minister. The parliament then elected **Abu Sayeed Chowdhury** president and, on his resignation in December 1973, the parliament chose **Mohammadullah** to replace him. In January 1975, Mujib caused an amendment to the **constitution** to be adopted changing the government to a presidential form with himself as president.

Following Mujib's assassination in August 1975, the senior member of the cabinet, **Khondakar Mushtaque Ahmed**, assumed the presidency. The military coup in November 1975 resulted in the assumption of the presidency by the chief justice, **Abu Sadat Muhammad Sayem**. He was displaced by **Ziaur Rahman** in April 1977. Zia had this assumption ratified through a referendum and then by a contested **election** in 1978. He appointed **Abdus Sattar** as **vice president**. Sattar became president on Zia's assassination in May 1981.

Hussain Muhammad Ershad overthrew Sattar in March 1982, but he did not initially proclaim himself president. Instead he looked to the judiciary and appointed **A. F. M. Ahsanuddin Chowdhury** president. However, Ershad dismissed Ahsanuddin in June 1984 and assumed the presidency, which he held until December 1990. He, too, called for a referendum in 1985.

The forced resignation of Ershad in December 1990 brought the restoration of the parliamentary system that had been absent since January 1975. The chief justice, **Shahabuddin Ahmad**, acted as president until parliament elected **Abdur Rahman Biswas** in October 1991, followed by Shahabuddin Ahmed in March 1997, **A. Q. M. Badruddoza Choudhury** in October 2001, **Iajuddin Ahmed** in September 2002, and **Zillur Rahman** in 2009. *See also* ELECTIONS; VICE PRESIDENT.

PRIME MINISTER. In a **parliamentary** system, the prime minister is the head of government. The prime minister is nominated by the party or coalition that holds the majority of the seats in parliament. This nomination must be confirmed through a vote of confidence in the parliament. The prime minister continues to hold office until he or she loses the confidence of the house or his or her party or coalition is defeated in an **election**. The prime minister heads the cabinet that is composed of members of the prime minister's party and possibly members of other parties in a coalition. Prime ministers under the parliamentary system have been **Mujibur Rahman** (1972–1975), **Khaleda Zia** (1991–1996 and 2001–2006), and **Hasina Wajid** (1996–2001 and 2009 to the present).

The title has also been used in presidential systems, a practice not usual in governments. The persons holding the title might be described as chairpersons of the cabinet, but in no way are considered heads of government. Those who have held the title in this meaning are **Tajuddin Ahmed, Mansur Ali, Shah Mohammad Azizur Rahman, Ataur Rahman Khan, Mizanur Rahman Chowdhury, Moudud Ahmed,** and **Kazi Zafar Ahmed.** *See also* ELECTIONS; PRESIDENT.

PRINCEP, JAMES (1799–1840). A servant of the **East India Company,** he was also a researcher. He deciphered the Pali script on the Asokan pillars and served as the secretary of the Asiatic Society of Bengal (its **Dhaka** section is now the **Asiatic Society of Bangladesh**).

PRIVATIZATION. Many of those who seek causes for Bangladesh's poor economic development look to the extensive government ownership of industrial firms and the resultant inefficiency and almost uninterrupted money-losing record. The prescription is ending government ownership and selling the assets of these firms to private investors. This view is supported by many international agencies such as the World Bank and the International Monetary Fund as well as many countries that provide economic assistance.

Although some **industries** have seen partial **privatization,** such as telecommunications, road and water **transport,** container handling in ports, and **tourism,** the record of privatization generally has been poor. Few firms have been sold. Private economic activity was permitted and even welcomed in almost all sectors, including **banking** in a limited way during the regime of **Hussain Muhammad Ershad.** Foreign private capital has been heavily involved in the exploration for natural gas. But the transfer of government-owned enterprises has been very limited and despite some political support appears unlikely to increase.

When privatization does take place, Bangladesh uses two methods: sale through tenders and sale by the public offering of shares. *See also* NATURAL RESOURCES.

PUKUR (POND). Dhaka city had several hundred ponds that were primarily used by the locals to bathe and to wash. Over the years most of these ponds have been filled due to the pressure of urban population and the need for living space. One of the last remaining is the Bangshal Pukur located at Haji Abdullah Sarkar Lane. It was evacuated about 50 years ago and is still in use. The pond serves over 3,000 marginalized people who pay 2 taka (about 0.02 U.S. cents) to take a bath. This pond is fast becoming **polluted** because it is also being used as a commercial fish farm. Another well-known pond was Shuritoal pond, but that was recently filled up and a girl's primary school now sits where the pond used to be.

PUNDRA, PUNDRANAGARA. *See* MAHASTHANGARH.

– Q –

QUADER, NOORUL (?–1997). He was the deputy commissioner of Pabna when the **War of Liberation** started in 1971. He went to India, taking with him whatever resources could be transferred. He later organized the resistance movement in Pabna. After the independence of Bangladesh he became the first secretary of the Ministry of Establishment. He was instrumental in establishing the **Tourism** Corporation of Bangladesh. His greatest contribution was in the **garment** sector, where he pioneered the start-up and later the growth of the garments industry of Bangladesh. It is his cooperative agreement with Daewoo Corporation of South Korea in 1978 that is credited with making the ready-made garment industry one of the largest contributors to Bangladesh export earnings. *See also* TRADE.

QUADRAT-E-KHUDA, MUHAMMAD TOFAZZIL (1900–1977). A prominent scientist who received 18 patents. Most of his patents are in the area of **agricultural** products. He served in a number of different capacities, including the first directorship of the Pakistan Scientific and Industrial Research Center. Soon after the independence of Bangladesh he was called to chair the first Educational Reform Committee.

QUAZI, DOWLAT (c. 1600–1638). Poet. Born in **Chittagong**, he worked at the court of the kings of **Arakan**. His *Shati Maina* and

Lore Chandrani are considered fine examples of middle Bengali poetry.

– R –

RABEYA KHATUN (1935–). Author of more than 100 books, from religious history to short stories and novels, she was first honored by the Bangla Academy in 1973 for her contribution to Bangla literature and its development. Since then she has received the Ekushey Padak in 1993, the Sher-e-Bangla Swarna Padak in 1996, and the Wrishiz Shahitya Padak in 1998. She was the editor of the monthly *Angana*. Her first novel was *Madhumati*. Many of her short stories were adapted for television and made into movies. *See also* LITERATURE.

RAHMAN, A. S. M. MOSTAFIZUR (1934–1996). He served in the Pakistani and Bangladeshi armies, retiring in 1973. He joined the cabinet of **Ziaur Rahman** as minister of home affairs in April 1978 and served under Zia and Abdus Sattar until December 1991. In the first **Khaleda Zia** government, Mostafiz was minister of foreign affairs.

RAHMAN, HABIBUR (1908–). President of the Dhaka **Muslim League** and member of the Working Committee of the **East Pakistan** Muslim League between 1948 and 1950. He served as Pakistan's ambassador to a number of countries, including Australia, New Zealand, Switzerland, Belgium, and Yugoslavia. During the **Muhammad Ayub Khan** regime Habibur Rahman served as minister of education, information and broadcasting, and minority affairs. He became a member of the National Assembly of Pakistan in 1962.

RAHMAN, HABIBUR (1922–1976). Journalist. He was assistant director of the National Book Centre from 1974 to 1976. Earlier he worked for several newspapers, and he wrote a number of books addressed to children.

RAHMAN, HABIBUR (1928–1988). An **architect**, he designed the Shahid Minar, the monument to those killed in the **language movement** in 1952. He was also a well-known painter.

RAHMAN, MUHAMMED MUSTAFIZUR (1941–2008). General Mustafizur Rahman was born in Ranjpur. For his service to the nation during the **War of Liberation** he received the title of *Bir Bikram*. He fought against the Pakistan army in Darshona, Jibannagar, Jhenidah, Magura, and Faridpur. He was wounded in November 1971. From December 1997 to December 2000, he was the chief of army staff. He was also principal staff officer of **Armed Forces** Division and general officer commanding of Infantry Division.

RAHMAN, S. M. MATIUR (1939–2008). He was a circle officer in Tentulia during the **War of Liberation**. He helped organize the freedom fighters and turned his office into a health clinic for those who were injured. On behalf of the Mujibnagar government Matiur Rahman was the first to hoist the **flag** of independent Bangladesh in Tentulia.

RAHMAN, SHAMSUR (1929–2006). The author of over 60 books of poems and many works of prose, he began his career as a journalist and from 1977 to 1987 was the editor of *Dainik Bangla*, a government-owned newspaper. His first love was poetry and in the 1950s he was part of a literary association called the Progressive Writers and Artists Association. His poems covered the **language movement** of 1952, and much later the **War of Liberation**. Through his poem *Swadhinata tumi* (Freedom You) he addressed the tragedies of the war. His first volume of poems published in 1960 was entitled *Prothom gan dition mrittur ageh* (First Song, before the Second Death). While his poems were political, he was never in politics, although he did join the political movement against President **Hussain Muhammad Ershad**. He integrated the **Dhaka** dialect into his poetry. Through his poems he addressed social issues of democracy and freedom, secularism and rule of law. In 1999 he was attacked by Islamists bent on silencing free thought, but he escaped. For his contribution to Bengali **literature** he was awarded the **Swadhinota Padak** in 1991.

RAHMAN, SHEIKH MUJIBUR. *See* MUJIBUR RAHMAN, SHEIKH.

RAHMAN, TARIQUE (1960–). Eldest son of former President **Ziaur Rahman** and former Prime Minister **Khaleda Zia**, he was appointed the senior joint secretary of BNP in 2002. He became a key player in the BNP-Jama'at alliance government of 2001–2006. He formed an alternate power structure to Prime Minster Khaleda Zia and became a very influential power broker in the country. He was arrested on 7 March 2007 on charges of corruption but was freed on bail on 3 September 2008. He left Bangladesh for medical treatment in England and is unlikely to return to the country in the immediate future. Cases pending against him include three extortion cases, a corruption case for amassing wealth illegally and concealing wealth information from the ACC, and a tax-evasion case filed by the National Board of Revenue (NBR).

RAHMAN, ZIAUR. *See* ZIAUR RAHMAN.

RAHMAN, ZILLUR (1929–). He was sworn in as the 19th **president** of Bangladesh on 12 January 2009. He is a lawyer and politician, having obtained his LL.B. and M.A. (Honors) in history from **Dhaka University** in 1954. He presided over a student gathering at Dhaka University on 19 February 1952 demanding Bangla be made a state **language** and on 20 February was one of the 11 student leaders who decided to violate the Section-144 rule that forbade the gathering of more than five persons in a public place. He served as the vice president of the Fazlul Huq Hall student union of Dhaka University. For his activism he was expelled from Dhaka University and his degree was withheld, although the university gave it to him after the provincial election of 1954. During the provincial election of 1954 Rahman served as the vice-chair of the **Mymensingh** district election steering committee. He became involved in political activism during the **Sylhet** referendum of the mid-1940s and took part in the mass movement against military rule of 1962, the Six-Point movement of 1966, and the mass movement of 1969. In 1970 he was elected a member of the National Assembly of Pakistan. During the **War of Liberation** he was associated with Swadhin Bangla Betar Kendra (Free Bangla Radio), and the Mujibnagar newspaper *Joy Bangla*. After 16 December 1971, he became a member of the Bangladesh

Constituent Assembly responsible for the **constitution** of Bangladesh. He was elected to the **parliament** of Bangladesh in 1973 and all subsequent elections, becoming minister of local government and rural development in 1996. During the 1996–2001 Awami League era he also served as the deputy leader in parliament, becoming the acting chief of the Awami League in 2007 when Sheikh Hasina was arrested by the **caretaker government**.

RAIHAN, ZAHIR (1933–1972). Writer and **film** director. He studied photography in Calcutta but ended up as a filmmaker. His first film was made in 1956 but was only released in 1961. The film was called *Kakhono Asheni.* His first English-language film, *Let There Be Light*, was not completed owing to the **War of Liberation**. He turned away from that project to create a documentary on the war, *Stop Genocide*, which is ranked as one of the 10 top documentaries of its kind in the world. In the Bangladesh film industry, his works such as *Jiban Thakey Neya* or *Kancher Deyal* are considered classics. *Jiban Thakey Neya* was a film about the repressive nature of the Pakistan army rule. He also made Urdu-language films. *Sangam* was the first colored film in undivided Pakistan. He directed another Urdu film, *Bahana*, which was made in cinemascope format. His films were based on his own writings. He was also a political activist. He was one of the first 10 students to take part in the 21 February 1952 **language movement** march. His political leaning was toward socialism. Raihan was killed by opponents of independence in 1972.

RAJMAHAL. Although it is located in the present Santal Parganas division of the Indian state of Jharkhand, it twice served as the capital of the Bengal province under the **Mughals**. Raja **Man Singh**, who was a governor under Emperor Akbar, chose the city as capital in 1595 primarily because of its command of the **Ganges**. In 1610, the capital was transferred to **Dhaka**. The capital was moved back to Rajmahal in 1639, but returned to Dhaka in 1659.

RAJSHAHI. A region, district, and district town in northern Bangladesh, it was once known as Rampur Boalia. The present name is said to mean the "royal territory," as it combines the words *raj* and *shah*. It lies on the **Ganges** (called the Padma in the area) about 120 miles northwest of Dhaka. It is the site of a university and of the **Varendra** Research Society, founded in 1910, which is devoted to the study of the ancient history of the area. The district was part of the kingdom of Pundra, whose capital was **Mahasthangarh**. During the **Sena** period, the area was known as Barendra Bhumi (the land of Varendra). During the 18th century, the extent of Rajshahi district was much greater than at present. During the 19th century various parts were detached to form **Murshidabad, Nadia, Jessore,** Malda, **Bogra,** and **Pabna** districts. The larger territory was under the control of the raja of **Nator.** Muslim-period monuments in Rajshahi city include the Chhota Sona Mosque and, from the **Hindu** period, the Govinda Temple. The region also contains the sites of **Paharpur, Gaur,** and a number of other **archeological** and historical locations. A Dutch monument, the Bara Kothi, is the centerpiece of the university.

The reorganization of **local government** during the **Hussain Muhammad Ershad** period divided the former Rajshahi district into Rajshahi, Nator, Naogaon, and Nawabganj districts.

RAMAKRISHNA MISSION. Founded in 1897 by Swami **Vivekananda** as a means for a group of devotees of **Ramakrishna Paramahamsa** to preach the latter's doctrines and serve humanity. The mission runs schools, colleges, and hospitals and teaches useful crafts to those who seek its assistance. Its branches in Bangladesh have remained open.

RAMAKRISHNA PARAMAHAMSA (1834–1886). An important **Hindu** spiritual leader in Bengal. He preached the concept that as various languages have different words for the same idea (e.g., water) so different religions have different names for God: Allah, Hari, Christ, Krishna, and so on. He preached compassion to all, and with this idea his successors established the **Ramakrishna Mission.** His most noted disciple was **Vivekananda.**

RANGPUR. A district and district town, the city lies on the Little Ghaghat River. It and its neighboring city of Saidpur (about 20 miles west) are major railway centers. The district's eastern boundary is the **Brahmaputra.** Several other rivers, including the **Tista,** cross the district. If a link canal is to be built between the Brahmaputra and the **Ganges** at **Farakka**, most of the canal would run through the Rangpur district.

In ancient times, Rangpur was a part of the kingdom of Kamarupa (**Assam**), described in the *Mahabharata*, the **Hindu** epic, as the most western part of Kamarupa. Assamese rule apparently continued until 1498, when the region was taken by the Afghan kings of **Gaur**, but it was again lost to the Koch rulers. Rangpur was formally annexed by the **Mughals** in 1584 but not completely subdued until 1661.

At Kamatapur are the ruins of an ancient fort whose origins have not been established. A temple at Sabramangala depicts scenes from the *Mahabharata* and *Ramayana*. The former district has now been divided into four districts: Rangpur, Nilphamari, Kurigaon, and Gaibandha. *See also* COOCH BEHAR.

RAPID ACTION BATTALION (RAB). A mixed force of the Bangladesh army and police services, it was established through the Armed Police Battalion (Amendment) Act of 2003. Its purpose is to provide the government of Bangladesh with skilled professionals who will be able to deter and combat dangerous law-and-order crises. Among its duties are gathering intelligence on crimes and criminal activities, and conducting investigations. In its pursuit of criminals it is guided by the Code of Criminal Procedure 1989 (Act V, 1989) and other applicable laws. RAB forces are divided into two wings, Cheetah and Cobra. For its success in reducing criminal activities RAB was awarded the **Swadhinota Padak** in 2006. A major blemish in its work is the number of criminals killed in crossfire, a term that refers to shooting exchanges that take place between RAB members and criminals. In 2004 the following criminal masterminds were killed by RAB as it attempted to arrest them: Pichchi Hannan, Killer Bhutto, Molla Shamim, Golakata Mojibar and Tokai Mizan of Dhaka, David of Narayanganj, Jane Alam, Ahmudya and Iqbal Bahar Chowdhury of Chittagong, outlawed partisan B. D. R. Altaf, and Asaduzzaman Litu, accused of killing journalist Shamsur Rahman in Khulna.

RAY, NANDA KUMAR. *See* NUNCOMAR.

RAZA, HASAN (1854–1922). He was a member of the *zamindar* family of Sunamganj in **Sylhet** district. He founded an English-language high school, but he is best known for the devotional songs he wrote. These songs focus on love, mysticism, and spiritual consciousness. They are still used by both the Muslim and the Hindu communities.

RAZAKAR BAHINI. A force structure set up by the Pakistani army to counter the **Mukti Bahini**. It was mainly composed of pro-Pakistani Bengalis and **Biharis**. Some were called Al-Shams and others Al-Badr. The purpose of the force was to maintain order through threat, intimidation, and brute force. Members of the force gained a ghastly reputation because they worked to suppress the people of Bangladesh and their legitimate demands. *See also* WAR OF LIBERATION.

RAZZAQUE, ABDUR (1932–2005). This painter-turned-sculptor is one of the most prominent leaders of the modern **art** movement of Bangladesh. An abstract expressionist painter, he was also the first to turn to sculpture after the **War of Liberation**. His watercolors and oil paintings were distinctive for their tone and texture. His sculpture pieces were both abstract and figures. He used a variety of mediums to present his artwork. He used cement, stone, steel, iron, bronze, and wood for his sculpture work.

RELIGION. Bangladesh is overwhelmingly Muslim, with about 88 percent of the population professing Islam as their religion. Another 11 percent are **Hindu**. The small remainder are **Christian, Buddhist**, and adherents of **tribal** religions.

There are no legal restrictions on any religion and little popular discrimination among the religious groups. The state takes no direct action on religious matters; for example, there is no ministry of religious affairs. Although there are occasional instances of what might be called discrimination, these are indeed rare and generally brief. Islamic militancy has become a force that threatens to disrupt the overall communal harmony that exists in the country. *See also* BRAHMO SAMAJ.

REMITTANCES. Between 2001 and 2008 remittances from Bangladeshi labor overseas rose from 2 percent of GDP to nearly 9 percent of GDP, exceeding foreign **aid** received by Bangladesh. Labor remittance started in the 1980s when Bangladeshis started to trickle out of

Bangladesh to become part of the international labor force. In 2002 the amount of remittances was $2 billion, which increased to $8 billion in 2008. In 2007, over 800,000 Bangladeshi citizens worked abroad, primarily in the **Middle East** and some in Southeast Asia, most of them as unskilled labor. By 2008 this figure reached nearly one million.

The primary source of international remittances is Saudi Arabia (30 percent) followed by the **United States** (17 percent). Remittances from all other Arab countries were 28 percent and from **Great Britain** 11 percent. International remittances will remain a function of global economic growth; they have rapidly spurred economic growth and provide a critical source of hard currency for Bangladesh. Most Bangladeshi workers going to the Middle East are between 17 and 30 years old. It will be interesting to see how Islamic fundamentalism impacts their stay in the Middle East, and their behavior upon their return to Bangladesh.

RICE. The food lifeline of Bangladesh is rice. Approximately 75 percent of the total agricultural land is utilized for rice cultivation. Of the population's total caloric intake, rice provides 70 percent. Bangladesh has consistently increased its total rice production and per-acre output. In 2007–2008 it produced approximately 28 million tons of rice. However, as the total population is high, Bangladesh has to also import rice.

Bangladesh has three growing seasons: *aman*, *aus*, and *boro*. Sown in spring, aman rice matures with the summer rains and is harvested in fall. Most of the seeds are high-yield or dwarf varieties and aman rice is less than 45 percent of the total rice production of the country. The traditional strain, aus, is grown during the April–May period. Aus is generally about 2 percent of total production. Boro rice production is primarily the outcome of the increased use of irrigation and the cultivation period is from October to March. Boro crop production is also from high-yield varieties and produces 16–18 million tons of rice out of a total of approximately 28 million tons. In 2009 rice production is estimated to be 33 million tons, of which boro rice will be 19 million tons.

Bangladesh has also been involved in the early activities of the International Rice Research Institute for introducing high-yield and disease-resistant varieties. In 1966, a rice research unit was established as part of the Cereals Section of the Agricultural Research Laboratory. In 1967, IR8, a widely distributed semi-dwarf rice variety, was introduced. Bangladesh has a large variety of rice. The latest research focuses on rice varieties that can survive longer under water. The Bangladesh Rice Knowledge Bank lists approximately 6,000 varieties of rice, of which nearly 25 percent are traditional and the rest are breeding lines. *See also* AGRICULTURE; ECONOMY; FAST FOOD OF OLD DHAKA; FOOD.

RIGHT TO INFORMATION ORDINANCE. In order to ensure that the public sector conducts itself in a transparent and accountable manner and to pursue the aims of good governance, the Right to Information ordinance was promulgated on 18 June 2008. Agencies of the public sector and other agencies receiving public funds now have to respond to a request for information from the public within 21 days of application. A three-member Information Commission serves as a review body in the case of a dispute between the public and the agency.

ROHINGYAS. *See* ARAKAN.

ROY, NIHARRANJAN (1903–1981). Art historian. Born in **Mymensingh**, he was educated in **Calcutta** and Leiden, the Netherlands. Among his works is *Metal Sculptures of Bengal.*

ROY, RAJA RAM MOHAN (1772–1833). A reformer, he was born in Hooghly district to a Brahmin family. He recognized that the British were to remain in control of Bengal and beyond and that the best course for Indians was to work with the British. He traveled several times to England and was in the employ of the **East India Company** from 1804 to 1814. His reforming **religious** views—opposition to idolatry and superstitions—formed the basis of a new religious body, the **Brahmo Samaj**, which, though drawn from the Hindu tradition, followed in many ways the congregational system of Christianity. The Brahmo Samaj would be in the forefront of the Bengal renaissance in the 19th century, including, among many other leaders, **Rabindranath Tagore.** Ram Mohan Roy was opposed to what he saw as social evils, including *sati* (the cremation of widows on the funeral pyres of their husbands), child marriage, polygamy, and caste distinctions. Although members of the Brahmo Samaj were generally drawn from upper castes, caste distinctions were not permitted within the organization. Raja Ram Mohan Roy is remembered as the first major Indian modernist reformer.

ROY, SIR PRAFULLA CHANDRA (1861–1944). Scientist. Born in **Khulna**, he studied in **Calcutta**, London, and Edinburgh. After teaching chemistry in Calcutta, he founded the Bengal Chemical and Pharmaceutical Works in 1901, the first such company in India. Roy continued his research and wrote *History of Hindu Chemistry*, which was the major publication of its kind at the time.

RUSSIA. Since the collapse in 1991 of the **Union of Soviet Socialist Republics**, the relations of Bangladesh with Russia have been almost exclusively in the area of **trade**. Bangladesh seeks Russian markets for its exports, principally garments, **jute**, and **tea**. Bangladesh has purchased Russian armaments. In 2005, Russia and Bangladesh signed a memorandum for Russia to build a nuclear power plant in Bangladesh. *See also* ARMED FORCES.

– S –

SAIFUR RAHMAN, MUHAMMAD (1932–2009). A chartered accountant, he served in the cabinets of **Ziaur Rahman** and **Khaleda Zia**. In the Ziaur Rahman cabinet he was minister of commerce (1977–1980) and minister of finance (1980–1982), continuing into the **Sattar** cabinet. Saifur Rahman has been minister of finance in both governments formed by Khaleda Zia. He is a spokesman for a market economy as the route for Bangladeshi development. In 2008, when Khaleda Zia was arrested, he attempted to take control of the **Bangladesh Nationalist Party** but failed. In September 2009 he died in a car accident while on his way to **Sylhet**.

SALAAM, ABDUS (1910–1976). Journalist. He joined the *Pakistan Observer*, owned by **Hamidul Haq Choudhury**, in 1949 and became editor in 1950. A bitter critic of the Pakistan government's

Urdu-language program, he was jailed in 1952 for his support of the **language movement**. Salaam was elected to the provincial assembly in 1954, but he did not remain in politics and continued to publish the *Observer*. The paper came under the control of the government after 1971. Salaam left the now *Bangladesh Observer* in 1972, but he worked for the *Bangladesh Times*, also government controlled, until his death.

SALIMULLAH KHAN, NAWAB SIR (1866–1915). Nawab of Dhaka, son of **Ahsanullah Khan**. A social activist and politician, he was known for his efforts to elevate the status of the Muslims of **India**. He was the founder of both **Dhaka University** and Ahsanullah Engineering College, which is now Bangladesh Engineering University. Salimullah was one of the founders of the All-India **Muslim League**; the founding meeting was held in his palace, Ahsan Manzil in **Dhaka**. He supported **Lord Curzon** in the latter's decision to partition Bengal in 1905. A number of organizations such as the Dhaka Orphanage, a medical school, and a Dhaka University dormitory are named in his honor. Salimullah served briefly as a nominated member of the East Bengal and Assam Legislative Council while that province existed.

SAMAD, LAILA (1928–1989). She was a trailblazer among **women** in journalism. She was assistant editor of the women's magazine *Begum* and was in charge of the women's section of the national daily *Sangbad*.

SAMATATA. Mentioned in inscriptions of the second **Gupta** emperor, Samudragupta (reigned c. AD 330–380), as a frontier state and as a kingdom he captured in eastern Bengal. Its capital is believed to have been Badkamta, in the vicinity of present-day **Comilla**. It is also mentioned in the work of the third-century Chinese **Buddhist** traveler Hiuen Tsiang.

SARFRAZ KHAN. The nawab of Bengal (1739–1740). He was a grandson of Nawab **Murshid Quli Jafar Khan** and was defeated and killed by a lieutenant, **Alivardi Khan**, who then became the nawab.

SARKAR, ABU HUSSAIN (1894–1969). He served as chief minister of **East Pakistan** from 1955 to 1956 and again briefly in 1958. He was a lawyer by profession. Arrested a number of times by the British, he took part in the Swadeshi movement and in the national movement for the independence of India. In 1935, Sarkar joined the **Krishak Praja Party (KPP)** of **Abul Kasem Fazlul Haq** and as a representative of KPP was elected to the Bengal Legislative Assembly in 1937. As a nominee of the **United Front**, he was elected to the East Pakistan Legislative Assembly in 1954. He also served as a central minister in 1955.

SARKAR, SIR JADUNATH (1870–1958). Historian. He was born in **Rajshahi** and educated in **Calcutta**. He was vice-chancellor of Calcutta University, 1926–1928. Sarkar's books on Indian history were among the standards of his time. He and **Romesh Chandra Majumdar** edited the classic two-volume *History of Bengal*.

SASANKA. The first ruler of Bengal (so far as is known) who was able to extend his rule outside Bengal. About the beginning of the seventh century, he became king of **Gaur**, with his seat at Karnasuvarna, which has been identified with Rangamati in the present **Murshidabad** district. He extended his rule over the Magadha region of Bihar and south to Chilka Lake in Orissa. He met opposition from rulers in north India in alliance with the ruler of Kamarupa (**Assam**), but retained the heart of his kingdom until his death, perhaps about 625. His coins indicate that he was a Shaivite; there are reports from Chinese pilgrims that he persecuted Buddhists.

SATTAR, ABDUS (1906–1985). President of Bangladesh, 1981–1982, he had a career both in law and in politics. Associated with the **United Front**, he was appointed a minister in the **Pakistan** government in 1956, a judge of the **East Pakistan** High Court in 1957, and a justice of the Pakistan Supreme Court in 1968. He was also chief election commissioner and conducted the elections of 1970 to the national and provincial assemblies. Sattar was able to flee Pakistan via **Afghanistan** in 1972 and held a number of posts in Bangladesh. He became a special assistant to president **A. S. M. Sayem** in 1975 and law minister in 1977, a post he retained after he was appointed

vice president the same year by President **Ziaur Rahman.** Sattar succeeded Zia as acting president when the latter was assassinated on 30 May 1981, and he was elected to the office on 15 November 1981. He was removed from the presidency by the coup led by **Hussain Muhammad Ershad** on 24 March 1982. Sattar headed **JAGODAL,** founded in 1978 as a party to support Zia and his program, and its successor, the **Bangladesh Nationalist Party (BNP),** until 1979, when, with a parliament in office, Zia assumed the chairmanship himself.

SAYEM, ABU SADAT MUHAMMAD (1916–2001). Sayem became the **president** of Bangladesh in November 1975, when a compromise took place between **Khalid Musharraf** and **Khondakar Mushtaque Ahmed** over who should lead Bangladesh. Sayem, who was the chief justice at that time, was chosen. He was a lawyer by profession who spent a considerable amount of time at the bar. While president, he held a number of important ministries, including those of defense and foreign affairs. He was also chief martial law administrator until November 1976. Sayem relinquished his presidency in April 1977 to **Ziaur Rahman.**

SEA BOUNDARY. Bangladesh is in dispute with both **India** and **Burma** over control of the northern reaches of the Bay of Bengal, a dispute which Bangladesh is unlikely to win. In terms of the law of the sea, Bangladesh is an adjacent state to each of the other two. The other two are opposite states to each other. Bangladesh stands at the northern head of the bay. Its claim to control is limited by its location. This is extenuated by the concave nature of the Bangladeshi coastline. The much larger area of the bay is divided on the principle of opposite states by Burma and India. These states, like Bangladesh, anticipate the possible exploitation of oil and gas, an anticipation heightened by the discovery of a major field in 2002 off the Andhra Pradesh coast of India.

SEASONS OF BANGLADESH. Instead of the traditional four seasons of the year, Bangladesh celebrates six seasons. These are *grishmo* (summer), *barsha* (monsoon), *sharat* (autumn), *hemanto* (late autumn), *sheeth* (winter), and *bashanto* (spring).

SEED PRODUCTION. Production of quality seeds has become increasingly vital for Bangladesh to maintain **agricultural** production for both cereal and **jute** production. With the decline of total **cultivable land** in Bangladesh, one critical means for increasing agricultural production significantly is to have quality seeds. Annually 4,000 tons of jute seeds are required for planting five million hectares of land. Bangladesh Agriculture Development Corporation (BADC) produces between 700 and 1,000 tons of seed, with an additional 500 to 700 tons being produced by individual farmers. Imported **Indian** seed meets the remaining demand, although the seed's quality and production per hectare is less than that of seed grown by BADC or local farmers. The Indian seed, however, tends to be cheaper and the credit mechanism makes this seed more attractive to farmers. Although hybrid rice seed production increased by 40 percent in 2008, a significant amount of rice seed is also imported. The **Bangladesh Rural Advancement Committee** (BRAC) and Supreme Seed are the two major producers of hybrid rice seed in Bangladesh. BRAC produces about 1,200 metric tons and Supreme Seed about 700 metric tons.

SEN, AMARTYA KUMAR (1933–). Winner of the Nobel Prize for Economic Science in 1998, he was born in Shantiniketan, the seat of the university founded by **Rabindranath Tagore**. His family home, however, is in the Wari area of **Dhaka**. Perhaps his best-known work is *Poverty and Famines*, in which he writes "in the terrible history of famines in the world, it is hard to find a case in which famine has occurred in a country with a free press and an active opposition within a democratic system." It can be noted that **famine** on a general scale has been absent from a democratic Bangladesh. Sen served as master of Trinity College, Cambridge University, but he has returned to his previous post at Harvard University.

SEN, DINESH CHANDRA (1866–1939). A folklorist, he collected folklore material from rural eastern Bengal. His publications include the *Folk Literature of Bengal* and two massive works, *Purbabanga gitika* (Songs of Eastern Bengal) and *Mymensingh gitika* (Songs of Mymensingh). He helped set up the Bengali department at Calcutta University. He wrote the first history of Bengali **literature**. He was a collector of Bengali folklore, primarily East Bengal *gitikas* or folk ballads. As a result he wrote a four-volume work on Bengali folklore, *Eastern Bengal Ballads*, that is considered a pioneering work. In his research on Bengali folklore he found that most of the ballads were sung by Muslims and low-caste **Hindus**. The language was pure Bengali, devoid of Sanskrit, Persian, or Arabic influences, making the work seminal in the understanding of Bengali language and literature. He also wrote *The Origin and Development of the Bengali Language*.

SEN, HIRALAL (1866–1917). Born in Manikganj, he was the first person to introduce moving pictures in Bengal. His entry into the film industry came with his organizing of the Royal Bioscope Company in 1900. He imported still **film** equipment, from which developed his early entry into moving pictures.

SEN, SURJA (1893–1934). A revolutionary who was hanged by the British because of his anti-British activities, he is noted for his organization of the **Chittagong** Armory raid of 1930. He formed his revolutionary group toward the end of World War I and for a time joined in the non-cooperation movement of Mahatma Gandhi. By 1923, Sen was disenchanted with nonviolence and began his radical movement, which included the attempt to murder a British judge. He was in prison from 1926 to 1928 and in 1930 served as the secretary of the Chittagong District Congress. He was betrayed in 1933, arrested by the British, and hanged in 1934.

SENA DYNASTY. It ruled Bengal from about 1095 to 1245, succeeding after consolidating the domains of the **Pala dynasty**. The dynasty apparently traces its ancestry to one Samantasena, who came to Bengal from Karnataka in south **India**. His grandson, Vijayasena, was the first to assume the royal title. His son, Vallalasena, wrote on **Hindu** religion and is said to have been the first proponent of hypergamy, the socially upward marriage of **women**, that is, marriage to men of higher caste, a system that he reestablished after the non-caste system of the preceding Pala Buddhists.

Vijayasena's grandson, **Lakshmana Sena**, extended the territories of the kingdom to Bihar and Orissa. In 1202, Lakshmana Sena was attacked at his capital, **Nadia**, by troops under the command of **Ikhtiyaruddin Muhammad Bakhtiyar Khalji**, the son of the ruler of the Delhi Sultanate, Bhakhtiyar Khalji, and forced to flee. The court of Lakshmana Sena supported literary figures, especially **Jayadeva**.

The Senas continued to rule in eastern Bengal until 1245, when that part of Bengal also came under Muslim rule. Unlike the Palas, the Senas were Brahmanical Hindus who perhaps set the stage for the rapid conversion of many in eastern Bengal to **Islam**, a casteless religion, as is the Buddhism the people once espoused.

SEPARATE ELECTORATES. A system of voting under which members of each religious community would vote separately for representatives from their own community in legislative bodies. The Muslims demanded this system in a meeting at Simla with Lord **Minto** in 1906. The system of separate electorates was opposed by many **Hindus**, who saw it as a means of divide-and-rule in **India**. The concept was included in the **Government of India Act of 1909** and was accepted in an agreement between the **Muslim League** and the Congress at Lucknow in 1916 in which the principal negotiators were **Muhammad Ali Jinnah** and Motilal Nehru. It remained an item high on the league agenda throughout the pre-independence period. After independence, India abolished separate electorates. Pakistan continued to use the system until the indirect elections of the **Ayub Khan** period were held. Separate electorates were used in the 1954 East Bengal election. Independent Bangladesh has not used separate electorates, but they were revived in Pakistan under Zia ul-Haq. In changes after 1909, several other groups gained separate representation, including Sikhs and Indian **Christians**. The opposite of separate electorates is termed joint electorates.

SERNIABAT, ABDUR RAB (?–1975). A lawyer and a politician, he was a member of the **National Awami Party** of **Maulana Bhashani**. He joined the **Awami League** in 1969 and became a minister in the Bangladesh provisional government-in-exile. After independence, Serniabat became minister for land reform and irrigation. A brother-in-law of Sheikh **Mujibur Rahman**, he was assassinated at the same time as Mujib.

SHAH JALAL MUJARRAD, HAZRAT (1271–1346). A religious preacher and soldier, he was probably born in Turkestan in 1271 and educated in Mecca. Reference to his death in 1346 was made by the great Arab traveler and historian Ibn Batuta. In 1303, Shah Jalal conquered **Sylhet** after having fought Gaur Govind and established his *khanqah* (**Sufi** hospice) there. He preached in Sylhet for 30 years and built a mosque that is in use today. A number of legends are associated with Shah Jalal, including the story that he crossed a river on his prayer rug in order to defeat Gaur Govind. His burial place in Sylhet is a pilgrimage site. The university in Sylhet has been named for him.

SHAHA, RONANDA PRASAD (1896–1971). A well-known social activist and philanthropist. He was a successful businessman who was initially involved in the supply of coal. He later expanded his business to include shipping, insurance, and **jute**. In 1938, he set up a 20-bed hospital and a residential girls' school. Both these enterprises have expanded and are well known throughout Bangladesh. During the great **famine** in Bengal in the early 1940s, Shaha donated generously to the Red Cross and maintained 250 free kitchens. After 1947, he chose to remain in **Pakistan** and was a leading member of the **Hindu** community. He and his only son were killed by the Pakistani army sometime in 1971. The now much larger hospital at Mirzapur in Tangail district remains a monument to the Shaha family.

SHAHABUDDIN, JUSTICE AHMAD (1895–1969). Governor of **East Bengal**, 1954–1955. A south Indian Muslim from Mysore state, he entered the civil service in 1921 and rose to the position of chief justice of East Bengal. After serving as governor, Shahabuddin became a justice of the Supreme Court and chief justice for a brief period in 1960.

SHAHABUDDIN, KHWAJA (1898–1977). A member of the **Nawab of Dhaka family** and younger brother of Sir **Khwaja Nazimuddin**, he had a long career in government service, often in the shadow of his elder brother. He was a member of the Bengal Legislative Assembly, 1937–1946, and a member of the Nazimuddin cabinet, 1943–1945.

Shahabuddin served as governor of the Northwest Frontier Province, 1951–1954, and as a member of the central cabinet, 1954–1955, and then undertook a number of diplomatic assignments. He returned to the central cabinet as minister of information under **Ayub Khan**, 1965–1969, thereby supporting a regime that was opposed by Nazimuddin. During this term of office he angered East Pakistanis by banning the works of Sir **Rabindranath Tagore** from Pakistan radio and television. After Bangladeshi independence, Shahabuddin stayed in Pakistan until his death.

SHAHIDULLAH, DR. MOHAMMAD (1885–1969). He is considered the foremost **educationist** of his time. He served in a number of educational institutions, including **Calcutta**, **Dhaka**, and **Rajshahi** Universities. Shahidullah is credited with writing more than 25 books, including *Essays on Islam*, *Traditional Culture in East Pakistan*, and *Hundred Sayings of the Holy Prophet*.

SHAKHARI BAZAR. Along with Tanti Bazar and Lakshmi Bazar, it is one of the oldest neighborhoods of **Dhaka** city. Some of the buildings date back to the late **Mughal** period. Most of the older buildings had ornamental facades but are currently in extremely dilapidated conditions. Most properties are owned by **Hindu** families and the two major craft industries of the area are gold ornaments and conch shell bangles. There is no serious conservation program, although some individuals are attempting to obtain a heritage status for the area and raise private funds for restoration of the buildings. There are 142 buildings in this area, of which 32 are listed as structurally vulnerable. Some of the old buildings have already collapsed.

SHAMSUDDIN, ABUL KALAM (1897–1978). Journalist and politician. As a college student he was active in the non-cooperation movement and the **Khilafat movement**. In 1923, he became an associate editor of the *Daily Mohammadi*, but was best known as editor of the important Muslim newspaper the *Daily Azad*, then published in **Calcutta** and now in **Dhaka**. Shamsuddin was elected to the Bengal Legislative Assembly in 1946. In 1952, he played a prominent role in the **language movement** and resigned his assembly seat. *See also* AKRAM KHAN, MAULANA MUHAMMAD.

SHAMSUDDIN MUZAFFAR SHAH. An **Abyssinian** originally named Sidi Badr, he rose to prominence during the rule of Nasiruddin Mahmud II of the **Ilyas Shahi dynasty.** In 1490, Sidi Badr murdered the ruler, usurped the throne, and assumed his royal title. He was a thoroughly cruel ruler, and the nobles under the leadership of **Alauddin Husain Shah** besieged the capital, **Gaur**, in 1493, in the course of which Shamsuddin Muzaffar Shah died. Alauddin Husain Shah assumed the throne as the first ruler of the **Husain Shahi dynasty.**

SHAMSUL HUDA, NAWAB SYED SIR (1862–1922). A jurist, educator, and political figure, he was born in **Comilla** district and educated at **Calcutta** University in law and in Persian. He attended the founding session of the **Muslim League** in 1906, but he withdrew from active politics when he became the first Muslim to serve on the Executive Council of the governor of Bengal in 1912, serving until 1917. Shamsul Huda earlier had been elected to the Imperial Legislative Council from **Eastern Bengal and Assam** in 1910. In 1917, he was appointed the first Muslim judge on the Calcutta High Court. Shamsul Huda left this position when he was elected to the Bengal Legislative Council in 1921, where he served as the first president of the council. He was one of the founders of Dhaka University.

SHAMSUZZOHA, MUHAMMAD (1934–1969). An educationist, he was born in Bankura district, now in West Bengal. He studied in **Dhaka** and was active in the **language movement.** He taught at Rajshahi University. In 1969, while students were protesting the government of **Ayub Khan**, Shamsuzzoha, who was provost of one of the residence halls, tried to stop the army from shooting at the students. The soldiers killed him.

SHARIATULLAH, HAJI (1779–1840). The founder of the **Faraizi movement**, he studied in Mecca and returned to Bengal after 20 years. While in Mecca he studied Wahhabi principles and practices. Upon his return, he began the movement based on his Islamic beliefs. The essential principles of the movement were political and economic freedom for peasants and workers, protection of peasants and workers from the suppression of the *zamindars* (landlords) and those who were involved in the cultivation of **indigo**, discouragement of certain forms of worship, including such "un-Islamic practices as veneration of saints," and avoidance of performing such important Islamic practices as the Friday prayers or the Eid prayers in India until **India** became a Muslim society.

SHARIF, AHMED (1921–1999). An expert in ancient and medieval Bengali literature, he had over 100 research publications and edited over 40 manuscripts of ancient and medieval Bengali literature. His two-volume (1979 and 1983) *Bangalee* and *Bangla shahitya* (Bengalee and Bangla **Literature**) are considered source books on Bengali literature. From Patiya in Chittagong, he was a controversial figure because of his stands against communalism and fascism. He received his Ph.D. from **Dhaka University** in 1967. He joined Dhaka University in 1950, prior to receiving his Ph.D., and retired in 1983. He was the first Kazi Nuzrul Islam Professor at Chittagong University (1984–1986). For his outstanding contribution to the understanding of Bengali literature he received an honorary doctorate of literature from Rabindra Bharati University of India.

SHEIKH HASINA WAJID (1947–). The daughter of Sheikh **Mujibur Rahman**, Sheikh Hasina was born on 28 September 1947, in Tungipara, Gopalganj district. She graduated from **Dhaka University** in 1973. Hasina was absent from Bangladesh on 15 August 1975, when the coup took place that took the lives of her father and many other members of the family. After being kept out of Bangladesh for some time, she returned on 17 May 1981 to a wide welcome from members of the **Awami League (AL)** and became the leader of the league. After the takeover of the government by **Hussain Muhammad Ershad**, Hasina was arrested several times, but in 1986 she was elected to **parliament** and became the leader of the opposition. She and her party left parliament in November 1987, and the league did not participate in the 1988 election held by Ershad. Hasina was a leader, along with **Khaleda Zia** of the **Bangladesh Nationalist Party (BNP)**, of the demonstrations that caused Ershad to resign and led to the election of February 1991.

In that election, the Awami League finished second, and she became the leader of the opposition in March 1991. She led the movement for a **caretaker government**. In the June 1996 election, the Awami League won a plurality (but not a majority) of the parliamentary seats. The Awami League gained the support of the **Jatiya Party** and formed a government with Sheikh Hasina as **prime minister**. In the October 2001 election the Awami League was trounced, but did finish second to the BNP and its allies; Sheikh Hasina returned to her earlier position as leader of the opposition. On 21 August 2004, an assassination attempt on her was made during an AL political rally. As part of the **Minus Two Politics**, she was barred from returning to Bangladesh from the **United States**, but she returned anyway. Upon her return she was arrested and after nearly a year was released on bail. Her party won the election of December 2008 and in January 2009 she became the prime minister once again. *See also* ELECTIONS.

SHELLEY, MIZANUR RAHMAN (1943–). A former member of the **Pakistan** and Bangladesh civil services, he was minister of information and broadcasting in the **Hussain Muhammad Ershad** regime as a non-political member of the cabinet. Before and since his cabinet service, Shelley has been the head of an important think tank, the Centre for Development Research Bangladesh.

SHER SHAH SURI (1472–1545). He rebelled against the Mughal emperor Humayun in 1539 and established himself as emperor of India until his death in 1545. His successors continued to rule north India until 1555, when Humayun reclaimed the throne. His descendants then continued to rule independently in Bengal until 1564, when they were overthrown by the **Karrani dynasty**. Among Sher Shah Suri's long-lasting achievements was the planning of the Grand Trunk Road.

SHIP BREAKING. Likely to have started in the early 1960s, by 2008 it was supplying between 80 and 90 percent of the steel needs of the country. About 1.5 million tons of scrap iron is produced every year by breaking up ships purchased from abroad. The scraps support the re-rolling mills and the steel mills of Bangladesh. There are 68 companies in the business, utilizing 36 ship-breaking yards in the **Chittagong** coastal area and employing anywhere from 10,000 to

30,000 workers. Ship breaking is still a relatively unregulated sector, although efforts are being made to subject the sector to **environmental** laws. The biggest danger comes from ships that were used for carrying toxic materials, primarily the unintended consequences of such scraps being used in construction materials and the **health** hazards of the workers in the shipyards.

SHIP BUILDING. A relatively new economic sector activity, the shipbuilding industry is expected to contribute approximately 5 percent of GDP by 2015. Bangladesh currently has nearly half a billion dollars' worth of ocean vessels under order to be delivered by 2010. Orders have come from the Netherlands, Germany, Denmark, and Mozambique. Bangladesh is attempting to carve out a market niche for itself for small vessels having a DWT range of 3,000–15,000, as more established ship-building countries such as Japan, **China**, South Korea, and Vietnam are not interested in this class. Its main competitor is India, which builds in the same weight class. Bangladesh has some labor advantages. While skilled labor is coming from Bangladeshi workers, higher levels of skills are coming from returning Bangladeshi workers who have worked in the shipyards of Singapore, South Korea, and Dubai. Ship building as a local industry employs over 100,000 workers and there are more than 300 small- and medium-scale docks in the country. Two companies (Ananda and Western Marine Shipyards) are leading the ship-building sector in Bangladesh. The total global ship-building sector is currently estimated to be $400 billion and Bangladeshi ship builders are aiming for an initial one percent market share.

SHUDDHA SANGEET PROSHAR GOSHTHI. Established in 1975, it is a cultural organization of classical musicians of Bangladesh. Its objectives are to promote classical **music** and to develop standards. The organization sponsors classical music performances and conferences. Students of classical music are divided into three groups, those below age 16, those between 16 and 25, and those above 25. Performances are regularly organized and students make vocal and instrumental presentations. Those under 16 are called *Protibha Sphuron*. The 16-to-25 group is called *Protibha Bikash*, and the 25 and above is called *Protibha Shondhan*.

SIKDAR, SIRAJ (1944–1975). A civil engineer by profession, he became involved with the labor movement in 1968. He was a member of the Communist Party and was a student leader. In June 1971 he formed the **East Bengal** Sarvohara (Proletariat) Party, which espoused a radical philosophy. Sikdar argued that **East Pakistan** was a colony of West Pakistan and similarly that Bangladesh was a colony of **India**. He called for the overthrow of the Sheikh **Mujibur Rahman** regime by force. Sikdar went underground in 1974 but was arrested and killed by the **Jatiyo Rakkhi Bahini** in 1975.

SIKDER, DEBEN (1917–1994). A communist leader, he was involved in the **Chittagong** Armory raid of 1930 and was jailed by the British. Sikder left terrorist organizations in 1937 and joined the Communist Party of India. He was a member of one of the factions of the **Communist Party of Bangladesh** at his death.

SIRAJI, ISMAIL HUSSAIN (1880–1931). Born in Sirajganj, he was active in the non-cooperation and **Khilafat movements**, but he made his career as a poet and novelist.

SIRAJUDDAULAH (1733–1757). Governor (nawab) of Bengal from April 1756 to June 1757. His birth name was Mirza Mahmud. He succeeded his maternal grandfather, **Alivardi Khan**, although the succession was contested by another grandson, Shaukat Jang, whom Sirajuddaulah defeated and killed. On 20 June 1756, he attacked **Calcutta** and was held responsible for the incident of the **Black Hole**. The British recaptured Calcutta on 2 January 1757, but they sought to replace Sirajuddaulah with a more pliable governor. Subverting officers on Sirajuddaulah's side, including **Mir Jafar**, the British under **Robert Clive** defeated Sirajuddaulah at the Battle of **Plassey** on 23 June 1757. Sirajuddaulah was captured and executed. His immediate successor was **Mir Jafar**.

SIRCAR, MOHAMMED JAMIRUDDIN (1931–). He served as acting **president** of Bangladesh from 21 July 2002, following the resignation of **Badruddoza Choudhury**, until the newly elected **Iajuddin Ahmed** was sworn in as president on 6 September 2002. He was elected speaker of **parliament** in October 2001, retaining that post while serving as acting president. He is a barrister and has served in several positions in the **Bangladesh Nationalist Party (BNP)**.

SIX POINTS. A plan for the accommodation of the grievances of East Pakistan put forward by Sheikh **Mujibur Rahman** in 1966. It became the platform of the **Awami League** in the 1970 **elections**. The six points were: (1) federal parliamentary government, with free and regular elections; (2) federal government that controls only foreign affairs and defense; (3) a separate **currency** or separate fiscal accounts for each province, to control movement of capital from east to west; (4) all power of taxation at the provincial level, with the federal government subsisting on grants from the provinces; (5) each federating unit could enter into foreign **trade** agreements on its own and control the foreign exchange earned; and (6) each unit could raise its own militia. These points are based on the **Twenty-one Point** program of the **United Front** in 1954. **Yahya Khan** issued a **legal framework order** prior to the 1970 elections that was a response and a challenge to several of the points. *See also* LEGAL FRAMEWORK ORDER.

SOBUR KHAN, ABDUL (1910–1982). A political leader associated with the **Muslim League**, he was a minister in the **Ayub Khan** government, 1962–1969. After Bangladeshi independence in 1971, the Muslim League was banned, but the party was permitted to return to political activity in 1976. As the leader of the **Bangladesh Muslim League**, Sobur was elected to **parliament** in 1979.

SONARGAON. In this **archeological** site located near **Dhaka**, in Narayanganj district, on the banks of the **Meghna** River, there have been found a number of seals that date from the **Deva dynasty**. It was a provincial center during the period of the **Delhi Sultanate** and **Ilyas Shahi** rule and a number of monuments remain. In the latter part of the 16th century, a neighboring town, Katrabo, was the seat of **Isa Khan**, the principal member of the **Bara Bhuiyan**, who resisted **Mughal** rule. It was a center of the cotton textile industry, including textile export. In the early 17th century it was overtaken by Dhaka, which had become the capital of the Mughal province of Bengal, and its importance greatly diminished. The city is the site of the Museum of Folk Art and Culture.

SOUTH ASIAN ASSOCIATION FOR REGIONAL COOPERATION (SAARC). The organization was formally established in **Dhaka** in December 1985, at a summit of the heads of government of the seven South Asian states. The summit was presided over by the Bangladesh president, **Hussain Muhammad Ershad**. The concept of a regional organization was first proposed in May 1980 by the then president, **Ziaur Rahman**. His name for the group was simply South Asia Regional Cooperation (SARC). In an effort to gain support for his idea, Zia visited each of the South Asian countries.

Member countries are Bangladesh, Bhutan, **India**, the Maldives, Nepal, **Pakistan**, and Sri Lanka. The purpose is to have a forum for discussing regional issues. In the agreement signed at Dhaka bilateral issues, such as the conflict between India and Pakistan over Kashmir, were excluded from the purview of SAARC. All decisions are to be on the basis of consensus rather than on the majority principle. Owing primarily to the hostility between India and Pakistan and also to disagreements between other pairs of states, SAARC has been ineffective in decision-making and meetings of the heads of government have been delayed or cancelled, including the one scheduled for Islamabad in January 2003. However, subordinate committees have usually met regularly. A secretariat is based in Kathmandu.

In December 1995, the states agreed to set up a South Asian Preferential Trading Arrangement (SAPTA) that is intended to reduce or eliminate **trade** barriers on agreed products among the countries. This has generally been an ineffective program. The states have also committed to establish a SAARC Free Trade Area (SAFTA). No progress has been made on this.

SOVIET UNION. *See* RUSSIA; UNION OF SOVIET SOCIALIST REPUBLICS.

SPECIAL POWERS ACT. An act passed during the Sheikh **Mujibur Rahman** government in 1974 to punish those engaged in "anti-social" acts. It empowered the government to detain anyone at any time without any reason. It has been used by governments as a means to restrict the activities of the political opposition.

ST. SCHOLASTICA'S GIRLS' HIGH SCHOOL. A missionary school established in 1883 by Euphrasie Barber, of the Sisters of Our Lady of the Missions, Religieuses de Notre Dame Missions, along with five Sisters—Marie du Sacré-Coeur, Marie de la Nativité, Marie St. Stanislaus, Marie Philippe, and Marie St. Verinique—who arrived in **Chittagong** on 24 March 1883 by an Austrian ship, the *Castor*, and set up place at Patherghata. The plight of the local **women**, young widows, and girls between the ages of 5 and 6 being readied to be married inspired the sisters to set up a school, an orphanage, and a hostel for young widows. The school, named St. Scholastica's Girls' High School, was born. It became one of the most well-known girls' schools in Chittagong for its quality **education**. The medium of instruction was English, although after the independence of Bangladesh the medium of instruction became Bengali or Bangla. It continues to be a major girl's school and maintains its standards.

STEEL RE-ROLLING INDUSTRIAL SECTOR. It was developed primarily to support the construction industry and the massive growth of high-rise building first in **Dhaka** and then in **Chittagong**. At present there are over 100 small- to medium-size steels mills in Bangladesh and another 250 re-rolling mills with a total annual capacity of 2.4 million tons. The market demand for steel is around 1.5 to 1.6 million tons. Steel manufacturing is hampered by the shortage of electricity. Modernization and new steel plants will double the total production in the next five years. Some of the larger corporations are located in Chittagong, such as the Bangladesh Steel Re-rolling Mills.

SUFISM. The spread of **Islam** into Bangladesh was largely the result of the preaching efforts of Sufis, many of them from Central Asia. Sufis are generally defined as Islamic mystics who emphasize the individual devotion to the divine. In various legends they are often described as having miraculous powers (e.g., **Hazrat Shah Jalal Mujarrad**). As Sufism developed in **India** and especially in Bengal, it took on some of the aspects of devotion and legends of **Hinduism**.

Many Bangladeshis invoke the blessings of *pirs* (a title often given to the heads of Sufi shrines) and visit the *khanqahs* (hospices) of living pirs and the *mazaars* (burial places) of those who have died and are still revered. Celebrations (*dargahs*) at the khanqahs or mazaars are often held to commemorate important dates in the life of the pir.

SUHRAWARDY, DR. LT. COL. SIR HASAN (1884–1946). He was born in **Dhaka**, the son of Maulana Obaidullah Suhrawardy, and educated at the **Kolkata** Medical School and in **Great Britain**. He was a member of the medical service and a professor of medicine at Calcutta University. Sir Hasan was a member of the Bengal Legislative Council, 1921–1924, and of the Central Legislative Assembly, 1945–1946.

SUHRAWARDY, DR. SIR ABDULLAH AL-M'AMUN (?–1935). A politician and educator, he received a doctorate from Edinburgh University and was called to the bar in London. He taught in Lahore and **Calcutta** after returning from **Great Britain**, but devoted much of his career to politics. He was a member of the Bengal Legislative Council, 1910–1920 and 1921–1926. In 1926 Sir Abdullah was elected to the Central Legislative Assembly, of which he remained a member until his death.

SUHRAWARDY, HUSAIN SHAHID (1893–1963). Founder of the **Awami League** in 1949, he had previously been a key member of the **Muslim League**. He was a member of a prominent Bengali Muslim family and was educated at Oxford and the Inns of Court in London. Suhrawardy was elected to the Bengal Legislative Council in 1921 and remained a member until 1936. He was also deputy mayor of **Calcutta**, 1923–1925, during the period that **Chittaranjan Das** was mayor. He entered the Bengal Legislative Assembly in 1937 and served in the **Fazlul Haq** coalition cabinet (1937–1941) and in the **Khwaja Nazimuddin** cabinet (1943–1945).

After the 1946 election, Suhrawardy successfully challenged Nazimuddin for the leadership of the Muslim League group in the assembly and became **prime minister** of Bengal, 1946–1947. The period was distinguished by the Great Calcutta Killing in August 1946, and then by Suhrawardy's working with Mahatma Gandhi to attempt (rather successfully) to tamp down the communal rioting. The period also saw Suhrawardy's floating of the concept of a third dominion to include Bengal and Assam as an eastern balance to **Pakistan** and "Hindustan." He had the support of some Congress party members (including Sarat Chandra Bose, brother of **Subhas Chandra Bose**), but he incurred the wrath of **Muhammad Ali Jinnah**. Jinnah effectively barred Suhrawardy from continuing in office as chief minister of East Bengal, a post to which Nazimuddin was elected.

In 1949, after a period of residence in India, Suhrawardy floated his concept of a party that would include non-Muslims as well as Muslims and founded the Awami League, although at first it was called the Awami Muslim League and did not include non-Muslims. This party, which never gained significant strength in the western wing of Pakistan, joined with the **Krishak Sramik Party** in the **United Front** to defeat the Muslim League in the 1954 East Bengal legislature **elections**. Suhrawardy left the legislative leadership in East Bengal to **Ataur Rahman Khan** of the provincial party so he could concentrate his attention on national politics. He was a minister in the cabinet of **Muhammad Ali Bogra**, 1954–1955, and was prime minister of Pakistan, 1956–1957. After martial law was instituted he opposed **Ayub Khan** and worked for the restoration of the parliamentary system. Suhrawardy died in Beirut on 5 December 1963. He, Fazlul Haq, and Nazimuddin are buried in adjacent graves in Dhaka. *See also* SUHRAWARDY FAMILY.

SUHRAWARDY FAMILY. A family of great prominence in government and intellectual circles in **Kolkata**. **Husain Shahid Suhrawardy** was the son of Sir Zahid Suhrawardy, a judge of the Calcutta High Court. Another branch of the family, that of Maulana Obaidullah Suhrawardy (a great-uncle of Husain Shahid), included this important religious figure and his sons Mahmud, a member of the Council of State, and Sir **Hasan Suhrawardy**, one-time vice-chancellor of Calcutta University. Sir Hasan's daughter, Shaista Suhrawardy Ikramullah, was a member of **parliament** (her book *From Purdah to Parliament* describes the change in her life; she has also written a biography of Husain Shahid Suhrawardy). Her husband, Ikramullah, was a foreign secretary of **Pakistan** (and his brother, Hidayatullah, a vice president of **India**). Their daughter, Sarwath, is married to Prince Hasan of Jordan, the brother of the late King Hussein. Through other connections, Husain Shahid Suhrawardy was related to **Abul Hashim**, Sir **Abdur Rahim** (his daughter was Husain Shahid's first wife), and **Fazlul Haq**.

SULTAN, MUHAMMAD (1928–1983). Founder-president of the East Pakistan Student Union, one of the most active student unions in the subcontinent. He joined the **National Awami Party** of **Bhashani** and was the secretary general of the party from 1966 to 1968. In 1970, Sultan retired from politics and returned to his earlier profession in the book printing and publishing world. He always fought for Bengali nationalism and for that reason his books were banned. For his contribution to Bengali nationalism he was awarded the **Ekushey Padak**. *See also* MARTYRS' DAY.

SULTAN, SHEIKH MOHAMMAD (1923–1994). Better known as Lal Mia, he was considered a master painter for his ability to illustrate the struggle of the masses in overcoming human ordeals and sufferings. He portrayed the dominance of man over nature and captured the natural serenity of his characters. He was a master of landscape painting. In his large canvas paintings he portrayed **agricultural** laborers, fishermen, and toiling men and women. A school dropout, he was patronized by a local *zamindar*, Dhirendranath Roy. He was later patronized by **Shahid Suhrawardy**. For a time he attended an **art** school in India but again dropped out. During World War II, he worked as a freelance artist drawing portraits of soldiers. He also spent time in Kashmir.

Born in Narial, he returned there after the partition of **India** but then spent time in the **United State**s and European countries. Toward the end of his career he spent all his time in Narial, where he had opened up Nanda Kanon primary and secondary schools. He also established the Nando Kanon Fine Arts College in Jessore. In 1982, Cambridge University conferred their Man of Achievement Award on him. Other awards he received include the **Ekushey Padak** in 1982 and the Independence Award in 1993.

SULTAN, SYED MAHMUD (1917–1991). He was a member of the constituent assembly of Pakistan. After 1971, Sultan was sent to the

United Nations when Bangladesh was trying to gain admission to the world body. He was the first Bangladeshi high commissioner to **Great Britain**. After the assassination of **Mujibur Rahman**, he resumed his law practice.

SUNDARBANS. A tract of mangrove swamp that lies along the coast of Bangladesh and West Bengal between the mouth of the **Meghna** in the west and that of the Hooghly in the east. It contains a vast number of streams that are tidal rivers and an uncountable number of islands. Except for a portion of the north of the region, the area is not cultivated. It is the home of the Bengal tiger and of crocodiles. It derives its name from the sundari mangrove that dominates the region.

Perhaps the earliest attempt to cultivate portions of the Sundarbans came in the 15th century when Khanja Ali made clearances at Bagerhat. There were predatory incursions by the **Portuguese** in the early 18th century. The shift of the **Ganges** outflow eastward deprived the Sundarbans of much of the water it once received. This has caused increased salinization. The restoration of the **Gorai River** and the development known as the **Ganga-Kobadak Project** have not yet restored the flow to its earlier levels. *See also* KHULNA.

SUPREME JUDICIAL COMMISSION (SJC). A nine-member body under the leadership of the chief justice of Bangladesh is entrusted with selecting and recommending candidates as judges of the High Court and Appellate Division of the Supreme Court. The SJC was created to ensure the independence of the judiciary from the executive branch. The SJC consists of the chief justice as chairperson and the law minister, two seniormost judges of the Appellate Division, the attorney general, a member of parliament from the government and one from the opposition, and the secretary of the Ministry of Law. The SJC recommends at least two candidates for each position through the Office of the **Prime Minister** to the **president**. The president of Bangladesh appoints one or may send back the recommendations for revision.

SURA DYNASTY. Tradition represents **Adisura** as the founder of the dynasty, but there is no contemporary evidence to support this. Literary tradition is the only support for the presumption that in about AD

700 he attempted the revival of Brahmanism in Bengal, which was dominated then by **Buddhism**. His supposed seat was **Gaur** or Lakshmanavati. He is said to have imported the Brahmins who are the ancestors of the Varendra (northern Bengal) and Radhiya (western Bengal) Brahmins. Whatever the historical basis, there is some evidence that the Sura family was powerful as late as the 11th century, as it is recorded that King Vijayasena of the **Sena dynasty** married a Sura princess. Southern Bengal (Radha) was ruled by a king named Ranasura when the Cholas invaded Bengal in 1023. *See also* HINDUISM; MAHIPALA I.

SURI DYNASTY. *See* SHER SHAH SURI.

SURMA RIVER. The river rises in the Indian state of Manipur and then flows through portions of **Assam** and Meghalya before entering the **Sylhet** region of Bangladesh. In Manipur and the Cachar district of Meghalya, it is known as the Barak River. After passing the city of Sylhet, it flows into **Mymensingh** district, where it joins the old channel of the **Brahmaputra**. In the rainy season it can be navigable to Silchar in Assam.

SWADESHI. Literally, "self country," the term was used during the opposition by **Hindus** to the partition of Bengal of 1905. They boycotted British-made goods in favor of goods made in India. Mahatma Gandhi also used the term during the struggle for the independence of India. *See also* BENGAL, PARTITION OF (1905).

SWADHINOTA PADAK (INDEPENDENCE AWARD). This is the highest civilian award of the government of Bangladesh. Established in 1977, it is given to individuals and organizations on the eve of Independence Day, which is observed on 16 December 1977. Awards are made to individuals and organizations. Ten individuals received the award the first year. Appendix 6 provides a list of award winners from 1977 to 2008.

SWARNIRVAR. A district-level effort to boost **agricultural** production begun in 1974. Swarnirvar means "self-reliance." It was initially organized around a village committee on which all segments of the village would be represented. Some of the slogans of the swarnirvar movement were "Let the hands of beggars turn into the hands of workers" and "We will beg no more, we will not allow the nation to beg."

SYLHET. Also known earlier as Srihatta, it is a region, district, and district town in the northeast of Bangladesh. Before the partition of 1947, the district was included in the province of **Assam**. The city is on the **Surma River**, which flows into the **Meghna**.

Sylhet has been a center of Islamic activity and many Muslim saints have shrines there, including **Hazrat Shah Jalal Mujarrad** and several of his followers. The Muslim occupation of Sylhet in 1303 was led by Shah Jalal. In its earlier history, Sylhet was divided into several small states that at times were under the control of the raja of Tippera (**Tripura**). Shah Jalal defeated (or perhaps outwitted, if the legends about him are to be believed) the ruler of Gor, or Sylhet proper. The British at first included Sylhet in Bengal, but in 1874 it was added to the newly created chief commissionership of Assam.

The district produces **tea** in the higher elevations. Rainfall is very heavy, averaging about 160 inches a year. The district is also a major center of **natural gas** production. *See also* NATURAL RESOURCES; SYLHET REFERENDUM.

SYLHET REFERENDUM. Held in 1947 in the Sylhet district of **Assam** to determine whether that district would go to **India** or **Pakistan** in the partition. It was agreed that if the district voted for Pakistan the boundary commission would delimit the contiguous areas of Muslim majority. The district did vote to go to Pakistan. The subdivisions of Sylhet, Moulvi Bazaar, Sunamganj, and Habiganj were awarded to Pakistan, with the subdivision of Karimganj going to India. *See also* SYLHET.

– T –

TAGORE, RABINDRANATH (SIR) (1861–1941). The most noted of modern Indian poets, winning the Nobel Prize for **literature** in 1913. His works are as well accepted by the Muslims of Bengal as they are by the **Hindus**. The banning of Tagore's works from **Pakistan** radio in 1965 by **Khawja Shahabuddin** was one of the straws that eventually broke the camel's back of Pakistan's unity. One of Tagore's poems, *Sonar Bangla* (Golden Bengal), serves as the national anthem of Bangladesh, and another of his poems is the national anthem of **India**. His work was not limited to poetry, as he wrote novels and plays and even took up painting in his last years. Tagore was active politically, especially when he urged moderate opposition to the 1905 partition of Bengal. He founded the Vishwa Bharati University at Shantiniketan ("the abode of peace") in rural Bengal in 1901. One of the principal characteristics of Tagore's writing was his understanding of rural Bengal despite his urban upbringing.

TAGORE FAMILY. A distinguished Brahmin family that contributed greatly to the intellectual development of Bengal ("the Bengal Renaissance"). Most famed of the family was the Nobel Prize–winner **Rabindranath Tagore**. The founder of the family in the period of note was Dwarkanath (1794–1846). He was a successful businessman who supported liberal movements of the day and was an early member of the **Brahmo Samaj**, based on the ideas of Raja **Ram Mohan Roy**. His son, Debendranath (1817–1905), continued the successful business and succeeded his father as leader of the Brahmo Samaj. Debendranath's son, Satyendranath (1842–1923), was the first Indian to pass the entry examination into the Indian Civil Service. The youngest son of Debendranath, Rabindranath, was the poet. Another member of the family, Abanindranath (1871–1951), was a noted artist and the founder of the Indian Society of Oriental Arts.

TALPATTY ISLAND. An uninhabited island that is in dispute between **India** and Bangladesh. It lies at the mouth of the Hariabhanga River, which is intended to form the boundary between the two countries, although the actual line of control has not yet been demarcated. The river drains the region of the **Sundarbans**. The question of sovereignty over the island, when and if decided, would be important to the final determination of the sea boundary between India and Bangladesh. Bangladesh has proposed that a study be made of the main flow of the river to determine whether it is to the west of the island, which would indicate that the ownership should belong to Bangladesh, or vice versa, in which case the ownership would be with India.

TAMIZUDDIN KHAN (1889–1963). He was born in **Faridpur** district and educated in law at Calcutta University. He was active in the Congress, the **Khilafat movement**, and the **Muslim League**, achieving his official positions as a member of the league. Tamizuddin was a member of the legislature in Bengal, 1926–1945, and was elected to the Central Legislative Assembly in 1946. He was a member of both the **Fazlul Haq** and **Khawja Nazimuddin** cabinets. After independence Tamizuddin became a member of the **Pakistan** Constituent Assembly and succeeded **Muhammad Ali Jinnah** as president of the assembly in 1948 on Jinnah's death. He held the office until the assembly was dissolved by Governor-General **Ghulam Muhammad** in 1954.

Tamizuddin challenged the dissolution in a notable case in which he maintained that the governor-general had no right to dissolve the assembly because the governor-general had caused a new assembly to be elected and, therefore, representative government had been restored. The judicial system agreed with Tamizuddin's position. Tamizuddin returned to public office as the speaker of the National Assembly elected in 1962, retaining that position until his death.

TANDA. Along with **Gaur**, this town served at various times as the capital of Bengal during the 16th century. The site, located in **Nadia** district of West Bengal, has been destroyed by the change of course of the Pagla River, a distributary of the **Ganges**. It was used as a capital during the **Karrani dynasty**, beginning in 1564 under Suleiman Karrani.

TANGTHA. Literally "Children of the Hills," this is what the tribal people known as the Bomang or Bom call themselves. The word Bom came from "Bomjao," meaning "united nation" and is formed from two different groups, Pangthaoye and Sunthola. They form the present-day Bom tribe. They are originally from China and came to reside in the Bandarban district of Bangladesh about 165 years ago. Approximately 10,000 Boms live in Bandarban and most of them have converted to **Christanity**. They are primarily hunters.

TARKABAGISH, MAULANA ABDUL RASHID (?–1986). A prominent member of the **Muslim League**, he left the league because of its policies in **East Pakistan** and joined the **Awami League**. He became the president of the East Pakistan Awami League in 1957. Tarkabagish relinquished his position when Sheikh **Mujibur Rahman** took over as the new leader. In 1976 he formed a new political party and named it the Gana Azad League (People's Freedom League).

TEA. Tea was imported to India from China in the 1820s. In 1834 the governor-general, Lord William Bentinck, had obtained tea seeds and skilled labor and set up a government plantation in Assam. This was sold to the Assam Tea Company in 1839, and the industry expanded rapidly. In the northeast, the principal tea-growing areas are in the Darjeeling district of West Bengal, Assam, and the Sylhet district of Bangladesh. In Bangladesh there are 163 tea estates, of which 28 belong to what are known as the sterling companies (foreign-owned). Bangladeshi owners have 58 estates. Other types of owners include the Bangladesh private limited companies (61), the National Tea Company (13), and the Bangladesh Tea Board (3). At one time, tea was the second-largest agricultural export of Bangladesh after **jute**. Today, however, tea production is declining. In 1997, 25.15 million kilograms of tea was produced. That is down to only 4.79 million kilograms in 2006. In 1997, tea export earned Bangladesh $38 million, but in 2006 Bangladesh earned only $6.69 million. Some efforts are being made to revive the tea industry, including a special emphasis on the development of excellent quality green tea.

TEBHAGA MOVEMENT. Celebrated by the indigenous peoples of Dinajpur, this day honors those who gave their lives protesting the repression of indigenous people during the British rule. On 4 January 1947 two tribals (Shibram Majhi and Shamir Uddin) were killed by the British police while demanding **agricultural** rights for indigenous farmers. This day has been officially celebrated by the Tebhaga Chetona Parishad (Tebhaga Awareness Committee) since 2004.

TERRORISM. The Jama'atul Mujaheddin Bangladesh (JMB), Harkat-ul-Jihad-al-Islam (HUJI-B), and Jagrata Muslim Janata Bangladesh

(JMJB), on the one hand, and the Gobo Mukti Fouz (GMF), Purbo Banglar Communist Party (PBCP), and New Biplobi Communist Party (NBCP), on the other, are the major groups involved in radicalism and extremism in Bangladesh. But the radicalism and extremism of the two broad groups are different. The first group is intolerant of religious minorities and demands conditions for an Islamic state guided by implementation of Sharia. The second group focuses its efforts on carving out a separate **Hindu** homeland and is also involved in transforming Bangladesh into a communist state.

Neither of these broad groups has a significant following, nor are they a broad-based movement in Bangladesh. However, the JMB, HUJI-B, and JMJB have caused considerable havoc in Bangladesh and have attracted the attention of the international community, which is mindful of terrorism that may have an international agenda. The near-simultaneous explosion of 450 small bombs in 63 of the 64 districts of Bangladesh in August 2005 forced the hand of the **Bangladesh Nationalist Party (BNP)** government. In 2006, the government of Bangladesh, often accused of soft-peddling on terroristic acts, extremism, and fundamentalism because of its coalition with **Jama'at-i-Islami**, banned the three parties and arrested their leaders. They were sentenced to death at the end of their trial. In March 2007, six high-profile members of the militant group JMB, including its leader Abdur Rahman and second-in-command Bangla Bhai, were executed by the **caretaker government**.

In September 2007, the caretaker government announced 12 steps to curb militancy in the country. These steps included a large-scale anti-militancy informational campaign by the Ministry of Information, anti-militancy sermons by imams after Friday prayers, increasing awareness among local government officials, an expanded intelligence watch on Qwami madrasa, and co-opting mosques and madrasas in the fight against militancy.

Perhaps the single greatest concern for the international community is whether Bangladesh is linked to international terrorism. While no definite links have been established, there is a higher degree of confidence that Bangladesh is linked to incidences of regional terrorism, some by choice and others because of regional conflicts and insurgency movements in the eastern provinces of **India** and western **Myanmar**. The most serious charge of complicity in the Indian insurgency movement is a result of the **Chittagong** arms seizure in 2004. The arms haul of 1,290 submachine guns of different varieties, almost 1,200 short-range rocket launchers, 400 semi-automatic rifles, and more than a million rounds of ammunitions was sufficient to arm several infantry brigades. Whether it indicates participation in international terrorism or involvement in the debilitating political machinations of India and Pakistan is difficult to assess. There are strong elements of radicalism, extremism, and fundamentalism in Bangladesh, but they are not so strong as to overcome the largely secular aspiration of the overwhelming majority of the citizens of Bangladesh. *See also* ISLAM; MILITANCY.

THEATRE. Perhaps the earliest operation of a theatre in what is now Bangladesh was in 1883 when *Neel Dharpan* by **Dinbondhu Mitra** was produced. The first professional theatre, the Diamond Jubilee Theatre, was established in the 1890s. Since liberation in 1971, a number of theatres and theatrical groups have been developed. Among these are the Bahubachan Theater in 1972 and the Nagrik Theater group in 1973. Now it is estimated that there are several hundred theatrical groups. An area in **Dhaka** is known as Theater Para (neighborhood). The Mahila Samiti (women's association) and the Guide House Auditorium offer regular theatre seasons. There is also folk theatre known as *jatra*, and spoken drama (the term *jatra* is also applied to musical folk drama). *See also* DEEN, SALEEM AL.

TIDAL BORE. The exceptionally high tides that enter the **Meghna** estuary and also affect some of the areas to the west of the river. The tides often exceed 18 feet and travel at 15 miles per hour, especially during the equinoxes. They can, and often do, cause major damage in the **coastal islands**.

TIKKA KHAN (1915–2002). A military officer, he was martial law administrator and governor of **East Pakistan** in 1971. In the latter office, he succeeded Admiral S. M. Ahsan and was replaced later in the year by **Abdul Muttalib Malik**. Described by Bangladeshis as the "butcher of Bangladesh," Tikka Khan administered the province during the worst period of the **War of Liberation**. After retirement, he entered politics in **Pakistan** as a member of the People's Party of Pakistan, the group founded by **Zulfiqar Ali Bhutto**.

TISTA. A river that flows through northwestern Bangladesh. It rises in Sikkim, flows rapidly through gorges, crosses the Jalpaiguri district of West Bengal and, in season, rushes violently through **Rangpur** district in Bangladesh to its confluence with the **Brahmaputra**. Formerly, the Tista flowed into the **Ganges**, but about 1787 it diverted to the Brahmaputra.

TITU MIR (?–1831). Born Mir Nisar Ali in 24 Parganas district, he studied in Mecca, where he became associated with Syed Ahmed of Bareilly, a town in the then United Provinces, now Uttar Pradesh, in India. Syed Ahmed followed closely the Wahhabi movement, a very strict version of **Islam** that is still practiced in Saudi Arabia. Syed Ahmed's current followers are known as Brelvis (after his home town) and are politically important in Pakistan today.

Titu Mir condemned the veneration of saints and the *pirs* who headed **Sufi** shrines. Turning violent after his return to Bengal, he and, after his death, his followers led movements against the British. He was killed in a clash with the British in 1831. His followers supported the **Blue Mutiny** of the **indigo** farmers, but by 1860 the movement had died out.

TOAHA, MOHAMMAD (1922–1987). Associated with the communist movement in Bengal since the early 1950s, he was a member of the **Awami League** and a close political associate of Sheikh **Mujibur Rahman**. He left the position of joint secretary of the Awami League in 1957 and joined the **National Awami Party** with **Maulana Bhashani**. He was imprisoned in 1958 and released in 1967. Toaha formed the Communist Party of **East Bengal** in 1969 and went underground in 1972. Returning to open politics in the late 1970s, he was elected to **parliament** in 1979 as a member of the Samyabadi Dal (Marxbadi, Leninbadi) (Communist Party). He was the only communist to be elected a member.

TOFAZZUL HUSSAIN (MOHAN MIA) (1911–1969). Editor and proprietor of the newspaper *Daily Ittefaq*, he started his career as a civil servant but resigned from the service in the late 1930s. His association with **Husain Shahid Suhrawardy** led to his connection with the **Muslim League**. In 1951 he established *Ittefaq*. He was a renowned columnist and used his paper to express the desires and expectations of the Bengali Muslims. His paper evolved into the mouthpiece of the **Awami League**, which brought together leaders of Bengali nationalism. The newspaper was banned and Tofazzul arrested during the **Ayub Khan** regime. Since his death the *Ittefaq* group has been managed by his sons. The paper did not support **Mujibur Rahman**'s authoritarian steps and was again proscribed. *Ittefaq* now has the largest circulation of any daily in Bangladesh. *See also* MEDIA.

TOURISM. Although there is significant potential for tourism in Bangladesh, the industry is poorly developed. Most tourist sites are difficult to reach, as the **transportation** sector is poor, and they are also deficient in accommodations that might attract foreign tourists. The government has developed a tourism master plan in the hope of utilizing private investment. The Bangladesh Parjatan [Tourism] Corporation was founded in 1972 for this purpose. The results so far have not been impressive.

As the capital and primary entry point for air travelers, **Dhaka** has the best facilities for tourists as well as a number of places of interest. Other centers that could be developed for historical and **archeological** tourism include **Rajshahi**, **Comilla**, **Sylhet**, and **Chittagong**. The **Sundarbans**, the home of the royal Bengal tiger, could also be developed. Cox's Bazaar, at the southern tip of Bangladesh, is most developed for attracting foreign tourists. The number of tourists has increased from 207,000 in 2005 to 467,000 in 2008. However, there are no reliable statistics on their impact on the **economy**. An overwhelming number of tourists come from **India**, followed by those from the **United States** and **Great Britain**.

TRADE. In 2000, Bangladesh exports totaled $5.9 billion and imports $8.1 billion, leaving an evident trade deficit of $2.2 billion. This deficit has been covered by borrowing and by remittances from Bangladeshi nationals working overseas, especially in the Persian Gulf area. In 2004, total exports were $7 billion and imports were $10 billion, but by 2008, exports went up to $14 billion and imports rose to $22 billion. Imports rose from 18.9 percent of GDP to 27.6 percent. During the same period exports as a percent of GDP rose from 13.1 percent to 18.9 percent.

Principal exports are ready-made **garments** and knitwear, frozen fish and seafood, **jute** products, and raw jute. Leather and leather products, **tea**, urea fertilizer, and ceramic tableware are also exported. Principal destinations for exports for 2008 were the **United States** (25.51 percent), Germany (15.20 percent), **Great Britain** (9.59 percent), and France (6.71 percent). Other countries receiving Bangladesh exports include Japan, Singapore, other European countries, and countries of the **Commonwealth**.

Major imports include food grains, capital goods, petroleum, textiles (especially for manufacture into garments), raw cotton, chemicals, and vegetable oils. The largest sources of imports for the same year were **China** (17.97 percent), **India** (13.81 percent), South Korea (3.64 percent), and the **United States** (3.48 percent).

TRADE UNIONS. There are no reliable statistics on the membership of trade unions in Bangladesh other than that they are important in many industries and in government employment. Unions, not unexpectedly, wish to ensure the **employment** of their members. From this is drawn the opposition of unions to **privatization**, which the unions feel, probably correctly, would result in unemployment—the new owners would attempt to increase productivity, resulting in job losses. Lower-level employees of the government are unionized and demand improved working conditions and benefits, occasionally through strikes.

TRANSPORTATION. While there are 2,818 kilometers (about 1,750 miles) of railroad, more than 19,000 kilometers (almost 12,000 miles) of paved roads, and 182,000 kilometers (more than 115,000 miles) of unpaved roads, the main means of transportation for the people of Bangladesh is the waterways. There are more than 8,000 kilometers (almost 5,000 miles) of waterways useable at times, primarily for smaller boats. Of these waterways, about 3,000 kilometers (about 1,850 miles) are the main cargo routes. **Chittagong** and Mongla are the only two seaports. There are also major river ports, such as **Dhaka**, Narayanganj, Chandpur, **Barisal**, and **Khulna**. Most of the river and road transportation is provided by private-sector organizations, although the state-owned Bangladesh Inland Waterways Corporation provides some service. Domestic and international air service is provided by the state-owned Bangladesh Biman, which is the national flag carrier. A number of foreign carriers also provide international service. Dhaka and Chittagong are the main airports but domestic service is provided to other places including **Sylhet, Rajshahi, Khulna, Jessore**, and Cox's Bazaar.

TRIBES. There are three distinct groups of tribals in Bangladesh. One of these groups is composed of tribes that are actually southern extensions of tribes whose main bodies are in the states of northeastern India. These include the Garos, Khasis, and others, residing principally in Mymensingh area. The second group is located primarily in the **Chittagong Hill Tracts** and the adjacent Chittagong region and is related to the peoples of Myanmar (Burma) and of areas of India such as the state of **Tripura**. The largest of these tribes are the Chakmas (48.1 percent of the tribal population of the Chittagong Hill Tracts), the Marmas (27.8 percent), and the Tripuras (12.3 percent); none of the other nine groups identified in the census comprises more than 4 percent of the tribal population of the Chittagong Hill Tracts. It is from these tribes that insurgency against the central government arises. One other tribal group, the Santals, originates from West Bengal, Bihar, and Orissa in India. It is the largest tribal group in South Asia and is second only to the Bengalis as an ethnic group in Bangladesh. They are predominantly **Hindu** and are often employed in **tea** estates. *See also* BUDDHISM; CHRISTIANITY; TANGTHA; WANNA FESTIVAL OF GARO.

TRIPURA. Now a state in India, it was a princely state and known until 1947 as Tippera. In earlier periods, Tripura controlled major portions of hill **Assam, Burma**, and Bengal. **Comilla** and **Noakhali** were joined in a single district under the name Tripura (Tippera), while the princely state was generally referred to as Hill Tippera. Noakhali became a separate district in 1822. The earliest mention of Tripura is believed to be in the 14th century work *Rajmala*, a record of the Manikya dynasty that ruled until 1947. Tribal groups in Tripura are waging a sporadic rebellion against Indian rule and in favor of an independent Tripura. **India** alleges that these groups find refuge in Bangladesh, a charge that is denied by Bangladesh. The boundary is hilly and forested, making control of movement difficult.

TRUTH AND ACCOUNTABILITY COMMISSION (TAC). Established in 2008 through an ordinance, it will permit those suspected of **corruption** to voluntarily go to the commission and seek its forgiveness. Such persons will avoid imprisonment but will have to confess and surrender their illegally obtained wealth or equivalent amount in cash to the state. Those coming before the commission will be disbarred from participating in any election for a period of five years. The TAC will have a tenure of five months with an additional five months to adjudicate pending cases.

TWENTY-ONE POINTS. The election manifesto of the **United Front** used during the **East Bengal** provincial election of 1954. Among the twenty-one points were: the recognition of Bengali as an official **language** of Pakistan; complete autonomy for East Bengal in all matters except defense, foreign affairs, and currency; the location of the headquarters of the navy in East Bengal; the institution of **land reform** and the distribution of surplus land to the landless; improvements to **irrigation**; the establishment of **agricultural** cooperatives; increases in agricultural production; the nationalization of the **jute** trade; the cessation of discrimination against Bengalis in the **armed forces**; the repeal of laws that allowed imprisonment without trial; and the implementation of the labor conventions of the International Labor Organization.

– U –

UKIL, ABDUL MALIK (1924–1987). A long-time stalwart of the **Awami League**, he was active in the **language movement** and in the **Democratic Action Committee** against **Ayub Khan**. Ukil was elected a member of the **East Pakistan** Provincial Assembly in 1954 and the National Assembly of Pakistan in 1962. He served as a minister in the cabinet of **Mujibur Rahman**. When the Awami League split prior to the 1979 parliamentary election, Ukil was the leader of the larger faction, although he lost his own election. After the 1986 election, he was named deputy leader of the opposition by the Awami League leader, **Sheikh Hasina Wajid**.

UNESCO WORLD HERITAGE LIST OF BANGLADESH. Three sites in Bangladesh are recognized as world heritage sites. These are the **Sundarbans** in southwest **Khulna**, a mangrove forest area home to the Bengal tigers, the historic mosque city of Bagerhat where the Sath Gambud (seven dome) mosque is located, and the **Buddhist** Vihara, also known as the Somapura Mahavihara, located at Paharpur in Naogoan.

UNION OF SOVIET SOCIALIST REPUBLICS. Initially, relations between Bangladesh and the Soviet Union were cordial, in recognition of Soviet support for Bangladeshi independence. Some members of the cabinet of **Mujibur Rahman**, such as **Tajuddin Ahmed**, were reported to have favored a treaty of friendship with the Soviet Union along the lines of the Indo-Soviet treaty of 1971.

The Soviets gave assistance to the rehabilitation of Bangladesh, especially the clearing of **Chittagong** Harbor. However, after the death of Mujib, the large Soviet presence became suspect in the eyes of the new leadership. Bangladesh strongly opposed the 1979 Soviet invasion of **Afghanistan**, and Soviet support to Vietnam's actions in Cambodia. In the 1983–1984 period, the **Hussain Muhammad Ershad** regime ousted a number of Soviet diplomats and officials on the grounds that they were acting against Bangladesh. Relations afterward were correct if not cordial. The Soviet Union supplied limited military assistance during the Mujib period and continued to give limited economic aid. It also sponsored a substantial number of scholarships for study in the Soviet Union.

Since the breakup of the Soviet Union in 1991, relations between Bangladesh and **Russia** have been correct, as Bangladesh wishes to continue and expand such markets as exist there. Generally, Bangladesh is too remote from the newly independent Central Asian republics to have a direct relationship with them, but there is some affinity resulting from **Islam** and from prospective **trade** relationships. *See also* FOREIGN POLICY.

UNITED EAST INDIA COMPANY OF THE NETHERLANDS. *See* DUTCH EAST INDIA COMPANY.

UNITED FRONT (UF). An umbrella political grouping consisting of the **Awami League**, the **Krishak Sramik Party (KSP)**, the **Nizam-i-Islam**, **Ganotantrik Dal**, and some smaller **political parties**. It was formed to oppose the Pakistan **Muslim League** in the **East Pakistan** provincial election of 1954. A **twenty-one point** manifesto, which included the importance of the Bengali **language**, regional autonomy, limitations on the powers of the central government, and rejection of the **Basic Principles Committee** report, won for the UF strong public support. The UF won an overwhelming victory and formed the first non-Muslim League government in April 1954. The East Pakistan Legislative Assembly had a total of 309 seats, of which the UF won 237 and the Muslim League won only 10. In May 1954 the UF government, led by **Fazlul Haq** as chief minister, was dismissed by the central government because of the purportedly anti-Pakistani statements of the UF leaders. By the time representative government was restored in 1955, under a KSP government led by **Abu Hussain Sarkar**, rivalries between the KSP and the Awami League had ended the UF. *See also* ELECTIONS; JATIYA JUKTA FRONT.

UNITED KINGDOM. *See* GREAT BRITAIN.

UNITED NATIONS. Bangladesh became a member of the United Nations in 1974, following the withdrawal of the veto by **China** that had been exercised at the request of **Pakistan**. Bangladesh was elected to the Security Council in 1978, winning election against Japan for the "Asian seat," and was elected again in 2000. In 1986, Bangladeshi foreign minister Humayun Rashid Chowdhury was elected president of the General Assembly. Bangladesh is also a member of the affiliated agencies of the United Nations. It chaired the Group of 77 in 1982 and 1983. *See also* FOREIGN POLICY.

UNITED NATIONS PEACEKEEPING OPERATIONS. In the 1990s Bangladesh **armed forces** increasingly became a major partner in the United Nations Peacekeeping Operations. In 2003, for its contribution to the peacekeeping effort of the United Nations, Bangladesh was made a member of the Organizational Committee of the Peacekeeping Commission. In 2007 Bangladesh had nearly 10,000 peacekeepers in 13 missions around the globe. Troops and/or civil officers have gone to places such as Cambodia, Somalia, Bosnia, and Haiti. Seventy-nine Bangladeshi peacekeepers have lost their lives during these operations.

UNITED STATES. Relations with the United States were difficult, initially, because of the American "tilt" toward **Pakistan** in the civil war. The United States delayed formal recognition of the new state until February 1972. However, American assistance for rehabilitation had already begun to flow from the U.S. government and from a wide range of private organizations. Bangladeshis also remembered the nearly unanimous support for their country from American academics and social organizations and from much of the press and many in Congress during the civil war. Despite opposition from some members of his cabinet like **Tajuddin Ahmed, Mujibur Rahman** saw the United States as a major source of the assistance he badly needed. He also visited the United States. Relations from the latter part of the Mujib period through the regimes of his successors were cordial and cooperative.

The United States is the largest overall donor of economic aid in the period since 1971, although in some recent years the annual commitments of Japan have exceeded those of the United States among national donors (in some years commitments by international financial organizations, such as the International Development Association, have been higher than bilateral arrangements). The United States has refused to give military assistance to Bangladesh other than a modest grant for training and some trainer jet aircraft. American activity in educational programs has been much less than that of the **Union of Soviet Socialist Republics.**

Relations during the post–Mujibur Rahman regimes have continued to be cordial, except for American protestations over the means used by **Hussain Muhammad Ershad** to gain power. The United States urged the restoration of elective democracy. Bangladeshi heads of government have visited the United States and president Bill Clinton made the first visit of a U.S. head of state to Bangladesh, however brief. Since 11 September 2001 there has been both civilian and military cooperation between the United States and Bangladesh in the fight against terrorism. United States is assisting Bangladesh in strengthening its intelligence systems and has implemented the Personal Identification Secure Comparison and Evaluation System to document passengers traveling into and out of the country. Closer cooperation between the two countries is expected in the future, especially in the areas of global climate change, financial crisis, food security, and peacekeeping. *See also* FOREIGN POLICY.

– V –

VANGA. The name used in ancient Hindu literature for central and southern Bengal. Vanga is mentioned in Sanskrit literature but there is no specific mention in the *Mahabharata*. It provided the name for all of Bengal. The Sanskrit "v" is interchangeable with "b."

VARENDRA. Ancient name applied to the northern region of present-day Bangladesh, centered on **Rajshahi**.

VARMAN DYNASTY. Rulers of southeastern Bengal from about 1045 to about 1150. Some historians believe that the Varmans arrived in Bengal, possibly from Orissa, in the train of the Kalachuris, invaders from central India. The Varmans were under the suzerainty of the **Palas** to about 1080, when they became independent. They were overthrown by the **Sena dynasty** in about 1150.

VERNACULAR ELITE. A term applied to the Bengali Muslim leadership that used Bengali as a family and political **language**, as opposed to the **national elite**, which generally used Urdu. Most prominent of this group both before and after Pakistani independence was **Fazlul Haq**. He used Bengali to appeal to the masses and formed the **Krishak Praja Party** to represent their interests. He and others in the group were concerned with the matters of Bengal first and of Muslims elsewhere in India second. After independence, Fazlul Haq was joined by **Suhrawardy**, whose **Awami League** was almost entirely an **East Bengal** party. **Mujibur Rahman** represented the group most prominently in the later years of the rule of **Ayub Khan** and in the first period of Bangladeshi independence.

VESTED PROPERTY ACT. An act that was initially introduced right after the partition of India in 1947 that permitted the government of **Pakistan** to take over properties abandoned by those who migrated to **India** from **East Pakistan**. The original act was entitled Requisition of Property Act (Act XIII of 1948). It was later renamed East Bengal Evacuees Act (1951), East Pakistan Disturbed Persons Rehabilitation Ordinance (1964), Enemy Property Order (1965), Bangladesh Vesting of Property and Assets Order (1972), and Vested and Non-resident Property Act (1974). The **Awami League** in 2001 passed a very narrowly defined law, the Vested Property Return Act, to return some of the confiscated property to their rightful owners and heirs. The law stated that property vested since 1969 will be returned only if claimants can show that they have resided continuously in Bangladesh and they put forth their claim within 90 days of publication of a list of vested properties. As of 2009 no such list has been published.

VICE PRESIDENT. This title has not been used when a **parliamentary** system has been the form of government, but it has occasionally been used during periods of rule dominated by the military. The duties of the office when it has existed have not been clearly defined, although in one case, that of **Abdus Sattar**, the holder of the vice presidency succeeded an assassinated **president, Ziaur Rahman**. Others who have held the title are **Syed Nazrul Islam, Mohammadullah, Mirza Nurul Huda**, A. K. M. Nurul Islam, and **Moudud Ahmed**.

VIDYASAGAR, ISVARCHANDRA (1820–1891). A Sanskritist and Bengali scholar who had a major impact on **education** in Bengal. He studied at Sanskrit College in **Calcutta** and rose to become a professor and later principal of the college. Vidyasagar worked for widespread education in Bengali and supported the more liberal causes of his time: widow remarriage, monogamy, and, especially, **women**'s education. Among his works was *Shakuntala*, based on a play by Kalidasa.

VIKRAMPUR. A site at Rampal near **Dhaka** that was ruled by several **Hindu** dynasties, including the **Chandra**, **Varman**, **Sena**, and **Deva**, serving as capital or alternate capital from the eighth to thirteenth centuries. It was the capital of the **Sena dynasty** after that dynasty's expulsion from **Nadia** in 1202. At the site of Vikrampur and its environs are the Rampal *dighi* (pond) and the remains of the palace of Valla-sena. An excavation called Agnikunda is held by tradition to be the burial place of the last Sena ruler at Vikrampur and his family, who killed themselves before the onslaught of the Muslims in the early 13th century. There is also the tomb of a noted *pir*, Baba Adam. *See also* LAKSHMANA SENA; SENA DYNASTY

VIVEKANANDA, SWAMI (1863–1902). A noted **Hindu** religious person who founded the **Ramakrishna Mission**. His original name was Narendranath Dutta. While he was studying law in **Calcutta**, he became a disciple of **Ramakrishna Paramahamsa**. Vivekananda traveled extensively, including to the United States in 1893, where he represented Hinduism at the Parliament of Religions held in connection with the Chicago World's Fair. He held that the West had declined spiritually and that the East held a religious message for the world. The Vedanta groups are another legacy of Vivekananda.

– W –

WAHIDUZZAMAN (1912–1976). A successful businessman, he entered politics as an associate of **Abul Kasem Fazlul Haq** and was elected to the Bengal Legislative Assembly in 1942. After Pakistani independence, however, Wahiduzzaman joined the **Muslim League** and was a member of the constituent assembly, 1951–1955. During the rule of **Ayub Khan** he was minister of commerce, 1962–1965. Wahiduzzaman left the Muslim League in 1969 and supported the movement against Ayub for the restoration of democracy.

WAJID, SHEIKH HASINA. *See* SHEIKH HASINA WAJID.

WALIULLAH, SYED (1922–1971). Novelist and journalist. He was born in **Chittagong**, studied in **Kolkata**, and began his work with

The Statesman. After partition in 1947, he worked with Radio Pakistan and served as press attaché at several embassies. Waliullah's novel *Tree without Roots* was widely acclaimed, was translated into English and French, and earned an award from the Bangla Academy. *See also* LITERATURE.

WANNA FESTIVAL OF GARO. Organized by the Mandi community of Garo tribal people of Modhupur forest, the festival honors their deities through celebration of traditional culture and social conventions. Held at the end of the harvest season, the festival includes **music** and **musical instruments** such as *dama*, *ghram*, *adury*, and *nagara*, which are played by the indigenous people to welcome their deities *Shushmi*, *Tatara*, *Bagba*, and *Goera*. Traditional songs and dances such as *Ajia*, *Ray-Ray*, and *Sherjing* are performed during the festival. This festival was downplayed during the Pakistan era but has seen its revival since 2003.

WAR CRIMES FACT FINDING COMMITTEE (WCFFC). An organization charged with identifying all the places in Bangladesh where mass killings were carried out by the Pakistani armed forces during the **War of Liberation**. A total of 5,000 small and large killing fields have been identified. Many places have been altered, making it almost impossible to gather any reliable information on the number of people killed. Nearly 1,000 fields have been properly identified and attempts are being made to place a plaque on each such site. Each site will be identified in a comprehensive GIS database and a publication of all sites is forthcoming. The committee also has compiled a list of 1,200 names of civilians and members of the Pakistani armed forces who should be tried for war crimes. A total of 13 researchers working from 1999 to 2006 collected the names. The committee organizes health and welfare programs to support freedom fighters and their families.

WAR OF LIBERATION. Known in Bangla as Muktijuddho (War of Liberation and Freedom) or Shadhinothar Juddho (War of Independence), it started at midnight 25 March 1971 and ended on 16 December 1971. On 25 March 1971 the Pakistan Army was ordered to launch a military operation in **East Pakistan**. The operation was called Search Light and its mission was to forcibly negate the results of the 1970 **election**. Major General Rao Farman Ali with 57 Brigade under Brigadier Arbab was responsible for operation in **Dhaka** city and its suburbs while Major General Khadim Raja was given the responsibility of the rest of the province. Lieutenant General Tikka Khan assumed the overall charge of the operation. The armed action led to mass killings of ordinary people and intellectuals, the looting and burning of cities, towns, and villages, and the exodus of over 10 million refugees to **India**. It also rapidly led to large-scale revolt and an uprising against the military action, a government-in-exile, a guerilla force composed of the Bengalis of the Pakistan Armed Forces, the local border and police forces, and hundred and thousands of civilians infuriated by the scale of killings and pillaging.

There are eight rare and popular movies on the War of Liberation. They are *Smritir Minar, Nine Months to Freedom, Stop Genocide, Joyjatra, Dateline Bangladesh, War Crimes File, Shei Rater Katha Bolte Eshechhi*, and *Arunodoyer Agnishakkhi*. Their respective directors are: Ahmed Muztaba Zamal, Shukhdev, Zahir Raihan, Tauquir Ahmed, Geeta Mehta, Howard Broadburn, Kawsar Chowdhury, and Subhash Dutta. *See also* WAR CRIMES FACT FINDING COMMITTEE.

WETLANDS OF BANGLADESH. The estimated total area of wetlands of Bangladesh consists of 7–8 million hectares that is about 50 percent of the land surface. The wetlands are made up of rivers, streams, freshwater lakes, and marshes, including *haor, baor*, and *beels*, cultivated fields, and estuarine systems with extensive mangrove swamps. Located mostly in the northeastern part of the country, in the greater **Sylhet** and **Mymensingh** district, the area is collectively known as haor basin.

WOMEN. The constitution of Bangladesh grants equal rights to women and men in all spheres of public life. Other laws, such as the **Family Law Ordinance** of 1961, the Family Courts Ordinance of 1985, the Dowry Prohibition Act of 1980, and the Cruelty to Women (Deterrent Protection) Act of 1983, provide special protection for women's rights. In the industrial sector, the rapid entry of women is the most significant recent change in Bangladesh. Approximately 90 percent of the laborers in the **garment industry** are women. Women are also employed in the pharmaceutical, electronic, and fish-processing industries in large numbers. With the assistance of **non-governmental organizations** such as the **Grameen Bank**, women in Bangladesh have had a strong impact on small business development. In addition, women in rural areas have established more than 500 organizations, such as **Nijera Kori**, with more than two million members to empower themselves for personal, social, economic, and political development. These organizations are significantly different from women's groups in urban areas, which are primarily social welfare units.

In the political area, there is increasing participation of women in the electorate and as members of political parties, as can be demonstrated by prime ministers **Khaleda Zia** and **Sheikh Hasina Wajid**, although each was the survivor of a deceased relative, a husband and father, respectively.

Despite such advances, women bear a disproportionately large share of the country's **poverty**. In most, if not all, development indicators, such as **education**, nutrition, and employment, women are invariably poorer than men. Even in social, economic, and political areas in which women have a significant presence, the wage and status differential continues to be a major barrier. In Bangladesh, a patriarchal society, women are still viewed mainly in their reproductive roles and are given subsidiary status as economically dependent liabilities and the cause of non-productive expenditures. *See also* WOMEN, OPEN PARLIAMENTARY SEATS CONTESTED.

WOMEN, OPEN PARLIAMENTARY SEATS CONTESTED. In the Bangladesh legislature, there are a number of seats reserved for women. Since its inception Bangladesh has reserved not fewer than 30 seats for women up to a high of 45 in the 2008 parliamentary **election**. Women's seats are distributed proportionately to the general election results. Women are, however, not barred from contesting the open seats. Over the years, the number of seats contested by women in Bangladesh has shown some increase. In the 1991 parliamentary election 46 women candidates ran in the election and a total of four won, including the two women leaders of the two principal parties. In 1996, only 36 women candidates took part in the election; five won, including the two party leaders. In the 2001 election 41 women candidates ran and only four won parliamentary seats, including the leader of the **Awami League** and the **Bangladesh Nationalist Party**. In the last parliamentary election of 2008, the largest number of women candidates (59) took part in the election and 18 of them won. In 1991 only 1.34 percent of the women who participated in the election won, however in 2008 6 percent of participating women won open seats.

– Y –

YAHYA KHAN, AGHA MUHAMMAD (1917–1980). A career military officer, he was president of **Pakistan,** 1969–1971, succeeding **Ayub Khan.** He entered the British Indian army in 1938. He was commander in **East Pakistan** from 1962 until 1966, when he became deputy commander in chief of the army. From that position, Yahya replaced Ayub as president in March 1969 in a palace coup. With the Pakistan army's loss to the **Mukti Bahini** and their Indian allies in December 1971, Yahya resigned the presidency and turned the government over to **Zulfiqar Ali Bhutto.**

YUNUS, MUHAMMAD (1940–). The founder of the **Grameen Bank,** Yunus received a Ph.D. from Vanderbilt University in 1969 as a Fulbright grantee. He joined the faculty of the University of **Chittagong** and became head of the Rural Economics Program. From this experience came his concept of **Gram Sarkar** and his eventual establishment of the Grameen Bank in 1976. He has been recognized in many ways for his rural development work, especially with **women**. He received the Magsaysay Award in 1984. In 1994, he was awarded the World Food Prize, in 2006 received the Nobel Peace Prize, and in 2009 received the Medal of Freedom from **United States** president Barak Obama.

– Z –

ZAFAR, SIKANDER ABU (1919–1975). A journalist by profession, he was the editor of *Samakaal*, a literary magazine. He also worked as a journalist for a number of newspapers, including the *Dainik Nabayug, Dainik Ittefaq,* and the *Daily Millat.* As a poet he is often viewed to be as great as **Kazi Nazrul Islam.** During a period when Bengali poetry tended to be romantic and nostalgic he wrote about the common people. In 1971 he followed up his collections of poems *Prashanna Prahar* and *Timirantik* with *Bangla Chharo* (Leave Bengal), which captured the revolutionary spirit of the times. In 1966 he received the Bangla Academy Award. For his immense contribution to **literature** he was posthumously awarded the **Ekushey Padak** and the **Swadhinota Padak.**

ZAHIR, SHAHEEDUL (1954–2008). Although a civil servant, Zahir was better known as the author of novels and other fiction exploring the world of the oppressed, the rural people of Bangladesh, and the poorest of the poor. One of his favorite subjects was the **War of Liberation**, through which he explored its ideals. He combined dreams and reality to create powerful symbolism to explore the lives of the poor, the downtrodden, and the urbanite. In 1985, he published his first collection of stories, *Parapar.* He published two other collections of stories, *Dumur Kheko Manush O Annanya Golpo* and *Dolu Nodir Hawa O Annanya Golpo.* His novel on the War of Liberation was entitled *Jibon O Rajnaitik Bastobota.* He was opposed to fundamentalism and communalism and covered these topics, along with the degeneration of society and the daily sufferings of the ordinary citizens of Bangladesh, in his writings.

ZAHURUL HUQUE (1935–1969). One of the co-accused in the **Agartala conspiracy case** against Sheikh **Mujibur Rahman.** In what was described as an attempt to escape, he was shot dead by the Pakistani army.

ZAINUL ABEDIN (1914–1976). A National Professor of the Arts, a title bestowed on him by Sheikh **Mujibur Rahman.** He became principal of the Art Institute, later the Art College, in 1949, and retired in 1967. He was instrumental in the founding of the Bangladesh Shilpakala Academy. Zainul Abedin is most famous for his more than 100 black-and-white sketches of the **Kolkata** famine of 1943. He is also well known for his abstract painting. Many of his works are on display in the Zainul Abedin Gallery of the Dhaka Museum.

ZAMINDAR. *See* PERMANENT SETTLEMENT.

ZIA, KHALEDA. *See* KHALEDA ZIA.

ZIA HYDER (1934–2008). He is credited with introducing **theatre** into the higher **education** curriculum in Bangladesh. From 1966 to 1968 he received a masters degree in fine **arts** from the University of Hawaii. In 1968, he took the initiative to establish the theatre group *Nagorik Natyasam-pradaya.* In 1970, he became a faculty member in the Department of Fine Arts, **Chittagong** University. Prior to joining Chittagong University he worked at **Pakistan** Television as a senior producer. He published five collections of essays on theatre, and four volumes on the history of world theatre. His works are used as reference sources on theatre in academic institutions of Bangladesh and **India.** He also translated such works as Jean Paul Sartre's *Huis clas* and co-authored a translation of Nikolai Gogol's *Zenit'ba.* Among the plays he directed were the translated works of Sophocles' *Oedipus,* Camus's *Le Malentendu,* Sarte's *Hus clas,* and Syed Waliullah's *Bohi Pir.* For his own play *Elebele,* he received the best production award from the Bangladesh Shilpakala Academy. He received the Shaheed Munier Chowdhury Award for his contribution to the development of theatre in Bangladesh.

ZIAUR RAHMAN (1936–1981). The effective leader of Bangladesh from 1975 to 1981. An army officer commissioned in 1953, he rose to the rank of major in 1971. In the **War of Liberation,** he led his unit (the "Z force") against the Pakistani army and with himself as provisional president proclaimed Bangladeshi independence in **Chittagong** on 27 March 1971. This act apparently earned him the displeasure of **Mujibur Rahman,** under whose regime Zia's career did not prosper to the extent that other **Mukti Bahini** leaders' careers did. Following the assassination of Mujib, Zia was appointed chief of staff of the army in August 1975. Although displaced briefly during the coup attempt by **Khalid Musharraf,** Zia emerged from the November 1975 coups as the dominant leader of the country. He was designated deputy chief martial law administrator and replaced **president A. S. M. Sayem** as chief martial law administrator in 1976.

After Sayem's retirement from the presidency for purported health reasons, Zia became president in April 1977. He had this confirmed through a referendum, but then won the post in a contested **election** in 1978, defeating **M. A. G. Osmany** and others. With his election as president, Zia resigned his army commission and was replaced as chief of staff by **Hussain Muhammad Ershad**. His favoring of Ershad, who was not a freedom fighter, earned him some opposition from passed-over freedom fighters. Zia remained president until his assassination on 30 May 1981 at the hands of a disgruntled freedom fighter, **Muhammad Abul Manzur**.

Not considered a likely candidate for a charismatic role, Zia nonetheless created one for himself and provided capable and pragmatic leadership emphasizing such points as rural development, **food** self-sufficiency, and **population planning**, as shown in his **Nineteen Points** program. The **Bangladesh Nationalist Party (BNP)** was founded as his political vehicle, although the actual leader of the party was **Abdus Sattar**. The BNP succeeded the earlier **JAGODAL**. Zia is also regarded as the "father" of the **South Asian Association for Regional Cooperation**. His widow, **Khaleda Zia**, was called to be the leader of the BNP and became **prime minister** of Bangladesh in March 1991. Her party lost the June 1996 election to the **Awami League** and Khaleda became leader of the opposition. However, she returned to the prime ministership in October 2001 when the BNP gained a substantial majority in **parliament**. *See also* ARMED FORCES; ELECTIONS.

ZOHRA, BEGUM KAZI (1912–2007). She was the first female Bengali Muslim doctor. She graduated from the Muslim Girls' Collegiate High School and the Aligarh College and University and obtained in 1935 her MBBS from the Lady Harding Medical College for **Women**, New Delhi, India. In 1948, after the partition of **India,** she joined the **Dhaka** Medical College and Hospital. She subsequently held the position of head of the Department of Obstetrics and Gynecology and also served as consultant to the Holy Family Red Crescent Hospital. She was also an honorary Colonel when attending patients at the Combined Medical Hospital of the Bangladesh **Armed**

Forces. For her dedication to the medical profession, especially women's health and increasing the number of women in medical science, she received the Taghma-e-Pakistan, the Begum Rokeya Padak, and **Ekushey Padak**. She comes from the Kazi family of Gopalpur, Madaripur district.

Appendix 1
Rulers of Selected Pre-Muslim Dynasties in Bengal

Note: Dates are approximate.

Pala Dynasty (c. 750–c. 1159)

750–770	Gopala
770–810	Dharmapala
810–850	Devapala
850–854	Vigrahapala (or Surapala)
854–908	Narayanapala
908–940	Rajyapala
940–960	Gopala II
960–988	Vigrahapala II
988–1038	Mahipala I
1038–1055	Nayapala
1055–1070	Vigrahapala III
1070–1075	Mahipala II
1075–1077	Surapala II
1077–1120	Ramapala
1120–1125	Kumarapala
1125–1140	Gopala III
1140–1155	Madanapala (loss of Bengal to the Senas)
1155–1159	Govindapala (loss of Bihar to the Delhi Sultanate)

Sena Dynasty (c. 1095–1245)

1095–1158	Vijayasena
1159–1178	Vallalasena
1178–1206	Laksmanasena (loss of Nadia in 1202)
1206–1220	Visvarupasena
1220–1223	Kesavasena

Appendix 2
Muslim Rulers of Bengal

Ilyas Shahi Dynasty (1342–1415)

1342–1357	Shamsuddin Ilyas Shah
1357–1389	Sikandar Shah
1389–1410	Ghiyasuddin Azam Shah
1410–1411	Saif Hamza Shah
1411–1414	Shihabuddin Bayazid Shah
1414	Alauddin Firoz Shah

Raja Ganesh Dynasty (1415–1433)

1415–1432	Jalaluddin Muhammad Shah
1432–1433	Shamsuddin Ahmad Shah

Ilyas Shahi Dynasty Restored (1433–1486)

1433–1459	Nasiruddin Mahmud
1459–1474	Ruknuddin Barbak Shah
1474–1481	Shamsuddin Yusuf Shah
1481	Sikandar
1481–1486	Jalaluddin Fath Shah

Abyssinians (1486–1493)

1486	Barbak Shahzada
1486–1490	Saifuddin Firoz Shah
1490–1493	Shamsuddin Muzaffar Shah

Husain Shahi Dynasty (1493–1538)

1493–1519	Alauddin Husain Shah
1519–1532	Nasiruddin Nusrat Shah
1532	Alauddin Firoz Shah
1532–1538	Ghiyasuddin Mahmud Shah

Suri Dynasty (1538–1564)

1538–1545	Sher Shah Suri
1545–1553	Islam Shah
1553–1555	Shamsuddin Muhammad Shah
1556–1560	Ghiyasuddin Bahadur Shah
1560–1563	Ghiyasuddin II
1563–1564	Ghiyasuddin III

Karrani Dynasty (1563–1575)

1563	Taj Khan Karrani
1563–1573	Sulaiman Karrani
1573	Bayazid Karrani
1573–1575	Daud Karrani

Appendix 3
Lieutenant Governors and Governors
of Bengal during the British Period

Lieutenant Governors

1898–1903	J. Woodburn
1903–1908	A. H. L. Fraser
1908–1912	E. N. Baker

Governors

1912–1917	Lord Carmichael
1917–1922	The Earl of Ronaldshay (later the Marquess of Zetland)
1922–1927	The Earl of Lytton
1927–1930	F. S. Jackson
1930–1932	H. L. Stephenson
1932–1937	Sir John Anderson
1937–1939	Lord Brabourne
1939–1944	Sir John Herbert
1944–1946	Lord Casey
1946–1947	F. J. Burrows

Lieutenant Governors of Eastern Bengal and Assam

1905–1906	J. B. Fuller
1906–1911	Sir Lancelot Hare
1911–1912	C. S. Bayley

Appendix 4
Governors and Chief Ministers
of East Bengal/East Pakistan

Note: Asterisks indicate individuals with entries in the dictionary.

Governors

1947–1950	Sir Frederick Bourne
1950–1953	Malik Sir Firoz Khan Noon*
1953–1954	Chaudhury Khaliquzzaman*
1954	Iskandar Mirza*
1954	Sir Thomas Ellis (acting)
1954–1955	Justice Shahabuddin*
1955–1956	Justice Amiruddin Ahmad
1956–1958	Moulvi Abul Kasem Fazlul Haq*
1958	Hamid Ali (acting)
1958	Sultannuddin Ahmed (acting)*
1958–1960	Zakir Husain
1960–1962	Muhammad Azam Khan*
1962	Ghulam Faruque
1962–1969	Abdul Monem Khan*
1969	Mirza Nurul Huda*
1969–1971	Syed Muhammad Ahsan
1971	Abdul Muttalib Malik*

Chief Ministers

1947–1948	Khwaja Sir Nazimuddin*
1948–1954	Nurul Amin*
1954	Moulvi A. K. Fazlul Haq*
1954–1955	(under central government rule)
1955–1956	Abu Hussain Sarkar*

1956–1958	Ataur Rahman Khan*
1958	Abu Hussain Sarkar*
1958	Ataur Rahman Khan*
1958–1971	(parliamentary system abolished)

Appendix 5
Principal Officers of the
Government of Bangladesh, 1971–2009

Source: The serial publication *Chiefs of State and Cabinet Members of Foreign Governments* produced by the Directorate of Intelligence, Central Intelligence Agency. The serial is either monthly or bimonthly. Dates entered in the list are those of the issue in which the name first appeared. It may not be the actual date on which the office was assumed by the individual.

In the early phase of the Ershad period many portfolios were not held separately but were grouped with other portfolios. There were also frequent vacancies during which Ershad or another of the military officers held charge of the ministries.

Note: Asterisks indicate individuals with entries in the dictionary.

MUJIB PERIOD (1971–1975)

President

Dec. 1971–Jan. 1972	Sheikh Mujibur Rahman* (Syed Nazrul Islam*, acting)
Jan. 1972–Dec. 1973	Abu Sayeed Chowdhury*
Jan. 1974–Jan. 1975	Mohammadullah*
Jan. 1975–Aug. 1975	Sheikh Mujibur Rahman*

Vice President

Jan. 1975–Aug. 1975	Syed Nazrul Islam*

Prime Minister

Dec. 1971–Jan. 1972   Tajuddin Ahmed*
Jan. 1972–Jan. 1975   Sheikh Mujibur Rahman*
Jan. 1975–Aug. 1975   Mansur Ali*

Minister of Agriculture

Jan. 1972–Feb. 1972   Phani Bhushan Majumdar*
Apr. 1973–Aug. 1975   Muhammad Abdus Samad Azad*

Minister of Commerce

Jan. 1972–Feb. 1972   Mansur Ali*
Feb. 1972–Mar. 1972   Syed Nazrul Islam*
Mar. 1972–Aug. 1975   Khondakar Mushtaque Ahmed*

Minister of Communications

Jan. 1972–Feb. 1972   Sheikh Abdul Aziz
Feb. 1972–Aug. 1975   Mansur Ali*

Minister of Defense

Dec. 1971–Jan. 1972   Muhammad Ataul Ghani Osmani*
Jan. 1972–Feb. 1972   Tajuddin Ahmed*
Feb. 1972–Aug. 1975   Sheikh Mujibur Rahman*

Minister of Education

Mar. 1973–Feb. 1975   Yusuf Ali
Feb. 1975–Aug. 1975   Muzaffar Ahmed Chowdhury*

Minister of Finance

Dec. 1971–Feb. 1972   Mansur Ali*
Feb. 1972–Nov. 1974   Tajuddin Ahmed*
Dec. 1974–Jan. 1975   (vacant)
Jan. 1975–Aug. 1975   Azizur Rahman Mallick

Minister of Food and Civil Supplies

Jan. 1972–June 1974   Phani Bhushan Majumdar*
July 1974–Aug. 1975   Abdul Monim

Minister of Foreign Affairs

Jan. 1972–Apr. 1973   Muhammad Abdus Samad Azad*
Apr. 1973–Aug. 1975   Kamal Hossain*

Minister of Foreign Trade (included with Minister of Commerce except below)

Apr. 1973–Feb. 1974   A. H. M. Kamruzzaman*

Minister of Forests, Fisheries, and Livestock

Apr. 1972–Mar. 1973   Muhammad Sohrab Hossain
Apr. 1973–Jan. 1974   Abdur Rab Serniabat*
Feb. 1974   Mollah Jalaluddin Ahmad*
Mar. 1974–June 1974   Sheikh Mujibur Rahman*
July 1974–Nov. 1974   Tajuddin Ahmed*
Dec. 1974   (vacant)
Jan. 1975–Aug. 1975   Abdur Rab Serniabat*

Minister of Health and Family Planning

Jan. 1972–Mar. 1972   Zahur Ahmad Chowdhury
Apr. 1972–Mar. 1973   Abdul Malik Ukil*
Apr. 1973–Aug. 1975   Abdul Mannan

Minister of Home Affairs

Dec. 1971–Feb. 1972   A. H. M. Kamruzzaman*
Feb. 1972–Mar. 1972   Sheikh Mujibur Rahman*
Apr. 1972–Mar. 1973   Abdul Mannan
Apr. 1973–June 1974   Abdul Malik Ukil*
July 1974–Aug. 1975   Mansur Ali*

Minister of Industries

Dec. 1972–Feb. 1972	Mansur Ali*
Feb. 1972–Mar. 1972	Syed Nazrul Islam*
Apr. 1972–Mar. 1973	Mustifizur Rahman Siddiqui
Apr. 1973–Feb. 1974	A. H. M. Kamruzzaman*
Mar. 1974–Aug. 1975	Syed Nazrul Islam*

Minister of Information and Broadcasting

Jan. 1972–Feb. 1972	Tajuddin Ahmed*
Feb. 1972–Mar. 1972	Sheikh Mujibur Rahman*
Apr. 1972–Mar. 1973	Mizanur Rahman Chowdhury*
Apr. 1973–Sep. 1973	Sheikh Abdul Aziz
Oct. 1973–Jan. 1975	Sheikh Mujibur Rahman*
Jan. 1975–Aug. 1975	Muhammad Korban Ali*

Minister of Jute

Apr. 1973–June 1974	Tajuddin Ahmed*
July 1974–Jan. 1975	Sheikh Mujibur Rahman*
Jan. 1975–Aug. 1975	Asaduzzaman Khan

Minister of Labor and Social Welfare

Jan. 1972–June 1974	Zahur Ahmad Chowdhury
July 1974–Jan. 1975	Abdul Mannan
Jan. 1975–Aug. 1975	Muhammad Yusuf Ali

Minister of Land Revenue (after Mar. 1974, titled Minister of Land Administration and Land Reform)

Jan. 1972–Mar. 1972	Khondakar Mushtaque Ahmed*
Apr. 1972–Feb. 1974	Abdur Rab Serniabat*
Mar. 1974–June 1974	Mollah Jalaluddin Ahmad*
July 1974–Jan. 1975	Phani Bhushan Majumdar*
Jan. 1975–Aug. 1975	Mohammadullah*

Minister of Law and Parliamentary Affairs

Jan. 1972–Feb. 1972	Khondakar Mushtaque Ahmed*
Feb. 1972–Mar. 1973	Kamal Hossain*
Apr. 1973–Aug. 1975	Manoranjan Dhar

Minister of Local Government, Rural Development, and Cooperatives

Jan. 1972–Feb. 1972	Phani Bhushan Majumdar*
Feb. 1972–Mar. 1972	Sheikh Abdul Aziz
Apr. 1972–Mar. 1973	Shamsul Haq
Apr. 1973–June 1974	Matiur Rahman
July 1974–Jan. 1975	Muhammad Abdus Samad Azad*
Jan. 1975–Aug. 1975	Phani Bhushan Majumdar*

Minister of Planning

Jan. 1972–Nov. 1974	Tajuddin Ahmed*
Dec. 1974–Jan. 1975	(vacant)
Jan. 1975–Aug. 1975	Syed Nazrul Islam*

Minister of Posts, Telephones, and Telegraph

Apr. 1972–Mar. 1973	Mollah Jalaluddin Ahmad*
Apr. 1973–Sep. 1973	Mohammad Ataul Ghani Osmany*
Oct. 1973–June 1974	Sheikh Abdul Aziz
July 1974–Aug. 1975	Mansur Ali*

Minister of Power, Natural Resources, Scientific and Technological Research, and Atomic Energy (title varied; "Power" dropped in Mar. 1974)

Apr. 1972–June 1974	Hafiz Ahmad Choudhury
July 1974–Jan. 1975	Kamal Hossain*
Jan. 1975–Aug. 1975	(remaining divisions included with Education)

Minister of Power, Flood Control, and Irrigation (title varied)

Feb. 1972–Feb. 1974   Khondakar Mushtaque Ahmad*
Mar. 1974–Aug. 1975   Abdur Rab Serniabat*

Minister of Public Works and Housing

Jan. 1972–Feb. 1972   Muhammad Yusuf Ali
Feb. 1972–Mar. 1972   Kamal Hossain*
Apr. 1972–Mar. 1973   Matiur Rahman
Apr. 1973–Aug. 1975   Mohammad Sohrab Hossain

Minister of Relief and Rehabilitation

Dec. 1971–Mar. 1973   A. H. M. Kamruzzaman*
Apr. 1973–May 1973   Mizanur Rahman Chowdhury*
June 1973–June 1974   Sheikh Mujibur Rahman*
July 1974–Aug. 1975   Abdul Monim

Minister of Shipping, Inland Waterways, and Water Transport

Apr. 1972–June 1974   Mohammad Ataul Ghani Osmany*
July 1974–Jan. 1975   Sheikh Mujibur Rahman*
Jan. 1975–Aug. 1975   Mansur Ali*
Aug. 1975   Abu Sayeed Choudhury*

MUSHTAQUE INTERREGNUM (AUGUST–NOVEMBER 1975)

President: Khondakar Mushtaque Ahmed*
Vice President: Mohammadullah*

Ministers

Agriculture: Abdul Monim
Defense: Khondakar Mushtaque Ahmad*
Education, Scientific and Technological Research, and Atomic Energy: Muzaffar Ahmad Choudhury
Finance: Azizur Rahman Mallick

Food: Abdul Monim
Foreign Affairs: Abu Sayeed Chowdhury*
Health and Family Planning: Abdul Mannan
Home Affairs: Khondakar Mushtaque Ahmed*
Law, Parliamentary Affairs, and Justice: Manoranjan Dhar
Local Government, Rural Development, and Cooperatives: Phani Bhushan Majumdar*
Planning: Muhammad Yusuf Ali
Ports, Shipping, and Inland Water Transport: Asaduzzaman Khan
Public Works and Urban Development: Mohammad Sohrab Hossain
Relief and Rehabilitation: Khitish Chandra Mondal

ZIA PERIOD (1975–1982, INCLUDING THE PERIOD OF ABDUS SATTAR)

President

Nov. 1975–Apr. 1977	Abu Sadat Muhammad Sayem*
Apr. 1977–May 1981	Ziaur Rahman*
May 1981–Mar. 1982	Abdus Sattar*

Vice President

June 1977–May 1981	Abdus Sattar*
Nov. 1981–Mar. 1982	Mirza Nurul Huda*
Mar. 1982	Mohammadullah*

Chief Martial Law Administrator

Nov. 1975–Nov. 1976	Abu Sadat Muhammad Sayem*
Nov. 1976–Mar. 1979	Ziaur Rahman*

Deputy Chief Martial Law Administrators

Nov. 1975–Nov. 1976	Ziaur Rahman*
Nov. 1975–Nov. 1977	Mosharraf Hossain Khan
Nov. 1975–Apr. 1976	Muhammad Ghulam Tawab

May 1976–Sep. 1976   Mohammad Khademul Bashar
Sep. 1976–Nov. 1977   Abdul Ghaffar Mahmud

Prime Minister

Mar. 1979–Mar. 1982   Shah Mohammad Azizur Rahman*

Deputy Prime Ministers

Apr. 1979–Aug. 1979   A. Q. M. Badruddoza Choudhury*
Apr. 1979–Dec. 1979   Moudud Ahmed*
Sep. 1979–Jan. 1982   Jamaluddin Ahmad
Sep. 1979–Dec. 1981   S. A. Bari A. T.

Minister of Agriculture (includes Forests except where separate entry is given)

Nov. 1975   Muhammad Ghulam Tawab
Dec. 1975–Jan. 1976   Abu Sadat Muhammad Sayem*
Feb. 1976–June 1976   Mirza Nurul Huda*
July 1976–Mar. 1979   Azizul Haq
Apr. 1979–Dec. 1981   Nurul Islam
Jan. 1982   Fasihuddin Mahtab
Feb. 1982   Abdul Kalim Chowdhury
Mar. 1982   Riazuddin Ahmad

Minister of Civil Aviation and Tourism

Nov. 1975–Jan. 1976   Muhammad Ghulam Tawab
Feb. 1976–Dec. 1976   (included with Communications)
Jan. 1977–June 1978   Abdul Ghaffar Mahmud
July 1978–Mar. 1979   Kazi Anwarul Huque*
Apr. 1979–Aug. 1979   M. A. Matin
Sep. 1979–Apr. 1980   Kazi Anwarul Huque*
May 1980–Dec. 1981   K. M. Obaidur Rahman
Jan. 1982–Mar. 1982   A. K. M. Moidul Islam

Minister of Commerce (included Foreign Trade until Feb. 1978)

Nov. 1975	Ziaur Rahman*
Dec. 1975–Dec. 1976	Mirza Nurul Huda*
Jan. 1977–Apr. 1980	Mohammad Saifur Rahman*
May 1980–Dec. 1981	(vacant)
Jan. 1982	A. S. M. Mostafizur Rahman*
Feb. 1982–Mar. 1982	Mirza Nurul Huda*

Minister of Communications

Nov. 1975	Musharraf Hossain Khan
Dec. 1975–Jan. 1976	Kazi Anwarul Huque*
Feb. 1976–Nov. 1977	Musharraf Hossain Khan (after Nov. 1977 divided into several ministries)

Minister of Defense

Nov. 1975–Apr. 1977	Abu Sadat Muhammad Sayem*
May 1977– May 1981	Ziaur Rahman*
May 1981–Mar. 1982	Abdus Sattar*

Minister of Education

Nov. 1975	Ziaur Rahman*
Dec. 1975–June 1977	Abul Fazal
July 1977–June 1978	Syed Ali Ahsan
July 1978–Oct. 1978	Kazi Zafar Ahmed*
Nov. 1978–Mar. 1979	Abdul Baten
Apr. 1979–Jan. 1982	Shah Mohammad Azizur Rahman*
Feb. 1982–Mar. 1982	Tofazzul Husain Khan

Minister in Charge of the Establishment Division

Nov. 1977–June 1978	Ziaur Rahman*
July 1978–Jan. 1982	Mohammad Majidul Huq
Feb. 1982–Mar. 1982	Abdus Sattar*

Minister of Finance

Nov. 1975–Nov. 1978	Ziaur Rahman*
Dec. 1978–Apr. 1980	Mirza Nurul Huda*
May 1980–Jan. 1982	Muhammad Saifur Rahman*
Feb. 1982–Mar. 1982	Fasihuddin Mahtab

Minister of Fisheries and Livestock

Nov. 1975–Jan. 1976	Mosharraf Hossain Khan (included Forests)
Feb. 1976–Nov. 1977	(included in Agriculture)
Dec. 1977–June 1978	M. R. Khan
July 1978–Apr. 1980	K. M. Obaidur Rahman
May 1980–Jan. 1982	S. A. Bari A. T.
Feb. 1982–Mar. 1982	(at minister of state level)

Minister of Food

Nov. 1975–Apr. 1976	Muhammad Ghulam Tawab
May 1976–Aug. 1976	Mohammad Khademul Bashar
Aug. 1976–June 1977	Abdul Ghaffar Mahmud
July 1977–Jan. 1982	Abdul Momen Khan
Feb. 1982–Mar. 1982	Abdul Halim Chowdhury

Minister of Foreign Affairs

Nov. 1975–Mar. 1977	Abu Sadat Muhammad Sayem*
Apr. 1977–Mar. 1982	Muhammad Shamsul Huq*

Minister of Health and Population Control

Nov. 1975	Muhammad Ghulam Tawab
Dec. 1975–Nov. 1977	Mohammad Ibrahim (from July 1977 to Aug. 1977, Ibrahim held only Population Control; Mohammad Masudul Haque held Health, Labor and Social Welfare)
Dec. 1977–Aug. 1979	A. Q. M. Badruddoza Choudhury*
Sep. 1979–Mar. 1981	M. A. Matin

May 1981–June 1981	(vacant)
July 1981–Dec. 1981	M. A. Matin
Jan. 1982	Abdur Rahman Biswas*
Feb. 1982–Mar. 1982	Khondker Abdul Hamid

Minister of Home Affairs

Nov. 1975–June 1978	Ziaur Rahman*
July 1978–Dec. 1981	A. S. M. Mustafizur Rahman*
Jan. 1982–Mar. 1982	M. A. Matin

Minister of Industries

Nov. 1975	Ziaur Rahman*
Dec. 1975–Jan. 1976	Mirza Nurul Huda*
Feb. 1976–June 1977	A. K. M. Hafizuddin
July 1977–Jan. 1982	Jamaluddin Ahmad
Feb. 1982	Mirza Nurul Huda*
Mar. 1982	Muhammad Yusuf Ali

Minister of Information and Broadcasting

Nov. 1975–Sep. 1976	Ziaur Rahman*
Oct. 1976–Oct. 1977	Akbar Kabir
Nov. 1977–June 1978	Shamsul Huda Choudhury*
July 1978–Apr. 1980	Habibullah Khan
May 1980–Jan. 1982	Shamsul Huda Choudhury*
Feb. 1982	Tofazzul Husain Khan
Mar. 1982	Shamsul Huda Choudhury*

Minister of Jute

Nov. 1975	Ziaur Rahman*
Dec. 1975–July 1977	Kazi Anwarul Huque*
Aug. 1977–Mar. 1979	A. M. Shafiul Azam
Apr. 1979–Apr. 1980	Abdur Rahman Biswas*
May 1980–Dec. 1981	Habibullah Khan
Jan. 1982–Mar. 1982	Muhammad Yusuf Ali

Minister of Labor (at times included Social Welfare)

Nov. 1975	Mosharraf Hossain Khan
Dec. 1975–Jan. 1976	Abul Fazal
Feb. 1976–June 1976	Mohammad Ibrahim
July 1976–Jan. 1977	Mohammad Masudul Haque
Feb. 1977–Aug. 1977	(included with Health)
Sep. 1977–June 1978	(included with Manpower Development)
July 1978–Apr. 1979	Shah Mohammad Azizur Rahman*
May 1979–Aug. 1979	(vacant)
Sep. 1979–Jan. 1982	Riazuddin Ahmad
Feb. 1982–Mar. 1982	Khondker Abdul Hamid

Minister of Land Administration and Land Reform

Nov. 1975	Mosharraf Hossain Khan
Dec. 1975–Jan. 1976	Mrs. Benita Roy
Feb. 1976–Nov. 1977	Kazi Anwarul Huque*
Dec. 1977–June 1978	Enayetullah Khan
July 1978–Mar. 1979	Mirza Ghulam Hafiz*
Apr. 1979–Mar. 1980	Mohammad Abdul Haque
Feb. 1982	Abdus Sattar*
Mar. 1982	Tofazzul Husain Khan

Minister of Law, Parliamentary Affairs, and Justice

Nov. 1975–Jan. 1977	Abu Sadat Mohammad Sayem*
Feb. 1977–Dec. 1981	Abdus Sattar*
Jan. 1982	Tofazzul Husain Khan
Feb. 1982–Mar. 1982	Shah Mohammad Azizur Rahman*

Minister of Local Government, Rural Development, and Cooperatives

Nov. 1975	Muhammad Ghulam Tawab
Dec. 1975–Jan. 1976	Mohammad Abdur Rashid
Feb. 1976–June 1978	Kazi Anwarul Huque*

July 1978–Jan. 1982	Abdul Halim Chaudhury
Feb. 1982–Mar. 1982	Shah Mohammad Azizur Rahman*

Minister of Manpower Development and Social Welfare

Nov. 1975–Aug. 1977	(under other ministries)
Sep. 1977–Nov. 1977	Mohammad Majidul Haque
Dec. 1977–June 1978	Zakaria Chowdhury
July 1978–Jan. 1982	S. A. Bari A. T.
Feb. 1982–Mar. 1982	(to ministry of Labor)

Minister of Petroleum and Natural Resources

Nov. 1975–Apr. 1976	Mohammad Ghulam Tawab
May 1976–Aug. 1976	Mohammad Khademul Bashar
Aug. 1976–June 1977	Abdul Ghaffar Mahmud
July 1977–June 1978	Ashfaque Hussain Khan
July 1978–Oct. 1978	Enayetullah Khan
Nov. 1978–June 1981	Akbar Hussain
July 1981–Jan. 1982	Kazi Anwarul Huque*
Feb. 1982–Mar. 1982	(vacant)

Minister of Planning

Nov. 1975	Abu Sadat Muhammad Sayem*
Dec. 1975–Apr. 1979	Mirza Nurul Huda*
May 1979–Dec. 1981	Fasihuddin Mahtab
Jan. 1982–Mar. 1982	Abdus Sattar*

Minister of Ports, Shipping, and Inland Water Transport

Nov. 1975–Jan. 1976	Mosharraf Hossain Khan
Feb. 1976–Nov. 1977	(included in Communications)
Dec. 1977–Dec. 1981	Nurul Huq
Jan. 1982	(vacant)
Feb. 1982	Shamsul Huda Choudhury*
Mar. 1982	Sultan Ahmad Choudhury

Minister of Posts, Telegraph, and Telephones

Nov. 1975–Jan. 1976	Muhammad Ghulam Tawab
Feb. 1976–Nov. 1977	(included in Communications)
Dec. 1977–Mar. 1979	Moudud Ahmed*
Apr. 1979–Feb. 1982	A. K. M. Moidul Islam
Mar. 1982	Sultan Ahmad Choudhury

Minister of Power, Flood Control, and Water Resources

Nov. 1975–Nov. 1977	Mosharraf Hossain Khan
Dec 1977–Mar. 1979	B. M. Abbas A. T.
Apr. 1979–Dec. 1979	Moudud Ahmed*
Jan. 1980–Dec. 1981	Kazi Anwarul Huque*
Jan. 1982	I. K. Siddiqui
Feb. 1982	(vacant)
Mar. 1982	Abdus Sattar*

Minister of Public Works and Urban Development

Nov. 1975	Muhammad Ghulam Tawab
Dec. 1975–June 1978	Mohammad Abdur Rashid
July 1978–Apr. 1980	Abdur Rahman
May 1980–May 1981	(vacant)
June 1981–Jan. 1982	Abul Hasnat
Feb. 1982–Mar. 1982	(vacant)

Minister of Railways, Roads, Highways, and Road Transport

Dec. 1975	Kazi Anwarul Huque*
Jan. 1976–Nov. 1977	(included with Communications)
Dec. 1977–June 1978	Mohammad Majidul Huq
July 1978–Feb. 1979	Mashiur Rahman*
Mar. 1979–Apr. 1979	(vacant)
May 1979–Jan. 1982	Abdul Alim
Feb. 1982–Mar. 1982	Shamsul Huda Choudhury*

Minister of Relief and Rehabilitation

Nov. 1975	Mohammad Ghulam Tawab
Dec. 1975–Jan. 1976	Muhammad Abdur Rashid
Feb. 1976–June 1978	Mrs. Benita Roy
July 1978–Mar. 1979	Rasa Raj Mondal
Apr. 1979–Jan. 1982	Imran Ali Sarkar
Feb. 1982–Mar. 1982	(vacant)

Minister of Science and Technology

Nov. 1975	Ziaur Rahman*
Dec. 1975–Jan. 1976	Abul Fazal
Feb. 1976–May 1981	Ziaur Rahman*
May 1981–Mar. 1982	Abdus Sattar*

Minister of Sports, Cultural Affairs, and Religion
(title varies; "Religion" added in May 1979)

July 1978–Jan. 1982	Shamsul Huda Choudhury*
Feb. 1982	Tofazzul Husain Khan
Mar. 1982	Shamsul Huda Choudhury*

Minister of Textiles

Nov. 1975–June 1977	(included with Industry)
July 1977–June 1978	Muzaffar Ahmad
July 1978–Mar. 1979	Abdul Alim
Apr. 1979–Mar. 1981	Mansur Ali
Apr. 1981–Mar. 1982	Muhammad Yusuf Ali

Minister of Women's Affairs

July 1978–Apr. 1980	Mrs. Amina Rahman
May 1980–Mar. 1982	(vacant)

Minister of Youth Development

July 1978–Mar. 1979	Kazi Anwarul Huque*
Apr. 1979–Apr. 1980	Khondakar Abdul Hamid
May 1980–Mar. 1981	Abdus Sattar*
Apr. 1981–Dec. 1981	M. A. Matin
Jan. 1982	Abul Qasim
Feb. 1982–Mar. 1982	(vacant)

ERSHAD PERIOD (MARCH 1982–DECEMBER 1990)

President

Mar. 1982–May 1984	A. F. M. Ahsanuddin Chowdhury*
June 1984–Dec. 1990	Hussain Muhammad Ershad*

Vice President

Jan. 1987–Sep. 1989	A. K. M. Nurul Islam
Sep. 1989–Dec. 1990	Moudud Ahmed*

Chief Martial Law Administrator

Mar. 1982–Jan. 1987	Hussain Muhammad Ershad*

Prime Minister

Mar. 1984–Jan. 1985	Ataur Rahman Khan*
July 1986–Jan. 1988	Mizanur Rahman Chowdhury*
Jan. 1988–Sep. 1989	Moudud Ahmed*
Sep. 1989–Dec. 1990	Kazi Zafar Ahmed*

Deputy Prime Ministers

Nov. 1988–Sep. 1989	Kazi Zafar Ahmed*
Nov. 1988–Jan. 1989	Moudud Ahmed*
Nov. 1988–Sep. 1989	M. A. Matin
Jan. 1988–Dec. 1990	Shah Moazzem Hussain

Minister of Agriculture

July 1982–June 1984	A. Z. M. Obaidullah Khan
Feb. 1984–Jan. 1985	Mahboob Ali Khan
Feb. 1985–Mar. 1987	Muhammad Abdul Munim
Mar. 1987–Sep. 1987	Mirza Ruhul Amin
Sep. 1987–Jan. 1988	M. Mahbubuzzaman
Jan. 1988–May 1989	Mahmudul Hasan
May 1989–May 1990	Muhammad Abdul Munim
May 1990–Dec. 1990	Sardar Amzad Hussain

Minister of Civil Aviation and Tourism

Aug. 1982–Jan. 1985	Hussain Muhammad Ershad*
Feb. 1985–Oct. 1985	A. R. Yusuf
July 1986–Mar. 1987	Shafiqul Ghani Swapan
Mar. 1987–Sep. 1987	M. A. Sattar
Sep. 1987–May 1989	(at minister of state level)
May 1989–Sep. 1989	Ziauddin Ahmed
Sep. 1989–Dec. 1990	H. M. A. Gaffar

Minister of Commerce

May 1982–Apr. 1984	Shafiul Azam
May 1984–Jan. 1985	M. A. Matin
Feb. 1985–May 1985	Sultan Mahmud
June 1985–Apr. 1986	Kazi Zafar Ahmed*
May 1986–June 1986	Sultan Mahmud
July 1986–Mar. 1987	Kazi Zafar Ahmed*
Mar. 1987–Jan. 1988	Mohammad Abdul Munim
Jan. 1988–May 1988	Abdus Sattar
May 1988–Jan. 1989	(at minister of state level)
Jan. 1989–May 1990	Abdus Sattar
May 1990–Dec. 1990	Shamsul Haq

Minister of Communications

Mar. 1982–June 1984	Mahboob Ali Khan
July 1984–Jan. 1985	A. Z. M. Obaidullah Khan

Feb. 1985–Oct. 1985	Sultan Ahmad
Nov. 1985–Apr. 1986	Moudud Ahmed*
May 1986–June 1986	Sultan Ahmad
July 1986–Mar. 1987	M. A. Matin
Mar. 1987–Jan. 1988	M. Motiur Rahman
Jan. 1988–Dec. 1990	Anwar Hussain Manju

Minister of Culture

Jan. 1988–Nov. 1989	Nur Mohammad Khan
Nov. 1989	Zafar Imam
Nov. 1989–Dec. 1990	(at minister of state level)

Minister of Defense

| Apr. 1982–Dec. 1990 | Hussain Muhammad Ershad* |

Minister of Education

June 1982–June 1984	Abdul Majeed Khan
July 1984–Jan. 1985	Shamsul Huda Choudhury*
Feb. 1985–Oct. 1985	Hussain Muhammad Ershad*
Nov. 1985–Feb. 1986	Shamsul Huda Choudhury*
Mar. 1986–Apr. 1986	M. A. Matin
May 1986–June 1986	Nurul Islam
July 1986–Mar. 1987	Mominuddin Ahmad
Mar. 1987–Jan. 1988	Mahbubur Rahman
Jan. 1988–May 1988	Sheikh Shahidul Islam
May 1988–Jan. 1989	Anisul Islam Mahmud
Jan. 1989–May 1990	Sheikh Shahidul Islam
May 1990–Dec. 1990	Kazi Zafar Ahmed*

Minister of Energy and Mineral Resources

Mar. 1982–Apr. 1982	Abdul Gaffar Mahmud
May 1982–July 1984	Sultan Mahmud
Feb. 1985–May 1985	Hussain Muhammad Ershad*
June 1985–Apr. 1986	Anwar Hossain Manju

May 1986–June 1986	Muhammad Abdul Munim
July 1986–Jan. 1988	Anwar Hossain Manju
Jan. 1988–Sep. 1989	A. B. M. Ghulam Mustafa
Sep. 1989–Dec. 1990	Ziauddin Ahmed Bablu

Minister of Establishment and Reorganization

Oct. 1983–Jan. 1985	Mohabbat Jan Chowdhury
Feb. 1985–Dec. 1990	Hussain Muhammad Ershad*

Minister of Finance

Mar. 1982–Jan. 1984	Abul Maal Abdul Muhith
Feb. 1984–Mar. 1987	Hussain Muhammad Ershad*
Mar. 1987–Jan. 1988	M. Syeduzzaman
Jan. 1988–May 1988	Wahidul Haq
May 1988–Sep. 1988	Mohammad Abdul Munim
Sep. 1988–May 1990	Wahidul Haq
May 1990–Dec. 1990	Mohammad Abdul Munim

Minister of Fisheries and Animal Husbandry

Nov. 1985–Apr. 1986	Sirajul Hussain Khan
May 1986–June 1986	Abdul Mannan Siddiqui
July 1986–Sep. 1987	Sirajul Hussain Khan
Sep. 1987–Jan. 1988	Mirza Rahul Amin
Jan. 1988–May 1988	Sardar Amzad Hussain
May 1988–Sep. 1988	Hussain Muhammad Ershad*
Sep. 1988–Jan. 1989	Sirajul Hussain Khan
Jan. 1989–Nov. 1989	Sardar Amzad Hussain
Nov. 1989–May 1990	Sunil Kumar Gupta
May 1990–Nov. 1990	M. A. Sattar
Nov. 1990–Dec. 1990	Mustafa Jamal Haider

Minister of Food

Apr. 1982–Jan. 1985	Abdul Gaffar Mahmud
Feb. 1985–Apr. 1986	Mohabbat Jan Chowdhury

May 1986 –June 1986	Abdul Mannan Siddiqui
July 1986–Mar. 1987	Mohabbat Jan Chowdhury
Mar. 1987–Jan. 1988	Sardar Amzad Hussain
Jan. 1988–May 1988	Iqbal Hussain Chowdhury
May 1988–Jan. 1989	Sardar Amzad Hussain
Jan. 1989–Jan. 1990	Iqbal Hussain Chowdhury
Jan. 1990–Dec. 1990	Shah Moazzem Hussain

Minister of Foreign Affairs

May 1992–June 1994	A. R. S. Doha
July 1984–May 1985	Hussain Muhammad Ershad*
June 1985–Jan. 1988	Humayun Rashid Choudhury
Jan. 1988–Dec. 1990	Anisul Islam Mahmud

Minister of Forests and Environment

Sep. 1988–Jan. 1990	A. K. M. Moyeedul Islam
Jan. 1990–Dec. 1990	Zafar Imam

Minister of Health and Family Planning

Mar. 1982–Apr. 1986	Shamsul Huq
July 1986–Jan. 1988	Salahuddin Qadir Chowdhury
Jan. 1988–May 1988	Mohammad Abdul Munim
May 1988–Sep. 1988	M. A. Matin
Sep. 1988–May 1989	Mohammad Abdul Munim
May 1989–Sep. 1989	M. A. Matin
Sep. 1989–Dec. 1990	Azizur Rahman

Minister of Home Affairs

Sep. 1982–Sep. 1983	Mohabbat Jan Chowdhury
Oct. 1983–Feb. 1986	Abdul Mannan Siddiqui
Mar. 1986–Mar. 1987	Mahmudul Hasan
Mar. 1987–May 1989	M. A. Matin
May 1989–Dec. 1990	Mahmudul Hasan

Minister of Industries

Mar. 1982–June 1984	Shafiul Azam
July 1984–June 1986	Sultan Mahmud
July 1986–Sep. 1990	Moudud Ahmed*
Sep. 1990–Dec. 1990	M. A. Sattar

Minister of Information and Broadcasting

Mar. 1982–May 1982	A. R. S. Doha
July 1982–Mar. 1984	Syed Najmuddin Hashim
Apr. 1984–Jan. 1985	Shamsul Huq
Feb. 1985–June 1985	A. R. Yusuf
July 1985–Oct. 1985	Serajul Hussain Khan
Nov. 1985–June 1986	Moazzem Hussain
July 1986–Nov. 1987	Anwar Zahid
Nov. 1987–Jan. 1988	Hussain Muhammad Ershad*
Jan. 1988–May 1988	Kazi Zafar Ahmed*
May 1988–Jan. 1989	Mahbubur Rahman
Jan. 1989–May 1990	Kazi Zafar Ahmed*
May 1990–Dec. 1990	Mizanur Rahman Shelley*

Minister of Irrigation, Water Development, and Flood Control

Mar. 1982–Apr. 1982	Abdul Gaffar Mahmud
May 1982–June 1983	Sultan Mahmud
July 1983–June 1984	A. Z. M. Obaidullah Khan
July 1984	A. R. S. Doha
Aug. 1984–Jan. 1985	Muhammad Aminul Islam Khan
Feb. 1985–June 1985	Sultan Ahmad
July 1985–Oct. 1985	Muhammad Aminul Islam Khan
Nov. 1985–Apr. 1986	Anisul Islam Mahmud
May 1986–June 1986	Sultan Ahmad
July 1986–Jan. 1988	Anisul Islam Mahmud
Jan. 1988–May 1988	Mahbubur Rahman
May 1988–Nov. 1988	(to minister of state level)
Nov. 1988–Jan. 1989	Anisul Islam Mahmud
Jan. 1989–Sep. 1989	Mahbubur Rahman

Sep. 1989–Nov. 1990   A. B. M. Ghulam Mustafa
Nov. 1990–Dec. 1990   Mizanur Rahman Shelley*

Minister of Jute and Textiles ("Jute" added only after September 1986; see Minister of Textiles)

July 1984   Muhammad Aminul Islam Khan
Aug. 1984–Jan. 1985   Muhammad Korban Ali*
Feb. 1985–June 1985   Sultan Ahmad
July 1985–Apr. 1986   Muhammad Abdus Sattar
May 1986–June 1986   Sultan Mahmud
July 1986–Mar. 1987   Hashimuddin Ahmad
Mar. 1987–Jan. 1988   Zafar Imam
Jan. 1988–May 1988   A. K. M. Moyeedul Islam
May 1988–Sep. 1988   Muhammad Korban Ali*
Sep. 1988–Sep. 1989   A. K. M. Moyeedul Islam
Sep. 1989–May 1990   Mahbubur Rahman
May 1990–Dec. 1990   Shahidul Islam

Minister of Labor and Manpower

Mar. 1982–June 1984   Muhammad Aminul Islam Khan
July 1984–Jan. 1985   Shah Moazzem Hossain
Feb. 1985–Oct. 1985   Anisul Islam Mahmud
Nov. 1985–June 1986   Muhammad Korban Ali*
July 1986–Mar. 1987   Muhammad Abdus Sattar
Mar. 1987–Sep. 1987   Abdur Rashid
Sep. 1987–Jan. 1988   Anwar Zahid
Jan. 1988–May 1988   Shah Moazzem Hussain
May 1988–Dec. 1990   Sirajul Hussain Khan

Minister of Land Administration and Land Reforms (name of ministry changed at various times)

Mar. 1982–Mar. 1984   Khondakar Abu Bakr
Apr. 1984–Jan. 1985   M. A. Haq
Feb. 1985–June 1985   T. I. M. Fazle Rabbi Chowdhury
July 1985–Oct. 1985   Muhammad Korban Ali*
Nov. 1985–Apr. 1986   A. K. M. Mayeedul Islam

May 1986–June 1986	Zakir Khan Chowdhury
July 1986–Mar. 1987	Mirza Rahul Amin
Mar. 1987–Sep. 1987	A. K. M. Moyeedul Islam
Sep. 1987–Jan. 1988	Sirajul Hussain Khan
Jan. 1988–May 1988	Sunil Kumar Gupta
May 1988–Jan. 1989	Mostafa Jamal Haider
Jan. 1989–Nov. 1989	Sunil Kumar Gupta
Nov. 1989–May 1990	Sardar Amzad Hussain
May 1990–Dec. 1990	Tajul Islam Chowdhury

Minister of Law and Justice

Mar. 1982–Mar. 1984	Khondakar Abu Bakr
July 1984–Jan. 1985	Ataur Rahman Khan*
Feb. 1985–Feb. 1986	A. K. M. Nurul Islam
Mar. 1986–Apr. 1986	A. K. M. Aminul Islam
May 1986–Nov. 1989	A. K. M. Nurul Islam
Nov. 1989–May 1990	Moudud Ahmed*
May 1990–Dec. 1990	Habibul Islam Bhuiyan

Minister of Local Government, Rural Development, and Cooperatives

Mar. 1982–Jan. 1985	Mahbubur Rahman
Feb. 1985–Feb. 1986	Mahmudul Hasan
Mar. 1986–Apr. 1986	Amanul Islam
May 1986–June 1986	Mahmudul Hasan
July 1986–Sep. 1988	Shah Moazzem Hossain
Sep. 1988–Sep. 1989	(to minister of state level)
Sep. 1989–Dec. 1990	Mohammad Naziur Rahman Manzur

Minister of Planning

Mar. 1982–Jan. 1984	Abul Maal Abdul Muhith
Apr. 1984–June 1984	Shamsul Huda Chowdhury
July 1984–Oct. 1985	Abdul Majeed Khan
Nov. 1985–Apr. 1986	Sultan Ahmad Chowdhury
July 1986–Mar. 1987	Muhammad Shamsul Haq*
Mar. 1987–July 1990	Abdul Karim Khondaker
July 1990–Dec. 1990	Moudud Ahmed*

Minister of Ports, Shipping, and Water Transport

Aug. 1984–Jan. 1985	Reazuddin Ahmad
Feb. 1985–Oct. 1985	Sultan Ahmad
Nov. 1985–Apr. 1986	Moudud Ahmed*
May 1986–June 1986	Sultan Ahmad
July 1986–Mar. 1987	A. K. M. Moyeedul Islam
Mar. 1987–Sep. 1987	Kazi Zafar Ahmed*
Sep. 1987–Nov. 1987	A. K. M. Moyeedul Islam
Nov. 1987–Jan. 1990	(see Minister of Shipping)
Jan. 1990–Mar. 1990	Mohammad Korban Ali*
Mar. 1990–Sep. 1990	(see Ministry of Shipping)
Sep. 1990–Dec. 1990	Mohdudur Rahman Chowdhury

Minister of Posts and Telecommunications

Nov. 1985–Feb. 1986	Mizanur Rahman Chowdhury*
May 1986–June 1986	Sultan Ahmad
July 1986–Mar. 1988	Mizanur Rahman Chowdhury*
Mar. 1988–Sep. 1989	(at minister of state level)
Sep. 1989–Dec. 1990	Qazi Firoz Rashid

Minister of Relief and Rehabilitation

Apr. 1982–July 1984	Abdul Gaffar Mahmud
Aug. 1984–Jan. 1985	Muhammad Yusuf Ali
Feb. 1985–June 1985	Hussain Muhammad Ershad*
July 1985–Oct. 1985	T. I. M. Fazle Rabbi Chowdhury
Nov. 1985–Feb. 1986	Salahuddin Qadir Chowdhury
Mar. 1986–June 1986	Abdul Mannan Siddiqui
July 1986–Sep. 1987	Muhammad Shamsul Haq
Sep. 1987–Jan. 1988	Maulana M. A. Mannan
Jan. 1988	Sirajul Hussain Khan
Jan. 1988–Jan. 1989	(at minister of state level)
Jan. 1989–Jan. 1990	Sirajul Hussain Khan
Jan. 1990–Sep. 1990	Mahdudur Rahman Chowdhury
Sep. 1990–Dec. 1990	Manzur Quader

Minister of Religious Affairs and Endowments

June 1982–May 1983	Abdul Majeed Khan
June 1983–June 1984	Mahbubur Rahman
July 1984–Jan. 1985	Khondakar Abu Bakr
Feb. 1985–June 1985	Hussain Muhammad Ershad*
July 1985–Oct. 1985	A. K. M. Nurul Islam
Nov. 1985–Feb. 1986	Muhammad Aminul Islam Khan
Mar. 1986–Apr. 1986	Shamsul Huda Choudhury*
May 1986–June 1986	A. K. M. Nurul Islam
July 1986–Jan. 1988	Maulana M. A. Mannan
Jan. 1988–May 1988	(at minister of state level)
May 1988–July 1988	Maulana M. A. Mannan
July 1988–Jan. 1989	Mufti Maulana Mohammad Wakkas
Jan. 1989–Jan. 1990	(at minister of state level)
Jan. 1990–May 1990	Nazimuddin al-Azad
May 1990–Dec. 1990	(vacant)

Minister of Social Welfare and Women's Affairs (Women's Affairs separated in January, 1990)

Apr. 1982–Jan. 1985	Shafia Khatun
Feb. 1985–June 1985	Hussain Muhammad Ershad*
July 1985–Sep. 1987	Rabia Bhuiyan
Sep. 1987–Jan. 1988	M. Shamsul Haq
Jan. 1988–Dec. 1990	Rezwanul Haq Chowdhury

Minister of Textiles (see Minister of Jute and Textiles)

July 1986–Mar. 1987	Hashimuddin Ahmed
Mar. 1987–Jan. 1988	Sunil Kumar Gupta
Jan. 1988–Nov. 1989	Zafar Imam
Nov. 1989–Jan. 1990	M. Abdul Malek
Jan. 1990–Dec. 1990	A. B. M. Ruhul Amin Havaldar

Minister of Women's Affairs

Jan. 1990–Dec. 1990	Syeda Razia Faiz

Minister of Works

Mar. 1982–Sep. 1983	Abdul Mannan Siddiqui
Oct. 1983–Jan. 1985	Mohammad Abdul Munim
Feb. 1985–June 1985	Mahmudul Hasan
July 1985–Feb. 1986	M. A. Matin
Mar. 1986–Apr. 1986	Salahuddin Qadir Chowdhury
May 1986–June 1986	Mohammad Abdul Munim
July 1986–Mar. 1987	A. K. M. Aminul Islam
Mar. 1987–Nov. 1987	Shafiqul Ghani Swapan
Nov. 1987–Jan. 1988	Hussain Muhammad Ershad*
Jan. 1988–May 1988	Mustafa Jamal Haider
May 1988–May 1989	Sheikh Shahidul Islam
May 1989–Nov. 1990	Mustafa Jamal Haider
Nov. 1990–Dec. 1990	Abul Hasnat

Minister of Youth and Sports

July 1985–June 1986	Zakir Khan Chowdhury
July 1986–Mar. 1987	Sunil Kumar Gupta
Mar. 1987–Sep. 1987	Sheikh Shahidul Islam
Sep. 1987–Jan. 1988	(at minister of state level)
Jan. 1988–May 1988	Iqbal Hossain
May 1988–Jan. 1989	Sunil Kumar Gupta
Jan. 1989–Sep. 1989	Iqbal Hossain
Sep. 1989–Jan. 1990	A. B. M. Havaldar
Jan. 1990–Dec. 1990	(vacant)

Ministers without Portfolio

Apr. 1984	Syed Najmuddin Hashim
Nov. 1984–Jan. 1985	Mizanur Rahman Chowdhury*

INTERIM GOVERNMENT (DECEMBER 1990–MARCH 1991)

Acting President: Chief Justice Shahabuddin Ahmed*

Advisers

Agriculture and Land: A. M. Anisuzzaman
Civil Aviation, Tourism, and Shipping: Mohammad Rafiqul Islam
Commerce: Imamuddin Ahmed
Communications, Posts, and Telecommunications: A. B. M. G. Kibria
Cultural Affairs and Food: Reazuddin Ahmed
Education: Zillur Rahman Siddique
Energy, Mineral Resources, and Works: Wahiduddin Ahmed
Finance: Kafiluddin Ahmed
Foreign Affairs: Fakhruddin Ahmed
Forest and Environment, Livestock and Fisheries: Qazi Fazlur Rahman
Health and Family Welfare: M. A. Majed
Industries, Jute, and Textiles: A. K. M. Musa
Irrigation, Water Development, and Flood Control: Qazi Fazlur Rahman
Labor and Manpower: A. K. M. Aminul Haq
Law and Justice: Mohammad Abdul Khaleque
Planning: Rahman Sobhan
Relief: B. K. Das
Social Welfare, Women's Affairs, Youth, and Sports: Alamgir M. A. Kabir

KHALEDA ZIA MINISTRIES (MARCH 1991–MAY 1996)

Acting President

Mar. 1991–Nov. 1991   Shahabuddin Ahmed*

President

Nov. 1991–May 1996   Abdur Rahman Biswas*

Prime Minister

Mar. 1991–May 1996   Khaleda Zia*

Minister of Agriculture, Irrigation, Flood Control, and Water Resources

Mar. 1991–May 1996   Majidul Haq

Minister of Commerce

Mar. 1991–Nov. 1991   M. Keramat Ali
Nov. 1991–Oct. 1993   M. K. Anwar
Oct. 1993–May 1996   Mohammad Shamsul Haq Khan

Minister of Communications, Railways, Roads, and Highways

Mar. 1991–May 1996   Oli Ahmed

Minister of Defense

Mar. 1991–Nov. 1991   Shahabuddin Ahmed*
Nov. 1991–May 1996   Khaleda Zia*

Minister of Education

Mar. 1991–Nov. 1991   A. Q. M. Badruddoza Chowdhury*
Nov. 1991–May 1996   Zamiruddin Sirkar

Minister of Energy and Mineral Resources

Mar. 1991–Nov. 1991   Khaleda Zia*
Nov. 1991–May 1996   Khondakar Mosharraf Hossain

Minister of Environment, Forests, Fisheries, and Livestock

Nov. 1991–Oct. 1993   Abdullah al-Noman
Divided Oct. 1993

Minister of Environment and Forests

Oct. 1993–Dec. 1995   Abdullah al-Noman
Jan. 1996–May 1996   Akbar Hossain

Minister of Establishment

Mar. 1991–May 1996   Khaleda Zia*

Minister of Finance

Mar. 1991–May 1996   Muhammad Saifur Rahman*

Minister of Fisheries and Livestock

Oct. 1993–Dec. 1995   Akbar Hussain
Jan. 1996–May 1996   Abdullah al-Noman

Minister of Food

Nov. 1991–Oct. 1993   Mohammad Shamsul Islam Khan
Oct. 1993–Dec. 1995   Mir Shawkat Ali
Jan. 1996–May 1996   Abdul Mannan Bhuiyan

Minister of Foreign Affairs

Mar. 1991–May 1996   A. S. M. Mustafizur Rahman

Minister of Health and Family Planning

Mar. 1991–May 1996   Chaudhury Kamal Ibne Yusuf

Minister of Home Affairs

Mar. 1991–Nov. 1991   Khaleda Zia*
Nov. 1991–May 1996   Abdul Matin Chowdhury

Minister of Industry

Mar. 1991–Oct. 1993   Mohammad Shamsul Islam Khan
Oct. 1993–Nov. 1995   Zahiruddin Khan

Minister of Information

Mar. 1991–Nov. 1991   Khaleda Zia*
Nov. 1991–Mar. 1995   Najmul Huda
Apr. 1995–May 1996   Mohammad Shamsul Islam

Minister of Jute

Nov. 1991–May 1996   Hannan Shah

Minister of Labor and Manpower

Nov. 1991–Dec. 1995   Abdul Mannan Bhuiyan
Jan. 1995–May 1996   Mir Shaukat Ali

Minister of Law and Justice

Mar. 1991–May 1996   Mirza Ghulam Hafiz*

Minister of Local Government, Rural Development, and Cooperatives

Mar. 1991–May 1996   Abdus Salam Talukdar

Minister of Planning

Mar. 1991–Nov. 1991   Saifur Rahman*
Nov. 1991–Nov. 1993   A. M. Zahiruddin Khan
Nov. 1993–May 1996   Khaleda Zia*

Minister of Posts and Telecommunications

Nov. 1991–Sep. 1993   M. Keramat Ali
Sep. 1993–May 1996   Tariqul Islam

Minister of Religious Affairs

Sep. 1993–Dec. 1995   M. Keramat Ali
Jan. 1996–May 1996   M. A. Mannan

Minister of Science and Technology

Sep. 1993–Nov. 1995   Abdul Mannan

Minister of Shipping

Mar. 1991–Nov. 1991   M. K. Anwar
Nov. 1991–Oct. 1993   (at minister of state level)
Oct. 1993–Dec. 1995   M. K. Anwar
Jan. 1996–May 1996   Khaleda Zia*

Minister of Social Welfare and Women's Affairs

Nov. 1991–Sep. 1993   Tariqul Islam
Divided Sept. 1993

Minister of Social Welfare

Sep. 1993–Nov. 1995   Fazlur Rahman Patel

Minister of Women's Affairs

Sep. 1993–Nov. 1995   Sarwari Rahman

Minister of Works

Nov. 1991–May 1996   Rafiqul Islam Mian

Minister of Youth Development and Sports

Nov. 1991–Nov. 1995   Sadiq Hussain Khan

Minister without Portfolio

Jan. 1996–May 1996   M. Karamat Ali

INTERIM GOVERNMENT (JUNE 1996)

President: Abdur Rahman Biswas*

Advisers

Chief Adviser: Muhammad Habibur Rahman
Agriculture, Irrigation, Flood Control, Water: A. Z. M. Naziruddin
Commerce: Shegufta Bakht Chowdhury
Communications: Syed Manzoor Elahi
Education, Science and Technology: Mohammed Yunus
Energy and Natural Resources: Jamilur Reja Chowdhury
Environment and Forests: Mohammed Yunus
Establishment: Muhammad Habibur Rahman
Finance: Mahmud Wahiduddin
Fisheries and Livestock: A. Z. M. Naziruddin
Food: A. Z. M. Naziruddin
Foreign Affairs: Muhammad Habibur Rahman
Health and Family Welfare: Abdur Rahman Khan
Home Affairs: Muhammad Habibur Rahman
Housing and Public Works: A. Z. M. Naziruddin
Information and Planning: Wahiduddin Mahmud
Jute: Shegufta Bakht Chowdhury
Land, Labor and Manpower: Nazima Chowdhury
Law: Syed Ishtiaq Ahmed
Local Government, Rural Development, Cooperatives: Syed Ishtiaq
    Ahmed
Post and Telecommunications: Syed Manzoor Elahi
Religious Affairs: Abdur Rahman Khan
Shipping: Syed Manzoor Elahi
Works: Rafiqul Islam Mian

SHEIKH HASINA WAJID MINISTRY (JULY 1996–JULY 2001)

President

| July 1996–Mar. 1997 | Abdur Rahman Biswas* |
| Apr. 1997–July 2001 | Shamsuddin Ahmed* |

Prime Minister

| July 1996–July 2001 | Sheikh Hasina Wajid* |

Minister of Agriculture, Irrigation, Flood Control, and Water

July 1996–July 2001   Matia Chowdhury

Minister of Cabinet Affairs

July 1996–July 2001   Sheikh Hasina Wajid

Minister of Chittagong Hill Tract Affairs

May 2000–July 2001   Kalpa Ranjan Chakma

Minister of Civil Aviation and Tourism

July 1996–Dec. 1997   Sheikh Hasina Wajid*
Jan. 1998–July 2001   Musharraf Hossain

Minister of Commerce

July 1996–Jan. 2000   Tofael Ahmed
Mar. 2000–July 2001   Abdul Jalil

Minister of Communications

July 1996–July 2001   Anwar Hossain Manju

Minister of Defense

July 1996–July 2001   Sheikh Hasina Wajid*

Minister of Education, Science, and Technology

July 1996–July 2001   A. S. H. K. Sadek

Minister of Energy and Mineral Resources

July 1996–May 1998   Nooruddin Khan
Mar. 2000–July 2001   Sheikh Hasina Wajid*

Ministry of Environment and Forests

July 1996–Mar. 2000   Sheikh Hasina Wajid*
May 2000–July 2001   Syeda Sajeda Chowdhury

Minister of Finance

July 1996–July 2001   S. A. M. S. Kibria

Minister of Fisheries and Livestock

July 1996–Sep. 1996   A. Z. M. Naziruddin
July 2000–July 2001   A. S. M. Abdur Rob

Minister of Food

July 1996–Jan. 2000   A. Z. M. Naziruddin
Mar. 2000–July 2001   Amir Hossain Amu

Minister of Foreign Affairs

July 1996–July 2001   Abdus Samad Azad

Minister of Health and Family Welfare

July 1996–Aug. 1996   Sheikh Hasina Wajid*
Sept. 1996–Jan. 2000   Salahuddin Yusuf
Mar. 2000–July 2001   Sheikh Fazalul Selim Karim

Minister of Home Affairs

July 1996–Jan. 2000   Rafiqul Islam
Mar. 2000–July 2001   Mohammad Nasim

Minister of Housing and Public Works

July 1996–Sep. 1996   A. Z. M. Naziruddin
Oct. 1996–Jan. 2000   Afsaruddin Ahmed Khan
Mar. 2000–July 2001   Mosharraf Hossain

Minister of Industries

Nov. 1996–July 2001   Tofael Ahmed

Minister of Information

July 1996–July 2001   Muhammad Habibur Rahman

Minister of Jute

July 1996–July 2001   Sheikh Hasina Wajid*

Minister of Land, Labor, and Manpower

July 1996–Jan. 1998   Sheikh Hasina Wajid*
Feb. 1998–July 2001   M. A. Mannan

Minister of Law and Justice

July 1996–Mar. 2000   Syed Ishtiaq Ahmed
May 2000–July 2001   Abdul Matin Khasru

Minister of Local Government, Rural Development, and Cooperatives

July 1995–July 2001   Zillur Rahman

Minister of Post and Telecommunications

July 1996–July 2001   Mohammad Nasim

Minister of Power

Apr. 1997–May 1998   Mohammad Nooruddin Khan

Minister of Religious Affairs

July 1996–Mar. 2000   Abdur Rahman Khan

Minister of Science and Technology

May 2000–July 2000   Nooruddin Khan

Minister of Shipping

July 1996–Aug. 1996   Sheikh Hasina Wajid*
Sept. 1996–Mar. 2000   A. S. M. Abdur Rob

Minister of Textiles

July 1996–July 2001   Sheikh Hasina Wajid*

Minister of Water Resources

Oct. 1996–July 2001   Abdur Rassaq

Minister of Works

Jul. 1996–Aug. 1996   Rafiqul Islam Mian

Ministers without Portfolio

July 1996–Jan. 1998   Jamilur Reja Chowdhury
Feb. 1998–Mar. 2000   Kalpa Ranjan Chakma
May 2000–July 2000   Salahuddin Yusuf

INTERIM GOVERNMENT (AUGUST 2001–OCTOBER 2001)

President: Shahabuddin Ahmed*

Advisers

Chief Adviser: Latifur Rahman
Agriculture: Syed Manzoor Elahi
Cabinet Division: Latifur Rahman

Chittagong Hill Tract Affairs: Latifur Rahman
Civil Aviation: Ishtiaq Ahmed
Commerce: Moinul Hossain Chowdhury
Communications: Anwar Hossain Manju
Cooperatives: B. B. Ray Chowdhury
Cultural Affairs: Rokeya Afzal Rahman
Defense: Shahabuddin Ahmed*
Education: A. S. M. Shahjahan
Election Commission: Latifur Rahman
Energy and Mineral Resources: A. K. M. Aminul Islam Chowdhury
Establishment: Latifur Rahman
Finance: M. Hafizuddin Khan
Fisheries and Livestock: Syed Manzoor Elahbi
Food, Forest, Environment and Land: Abdul Muyeed Chowdhury
Foreign Affairs: Latifur Rahman
Health and Family Welfare: M. A. Malek
Home Affairs: Latifur Rahman
Housing and Public Works: Abdul Muyeed Chowdhury
Industries: Moinul Hossain Choudhury
Information: Abdul Muyeed Chowdhury
Jute and Textiles: M. Hafizuddin Khan
Labor and Manpower: M. A. Rahman
Law and Justice: Syed Ishtiaq Ahmed
Local Government: B. B. Ray Choudhury
Parliament: Syed Ishtiaq Ahmed
Planning: M. Hafizuddin Khan
Post and Telecommunications: Moinul Hossain Chowdhury
Relief: B. B. Ray Chowdhury
Religious Affairs: M. A. Malek
Roads and Railways: A. K. M. Aminul Islam Choudhury
Rural Development: B. B. Ray Chowdhury
Science and Technology: A. S. M. Shahjahan
Shipping: Syed Manzoor Elahi
Social Affairs: Rokeya Afzal Rahman
Tourism: Syed Ishtiaq Ahmed
Water Resources: A. K. M. Aminul Islam Choudhury
Women and Children: Rokeya Afzal Rahman
Youth and Sports: A. S. M. Shahjahan

KHALEDA ZIA MINISTRY (OCTOBER 2001–OCTOBER 2006)

President

Oct. 2001–June 2002   A. Q. M. Badruddoza Choudhury*
July 2002–Sep. 2002   Mohammad Jamiruddin Sircar (acting)*
Sep. 2002–Oct. 2006   Iajuddin Ahmed*

Prime Minister

Oct. 2001–Oct.2006   Khaleda Zia

Minister of Agriculture

Oct. 2001–May 2003   Maulana Matiur Rahman Chowdhury
May 2003–Oct. 2006   M. K. Anwar

Minister of Commerce

Oct. 2001–Mar. 2004   Amir Khasru Mahmud Chowdhury
Mar. 2004–June 2006   Altaf Hussain Chowdhury
June 2006–Oct. 2006   M. Hafizuddin Ahmed

Minister of Communications

Oct. 2001–Oct. 2006   Najmul Huda

Minister of Defense

May 2003–Oct. 2006   Khaleda Zia

Minister of Disaster Management and Relief

Oct. 2001–May 2004   Chowdhury Kamal Ibne Yusuf
May 2004 merged with Ministry of Food

Minister of Education

Oct. 2001–Oct. 2006   Osman Faruk

Minister of Energy and Resources

May 2003–Oct. 2006   Khaleda Zia

Minister of Environment and Forest

Oct. 2001–June 2005   Shahjahan Siraj
June 2005–Oct. 2006   Tariqul Islam

Minister of Finance and Planning

Oct. 2001–Oct. 2006   M. Saifur Rahman*

Minister of Fisheries and Livestock

Oct. 2001–May 2003   Sadeq Hossain Khoka
May 2003–May 2004   (vacant)
May 2004–Oct. 2006   Abdullah Al Noman

Minister of Food (and Disaster Management, after May 2004)

Oct. 2001–May 2004   Abdullah Al Noman
May 2004–Oct. 2006   Chowdhury Kamal Ibne Yusuf

Minister of Foreign Affairs

Oct. 2001   A. Q. M. Badruddoza Choudhury*
Oct. 2001–Oct. 2006   Murshed Khan

Minister of Health and Family Welfare

Oct. 2001–Oct. 2006   Khandaker Mosharraf Hossain

Minister of Home Affairs (demoted to state minister level in 2005)

Oct. 2001–May 2004   Altaf Hossain Chowdhury
May 2004–May 2005   Lutfuzzaman Babor (acting)

Minister of Housing and Public Works

Oct. 2001–Oct. 2006   Mirza Abbas

Minister of Industry

Oct. 2001–May 2003   M. K. Anwar
May 2003–Oct. 2006   Maulana Matiur Rahman

Minister of Information

Oct. 2001–June 2005   Tariqul Islam
June 2005–Oct. 2006   M. Shamsul Islam

Minister of Jute (Textile was merged in 2004)

Oct. 2001–June 2005   M. Hafizuddin Ahmed
June 2005–Oct. 2006   Shahjahan Siraj

Minister of Labor and Employment

Oct. 2001–May 2003   Abdullah al-Noman
May 2003–June 2005   Amanullah Aman
June 2005–Oct. 2006   (vacant)

Minister of Land (demoted to state minister level in 2005)

Oct. 2001–June 2005   M. Shamsul Islam

Minister of Law and Justice (also Parliamentary Affairs in 2004)

Oct. 2001–Oct. 2006   Moudud Ahmed*

Minister of Local Government, Rural Development, and Cooperatives

Oct. 2001–Oct. 2006   Abdul Mannan Bhuiyan

Minister of NGO (established in 2004 and demoted to state minister level in 2005)

May 2004–June 2005   Lutfur Rahman Khan Azad

Minister of Post and Telecommunications

Oct. 2001–Oct. 2006   Aminul Huq

Minister of Science and Information and Communications Technology

Oct. 2001–Oct. 2006   Abdul Moyeen Khan

Minister of Shipping

Oct. 2001–Oct. 2006   Akbar Hossain

Minister of Social Welfare

Oct. 2001–Oct. 2006   Ali Ahsan Mujahid

Minister of Textiles (merged with Jute in 2004)

Oct. 2001–May 2004   Abdul Matin Chowdhury

Minister of Water Resources

Oct. 2001–May 2003   L. K. Siddiqui
May 2003–Oct. 2006   Hafizuddin H. Ahmed

Minister of Women's and Children's Affairs

Oct. 2001–Oct. 2006   Khurshid Jahan Huq

Ministers without Portfolio

Oct. 2001–May 2003   Harunur Rashid Khan Monno
May 2003–May 2004   (vacant)
May 2004–Oct. 2004   Abdul Matin Chowdhury

INTERIM GOVERNMENT (OCTOBER 2006–JANUARY 2007)

President: Iajuddin Ahmed

Advisers

Chief Adviser: Iajuddin Ahmed
Agriculture, Cultural Affairs, Youth Sports Adviser: C.M. Shafi Sami
Finance, Planning, Commerce, Post, Telecommunication Adviser: Akbar Ali Khan
Fisheries, Livestock, Housing, Public Works, Liberation War Affairs Adviser: Dhiraj Kumar Nath
Health Adviser: Sultana Kamal
Industries, Science, Information, Communication, Textiles, Jute Adviser: Sufia Rahman
Law, Justice, Land, Environment, Forest Adviser: Justice Fazlul Haque
Local Government, Shipping, Civil Aviation Adviser: M. Azizul Haque
Power, Energy, Food, Disaster Management, Communications, CHT Adviser: Hasan Mashhud Chowdhury*
Water Resources Information, Religious Affairs Adviser: Mahbubul Alam
Women and Children Affairs, Primary Mass Education, Social Welfare Adviser: Yasmin Murshed

(Four advisers resigned in December 2006, and the caretaker government under Chief Adviser Iajuddin Ahmed resigned 11 January 2007.)

INTERIM GOVERNMENT (JANUARY 2007–JANUARY 2009)

President: Iajuddin Ahmed

Initial Advisers

Chief Adviser: Fakhruddin Ahmed*
Agriculture, Environment, Forest, Fisheries, Livestock Adviser: Sajjadul Karim

Commerce, Finance, Planning, Post, Telegraph Adviser: Mirza Azizul Islam

Communication, Shipping, Civil Aviation and Tourism, Liberation
War Adviser: M. A. Matin

Education, Cultural Affairs, Primary Mass Education Adviser: Ayub
Quadri

Energy, Mineral Resources, Food, Disaster Management, Power,
Science, Information, Communication, Technology Adviser: Tap-
pan Chowdhury

Foreign Affairs, Overseas Employment, Expatriate Welfare, CHT
Adviser: Iftekhar Ahmed Chowdhury

Health, Religious Affairs, Water Adviser: Motiur Rahman

Industries, Jute, Textiles, Social Welfare, Women and Children Adviser: Geetiara Safiya Chowdhury

Law, Justice, Parliamentary Affairs, Information, Housing, Land
Adviser: Mainul Hossain

Local Government, Rural Development, Cooperatives, Labor, Employment Adviser: Anwarul Iqbal

SHEIKH HASINA WAJID MINISTRY
(JANUARY 2009–)

President

Jan. 2009–   Zillur Rahman

Prime Minister

Jan. 2009–   Sheikh Hasina Wajid

Minister of Agriculture

Jan. 2009–   Matia Chowdhury

Minister of Civil Aviation and Tourism

Jan. 2009–   G. M. Quader

Minister of Commerce

Jan. 2009–   Faruq Khan

Minister of Communications

Jan. 2009–   Syed Abul Hossain

Minister of Cultural Affairs

Jan. 2009–   Abul Kalam Azad

Minister of Defense

Jan. 2009–   Sheikh Hasina Wajid

Minister of Education

Jan. 2009–   Nurul Islam Nahid

Minister of Electricity, Oil & Mineral Resources

Jan. 2009–   Sheikh Hasina Wajid

Minister of Establishment

Jan. 2009–   Sheikh Hasina Wajid

Minister of Finance

Jan. 2009–   Abu Maal Abdul Muhith

Minister of Fisheries & Livestock

Jan. 2009–   Abdul Latif Biswas

Minister of Food and Disaster Management

Jan. 2009–   Abdur Razzak

Minister of Foreign Affairs

Jan. 2009–   Dipu Moni

Minister of Health & Family Planning

Jan. 2009–   A. F. M. Ruhul Huque

Minister of Home Affairs

Jan. 2009–   Sahara Khatun

Minister of Housing and Public Works

Jan. 2009–   Sheikh Hasina Wajid

Minister of Industries

Jan. 2009–   Dilip Barua

Minister of Information

Jan. 2009–   Abdul Kalam Azad

Minister of Jute and Textiles

Jan. 2009–   Abdul Latif Siddiqui

Minister of Labor & Employment

Jan. 2009–   Khandakar Mosharraf Hossain

Minister of Land

Jan. 2009–   Rezaul Karim Hira

Minister of Law, Justice & Parliamentary Affairs

Jan. 2009–   Shafique Ahmed

Minister of Local Government, Rural Development & Cooperatives

Jan. 2009–   Syed Ashraful Islam

Minister of Overseas Employment & Expatriate Welfare

Jan. 2009–   Khandakar Mosharraf Hossain

Minister of Planning

Jan. 2009–   A. K. Khandekar

Minister of Post & Telecommunications

Jan. 2009–   Raziuddin Ahmed Raju

Minister of Primary & Mass Education

Jan. 2009–   Nurul Islam Nahid

Minister of Religious Affairs

Jan. 2009–   Sheikh Hasina Wajid

Minister of Shipping

Jan. 2009–   Afsarul Amin

Minister of Social Welfare

Jan. 2009–   Enamul Haq Mostafa Shahid

Minister of Water Resources

Jan. 2009–   Ramesh Chandra Sen

Minister of Women's and Children's Affairs

Jan. 2009–   Sheikh Hasina Wajid

Appendix 6
Swadhinata Padak (Independence Day Award) Winners 1977–2008

Note: Asterisks indicate individuals with entries in the dictionary.

1977 Award Winners

Mawlana Abdul Hamid Khan Bhashani (Social work; posthumous)*
Kazi Nazrul Islam (Literature; posthumous)*
Dr. Mokarram Hussain Khundker (Science and Technology; posthumous)
Zainul Abedin (Arts; posthumous)*
Mahbub Alam Chashi (Rural Development)
Brig. Mahmudur Rahman Chowdhury (Medical Science)*
Dr. Md. Zafrullah Chowdhury (Population Control)
Begum Runa Laila (Music)
Habildar Mostak Ahmad (Sports)
Enayet Karim (Welfare; posthumous)*

1978 Award Winners

Poet Jasimuddin (Literature; posthumous)*
Dr. Mazharul Haque (Education; posthumous)
Ranada Prasad Saha (Social Welfare; posthumous)
Dr. Muhammad Ibrahim (Social Welfare)
Dr. Shah Muhammad Hasanuzzaman (Science and Technology)
Abdul Ahad (Music)*
Mahfuzul Haque (Rural Development)
Alamgir M. A. Kabir (Population Control)

1979 Award Winners

Abul Mansur Ahmed (Literature; posthumous)
Dr. Qazi Motahar Hossain (Science and Technology)*

Dr. Muzaffar Ahmed Choudhury (Education; posthumous)
Feroza Begum (Music)
Samar Das (Music)*
Fuljhuri Khan (Music)
Kamrul Hassan (Arts)
Begum Tahera Kabir (Social Welfare)
Nur Mohammad Mandal (Population Control)

1980 Award Winners

Dr. Muhammad Shahidullah (Education; posthumous)
Mawlana Abu Zafar Mohammad Saleh (Education)
Al-Haj Zahir Uddin (Social Work; posthumous)
Poet Farrukh Ahmed (Literature; posthumous)*
Munir Chowdhury (Science and Technology; posthumous)*
Sohrab Hossain (Music)
Dr. Khondokar Ameer Hasan (Science and Technology)

1981 Award Winners

Maulana Mohammad Akram Khan (Journalism; posthumous)*
Abbas Uddin Ahmed (Music; posthumous)*
Major Abdul Ghani (Social Work; posthumous)
Begum Samsun Nahar Mahmud (Social Work; posthumous)
Abbas Mirja (Sports; posthumous)
Dewan Mohammad Azraf (Literature)
Waliullah Patwari (Education)
Ustad Khadem Hossain Khan (Music)

1982 Award Winners

Dr. Abdur Rashid (Education; posthumous)
Kazi Mohammad Mosharraf Hossain (Social Work; posthumous)
Syed Murtaza Ali (Literature; posthumous)
Anwarul Haque (Fine Arts; posthumous)
Begum Feroza Bari (Social Service)

1983 Award Winners

Poet Abdul Kadir (Literature)
Dr. Muhammad Enamul Haque (Education; posthumous)

Dr. Sirajul Haque (Education)
Bangladesh Institute of Research and Rehabilitation for Diabetes, Endocrine and Metabolic Disorders (Medical Science)

1984 Award Winners

Dr. Muhammad Qudrat-i-Khuda (Science and Technology)*
Mohammad Nasir Uddin (Journalism)
Professor Muhammad Mansur Uddin (Literature)
Shah Abul Hasnat Mohammad Ismail (Literature)
Ustad Ayet Ali Khan (Music)
Rashid Uddin Choudhury, Bulbul Choudhury (Dance; posthumous)*
Didar Sarbik Gram Unnayan Samabay Somity (Rural Development)
Kumudini Welfare Trust (Social Service)

1985 Award Winners

General Mohammad Ataul Gani Osmani (Social Welfare; posthumous)

1986 Award Winners

Bangladesh Academy for Rural Development, Comilla (Rural Development)*
Professor Mofiz-Ud-Din Ahmed (Science and Technology)
Md. Mosharraf Hossain (Sports)

1987 Award Winners

M. Hossain Ali (Social Work)
Professor Syed Ali Ahsan (Literature)
Professor Muhammad Yunus (Rural Development)*
Armed Forces Institute of Pathology and Transfusion (Medical Science)

1988 Award Winners

Aminul Islam (Fine Arts)
Md. Nurul Alam (Social Work)

1989 Award Winners

Professor Dr. Md. Mostafizur Rahman (Medical Science and Social Work)
Niaz Morshed (Sports)

1990 Award Winners

Professor Aminul Islam (Science and Technology)
Muhamad Yasin (Rural Development)

1991 Award Winners

Naib Subedar Shah Alam (Sports)
Poet Shamsur Rahman (Literature)*
Professor Md. Innas Ali (Science and Technology)

1992 Award Winners

Bangladesh Rice Research Institute (Science and Technology)
Professor Kazi Jaker Hossain (Education)
Zahir Raihan (Literature; posthumous)*

1993 Award Winners

Kazi Abdul Alim (Sports)
Principal Abul Kashem (Education)
S. M. Sultan (Fine Arts)*
Zahanara Begum (Rural Development)
A. Q. M. Badruddoza Chowdhury (Medical Science)*

1994 Award Winners

Directorate of the Geological Survey of Bangladesh (Science and Technology)
Ahsan Habib (Literature; posthumous)
Atiqur Rahman (Sports)
Mobarak Hossein Khan (Music)
Grameen Bank (Rural Development)*

1995 Award Winners

Dr. Abdullah Al-Muti Sharfuddin (Science and Technology)
Al-haj Moulavi Kazi Ambar Ali (Education)
Abdul Karim Sahitya Bisharad (Literature; posthumous)
Begum Ferdousy Rahman (Music)
Begum Syed Iqbal Mand Banu (Social Service)
Mohammad Zakaria Pintu (Sports)
Syed Mohammad Ali (Journalism)

1996 Award Winners

Moulavi Abdul Hashim (Literature)
Anjuman Mufidul Islam (Social Work)*
Mohammad Abdul Jabbar (Music)*
Sabina Yasmin (Music)
Professor A. M. Zahurul Haq (Science and Technology)
Dr. Kazi Abul Mansur (Medical Science)
Kazi Md. Salahuddin (Sports)
Safiuddin Ahmed (Fine Arts)

1997 Award Winners

Dr. Munshi Siddique Ahmed (Science and Technology)
Dr. Nurul Islam (Medical Science)
Professor Kabir Chowdhury (Education)
Professor Abdul Matin (Education)
Begum Sufia Kamal (Literature)
Shawkat Osman (Literature)*
Abdul Alim (Music; posthumous)*
Jahanara Imam (Social Work)
Justice Syed Mohammad Hossein (Social Work)
Dhirendranath Datta (Language and Independence Movements; posthumous)

1998 Award Winners

Shahidullah Kaiser (Literature)
Dr. Abdul Mosabber Chowdhury (Science and Technology)
Sheikh Fazilatunnisa Mujib (Liberation War)

Syed Nazrul Islam (Liberation War)*
Tajuddin Ahmed (Liberation War)*
Captain Monsur Ali (Liberation War)*
A. H. M. Kamruzzaman (Liberation War)*
Abdur Rab Serniabad (Liberation War)*
Sheikh Fazlul Huq Moni (Liberation War)
Sheikh Kamal (Sports)

1999 Award Winners

Mazharul Islam (Architecture)
Fazlur Rahman Khan (Architecture)
Mohammad Kibria (Fine Arts)
Sikandar Abu Jafar (Literature)
Brojen Das (Sports)
Begum Badrunnesa Ahmed (Social Work)
Kalim Sharafi (Music)
Professor A. Q. M. Bazlul Karim (Education)
Professor A. F. Salahuddin Ahmed (Education)
Abdus Samad Azad (Liberation War)*
Professor Rashiduddin Ahmed (Medical Science)

2000 Award Winners

Syed Shamsul Haque (Literature)
Binodbihari Chowdhury (Social Work)
Ajit Ray (Music)
Ustad Khursheed Khan (Music)
Sardar Fazlul Karim (Education)
Shahabuddin (Painting)
Maulana Abdur Rashid Tarkabagish (Literature)*
Major Gen. Mohammad Abdur Rab (Bir Uttom) (Liberation War)
Sultana Kamal (Sports)
Rokonuzzaman Khan (Children's Organizer)

2001 Award Winners

Sayeda Motahera Banu (Literature)
Shaheed Mashiur Rahman (Independence and Liberation War)

Al-haj Zahur Ahmed Chowdhury (Independence and Liberation War)*

M. A. Aziz (Independence and Liberation War)

Muhammad Mayezuddin (Independence and Liberation War)

Ruhul Quddus (Independence and Liberation War)

Aminuddin (Independence and Liberation War)

Dr. Zikrul Haque (Independence and Liberation War)

Ashfaqur Rahman Khan (Independence and Liberation War)

M. R. Akhtar Mukul (Journalism)*

Bangladesh Cricket Board (Sports)

2002 Award Winners

Hasan Hafizur Rahman (Literature)

Barin Majumder (Music)

Abdul Latif (Music)

S. A. Bari (Liberation War)

Dhaka Ahsania Mission (Social Work)

2003 Award Winners

Sheikh Mujibur Rahman (Independence and Liberation War; posthumous)*

Ziaur Rahman (Independence and Liberation War; posthumous)*

2004 Award Winners

Oli Ahad (Liberation war)

Comrade Moni Singh (Liberation war; posthumous)*

Brig. (retd) Prof. Abdul Malik (Medical Science)

Muhammad Siddiq Khan (Education; posthumous)

Abu Ishaque (Literature; posthumous)

Altaf Mahmud (Culture; posthumous)

Valrie Ann Taylor (Social Work)

Bangladesh Ansar and VDP (Sports)

Rural Development Academy (Rural Development)*

Sandhani (Social Work)

2005 Award Winners

Mujibul Huq
International Centre for Diarrhoeal Disease Research, Bangladesh*

2006 Award Winners

Rapid Action Battalion (Social Work)*
Bangladesh Betar (Bangladesh Liberation War)

2007 Award Winners

Bangladesh Army (Bangladesh Liberation War)
BRAC (Social Work)*

2008 Award Winners

Dr. Syed Muhammad Shamsuzzoha (Liberation War)
Dr. Govinda Chandra Dev (Liberation War)*
Rehman Sobhan (Research and Training)
Bangladesh Rifles (Bangladesh Liberation War)*

Bibliography

This bibliography is arranged generally in accordance with the topics used by the *Bibliography of Asian Studies*, published annually by the Association for Asian Studies.

CONTENTS

INTRODUCTION

This bibliography is a compilation of books in English on eastern Bengal, East Pakistan, and Bangladesh. It concentrates, although not exclusively, on works that have been published relatively recently. It has drawn to a large extent on the *Bibliography of Asian Studies* prepared and published annually by the Association for Asian Studies. This series is now online and available only by subscription. It is usually available at college libraries and other larger libraries for use by those who are doing research. The *Bibliography of Asian Studies* is not limited to American sources, but covers the world at large. It also includes articles and chapters in books that are not included here.

There is an increasing amount of scholarly literature in Bangla, but it must also be said that authors who wish their work to be available worldwide more often write in English. There are several major publishers in Bangladesh who publish many or all of their books in English. Catalogs are available in advertisements in such publications as *Dhaka Courier*, a weekly, as well as on the websites of such publishers as University Press (successor to Oxford University Press, Dhaka) and Academic Publishers. The University Press stock list is available online at www.upl.com.

Before the independence of India, the principal center for both English and Bangla publications on Bengal was Calcutta. As far as Bangladesh (the eastern portion of the former Bengal) is concerned, since independence, Dhaka has been the principal center for publication. Thus this bibliography contains many books that were published in Calcutta. The spelling for Dhaka (formerly Dacca) and Calcutta (now Kolkata) in this bibliography is the spelling of the location at the time of publication and used in the publishing details in the book itself.

Users of the bibliography will also note that some books cited are about Bengal in general and not specifically about eastern Bengal. This, of course, is more often the case for works published before 1947, but there remain writers in West Bengal who maintain an interest in Bangladesh. Also a number of works have been published elsewhere in India, most of them in New Delhi, even ones that have been written by Bangladeshi authors. For some time after Bangladeshi independence it was thought that Indian publishers had greater skills and greater marketing capability than those in Dhaka. This has changed markedly as the publishing industry in Bangladesh has grown. There are also works published in Pakistan, mainly in Karachi, both before and after Bangladeshi independence.

Although the citations for earlier works are limited in this bibliography, there are in larger library collections works by British and other European travelers and administrators dating from the 18th and especially the 19th centuries. The citations for these memoirs and other writings can be found in Internet catalogs, most notably those of the Library of Congress. The Library of Congress catalog can be accessed by typing simply "loc" (without the quotation marks) into a search engine such as Google.

There is no national library in Bangladesh that has the role of the Library of Congress or the British Museum. Lack of funds has made it difficult for university libraries, such as Dhaka University, to preserve materials and to remain current on new publications. Further, accessing the library collections is often difficult. The district libraries are often underutilized, and are sometimes surprisingly rich sources of information, especially historical.

For specific subjects there may be collections that would be useful for research, but it takes the researcher time to ferret them out. An exception for historians is the library of the Asiatic Society of Bangladesh. For other subjects, ministries dealing with the field may have materials that would be useful, but gaining access to these is likely to be cumbersome and often requires an advocate in the ministry. Parliamentary papers are available, but these most often are in Bangla. Newspaper archives tend to be disorganized and not well preserved. Archeological records that have been acquired can be found at the Bangladesh National Museum.

Financial information since independence is sometimes available at the local offices of aid-giving organizations, but materials for such groups as the World Bank, the International Monetary Fund, and the United Nations Development Program, as well as many non-governmental organizations, are more likely to be available at the home offices of the organizations or even in the Library of Congress, whose Internet catalog can be used.

There are very few published bibliographies for South Asia. A relatively recent one is David N. Nelson, *Bibliography of South Asia* (Metuchen, N.J.: Scarecrow Press, 1994). It catalogs books by the Library of Congress catalog numbers rather than more broadly topically. One might as well search the Library of Congress catalog by subject, a process that is rather slow, but which does have the advantage of providing the most recent works. The bibliography in *Bangladesh, a Country Study*, edited by James Heitzman and Robert Worden (Washington D.C.: Federal Research Division, Library of Congress, 1989) lists a number of basic works. The Bangladesh Development Research Center in 2007 published the *Bangladesh Development Bibliography*, which attempts to comprehensively catalog books, articles, and reports on development. The University of Texas at Austin has the *Bangladesh WWW Virtual Library*, which is an additional source.

Both as East Pakistan and as Bangladesh, the country has been a participant in the Library of Congress publication acquisition program. This means that books are available at many American universities that have South Asia programs. These include the University of Pennsylvania, Columbia University, the University of Chicago, the University of California (Berkeley and Los Angeles), the University of Texas, the University of Washington, and the University of Wisconsin, among others. Catalogs of these and other universities and colleges can be consulted through the Internet.

Enauyetullah Khan's *Bangladesh: Splendours of the Past*, James Novak's *Bangladesh: Reflections on the Water*, and Craig Baxter's *Bangladesh: A New Nation in an Old Setting* will provide the reader with a general sense of the country, its challenges, and its opportunities. Readers can complement their knowledge about Bangladesh by reading more recent works such as those by Mahfuzul Huq Chowdhury, Masud Chowdhury, and Nurul Islam. Hamida Hossain's assessment of human rights, Intiaz Ahmed's book on terrorism, Abu Nasar Saied Ahmed's on fundamentalism, and Taj-ul-Islam Hashmi's work on Islam and women should also be of interest to the general reader. Waresul Karim's *Election under a Caretaker Government* and Fakhruddin Ahmed's *The Caretakers: A First-Hand Account of the Interim Government of Bangladesh* will give readers an opportunity to realize the innovative approach to democratic governance in Bangladesh.

Father Richard Timm's work on the indigenous peoples of Bangladesh, *The Adivasis of Bangladesh*; Mohammad Afsaruddin's book, *Rural Life in Bangladesh*; and B. M. Abbas' book, *The Ganges Water Dispute*, are classics for readers who are interested in these topics. In folklore, Mustafa Zaman, Kabir Chowdhury, and Jasimuddin are noteworthy for their contributions. The Bangladesh War of Liberation has many contributors. Jahanara Imam's *Of Blood and Fire*, Richard Sisson and Leo Rose's *War and Independence*, Montassir Mamoon's *Vanquished Generals and the War of Liberation of Bangladesh*, and Anthony Mascarenhas' *The Rape of Bangladesh* cover a wide span of thoughts, experiences, and perspectives. Nazimuddin Ahmed's contribution to archeology, Sirajul Islam's to history, Nafis Ahmed's to geography, Syed Ashraf Ali's to literature, and Mohammad Mohabbat Khan's to public administration are a small sampling of works included in this bibliography.

Scholars whose works extend over many decades in Bangladesh include Rehman Sobhan, Emajuddin Ahemad, Burhanuddin Khan Jahangir, Rounaq Jehan, Zillur Rahman Khan, Talukder Maniruzzaman, A. M. A. Muhith, Mohammad Rashiduzzaman, William van Schendel, and Mizanur Rahman Shelley.

GENERAL AND MISCELLANEOUS

Afsaruddin, Mohammad. *Society and Culture in Bangladesh*. Dhaka: Book House, 1990.

Ahamed, Emajuddin, ed. *Golden Jubilee Volume: Asiatic Society of Bangladesh (1952–2002)*. Dhaka: Asiatic Society of Bangladesh, 2005.

Ahamed, Emajuddin, and Harun-or-Rashid, eds. *State and Culture*. Dhaka: Asiatic Society of Bangladesh, 2007.

Ahmad, Mokbul Morshed. *Donor NGOs, the State and Their Clients in Bangladesh*. Dhaka: Maniruddin Ahmed and Lutfun Nahar, 2000.

Ahmar, Moonis, ed. *Paradigms of Conflict Resolution in South Asia*. Dhaka: University Press Limited, 2003.

Ahmed, A. F. Salahuddin. *Bangladesh Tradition and Transformation*. Dhaka: University Press, 1987.

Ahmed, Imtiaz, ed. *Women, Bangladesh and International Security*. Dhaka: University Press Limited, 2008.

Ahmed, Moeen U. *Shantir Swapney: Samayer Smriticharan* (Dream for Peace: Reminiscence of Time). Dhaka: Bangladesh Army, 2008.

Ahmed, Moudad. *South Asia: Crisis of Development: The Case of Bangladesh*. Dhaka: University Press, 2002.

Ahmed, Rafiuddin, ed. *Bangladesh: Society, Religion, and Politics*. Chittagong: South Asia Studies Group, 1985.

Ahmed, Sufia, ed. *Justice Muhammad Ibrahim, (1898–1966): Memorial Volume*. Dhaka: Academic Press, 2006.

Ahmed, Syed Ishtiaq. *The Ishtiaq Papers*. Dhaka: University Press Limited, 2008.

Ali Reza, A. H. M., et al. *Bengal Tiger in the Bangladesh Sundarbans*. Dhaka: IUCN–World Conservation Union, 2004.

Ara, Shawkat. *Socio-Political Attitude, Values and Personality: A Study of Activists in Bangladesh and India*. Dhaka: Jhinuk Prokash, 2008.

Asaduzzaman, A. The *'Pariah' People: An Ethnography of the Urban Sweepers in Bangladesh*. Dhaka: University Press Limited, 2001.

Baxter, Craig. *Bangladesh: A New Nation in an Old Setting*. Boulder, Colo.: Westview Press, 1984.

———. *Bangladesh: From a Nation to a State*. Boulder, Colo.: Westview Press, 1997.

Chakraberty, C. *Racial Basis of Indian Culture (Including Pakistan, Bangladesh, Sri Lanka and Nepal)*. New Delhi: Aryan, 1997.

Chakravarty, Gita. *The Bangladesh Movement 1947–1971: A Bibliography of English and Bengali Sources*. Calcutta: Firma KLM, 1998.

Chakravarty, S. B., and Virendra Narain, eds. *Bangladesh*. 3 vols. New Delhi: South Asian Publishers, 1986.

Chowdhury, A. M., and Fakrul Alam, eds. *Bangladesh: On the Threshold of the Twenty-first Century*. Dhaka: Asiatic Society of Bangladesh, 2002.

The Common Country Assessment Bangladesh. Dhaka: University Press Limited, 2000.

Conservation of Asian Elephants in Bangladesh. Dhaka: IUCN–World Conservation Union, 2004.

Dey, Tapan Kumar. *Deer Population in the Bangladesh Sundarbans.* Dhaka: Ad Communication, 2007.

Economics and Governance of Nongovernmental Organizations in Bangladesh: World Bank Country Study. Dhaka: University Press Limited, 2007.

Fishwick, Marshall W., ed. *Bangladesh: Inter-Cultural Studies.* Dhaka: Ananda, 1983.

Glassie, Henry, and Firoz Mahmud. *Living Traditions.* Dhaka: Asiatic Society of Bangladesh, 2007.

Haque, A. T. M. Shamsul. *Mosaic of Memories: Varied Experiences of a Member of the Civil Service.* Dhaka: Pathak Shamabesh, 2007.

Haque, Zahirul. *Bangladesh Mosaic in Green.* Dhaka: External Publicity Wing, 2008.

Hasan, Faruque. *Development of Tourism in Bangladesh: Strategy and Beyond.* Dhaka: Charusheelon, 2008.

Heitzman, James, and Robert L. Worden, eds. *Bangladesh, A Country Study.* Washington, D.C.: Federal Research Division, Library of Congress, 1989.

Hena, Abu. *Not without Purpose: Essays and Writings on the State of Affairs in Bangladesh and the Present Day World.* Dhaka: Dizzy Publishers, 2005.

Holloway, Richard. *Supporting Citizens' Initiatives: Bangladesh's NGOs and Society.* Dhaka: University Press, 1998.

Hossain, Shamsul, ed. *Abdul Karim: Commemoration Volume.* Dhaka: Adorn Publishers, 2008.

Hundred Years of Bangabhaban 1905–2005. Dhaka: Press Wing Bangabhaban, 2006.

Huq, Farida. *Journey through 1971: My Story.* 2nd rev. ed. Dhaka: Academic Press and Publishers Library, 2008.

Islam, K. A. *In the Wonderland of Bangladeshi Managers: A Sensational Book Revealing Managerial Lapses in Bangladesh.* Dhaka: Boi Bazaar, 2006.

Islam, M. Shahidul. *Sea-Level Changes in Bangladesh: The Last Ten Thousand Years.* Dhaka: Asiatic Society of Bangladesh, 2001.

Islam, Manu. *Who's Who in Bangladesh.* Dhaka: Centre for Bangladesh Culture, 2001.

Islam, Md. Anwarul, Mahmud-ul Ameen, and Ainun Nishat, eds. *Red Book of Threatened Birds of Bangladesh.* Dhaka: IUCN, 2000.

Islam, Sirajul. *Banglapedia: National Encyclopedia of Bangladesh.* Dhaka: Asiatic Society of Bangladesh, 2003.

Jahan, N. S. Nowroz. *A Field Guide to Bangladeshi Flowers*. Dhaka: Asiatic Society of Bangladesh, 2005.

Jahan, Rounaq, ed. *Bangladesh: Promise and Performance*. Dhaka: University Press, 2000.

Kalam, Abul, ed. *Bangladesh in the New Millennium: A University of Dhaka Study*. Dhaka: University Press, 2004.

Karlekar, Hiranmay. *Bangladesh: The Next Afghanistan?* New Delhi: Sage, 2005.

Khan, Mohammad Mohabbat, and John P. Thorp, eds. *Bangladesh: Society, Politics, and Bureaucracy*. Dhaka: Centre for Administrative Studies, 1984.

Khan, Rubaiyet Hasan, Dewan Muhammad, and Nur A. Yazdani. *An Introduction to Business: Practices in Bangladesh*. Dhaka: A. H. Development Pub., 2008.

Khanna, S. K., and K. N. Sudarshan. *Encyclopedia of South Asia: Bangladesh*. New Delhi: A. P. H., 1998.

Kumar, B. B., ed. *Illegal Migration from Bangladesh*. New Delhi: Concept, 2006.

Larsen, Torben B. *Butterflies of Bangladesh: An Annotated Checklist*. Dhaka: IUCN–World Conservation Union, 2004.

Lasnier, France. *Rickshaw Art in Bangladesh*. Dhaka: University Press, 2002.

Mahbub Ullah. *Globalisation and Beyond: Search for Identity*. Dhaka: Adorn Publishers, 2003.

Mahmud-ul-Ameen, Md. Anwarul Islam, and Ainun Nishat, eds. *Red Book of Threatened Fishes of Bangladesh*. Dhaka: IUCN–World Conservation Union, 2000.

Mintoo, Abdul Awal. *Bangladesh: Anatomy of Change*. Dhaka: University Press, 2004.

Muhith, Abul Maal Abdul. *Bangladesh in the 21st Century*. Dhaka: University Press, 1999.

Mukhopadhyay, Kali Prasad. *Partition, Bengal and After: The Great Tragedy of India*. New Delhi: Reference Press, 2007.

Muqtada, Muhammed, Andrea M. Singh, and Mohammed Ali Rashid, eds. *Bangladesh: Economic and Social Challenges of Globalisation*. Dhaka: University Press Limited, 2002.

Mustafa Majid, Mustafa. *The Rakhaines*. Dhaka: GP, 2008.

Novak, James J. *Bangladesh: Reflections on the Water*. Bloomington: Indiana University Press, 1993.

O'Donnell, Charles Peter. *Bangladesh: Biography of a Muslim Nation*. Boulder, Colo.: Westview Press, 1984.

Paul-Majumdar, Pratima, and Anwara Begum. *Engendering Garment Industry: The Bangladesh Context*. Dhaka: University Press Limited, 2006.

Rahim, Enayetur, and Henry Schwartz, eds. *Contributions to Bengal Studies: An Interdisciplinary and International Approach*. Dhaka: University Press, 1998.

Rahman, A. T. R. *Bangladesh in the Mirror: An Outsider Perspective on a Struggling Democracy*. Dhaka: University Press Limited, 2006.

Rahman, Khan Ferdousour. *Unbundling Human Rights*. Dhaka: Academic Press and Publishers, 2008.

Rashid, Harun-er. *An Introduction to Peace and Conflict Studies*. Dhaka: University Press, 2005.

Rizal Dhurba, and Yozo Yokota. *Understanding Development, Conflict and Violence: The Cases of Bhutan, Nepal, North-East India and the Chittagong Hill Tracts of Bangladesh*. New Delhi: Adroit Publisher, 2006.

Roy, Raja Devasish. *Land and Forest Rights in the Chittagong Hill Tracts, Bangladesh*. Kathmandu: International Centre for Integrated Mountain Development, 2002.

Roy, Samaren. *The Roots of Bengali Culture*. Calcutta: Firma KLM, 1981.

Saigal, J. R. *Pakistan Splits: The Birth of Bangladesh*. Delhi: Manas, 2000.

Shashi, S. S., ed. *Encyclopaedia Indica: India, Pakistan, Bangladesh*. New Delhi: Anmol, 1998.

Shehabuddin, K. M. *There and Back Again: A Diplomat's Tale*. Dhaka: University Press, 2006.

Siddique, Kamaluddin, and Zia Uddin Ahmed, eds. *Encyclopedia of Flora and Fauna of Bangladesh*. 26 vols. Dhaka: Asiatic Society of Bangladesh, 2007–2008.

Singh, Nagendra, Kr., ed. *Encyclopaedia of Muslim Biography: India, Pakistan and Bangladesh*. Delhi: A. P. H., 2001.

——, ed. *Encyclopaedia of Women Biography: India, Pakistan, Bangladesh*. New Delhi: A. P. H., 2001.

Tagore, Rabindranath, Sir. *Glimpses of Bengal, Selected from the Letters of Sir Rabindranath Tagore*. London: Macmillan, 1921.

Thanki, Mridu Shailaj, and Jyoti Dhingra. *Our Lives and Hopes: Beyond Statistics and Reports*. Dhaka: University Press Limited, 2006.

Bibliography

Gustafson, W. Eric, ed. *Pakistan and Bangladesh: Bibliographic Essays in Social Science*. Islamabad: University of Islamabad Press, 1976.

Kozicki, Richard J. *International Relations of South Asia, 1947–1980: A Guide to Information Sources*. Detroit, Mich.: Gale Research, 1981.

Nelson, David N. *Bibliography of South Asia*. Metuchen, N.J.: Scarecrow Press, 1994.

Rahim, Joyce, and Enayetur Rahim. *Bangladesh: A Select Bibliography of English Language Periodical Literature, 1971–1986.* Dhaka: Asiatic Society of Bangladesh, 1986.

Razzak, Mohammad Abdur. *Bangladesh: A Select General Bibliography.* Rajshahi, Bangladesh: Razzaque, 1987.

Shamsuddoulah, A. B. M. *Introducing Bangladesh through Books: A Select Bibliography with Introductions and Annotations, 1855–1976.* Dhaka: Great Eastern Books, 1976.

ANTHROPOLOGY AND SOCIOLOGY

Bibliography

Qadir, S. A. *Social Science Research in Bangladesh.* Dhaka: National Institute of Local Government, 1987.

Folklore

Bradley-Birt, Francis Breadley. *Bengal Fairy Tales.* London: John Lane, 1920.

Chowdhury, Kabir. *Folktales of Bangladesh.* Dacca: Bangla Academy, 1972.

Chowdhury, Kabir, Serajul Islam Chowdhury, and Khondakar Ashraf, trans. *Folk Poems from Bangladesh.* Dhaka: Bangla Academy, 1985.

Damant, Gaborn Henry. *Tales from Bangladesh.* Dacca: Bangladesh Books International, 1976.

Hafiz, Abdul. *Folktales of Bangladesh.* Dhaka: Bangla Academy, 1985.

Jasimuddin. *Folktales of Bangladesh.* Dacca: Oxford University Press, 1974.

Karima, Anoyarula. *The Myths of Bangladesh.* Kushtia: Folklore Research Institute, 1988.

Khan, Shamsuzzaman, ed. *Folklore of Bangladesh.* 2 vols. Dhaka: Bangla Academy, 1987–1992.

Roy Choudhury, Pranab Chandra. *Folk Tales of Bangladesh.* New Delhi: Sterling, 1982.

Sen, Dineshchandra. *Bengali Folklore: Collections and Studies, 1800–1947.* Dhaka: Bangla Academy, 1997.

——. *Bhombal Dass: The Uncle of Lion; A Folk Tale from Bangladesh.* New York: Macmillan, 1995.

——. *The Folk Literature of Bengal.* New Delhi: D. K. Publishers, 1985.

Siddiqui, Ashraf. *Folkloric Bangladesh.* Dacca: Bangla Academy, 1976.

——. *Our Folk-Literature: Ballad Stories.* Dacca: Bureau of National Reconstruction, 1968.

——. *Our Folklore, Our Heritage.* Dacca: Bangladesh Books International, 1977.

Zaman, Mustafa. *Folkloric Bangladesh.* Dacca: Bangladesh Folk Lore Parishad, 1979.

Population

Afsar, Rita. *Rural-Urban Migration in Bangladesh: Causes, Consequences and Challenges.* Dhaka: University Press, 2001.

Ahmad, Alia. *Women and Fertility in Bangladesh.* Newbury Park, Calif.: Sage Publications, 1991.

Akhter, Farida. *Depopulating Bangladesh: Essays on the Politics of Fertility.* Dhaka: Narigrantha Prabartana, 1992.

Banerjee, Sumanta. *Bangladesh.* New York: United Nations Fund for Population Activities, 1982.

Blanchet, Therese. *Meanings and Rituals of Birth in Rural Bangladesh: Women, Pollution, and Marginality.* Dhaka: University Press, 1984.

Blanchet, Therese, and Sabina Faiz Rashid. *Discoursing Birthing Care: Experiences from Bangladesh.* Dhaka: University Press Limited, 2000.

Faraizi, Aminul Haque. *Bangladesh: Peasant Migration and World Capitalism.* New Delhi: Sterling, 1993.

Ghulam Rabbani, A. K. M. *Bangladesh Population Census, 1981: Analytical Findings and National Tables.* Dhaka: Bangladesh Bureau of Statistics, 1984.

Haider, Muhiuddin. *Village Level Integrated Population Education: A Case Study of Bangladesh.* Lanham, Md.: University Press of America, 1982.

Hye, Hasnat Abdul. *Community Participation: Case Studies of Population Health Programmes in Bangladesh.* Comilla, Bangladesh: Bangladesh Academy for Rural Development, 1989.

Kaosar, Afsana. *Disciplining Birth Power, Knowledge and Childbirth Practices in Bangladesh.* Dhaka: University Press Limited, 2005.

Maloney, Clarence. *Beliefs and Fertility in Bangladesh.* Dacca: International Centre for Diarrohoeal Disease Research, 1981.

Miranda, Armindo. *The Demography of Bangladesh: Data and Issues.* Fantoft, Bergen, Norway: Chr. Michelson Institute, 1982.

Noman, Ayesha. *Status of Women and Fertility in Bangladesh.* Dhaka: University Press, 1983.

Rashiduzzaman, M. *Rural Leadership and Population Control in Bangladesh.* Lanham, Md.: University Press of America, 1982.

Samaddar, Ranabir. *The Marginal Nation: Transborder Migration from Bangladesh to West Bengal.* Thousand Oaks, Calif.: Sage, 1999.

Stoeckel, John E., and Moqbul A. Choudhury. *Fertility, Infant Mortality, and Family Planning in Rural Bangladesh.* Dacca: Oxford University Press, 1973.

Bibliography

Alauddin, Mohammad. *Population and Family Planning in Bangladesh: A Survey of the Research.* Washington, D.C.: World Bank, 1983.

Overseas Communities

Ali, Syed Ashraf. *Labor Migration from Bangladesh to the Middle East.* Washington, D.C.: World Bank, 1981.

Asghar, Mohammad Ali. *Bangladesh Community Organizations in East London.* London: Bangla Heritage, 1996.

Eade, John. *The Politics of Community: The Bangladeshi Community in East London.* Aldershot, UK: Avebury, 1990.

Islam, Muinul, et al., eds. *Overseas Migration from Rural Bangladesh: A Micro Study.* Chittagong: University of Chittagong, 1987.

Rural Conditions

Afsaruddin, Mohammad. *Rural Life in Bangladesh: A Study of Five Selected Villages.* Dacca: Nawrose Kitabistan, 1979.

Ahmad, Qazi Kholiquzzaman, ed. *Socio-Economic and Indebtedness-Related Impact of Micro-Credit in Bangladesh.* Dhaka: University Press, 2007.

Anisuzzamam, Mohammad. *Planning for Local Development: An Evaluation of Three Training Courses on Local Level Planning and Management.* Comilla: Bangladesh Academy for Rural Development, 1989.

Baqee, Abdul, and Mujibur Rahman Khan. *Peopling in the Land of Allah Jaane: Power, Peopling, and Environment: The Case of the Charlands of Bangladesh.* Dhaka: University Press, 1998.

Barman, Dalem Ch. *Emerging Leadership Patterns in Rural Bangladesh: A Study.* Dhaka: Centre for Social Studies, 1988.

Bhattacharya, Ranjit Kumar. *The Moslems of Rural Bengal.* Calcutta: Subarnarekha, 1991.

Bleie, Tone. *Tribal Peoples, Nationalism and the Human Rights Challenge: The Adivasis of Bangladesh.* Dhaka: University Press, 2005.

Bose, Sugata. *Agrarian Bengal: Economy, Social Structure, and Politics, 1919–1947.* New York: Cambridge University Press, 1986.

———. *Peasant Labour and Colonial Capital: Rural Bengal since 1770.* New York: Cambridge University Press, 1993.

Chowdhury, Anwarullah. *Agrarian Social Relations and Development in Bangladesh.* New Delhi: Oxford, 1982.

Dutt, Romesh Chunder. *The Peasantry of Bengal.* Calcutta: Thacker, Spink, 1874; reprint, Calcutta: Manisha, 1980.

Duyne, Jennifer E. *Local Initiatives: Collective Water Management in Rural Bangladesh.* New Delhi: D. K. Printworld, 2004.

Hartmann, Betsy, and James K. Boyce. *A Quiet Violence: View from a Bangladesh Village.* London: Zed Press, 1983.

Islam, A. K. M. Aminul. *A Bangladesh Village, Conflict and Cohesion: An Anthropological Study of Politics.* Cambridge, Mass.: Schenkman, 1974.

———. *Victorious Victims: A Political Transformation in the Transitional Society of Bangladesh.* Cambridge, Mass.: Schenkman, 1978.

Islam, Jane. *Shailan: Portrait of a Village.* Dhaka: University Press, 2002.

Islam, M. Rafiqul. *Human Resource Development in Rural Bangladesh.* Dhaka: National Institute of Local Government, 1990.

Khan, Iqbal Alam, and Janet Seeley. *Making a Living: The Livelihoods of the Rural Poor in Bangladesh.* Dhaka: University Press, 2005.

Makita, Rie. *Livelihood Diversification and Landlessness in Rural Bangladesh.* Dhaka: University Press Limited, 2007.

Rahman, P. K. Md. Motiur. *Poverty Issues in Rural Bangladesh.* Dhaka: University Press Limited, 1994.

Sadeque, Mohammed. *Survival Pattern of the Rural Poor: A Case Study of Meherchandi, a Village in Bangladesh.* New Delhi: Northern Book Centre, 1990.

Schendel, Willem van. *Three Deltas: Accumulation and Poverty in Rural Burma, Bengal, and South India.* Newbury Park, Calif.: Sage, 1991.

Seraj, Toufiq M. *The Role of Small Towns in Rural Development: A Case Study of Bangladesh.* Dhaka: National Institute of Local Government, 1989.

Thorp, John P. *Power among the Farmers of Daripalla: A Bangladesh Village Study.* Dacca: Caritas Bangladesh, 1978.

Bibliography

Saqui, Q. M. Afsar Hossain. *Village Studies in Bangladesh: An Annotated Bibliography.* Dhaka: National Institute of Local Government, 1987.

Schendel, Willem van. *Bangladesh: A Bibliography with Special Reference to the Peasantry.* Amsterdam: Antropologisch-Sociologisch Centrum, Universiteit van Amsterdam, 1976.
Shaukat Ali, A. M. M. *A Comprehensive Bibliography on Agriculture and Rural Development.* Dhaka: University Press, 1994.

Social Conditions

Ahmed, Saifuddin. *NGO Perception of Poverty in Bangladesh: Myth and Reality.* Dhaka: Osder Publishers, 2007.
Ahsan Ullah, A. K. M., Abdar Rahman, and Munira Murshed. *Poverty and Migration: Slums of Dhaka City.* Dhaka: Association for Rural Development and Studies, 1999.
Ali, A. F. Imam. *Hindu-Muslim Community in Bangladesh: Caste and Social Structure.* Delhi: Kanishka, 1992.
Amin, Rahul. *Giving Voice to the Poor: Poverty Alleviation in West Bengal and Bangladesh.* Dhaka: University Press, 2002.
Asaduzzaman, A. *The 'Pariah' People: An Ethnography of the Urban Sweepers in Bangladesh.* Dhaka: University Press, 2001.
Bal, Ellen. *They Ask if We Eat Frogs: Social Boundaries, Ethnic Categories and the Garo People of Bangladesh.* Delft, Netherlands: Eburon, 2000.
Bal, Ellen, and Yasuhiro Takami. *Manderangni Jagring: Images of the Garos in Bangladesh.* Dhaka: University Press, 1999.
Bandyopadhyay, Sekher, Abhijit Dasgupta, and Willem van Schendel. *Bengal: Communities, Development and States.* New Delhi: Manohar, 1994.
Barkat, Abul, et al. *Deprivation of Hindu Minority in Bangladesh: Living with Vested Property.* Dhaka: Pathak Shamabesh, 2008.
Bhattacharya, Ranjit Kumar. *Moslems of Rural Bengal: A Study in Social Stratification and Socio-Cultural Boundary Maintenance.* Calcutta: Subarnarekha, 1991.
Blanchet, Therese. *Lost Innocence: Stolen Childhoods.* Dhaka: University Press, 1996.
Cumming, David. *The Ganges Delta and Its People.* New York: Thompson Learning, 1994.
Elahi, Maudood K., and Iffat Ara. *Understanding the Monga in Northern Bangladesh.* Dhaka: Academic Press and Publishers Library, 2008.
Hossain, Naomi. *Elite Perceptions of Poverty in Bangladesh.* Dhaka: University Press, 2005.
Karim, A. K. Nazmul. *The Dynamics of Bangladesh Society.* New Delhi: Vikas, 1980.

Rahman, A. T. R. *Volunteerism and Nation-Building for Bangladesh*. Dhaka: Academic Publishers, 1993.

Shahidullah, Muhammad. *Better Days, Better Lives: Towards Strategy for Implementing the Convention on the Rights of the Child in Bangladesh*. Dhaka: University Press, 2001.

———. *Jagatpur 1977–9: Poverty and Social Change in Rural Bangladesh*. Dhaka: University Press, 2000.

———. *Traditional Culture in East Pakistan*. Dacca: Department of Bengali, University of Dacca, 1963.

Siddiqui, Kamal. *Social Formation in Dhaka City*. Dhaka: University Press, 1993.

Source Book: Health, Nutrition and Population Sector. Dhaka: Human Resources Management, Planning and Development Unit, 2005.

Sufia M. Uddin. *Constructing Bangladesh: Religion, Ethnicity and Language in an Islamic Nation*. Chapel Hill: University of North Carolina Press: 2006.

Zehadul Karim, A. H. M. *The Pattern of Rural Leadership in an Agrarian Society: A Case Study of the Changing Power Structure in Bangladesh*. New Delhi: Northern Book Centre, 1990.

Social Structure

Ahmed, Rahnuma. *Brides and the Demand System in Bangladesh: A Study*. Dhaka: Centre for Social Studies, Dhaka University, 1987.

Ali, A. F. Imam. *Changing Social Stratification in Rural Bangladesh: A Case Study of Two Selected Villages*. Chittagong: University of Chittagong, 1990.

Aziz, K. M. Ashraful. *Kinship in Bangladesh*. Dacca: International Centre for Diarrhoeal Disease Research, 1979.

Barkat-e-Khuda. *Power Structure in Rural Bangladesh*. Canberra: ANU Press, 1981.

Barua, Tushar Kanti. *Political Elite in Bangladesh: A Socio-Anthropological and Historical Analysis of the Processes of Their Formation*. Bern: P. Lang, 1978.

Brauns, Claus-Dieter. *Mru: A Hill People on the Border of Bangladesh*. Basel: Birkhauser Verlag, 1989.

Choudhury, Anwarullah, Qamrul Ahsan Chowdhury, and Kibriaul Khaleque, eds. *Sociology of Bangladesh: Problems and Prospects*. Dhaka: Bangladesh Sociology Association, 1987.

Chowdhury, Bazlul Mobin, and Syed Zahur Sadeque, eds. *Bangladesh Social Structure and Development*. Dhaka: Bangladesh Sociological Association, 1989.

Gomes, Stephen G. *The Paharias: A Glimpse of Tribal Life in Northwestern Bangladesh.* Dhaka: Caritas Bangladesh, 1988.

Gupta, Dipankar, ed. *Social Stratification.* New York: Oxford University Press, 1992.

Inden, Ronald B. *Marriage and Rank in Bengali Culture: A History of Caste and Clan in Middle Period Bengal.* Berkeley: University of California Press, 1976.

Jahangir, Burhanuddin Khan. *Rural Society, Power Structure, and Class Practice.* Dacca: Centre for Social Studies, 1982.

Karim, M. Bazlul. *Participation, Development, and Social Structure.* Lanham, Md.: University Press of America, 1993.

Laure, Jason, and Ettagale Laure. *Joi Bangla! The Children of Bangladesh.* New York: Farrar, Straus and Giroux, 1974.

Risley, Herbert Hope. *The Tribes and Castes of Bengal: Ethnographic Glossary.* Calcutta: Firma KLM, 1981.

Sattar, Abdus. *Tribal Culture in Bangladesh.* Dacca: Muktadhara, 1975.

Talukdar, S. P. *The Chakma Life and Struggle.* Delhi: Gain Publishing, 1988.

Timm, Richard W. *The Adivasis of Bangladesh.* London: Minority Rights Group, 1991.

White, Sarah C. *Arguing with the Crocodile: Gender and Class in Bangladesh.* London: Zed Books, 1992.

Zehadul Karim, A. H. M. *The Pattern of Rural Leadership in an Agrarian Society: A Case Study of the Changing Power Structure in Bangladesh.* New Delhi: Northern Book Centre, 1990.

Social Work

A Directory of NGO Networks in Bangladesh and an Introduction to Networks. Dhaka: PACT Bangladesh/PRIP, 1992.

Women

Abdullah, Tahrunnessa Ahmed. *Village Women of Bangladesh: Prospects for Change, a Study.* New York: Pergamon Press, 1982.

Afsana, Kaosar, and Sabina Faiz Rashid. *Discovering Birthing Care: Experiences from Bangladesh.* Dhaka: University Press, 2001.

Ahmad, Perveen. *Income Earning as Related to the Changing Status of Village Women in Bangladesh.* Dacca: Women for Women, Study and Research Group, 1980.

Ahmed, Niaz. *Divorced Women in Bangladesh: Psycho-Social and Economic Conditions.* Dhaka: A. H. Development Publishers, 2007.

Akanda, Latifa, and Roushan Jahan, eds. *Women for Women: Collected Articles.* Dhaka: Women for Women, 1983.

Azim, Ferdous, and Niaz Zaman, eds. *Different Perspectives: Women Writing in Bangladesh.* Dhaka: University Press, 1998.

Bangladesh: Strategies for Enhancing the Role of Women in Economic Development. Washington, D.C.: World Bank, 1990.

Begum, Asma. *Village Women and Grameen Bank in Bangladesh.* New Delhi: Gyan Publishers, 2007.

Begum, Hamida A., et al., eds. *Women and National Planning in Bangladesh.* Dhaka: Women for Women, 1990.

Blanchet, Therese, Abdur Razzaque, and Hannan Biswas. *Documenting the Undocumented: Female Migrant Workers from Bangladesh.* Dhaka: Pathak Shamabesh, 2008.

Borthwick, Meredith. *The Changing Role of Women in Bengal, 1849–1905.* Princeton, N.J.: Princeton University Press, 1984.

Chen, Martha Alter. *A Quiet Revolution: Women in Transition in Rural Bangladesh.* Cambridge, Mass.: Schenkman, 1983.

Dannecker, Petra. *Between Conformity and Resistance: Women Garment Workers in Bangladesh.* Dhaka: University Press, 2002.

Engels, Dagmar. *Beyond Purdah? Women in Bengal, 1890–1919.* London: Oxford University Press, 1996.

Evers, Barbara, and Kaniz Siddique, eds. *Who Gets What: A Gender Analysis of Public Expenditure in Bangladesh.* Dhaka: University Press Limited, 2006.

Firoj, Jalal. *Women in Bangladesh Parliament: A Study on Opinions of the Women MPs.* Dhaka: A. H. Development Publishers, 2007.

Folk Medicine and Rural Women in Bangladesh. Dacca: Women for Women, 1980.

Ghulam Murshid. *Reluctant Debutante: Response of Bengali Women to Modernization, 1849–1905.* Rajshahi, Bangladesh: Sahitya Samsad, Rajshahi University, 1983.

Goetz, Anne Marie. *Women Development Workers: Implementing Rural Credit Programmes in Bangladesh.* Thousand Oaks, Calif.: Sage, 2001.

Hamid, Shamim. *Why Women Count: Essays on Women in Development in Bangladesh.* Dhaka: University Press, 1996.

Hashmi, Taj ul-Islam. *Women and Islam: Beyond Subjection and Tyranny.* New York: St. Martin's, 2000.

Hossain, Hameeda, Roushan Jahan, and Salma Sobhan. *No Better Option? Industrial Women Workers in Bangladesh.* Dhaka: University Press, 1990.

Islam, Shamima, ed. *Exploring the Other Half: Field Research with Rural Women in Bangladesh.* Dacca: Women for Women, 1982.

Jahan, Rounaq. *Elusive Agenda: Mainstreaming Women in Development*. London: Zed, 1995.

Kabeer, Naila. *Bangladeshi Women Workers and Labour Market Decisions: The Right to Choose*. Dhaka: University Press, 2001.

———. *The Quest for National Identity: Women, Islam, and the State in Bangladesh*. Brighton, England: Institute of Development Studies, University of Sussex, 1989.

Kafi, Sharif Abdullahel. *Disaster and Destitute Women: Twelve Case Studies*. Dhaka: Bangladesh Development Partnership Centre, 1992.

Khan, Saira Rahman. *The Socio-Legal Status of Bengali Woman in Bangladesh: Implications for Development*. Dhaka: University Press, 2001.

Khan, Salma. *The Fifty Percent: Women in Development and Policy in Bangladesh*. Dhaka: University Press, 1988.

Khan, Zarina Rahman. *Women, Work, and Values: Contradictions in the Prevailing Notions and the Realities of Women's Lives in Rural Bangladesh*. Dhaka: Dana Publishers, 1992.

Kotalova, Jitka. *Belonging to Others: Cultural Construction of Womanhood among Muslims in a Village in Bangladesh*. Stockholm: Almqvist and Wiksell International, 1993.

Mahtab, Nazmunnessa. *Women in Bangladesh: From Inequality to Empowerment*. Dhaka: A. H. Development Publishing House, 2007.

Monsoor, Taslima. *From Patriarchy to Gender Equity: Family Law and Its Impact on Women in Bangladesh*. Dhaka: University Press, 1999.

Muna, Lazeena. *Romance and Pleasure: Understanding the Sexual Conduct of Young People in Dhaka in the Era of HIV and AIDS*. Dhaka: University Press, 2005.

Nahar, Nilufar. *Aged Women in Urban Area of Dhaka City in Bangladesh*. Dhaka: A. H. Development Publishers, 2006.

Naz, Farzana. *Pathways to Women's Empowerment in Bangladesh*. Dhaka: A. H. Development, 2006.

Nilufar Banu. *Some Socio-Economic Problems of the Educated Working Women of Dhaka City: Socio-Economic Survey, 1983–84*. Dhaka: Bureau of Economic Research, University of Dhaka, 1988.

Quddus, Mohammad Abdul. *Rural Women in Households in Bangladesh: With a Case Study of Three Villages in Comilla*. Comilla: Bangladesh Academy for Rural Development, 1985.

Rozario, Santi. *Purity and Communal Boundaries: Women and Social Change in a Bangladeshi Village*. Dhaka: University Press, 2001.

Scott, Gloria L. *The Impact of Technology Choice on Rural Women in Bangladesh: Problems and Opportunities*. Washington, D.C.: World Bank, 1985.

Shehebuddin, Elora. *Reshaping the Holy Democracy, Development and Muslim Women in Bangladesh.* New York: Columbia University Press, 2008.

Siddiqui, Tasneem. *Transcending Boundaries: Labour Migration of Women from Bangladesh.* Dhaka: University Press, 2001.

The Situation of Women in Bangladesh. Dacca: Women for Women, 1979.

Sobhan, Rehman, and Nasreen Khundker, eds. *Globalisation and Gender: Changing Patterns of Women's Employment in Bangladesh.* Reprint. Dhaka: University Press Limited, 2004.

Todd, Helen. *Women at the Center: Grameen Bank Borrowers after One Decade.* Dhaka: University Press, 1996.

Wallace, Ben, et al. *The Invisible Resource: Women and Work in Rural Bangladesh.* Boulder, Colo.: Westview Press, 1987.

Westergaard, Kirsten. *Pauperization and Rural Women in Bangladesh: A Case Study.* Comilla: Bangladesh Academy for Rural Development, 1983.

Women, Health, and Culture: A Study of Beliefs and Practices Connected with Female Diseases in a Bangladesh Village. Dhaka: Women for Women, 1985.

Bibliography

McCarthy, Florence E. *Bibliography and Selected References regarding Rural Women in Bangladesh.* Dacca: Women's Section, Planning and Development Division, Ministry of Agriculture, 1978.

ARTS

Ahmad, Perveen. *The Aesthetics and Vocabulary of Nakshi Kantha: Bangladesh National Museum Collection.* Dhaka: Bangladesh National Museum, 1997.

Al Zaman, Mahmud. *Safiuddin Ahmed: Art of Bangladesh*, series 2. Dhaka: Bangladesh Shilpakala Academy, 2002.

Anisuzzaman. *Debdas Chakraborty: Art of Bangladesh* series, 8. Dhaka: Bangladesh Shilpakala Academy, 2003.

Asher, Frederick M. *The Art of Eastern India: 300–800.* Minneapolis: University of Minnesota Press, 1980.

——. *Contemporary Art of Bangladesh.* Dacca: Shilpakala Academy, 1978.

Biswas, S. S. *Terracotta Art of Bengal.* Delhi: Agam, 1981.

Dunham, Mary Frances. *Jarigan: Muslim Epic Songs of Bangladesh.* Dhaka: University Press, 1997.

Freedman, Matthew S. *Bangladesh Metal Casting: Five Techniques*. Dhaka: University Press, 2001.

Glassie, Henry H. *Art and Life in Bangladesh*. Bloomington: Indiana University Press, 1997.

Haque, Enamul. *The Art Heritage of Bangladesh*. Dhaka: International Centre for Study of Bengal Art, 2007.

———. *Islamic Art Heritage of Bangladesh*. Dhaka: Bangladesh National Museum, 1983.

———, ed. *An Anthology of Crafts in Bangladesh*. Dhaka: National Crafts Council of Bangladesh, 1987.

Haque, Zulekha. *Gahana, Jewellery of Bangladesh*. Dhaka: Bangladesh Small and Cottage Industries Corp., 1984.

Huq, Syed Azizul. *Quamrul Hassan: Art of Bangladesh*, series 3. Dhaka: Bangladesh Shilpakala Academy, 2003.

Huque, Mofidul. *Qayyum Chowdhury: Art of Bangladesh*, series 6. Dhaka: Bangladesh Shilpakala Academy, 2003.

———. *Terracotta Decorations of Late Mediaeval Bengal: Portrayal of a Society*. Dacca: Asiatic Society of Bangladesh, 1980.

Huntington, Susan L., and John C. Huntington. *Leaves from the Bodhi Tree: The Art of Pala India (8th–12th Centuries) and Its International Legacy*. Dayton, Ohio: Dayton Art Institute in association with the University of Washington Press, 1990.

Hye, Hasnat Abdul. *Murtaja Baseer: Art of Bangladesh*, series 11. Dhaka: Bangladesh Shilpakala Academy, 2004.

Islam, Nazrul. *Abdur Razzaque: Art of Bangladesh*, series 7. Dhaka: Bangladesh Shilpakala Academy, 2003.

———. *Zainul Abedin: Art of Bangladesh*, series 1. Reprint. Dhaka: Bangladesh Shilpakala Academy, 1997.

Islam, Syed Manzoorul. *Mohammad Kibria: Art of Bangladesh*, series 9. Dhaka: Bangladesh Shilpakala Academy, 2004.

Jamal, Osman. *Aminul Islam: Art of Bangladesh Series*. Dhaka: Bangladesh Shilpakala Academy, 2004.

Khan, Enayetullah. *Bangladesh: Splendours of the Past*. Dhaka: Cosmos, 2001.

Khan, Sadeq, ed. *S. M. Sultan: Art of Bangladesh*, series 4. Dhaka: Bangladesh Shilpakala Academy, 2003.

Lasnier, France. *Rickshaw Art in Bangladesh*. Dhaka: University Press, 2002.

Mahmud, Firoz. *The Museums in Bangladesh*. Dhaka: Bangla Academy, 1987.

Mansur, Abul. *Brick Temples of Bengal: From the Archives of David McCutchion*. Princeton, N.J.: Princeton University Press, 1983.

——. *Rashid Choudhury: Art of Bangladesh*, series 5. Dhaka: Bangladesh Shilpakala Academy, 2003.

Michell, George, ed. *The Islamic Heritage of Bengal*. Paris: UNESCO, 1984.

Sirajuddin, Muhammad. *Living Crafts in Bangladesh*. Dhaka: Markup International, 1992.

Tofayell, Z. A. *Bangladesh: Antiquities and Museums*. Dacca: Atikullah, 1972.

Zaman, Niaz. *The Art of Kantha Embroidery*. Dacca: Bangladesh Shilpakala Academy, 1981.

Architecture

Ahmed, Khondhokar Iftekhar. *Up to the Waist in Mud: Earth-Based Architecture in Rural Bangladesh*. Dhaka: University Press, 1994.

Ahmed, Nazimuddin. *The Buildings of Khan Jahan in and around Bagerhat*. Dhaka: University Press, 1989.

Ahmed, Nazimuddin, and John Sanday. *Buildings of the British Raj in Bangladesh*. Dhaka: University Press, 1986.

——. *Discover the Monuments of Bangladesh: A Guide to Their History, Location and Development*. Dhaka: University Press, 1984.

Asher, Catherine B. *Architecture of Mughal India*. New York: Cambridge University Press, 1982.

Banerji, Anupam. *The Architecture of Corbusier and Kahn in the East: A Philosophical Inquiry*. Lewiston, N.Y.: E. Mellen Press, 2001.

Basu, Dwijendra Nath. *Functional Analysis of Old Bengali Structures*. Calcutta: Basudha, 1976.

Dani, Ahmed Hasan. *The Adina Masjid, the Largest Mosque Ever Built in Indo-Pak Sub-continent at Hazrat Pandua, A.H.776/A.D.1374/1375: A Monograph*. Dacca: Society for Pakistan Studies, 1970.

——. *Buddhist Sculptures in East Pakistan*. Karachi: Department of Archaeology, 1959.

——. *A Guide to the Ancient Monuments of East Pakistan*. Dacca: Society for Pakistan Studies, 1970.

——. *Mosque Architecture of Pre-Mughal Bengal*. Dacca: University Press, 1979.

——. *Muslim Architecture in Bengal*. Dhaka: n.p., 1961.

Hasan, Sayed Mahmudul. *Gaud and Hazrat Pandua: Romance in Brick and Stone*. Dhaka: Islamic Foundation Bangladesh, 1987.

——. *Glimpses of Muslim Art and Architecture*. Dhaka: Islamic Foundation Bangladesh, 1983.

——. *Muslim Monuments of Bangladesh.* Dhaka: Islamic Foundation Bangladesh, 1987.

Husain, A. B. M., ed. *Architecture: A History through the Ages.* Dhaka: Asiatic Society of Bangladesh, 2007.

Khan, Ahmed Nabi. *Islamic Architecture in South Asia: Pakistan–India–Bangladesh.* New Delhi: Oxford University Press, 2003.

Khan, Muhammad Hafizullah. *Terracotta Ornamentation in Muslim Architecture of Bengal.* Dhaka: Asiatic Society of Bangladesh, 1988.

Zahiruddin, Shah Alam, Abu H. Imamuddin, and M. Mohiuddin Khan, eds. *Contemporary Architecture, Bangladesh.* Dhaka: University Press, 1990.

Painting

Abedin, Zainul. *Zainul Abedin.* Dacca: Bangladesh Shilpakala Academy, 1977.

Chowdhury, Qayyum. *Qayyum Chowdhury.* Dacca: Bangladesh Shilpakala Academy, 1977.

Gallagher, Rob. *The Rickshaws of Bangladesh.* Dhaka: University Press, 1992.

Islam, Muhammad Sirajul, ed. *Zainul Abedin.* Dacca: Bangladesh Shilpakala Academy, 1977.

Jehangir, Burhanuddin Khan. *Contemporary Painters, Bangladesh.* Dacca: Bangla Academy, 1974.

McCutchion, David, and S. K. Bhowmik. *Patuas and Patua Art in Bangladesh.* Calcutta: Firma KLM, 1999.

Nandi, Sudhirakumara. *Art and Aesthetics of Abanindranath Tagore.* Calcutta: Rabindra Bharati University, 1983.

Roy, Kshitis. *Rabindranath Tagore.* New Delhi: National Gallery of Modern Art, 1988.

Sultan, S. M. *S. M. Sultan.* Dacca: Bangladesh Shilpakala Academy, 1976.

Zaman, Mahmud Al. *Kazi Abdul Baset: Art of Bangladesh*, series 12. Dhaka: Bangladesh Shilpakala Academy, 2004.

Sculpture

Chattopadhya, Pranab K. *Metalcrafts of Eastern India and Bangladesh.* Jaipur: Publication Scheme, 2005.

Friedman, Matthew S. *Bangladesh Metal Casting: Five Techniques.* Dhaka: University Press, 2001.

Haque, Enamul, and Adalbert J. Gail, eds. *Sculptures in Bangladesh: An Inventory of Select Hindu, Buddhist and Jain Stone and Bronze Images in*

Museums and Collections of Bangladesh (Up to the 13th Century). Dhaka: International Centre for Study of Bengal Art, 2008.

Huntington, Susan L. *The Pala and Sena Schools.* Leiden, Netherlands: Brill, 1984.

Shamsul Alam, A. K. M. *Sculptural Art of Bangladesh: Pre-Muslim Period.* Dhaka: Department of Archaeology and Museums, 1985.

Theatre

Ahmed, Syed Jamil. *Acinpakhi Infinity: Indigenous Theatre of Bangladesh.* Dhaka: Dhaka University Press, 2000.

Al-Mamun, Abdullah. Trans. Kabir Chowdhury. *Kokilas: A Play in Three Parts.* Dhaka: University Press, 1993.

Banerjee, Brajendra Nath. *Bengali Stage, 1795–1873.* Calcutta: Ranjan Publishing House, 1943.

Banerji, Himani. *Mirror of Class: Essays on Bengali Theatre.* Calcutta: Papyrus, 1998.

Bharucha, Rustom. *Rehearsals of Revolution: The Political Theatre of Bengal.* Honolulu: University of Hawaii Press, 1983.

Das Gupta, Hemendra Nath. *The Indian Stage.* Calcutta: Metropolitan Printing and Publishing, 1934.

Guha-Thakurta, Prabhucharan. *The Bengali Drama.* London: K. Paul, Trench, Trubner, 1930.

———. *The Bengali Drama: Its Origin and Development.* Westport, Conn.: Greenwood Press, 1974.

Mamoon, Montassir. *Festivals of Bangladesh.* Trans. Rajoshi Ghosh. Dhaka: International Centre for Bangladesh Studies, 1996.

COMMUNICATIONS AND MEDIA

Begum, Anwara. *Magical Shadows: Women in the Bangladeshi Media.* New Delhi: South Asian Publishers, 2008.

Kabir, Alamgir. *This Was Radio Bangladesh, 1971.* Dhaka: Bangla Academy, 1984.

Kibriya, Golam. *The Press in Bangladesh and Issues of Mass Media.* Dhaka: Sunday Publications, 1985.

Mamoon, Muntassir, ed. *Media and the Liberation War of Bangladesh*, vol. 2, *Selections from the Frontier.* Dhaka: Centre for Bangladesh Studies, 2002.

Rahman, Farhana Haque. *Stalking Serendipity and Other Pasquinades*. Dhaka: University Press, 1990.

Rahman, M. Golam. *Communications Issues in Bangladesh*. New Delhi: Har-Anand, 1998.

ECONOMICS

Agriculture

Abul Kassem, A. B. M. *Jute and Its Diversification*. Ashar Kota, Comilla District: Hosene Ara Kassem, 1992.

Ahmad, Alia. *Agricultural Stagnation under Population Pressure: The Case of Bangladesh*. New Delhi: Vikas, 1984.

Ahmed, Jasimuddin. *Agriculture Development Strategies, Bangladesh: A Comparative Analysis of Effects on Production and Distribution*. Gutting: Edition Herodot, 1984.

Ahmed, Residing. *Retrospects and Prospects of the Rice Economy in Bangladesh*. Dhaka: University Press, 2001.

Alamgir, Mohiuddin. *Famine in South Asia: Political Economy of Mass Starvation*. Cambridge, Mass.: Oelgeschleger, Gunn and Hain, 1980.

Alauddin, Mohammad, and T. A. Tisdell. *The "Green Revolution" and Economic Development: The Process and Its Impact on Bangladesh*. New York: St. Martin's Press, 1991.

Ali, Altaf. *Bangladesh Agriculture: Its Potential and Development*. Tokyo: Association for International Cooperation of Agriculture and Forestry, 1984.

Ali, M. Yousouf. *Fish, Water and People: Reflections on Inland Openwater Fisheries Resources in Bangladesh*. Dhaka: University Press, 1997.

Alim, Abdul. *A Handbook of Bangladesh Jute*. Dacca: Effat Begum, 1978.

Ashrafi, Siddiqur Rahman, ed. *Guide to Bangladesh Agriculture*. Dhaka: Banglar Mukh Publications, 1982.

Banic, Arindam, ed. *New Technology and Land Elevations: Small Farms in Bangladesh*. Dhaka: University Press, 1998.

Boyce, James K. *Agrarian Impasse in Bengal: Institutional Constraints to Technological Change*. New York: Oxford University Press, 1987.

Brammer, Hugh. *Agricultural Development Possibilities in Bangladesh*. Dhaka: University Press, 1997.

——. *Agriculture Disaster Management in Bangladesh*. Dhaka: University Press, 1999.

——. *Agroecological Aspects of Agricultural Research in Bangladesh*. Dhaka: University Press, 2001.

Faruqee, Rashid, ed. *Bangladesh Agriculture in the 21st Century*. Dhaka: University Press, 1998.

Ghosh, Tushar Kanti. *The Bengal Tragedy*. Lahore: Hero Publications, 1944.

Greeley, Martin. *Postharvest Losses, Technology, and Employment: The Case of Rice in Bangladesh*. Boulder, Colo.: Westview Press, 1987.

Hossain, Hameeda, ed. *From Crisis to Development: Coping with Disasters in Bangladesh*. Dhaka: University Press, 1992.

Hossain, Mahabub. *Nature and Impact of the Green Revolution in Bangladesh*. Washington, D.C.: International Food Policy Research Institute, 1988.

Hossain, Mosharaff. *Agriculture in Bangladesh: Performance, Problems, and Prospects*. Dhaka: University Press, 1991.

Howlader, Sushil Ranjan. *Agricultural Involution, Rural Differentiation and Economic Impasse*. New Delhi: Har-Anand, 1996.

———. *Bangladesh: Agricultural Involution, Rural Differentiation and Economic Impasse*. New Delhi: Har-Anand, 1997.

Huq, Saleemul, A. Atiq Rahman, and Gordon R. Conway. *Environmental Aspects of Agricultural Development in Bangladesh*. Dhaka: University Press, 1990.

Huque, Azizul, Sir. *The Man behind the Plow*. Dacca: Bangladesh Books International, 1980.

Hussain, Mohammad Sultan. *Soil Classification with Special Reference to the Soils of Bangladesh*. Dhaka: University of Dhaka, 1992.

Irfanullah, Haseeb Md., and Rashiduzzaman Ahmed, eds. *Promoting Eco-Friendly Agricultural Practices in the Chanda Beel Area*. Dhaka: IUCN World Conservation Union, 2005.

Jannuzi, F. Thomasson, and James T. Peach. *The Agrarian Structure of Bangladesh: An Impediment to Development*. Boulder, Colo.: Westview Press, 1980.

Khan, Shakeeb Adnan. *The State and Village Society: The Political Economy of Agricultural Development in Bangladesh*. Dhaka: University Press, 1989.

Masum, Muhammad. *Unemployment and Underemployment in Agriculture: A Case Study of Bangladesh*. Delhi: B. R. Publishing Corp., 1982.

Negi, Sharad Singh. *Forests and Forestry in SAARC Countries*. Delhi: Periodical Experts Book Agency, 1992.

Nuruzzaman, A. K. M. *Aquaculture in Bangladesh: Challenges and Opportunity*. Dhaka: Bangladesh Agricultural Research Council, 1991.

Parikh, Ashok K. *The Economics of Fertilizer Use in Developing Countries: A Case Study of Bangladesh*. Aldershot, UK: Avebury Gower, 1990.

Rahman, A. Atiq, et al., eds. *Shrimp Farming and Industry: Sustainability, Trade and Livelihoods*. Dhaka: University Press Limited, 2006.

Rahman, Atiur. *Peasants and Classes: A Study in Differentiation in Bangladesh.* Dhaka: University Press, 1986.

Rogaly, Ben, Barbara Hariss-White, and Sugata Bose: *Sonar Bangla?* New Delhi: Sage, 1999.

Saha, Bimal Kumar, ed. *Agricultural Structure and Productivity in Bangladesh and West Bengal: A Study in Comparative Perspective.* Dhaka: University Press, 1999.

Sarkar, Md. Ruhul Amin. *Rural Financing and Agricultural Credit in Bangldesh: Future Development Strategies for Formal Sector Banks.* Dhaka: University Press Limited, 2006.

Shahabuddin, Quazi. *Peasant Behaviour under Uncertainty: Decision-Making among Low-Income Farmers in Bangladesh.* Dhaka: Q. Shahabuddin, 1989.

Shibli, M. Abdullah. *Investment Opportunities, Household Savings, and Rates of Return on Investment: A Case Study of the Green Revolution in Bangladesh.* Lanham, Md.: University Press of America, 1991.

Sikdar, Mohammad Firoze Shah. *Jute Cultivation in India and Bangladesh: A Comparative Study.* New Delhi: Mittal Publications, 1990.

Wennergren, E. Boyd. *Agricultural Development in Bangladesh.* Boulder, Colo.: Westview Press, 1984.

Irrigation

Howes, Michael. *Whose Water?* Dhaka: Bangladesh Institute of Development Studies, 1985.

Huq, Saleemul, Gordon R. Conway, and A. Atiq Rahman. *Environmental Aspects of the Surface Water System in Bangladesh.* Dhaka: University Press, 1990.

Ganges Flood Plain

Adnan, Shapan. *Floods, People, and the Environment: Institutional Aspects of Flood Protection Programmes in Bangladesh, 1990.* Dhaka: Research and Advisory Services, 1990.

Ahmad, Qazi Kholiquzzaman. *Ganges-Brahmaputra-Megna Region: A Framework for Sustainable Development.* Dhaka: University Press, 2001.

Berkoff, D. J. W. *Irrigation Management in the Indo-Gangetic Plain.* Washington, D.C.: World Bank, 1990.

Biswas, M. R., and M. A. S. Mandal, eds. *Irrigation Management for Crop Diversification in Bangladesh.* Dhaka: University Press, 1993.

Dorosh, Paul, Carlo del Ninno, and Quazi Shahabuddin, eds. *The 1998 Floods and Beyond: Towards Comprehensive Food Security in Bangladesh*. Dhaka: University Press Limited, 2004.

Farouk, A. *Irrigation in a Monsoon Land: Economics of Farming in the Ganges-Kobadak*. Dacca: Bureau of Economic Research, Dacca University, 1968.

Islam, Naibul K. M. *Impacts of Flood in Urban Bangladesh: Micro and Macro Level Analysis*. Dhaka: A. H. Development Pub., 2006.

Miah, M. Maniruzzaman. *Flood in Bangladesh: A Hydromorphological Study of the 1987 Flood*. Dhaka: Academic Publishers, 1988.

Siddiqui, Kamal Uddin, and A. N. H. Akhtar Hossain, eds. *Options for Flood Risk and Damage Reduction in Bangladesh*. Dhaka: University Press Limited, 2006.

Upreti, B. C. *Politics of the Himalayan Waters: An Analysis of the Water Issues of Nepal, India and Bangladesh*. Jaipur, India: Nirala, 1993.

Ganges Water Dispute

Abbas, B. M. *The Ganges Water Dispute*. New Delhi: Vikas, 1982.

Basic Documents on Farakka Conspiracy from 1951 to 1976. Dacca: Khoshroz Kitab Mahal, 1976.

Crow, Benjamin, and Alan Lindquist. *Sharing the Ganges: The Politics and Technology of River Development*. Thousand Oaks, Calif.: Sage, 1994.

The Ganges-Brahmaputra Basin: Water Resource Cooperation between Nepal, India, and Bangladesh. Austin, Tex.: Lyndon B. Johnson School of Public Affairs, 1992.

Islam, M. Rafiqul. *The Ganges Water Dispute: International Legal Aspects*. Dhaka: University Press, 1987.

Khurshida Begum. *Tension over the Farakka Barrage: A Techno-Political Tangle in South Asia*. Calcutta: K.P. Bagchi, 1988.

Nazem, Nurul Islam. *Indo-Bangladesh Common Rivers and Water Diplomacy*. Dhaka: Bangladesh Institute of International and Strategic Studies, 1986.

Verghese, B. G. *Waters of Hope: Integrated Water Resource Development and Regional Cooperation within the Himalayan-Ganga-Brahmaputra-Barak Basin*. New Delhi: Oxford University Press, 1990.

Water Resource Challenges in the Ganges-Brahmaputra Basin. Austin: University of Texas Press, 1993.

White Paper on the Ganges Water Dispute. Dacca: Government of the People's Republic of Bangladesh, 1976.

Bibliography

Bangladesh Agricultural Bibliography, 1983–1984. Dhaka: Bangladesh Agricultural Research Council, 1985.

Economic Conditions

Abu, Abdullah, ed. *Modernisation at Bay: Structure and Change in Bangladesh*. Dhaka: University Press, 1991.

Ahmed, A. K. N. *Of Deregulation and Central Bank Autonomy: Essays on Economic Issues in Bangladesh*. Dhaka: University Press, 1997.

Ahmed, Raisuddin. *Retrospects and Prospects of the Rice Economy of Bangladesh*. Dhaka: University Press, 2001.

Alamgir, Mohiuddin. *Bangladesh: A Case of below Poverty Level Equilibrium Trap*. Dacca: Bangladesh Institute of Development Studies, 1978.

Bangladesh Development Debates: Perspectives from Policy Dialogues, vol. 1, *Macroeconomic Issues Governance and Regional Perspectives*. Dhaka: Pathak Shamabesh Book, 2001.

Barkat, Abul, et al. *Development as Conscientization: The Case of Nijera Kori in Bangladesh*. Dhaka: Pathak Shamabesh Book, 2008.

Barkat, Abul, Prosanta K. Roy, and Md. Shahnewaz Khan. *Charland in Bangladesh: Political Economy of Ignored Resource*. Dhaka: Pathak Shamabesh Book, 2007.

Crewe, Emma, and Elizabeth Harrison. *Whose Development? An Ethnography of Aid*. London: Zed, 1998.

End of MFA Quotas: Key Issues and Strategic Options for Bangladesh Readymade Garment Industry. Bangladesh Development Series, paper no. 2. Dhaka: World Bank Office Dhaka, 2005.

Farouk, A. *Changes in the Economy of Bangladesh*. Dacca: University Press, 1982.

Garry, Marion L. *A People's History of Development: 25 Years in Northern Bangladesh*. Dhaka: University Press, 1999.

Habibullah, M. *Growth Problems of a Developing Economy*. Dhaka: Ruprekha Publishers, 1990.

Herbon, Dietmar. *The System of Exchange and Distribution in a Village in Bangladesh*. Groninghem, Netherlands: Herodot, 1985.

Huda, K. M. Nurul. *Municipal Solid Waste Management: Bangladesh Perspective*. Dhaka: Academic Press and Publishers Library, 2008.

Imam, Badrul. *Energy Resources of Bangladesh*. Dhaka: University Grants Commission of Bangladesh, 2005.

Islam, M. Faizul, and Syed Saad Andaleeb, eds. *Development Issues of Bangladesh–III: Human Development and Quality of Life*. Dhaka: University Press Limited, 2007.

Jaccard, Mark, Mujibur Rahman Khan, and John Richards. *Natural Gas Options for Bangladesh: Spring 2001*. Dhaka: IUBAT—International University of Business Agriculture and Technology, 2001.

Jansen, Eirik G. *Rural Bangladesh: Competition for Scarce Resources*. Oslo: Norwegian University Press, 1986.

Khan, Azizur Rahman. *The Economy of Bangladesh*. New York: St. Martin's Press, 1972.

Maloney, Clarence. *Behavior and Poverty in Bangladesh*. Dhaka: University Press, 1988.

Momin, M. A. *Rural Poverty and Agrarian Structure in Bangladesh*. New Delhi: Vikas, 1992.

Osmani, Siddiqur Rahman. *Economic Inequality and Group Welfare: A Theory of Comparison with Application to Bangladesh*. New York: Oxford University Press, 1982.

Quibria, M. A. *The Bangladesh Economy in Transition*. London: Oxford University Press, 1997.

Rahim, A. M. A., ed. *Bangladesh Economy: Problems and Issues*. Dacca: University Press, 1977.

———, ed. *Bangladesh Economy: Problems and Policies*. Dacca: Barnamala Press, 1980.

Rahman, Hossain Zillur, and Mahbub Hassan, eds. *Rethinking Rural Poverty: Bangladesh as a Case Study*. Thousand Oaks, Calif.: Sage, 1994.

Raihan, Selim. *Dynamics of Trade Liberalization in Bangladesh: Analyses of Policies and Practices*. Dhaka: Pathak Shamabesh, 2007.

Rao, V. K. R. V., ed. *Bangla Desh Economy: Problems and Prospects*. Delhi: Vikas, 1972.

Rashid, Haroun-er. *Economic Geography of Bangladesh*. Reprint. Dhaka: University Press, 2005.

Schendel, Willem van. *Peasant Mobility: The Odds of Life in Rural Bangladesh*. Atlantic Highlands, N.J.: Humanities Press, 1981.

Seth, Krishnan Lal. *Economic Prospects of Bangla Desh*. New Delhi: Trimurti Publications, 1972.

Sobhan, Rahman. *The Decade of Stagnation: The State of the Bangladesh Economy in the 1980s*. Dhaka: University Press, 1991.

Stepanek, Joseph F. *Bangladesh: Equitable Growth?* New York: Pergamon Press, 1979.

Targeting Resources for the Poor in Bangladesh. Bangladesh Development Series, paper no. 5. Dhaka: World Bank Office Dhaka, 2005.

Tsai, Chu-fa, and M. Youssouf Ali, eds. *Openwater Fisheries of Bangladesh.* Dhaka: University Press, 1997.

Vivekananda, Franklin, ed. *Bangladesh Economy: Some Selected Issues.* Stockholm: Bethany Books, 1986.

Wahid, Abu N. M., and Charles E. Weis, eds. *The Economy of Bangladesh: Problems and Prospects.* Westport, Conn.: Praeger, 1996.

Economic History

Anisuzzaman. *Factory Correspondence and Other Bengali Documents in the India Office Library and Records: Supplementary to J. F. Blumhardt's Catalogue of the Bengali and Assamese MSS in the Library of the India Office (1924).* London: India Office Library and Records, 1981.

Barui, Balai. *The Salt Industry of Bengal, 1757–1800: A Study in the Interaction of British Monopoly Control and Indigenous Enterprise.* Calcutta: K. P. Bagchi, 1985.

Bhattacharya, Sukumar. *The East India Company and the Economy of Bengal from 1704 to 1740.* London: Luzac, 1954.

Chakrabarty, Dipesh. *Rethinking Working-Class History: Bengal, 1890–1940.* Princeton, N.J.: Princeton University Press, 1989.

Chowdhury, Benoy. *Growth of Commercial Agriculture in Bengal, 1757–1900.* Calcutta: R. K. Maitra, 1964.

Chowdhury, Mahfuz R. *Economic Exploitation of Bangladesh.* Dhaka: Shraban Prokashoni, 2004.

Gain, Philip. *The Last Forests of Bangladesh.* Dhaka: Society for Environment and Human Development, 2002. Reprint.

Garry, Marion L. *A People's History of Development: 25 Years in Northern Bangladesh.* Dhaka: University Press, 1999.

Ghosal, Hari Ranjan. *Economic Transition in the Bengal Presidency, 1793–1833.* Calcutta: Firma KLM, 1966.

Guha, Ranajit. *A Rule of Property for Bengal: An Essay on the Idea of Permanent Settlement.* Paris: Mouton, 1963.

Hossain, Hameeda. *The Company Weavers of Bengal: The East India Company and the Organization of Textile Production in Bengal, 1750–1813.* New York: Oxford University Press, 1988.

Huq, Mazharul. *The East India Company's Land Policy and Commerce in Bengal, 1698–1784.* Dacca: Asiatic Society of Pakistan, 1964.

Islam, M. Mufakharul. *Bengal Agriculture, 1920–1946: A Quantitative Study.* New York: Cambridge University Press, 1978.

Mitra, Debendra Bijoy. *The Cotton Weavers of Bengal, 1757–1833.* Calcutta: Firma KLM, 1978.

———. *Monetary System in the Bengal Presidency, 1757–1835*. Calcutta: K. P. Bagchi, 1991.

Mukerji, Karuna Moy. *The Problem of Land Transfer: A Study of Land Alienation in Bengal*. Shantiniketan, West Bengal: Bidyut Ranjan Basu, 1957.

Mukherjee, Radhakamal. *The Changing Face of Bengal: A Study in Riverine Economy*. Calcutta: University of Calcutta, 1938.

Nakazaro, Nariaki. *Agrarian System of Eastern Bengal*. Calcutta: Bagchi, 1994.

Ray, Ratnalekha. *Change in Bengal Agrarian Society, c. 1760–1850*. New Delhi: Manohar, 1979.

Schendel, Willem van, and Aminul Haque Faraizi. *Rural Labourers in Bengal, 1880 to 1980*. Rotterdam: Comparative Asian Studies Program, Erasmus University, 1984.

Sen, Sunil Kumar. *Agrarian Struggle in Bengal, 1946–47*. New Delhi: People's Publishing House, 1972.

Sinha, Jogis Chandra. *Economic Annals of Bengal*. London: Macmillan, 1927.

Sinha, Narendra Krishna. *Economic History of Bengal*, 3 vols. Calcutta: Firma KLM, 1956–70.

Sobhan, Rehman, ed. *Privatisation in Bangladesh: An Agenda in Search of a Policy*. Dhaka: University Press, 2005.

Tripathi, Amales. *Trade and Finance in the Bengal Presidency, 1793–1833*. Calcutta: Oxford University Press, 1979.

Economic Planning

Afsar, Rita. *Swanirvar as a Strategy for Endogenous Rural Development*. Dhaka: Bangladesh Institute for Development Studies, 1988.

Ahmad, Qazi Kholiquzzaman, ed. *Ganges-Brahmaputra-Meghna Region: A Framework for Sustainable Development*. Dhaka: University Press, 2001.

Ahmed, Salahuddin, ed. *Dimensions of Development in Islam*. Dhaka: Islamic Economics Research Bureau, 1991.

———. *Dualistic Economic Development in Bangladesh*. Dhaka: Parveen Ahmed, 1990.

Alamgir, Mohiuddin Khan. *Development Strategy for Bangladesh*. Dacca: Centre for Social Studies, 1980.

Ali, Ashraf, M. Faizul Islam, and Ruhul Quddus. *Development Issues of Bangladesh*. Dhaka: University Press, 1996.

Ejazul Huq, K. M. *Planning for Core Needs in Bangladesh: Basic Needs Approach*. Dhaka: University Press, 1984.

Islam, Nazrul, and Muhammad Z. Mamun. *Entrepreneurship Development*. Dhaka: University Press, 2001.

Islam, Nurul. *Development Planning in Bangladesh: A Study in Political Economy*. New York: St. Martin's Press, 1977.

———. *Development Strategy of Bangladesh*. New York: Pergamon Press, 1978.

Khan, Azizur Rahman, and Mahabub Hossain. *The Strategy of Development in Bangladesh*. New York: St. Martin's Press, 1990.

Lovell, Catherine H. *Breaking the Cycle of Poverty: The BRAC Strategy*. West Hartford, Conn.: Kumarian Press, 1992.

Norbye, Ole David Koht, ed. *Bangladesh Faces the Future*. Dhaka: University Press, 1990.

Rahman, Golam. *Town Planning and the Political Culture of Planning in Bangladesh*. Dhaka: AH Development Publishing House, 2008.

Rahman, Sultan Hafeez. *Macroeconomic Performance, Stabilization, and Adjustment: The Experience of Bangladesh in the 1980s*. New Delhi: Indus Publishing, 1992.

Report of the Task Forces on Bangladesh Development Strategies for the 1990s. Dhaka: University Press, 1991.

Robinson, E. A. G, and Keith Griffin, eds. *The Economic Development of Bangladesh within a Socialist Framework*. London: Macmillan, 1974.

Samad, Abdus. *Bangladesh, Facing the Future*. Dhaka: Samad, 1983.

Sharif, M. Raihan. *Planning with Social Justice: The Bangladesh Case*. Dacca: Bangladesh Books International, 1979.

Sobhan, Rahman. *Changes and Challenges: A Review of Bangladesh's Development, 2000*. Dhaka: University Press, 2001.

———. *Rethinking the Role of the State in Development: Asian Perspectives*. Dhaka: University Press, 1993.

Bibliography

Sharma, Prakash C. *Rural and Economic Development Planning in Bangladesh (Formerly East Pakistan), 1950–1972: A Selected Research Bibliography*. Monticello, Ill.: Council of Planning Librarians, 1975.

Talukder, Alauddin. *Ten Years of BDS Articles and BIDS Publications: A Cumulative Index; Supplement, 1971–1980*. Dacca: Bangladesh Institute of Development Studies, 1980.

Economic Theory

Ahmad, Shamsuddin. *Dual Gap Analysis for Bangladesh*. Dhaka: Bureau of Economic Research, University of Dhaka, 1992.

Faaland, Just, and J. R. Parkinson. *Bangladesh: The Test Case of Development.* Boulder, Colo.: Westview Press, 1976.

Haque, Wahidul. *An Optional Macro-Economic Planning Model for the Bangladesh Economy: Strategies for Self-Reliant Development.* Dhaka: Bangladesh Institute of Development Studies, 1988.

Thomas, Winburn Townshed. *Bangladesh: Views on Development Planning.* Dhaka: Maleka Rahman, 1983.

Finance

The Grameen Reader: Training Materials for the International Replication of the Grameen Bank Financial System for Reduction of Rural Poverty. Dhaka: Grameen Bank, 1992.

Hassan, Kabir. *Banking and Finance in Bangladesh.* Dhaka: Academic Publishers, 1995.

Hossain, Akhtar. *Exchange Rates, Capital Flows and International Trade: The Case of Bangladesh.* Dhaka: University Press, 2000.

Hossain, Mahabub. *Credit for the Rural Poor: The Experience of the Grameen Bank in Bangladesh.* Dhaka: Bangladesh Institute of Development Economics, 1984.

Hussain, Motahar. *The System of Government Budgeting in Bangladesh.* 5th ed. Dhaka: AH Development, 2008.

Patwary, S. U. *Financial Administration in Bangladesh.* Dhaka: Book Syndicate, 1983.

Ray, Jayanta Kumar. *To Chase a Miracle: A Study of the Grameen Bank of Bangladesh.* Dhaka: University Press, 1987.

Shah Alam, Muhammad, and Anil Bhuimali. *Consumer Credit Programme of Commercial Banks in Bangladesh.* New Delhi: Abhijeet Pub., 2007.

Sharif, Iffath. *Challenges for Second Generation Microfinance: Regulation, Supervision and Resource Mobilization.* Dhaka: University Press, 2001.

Taheruddin, M. *Essays on Banking and Development.* Dhaka: Academic Publishers, 1986.

Wahid, Abu N. M., ed. *The Grameen Bank: Poverty Relief in Bangladesh.* Boulder, Colo.: Westview Press, 1993.

Watanabe, Tatsuya. *The Ponds and the Poor: The Story of the Grameen Bank's Initiative.* Dhaka: Grameen Bank, 1993.

Wood, Geogrey, and Iffath A. Sharif, eds. *Who Needs Credit? Poverty and Finance in Bangladesh.* Dhaka: University Press, 1997.

Wright, Graham A. N. *Microfinance Systems: Designing Quality Financial Services for the Poor.* Dhaka: University Press, 2001.

Yunus, Muhammad. *Banker to the Poor: The Autobiography of Muhammad Yunus, Founder of Grameen Bank.* Karachi: Oxford University Press, 2001.

Industry

Ahmad, Muzaffer. *State and Development: Essays on Public Enterprise.* Dhaka: University Press, 1987.

Ahmed, Momtaz Uddin. *The Financing of Small-Scale Industries: A Study of Bangladesh and Japan.* Dhaka: University of Dhaka, 1987.

Ahmed, Rakibuddin. *The Progress of the Jute Industry and Trade, 1855–1966.* Dacca: Pakistan Central Jute Committee, 1966.

Ali, Muhammad Raushan. *Achievement Motivation and Industrial Productivity in Bangladesh.* Dacca: University of Dacca, 1979.

DeLucia, Russell J. *Energy Planning for Developing Countries: A Study of Bangladesh.* Baltimore, Md.: Johns Hopkins University Press, 1982.

Humphrey, Clare E. *Privatization in Bangladesh: Economic Transition in a Poor Country.* Dhaka: University Press, 1992.

Huq, M. Mozammel, and Jim Love, eds. *Strategies for Industrialisation: The Case of Bangladesh.* Dhaka: University Press, 2001.

Islam, Sadequl. *The Textile and Clothing Industry of Bangladesh in a Changing World.* Dhaka: University Press, 2001.

Latif, Muhammad Abdul. *Handloom Industry of Bangladesh, 1947–90.* Dhaka: University Press, 1997.

Quddus, Munir. *Entrepreneurs and Economic Development: The Remarkable Story of Garment Exports from Bangladesh.* Dhaka: University Press, 2000.

Rahman, Atiur, ed. *The Budget-Making Process.* Dhaka: University Press, 2002.

Razzaque, Abdur, and Selim Raihan, eds. *Trade and Industrial Policy Environment in Bangladesh with Special Reference to Some Non-traditional Export Sectors.* Dhaka: Pathak Shamabesh, 2007.

Reza, Sadrel, and Mizanur Rahman Shelley. *Privatizing Industrial Regulatory Functions in Bangladesh.* Dhaka: University Press, 1994.

Shamsul Islam. *Public Corporations in Bangladesh.* Dacca: Local Government Institute, 1975.

Siddiqi, Hafiz G. A. *Industrial Policies and Export Incentives.* Dhaka: Dana Prokashan, 1984.

Sobhan, Rahman, and Muzaffar Ahmad. *Public Enterprise in an Intermediate Regime: A Study of the Political Economy of Bangladesh.* Dacca: Bangladesh Institute of Development Studies, 1980.

International Economics

Ahmed, Nasiruddin. *Trade Liberalization in Bangladesh: An Investigation into Trends.* Dhaka: University Press, 2001.

Chadha, I. S. *Managing Projects in Bangladesh: A Scenario Analysis of Institutional Environment for Development Projects.* Dhaka: University Press, 1989.

Choudhury, Khashruzzaman. *Foreign Aid, Government Sector, and Bangladesh.* Dhaka: National Institute of Local Government, 1990.

Das, Gurudas, and C. Joshua Thomas, eds. *Indo-Bangladesh Border Trade: Benefiting From Neighbourhood.* New Delhi: Akansha Publishing House, 2008.

Eusufzai, Zaki. *Liberalization in the Shadow of a Large Neighbour: A Case of Bangladesh-India Economic Relations.* Dhaka: University Press, 2000.

Faaland, Just. *Aid and Influence: The Case of Bangladesh.* New York: St. Martin's Press, 1981.

Huq, Muhammad Shamsul, and Chowdhury Rafiqul Abrar. *Aid, Development and Diplomacy: Need for an Aid Policy.* Dhaka: University Press, 1999.

Raihan, Selim, and Abdur Razzaque, eds. *WTO and Regional Trade Negotiation Outcomes: Quantitative Assessments of Potential Implications on Bangladesh.* Dhaka: Pathak Shamabesh, 2007.

Reza, Sadrel. *The Export Trade of Bangladesh, 1950–1978.* Dacca: University of Dacca, 1981.

———. *Private Foreign Investment in Bangladesh.* Dhaka: University Press, 1987.

———. *Transnational Corporations in Bangladesh: Still at Bay?* Dhaka: University Press, 1995.

Sobhan, Rahman. *The Crisis of External Dependence: The Political Economy of Foreign Aid to Bangladesh.* London: Zed Press, 1982.

———, ed. *From Aid Dependence to Self Reliance: Development Options for Bangladesh.* Dhaka: University Press, 1990.

Labor

Ahmad, Alia. *Child Labour in Bangladesh.* Dhaka: Bangladesh Institute of Development Studies, 1991.

Gardner, Katy. *Global Migrants, Local Lives: Travel and Transformation in Rural Bangladesh.* New York: Oxford University Press, 1995.

Hossain, Hameeda. *No Better Option? Industrial Women Workers in Bangladesh.* Dhaka: University Press, 1990.

Jensen, Kurt Morck. *Non-agricultural Occupations in a Peasant Society: Weavers and Fishermen in Noakhali, Bangladesh*. Copenhagen: Centre for Development Research, 1987.

Mannan, M. A. *Workers' Participation in Managerial Decision-Making: A Study in a Developing Country*. Delhi: Daya Publishing House, 1987.

Land Development and Settlement

Alamgir, Mohiuddin Khan, ed. *Land Reform in Bangladesh*. Dacca: Centre for Social Studies, 1981.

Brammer, Hugh. *Land Use and Land Use Planning in Bangladesh*. Dhaka: University Press, 2002.

Choudhury, A. K. M. Kamaluddin. *Land Use Planning in Bangladesh*. Reprint. Dhaka: AH Development Publishing House, 2008.

Hussain, Tafazzal. *Land Rights in Bangladesh: Problems of Management*. Dhaka: University Press, 1995.

Roy, Prosanta K. *Bangladesh Dark Facets of Land Rights and Management with Directions to Agrarian Reform*. Dhaka: AH Development Publishing House, 2008.

Siddiqui, Kamal, ed. *Land Reforms and Land Management in Bangladesh and West Bengal: A Comparative Study*. Dhaka: University Press, 1988.

Wilde, Keon de, ed. *Out of the Periphery: Development of Coastal Chars in Southeastern Bangladesh*. Dhaka: University Press Limited, 2000.

Rural Development

Adnan, Shapan. *Annotation of Village Studies in Bangladesh and West Bengal: A Review of Socio-Economic Trends over 1942–88*. Comilla: Bangladesh Academy for Rural Development, 1990.

Ahmad, Nasiruddin. *Landlessness in Bangladesh*. Dhaka: University Press, 1988.

Ahmad, Nasreen. *Slip Trip Tumble: Determining Landlessness in Rural Bangladesh*. Dhaka: University Press, 2005.

Ahmad, Razia. *Financing the Rural Poor: Obstacles and Realities*. Dhaka: University Press, 1983.

Alim, Abdul. *Agriculture Credit Financing in Bangladesh*. Dhaka: Bangladesh Books International, 1981.

———. *Land Reforms in Bangladesh: Social Changes, Agricultural Development, and Eradication of Poverty*. Dhaka: Samina, 1979.

Ameer, K. M. *Rain and River*. Dhaka: Nabeela Books, 1991.

Andaleeb, Syed Saad, *The Bangladesh Economy: Diagnoses and Prescriptions: Selections from the Journal of Bangladesh Studies*. Dhaka: University Press Limited, 2008.

Anisuzzaman, M., ed. *Comilla Models of Rural Development: A Quarter Century of Experience*. Comilla: Bangladesh Academy for Rural Development, 1986.

Anisuzzaman, M., and Kirsten Westergaard, eds. *Growth and Development in Rural Bangladesh: A Critical Review*. Dhaka: University Press, 1993.

Bangladesh Development Series. *Bangladesh: A Proposed Rural Development Strategy—A World Bank Study*. Dhaka: University Press, 2000.

Barkat-e-Khuda. *Rural Development and Change: A Micro Study*. Dhaka: University Press, 1988.

Blair, Harry W. *Can Rural Development Be Financed from Below?* Dhaka: University Press, 1989.

Chashi, Mahbub Alam. *In Quest of Shawnirvar*. Dhaka: Shawnirvar Workers Trust, 1984.

Chowdhury, Anwarullah. *Agrarian Social Relations and Rural Development in Bangladesh*. Totowa, N.J.: Allenheld, Osman, 1982.

Chowdhury, Pijush Kumar, M. Ameerul Huq, and Syed Aminur Rahman. *Cooperatives as Institutions for the Development of the Rural Poor*. Comilla: Bangladesh Academy for Rural Development, 1987.

Datta, Rajat. *Society, Economy and the Market: Commercialization in Rural Bangladesh, c. 1760–1800*. Delhi: Manohar, 2000.

Herbon, Dietmar. *Agrarian Reproduction in Bangladesh: Studies of Attempts to Ensure a Livelihood in a Rural Region*. Aachen: Alano/Herodot, 1992.

Hossain, Zillur Rahman, and Mahabub Hossain, eds. *Rethinking Rural Poverty*. Thousand Oaks, Calif.: Sage, 1994.

Hye, Hasnat Abdul. *Below the Line: Rural Poverty in Bangladesh*. Dhaka: University Press, 1996.

Islam, M. Rafiqul. *Human Resource Development in Rural Development in Bangladesh*. Dhaka: National Institute of Local Government, 1990.

Khan, Akhter Hameed. *Bengal Reminiscences*. Comilla: Bangladesh Academy for Rural Development, 1981.

———. *The Works of Akhter Hameed Khan*. Comilla: Bangladesh Academy for Rural Development, 1983.

Khan, Azizur Rahman, and Rahman Sobhan. *Trade, Planning, and Rural Development: Essays in Honor of Nurul Islam*. New York: St. Martin's Press, 1990.

Khan, Mohammad Mohabbat, and Habib Mohammad Zafrullah, eds. *Rural Development in Bangladesh: Trends and Issues*. Dacca: Centre for Administrative Studies, 1981.

Mahbub, Ullah. *Bangladesh Economy: Turns of the Decades.* Dhaka: Adorn Publishers, 2003.

——. *Land Livelihood and Change in Rural Bangladesh.* Dhaka: University Press, 1996.

Maloney, Clarence. *Rural Savings and Credit in Bangladesh.* Dhaka: University Press, 1988.

Mozammel Hossain, A. M. *Rural Development at the Cross Roads in Bangladesh.* Dhaka: Prottasha Prokashon, 1993.

Rafi, Mohammad. *Counting the Hills: Assessing Development in the Chittagong Hill Tracts.* Dhaka: University Press, 2001.

Rahman, Motiur. *Poverty Issues in Rural Bangladesh.* Dhaka: University Press, 1994.

Ray, Jayanta Kumar. *Organizing Villagers for Self-Reliance: A Study of Deedar in Bangladesh.* Comilla: Bangladesh Academy for Rural Development, 1983.

——. *Organizing Villagers for Self-Reliance: A Study of Gonoshasthya Kendra in Bangladesh.* Calcutta: Orient Longmans, 1986.

Sabiha Sultana. *Co-operative Farming in Bangladesh.* Comilla: Bangladesh Academy for Rural Development, 1972.

——. *Rural Settlements in Bangladesh: Spatial Pattern and Development.* Dhaka: Graphosman, 1993.

Sobhan, Rahman, ed. *Public Allocative Strategies, Rural Development, and Poverty Alleviation: A Global Perspective.* Dhaka: University Press, 1991.

Stevens, Robert D., Hamza Alavi, and Peter J. Bertocci, eds. *Rural Development in Bangladesh and Pakistan.* Honolulu: University Press of Hawaii, 1976.

Westergaard, Kirsten. *State and Rural Society in Bangladesh: A Study in Relationship.* London: Curzon Press, 1985.

Yousoof, M. A. *Agricultural Credit and Rural Financing in Bangladesh: Problems and Prospects.* Dhaka: Manju and Khosru, 1983.

Bibliography

Akhter, Nilufar. *Rural Development of Bangladesh: A Select Bibliography.* Dacca: Bangladesh Institute of Development Studies, 1981.

Ali, A. A. M. Shaukat, and Mujibur Rahman Khan, eds. *A Comprehensive Bibliography on Agriculture and Rural Development.* Dhaka: University Press, 1994.

Cain, Mead. *Landlessness in India and Bangladesh: A Critical Review of Data Sources.* New York: Population Council, 1981.

Hye, Hasnat Abdul. *Village Studies in Bangladesh*. Comilla: Bangladesh Academy for Rural Development, 1985.

Schendel, Willem van. *Bangladesh: A Bibliography with Special Reference to the Peasantry*. Amsterdam: Antropologisch-Sociologisch Centrum, Universiteit Amsterdam, 1976.

Transportation

Jansen, Eirik G. *The Country Boats of Bangladesh: Social and Economic Development and Decision Making in Inland Water Transport*. Dhaka: University Press, 1989.

——. *Sailing against the Wind: Boats and Boatmen of Bangladesh*. Dhaka: University Press, 1982. Photographs by Trygve Bolstad.

Urban Development

Atiqullah, Mohammad. *Growth of Dacca City: Population and Area, 1608–1981*. Dacca: Social Science Research Project, Department of Statistics, University of Dacca, 1965.

Qadir, Sayeeda. *Bastees of Dacca: A Study of Squatter Settlements*. Dacca: Local Government Institute, 1975.

Siddiqui, Kamal. *Social Formation in Dhaka City: A Study in Third World Urban Sociology*. Dhaka: University Press, 1990.

Bibliography

Islam, Nazrul. *Bibliography on Bangladesh Urbanization*. Dacca: Centre for Urban Studies, 1982.

EDUCATION

Ahmad, Qazi Kholiquzzaman. *Financing Primary and Secondary Education in Bangladesh*. Bangladesh, Campaign for Popular Education, 2007.

Ahmed, Samir, et al. *The State of Secondary Education: Progress and Challenges*. Dhaka, Bangladesh: Campaign for Popular Education, 2006.

Alam, Mahmudul. *Bangladesh Education in Transition: Policy, Performance and Way Forward*. Dhaka: A. H. Development, 2008.

Ara, Shawkat. *Ideology and Student Activism*. Rajshahi: University of Rajshahi, 1988.

Ayyub Ali, A. K. M. *History of Traditional Islamic Education in Bangladesh, Down to A.D. 1980*. Dhaka: Islamic Foundation Bangladesh, 1983.

Azher, Sakina. *An Islamic Philosophy of Education and Its Role in Bangladesh Education*. Dhaka, Hakkani Pub., 2001.

Choudhury, Azharul Huq. *Private Universities Facing the Future*. Dhaka: Quest, 1990.

Chowdhury, A. Mustaque R., et al. *A Question of Quality: State of Primary Education in Bangladesh*. Dhaka: University Press Limited, 2001.

Chowdhury, A. Mustaque R., Rasheda K. Choudhury, and Samir R. Nath, eds. *Hope Not Complacency: State of Primary Education in Bangladesh*. Dhaka: University Press, 1999.

Duza, Asfia, et al., eds. *Education and Gender Equity*. Dhaka: Women for Women, 1992.

Eshan, Mohammad. *Higher Education Governance in Bangladesh: The Public Private Dilemma*. Dhaka: A. H. Development Pub., 2008.

Greaney, Vincent, Shahidur R. Khandker, and Mahmudul Alam. *Bangladesh: Assessing Basic Learning Skills*. Dhaka: University Press, 1998.

Gustavsson, Styrbjorn. *Primary Education in Bangladesh: For Whom?* Dhaka: University Press, 1990.

Huq, M. Shamsul, et al. *Higher Education and Employment in Bangladesh*. Dhaka: University Press, 1983.

Ibrahimy, Sekander Ali, ed. *Reports on Islamic Education and Madrasah Education in Bengal, 1861–1977*. Dhaka: Islamic Foundation Bangladesh, 1990.

Jalaluddin, A. K., and A. Mushtaque R. Chowdhury. *Getting Started: Universalising Quality Primary Education in Bangladesh*. Dhaka: University Press, 1997.

Nath, Samir Rajan, and Amina Mahbub. *Inside Schools*. Dhaka: Academic Press and Publishers, 2008.

Rahim, Muhammad Abdur. *The History of the University of Dacca*. Dacca: University of Dacca, 1981.

Sattar, Ellen. *Universal Primary Education in Bangladesh*. Dacca: University Press, 1982.

Shaidai, Shamsul Haque. *The Light of Other Days: A Teacher's Tale*. Dhaka: Pabna Samiti, 1988.

Siddique, Zillur Rahman. *Visions and Revisions: Higher Education in Bangladesh, 1947–1992*. Dhaka: University Press, 1997.

Sillitoe, Paul, ed. *Indigenous Knowledge Development in Bangladesh*. Dhaka: University Press, 2001.

GEOGRAPHY

Ahmad, Nafis. *A New Economic Geography of Bangladesh.* New Delhi: Vikas, 1976.

Ahmed, Noazesh. *Bangladesh.* Dacca: Bangladesh Books International, 1977.

Bhattacharyya, Amitabha. *Historical Geography of Ancient and Early Mediaeval Bengal.* Calcutta: Sanskrit Pustak Bandar, 1977.

Brammer, Hugh. *The Geography of the Soils of Bangladesh.* Dhaka: University Press, 1996.

Chapman, Graham P. *The Geopolitics of South Asia.* Aldershot, UK: Ashgate, 2000.

Chatterjee, Shiba Prasad. *Bengal in Maps.* Bombay: Orient Longmans, 1949.

Das, Amal Kumar, Sankarananda Mukerji, and Manas Kamal Chowdhuri, eds. *A Focus on Sundarban.* Calcutta: Editions India, 1981.

De, Rathindranath. *The Sundarbans.* New York: Oxford University Press, 1990.

Hossain, Anwar. *A Journey through Bangladesh.* Dhaka: Classic Books International, 1988.

Islam, M. Aminul, and M. Maniruzzaman Miah, eds. *Bangladesh in Maps.* Dacca: University of Dacca, 1981.

Khan, M. Salar. *Wetlands of Bangladesh.* Dhaka: Bangladesh Centre for Advanced Studies, 1994.

Mamun, Muhammad Z. *Densification: A Strategic Plan to Mitigate Riverbank Erosion in Bangladesh.* Dhaka: University Press, 1999.

Rafi, Mohammad. *Counting the Hills: Assessing Development in the Chittagong Hills Tracts.* Dhaka: University Press, 2001.

Rashid, Harouner. *Geography of Bangladesh.* Dhaka: University Press, 1991.

Schendel, Willem van, Wolfgang Mey, and Aditya Kumar Dewan. *The Chittagong Hill Tracts: Living in Borderland.* Dhaka: University Press, 2001.

Yeo, Dan. *Bangladesh: A Traveller's Guide.* Cambridge, Mass.: Bradt Enterprises, 1982.

Bibliography

Sukhwal, B. L. *A Systematic Geographic Bibliography on Bangla Desh.* Monticello, Ill.: Council of Planning Librarians, 1973.

HISTORY

General History

Ahmad, Kamruddin. *A Social History of Bengal.* Dhaka: Progoti Publishers, 1970.

Ahmed, A. F. Salahuddin. *History and Heritage: Reflections on Society Politics and Culture of South Asia.* Dhaka: University Press Limited, 2007.

Campbell, A. Claude. *Glimpses of Bengal: A Comprehensive Archaeological, Biographical and Pictorial History of Bengal, Behar and Orissa.* New Delhi: Sundeep Prakashan, 2003.

Dhaka Chamber of Commerce and Industry. *Commercial History of Dhaka.* Dhaka: Academic Press and Publishers Library, 2009.

Islam, Sirajul, ed. *History of Bangladesh 1704–1971.* Reprint. Dhaka: Asiatic Society of Bangladesh, 2007.

Kejariwal, O. P. *The Asiatic Society of Bengal and the Discovery of India's Past.* London: Oxford University Press, 1988.

Majumdar, Romesh Chandra, and Jadunath Sarkar, eds. *The History of Bengal.* Dacca: University of Dacca, 1963.

Mondal, Sushila. *History of Bengal.* Calcutta: Prakash Mandir, 1970.

Moshin, K. M., and Sharifuddin Ahmed, eds. *Cultural History.* Dhaka: Asiatic Society of Bangladesh, 2007.

Rabbani, Golam. *Dhaka: From Mughal Outpost to Metropolis.* Dhaka: University Press, 1997.

Rahim, Muhammad Abdur. *Social and Cultural History of Bengal.* Karachi: Pakistan Historical Society, 1963.

Ray, Niharranjan. *History of the Bengali People.* Calcutta: Orient Longmans, 1994.

Sengupta, Nitish. *Bengal Divided: The Unmaking of a Nation (1905–1971).* New Delhi: Penguin/Viking 2007.

———. *History of the Bengali-Speaking People.* New Delhi: UBS Publishers, 2001.

Sur, Atul Krishna. *History and Culture of Bengal.* Calcutta: Chuckervertti, Chatterjee, 1963.

Ancient, Buddhist, and Hindu Periods

Acharyya, N. N. *History of Medieval Assam.* Gauhati, Assam: Dutta Baruah, 1966.

Ahmed, Nazimuddin. *Mahasthan: A Preliminary Report on the Recent Archaeological Excavation at Mahasthangarh.* Karachi: Department of Archaeology and Museums, 1964.

Ali, Mohammed. *Archaeological Survey Report of Bogra District.* Dhaka: Directorate of Archaeology and Museums, 1986.

Bagchi, Jhunu. *The History and Culture of the Palas of Bengal and Bihar.* New Delhi: Abhinav, 1993.

Chakrabarti, Amita. *History of Bengal, c. A.D. 550 to c. A.D. 750.* Burdwan: University of Burdwan, 1991.

Choudhury, Pratap Chandra. *Assam-Bengal Relations from the Earliest Times to the Twelfth Century A.D.* Guwahati, Assam: United Publishers, 1988.

Chowdhury, Abdul Momin. *Dynastic History of Bengal.* Dacca: Asiatic Society of Pakistan, 1967.

Dani, Ahmad Hasan. *Bibliography of the Muslim Inscriptions of Bengal.* Dacca: n.p., 1957.

———. *Prehistory and Protohistory of Eastern India, with a Detailed Account of the Neolithic Cultures in Mainland South East Asia.* Calcutta: Firma KLM, 1960.

Maitreya, Akshayakumara. *The Fall of the Pala Empire.* Rajarammohunpur, District Darjeeling: University of North Bengal, 1987.

Majumdar, Romesh Chandra. *History of Ancient Bengal.* Calcutta: G. Bharadwaj, 1971.

———. *History of Mediaeval Bengal.* Calcutta: G. Bharadwaj, 1973.

Monahan, Francis John. *The Early History of Bengal.* Varanasi: Bhartiya Publishing House, 1974.

Mondal, Sushila. *History of Bengal.* Calcutta: Prakash Mandir, 1970ff.

Morrison, Barrie M. *A Cultural Center of Early Bengal: An Archaeological Report and Historical Analysis.* Seattle: University of Washington Press, 1974.

———. *Lalmai, Political Centers and Cultural Regions in Early Bengal.* Tucson: University of Arizona Press, 1970.

Mukherjee, B. N. *Coins and Currency System in Gupta Bengal.* New Delhi: Harman, 1992.

Paul, Pramode Lal. *The Early History of Bengal, from the Earliest Times to the Muslim Conquest.* Calcutta: Indian Research Institute, 1939.

Roychoudhuri, Bani. *The Political History of Bengal to the Rise of the Pala Dynasty, c. 326 B.C. to A.D. 750.* Calcutta: Sanskrit Pustak Bhandar, 1990.

Shahanara Husain. *Everyday Life in the Pala Empire.* Dacca: Asiatic Society of Pakistan, 1968.

———. *The Social Life of Women in Early Medieval Bengal.* Dhaka: Asiatic Society of Bangladesh, 1985.

Tripathi, Ratikanta. *Social and Religious Aspects in Bengal Inscriptions.* Calcutta: Firma KLM, 1987.

Muslim Period

Akanda, Latifa. *Social History of Muslim Bengal.* Dhaka: Islamic Cultural Centre, 1981.

Ali, Muhammad Mohar. *History of the Muslims of Bengal*. Riyadh: Imam Muhammad ibn Sa'ud Islamic University, Department of Culture and Publications, 1988.

Azraf, Muhammad. *The Background of the Culture of Muslim Bengal*. Dacca: Society for Pakistan Studies, 1970.

Banerjee, Brajendra Nath. *Begams of Bengal*. Calcutta: S. K. Mitra and Brothers, 1942.

Chatterjee, Anjali. *Bengal in the Reign of Aurangzib, 1658–1707*. Calcutta: Progressive Publishers, 1967.

Chattopadhyay, Subhas Chandra. *Diwani in Bengal, 1765: Career of Nawab Najm-ud-daulah*. Varanasi: Vishwavidyalaya Prakashan, 1980.

Dasa Gupta, Yogendra-Natha. *Bengal in the Sixteenth Century A.D.* Calcutta: University of Calcutta, 1914.

Dasgupta, Biplah. *European Trade and Colonial Conquest*. London: Anthem Press, 2002.

Datta, Kalikinkar. *Alivardi and His Times*. Calcutta: World Press, 1963.

———. *Studies in the History of the Bengal Subah*. Calcutta: University of Calcutta, 1936.

Eaton, Richard M. *The Rise of Islam and the Bengal Frontier, 1204–1760*. Berkeley: University of California Press, 1993.

Fuzli Rubbee, Khondkar. *The Origin of the Musalmans of Bengal*. Dacca: Society for Pakistan Studies, 1970.

Ghosh, Jamini Mohan. *Magh Raiders in Bengal*. Calcutta: Bookland, 1960.

Habibullah, Abul Barkat Muhammad. *Foundation of Muslim Rule in India: A History of the Establishment and Progress of the Turkish Sultanate of Delhi, 1206–1280 A.D.* Allahabad, India: Central Book Depot, 1961.

Hardy, Peter. *Historians of Medieval India: Studies in Indian Muslim Historical Writing*. London: Luzac, 1960.

Karim, Abdul. *Corpus of the Arabic and Persian Inscriptions of Bengal*. Dhaka: Asiatic Society of Bangladesh, 1992.

———. *History of Bengal: Mughal Period*. Rajshahi: Institute of Bangladesh Studies, University of Rajshahi, 1992.

———. *Murshid Quli Khan and His Times*. Dacca: Asiatic Society of Pakistan, 1963.

———. *The Provinces of Bihar and Bengal under Shahjahan*. Dacca: Asiatic Society of Bangladesh, 1974.

———. *Social History of the Muslims in Bengal, Down to A.D. 1538*. Chittagong: Baitush Sharaf Islamic Research Institute, 1985.

Karim, Khondkar Mahbubul. *The Provinces of Bihar and Bengal under Shah Jehan*. Dhaka: Asiatic Society of Bangladesh, 1974.

Raychaudhuri, Tapankumar. *Bengal under Akbar and Jehangir.* Calcutta: A. Mukherjee, 1953.

Roy, Atul Chandra. *The Career of Mir Jafar Khan (1757–65 A.D.).* Calcutta: Das Gupta, 1953.

———. *History of Bengal: Mughal Period, 1526–1765.* Calcutta: Nababharat Publishers, 1968.

———. *History of Bengal: Turko-Afghan Period.* New Delhi: Kalyani Publishers, 1986.

Saran, Parmatma. *The Provincial Government of the Mughals.* Allahabad: Kitabistan, 1941.

Sarkar, Jadu Nath, ed., trans. *Bengal Nawabs, Containing Azad-al-Husaini's Naubahar-i Murshid Quli Khani, Karam 'Ali's Muzaffarnamah, and Yusuf 'Ali's Ahwal-i-Mahabat Jang.* Calcutta: Asiatic Society, 1985.

Sarkar, Jagadish Narayan. *Hindu-Muslim Relations in Bengal: Medieval Period.* Delhi: Idarah-i Adabiyat-i Delhi, 1985.

Srivastava, Ashirbadi Lal. *Shuja-ud-daulah.* Calcutta: S. N. Sarkar, 1939, 1945.

Stewart, Charles. *The History of Bengal from the First Mohammedan Invasion until the Virtual Conquest of That Country by the English, A.D. 1757.* Delhi: Oriental Publishers, 1971.

Tarafdar, Momtazur Rahman. *Husain Shahi Bengal, 1494–1538 A.D.: A Socio-Political Study.* Dacca: Asiatic Society of Pakistan, 1965.

British Period

Abdul Latif. *Autobiography and Other Writings of Nawab Abdul Latif Khan Bahadur.* Chittagong: Mehrub Publications, 1968.

Abdur Rab, A. S. M. *A. K. Fazlul Haq.* Lahore: Ferozsons, 1967.

Abul Hashim. *In Retrospection.* Dacca: Subarna Publishers, 1974.

Ahmad Khan, Muin-ud-din. *Muslim Struggle for Freedom in Bengal: From Plassey to Pakistan, A.D. 1757–1947.* Dhaka: Islamic Foundation of Bangladesh, 1982.

———. *Titu Mir and His Followers in British Indian Records, 1831–1833 A.D.* Dhaka: Islamic Foundation of Bangladesh, 1980.

Ahmed, A. F. Salahuddin. *Social Ideas and Social Change in Bengal, 1818–1835.* Leiden: E. J. Brill, 1965.

Ahmed, Rafiuddin. *The Bengal Muslims, 1871–1906: A Quest for Identity.* New York: Oxford University Press, 1981.

Ahmed, Sufia. *Muslim Community in Bengal, 1884–1912.* Dacca: Oxford University Press, 1974.

Akanda, S. A., ed. *Studies in Modern Bengal*. Rajshahi: Institute of Bangladesh Studies, University of Rajshahi, 1981.

Akhtar, Shirin. *The Role of the Zamindars in Bengal, 1707–1772*. Dacca: Asiatic Society of Bangladesh, 1982.

Banerjea, Surendranath. *A Nation in Making: Being the Reminiscences of Fifty Years of Public Life*. New York: Oxford University Press, 1925.

Banerjee, Tarasankar. *Various Bengal: Aspects of Modern History*. Calcutta: Ratna Prakashan, 1985.

Bhattacharya, Bhabani. *Socio-Political Currents in Bengal: A Nineteenth Century Perspective*. New Delhi: Vikas, 1980.

Bose, Nemai Sadhan. *Indian Awakening and Bengal*. Calcutta: Firma KLM, 1976.

Broomfield, John H. *Elite Conflict in a Plural Society: Twentieth Century Bengal*. Berkeley: University of California Press, 1968.

———. *Mostly about Bengal: Essays in Modern South Asian History*. New Delhi: Manohar, 1982.

Buckland, Charles Edward. *Bengal under the Lieutenant-Governors*. Calcutta: K. Bose, 1902.

Campos, J. J. A. *History of the Portuguese in Bengal*. New York: AMS Press, 1975.

Chakravarti, Ranjan. *Authority and Violence in Colonial Bengal, 1800–1860*. Calcutta: Bookland, 1997.

Chakravorty, Jagannath. *Studies in the Bengal Renaissance*. Calcutta: National Council of Education, 1977.

Chatterjee, Manini. *Do or Die: The Chittagong Uprising, 1930–34*. New Delhi: Penguin, 1999.

Chatterjee, Partha. *Bengal, 1920–1947: The Land Question*. Calcutta: K. P. Bagchi, 1984.

Chatterjee, Pranab Kumar. *Struggle and Strife in Urban Bengal, 1937–47: A Study of Calcutta-Based Urban Politics in Bengal*. Calcutta: Das Gupta, 1991.

Chatterjee, Shiba Prasad. *The Partition of Bengal: A Geographical Study with Maps and Diagrams*. Calcutta: D. R. Mitra, 1947.

Chatterjee, Srilata. *Congress Politics in Bengal, 1919–1939*. London: Anthem Press, 2002.

Chatterji, Bhola. *Aspects of Bengal Politics in the Early Nineteen-thirties*. Calcutta: World Press, 1969.

Chatterji, Joya. *Bengal Divided: Hindu Communalism and Partition, 1932–1947*. New York: Cambridge University Press, 1964.

Chattopadhya, Basudeb. *Crime and Control in Early Colonial Bengal, 1770–1860*. Calcutta: Bagchi, 2000.

Chattopadhyay, Dilipkumar. *Dynamics of Social Change in Bengal, 1817–1851*. Calcutta: Punthi Pustak, 1990.

Chattopadhyay, Manju. *Petition to Agitation: Bengal, 1857–1885*. Calcutta: K. P. Bagchi, 1985.

Chattopadhyaya, Gautam, ed. *Awakening in Bengal in Early Nineteenth Century: Selected Documents*. Calcutta: Progressive Publishers, 1965.

——. *Bengal Electoral Politics and the Freedom Struggle, 1862–1947*. New Delhi: Indian Council of Historical Research, 1984.

Chaudhuri, K. N. *The English East India Company*. London: F. Cass, 1965.

Chaudhury, Sushil. *From Prosperity to Decline: Eighteenth Century Bengal*. New Delhi: Manohar, 1995.

Choudhury, Indira. *Frail Hero and Virile History: Gender and the Politics of Culture in Colonial Bengal*. London: Oxford University Press, 1998.

Choudhury, Serajul Islam. *Middle Class and the Social Revolution in Bengal: An Incomplete Agenda*. Dhaka: University Press, 2002.

Cronin, Richard P. *British Policy and Administration in Bengal, 1905–1912: Partition and the New Province of Eastern Bengal and Assam*. Calcutta: Firma KLM, 1977.

Daly, F. C. *First Rebels: A Strictly Confidential Note on the Growth of the Revolutionary Movement in Bengal*. Calcutta: Riddhi-India, 1981.

Das, Binod Sankar. *Changing Profile of the Frontier Bengal, 1751–1833*. Delhi: Mittal Publications, 1984.

Das, Suranjan. *Communal Riots in Bengal, 1905–1947*. Delhi: Oxford University Press, 1991.

Das, Tarakchandra. *Bengal Famine (1943) as Revealed in a Survey of the Destitutes in Calcutta*. Calcutta: University of Calcutta, 1949.

Datta, Kalikinkar. *The Dutch in Bengal and Bihar, 1740–1825 A.D.* Delhi: Motilal Banarsidas, 1968.

——. *The Santhal Insurrection of 1855–57*. Calcutta: University of Calcutta, 1989.

De, Amalendu. *Roots of Separatism in Nineteenth-Century Bengal*. Calcutta: Ratna Prakashan, 1974.

De, Dhurjati Prasad. *Bengal Muslims in Search of Social Identity*. Dhaka: University Press, 1998.

De, Soumitra. *Nationalism and Separatism in Bengal: A Study of India's Partition*. New Delhi: Vikas, 1992.

Dutt, Kalpana. *Chittagong Armoury Raiders: Reminiscences*. Bombay: People's Publishing House, 1945.

Dutta, Abhijit. *Muslim Society in Revolt: Titu Meer's Revolt, 1831; A Study*. Calcutta: Minerva Associates, 1987.

Edwardes, Michael. *The Battle of Plassey and the Conquest of Bengal.* New York: Macmillan, 1963.

Forbes, Geraldine H. *Positivism in Bengal: A Case Study in the Transmission and Assimilation of an Ideology.* Calcutta: Minerva, 1975.

Fuller, Bampfylde. *Some Personal Experiences.* London: J. Murray, 1935.

Ghosh, Kali Charan. *Famines in Bengal, 1770–1943.* Calcutta: National Council of Education, 1987.

Ghosh, Niranjan. *The Role of Women in the Freedom Movement in Bengal, 1919–1947.* Calcutta: Firma KLM, 1988.

Ghosh, Suresh Chandra. *The British in Bengal: A Study of the British Society and Life in the Late Eighteenth Century.* New Delhi: Munshiram, 1998.

———. *The Social Condition of the British Community in Bengal, 1757–1800.* Leiden: E. J. Brill, 1970.

Ghosha, Binayajibana. *Revolt of 1905 in Bengal.* Calcutta: G. A. E. Publishers, 1987.

Gopal, Ram. *How the British Occupied Bengal.* New York: Asia Publishing House, 1964.

Gopal, Sarvepalli. *The Permanent Settlement in Bengal and Its Results.* London: George Allen and Unwin, 1949.

Gordon, Leonard A. *Bengal: The Nationalist Movement, 1876–1940.* New York: Columbia University Press, 1973.

Greenough, Paul R. *Prosperity and Misery in Modern Bengal: The Famine of 1943–1944.* New York: Oxford University Press, 1982.

Gupta, Brijen Kishore. *Sirajuddaullah and the East India Company, 1756–1757: Background to the Foundation of British Power in India.* Leiden: E. J. Brill, 1966.

Hamilton, Francis. *Francis Buchanan in Southeast Bengal, 1798: His Journey to Chittagong, Chittagong Hill Tracts, Noakhali, and Comilla.* Dhaka: University Press, 1992.

Haque, Enamul, comp. *Nawab Bahadur Abdul Latif: His Writings and Related Documents.* Dacca: Samudra Prokashani, 1968.

Harun-or-Rashid. *The Foreshadowing of Bangladesh: Bengal Muslim League and Muslim Politics, 1936–1947.* Dhaka: Asiatic Society of Bangladesh, 1987.

Hashmi, Taj ul-Islam. *Pakistan as a Peasant Utopia: The Communalization of Class Politics in East Bengal, 1920–1947.* Boulder, Colo.: Westview Press, 1992.

Hill, S. C. *Bengal in 1756–1757: A Selection of Papers Dealing with the Affairs of the British in Bengal during the Reign of Siraj-ud-Daula with Notes and Historical Introduction.* Delhi: Manas Publications, 1985.

Hunter, William Wilson. *Annals of Rural Bengal*. Reprint. New York: Johnson Reprint, 1970.

Iftikhar-ul-Awwal, A. Z. M. *The Industrial Development of Bengal, 1900–1939*. New Delhi: Vikas, 1982.

Ikramullah, Shaista Suhrawardy. *From Purdah to Parliament*. Reprint. Karachi: Oxford University Press, 1998.

Islam, Mustafa Nurul. *Bengali Muslim Public Opinion as Reflected in the Bengali Press, 1901–1930*. Dhaka: Bangla Academy, 1970.

Islam, Sirajul. *Bengal Land Tenure: The Origin and Growth of Intermediate Interests in the 19th Century*. Calcutta: K. P. Bagchi, 1988.

———. *The Permanent Settlement in Bengal: A Study of Its Operation, 1790–1819*. Dacca: Bangla Academy, 1979.

———. *Rent and Raiyat: Society and Economy of Eastern Bengal, 1859–1928*. Dhaka: Asiatic Society of Bangladesh, 1989.

———. *Rural History of Bangladesh: A Source Study*. Dacca: Titot Islam, 1977.

Jahanara Begum. *The Last Decades of Undivided Bengal*. Calcutta: Minerva, 1984.

Jones, Mary Evelyn Monckton. *Warren Hastings in Bengal, 1772–1774*. Oxford: Clarendon Press, 1918.

Kabeer, Rokeya Rahman. *Administrative Policy of the Government of Bengal, 1870–1890*. Dacca: National Institute of Public Administration, 1965.

Kabir, Humayun. *Muslim Politics, 1906–47, and Other Essays*. Calcutta: Firma KLM, 1969.

Kaviraj, Narahari. *A Peasant Uprising in Bengal, 1783: The First Formidable Peasant Uprising against the Rule of East India Company*. New Delhi: People's Publishing House, 1972.

———. *Wahabi and Faraizi Rebels of Bengal*. New Delhi: People's Publishing House, 1982.

Kejariwal, O. P. *The Asiatic Society of Bengal and the Discovery of India's Past, 1784–1838*. New York: Oxford University Press, 1988.

Khan, Abdul Majed. *The Transition of Bengal, 1756–1775: A Study of Seiyid Muhammad Reza Khan*. London: Cambridge University Press, 1969.

Khan, Akbar Ali. *Some Aspects of Peasant Behaviour in Bengal, 1890–1914: A Neo-Classical Analysis*. Dhaka: Asiatic Society of Bangladesh, 1982.

Khan, Bazlur Rahman. *Politics in Bengal, 1927–1936*. Dhaka: Asiatic Society of Bangladesh, 1987.

Kling, Blair. *The Blue Mutiny: The Indigo Disturbances in Bengal, 1859–1862*. Philadelphia: University of Pennsylvania Press, 1966.

———. *Partner in Empire: Dwarkanath Tagore and the Age of Enterprise in Eastern India*. Berkeley: University of California Press, 1976.

Kopf, David. *The Brahmo Samaj and the Shaping of the Modern Indian Mind.* Princeton, N.J.: Princeton University Press, 1979.

———. *British Orientalism and the Bengal Renaissance.* Berkeley: University of California Press, 1969.

Kopf, David, and Saifuddin Joarder, eds. *Seminar of Perspectives of the Bengal Renaissance.* Dacca: Bangladesh Books International, 1977.

Laushey, David M. *Bengal Terrorism and the Marxist Left: Aspects of Regional Nationalism in India, 1905–1943.* Calcutta: Firma KLM, 1975.

Maitra, Jayanti. *Muslim Politics in Bengal, 1855–1906: Collaboration and Confrontation.* Calcutta: K. P. Bagchi, 1984.

Majumdar, Romesh Chandra. *Glimpses of Bengal in the Nineteenth Century.* Calcutta: Firma KLM, 1960.

———. *Renascent India: First Phase.* Calcutta: G. Bharadwaj, 1976.

———. *The Revolutionary Movement in Bengal and the Role of Surya Sen.* Calcutta: University of Calcutta, 1978.

Mallick, Azizur Rahman. *British Policy and the Muslims in Bengal, 1757–1856.* Dacca: Bangla Academy, 1977.

Mallikarjuna Sharma, I. *Easter Rebellion in India: The Chittagong Uprising.* Hyderabad, India: Marxist Study Forum, 1993.

Mandal, Tirtha. *Women Revolutionaries of Bengal, 1905–1939.* New Delhi: Minerva, 1991.

Mannan, Mohammad Siraj. *The Muslim Political Parties in Bengal, 1936–1947: A Study of Their Activities and Struggle for Freedom.* Dhaka: Islamic Foundation Bangladesh, 1987.

Marshall, Peter James. *Bengal—The British Bridgehead: Eastern India, 1740–1828.* New York: Cambridge University Press, 1987.

———. *East Indian Fortunes: The British in Bengal in the Eighteenth Century.* Oxford: Clarendon Press, 1976.

———. *The Impeachment of Warren Hastings.* London: Oxford University Press, 1965.

Mazumdar, Durga Prasad. *Dimensions of Political Culture in Bengal, 1814–1857, with Special Reference to Raja Ram Mohan Roy.* Calcutta: Calcutta University, 1993.

Mitra, Lalit Mohan. *The Danes in Bengal.* Calcutta: Prabartak Publishers, 1951.

Molla, M. K. U. *The New Province of Eastern Bengal and Assam.* Dhaka: University Press, 1981.

Momen, Humaira. *Muslim Politics in Bengal: A Study of Krishak Praja Party and the Elections of 1937.* Dacca: Sunny House, 1972.

Mukherjee, Arun. *Crime and Public Disorder in Colonial Bengal.* Calcutta: Bagchi, 1995.

Mukhopadhyay, Amar Kumar, ed. *The Bengali Intellectual Tradition, from Rammohun Roy to Dhirendranath Sen.* Calcutta: K. P. Bagchi, 1979.

Mukhopadhyaya, Amitabha. *Reform and Regeneration in Bengal, 1774–1823.* Calcutta: Rabindra Bharati University, 1968.

Neogy, Ajit K. *Partitions of Bengal.* Calcutta: A. Mukherjee, 1987.

Oddie, Geoffrey. *Missionaries, Rebellion and Proto-Nationalism.* London: Curzon Press, 1999.

O'Malley, Lewis Sydney Steward. *History of Bengal, Bihar and Orissa under British Rule.* Calcutta: Bengal Secretariat Book Depot, 1925.

Palit, Chittabrata. *New Viewpoints on Nineteenth Century Bengal.* Calcutta: Progressive Publishers, 1980.

———. *Tensions in Rural Bengal Society: Landlords, Planters and Colonial Rule, 1830–1860.* Calcutta: Orient Longmans, 1975.

Panda, Chitta. *The Decline of the Bengal Zamindars: Midnapore, 1870–1920.* Delhi: Oxford University Press, 1996.

Poddara, Arabinda. *Renaissance in Bengal: Quests and Confrontations, 1800–1860.* Simla: Indian Institute of Advanced Study, 1970.

———. *Renaissance in Bengal: A Search for Identity.* Simla: Indian Institute of Advanced Study, 1977.

Prakash, Om. *The Dutch East India Company and the Economy of Bengal, 1630–1720.* Princeton, N.J.: Princeton University Press, 1985.

Prakash, Om, and Denys Lombard, eds. *Commerce and Culture in the Bay of Bengal, 1500–1800.* Delhi: Manohar, 1999.

Rahim, Enayetur. *Provincial Autonomy in Bengal, 1937–1943.* Dhaka: University Press, 1981.

Rahim, Enayetur, and Joyce L. Rahim. *Bengal Politics: Documents of the Raj.* 3 vols. Dhaka: University Press, 1996, 1999, 2000.

Rahman, Hossainur. *Hindu-Muslim Relations in Bengal, 1905–1947: A Study in Cultural Confrontation.* Bombay: Nachiketa Publications, 1974.

Ram Gopal. *How the British Occupied Bengal.* New York: Asia Publishing House, 1963.

Rao, Amiya. *The Blue Devil: Indigo and Colonial Bengal.* London: Oxford University Press, 1992.

Ray, Dalia. *The Bengal Revolutionaries and Freedom Movement.* New Delhi: Cosmo Publications, 1990.

Ray, Nitish, and Ranjit Roy. *Bengal Yesterday and Today: Collection of Eight Essays on the 19th and 20th Centuries.* Calcutta: Papyrus, 1991.

Ray, Rajat Kanta. *Social Conflict and Political Unrest in Bengal, 1875–1927.* Delhi: Oxford University Press, 1984.

Raychaudri, Tapan. *Europe Reconsidered: Perceptions of the West in Nineteenth Century Bengal.* Delhi: Oxford University Press, 1988.

Roy, Samaren. *The Bengalees: Glimpses of History and Culture.* New Delhi: Allied Publishers, 1999.

Rule, Pauline. *The Pursuit of Progress: A Study of the Intellectual Development of Romesh Chunder Dutt, 1848–1888.* Calcutta: Editions Indian, 1977.

Samanta, Arabinda. *Malarial Fever in Colonial Bengal, 1820–1939: Social History of an Epidemic.* Kolkata: Firma KLM, 2002.

Sanyal, Rajat. *Voluntary Associations and the Urban Public Life in Bengal, 1815–1876: An Aspect of Social History.* Calcutta: Riddhi-India, 1980.

Sarkar, Chandiprasad. *The Bengal Muslims: A Study in Their Politicization, 1912–1929.* Calcutta: K. P. Bagchi, 1991.

Sarkar, Kamala. *Bengal Politics, 1937–1947.* Calcutta: A. Mukherjee, 1990.

Sarkar, Sumit. *The Swadeshi Movement in Bengal, 1903–1908.* New Delhi: People's Publishing House, 1973.

Sarkar, Tanika. *Bengal, 1928–1934: The Politics of Protest.* New York: Oxford University Press, 1987.

Saxena, Vinod Kumar, ed. *The Partition of Bengal, 1905–1911: Select Documents.* Delhi: Anishka Publishing House, 1987.

Scrafton, Luke. *A History of Bengal before and after Plassey, 1739–1758.* Calcutta: Firma KLM, 1975; reprint of London edition, 1763.

Sen, Amiya P. *Hindu Revivalism in Bengal, 1872–1905.* London: Oxford University Press, 2001.

Sen, Asoka Kumar. *The Educated Middle Class and Indian Nationalism: Bengal during the Pre-Congress Decades.* Calcutta: Progressive Publishers, 1988.

———. *The Popular Uprising and the Intelligentsia: Bengal between 1855–1873.* Calcutta: Firma KLM, 1992.

Sen, Ranjit. *New Elite and New Collaboration: A Study of Social Transformations in Bengal in the Eighteenth Century.* Calcutta: Papyrus, 1985.

Sen, Shila. *Muslim Politics in Bengal, 1937–1947.* New Delhi: Impex India, 1976.

Sen, Suranjit. *Metamorphosis of Bengal Polity, 1700–1793.* Calcutta: Rabindra Bharati University, 1987.

Sengupta, Kalyan Kumar. *Pabna Disturbances and the Politics of Rent, 1873–1885.* New Delhi: People's Publishing House, 1974.

Sensarma, P. *The Military History of Bengal.* Calcutta: Naya Prokash, 1977.

Shan Muhammad. *The Right Honourable Syed Ameer Ali: Personality and Achievements.* New Delhi: Uppal House, 1991.

Sharma, Ram Suresh. *Bengal under John Peter Grant, 1859–1862.* Delhi: Captial Publishing House, 1989.

Sinha, Devi P. *The Educational Policy of the East India Company in Bengal to 1854.* Calcutta: Punthi Pustak, 1964.

Sinha, Narendra Krishna. *Ashutosh Mookerjee: A Biographical Study.* Calcutta: Ashutosh Mookerjee Centenary Committee, 1966.
——, ed. *The History of Bengal, 1757–1905.* Calcutta: University of Calcutta, 1967.
Sinha, Pradip. *Nineteenth Century Bengal: Aspects of Social History.* Calcutta: Firma K. L. Mukhopapdyay, 1965.
Southard, Barbara. *The Women's Movement and Colonial Politics in Bengal, 1921–36.* Delhi: Manohar, 1995.
Thankappan Nair, P. *British Beginnings in Bengal, 1600–1660.* Calcutta: Punthi Pustak, 1991.
Tripathi, Amales. *Trade and Finance in the Bengal Presidency, 1793–1885.* London: Oxford University Press, 1979.
Vansittart, Henry. *A Narrative of the Transactions in Bengal, 1760–1764.* Calcutta: K. P. Bagchi, 1976.
Wasti, Syed Razi. *Lord Minto and the Indian Nationalist Movement, 1905–1910.* Oxford: Clarendon Press, 1964.
Wilson, Charles Robert. *The Early Annals of the British in Bengal.* New Delhi: Bimla Publishing House, 1983.

Bibliography

Mamoon, Muntasir. *Index to Articles in Bengal: Past and Present, Volumes 1–85, 1907–1966.* Dhaka: Dhaka University Library, 1986.

Pakistan Period and the War of Liberation

Ahmad, Abul Mansur. *End of a Betrayal and Restoration of the Pakistan Resolution.* Dacca: Koshroz Kitab Mahal, 1975.
Ahmad, Kabir Uddin. *Breakup of Pakistan: Background and Prospects of Bangladesh.* London: Social Science Publishers, 1972.
Ahmed, Akhtar. *Advance to Contact: A Soldier's Account of the Bangladesh Liberation War.* Dhaka: University Press, 2000.
Ahmed, Moudud. *Bangladesh: A Constitutional Quest for Autonomy.* Dacca: University Press, 1979.
Ahsan, Qamarul. *Politics and Personalities in Pakistan.* Dacca: Mohiuddin, 1969.
Akbar Khan, Mohammed. *The Mystery of the Debacle of Pakistan, 1971, and Myth of Exploitation since 1947, and Secret of the Covert War Unmasked.* Karachi: Islamic Military Science Association, 1972 or 1973.
Alama, Jagalula. *Emergence of Bangladesh and Big Power Role in 1971.* Dhaka: Progoti Prakashani, 1990.

Ayoob, Mohammed, et al. *Bangla Desh: A Struggle for Nationhood.* Delhi: Vikas, 1971.

Banerjee, Debendra Nath. *East Pakistan: A Case-Study in Muslim Politics.* Delhi: Vikas, 1969.

The Bangla Desh Papers: The Recorded Statements of Z. A. Bhutto, Mujeeb-ur-Rahman, Gen. Yahya Khan, and Other Politicians of United Pakistan, 1969–1971. Lahore: Vanguard Books, 1978.

Bangladesh Documents. New Delhi: Ministry of External Affairs, 1971.

Bangladesh Establishment Illegal: A Legal Study by International Commission of Jurists. Lahore: Fazalsons, 1972.

Bergsaker, Robert. *Storm over Bangla Desh.* Oslo: Filadelfiaforlaget, 1972.

Bhatnagar, Yatindra. *Bangladesh: Birth of a Nation.* New Delhi: Publication Division, 1971.

———. *Mujib, the Architect of Bangla Desh: A Political Biography.* Delhi: Indian School Supply Depot, 1971.

Bhattacharjea, Ajit, comp. *Dateline Bangla Desh.* Bombay: Jaico Publishing House, 1971.

Bhuiyan, Muhammad Abdul Wadud. *Emergence of Bangladesh and Role of Awami League.* New Delhi: Vikas, 1982.

Chakrabarti, S. K. *The Evolution of Politics in Bangladesh, 1947–1978.* New Delhi: Associated, 1978.

Chandra, Prabodh. *Bloodbath in Bangla Desh.* New Delhi: Adarsh Publications, 1971.

Chatterjee, Sisir. *Bangladesh: The Birth of a Nation.* Calcutta: The Book Exchange, 1972.

Chaudhuri, Kalyan. *Genocide in Bangladesh.* Bombay: Orient Longman, 1972.

Choudhury, A. K. *The Independence of East Bengal: A Historical Process.* Dhaka: Jatiya Grantha Kendra, 1984.

Choudhury, G. W. *Constitutional Development in Pakistan.* Vancouver: Publications Centre, University of British Columbia, 1969.

———. *Democracy in Pakistan.* Dacca: Green Book House, 1967.

———. *The Last Days of United Pakistan.* Bloomington: Indiana University Press, 1974.

Chowdhury, Hamidul Haq. *Memoirs.* Dhaka: Associated Printers, 1989.

Chowdhury, Namja. *The Legislative Process in Bangladesh: Politics and Functioning of the East Bengal Legislature, 1947–58.* Dacca: University of Dacca, 1980.

Das, Mitra. *From Nation to Nation: A Case Study of Bengali Independence.* Calcutta: Minerva, 1981.

Dasgupta, R. K. *Revolt in East Bengal.* Delhi: A. Dasgupta, 1971.

Dasgupta, Sukharanjan. *Midnight Massacre in Dacca.* New Delhi: Vikas, 1978.

Feldman, Herbert. *The End and the Beginning: Pakistan, 1969–1971.* London: Oxford University Press, 1975.

Gandhi, Indira. *India and Bangladesh: Selected Speeches and Statements, March to December 1971.* New Delhi: Orient Longman, 1972.

Garg, S. K. *Spotlight: Freedom Fighters of Bangladesh; A New Outlook.* New Delhi: Allied, 1984.

Ghosh, Sucheta. *The Role of India in the Emergence of Bangladesh.* Calcutta: Minvera, 1983.

Hossain, Ishtiaq. *India and the War of Liberation in Bangladesh.* Dacca: Forum for International Affairs, 1978.

Huq, Ghaziul. *Bangla Desh Unchained.* Calcutta: Indian Associated Publishing Co., 1971.

Hussain, Syed Shabir. *The Death Dance.* Islamabad: Kamran Publishing House, 1979.

Ikramullah, Shaista Suhrawardy. *Huseyn Shaheed Suhrawardy, a Biography.* Karachi: Oxford University Press, 1991.

Imam, Jahanara. *Of Blood and Fire: The Untold Story of Bangladesh's War of Independence.* New Delhi: Sterling Publishers, 1989.

Islam, M. Rafiqul. *The Bangladesh Liberation Movement: International Legal Implications.* Dhaka: University Press, 1987.

———, ed. *Genocide in Bangladesh: Harrowing Accounts of Some Eye-Witnesses and the Extracts from the Press.* Dhaka: Noman Brothers, 1991.

———. *A Tale of Millions: Bangladesh Liberation War, 1971.* Dacca: Bangladesh Books International, 1981.

Jackson, Robert Victor. *South Asian Crisis: India, Pakistan, Bangla Desh.* London: Chatto and Windus, 1975.

Jacob, J. F. R. *Surrender at Dhaka.* Delhi: Manohar, 1997.

Jafar, Abu. *Maulana Akram Khan: A Versatile Genius.* Dhaka: Islamic Foundation Bangladesh, 1984.

Jagdev Singh. *Dismemberment of Pakistan: 1971 Indo-Pak War.* New Delhi: Lancer, 1988.

Jahan, Rounaq. *Pakistan: Failure in National Integration.* New York: Columbia University Press, 1972.

Kamal, Kazi Ahmed. *Politicians and Inside Stories: A Glimpse Mainly into Lives of Fazlul Haq, Shaheed Suhrawardy, and Moulana Bhashani.* Dacca: Kazi Giasuddin Ahmed, 1970.

———. *Sheikh Mujibur Rahman and Birth of Bangladesh.* Dacca: Kazi Giasuddin Ahmed, 1972.

———. *Sheikh Mujibur Rahman: Man and Politician*. Dacca: Kazi Giasuddin Ahmed, 1970.

Karim, Nehal. *The Emergence of Nationalism in Bangladesh*. Dhaka: University of Dhaka, 1992.

Khan, Fazal Muqueem. *Pakistan's Crisis in Leadership*. Islamabad: National Book Foundation, 1973.

Khan, Rao Farman Ali. *How Pakistan Got Divided*. Lahore: Jang Publishers, 1992.

Khan, Roedad. *The American Papers: Secret and Confidential India, Pakistan and Bangladesh Documents, 1965–1973*. Karachi: Oxford, 1999.

Khan, Zillur R. *Third World Charismat: Sheikh Mujib and the Struggle for Freedom*. Dhaka: University Press, 1996.

Khan, Zillur R., and A. T. R. Rahman. *Provincial Autonomy and Constitution Making: The Case of Bangladesh*. Dhaka: Green Book House, 1973.

Lachhman Singh. *Indian Sword Strikes in East Pakistan*. New Delhi: Vikas, 1979.

———. *Victory in Bangladesh*. Dehra Dun: Natraj Publishers, 1991.

Mahmood, Safdar. *The Deliberate Debacle*. Lahore: Sheikh Muhammad Ashraf, 1976.

———. *Pakistan Divided*. Lahore: Ferozsons, 1984.

Malik, Amita. *The Year of the Vulture*. New Delhi: Orient Longman, 1972.

Mamoon, Montassir. *Vanquished Generals and the War of Liberation of Bangladesh*. Trans. Kushal Ibrahim. Dhaka: Samoy Prakashan, 2000.

Maniruzzaman, Talukder. *Group Interests and Political Change: Studies of Pakistan and Bangladesh*. New Delhi: South Asian Publishers, 1982.

———. *Radical Politics and the Emergence of Bangladesh*. Dacca: Bangladesh Books International, 1975.

Mascarenhas, Anthony. *The Rape of Bangla Desh*. Delhi: Vikas, 1971.

Maswani, A. M. K. *Subversion in East Pakistan*. Lahore: Amir Publications, 1979.

Mirza, Sarfaraz Hussain, comp. *Not the Whole Truth: East Pakistan Crisis (March–December, 1971): The Foreign Press*. Lahore: Centre for South Asian Studies, University of Punjab, 1989.

Moraes, Dom. *The Tempest Within: An Account of East Pakistan*. Delhi: Vikas, 1971.

Muhith, A. M. A. *American Response to the Bangladesh Liberation War*. Dhaka: University Press, 1996.

———. *Bangladesh: Emergence of a Nation*. Dhaka: University Press, 1992.

Mujibur Rahman, Sheikh. *Bangladesh, My Bangladesh. Selected Speeches and Statements, October 28, 1970 to March 26, 1971*. New Delhi: Orient Longmans, 1972.

Nair, M. Bhaskaran. *Politics in Bangladesh: A Study of the Awami League, 1949–58*. New Delhi: Northern Book Centre, 1990.

Niazi, A. A. K. *The Betrayal of East Pakistan*. Karachi: Oxford University Press, 1998.

Nicholas, Marta, and Philip Oldenburg. *Bangladesh: The Birth of a Nation: A Handbook of Background Information and Documentary Sources*. Madras: M. Seshachalam, 1972.

O'Connor, Noel G. *The Soldier Is Afraid: An Account of Operation Sikander, Bangladesh War, 1971*. Bhopal: Services Publishing House, 1981.

Osmany, Shireen Hasan. *Bangladeshi Nationalism: History of Dialectics and Dimensions*. Dhaka: University Press, 1992.

Pakistan from 1947 to the Creation of Bangladesh. New York: Scribner, 1973. [From Keesing's archives.]

Payne, Robert. *Massacre*. New York: Macmillan, 1973.

Qutubuddin Aziz. *Blood and Tears*. Karachi: United Press of Pakistan, 1974.

Rahamana, Phajalura. *Culture Conflicts in East Pakistan, 1947–1971: A Study in the Attitude of Bengali Muslim Intelligentsia towards Bengali Literature and Islam*. Dhaka: Sejuty Prakashan, 1990.

Rahim, Enayetur, and Joyce L. Rahim. *Bangladesh Liberation War and the Nixon White House*. Dhaka: Pustaka, 2000.

Rahman, Choudhury Shamsur. *Life in East Pakistan*. Chittagong: Pakistan Cooperative Book Society, 1956.

Rahman, Matiur. *The Role of India and the Big Powers in the East Pakistan Crisis of 1971*. London: R. Rahman, 1984.

Rama, Sivalenka. *Role of India in Bangladesh Liberation Movement*. Hyderabad, India: Rama, 1978.

Ray, Jayanta Kumar. *Democracy and Nationalism on Trial: A Study of East Pakistan*. Simla: Indian Institute of Advanced Study, 1968.

Rizvi, Hasan-Askari. *Internal Strife and External Intervention: India's Role in the Civil War in East Pakistan (Bangladesh)*. Lahore: Progressive Publishers, 1981.

———. *The Military and Politics in Pakistan, 1947–86*. Lahore: Progressive Publishers, 1986.

Roy Chowdhury, Subrata. *The Genesis of Bangladesh: A Study in International Legal Norms and Permissive Conscience*. London: Asia Publishing House, 1972.

Rushbrook Williams, L. F. *Pakistan under Challenge*. London: Stacey International, 1975.

Saadullah Khan. *East Pakistan to Bangla Desh*. Lahore: Lahore Law Times Publications, 1975.

Saigal, J. R. *Pakistan Splits: The Birth of Bangladesh*. Delhi: Manas, 2000.

Salunke, S. P. *Pakistani POWs in India*. New Delhi: Vikas, 1977.

Sen Gupta, Jyoti. *Bangladesh in Blood and Tears*. Calcutta: Naya Prokash, 1981.

——. *History of Freedom Movement in Bangladesh, 1943–1973: Some Involvement*. Calcutta: Naya Prokash, 1974.

Sethi, Surinder Singh. *The Decisive War: Emergence of a New Nation*. New Delhi: Sagar Publications, 1972.

Sharma, Shri Ram. *Bangladesh Crisis and Indian Foreign Policy*. New Delhi: Young Asia, 1978.

Shelley, Mizanur Rahman. *Emergence of a New Nation in a Multi-Polar World: Bangladesh*. Dacca: University Press, 1979.

Siddiq, Salik. *Witness to Surrender*. Karachi: Oxford University Press, 1977.

Siddiqui, Kalim. *Conflict, Crisis and War in Pakistan*. London: Macmillan, 1972.

Singh, Swaran. *Bangla Desh and Indo-Pak War: India Speaks at the U.N.* New Delhi: Publications Division, 1972.

Sisson, Richard, and Leo Rose. *War and Secession: Pakistan, India and the Creation of Bangladesh*. Berkeley: University of California Press, 1990.

Sodhi, Harinder Singh. *"Operation Windfall": Emergence of Bangladesh*. New Delhi: Allied, 1980.

Subrahmanyam, K. *Bangla Desh and India's Security*. Dehra Dun: Palit and Dutt, 1972.

Suhrawardy, Huseyn Shaheed. *Memoirs of Huseyn Shaheed Suhrawardy with a Brief Account of His Life and Work*. Dhaka: University Press, 1987.

Tiwary, I. N. *War of Independence in Bangla Desh: A Documentary Study with an Introduction*. Varanasi: Navachetna Prakashan: 1971.

Uban, Sujan Singh. *Phantoms of Chittagong: The "Fifth Army" in Bangladesh*. New Delhi: Allied Publishers, 1985.

Umar, Badruddin. *The Emergence of Bangladesh: Class Struggles in East Pakistan (1947–1958)*. New York: Oxford University Press, 2004.

——. *Politics and Society in East Pakistan and Bangladesh*. Dacca: Mowla Bros., 1974.

Wilcox, Wayne Ayres. *The Emergence of Bangladesh: Problems and Opportunities for a Redefined American Policy in South Asia*. Washington, D.C.: American Enterprise Institute for Public Policy Research, 1973.

Zafar, S. M. *Through the Crisis*. Lahore: Book Centre, 1970.

Zaheer, Hasan. *The Separation of East Pakistan: The Rise and Realization of Bengali Muslim Nationalism*. New York: Oxford University Press, 1994.

Zaman, Hasan, comp. *East Pakistan Crisis and India*. Dacca: Pakistan Academy, 1971.

Bibliography

Chakravarty, Gita. *The Bangladeshi Movement, 1947–1971: A Bibliography of English and Bengali Sources*. Calcutta: Firma KLM, 1998.

Local History

Ahmed, Sharif Uddin. *Dacca: A Study in Urban History and Development*. Riverdale, Md.: Riverdale, 1986.

———. *Dhaka: Past, Present, and Future*. Dhaka: Asiatic Society of Bangladesh, 1991.

Akanda, S. A., ed. *The District of Rajshahi: Its Past and Present*. Rajshahi: Institute of Bangladesh Studies, University of Rajshahi, 1983.

Ali, Syed Murtaza. *History of Chittagong*. Dacca: Standard Publishers, 1964.

Dani, Ahmad Hasan. *Dacca: A Record of Its Changing Fortunes*. Dacca: Mrs. S. S. Dani, 1962.

D'Oyly, Charles, Sir. *Antiquities of Dacca*. London: J. Landseer, 1814–27.

Hasan, Sayed Mahmudul. *Dhaka: The City of Mosques*. Dacca: Islamic Foundation Bangladesh, 1981.

Hossain, Anwar. *Dhaka Portrait: 1967–1992; Images, Concept, Photographs, Designs and Layout*. Dhaka: AB Publishers, 1992.

Hutchinson, Robert H. S. *Chittagong Hill Tracts*. Delhi: Vivek, 1978.

Islam, Sirajul, ed. *Bangladesh District Records: Dacca District*. Dacca: University of Dacca, 1981.

Kanunago, Suniti Bhushana. *A History of Chittagong*. Chittagong: Signet Library, 1988.

Karim, Abdul. *Dacca: The Mughal Capital*. Dacca: Asiatic Society of Pakistan, 1964.

Mohsin, K. M. *A Bengal District in Transition: Murshidabad, 1765–1793*. Dacca: Asiatic Society of Bangladesh, 1973.

Mukherjee, Nilmani. *A Bengal Zamindar: Jaykrishna Mukherjee of Uttarpara and His Times, 1808–1888*. Calcutta: Firma KLM, 1975.

Taifoor, Syed Muhammed. *Glimpses of Old Dacca*. Dacca: S. M. Perwez, 1952.

Archeology and Prehistory

Ahmed, Nazimuddin. *Discover the Monuments of Bangladesh*. Dhaka: University Press, 1984.

Akman, Afroz. *Mahasthan*. Dhaka: Bangladesh National Museum, 2006.

Alam, A. K. M. Shamsul. *Mainamati*. Dhaka: Department of Archaeology, 1982.

Alam, Md. Shafiqul, and Jean-Francois Salles, eds. *First Interim Report, 1993–1999: France-Bangladesh Joint Venture Excavations at Mahasthangarh*. Dhaka: Department of Archaeology, 2005.

Bangladesh: An Album of Archaeological Relics. Dhaka: Directorate of Archaeology and Museums, 1984.

Bhattacharya, Gouriswar, et al. *Kalhar (White Water-Lily): Studies in Art, Iconography, Architecture and Archaeology of India and Bangladesh*. Professor Enamul Haque felicitation volume. New Delhi: Kaveri Books, 2007.

Chakrabarti, Dilip K. *Ancient Bangladesh: A Study of the Archaeological Sources with an Update on Bangladesh Archaeology, 1990–2000*. Dhaka: University Press, 2001.

Chittagong University Museum. *Catalogue of Coins in the Cabinet of the Chittagong University Museum*. Chittagong: Chittagong University Museum, 1979.

Ghosh, Shankar Prosad. *Terracottas of Bengal, with Special Reference to Nadia*. New Delhi: D. K. Publishers, 1986.

Hasan, Sayed Mahmudul. *Dacca: Gateway to the East*. Dacca: Research Centre for Islamic Art and Culture, 1982.

———. *A Guide to Ancient Monuments of East Pakistan*. Dacca: Society for Pakistan Studies, 1970.

———. *Muslim Monuments of Bangladesh*. Dhaka: Islamic Foundation Bangladesh, 1988.

———. *Sonargaon*. Dhaka: Bangladesh Folk Art and Crafts Foundation, 1982.

Khan, F. A. *Mainamati: Recent Archaeological Discoveries in East Pakistan*. Karachi: Pakistan Publications, 1955.

Majumdar, Nani Gopal, ed. *Inscriptions of Bengal*, vol. 3. Rajshahi: Varendra Research Society, 1929.

Sen, Benoychandra. *Some Historical Aspects of the Inscriptions of Bengal: Pre-Muhammadan Epochs*. Calcutta: University of Calcutta, 1942.

Siddiq, Mohammed. *The Epigraphy of Muslim Bengal*. Abingdon, Oxford, England: Routledge/Curzon, 2003.

LANGUAGE

Alam, Fakrul, ed. *Revisioning English in Bangladesh*. Dhaka: University Press, 2001.

Azad, Humayun. *Pronominalization in Bengali*. Dhaka: University of Dhaka, 1983.

Banerji, Rakhal Das. *The Origin of the Bengali Script*. Reprint. Calcutta: Nababharat Publishers, 1973.

Chatterjee, Suniti Kumar. *The Origin and Development of the Bengali Language*. London: Allen and Unwin, 1970–72.

Gangopadhyay, Malaya. *The Noun Phrase in Bengali: Assignment of Role and the Karaka Theory*. Delhi: Motilal Banarsidas, 1990.

Haldar, Gopal. *A Comparative Grammar of East Bengal Dialects*. Calcutta: Puthipatra, 1986.

Jahan-Ara, Begum. *Pronominal Usage and Appellatives in Bangla*. Dhaka: Karim Book Corporation, 1991.

Khondkar, Abdur Rahim. *The Portuguese Contribution to Bengali Prose, Grammar, and Lexicography*. Dacca: Bangla Academy, 1976.

Morshed, Abul Kalam Manzur. *A Study of Standard Bengali and the Noakhali Dialect*. Dhaka: Bangla Academy, 1985.

Muhammad, Kazi Dina. *The Verbal Structure in Colloquial Bengali*. Dhaka: Bangla Academy, 1985.

Qayyum, Mohammad Abdul. *A Critical Study of the Early Bengali Grammars: Halhed to Haughton*. Dhaka: Asiatic Society of Bangladesh, 1982.

Sen, Sukuman. *Women's Dialect in Bengali*. Calcutta: Jijnasa, 1979.

Zbavitel, Dusan. *Non-finite Verbal Forms in Bengali*. Prague: Oriental Institute, 1970.

LITERATURE

Ashraf, Syed Ali. *Muslim Traditions in Bengali Literature*. Dhaka: Islamic Foundation Bangladesh, 1983.

Azim, Firdous, and Niaz Zaman, eds. *Different Perspective: Women Writing in Bangladesh*. Dhaka: University Press, 1998.

——, eds. *Galpa: Short Stories by Women from Bangladesh*. Dhaka: Writers. ink, 2006.

——, eds. *Infinite Variety: Women in Society and Literature*. Dhaka: University Press, 1994.

Bandhopadhyaya, Asitakumara. *History of Modern Bengali Literature: Nineteenth and Twentieth Centuries*. Calcutta: Modern Book Agency, 1986.

Bose, Amalendu. *Michael Madhusudan Dutt*. New Delhi: Sahitya Akademi, 1981.

Capwell, Charles. *The Music of the Bauls of Bengal*. Kent, Ohio: Kent State University Press, 1986.

Chakraborty, Asoke Kumar. *Muslim Literati and the Development of the Muslim Community in Bengal*. Simla, India: Indian Institute of Advanced Study, 2002.

Chakravarty, Basudha. *Kazi Nazrul Islam.* New Delhi: National Book Trust, India, 1968.

Chatterjee, Santa. *Tales of Bengal.* Thompson, Conn.: Inter Culture Associates, 1979.

Chatterji, Suniti Kumar. *The Various "Matters" in New or Modern Indian Literature and the Romances of Medieval Bengal: Gauda Banga Ramya Katha.* Calcutta: Asiatic Society, 1982.

Chaudhary, Sagar, ed. *Vintage Short Fiction from Bangladesh.* Dhaka: University Press Limited, 2008.

Chaudhuri, Rosinka. *Gentlemen Poets in Colonial Bengal: Emergent Nationalism and the Orientalist Project.* Calcutta: Seagull Books, 2002.

Chowdhury, Kabir, and Saikat Chowdhury. *Taslima Nasreen and the Issue of Feminism.* Dhaka: Pratyasha Prakashan, 1997.

De, Kali Kumar. *Bengal's Contribution to Sanskrit Literature.* Calcutta: Sanskrit College, 1960.

De, Sushil Kumar. *History of Bengali Literature in the Nineteenth Century, 1800–1825.* Calcutta: University of Calcutta, 1919.

Ghosh, J. C. *Bengali Literature.* London: Oxford University Press, 1948.

Gosvami, Karunamaya. *Aspects of Nazrul Songs.* Dhaka: Nazrul Institute, 1990.

Haldar, Gopal. *Kazi Nazrul Islam.* New Delhi: Sahitya Akademi, 1973.

Islam, Manu, ed. *Literary Personalities of Bangladesh.* Dhaka: Baktittya Prokashani, 1985.

Kampchen, Martin, ed. *My Broken Love: Gunter Grass in India and Bangladesh.* New Delhi, Viking, 2001.

Kripalani, Krishna. *Rabindranath Tagore: A Biography.* Calcutta: Visva-Bharati, 1980.

Krsndasa Kaviraja Gosvami. *Sri Sri Chaitanya Charitamrita.* English translation. Calcutta: Sri Sri Chaitanya-Charitamrita Karyalaya, 1954–1956.

Lago, Mary M. *Rabindranath Tagore.* Boston: Twayne Publishers, 1976.

Mahfuzullah, M. *The Distinctive Features of Our Literature.* Dacca: Society for Pakistan Studies, 1970.

Mostapha Kamala, Abu Hena. *The Bengali Press and Literary Writing, 1818–31.* Dacca: University Press, 1977.

Moudud, Hasna Jasimuddin. *A Thousand Year Old Bengali Mystic Poetry.* Dhaka: University Press, 1992.

Mukhia, Banani. *Women's Images, Men's Imagination: Female Characters in Bengali Fiction in the Late 19th Century and Early 20th Century.* New Delhi: Manohar, 2002.

Murshid, Khan Sarwar, ed. *Contemporary Bengali Writing: Bangladeshi Period.* Dhaka: University Press, 1996.

——, ed. *Contemporary Bengali Writing: Pre-Bangladesh Period*. Dhaka: University Press, 1996.

Naravane, Vishwanath S. *Sarat Chandra Chatterji: An Introduction to His Life and Work*. Delhi: Macmillan, 1976.

Openshaw, Jeanne. *Seeking Bauls of Bengal*. Cambridge: Cambridge University Press, 2002.

Quader, Abedin, ed. *An Anthology of Modern Literature from Bangladesh*. Dhaka: Swaptapadi Publications, 1986.

Ramaswami Shastri, K. S. *Sir Rabindranath Tagore: His Life, Personality, and Genius*. Delhi: Akashdeep, 1988.

Rhys, Ernest. *Rabindranath Tagore: A Biographical Study*. New York: Haskell House, 1970.

Ross, Fiona G. E. *Printed Bengal Character and Its Evolution*. London: Curzon, 1999.

Roy, Basanta Kumar. *Rabindranath Tagore: The Man and His Poetry*. Norwood, Pa.: Norwood Editions, 1978.

Salkar, K. R. *Rabindranath Tagore: His Impact on Indian Education*. New Delhi: Sterling Publishers, 1990.

Sen, Dinesh Chandra. *History of Bengali Language and Literature*. Calcutta: University of Calcutta, 1911.

Sen, Sukumar. *Folk Music of Eastern India with Special Reference to Bengal*. Calcutta: Naya Prakash, 1988.

Siddiqui, Zillur Rahman. *Literature of Bangladesh and Other Essays*. Dhaka: Bangladesh Books International, 1982.

Yarrington, Matt. *Crocodile in the Water, Tiger on the Bank: Common Bengali Proverbs*. Dhaka: University Press Limited, 2008.

Zaman, Niaz, ed. *From the Delta: English Fiction from Bangladesh*. Dhaka: University Press, 2005.

——, ed. *Under the Krishnachura: Fifty Years of Bangladeshi Writing*. Dhaka: University Press Limited, 2003.

Zaman, Niaz Ali. *Animal Tales from Bangladesh*. Dhaka: Bangla Academy, 1985.

Fiction

Awwal, Mohammad Abdul. *The Prose Works of Mir Masarraf Hosen, 1869–1899*. Chittagong: University of Chittagong, 1975.

Marre, Runa Khan. *The Flower Maiden and Other Stories: Fairy Tales from Bangladesh*. Dhaka: University Press, 2001.

——. *Rani Kachan Mala and Other Stories*. Dhaka: University Press, 2001.

Samasujjamana, Abula Phajala. *The Trembling Flame (A Collection of Short Stories).* Dhaka: Tribhuj Praksasani, 1992.

Zaman, Niaz. *Literature in Bangladesh: Selected Short Stories.* Dhaka: University Press, 1998.

Poetry

Al Mahmud. *Beyond the Blue, Beneath the Bliss: Adventure, Oppression, Serenade, Destruction, Temptation, Salvation, Prayer.* Translated from Bengali by Mahbubul Alam Akhand. Dhaka: Pathak Shamabosh, 2000.

Chandidas. *Love Songs of Chandidas, the Rebel Poet-Priest of Bengal.* New York: Grove Press, 1967.

Hashim, Syed Najmuddin, ed. and trans. *The Devotee, the Combatant: Select Poems of Shamsur Rahman.* Dhaka: Pathak Shamabesh, 2000.

Huda, Muhammad Nurul. *Flaming Flowers: Poets' Response to the Emergence of Bangladesh.* Dhaka: Bangla Academy, 1986.

Jasimuddin. *Gipsy Wharf.* London: Allen and Unwin, 1969.

——. *Selected Poems of Jasimuddin.* Dacca: Oxford University Press, 1975.

Kamal, Sufia. *Mother of Pearls and Other Poems.* Translated and edited by Sajed Kamal. Dhaka: Bangla Academy, 2001.

——. *Where My Darlings Lie Buried: Memoirs of the Genocide.* Translated and edited by Sajed Kamal. New York: Vantage, 1975.

Lalon Shah. *Songs of Lalon.* Dhaka: University Press, 1987.

——. *Songs of Lalon Shah.* Dhaka: Bangla Academy, 1991.

Mukhopadhyay, Manik, ed. *The Golden Book of Saratchandra* [Chattopadhyay]. Bombay: Allied Publishers, 1977.

Nazrul Islam, Kazi. *The Fiery Lyre of Nazrul Islam.* Dacca: Bangla Academy, 1974.

——. *The Morning Shinai: Twenty Poems of Kazi Nazrul Islam.* Translated and introduced by Kabir Chowdhury. Dhaka: Nazrul Institute, 1991.

——. *A New Anthology.* Dhaka: Bangla Academy, 1990.

——. *The Rebel and Other Poems.* New Delhi: Sahitya Akademi, 1974.

Rashid, M. Harunur, ed. *A Choice of Contemporary Verse from Bangladesh.* Dhaka: Bangla Academy, 1986.

——. *Three Poets: Shamsur Rahman, Al Mahmud, Shaheed Quaderi.* Dacca: Bangladesh Books International, 1976.

Saif, Hayat, and Mahbub Talukdar, eds. *A Selection of Contemporary Verse from Bangladesh.* Dhaka: Second Asian Poetry Festival, 1989.

Tofayell, Z. A. *Lalon Shah and Lyrics of the Padma.* Dacca: Ziaunnahar, 1968.

PHILOSOPHY AND RELIGION

Bamladesa Hindu Bauddha Khrishtana Aikya Parishad. *Communal Persecution and Repression in Bangladesh, Some Facts.* Dhaka: Bangladesh Hindu Bouddha Christian Okhya Parishad, 1993.

Buddhism

Khan, Abdul Mabud. *The Maghs: A Buddhist Community in Bangladesh.* Dhaka: University Press, 1999.

Christianity

Ali, Muhammad Mohar. *The Bengali Reaction to Christian Missionary Activities, 1833–1857.* Chittagong: Mehrub Publications, 1965.

Dutta, Abhijit. *Nineteenth Century Bengal Society and Christian Missionaries.* Calcutta: Minerva Associates, 1992.

Hefley, James C. *Christ in Bangladesh.* New York: Harper and Row, 1973.

Lockerbie, Jeannie. *On Duty in Bangladesh.* Grand Rapids, Mich.: Zondervan, 1973.

———. *Write the Vision.* South Pasadena, Calif.: William Carey Library, 1989.

McKinley, Jim. *Death to Life, Bangladesh: The Experience of an American Missionary Family.* Dacca: Immanuel Baptist Church, 1979.

McNee, Peter. *Crucial Issues in Bangladesh: Making Missions More Effective in the Mosaic of Peoples.* South Pasadena, Calif.: William Carey Library, 1976.

Olsen, Viggo. *Daktar II.* Chicago: Moody Press, 1990.

Olsen, Viggo, and Jeannie Lockerbie. *Daktar: Diplomat in Bangla-desh.* Chicago: Moody Press, 1973.

Soddy, Gordon. *Baptists in Bangladesh: An Historical Sketch of More Than One Hundred Years' Work of the Baptist Missionary Society in Bengal.* Khulna: National Council of Churches, Bangladesh, 1987.

Walsh, Jay, and Patricia C. Oviatt. *Ripe Mangoes: Miracle Missionary Stories from Bangladesh.* Schaumburg, Ill.: Regular Baptist Press, 1978.

Zene, Cosimo. *The Rishi of Bangladesh: A History of Christian Dialogue.* Abingdon, Oxfordshire, England: Routledge/Curzon, 2002.

Hinduism

Kamra, A. J. *The Prolonged Partition and Its Pogroms: Testimonials on Violence against Hindus in East Bengal, 1946–64.* New Delhi: Voice of India, 2000.

Roy, Tathagata. *My People, Uprooted: A Saga of the Hindus of Eastern Bengal*. Kolkata: Ratna Prakashan, 2002.

Sastri, Sibnath. *History of the Brahmo Samaj*. Calcutta: Sadharan Brahmo Samaj, 1974.

Sen, Amiyakumar. *Tattwabodhini Sabha and the Bengal Renaissance*. Calcutta: Sadharan Brahmo Samaj, 1979.

Sen, Priyaranjan. *The Story of Chandidas: A Poetic Representation of the Fusion of Sakta and Vaishnava Cultures*. Calcutta: Indian Publications, 1963.

Islam

Ahmad Khan, Muin-ud-din. *History of the Fara'idi Movement in Bengal, 1818–1906*. Karachi: Pakistan Historical Society, 1965.

——. *Selections from Bengal Government Records on Wahhabi Trials (1863–1870)*. Dacca: n.p., 1961.

Ahmed, Rafiuddin, ed. *Islam in Bangladesh: Society, Culture, and Politics*. Dhaka: Elite Printing and Packages, 1983.

——, ed. *Understanding the Bengal Muslim: Interpretive Essays*. New Delhi: Oxford University Press, 2001.

Akramuzzaman. *A Sociological Profile of Islam*. Dacca: Islamic Foundation Bangladesh, 1979.

Ali, Syed Murtaza. *Saints of East Pakistan*. Dacca: Oxford University Press, Pakistan Branch, 1971.

Ameer Ali, Syed. *Memoirs and Other Writings of Syed Ameer Ali*. Delhi: Renaissance Publishing House, 1985.

——. *The Spirit of Islam: A History of the Evolution and Ideals of Islam, with a Life of the Prophet*. London: Christophers, 1955.

Banu, U. A. B. Razia Akhter. *Islam in Bangladesh*. Leiden: E. J. Brill, 1991.

Ghazi, Shamsur Rahman. *Islamic Law as Administered in Bangladesh*. Dacca: Islamic Foundation Bangladesh, 1981.

Haq, Muhammad Enamul. *A History of Sufi-ism in Bengal*. Dacca: Asiatic Society of Bangladesh, 1975.

Haq, Muhammad Mazammil. *Some Aspects of the Principal Sufi Orders in India*. Dhaka: Islamic Foundation Bangladesh, 1985.

Jafar, Abu. *Muslim Festivals in Bangladesh*. Dacca: Islamic Foundation, 1980.

Lahiri, Pradip Kumar. *Bengali Muslim Thought, 1818–1947: Its Liberal and Rational Trends*. Calcutta: Bagchi, 1991.

Latif, Abdul, Sheikh. *The Muslim Mystic Movement in Bengal, 1301–1550*. Calcutta: K. P. Bagchi, 1993.

Meerza, Delawar Hosaen Ahamed. *Muslim Modernism in Bengal: Selected Writings of Delawar Hosaen Ahamed Meerza, 1840–1913*. Dacca: Centre for Social Studies, 1980.

Murshed, Tazeen M. *The Sacred and the Secular: Bengali Muslim Discourses, 1871–1977*. Calcutta: Oxford Univesity Press, 1995.

Quasem, Abul. *Islam, Science, and Modern Thoughts*. Dacca: Islamic Foundation Bangladesh, 1980.

Roy, Asim. *The Islamic Syncretist Tradition in Bengal*. Princeton, N.J.: Princeton University Press, 1983.

Sarkar, Jagadish Narayan. *Islam in Bengal (Thirteenth to Nineteenth Century)*. Calcutta: Ratna Prakashan, 1972.

POLITICS AND GOVERNMENT

Ahamed, Emajuddin. *Military Rule and the Myth of Democracy*. Dhaka: University Press, 1988.

——, ed. *Society and Politics in Bangladesh*. Dhaka: Academic Publishers, 1989.

Ahmed, Abu Nasar Saied. *Fundamentalism in Bangladesh: Its Impact on India*. New Delhi: Akansha, 2008.

Ahmed, Fakhruddin. *The Caretakers: A First Hand Account of the Interim Government of Bangladesh (1990–91)*. Dhaka: University Press, 1998.

Ahmed, Imtiaz, ed. *Terrorism in the 21ˢᵗ Century: Perspectives from Bangladesh*. Dhaka: University Press Limited, 2005. Revised 2009.

Ahmed, Moudud. *Bangladesh: Era of Sheikh Mujibur Rahman*. Dhaka: University Press, 1983.

——. *Democracy and the Challenge of Development: A Study of Politics and Military Intervention in Bangladesh*. Dhaka: University Press, 1995.

Ahmed, Nizam. *Limits of Parliamentary Control: Public Spending in Bangladesh*. Dhaka: University Press Limited, 2006.

——. *The Parliament of Bangladesh*. Aldershot, UK: Ashgate, 2002.

Ahmed, Nizam, and A. T. M. Obaidullah, eds. *The Working of Parliamentary Committees in Westminster Systems: Lessons for Bangladesh*. Dhaka: University Press Limited, 2007.

Ahmed, Rafiuddin, ed. *Religion, Nationalism, and Politics in Bangladesh*. New Delhi: South Asian Publishers, 1990.

Ahmed, Salahuddin. *Bangladesh: Past and Present*. New Delhi: APH, 2004.

Alam, Habibul. *Brave of Heart: The Urban Guerilla Warfare of Sector-2, during the Liberation War of Bangladesh*. Dhaka: Academic Press and Publishers Library, 2006.

Ali, A. F. Imam. *Hindu-Muslim Community in Bangladesh.* Delhi: Kanishka Publishing House, 1992.

Ali, S. M. *After the Dark Night: Problems of Sheikh Mujibur Rahman.* Delhi: Thompson Press, 1973.

———. *Awami League Rule: Glimpses from the International Press.* Dhaka: Oasis Press, 1992.

Andaleeb, Syed Saad, ed. *Political Culture in Bangladesh: Perspectives and Analyses: Selections from the Journal of Bangladesh Studies.* Dhaka: University Press Limited, 2007.

Badruddin Umar. *Towards the Emergency.* Dacca: Muktadhara, 1980.

Banerjee, Subrata. *Bangladesh.* New Delhi: National Book Trust, India, 1981.

Bauer, Caroline Feller. *Bangladesh at Work.* Dhaka: University Press, 2006.

Brace, Steve. *Bangladesh.* New York: Thompson Learning, 1995.

Chakravarti, S. R. *Bangladesh under Mujib, Zia and Ershad: Dilemmas of a New Nation.* New Delhi: HarAnand, 1995.

Chitkara, M. G. *Bangladesh: Mujib to Hasina.* New Delhi: APH Publishing, 1997.

Chopra, J. K. *Bangladesh as a New Nation.* Jaipur, India: Sublime, 2000.

Choudhury, Dilara. *Constitutional Development in Bangladesh: Stress and Strains.* Karachi: Oxford University Press, 1994.

Chowdhury, Mahfuzul Huq, ed. *Thirty Years of Bangladesh Politics: Essays in Memory of Dr. Mahfuzul Huq.* Dhaka: University Press Limited, 2002.

Chowdhury, Masud A. T. M. *Reminiscence of a Few Decades and Problems of Democracy in Bangladesh.* Dhaka: GM Academic Press and Publishers, 2008.

Dasgupta, Sukharanjan. *Midnight Massacre in Dacca.* New Delhi: Vikas, 1978.

De, Barun, and Ranabir Samaddar, eds. *Development and Political Culture: Bangladesh and India.* New Delhi: HarAnand, 1996.

Franda, Marcus F. *Bangladesh Nationalism and Ziaur Rahman's Presidency.* Hanover, N.H.: American Universities Field Staff, 1981.

———. *Bangladesh: The First Decade.* New Delhi: South Asian Publishers, 1982.

Hafiz, M. Abdul, and Abdur Rob Khan, eds. *Nation Building in Bangladesh: Retrospect and Prospect.* Dhaka: Bangladesh Institute of International and Strategic Studies, 1986.

Hakim, Muhammad A. *Bangladesh Politics: The Shahabuddin Interregnum.* Dhaka: University Press, 1993.

Hakim, S. Abdul. *Begum Khaleda Zia of Bangladesh: A Political Biography.* New Delhi: Vikas, 1992.

Harun, Shamsul Huda. *Bangladesh Voting Behaviour: A Psephological Study, 1973*. Dhaka: Dhaka University, 1986.

Hasanuzzaman, al-Masud, ed. *Bangladesh: Crisis of Political Development*. Savar, Bangladesh: Jahangirnagar University, 1988.

———. *Role of Opposition in Bangladesh Politics*. Dhaka: University Press, 1998.

Hossain, Golam. *General Ziaur Rahman and the BNP: Political Transformation of a Military Regime*. Dhaka: University Press, 1988.

Hossain, Hamida, ed. *Human Rights in Bangladesh 2005*. Dhaka: Ain o Salish Kendra (ASK), 2006.

———. *Human Rights in Bangladesh 2006*. Dhaka: Ain o Salish Kendra (ASK), 2007.

Huque, Kazi Anwarul. *Under Three Flags: Reminiscences of a Public Servant*. Dhaka: Islamic Foundation, 1986.

Hussain, Motahar. *Development Administration in Bangladesh*. Reprint. Dhaka: A. H. Development, 2005.

Islam, Nurul. *Making of a Nation: Bangladesh; An Economist's Tale*. Dhaka: University Press, 2003.

Jahan, Rounaq. *Bangladesh Politics: Problems and Issues*. Dhaka: University Press, 1980.

———, ed. *Bangladesh: Promise and Performance*. Dhaka: University Press, 2000.

Jahangir, Burhanuddin Khan. *Problematics of Nationalism in Bangladesh*. Dhaka: Centre for Social Studies, 1986.

Jamil, Ishtiaq. *Administrative Culture in Bangladesh*. Dhaka: A. H. Development Pub., 2007.

Kabir, Muhammad Ghulam. *Minority Politics in Bangladesh*. New Delhi: Vikas, 1980.

Karim, S. A. *Sheikh Mujib: Triumph and Tragedy*. Dhaka: University Press Limited, 2005.

Karim, Waresul. *Election under a Caretaker Government: An Empirical Analysis of the October 2001 Parliamentary Election in Bangladesh*. Dhaka: University Press, 2004.

Khan, Iqbal Ansari. *The Third Eye: Glimpses of the Politicos*. Dhaka: University Press, 1991.

Khan, M. Salimuddin, ed. *Politics and Stability in Bangladesh: Problems and Prospects*. Dhaka: Jahangirnagar University, 1985.

Khan, Mohammad Mohabbat, and Syed Anwarul Husain, eds. *Bangladesh Studies: Politics, Administration, Rural Development, and Foreign Policy*. Dhaka: Centre for Administrative Studies, University of Dhaka, 1985.

Khan, Zillur Rahman. *Leadership Crisis in Bangladesh: Martial Law to Martial Law*. Dhaka: University Press, 1983.

———. *Leadership in the Least Developed Nation: Bangladesh*. Syracuse, N.Y.: Maxwell School of Citizenship and Public Affairs, 1983.

Khanam, Rashida. *The Nature of Legitimacy and the Crisis of Bangladesh Politics 1972–1990*. Dhaka: AH Development Publishing House, 2008.

Kochanek, Stanley A. *Patron-Client Politics and Business in Bangladesh*. Thousand Oaks, Calif.: Sage, 1993.

Lifschultz, Lawrence. *Bangladesh: The Unfinished Revolution*. London: Zed Press, 1979.

Maleque, Md. Abdul. *Pressure Groups: Dynamics of Bangladesh Politics*. Dhaka: Academic Press and Publishers Library, 2007.

Mamoon, Muntasir, ed. *Civil Society in Bangladesh*. Calcutta: Firma KLM, 1996.

Maniruzzaman, Talukder. *The Bangladesh Revolution and Its Aftermath*. Dacca: Bangladesh Books International, 1980.

Mannan, Md. Abdul. *Elections and Democracy in Bangladesh*. Dhaka: Academic Press and Publishers Library, 2005.

Mascarenhas, Anthony. *Bangladesh: A Legacy of Blood*. London: Hodder and Stoughton, 1986.

May, R. J., and Binayak Ray, eds. *Corruption, Governance and Democracy in South Asia: Bangladesh, India and Pakistan*. Kolkata: Towards Freedom, 2006.

Mishra, S. K. *Bangladesh: A Silent Security Threat*. New Delhi: Radha, 2008.

Momen, Nurul. *Bangladesh: The First Four Years (from 16 December 1971 to 15 December 1975)*. Dacca: Bangladesh Institute of Law and International Affairs, 1980.

Muhith, A. M. A. *Issues of Governance in Bangladesh*. Dhaka: Mowla Brothers, 2000.

Nawaz, Mohammed. *Bangladesh through the Period of Turmoil and Reconstruction*. Lahore: Progressive Publishers, 1974.

Nurujjamana, Mohammada. *Prof. Ghulam Azam: A Profile of Struggle in the Cause of Allah*. Dhaka: Prachi Prakashani, 1992.

Osmany, Mufleh R. *Wither National Security Bangladesh 2007*. Dhaka: University Press Limited, 2008.

Panday, Pranab Kumar. *Problems of Urban Governance in Bangladesh*. New Delhi: Serials, 2009.

Puchkov, V. P. *Political Development of Bangladesh*. New Delhi: Patriot Publishers, 1989.

Rahman, Matiur. *Bangladesh Today: An Indictment and a Lament*. London: News and Media, 1978.

Rahman, Muhammad Anisur. *The Lost Moment: Dreams with a Nation Born through Fire; Papers on Political Economy of Bangladesh.* Dhaka: University Press, 1993.

RAW in Bangladesh: Portrait of an Aggressive Intelligence. Dhaka: Abu Rushd, 2005.

Ray, Jayanta Kumar, and Muntassir Mamoon. *Essays on Politics and Governance in Bangladesh, India, Pakistan and Thailand.* Kolkata: Towards Freedom, 2007.

Sadik, Musa. *Bangladesh Wins Freedom.* Dhaka: Gholam Moyenuddin, 2005.

Saha, B. P. *Liberation Struggle and After.* New Delhi: Vikas, 1985.

Samaddar, Ranabir. *Paradoxes of the Nationalist Time: Political Essays on Bangladesh.* Dhaka: University Press, 2002.

Sayem, Abusadat Mohammad. *At Bangabhaban: Last Phase.* Dhaka: Hakkani Publishers, 1988.

Seabrook, Jeremy. *Freedom Unfinished: Fundamentalism and Resistance in Bangladesh.* London: Zed Books, 2001.

Sector Commanders Forum. *Bangladesh Genocide 1971: The Trial of War Criminals.* Dhaka, 2008.

Sen, Achintya. *People, Power, Politics, 1972–1991.* Dhaka: Pinaki Das, 1991.

Sen, Rangalal. *Political Elites in Bangladesh.* Dhaka: University Press, 1986.

Sengupta, Dipankar, and Sudhir Kumar Singh. *Insurgency in North-East India: The Role of Bangladesh.* Delhi: Authorspress, 2004.

Shamsuddin, Abu Zafar. *Sociology of Bengal Politics and Other Essays.* Dacca: Bangla Academy, 1973.

Shawkat Ali, A. M. M. *Bangladesh Civil Service: A Political-Administrative Perspective.* Dhaka: University Press Limited, 2004.

——. *The Lore of the Mandarins: Towards a Non-partisan Public Service in Bangladesh.* Dhaka: University Press, 2002.

Siddiqi, Dina M., ed. *Human Rights in Bangladesh 2000.* Dhaka: Ain o Salish Kendra (ASK), 2004.

Siddiqui, S. A. *The Pattern of Secularism in India and Bangladesh.* Chittagong: Siddiqui, 1974.

Sobhan, Farooq, ed. *Countering Terrorism in Bangladesh.* Dhaka: University Press Limited, 2008.

Sobhan, Rahman. *Bangladesh: Problems of Governance.* Delhi: Konark, 1993.

Umar, Badruddin. *The Emergence of Bangladesh: Class Struggles in East Pakistan (1947–1958).* New York: Oxford University Press, 2004.

Zafarullah, Habib, ed. *The Zia Episode in Bangladesh Politics.* New Delhi: South Asia Publications, 1996.

Zafarullah, Habib, and M. M. Khan. *The Bureaucratic Ascendancy: Public Administration in Bangladesh: The First Three Decades*. New Delhi: South Asian Pub., 2005.

Ziring, Lawrence. *Bangladesh: From Mujib to Ershad: An Interpretive Study.* Karachi: Oxford University Press, 1992.

Bibliography

Zahiruddin, Habib Mohammad. *Government and Politics in Bangladesh: A Bibliographical Guide*. Dacca: Centre for Administrative Studies, 1981.

Armed Forces

Ahmad, Borhanuddin. *The Generals of Pakistan and Bangladesh*. New Delhi: Vikas, 1993.

Bangladesh Army. *Bangladesher Muktijudhha*. A seven-volume publication on the major and minor battles during the War of Liberation. Dhaka: Asia Publication, 2008.

Gautam, P. K. *Operation Bangladesh*. New Delhi: Manas Publishers, 2007.

Hasanuzzaman. *Search for a New Dimension: Politico-Constitutional and Military Tangle in Bangladesh*. Dhaka: Bangladesh Book House, 1992.

Hossain, Golam. *Civil-Military Relations in Bangladesh*. Dhaka: Academic Publishers, 1991.

Kabir, Bhuian. *Politics of Military Rule and the Dilemmas of Democratization in Bangladesh*. Denver, Colo.: Academic Books, 2000.

Kukreja, Veena. *Civil-Military Relations in South Asia: Pakistan, Bangladesh and India*. New Delhi: Sage, 1991.

Rezwan-ul-Alam. *Military-Media Relations in Bangladesh 1975–1990*. Dhaka: Palok Publishers, 2008.

Defense

Buzan, Barry. *South Asian Insecurity and the Great Powers*. New York: St. Martin's Press, 1986.

Jain, B. M. *South Asian Security: Problems and Prospects*. New Delhi: Radiant Publishers, 1985.

Narain, Jai. *Economics of Defence: A Study of SAARC Countries*. New Delhi: Lancers Books, 1989.

Sinha, K. K. *Problems of Defence of South and East Asia*. Bombay: Manaktalas, 1969.

Elections

Ahmed, Fakhruddin, ed. *Union Parishad Election, 1997*. Dhaka: Fair Election Monitoring Alliance, 1998.

Akhter, Muhammad Yeahia. *Electoral Corruption in Bangladesh*. Aldershot, UK: Ashgate, 2001.

Blair, Harry W. *Voting, Caste, Community, Society: Explorations in Aggregate Data Analysis in India and Bangladesh*. Delhi: Young Asia, 1979.

Chakravarty, S. R. *Bangladesh: The Nineteen Seventy-Nine Elections*. New Delhi: South Asian Publishers, 1988.

Coordinating Council for Human Rights in Bangladesh (CCHRB). *Parliamentary Election 1991: Observation Report*. Dhaka: The Council, 1991.

Kajal, Iftikhar. *National Parliament Election, 1991: Some Reflections*. Dhaka: Raktoreen, 1991.

Thiagarajah, Jeevan, ed. *Governance and Electoral Process in Bangladesh: Report of the SAARC-NGO Observers*. New Delhi: Vikas, 1997.

International Relations

Abdur Razzak. *Foreign Powers and Bangladesh*. London: Bangladesh Krishak Sramik Awami League, 1977.

Ahamed, Emajuddin, ed. *Foreign Policy of Bangladesh: A Small State's Imperative*. Dhaka: University Press, 1984 and 2004.

Ahamed, Emajuddin, and Abul Kalam, eds. *Bangladesh, South Asia, and the World*. Dhaka: Academic Publishers, 1992.

Ahmad, Muzaffer, and Abul Kalam, eds. *Bangladesh Foreign Relations: Changes and Directions*. Dhaka: University Press, 1989.

Ahmed, Fakhruddin. *Critical Times: Memoirs of a South Asian Diplomat*. Dhaka: University Press, 1994.

Ahmed, Kamal Uddin. *Bangladesh and Its Neighbours*. Dhaka: Asiatic Society of Bangladesh, 2008.

Arshad-uz-Zaman. *Privileged Witness: Memoirs of a Diplomat*. Dhaka: University Press, 2000.

Ayoob, Mohammed. *India, Pakistan and Bangladesh: Search for New Relationship*. New Delhi: Indian Council of World Affairs, 1975.

Azad, Salam. *Role of Indian People in Liberation War of Bangladesh*. Delhi: Bookwell, 2008.

Bhardwaj, Sanjay. *Bangladesh–US Relations: From Cooperation to Partnership*. Delhi: Kalinga, 2002.

Bhasin, Avtar Singh, ed. *India–Bangladesh Relations: Documents 1971–2002*. New Delhi: Geetika Publishers, 2003.

Bindra, Sukhwant Singh. *Indo–Bangladesh Relations*. New Delhi: Deep and Deep Publications, 1982.

Chakravarti, S. R. *Foreign Policy of Bangladesh*. New Delhi: HarAnand, 1994.

Choudhury, Dilara. *Bangladesh and the South Asian International System*. Dhaka: Academic Publishers, 1992.

Choudhury, G. W. *India, Pakistan, Bangladesh, and the Major Powers: Politics of a Divided Subcontinent*. New York: Free Press, 1975.

Debbarma, P. K. *The Chakma Refugees in Tripura*. New Delhi: South Asian Publishers, 1993.

Deora, M. S. *India and the Freedom Struggle of Bangladesh*. New Delhi: Discovery, 1995.

Dixit, J. N. *Liberation and Beyond: Indo-Bangladesh Relations*. Delhi: Konark, 1999.

Eusufzai, Zaki. *Liberalisation in the Shadow of a Large Neighbour: A Case of Bangladesh-India Economic Relations*. Dhaka: University Press Limited, 2000.

Ghosh, Suchita. *China, Bangladesh, India Tangle Today*. New Delhi: Sterling, 1995.

Gulati, Chandrika J. *Bangladesh: Liberation to Fundamentalism: A Study of Volatile Indo-Bangladesh Relations*. New Delhi: Commonwealth Publishers, 1988.

Haendel, Dan. *The Process of Policy Formulation: U.S. Foreign Policy in the Indo-Pakistan War of 1971*. Boulder, Colo.: Westview Press, 1977.

Hafiz, M. Abdul, and Abdur Rob Khan, eds. *Security of Small States*. Dhaka: University Press, 1987.

Haider, Zaglul. *The Changing Pattern of Bangladesh Foreign Policy: A Comparative Study of the Mujib and Zia Regimes*. Dhaka: University Press Limited, 2006. Rev. edition, 2008.

Hazarika, Sanjoy. *Rites of Passage: Border Crossings, Imagined Homelands, India's East and Bangladesh*. New Delhi: Penguin, 2000.

Islam, M. Rafiqul. *The Ganges Water Dispute: International Legal Aspects*. Dhaka: University Press, 1987.

Jain, Jagdish P. *China, Pakistan, and Bangladesh*. Delhi: Radiant Publishers, 1974–76.

Kabir, Muhammad Ghulam. *Changing Face of Nationalism: The Case of Bangladesh*. Denver, Colo.: Academic Books, 2001.

Kalam, Abul. *Subregionalism in South Asia: ASEAN and SAARC Experiences*. New Delhi: UBS Publications, 2001.

Khan, Ataur R. *India, Pakistan and Bangladesh: Conflict or Co-operation?* Dacca: Sindabad, 1976.

Khan, Rumana S. *Non-military Security of Bangladesh: External Determinants.* Dhaka: University Press, 1996.

Khan, Zillur Rahman, ed. *SAARC and the Superpowers.* Dhaka: University Press, 1991.

Khurshida Begum. *Tension over the Farakka Barrage: A Techno-Political Tangle in South Asia.* Dhaka: University Press, 1987.

Lal, Shiv. *Bangla-Pak Polities.* New Delhi: Election Archives, 1985.

Malhotra, Inder. *Dynasties of India and Beyond: Pakistan, Sri Lanka, Bangladesh.* New Delhi: HarperCollins, 2003.

Maniruzzaman, Talukder. *Politics and Security in Bangladesh.* Dhaka: University Press, 1994.

Momen, Nurul. *Bangladesh in the United Nations: A Study in Diplomacy.* Dhaka: University Press, 1987.

Mostafa, Golam. *National Interest and Foreign Policy: Bangladesh's Relations with the Soviet Union and Its Successor States.* Denver, Colo.: iAcademic Books, 2001.

Nair, Sukumaran, P. *Indo-Bangladesh Relations.* New Delhi: APH, 2008.

Narain, Virendra. *Foreign Policy of Bangladesh, 1971–1981: The Context of National Liberation Movement.* Jaipur: Aalekh Publishers, 1987.

Oliver, Thomas W. *The United Nations in Bangladesh.* Princeton, N.J.: Princeton University Press, 1978.

Rai, Baljit. *Demographic Aggression against India: Muslim Avalanche from Bangladesh.* Chandigarh, India: BS Publishers, 1993.

Rashid, Harun ur. *The Diary of a Diplomat.* Dhaka: Ekushey, 1999.

———. *Foreign Relations of Bangladesh.* Varanasi, India: Rishi Publications, 2001.

———. *Indo-Bangladesh Relations: An Insider's View.* New Delhi: Har-Anand, 2002.

Reddy, K. C., and T. Nirmala Devi, eds. *Regional Cooperation in South Asia: New Dimensions.* New Delhi: Kanishka, 2002.

Saha, Rekha. *India-Bangladesh Relations.* Calcutta: Minerva, 2000.

Shamsul Huq, Muhammad. *Bangladesh International Politics: The Dilemmas of the Weak States.* New Delhi: Sterling, 1993.

———. *International Politics: A Third World Perspective.* New Delhi: Sterling, 1987.

Sharma, Sarbjit. *U.S.-Bangladesh Relations: A Critique.* New Delhi: UBS Publishers, 2001.

Singh, Kuldeep. *India and Bangladesh.* New Delhi: Anupama Publishers, 1987.

Sobhan, Farooq, ed. *Bangladesh-India Dialogue: Vision of Young Leaders.* Dhaka: University Press Limited, 2006.

———, ed. *Dynamics of Bangladesh-India Relations: Dialogue of Young Journalists across the Border*. Dhaka: University Press, 2005.

Sobhan, Rehman, ed. *Bangladesh-India Relations: Perspectives from Civil Society Dialogues*. Dhaka: University Press, 2002.

Tajuddin, Muhammad. *Foreign Policy of Bangladesh: Liberation War to Sheikh Hasina*. New Delhi: National Books, 2001.

Tayyeb-ur Rahman, Syed. *Global Geo-strategy of Bangladesh, OIC, and Islamic Umma*. Dhaka: Islamic Foundation Bangladesh, 1985.

Trivedi, Rabindranath. *International Relations of Bangladesh and Bangabandhu Sheikh Mujibur Rahman: Documents, Messages and Speeches 1971–1973*. Dhaka: Parama, 1999.

Wright, Denis. *Bangladesh: Origins and Indian Ocean Relations, 1971–1975*. New Delhi: Sterling Publishers, 1988.

Law

Bhattacharya, Debesh Chandra. *Enemy (Vested) Property Laws in Bangladesh: Nature and Implications*. Dhaka: Chitra Bhattacharya, 1991.

Dipankar, Sengupta, and Sudhir Kumar Singh, eds. *Minorities and Human Rights in Bangladesh*. New Delhi: Authorspress 2003.

Islam, Mahmudul. *Constitutional Law of Bangladesh*. Dhaka: Bangladesh Institute of Law and International Affairs, 1995.

Mahmood, Tahir, ed. *Cases in the Muhammadan Law of India, Pakistan and Bangladesh*. Reprint. New Delhi: Oxford University Press, 2005.

Munim, F. K. M. A. *Rights of the Citizen under the Constitution and Law*. Dhaka: Bangladesh Institute of Law and International Affairs, 1975.

Patwari, A. B. M. Mafizul Islam. *Legal System of Bangladesh*. Dhaka: Aligarh Library, 1991.

Pereira, Faustina. *The Fractured Scales: Search for a Uniform Personal Code*. Calcutta: Stree, 2002.

Rahman, Rafiqur. *Law of Evidence*. Dhaka: Nuruzzaman Choudhury, 1993.

Zahir, M. *Company and Securities Laws*. Dhaka: University Press, 2001.

———. *Delay in Courts and Court Management*. Dhaka: Bangladesh Institute of Law and International Affairs, 1988.

Local Government

Ahmed, Tofail. *Decentralization and the Local State under Peripheral Capitalism: A Study in the Political Economy of Local Government in Bangladesh*. Dhaka: Academic Publishers, 1993.

Ali, Qazi Azher. *District Administration in Bangladesh*. Dacca: National Institute of Public Administration, 1978.

Ali, Sheikh Maqsood. *Decentralization and People's Participation in Bangladesh*. Dhaka: National Institute of Local Government, 1983.

Aziz, Mohammed Abdul. *The Union Parishad in Bangladesh: An Analysis of Problems and Directions of Reform*. Dhaka: National Institute of Local Government, 1991.

Belal, Khalid, ed. *The Chittagong Hill Tracts: Falconry in the Hills*. Chittagong: Codec, 1992.

Chaudhuri, Muzaffar Ahmed. *Rural Government in East Pakistan*. Dacca: Puthighar, 1969.

Choudhury, Lutful Hoq. *Local Self-Government and Its Reorganization in Bangladesh*. Dhaka: National Institute of Local Government, 1987.

Faizullah, Mohammad. *Development of Local Government in Bangladesh*. Dhaka: National Institute of Local Government, 1987.

Hasnat, Abdul Hye, ed. *Decentralization, Local Government Institutions and Resource Mobilization*. Comilla: Bangladesh Academy for Rural Development, 1985.

Karim, Muhammad Abdul. *Upazila System in Bangladesh: A Political and Administrative Analysis*. Dhaka: National Institute of Local Government, 1991.

Khandaker, Mushtaque Ahmad. *Paurashava (Municipal) Services: A Case Study of Narayanganj*. Dhaka: National Institute of Local Government, 1990.

Mallick, Bishawjit. *Local Government: Local Peoples' Institution; A Compilation on Local Government Issues*. Dhaka: AH Development Publishing House, 2004.

Mey, Wolfgang, ed. *They Are Now Burning Village after Village: Genocide in the Chittagong Hill Tracts, Bangladesh*. Copenhagen: International Work Group for Indigenous Affairs, 1984.

Mohsin, Ameena. *The Politics of Nationalism: The Case of the Chittagong Hill Tracts, Bangladesh*. Dhaka: University Press, 1997.

Morshed, M. Mahbubur Rahman. *Bureaucratic Response to Administrative Decentralization*. Dhaka: University Press, 1997.

Rahman, A. H. M. Aminur. *Politics of Rural Self-Government in Bangladesh*. Dhaka: University of Dhaka, 1990.

Rahman, Atiur. *Rural Power Structure: A Study of the Local Level Leaders in Bangladesh*. Dacca: Bangladesh Books International, 1981.

Rahman, Hossain Zillur, and S. Aminul Islam. *Local Governance and Community Capacities: Search for New Frontiers*. Dhaka: University Press, 2002.

Rahman, Mohammad Shafiqur. *Planning and Development of Upazila in Bangladesh*. Dhaka: National Institute of Local Government, 1991.

Shamsul Hoque, A. N. *Subnational Administration in Bangladesh and Its Role in Development: An Overview*. Rajshahi: Department of Political Science, Rajshahi University, 1982.

Shawkat Ali, A. M. M. *Politics, Development and Upazila*. Dhaka: National Institute of Local Government, 1986.

Shelley, Mizanur Rahman, ed. *The Chittagong Hills Tracts of Bangladesh: The Untold Story*. Dhaka: Centre for Development Research, Bangladesh, 1992.

Siddiqui, Kamal. *Local Governance in Bangladesh: Leading Issues and Major Challenges*. Dhaka: University Press, 2001.

———. *Local Government in Bangladesh*. Dhaka: National Institute of Local Government, 1984. Reprint, 2005.

Political Parties

Ghosh, Shyamali. *The Awami League, 1949–1971*. Dhaka: Academic Publishers, 1990.

Hasanuzzaman, Al Masud. *Role of Opposition in Bangladesh Politics*. Dhaka: University Press, 1998.

Kabir, Bhuian Md. Monoar. *The Politics and Development of the Jamaat-E-Islami Bangladesh*. Dhaka: A. H. Development Pub., 2006.

Mohaimena, Mohammad Abdulla. *Awami League in the Politics of Bangladesh*. Dhaka: Pioneer Publications, 1990.

Shelley, Mizanur Rahman. *Pakistan, the Second Republic: Politics and Parties*. Dacca: Concept Publications, 1970.

Public Administration

Abedin, Mohammad Jainul. *Papers on Administration and Related Issues*. Dhaka: Academy for Planning and Development, 1991.

Anisuzzaman, Mohammad. *Bangladesh Public Administration and Society*. Dhaka: Bangladesh Books International, 1979.

Barenstein, Jorge. *Overcoming Fuzzy Government in Bangladesh: Policy Implementation in Least Developed Countries*. Dhaka: University Press, 1994.

Chadha, I. S. *Managing Projects in Bangladesh: A Scenario Analysis of Institutional Environment for Development Projects*. Dhaka: University Press, 1990.

Giasuddin Ahmed, Syed. *Bangladesh Public Service Commission*. Dhaka: University of Dhaka, 1990.

Hayadara, Iusupha. *Development, the Upazila Way*. Dhaka: Dhaka Prokashan, 1986.

Huq, M. Enamul. *Readings on Policing*. Dhaka: Sumi, 1992.

Khan, Mohammad Mohabbat. *Politics of Administrative Reform: A Case Study of Bangladesh*. New Delhi: Ashish Publishing House, 1991.

Kibria, A. B. M. G. *Police Administration in Bangladesh*. Dacca: Khoshroz Kitab Mahal, 1976.

Rahman, M. Shamsur. *Administrative Elite in Bangladesh*. New Delhi: Manak Publications, 1991.

Seraj, Toufiq M. *The Role of Small Towns in Rural Development: A Case Study of Bangladesh*. Dhaka: National Institute of Local Government, 1989.

Shawkat Ali, A. M. M. *An Analysis of the Working of Basic Democracy Institutions in East Pakistan*. Comilla: Bangladesh Academy for Rural Development, 1963.

————. *Civil Service Management in Bangladesh*. Dhaka: University Press Limited, 2008.

Sirajuddin, Muhammad. *Institutional Support for Planning and Project Management*. Dhaka: Study Group, 1982.

Regional Associations

Ahamed, Emajuddin. *SAARC: Seeds of Harmony*. Dhaka: University Press, 1985.

Ahsan, Abul. *SAARC: A Perspective*. Dhaka: University Press, 1992.

Aminuzzaman, M. Salahuddin, ed. *Governance and Development: Bangladesh and Regional Experiences*. Dhaka: Shrabon Prokashani, 2006.

Anand, Ram Prakash. *South Asia in Search of a Regional Identity*. New Delhi: Banyan Publications, 1991.

ASEAN Experiences of Regional and Inter-Regional Cooperation: Relevance for SAARC. Dhaka: Bangladesh Institute for International and Strategic Studies, 1988.

De, Prabir Kumar, *Regionalism and National Security: Bangladesh and SAARC*. Kolkata: Sujan Publishers, 2005.

Devi, T. Nirmala, ed. *India and Bay of Bengal Community: The BIMSTEC Experiment (Bangladesh-India-Myanmar-Sri Lanka-Thailand Economic Cooperation)*. New Delhi: Gyan Publishers, 2007.

Hafiz, M. Abdul, ed. *South Asian Regional Cooperation: A Socio-Economic Approach to Regional Stability*. Dhaka: Bangladesh Institute of International and Strategic Studies, 1985.

Kabir, Mohammad Humayun, ed. *Small States and Regional Stability in South Asia*. Dhaka; University Press, 2005.

Mendis, Vernon L. B. *SAARC: Origins, Organization, and Prospects.* Perth, Western Australia: Indian Ocean Centre for Peace Studies, 1991.

Mishra, Pramod Kumar. *South-South Cooperation: A SAARC Perspective.* Calcutta: Chatterjee Publishers, 1990.

Rahman, Atiur. *Political Economy of SAARC.* Dhaka: Papari Prakasani, 1983.

Satyamurty, K. *South Asian Regional Cooperation.* Hyderabad, India: Booklinks, 1982.

Wadhva, Charan D., ed. *Regional Economic Cooperation in South Asia.* Ahmedabad: Allied Publishers, 1987.

SCIENCE AND TECHNOLOGY

Dasgupta, Subrata. *Jagdish Chandra Bose and the Indian Response to Western Science.* New Delhi: Oxford University Press, 1999.

Eusuf, M., ed. *Solar Photovoltaic Systems in Bangladesh: Experiences and Opportunities.* Dhaka: University Press, 2005.

Farouk, A. *A Study of Occupations Where Qualifications in Natural Sciences and Mathematics Are Required in East Pakistan.* Dacca: Bureau of Economic Research, 1970.

Huq, Mozammel, ed. *Building Technological Capability: Issues and Prospects; Nepal, Bangladesh and India.* Dhaka: University Press, 2003.

Khan, F. H. *The Geology of Bangladesh.* Dhaka: University, 2001.

Environmental Science

Adrika, Ahana. *A Plan for Ensuring Sustainability of Community Based Haor and Floodplain Resource Management Projects.* Dhaka: IUCN—World Conservation Union, 2005.

Ahmed, Imtiaz, ed. *Living with Floods: An Exercise in Alternatives.* Dhaka: University Press, 1999.

Ahmed, Rashiduzzaman, and Ainun Nishat, eds. *Participatory Problem Census in Pagnar and Sanuar-Dakuar Haors.* Dhaka: IUCN—World Conservation Union, 2005.

Ahmed, Ziauddin. *The Fading Horizon: Science and Technology in Bangladesh.* Dhaka: Hassan Book House, 2007.

Alauddin, Muhammad, and Clement Allen Tisdell. *The Environment and Economic Development in South Asia: An Overview Concentrating on Bangladesh.* New York: St. Martin's Press, 1998.

Amin, Shahalam M. N., ed. *Studies on Coastal Environments in Bangladesh.* Dhaka: A. H. Development Pub., 2008.

Anwar, Jamal. *Bangladesh: The State of the Environment*. Dhaka: Shahitya Prakash, 1993.

Choudhury, Junaid, K., et al. *Eco-restoration Nursery for the Hilly Areas of Bangladesh: A Community Based Approach*. Dhaka: IUCN—World Conservation Union, 2004.

De Wilde, Koen, ed. *Out of the Periphery: Development of Chars in Southeastern Bangladesh*. Dhaka: University Press, 2001.

Elahi, K. Maudood, Sharif A. H. M. Raihan, and A. K. M. Abul Kalam, eds. *Bangladesh: Geography, Development, and Environment*. Dhaka: Bangladesh National Geographic Association, 1992.

Gaan, Narottam. *Environmental Degradation: The Case of Bangladesh-India*. New Delhi: South Asian Publishers, 1998.

Hassan, Mahabubul, Arif Mohammad Faisal, and M. Anisul Islam. *Reexcavation: A Major Step in Wetland Restoration in the Haors*. Dhaka: IUCN—World Conservation Union, 2005.

Irfanullah, Haseeb Md. Ainun Nishat, and Rashiduzzaman Ahmed, eds. *Socio-Economic Baseline Survey of Pagnar and Sanuar-Dakuar Haors*. Dhaka: IUCN—World Conservation Union, 2005.

Islam, M. Aminul, Md. Rakibul Haque, and Sharoar Jahan. *Participatory Landuse Survey of Pagnar and Sanuar-Dakuar Haors*. Dhaka: IUCN—World Conservation Union, 2005.

Kabir, Md. Humayun, and Shahalam N. M. Amin. *Tanguar Haor: A Diversified Freshwater Wetland: Local People's Dependence of Resources and Participation in Conservation Practices*. Dhaka: Academic Press and Publishers Library, 2007.

Monitoring and Evaluation Guidelines for Community Based Wetland Resource Management. Dhaka: IUCN—World Conservation Union, 2003.

Nishat, Ainun, ed. *A Plan for Sustainable Wetland Resource Management*. Dhaka: IUCN—World Conservation Union, 2005.

Nishat, Ainun, Mir Waliuzzaman, and Munjurul Hannan Khan, eds. *Introduction to Community Based Haor and Floodplain Resource Management*. Dhaka: IUCN—World Conservation Union, 2004.

Nishat, Ainun, S. M. Munjural H. Khan, and Rashiduzzaman Ahmed, eds. *Poverty Status of a Critical Wetland Area: Hakaluki Haor*. Dhaka: IUCN—World Conservation Union, 2005.

Rahman, A. Atiq, et al., eds. *Environment and Development in Bangladesh*. Dhaka: University Press, 1994.

Rahman, A. Atiq, and Mujibur Rahman Khan, eds. *Environment and Poverty: Key Linkages for Global Sustainable Development*. Dhaka: University Press, 1998.

Rahman, Atiur, M. Ashraf Ali, and Farooque Chowdhury, ed. *People's Report on Bangladesh Environment 2001*. Dhaka: University Press, 2001.

Rahman, Matiur, ed. *Globalisation, Environmental Crisis and Social Change in Bangladesh*. Bangladesh: University Press Limited, 2003.

Rasheed, K. B. Sajjadur. *Bangladesh: Resource and Environmental Profile*. Dhaka: AH Development Publishing House, 2008.

Riverine Chars in Bangladesh: Environmental Dynamics and Management Issues. Dhaka: University Press Limited, 2000.

Roy, Raja Devasish, et al. *The Chittagong Hill Tracts: Life and Nature at Risk*. Dhaka: Society for Environment and Human Development (SEHD), 2000.

Seminar on Women and Environment (1991: Dhaka) Proceedings. Dhaka: Geographic Society, 1992.

Zaker Husain, Kazi. *An Introduction to the Wildlife of Bangladesh*. Dacca: F. Ahmed, 1974.

Public Health

Akmam, Wardatul. *Arsenic Mitigation in Rural Bangladesh: A Policy-Mix for Supplying Safe Water in Badly Affected Areas of Meherpur District*. Dhaka: Gatidhara, 2008.

Alam, Md. Jahangir. *Traditional Medicine in Bangladesh: Issues and Challenges*. Dhaka: Asiatic Society of Bangladesh, 2007.

Comparative Advantages of Public and Private Health Care Providers in Bangladesh. Bangladesh Development Series, paper no. 4. Dhaka: World Bank Office Dhaka, 2005.

Dayal, Edison. *Food, Nutrition and Health in Bangladesh*. Brookfield, Vt.: Avebury, 1997.

Harun-ar-Rashid. *Research Studies on Health Impact of Arsenic Exposure*. Bangladesh: Bangladesh Medical Research Council (BMRC), 2002.

Nazneen, Khaleda. *Governance of the Health Care Sector in Bangladesh*. Dhaka: University Press, 2001.

Perry, Henry B. *Health for All in Bangladesh: Lessons in Primary Health Care for the Twenty-first Century*. Dhaka: University Press, 2000.

UNICEF. *Assessment of Risk and Vulnerability of Children and Women to HIV in Bangladesh*. Dhaka: UNICEF, 2008.

INTERNET SOURCES

Ain O Shalish Kendra: www.askbd.org/web

Anti-Corruption Commission: www.acc.org.bd

Association for Social Advancement: www.asa.org.bd
Awami League: www.albd.org
Bangladesh Bureau of Statistics: www.bbs.gov.bd
Bangladesh Genocide: www.genocidebangladesh.org
Bangladesh Jamaat-e-Islami: www.jamaat-e-islami.org
Bangladesh Nationalist Party: www.bnpbd.org
Bangladesh Parliament: www.parliamentofbangladesh.org
Bangladesh Rural Advancement Committee (BRAC): www.brac.net
Bangladesh Yellow Book: www.bdyellowbook.com
Comprehensive Portal for Government of Bangladesh: www.bangladesh.gov.
    bd
Dhaka Stock Exchange: www.dsebd.org
Election Commission: www.esc.gov.bd
Export Promotion Bureau: www.epb.gov.bd
Federation of Bangladesh Chambers of Commerce and Industry (FBCCI):
    www.fbcci-bd.org
Government of Bangladesh Digitized Forms (English): www.forms.gov.bd/
    eng
Grameen Foundation: www.grameenfoundation.org
International Centre for Diarrhoeal Disease Research, Bangladesh (ICDDRB):
    www.icddrb.org
National Tourism Organization: www.bangladeshtourism.gov.bd
University Grants Commission: www.ugc.gov.bd
World Bank Bangladesh Resources: www.worldbank-bangladesh.com

Newspaper

First Bangladesh Online Newspaper: www.bdnews24.com

Business Newspapers

Bangladesh Business News: www.bizbangladesh.com
Bangladesh Business Online: www.bdbusinessonline.com

English Newspapers

The Daily Star: www.thedailystar.net
The Financial Express: www.thefinancialexpress-bd.com
The Independent: www.theindependent-bd.com
New Age: www.newagebd.com

Bengali Newspapers

Prothom Alo: www.prothom-alo.com
The Daily Ittefaq: www.ittefaq.com
The Daily Inqilab: www.dailyinqilab.com

English Weekly

Dhaka Courier: www.dhakacourier.net

About the Author

Syedur Rahman (Ph.D., Syracuse University) is the retired director of international programs in the College of Education at Pennsylvania State University. In 1969 he received his B.A. (honors) degree in political science from Dhaka University. He received his M.A. in public administration in 1972 from Dhaka University and joined Dhaka University as a lecturer in the Department of Public Administration in April. In September 1972, he was awarded an international scholarship for higher education abroad. Upon completion of his Ph.D. in 1977, he returned to Dhaka University. In 1978, he became the budget director of the National Iranian Copper Mines. In 1982, he served for a brief period in the Permanent Mission of Bangladesh to the United Nations before joining the staff of the Institute of Public Administration at Pennsylvania State University.

He was president of the American Institute of Bangladesh Studies from 1998 to 2005. He is the co-author of *Government and Politics of South Asia*. In 2008, he completed a study on building the administrative capacity of Bangladeshi institutions of higher education, which was funded by the Educational and Cultural Affairs Division of the United States Department of State. He is the principal author of two reports: "Changing Perspectives on Human Resources Development" and "Strengthening Local Government in Bangladesh," both funded by the United Nations Department of Development Support and Management Services. His articles on Bangladesh include "Towards Institution Building in Bangladesh: Trends in Democracy and Human Rights," "Good Governance and Local Government System in Bangladesh," "Political Boundary Building in Bangladesh," "Issues and Agenda for Regional Cooperation in South Asia," and "The Bangladesh Military and Economic Development."

Dr. Rahman was also the director of a leadership and management development program for mid-career officials from developing countries. In that capacity he was responsible for the professional development of some 300 policy and program managers from 107 different countries. His focus on management led to such publications as "The Growth of Information Technology in the Public Sector of Developing Countries," "Managerial Thinking: A Study of Public Managers from Developing Countries," and "Improved Budgeting and Financial Management as a Tool for Enhancing the Role of Local Government in Developing Countries."

Breinigsville, PA USA
14 April 2010
236130BV00001B/2/P